Making Sense

C000071869

The phenomenon of multimodality is central to our everyday interaction. Hybrid modes of communication that combine traditional uses of language with imagery, tagging, hashtags, and voice-recognition tools have become the norm. Bringing together concepts of meaning and communication across a range of subject areas, including education, media studies, cultural studies, design, and architecture, the authors uncover a multimodal grammar that moves away from rigid and language-centered understandings of meaning. They present the first framework for describing and analyzing different forms of meaning across text, image, space, body, sound, and speech. Succinct summaries of the main thinkers in the fields of language, communications, and semiotics are provided alongside rich examples to illustrate the key arguments. A history of media including the genesis of digital media is covered. This book will stimulate new thinking about the nature of meaning, and life itself, and will serve practitioners and theorists alike.

BILL COPE is a Professor in the College of Education at the University of Illinois, Urbana-Champaign.

MARY KALANTZIS was from 2006 to 2016 Dean of the College of Education at the University of Illinois, Urbana-Champaign.

They are co-authors of multiple books including the companion to this volume, *Adding Sense: Context and Interest in a Grammar of Multimodal Meaning* (Cambridge, 2020), *New Learning: Elements of a Science of Education* (Cambridge, 2008, 2012), *Literacies* (Cambridge 2012, 2016) and *e-Learning Ecologies* (2017).

Making Sense

Reference, Agency, and Structure in a Grammar of Multimodal Meaning

Bill Cope

University of Illinois at Urbana-Champaign

Mary Kalantzis

University of Illinois at Urbana-Champaign

CAMBRIDGE
UNIVERSITY PRESS

CAMBRIDGE
UNIVERSITY PRESS

University Printing House, Cambridge CB2 8BS, United Kingdom

One Liberty Plaza, 20th Floor, New York, NY 10006, USA

477 Williamstown Road, Port Melbourne, VIC 3207, Australia

314-321, 3rd Floor, Plot 3, Splendor Forum, Jasola District Centre, New Delhi - 110025, India

103 Penang Road, #05-06/07, Visioncrest Commercial, Singapore 238467

Cambridge University Press is part of the University of Cambridge.

It furthers the University's mission by disseminating knowledge in the pursuit of education, learning and research at the highest international levels of excellence.

www.cambridge.org
Information on this title: www.cambridge.org/9781107589797
DOI: 10.1017/9781316459645

First published 2020
First paperback edition 2022

A catalogue record for this publication is available from the British Library

Library of Congress Cataloging in Publication data
Names: Cope, Bill, author. | Kalantzis, Mary, author.
Title: Making sense : reference, agency, and structure in a grammar of multimodal meaning / Bill Cope, Mary Kalantzis.
Description: Cambridge, United Kingdom ; New York, NY: Cambridge University Press, 2018. | Includes bibliographical references.
Identifiers: LCCN 2019018407 | ISBN 9781107133303 (hardback)
Subjects: LCSH: Modality (Linguistics) | Semiotics. | Functionalism (Linguistics)
Classification: LCC P99.4.M6 C67 2018 | DDC 415/.6–dc23
LC record available at https://lccn.loc.gov/2019018407

ISBN 978-1-107-13330-3 Hardback
ISBN 978-1-107-58979-7 Paperback

For Sophia and William.

Contents

List of Figures   *page* xiv
Key to In-text Markers   xv

ELEMENTS OF A THEORY	EXAMPLES AND DISCUSSION	

Part 0		1
Making Sense: An Overview §0.0		1
	§0.0a *Big Yam Dreaming*, By an Artist We Don't (at First) Name	6
Meaning §0		11
	§0a Andy Warhol's *Water Heater*	13
	§0b Walter Benjamin's *Arcades*	14
	§0c Bundling	17
	§0d Supermarket Order	18
Participation §0.1		20
Representation §0.1.1		20
Communication §0.1.2		21
Interpretation §0.1.3		22
Meaning Form §0.2		22
Text §0.2.1		23
	§0.2.1a Unicode	23
	§0.2.1b Learning to Read	25
Image §0.2.2		26
Space §0.2.3		27
Object §0.2.4		27
Body §0.2.5		28
Sound §0.2.6		29
Speech §0.2.7		29

§0.2.7a M.A.K. Halliday on the   30
Differences Between Speech and
Writing

Multimodality §0.2.8   33
Synesthesia §0.2.9   34
§0.2.9a Alexander Bogdanov's   34
Philosophy of Living Experience

Transposition of Forms   39
§0.2.10
Meaning Function §0.3   42
§0.3a M.A.K. Halliday and   43
Ruqaiya Hasan's *Systemic-
Functional Grammar*

Reference §0.3.1   45
Agency §0.3.2   45
Structure §0.3.3   46
Context §0.3.4   47
Interest §0.3.5   48
Transposition of   48
Functions §0.3.6
Grammar §0.4   49
§0.4a Pāṇini's *Aṣṭādhyāyī*   50
§0.4b Michael Reddy's *Conduit*   55
Metaphor
§0.4c Edmund Husserl's *Pure*   58
Phenomenology
§0.4d Jacques Derrida's *Of*   61
Grammatology
§0.4e Mr. He's *Gypsy China Chairs*   64
Design §0.4.1   68
To Parse §0.4.2   72
Part 1   77
Overview of Part 1 §1.0   77
Reference §1   78
§1a Gottlob Frege's *Sense and*   79
Reference
Specification §1.1   83
Instance §1.1.1   83
§1.1.1a Henri Cartier-Bresson's   87
The Decisive Image
§1.1.1b The Leica M3   88
§1.1.1c Everyday "Identifiers"   89
§1.1.1d Numbers as Text   91

Contents

§1.1.1e Penelope Umbrico's *Sunset Portraits* ... 92

§1.1.1f URLs and TCP/IP ... 93

§1.1.1g The Internet of Things ... 94

§1.1.1h Lewis Carroll's *Alice* ... 96

§1.1.1i "Big Data" ... 96

§1.1.1j Joseph Kusuth's *Real* ... 98

Absence §1.1.2 ... 99

§1.1.2a John Cage's *4'33"* ... 100

Concept §1.1.3 ... 101

§1.1.3a Lev Vygotsky and Aleksandr Luria's *Higher Psychological Processes* ... 103

§1.1.3b Lev Vygotsky and Aleksandr Luria on Children's Concept Development ... 105

§1.1.3c Aleksei Leontyev on the Psyche ... 107

§1.1.3d Aleksandr Luria in Uzbekistan ... 108

§1.1.3e Aleksandr Luria on Cognitive Development ... 110

§1.1.3f Sergei Eisenstein's *Battleship Potemkin* ... 111

§1.1.3g Lev Rudinev's Moscow State University ... 112

§1.1.3h Otto Neurath's Pictorial Statistics ... 114

§1.1.3i The Vienna Circle's *Scientific Conception of the World* ... 117

§1.1.3j Marie Reidemeister's *Isotype* ... 118

Circumstance §1.2 ... 119

§1.2a Gottlob Frege's "Aristotle" ... 120

§1.2b Unified Modeling Language ... 122

§1.2c Object-oriented Software Development ... 125

Entity §1.2.1 ... 126

Action §1.2.2 ... 127

§1.2.2a Leonard Bloomfield on Nouns and Verbs in Tagalog ... 127

§1.2.2b Henri Bergson's "Integral Experience" ... 129

x   Contents

§1.2.2c Alfred North Whitehead's   130
Process and Reality
§1.2.2d Citroën DS and Bézier   132
Curves
§1.2.2e Scalable Vector Graphics   134
Property §1.3   135
§1.3a René Descartes and John   138
Locke on Color
Quality §1.3.1   140
§1.3.1a Berlin and Kay's *Basic*   141
Color Terms
§1.3.1b C.L. Hardin's *Color for*   143
Philosophers
§1.3.1c Isaac Newton's Spectral   144
Decomposition of Light
§1.3.1d Leonardo da Vinci's Color   147
Mixing
§1.3.1e Pantone Matching and   148
Digitized Color
§1.3.1f The Colors "Greige" and   149
"YInMin Blue"
§1.3.1g Alfred Munsell's *Color*   151
Notation
§1.3.1h ICC Color Profiles   152
Quantity §1.3.2   153
§1.3.2a Ada Lovelace's Notes   156
on the Analytical Engine
§1.3.2b Alan Turing's   159
"Mechanical Intelligence"
§1.3.2c The "Turing Test"   163
§1.3.2d Gottfried Leibniz: "Let us   169
Calculate"
Part 2   173
Overview of Part 2 §2.0   173
§2.0a Errol Morris' *Fog of War*   174
Agency §2   175
§2a J.M.W. Turner's *Rain, Steam*   176
and Speed
Event §2.1   180
Predication §2.1.1   180
§2.1.1a Ludwig Wittgenstein's   182
Tractatus
§2.1.1b Wittgenstein's Handles   186

Contents   xi

                        §2.1.1c HandleSets.com   188
                        §2.1.1d Picture Theory in Vienna   192
Transactivity §2.1.2   198
                        §2.1.2a Charles Fillmore on Case   198
                        §2.1.2b Jacques Tati's *Mon Oncle*   202
                        §2.1.2c Dyirbal *Scrub Hen* Song   204
                        §2.1.2d R.M.W. Dixon's *Ergativity*   207
                        §2.1.2e Paddy Biran and Jack   211
                            Murray Sing *Destruction of Our
                            Country*
        Role §2.2   212
                        §2.2a Four Marys   215
                        §2.2b Leon Battista Alberti's   217
                            Commentaries
                        §2.2c Erwin Panofsky's   218
                            Perspective as Symbolic Form
        Self §2.2.1   222
                        §2.2.1a Al-Hasan ibn al-   222
                            Haytham's *Book of Optics*
                        §2.2.1b Islam's Imaging   224
        Other §2.2.2   228
                        §2.2.2a John Berger's   228
                            Understanding the Photograph
                        §2.2.2b Susan Sontag's *On   230
                            Photography*
                        §2.2.2c Félix Nadar's *When I was a   232
                            Photographer*
        Thing §2.2.3   235
                        §2.2.3a Eadweard Muybridge's   235
                            Images of Movement
Conditionality §2.3   237
                        §2.3a Isaac Newton's *Opticks*   239
        Assertion §2.3.1   241
                        §2.3.1a J.L. Austin's *How to Do   243
                            Things with Words*
                        §2.3.1b John R. Searle's *Reply to   246
                            Derrida*
Requirement §2.3.2   251
                        §2.3.2a Elizabeth Anscombe's   253
                            Compilation of Wittgenstein
                            Notes, *On Certainty*
        Possibility §2.3.3   257

Part 3   259
    Overview of Part 3 §3.0   259
        §3.0a Ibn Jinnî's *Kha â'i* (Origins   260
        of Speech)
        ***Structure* §3**   261
        §3a Sîbawayh's *Kitâb* (Grammar)   262
        §3b Mattâ ibn Yûnus' "Logic"   263
        §3c Al Fārābī's "Meaning"   264
        §3d Ferdinand de Saussure's   266
        Course in General Linguistics
        §3e Sebastiano Timpanaro's   269
        "Structuralism and its
        Successors"
    Ontology §3.1   271
        §3.1a Roy Bhaskar   272
        and Mervyn Hartwig's
        Enlightened Common Sense
Material Structures §3.1.1   275
        §3.1.1a Elizabeth Grosz's   276
        Incorporeal
        §3.1.1b Gilles Deleuze's *Logic of*   277
        Sense
    Ideal Structures §3.1.2   280
        §3.1.2a Errol Morris' *Unknown*   281
        Known
        §3.1.2b Colin McGinn's *Mindsight*   282
        §3.1.2c John Watson's *Behavior*   286
        §3.1.2d B.F. Skinner's *Verbal*   287
        Behavior
        §3.1.2e Noam Chomsky's   288
        Review of *Verbal Behavior*
        §3.1.2f Noam Chomsky's   290
        Syntactic Structures
        §3.1.2g René Descartes' "Cogito"   293
        §3.1.2h Kenneth MacCorquodale's   294
        Reply to Chomsky
        §3.1.2i B.F. Skinner's *Beyond*   295
        Freedom
        §3.1.2j Noam Chomsky's *Kinds of*   298
        Creatures
    Design §3.2   301
        §3.2a Intelligent Medical Objects   303
    Relation §3.3   307
        §3.3a Thomas Gruber's "Ontology"   310

Contents   xiii

	§3.3b Extensible Markup Language	313
	§3.3c Tim Berners-Lee's *Semantic Web*	316
	§3.3d Debiprasad Chattopadhyaya's *Lokayata*	318
	§3.3e Immanuel Kant's *Critique of Pure Reason*	321
Metaontology §3.4		322
	§3.4a Ramanathan Guha's Schema.org	323
	§3.4b The Meaning of Everything	326

References	329
Index	355

Figures

0.0	Meaning and its functions	*page* 2
0d(i)	Meaning functions	18
0d(ii)	Meaning forms	19
0.3	Matrix for a transpositional grammar	42
0.4.1a(i)	Five questions about meaning	72
0.4.1a(ii)	A transpositional grammar	74
1.0	Functions of reference	77
1.1.1	Specification	86
1.1.2	Absence	100
1.2(i)	Circumstances specified	120
1.2(ii)	Circumstances	120
1.3(i)	Properties specified	136
1.3(ii)	Properties	137
2.0	Functions of Agency	173
2.1	Event	180
2.1.2a	Transactivity	199
2.2(i)	Roles over time and place	213
2.2(ii)	Roles	214
2.3	Conditionality	238
3.0	Functions of structure	259
3.1	Ontology	271
3.2	Designs in the meeting of material and ideal structures	302
3.3	Relations	310
3.4b	Some digital ontologies	326

Key to In-text Markers

Footnote to a source[123]

Cross-reference to ideas discussed or lives described in another section of this book[§1.2.3] or its companion volume, *Adding Sense*[§AS1.2.3]

Related media to be found online at meaningpatterns.net[*]

Part 0   Meaning

§0.0   *Making Sense*: An Overview

> A grammar is a resource for meaning, the critical functioning semiotic by means of which we pursue our everyday life. It therefore embodies a theory of everyday life; otherwise it cannot function in this way ... A grammar is a theory of human experience. *M.A.K. Halliday.*[1]

Making Sense is a grammar of everyday life. In our old-fashioned schoolish understandings, "grammar" was the syntax of language, rules for correct speaking and writing. Following Michael Halliday's suggestion, we want to use this word in a wider sense, to develop an account of grammar as patterns in meaning.

Our reasons for wanting an expanded definition of grammar are twofold. First, the meanings of speech and writing have never made sense outside a wider understanding of the relations of text and speech to image, sound, body, space, and object. It makes even less sense to make such a separation today, in an era of pervasive digital media where these forms of meaning are so profoundly overlaid. This phenomenon we call "multimodality." The activity of reframing a meaning in one form, then another, or several together at the same time, we call "transposition."

The second reason for our broader definition of grammar is to challenge their very mode of operation, and more generally structuralist approaches to linguistics which classify and categorize meanings – singular versus plural, noun versus verb, first person versus third, and a myriad of such distinctions. Defying the neat separations, we want to say that meanings are always ready

---

[1] M.A.K. Halliday, 2000 [2002], "Grammar and Daily Life: Concurrence and Complementarity," pp. 369–83 in *On Grammar*, The Collected Works of M.A.K. Halliday, Volume 1, edited by J.J. Webster, London, UK: Continuum, pp. 369–70. A note on the dates of references: we're incidentally interested in the history of ideas, so when there are two dates, the older is the date when the edition we are referencing was first published and, if not in English, in its original language. The newer is the date of the edition we have at hand, for the purposes of page referencing.

to move. Their meanings are not just in what they are, but the possibilities in their imminent transposability.

To take the three examples that we have just mentioned from a conventional understanding of syntax: multiple things can be instantiated one by one, but their meanings in multiplicity (concepts) are very different from their meanings as instances. Entities have been constituted in action, and action configures entities. By empathy, I put myself in the position of an other.

The meaning is as much in the dynamics of movability as fixed categories – after multimodality, a second dimension of this transpositional grammar. We call this "functional transposition." We set out to develop concepts for a functional theory of meaning that will work across all the forms of meaning.

We propose in this grammar that there are five functions of meaning, five things that meaning does in everyday life, in human experience: reference, agency, structure, context, and interest. These are five ways "to parse" any act or artifact of meaning (see Fig. 0.0).

§0 Meaning	
	§1 Reference
	§2 Agency
	§3 Structure
	§AS1 Context
	§AS2 Interest

Fig. 0.0: Meaning and its functions

The first three – reference, agency, and structure – are addressed in conventional accounts of language. In his functional grammar, Michael Halliday calls these ideational, interpersonal, and textual metafunctions,[0.3a] although we mean something somewhat different for each of the three, and we want to create a conceptual framework which will work for image, sound, body, space, and object as well as speech and text. *Making Sense* addresses these three.

The remainder of our transpositional grammar, the functions of context and interest, we address in a companion book, *Adding Sense*. This is the conventional domain of a philosophy of meaning and a subdiscipline of linguistics that is frequently called "pragmatics." However, once again, we want to escape the narrowness of language-centered accounts of meaning in order to create a grammar of the multimodal transpositions in context and the expression of interest.

Of course, this is too much even for two books, so we present our case around the theoretical skeleton of a grammar of multimodality, tangentially discussing relevant theorists and their thinking, and offering symptomatic examples of meaning-making activities. Our method is to weave between practices drawn from the scholarly disciplines of linguistics (mainly of the social, functional, and pragmatic varieties), philosophy, and history. In a time when the disruptions in ordinary life are so disorienting, a wide-ranging interdisciplinary approach is necessary.

Around its unfolding theoretical schema, the book has two supplementary devices: discussion of key theorists; and parsing examples of multimodal meaning practices. The theorists we have selected offer us the support we have found we need to think through the grammar as it unfolds in this book. We pass by them, one by one, mentioning them when their ideas seem germane to an idea of ours. We come to these folks at points where we feel it would be illuminating to bring them into the conversation. Each time we come back to them, it seems like we know them as friends. These people are the inspiration of our ideas, directly or indirectly; we need to acknowledge them as our sources. We also want to draw distinctions, because we have come to know and love them for their limitations as well as their virtuous insights.

In the selection of examples of multimodal meanings, we cross histories and cultures. Historically, we can't know the specificity of the present except in the continuities and contrasts with its pasts. So, the book traces the origins and parses a number of practices and artifacts of the digital era, the historical evolution of textual practices in media such as writing and imaging over thousands of years, and also the meaning practices of "first peoples," at which point our frame of reference becomes tens of thousands of years.

Our cultural range includes: indigenous or first peoples, with a focus on Australian peoples with whom we have worked at earlier stages in our research careers; the historical evolution of meaning practices in the Indian, Chinese, Arab, and European traditions; and the globalized social practices and cultural sensibilities of the digital age. So, the frame of reference for our grammar is global-wide and species-long. This means that, from a practical point of view, all we can do is offer pertinent and we hope also poignant examples.

In both of these supplementary devices, our method of presentation is essentially historical, so narrative in form. We want to connect the thinkers into the context of their thinking, and their interests as persons. We want to understand their meanings, not just in what they said, but in what we can now make of the meanings of their lives. In the examples, we want to find decisive or symptomatic moments in the development of meaning-making tools and practices, and tell these as stories. So, this book is part history of ideas, part philosophy of history.

We've worked over the ground covered in this book several times before in publications connected with the development of our pedagogy of "Multiliteracies," starting with the work[2] we did in the New London Group[*] with Courtney Cazden,[3] Norman Fairclough,[4] James Paul Gee,[5] Gunther Kress,[6] Allan Luke,[7] Carmen Luke,[8] Sarah Michaels,[9] and Martin Nakata.[10] The version we present is more or less the same in terms of its conceptual framework, though we've refined the terminology and made our central organizing principle the functions of meaning (reference, agency, structure, context, and interest) rather than its forms (text, image, space, object, body, sound, speech) as we did in our *Literacies* book. We've also done a lot of work designing, developing, and

[*] http://meaningpatterns.net/new-london-group

[2] Bill Cope and Mary Kalantzis, 2009a, "A Grammar of Multimodality," *International Journal of Learning* 16(2):361–425; Bill Cope and Mary Kalantzis, 2009b, "'Multiliteracies': New Literacies, New Learning," *Pedagogies: An International Journal* 4:164–95; Mary Kalantzis, Bill Cope, Eveline Chan, and Leanne Dalley-Trim, 2016, *Literacies* (Edn 2), Cambridge, UK: Cambridge University Press.

[3] Courtney B. Cazden, 2001, *Classroom Discourse: The Language of Teaching and Learning*, Portsmouth, NH: Heinemann; Courtney Cazden, 2018, *Communicative Competence, Classroom Interaction, and Educational Equity: The Selected Works of Courtney B. Cazden*, New York, NY: Routledge.

[4] Norman Fairclough, 1992, *Discourse and Social Change*, Cambridge UK: Polity Press; Norman Fairclough, 2001, *Language and Power*, London: Longmans.

[5] James Paul Gee, 2017, "A Personal Retrospective on the New London Group and Its Formation," pp. 32–45 in *Remixing Multiliteracies: Theory and Practice from New London to New Times*, edited by F. Serfini and E. Gee, New York, NY: Teachers College Press; James Paul Gee, 1992 [2013], *The Social Mind: Language, Ideology, and Social Practice*, Champaign, IL: Common Ground; James Paul Gee, 1996, *Social Linguistics and Literacies: Ideology in Discourses*, London, UK: Taylor and Francis.

[6] Gunther Kress, 2009, *Multimodality: A Social Semiotic Approach to Contemporary Communication*, London, UK: Routledge; Gunther Kress and Theo van Leeuwen, 2006, *Reading Images: The Grammar of Visual Design*, London, UK: Routledge.

[7] Antero Garcia, Allan Luke, and Robyn Seglem, 2018, "Looking at the Next Twenty Years of Multiliteracies: A Discussion with Allan Luke," *Theory into Practice* 57(1):72–78; Allan Luke, 1996, "Text and Discourse in Education: An Introduction to Critical Discourse Analysis," *Review of Research in Education* 21:3–48.

[8] Carmen Luke and Jennifer Gore, eds., 1992, *Feminisms and Critical Pedagogy*, New York, NY: Routledge; Carmen Luke, 2003, "Pedagogy, Connectivity, Multimodality, and Interdisciplinarity," *Reading Research Quarterly* 38(3):397–403.

[9] Sarah Michaels and Richard Sohmer, 2000, "Narratives and Inscriptions: Culture Tools, Power, and Powerful Sensemaking," pp. 267–88 in *Multiliteracies: Literacy Learning and the Design of Social Futures*, edited by B. Cope and M. Kalantzis, London, UK: Routledge; Richard Sohmer and Sarah Michaels, 2002, "Re-Seeing Science: The Role of Narratives in Mediating between Scientific and Everyday Understanding and Explanation," pp. 167–208 in *Learning for the Future*, edited by M. Kalantzis, G. Varnava-Skoura and B. Cope, Melbourne, AU: Common Ground.

[10] Martin Nakata, 2000, "History, Cultural Diversity and English Language Teaching," pp. 106–20 in *Multiliteracies: Literacy Learning and the Design of Social Futures*, edited by B. Cope and M. Kalantzis, London, UK: Routledge; Martin Nakata, 2007, *Disciplining the Savages: Savaging the Disciplines*, Canberra, Australia: Aboriginal Studies Press.

testing online multimodal writing environments for the purposes of knowledge work[11] and learning.[12]

A note about the form of this book and its companion, *Adding Sense*: they are written as if they were like a non-fiction novel that can be read from the beginning to the end. They have a cast of main characters who periodically come back onto the scene. However, realistically, many readers will dart all over the place, so the sectioning has been designed for that. Each section can be read separately. We try to help non-linear readings with cross-references marked thus[§0.0] when another relevant section will elaborate on an idea, provide an example, or describe a life. In this kind of reading, the text serves more as a dictionary of concepts or encyclopedia of illustrative examples, where matters of interest can be "looked up."

And another note: this is just a work of writing. The reason is in part practical. We could have included images, but we wanted to use too many. We also wanted to include moving image, and sound, and other embedded media from the web. This might render on some e-book devices, but not all, and not in the print version. So, we have decided to put illustrative media in a slideshow on the web at meaningpatterns.net. We refer to the slides in this text thus,[*] but they are not essential to its reading. This may seem a contrary move for a book on multimodality. But it is a pragmatic one given the affordances of the book as a medium.

In any event, writing is a habit of social theory. For the purposes of theorizing, text is a nicely old-fashioned form, and one that has for a long time well served social theorists, philosophers, and historians. Books are still good old things.

And finally, about us, our interest. Our profession is education, where the greatest challenges of our time are inequality of outcomes, learner diversity, and the transformative potentials of new technologies. This grammar does not directly address these specifically educational challenges – we have done that elsewhere.[13] Rather, we want to cast these challenges in a broader frame of

---

[*] http://meaningpatterns.net

[11] Bill Cope, Mary Kalantzis, and Liam Magee, 2011, *Towards a Semantic Web: Connecting Knowledge in Academic Research*, Cambridge, UK: Elsevier; Bill Cope and Angus Phillips, eds., 2014, *The Future of the Academic Journal*, Oxford, UK: Elsevier.

[12] US Department of Education, Institute of Education Sciences: "The Assess-as-You-Go Writing Assistant" (R305A090394); "Assessing Complex Performance" (R305B110008); "u-Learn.net: An Anywhere/Anytime Formative Assessment and Learning Feedback Environment" (ED-IES-10-C-0018); "The Learning Element" (ED-IES-lO-C-0021); and "InfoWriter: A Student Feedback and Formative Assessment Environment" (ED-IES-13-C-0039). Bill and Melinda Gates Foundation: "Scholar Literacy Courseware." National Science Foundation: "Assessing 'Complex Epistemic Performance' in Online Learning Environments" (Award 1629161).

[13] Mary Kalantzis and Bill Cope, 2012b, *New Learning: Elements of a Science of Education* (Edn 2), Cambridge, UK: Cambridge University Press; Mary Kalantzis and Bill Cope, 2016, "Learner Differences in Theory and Practice," *Open Review of Educational Research* 3(1):85–132; Bill Cope and Mary Kalantzis, eds., 2017, *E-Learning Ecologies: Principles for New Learning and Assessment*, New York, NY: Routledge.

reference, where we hope that the terms of our discussion may be helpful not only to educators as designers of learning ecologies, but designers of all kinds, people who in their work and community lives make meanings in the social and material world in a myriad of ways.

It is now a truism – and also a cliché – to say that we live in a time of "disruptive" change. It's a matter of conjecture how long we have lived in the disruption. Perhaps modernity has been disruptive for its duration, or perhaps we humans have been disruptive of the earth since our emergence as a species which, for better but often for worse, quickly made its presence felt everywhere in the geosphere.

Of today's disruptions, in this book and its companion, *Adding Sense*, we will among other things explore some of the transformations in our modes of social participation in the digital era – investigating elements of a grammar of digital modernity. To set this in context, we will trace the ways in which earlier grammars of meaning have in their own time also been disruptive. We will also engage with human diversity as manifest in divergent practices of meaning-making. And we will ponder the confounding of each other's meanings in societies of inequality. In each case, our focal interest is the nature of the social. The implications are not just descriptive-analytical, but ethical-political.

§0.0a   Big Yam Dreaming, *By an Artist We Don't (at First) Name*

Be advised, warns the 2008 introduction to a catalogue for an exhibition of her paintings, that this publication may contain the name of the artist, and there may be images of her. So reader, go no further if you may be shocked or offended, if this is the way of your meaning.

In accordance with her custom, our artist's name must be suppressed after death. Images of her person are forbidden. Her powerful spectral presence, her meaning to the living, is now to be referenced in an effort never-to-forget by never naming, never picturing.

If you are from a place where the habit is to enumerate dates, this much is certain, she died on September 2, 1996. But nobody knows quite when she was born, perhaps 1910, because no-one in her lifeworld found enumeration to be meaningful. To the extent that her life is now at least roughly calculable, she was about 86 when she died. Of the place of birth and death of this artist, we know and can speak thus much without fear of offending custom: Utopia.

Utopia was the name given to a cattle station established in 1928 in the Australian desert, perhaps in a moment of white man's irony. In this most marginal of agricultural land, the station was able to support only a few head of cattle per square mile. Those colonizers only ever half owned this land, having been granted the strange property title of a "pastoral lease," a rationalization of what at the time seemed to the authorities to be unstoppable theft. The property was sold to the Aboriginal Land Fund in 1976. About 1000 speakers of Anmatyerre live today on these, their ancestral lands, in family groups of 20 or 30 on outstations scattered across hundreds of square kilometers.

The artist we are writing about started to paint at the age of 78, and in the last eight years of her life, she produced over 3000 canvases, approximately one per day in the calculation of her curators, for whom such calculation produces a result that is notable.

Hers was an "impossible modernism," said Akira Tatehata, Director, National Museum of Art, Osaka, when an exhibition of her works toured there – this and an exhibition in Australia soon after were the reason for a 2008 catalogue where several art-historical luminaries speak to her work. Maybe she was "one of the twentieth century's most important abstract artists," or perhaps such an accolade is impossible for "a quintessential outsider." She could neither read nor write, and only once or twice travelled beyond her place of birth and death. Would that she were to "be accorded the legendary status granted to . . . Mark Rothko, Andy Warhol and Georgia O'Keefe," says curator Margot Neale in her introduction to the catalogue. Her work is like as it was unlike Monet and Pollock, resonating with "multiple modernisms," perhaps abstract expressionism, or minimalism, or conceptualism, or the modernism that is postmodernism?

But how so, when these movements are so completely alien to the artist? What gives anyone a right to ascribe meaning to another? Or in an ethnographic mode, should we try to work out what her meanings were, and so differently?

Now we've reached a point in our narrative where we can't help ourselves but to transgress the painter's protocols of meaning. If you are in a culture where you need to name the artist of a work, for the sake of its provenance, its "genius" (to take a word from the title of the catalogue), our commentators will, out of awkward cross-cultural necessity, give you an official artist's name if not a "real" name: Emily Kame Kngwarreye. This may have been altered as a mark of respect, the catalogue says, and besides, there are many spellings, even in this catalogue. It's a "professional name," created so her art can enter into the world of the market economy. There are also some photos of her, but discreetly placed near the back of the book, hence the page of warnings at the start.[14]

Before she began to paint, Emily Kame Kngwarreye already had things that she had said, some of these secret and sacred "women's business," but these are only known by people who now cannot speak her name or view her likeness.

---

[14] Margot Neale, ed., 2008, *Utopia: The Genius of Emily Kame Kngwarreye*, Canberra, Australia: National Museum of Australia Press, pp. 11, 31, 13, 16, 25.

She had sung these things in Anmatyerre, painted them onto her body, danced them with the other women.

Emily Kame Kngwarreye had been an elder, an owner of land defined by its narrative focal points but without surveyed boundaries. Alhalkere was her "country," a nice usage in Aboriginal English because in dictionary English it connotes both sovereignty of a certain kind and landscape. We need to push this further than an ambiguity in English, because the people called Alhalkere were not just in or of a country of that name, they were the country Alhalkere. Not "property" – though that's what Utopia station had been, "a property" – nor country in the sense of a nation-space to which she belonged, but more a country that belonged the people. In English, we need to become ungrammatical, and even then, it is hard to get close to the meaning. Translation at a certain point fails us, though we can struggle to get closer by fumbling with qualifications.

Big Yam Dreaming is a giant canvas in the permanent collection of the National Gallery of Victoria. In the world where truth and property are mundanely material, we are told that it is synthetic polymer on canvas, 291.1 cm × 801.8 cm. (As paintings go, it's big; the enumeration to a decimal point of a centimeter is a modern absurdity.) We'll never be able to see this so long as it is on the wall of a gallery, but we are told that the following is inscribed in black fiber-tipped pen on the reverse:

959130 / Emily Kngwarreye / Commissioned by THE HOLT FAMILY/ OF DELMORE SPRINGS N.T. / 22/23/7/95
     EM/EMILY[15]

Big Yam Dreaming was completed in two days in 1995, the year before she died, on July 22–23 according to the empirically fastidious, provenance-conscious notation on the back of the canvas. Two assistants had painted a black background. The canvas was laid out on the ground in an open-sided shelter shaded with corrugated iron, the dogs and flies of the desert buzzing around. Emily sat cross-legged on the canvas, painting white lines from the middle of the canvas to the edge.

"I am Kame now," Emily is said to have said, just one of the only dozen or so of her sentences that have been recorded in English. Kame is a desert yam, Emily's totem. She was the yam, a creeper that spreads its shoots and roots across the cracked desert earth. When the tuber ripens, you can dig down into the cracks to locate the edible yam seeds. Harvesting is women's work. From higher up, the *Big Yam Dreaming* might also be a map of the country. Or on another scale, the white lines on a black ground are the white ocher markings

---

[15] www.ngv.vic.gov.au/explore/collection/work/57498/

applied to black bodies for ceremony – though only such imagery as was publicly allowable, not sacred and secret meanings. Without this narrative, the painting is just a beautiful mesh of white lines, just minimalism, and so to us moderns, just modernism, and also perhaps more.

In this book, when we talk about an object like *Big Yam Dreaming*, we are addressing meaning – the "grammar of multimodality" – at two levels. One is simply to make sense; the other is to make sense of our making sense. When grammar was just for sentences, we called the first level of analysis "parsing." In our multimodal grammar, we want to parse a world beyond the text.

Making sense of *Big Yam Dreaming* we have:

> *Reference:* yam, land, person, person, people (one of each, *this*, and in general).
>
> *Agency:* the land speaks, the country belongs, the yam lives the person, and more.
>
> *Structure:* the shoots and roots of the yam creeper, painted lines, cracks in the desert soil, Anmatyerre language, Aboriginal English, and more.
>
> *Context:* Alhalkere people, galleries, tradition, modernism, and more.
>
> *Interest:* the land to which Kame speaks, to connect with Emily, to address the politics of theft and the historical pain that Indigenous Peoples have endured and continue to endure, to make some money, and more.

The ". . . and more" indicates that although these things may have become focal points of our attention based on our interest, meanings are inexhaustible. These are some of the distinguishable elements of a grammar of multimodality, pointers to the kinds of work we need to do to begin to make sense of this image. If we are not Alhalkere, our viewing and talking will necessarily be different from Emily's, and so require of us greater attention. Nevertheless, we do mean to connect with her. So, we parse the canvas; we parse our talking around the canvas; we parse the history of our meanings in relation to Emily's.

If one level of analysis in the grammar of multimodality is to parse in order to make sense, another level is to make sense of our making sense. What are the meanings of meanings? We must, of necessity, experience a disorientation because Emily's and our frames of reference are so different. We want to speak to the person of the artist and to envision her living, but we can't have names or pictures for her. (We thought for a moment we might put a photo of her at meaningpatterns.net, the web slideshow that accompanies this book, because the National Museum's catalogue does that, albeit with a warning, but we decided after a while that we shouldn't.) Though we don't really buy the "professional name" argument, we have used her name. To speak of an artist in the ways we know, we must at least to some extent transgress.

Then, if we dare to name, "Kame" is a person, is a plant, is the land, is a totem, and more. These are not mere metaphors,$^{§AS1.4.4a}$ they are realer than that. And when the country belongs you, there are not actives and passives that are found in our dichotomous ontology of acting and being acted upon.$^{§2.1.2}$ The more we work at our parsing, the more we get a sense that Emily's meanings and ours are incommensurable. It is hard to grasp the differences when the meanings of the meanings might be so different. This is where our making sense begins to fail us. But the difference is the point. Can we develop a grammar of the patterns of differing, rather than a grammar of similarity? What is the scope of human difference? What are the limits of our mutual understanding? Why do we have an interest in understandability? These are some of the questions we want to address in this book.

We have been back to Utopia a number of times, driving there across the thousand-odd kilometers of dirt track that by a modern reckoning is just a wobbly line in the desert from Mount Isa to Alice Springs. We were working with teachers in the schools to develop literacy as policy and practice in the training of Aboriginal teachers, in projects funded by the Australian Government.[16] Little one-room schools have been set up at each of the out-stations on Utopia. But what was more striking than the writing – or, for a school, the fact that not much writing was happening – was the prolific painting, on every surface, from the panels of wrecked cars to the walls of the school itself.[*]

You can buy "Emilies" online at the Delmore Gallery. Because she is dead and famous you will have to contact the gallery to find out what they will cost.

Delmore Gallery represents a distinguished and talented list of emerging and acclaimed artists from Utopia ... Established by the Holt family in 1989, Delmore Gallery was originally situated 250 kilometers northeast of Alice Springs in the Northern Territory of Australia. The Holt's property, Delmore Downs Station, bordered Utopia, a former cattle station that has been under the management of its traditional owners since 1976, located very close to the exact centre of Australia. The Holt family owned properties in

---

[*] http://meaningpatterns.net/big-yam-dreaming

[16] Mary Kalantzis, Bill Cope, Nicky Solomon, Allan Luke, Bob Morgan, and Martin Nakata, 1994, "Batchelor College Entry Profile and Stage Level Assessment Scales," Batchelor, NT: Batchelor College; Bill Cope, Mary Kalantzis, Michael McDaniel, Sue McGinty, Martin Nakata, Ailsa Purdon, Nicky Solomon, and Ron Stanton, 1995, "Assessment and Access to Adult Literacy Programs for Aboriginal and Torres Strait Islander People Wishing to Participate in Vocational Education and Training," Canberra: Department of Employment, Education and Training; Bill Cope, 1998, "The Language of Forgetting: A Short History of the Word," pp. 192–223 in *Seams of Light: Best Antipodean Essays*, edited by M. Fraser, Sydney, Australia: Allen and Unwin.

this area, including Macdonald Downs, Dneiper, Delny and Delmore Downs since 1924. ... The Delmore name on the back of a canvas is recognised as one of the best provenances available. FREE SHIPPING WORLDWIDE. Copyright © 2017 Delmore Gallery. Powered by Shopify.[17]

§0 MEANING

> **Meaning.** *The processes of making sense of the world using material media and their associated cognitive architectures; making sense of what we encounter in the natural and human-historical worlds; making sense to each other; our social and personal means of intending and acting; the patterns in these meanings and the traces they leave in the form of media artifacts; and the transpositions of meaning across different forms (text, image, space, body, sound, and speech) and different attentions to meaning according to its functions (reference, agency, structure, context, and interest).*

Here is our grammar, just in text. We make meaning as an integral part of our experience of life, as we see things, feel things, understand things, express things, plan things, and act in ways that could have effect. Meaning is in one moment contemplative. We see, hear, and feel meanings in our encounters in the natural and human-historical worlds. In the human world, in other moments meanings animate our actions. We mean to do things in our lives and in the world. Then sometimes we do them, meaningfully – or thoughtlessly, in which case there is meaning even in the thoughtlessness. We perform acts of meaning. To mean is also to act. Meaning is how we make sense and act sensibly. This meaning happens in history, in circumstances that are always changing, always different, given our nature as a species that is as much self-made as it is a creature of natural history.

Meaning can manifest itself in a variety of forms:[§AS0.1] text, image, space, object, body, sound, and speech – the means by which meaning is made. This is where representation and communication occurs, where thinking or thinkable things are expressed.

These forms are closely interwoven. In fact, no form of meaning ever occurs by itself, without at least some of the others overlaid or juxtaposed. Written text is also a kind of imaging, and images and text are often set together in a tightly woven, multimodal meaning. Speech uses sound. Our interactions with objects almost invariably entail our bodies.

So why bother to make these distinctions between different forms of meaning? We do so in this book because we want to analyze the characteristic affordances of each of these forms, or their sense-making potentials.

---

[17] http://delmoregallery.com.au/pages/about

Each meaning form is constituted in a relatively discrete system. Patterns of meaning in text, for instance, are distinct and different from patterns of meaning in image. From one meaning form to another, the potentials for meaning are different in some significant ways. These differences are also the reason why we often overlay and juxtapose forms, for instance image with text, because the two can reinforce each other to make a shared message, each contributing something that complements the other in the combined effort. Indeed, much of the time for practical purposes meaning forms are inseparable – text from visual design, speech from sound, object from space. Nevertheless, the analytical distinctions help us see what kinds of meaning each form peculiarly achieves, and how it is achieved.

We are proposing in this grammar that every act and artifact of meaning, no matter what its form or patterns of multimodal combination, always expresses meaning simultaneously in five ways: reference, agency, structure, context, and interest. These are the kinds of use to which any meaning can be put. They are perspectives from which to analyze and interpret meaning.

If differences come into view with the parsing of meaning forms, parallels can be traced across meaning functions.[§AS0.2] Almost everything that can be meant in one form can also be meant in some or all of the others.

"The mountains loomed large," one of us can type here for you to read. Or we can show you a photo that one of us took.[*] It's the same mountains that we mean, but the form of that meaning is different – and the two forms of meaning are complementary when the writing and image appear together in multimodal communication. The forms of text and image may be different, but the meaning function is shared. In this case, we might want to highlight the function of reference – these there mountains. And we could go on to discuss the other functions at work to deal with the meaning in these mountains: agency (our relations in the act of meaning – in the center of the picture is the house where Mary was born); structure (the different ways the meaning is arranged in image compared to text); context (relevant surrounding meanings); and interest (the purposes of the meaning for its participants). All of these functions are there in every act of meaning, always, inevitably.

To tie these ideas together into a dynamic, ever-changing whole, meanings can always be transposed. Something can be meant in one form then another, though the re-meaning is never quite the same – in, for instance, the transposition from text to image in the case of our mountains. This never-quite-the-sameness is the reason we reach for multimodality so often and with such ease. This is transposition of meaning form.

One meaning function can also transpose into another. The functions are alternative meaning perspectives on the same thing, but what is "seen" from

---

[*] http://meaningpatterns.net/mountains

each perspective is both one-and-the-same and never the same. Reference: these mountains for the knowing. Interest: still these mountains but this time the reason we are showing you them.

And within each function, there is constant movement. In reference, one mountain is always ready to be counted as one of many. In interest, our mountains become yours as well, as they are added to your repertoire of meanings. Meanings are always ready to become something else. They are not stable or fixed points, as the neat categorical structuralism of traditional grammars would have us believe.

This idea of immanent movability and imminent movement is fundamental to our analysis. For this reason, we call this a "transpositional grammar."[§0.2.10]

§0a   Andy Warhol's Water Heater

"I just happen to like ordinary things," said Andy Warhol.[18] Moving from Pittsburgh to New York in 1949, Warhol worked for over a decade as a successful commercial artist. The fashionable shoe in the advertisement, he complained "was called a 'creation' but the drawing of it was not."[19] In *Water Heater* (1961),[*] he brought the commercial artist out of the shadows of representational invisibility, taking as his subject a boring black and white advertisement from the *New York Daily News*. Putting it on a canvas, he magnified its ordinariness. More than ordinary, his rendering is incomplete, messy with the paint dripping from the badly executed lettering. The ordinariness of the water heater is accentuated because it is – kind of – worse than ordinary.

Ten years later, the painting ended up in the Museum of Modern Art in New York for its insightfully exaggerated ordinariness. Warhol's interest? It seems, to recover the overlooked work of the ordinary image maker in a world where not all image makers are equal. The so-ordinary advert on which the painting was based, whose artist and artistry – ironically perhaps – remains as invisible today as it was then. And perhaps also the water heater itself, and its user, and the maker of the water heater – to call attention to a network of ordinary things that may otherwise have been overlooked for their ordinariness.

Our grammar of multimodality is a philosophy of ordinary meanings. However, here is Ludwig Wittgenstein's[§2.1.1a] challenge for our knowing: "The aspects of things that are most important for us are hidden because of

---

[*] http://meaningpatterns.net/warhol

[18] Andy Warhol, 2006, *"Giant" Size*, London, UK: Phaidon, p. 91.
[19] Carolyn Lanchner, 2008, *Andy Warhol*, New York, NY: Museum of Modern Art, p. 5.

their simplicity and familiarity. (One is unable to notice something – because it is always before one's eyes.)"[20]

§0b   *Walter Benjamin's* Arcades

In this book, we're going to look at things whose meanings are at times so ordinary that they tend to disappear from sight. "Quotidian" is the word we like – mundane, unexceptional, but also omnipresent, dependable.

A: Arcades
B: Fashion
D: Boredom
F. Iron Construction
O: Gambling
P: The Streets of Paris
R: Mirrors
U: Railroads
V: Conspiracies
Y: Photography[21]

These are some quotidian things mentioned in the index to thirty-something folders of notes on cards by a man who had been spending his days in the *Bibliothèque Nationale* in Paris – reading, copying quotations onto cards, taking down references and writing down ideas as they sprang to his mind. Walter Benjamin,[*] German Jewish writer and intellectual, had fled from Berlin to Paris in 1933 when the Nazis came to power.

The card index marks the conquest of three-dimensional writing ... Today the book is already, as the present mode of scholarly production demonstrates, an outdated mediation between two different filing systems. For everything that matters is to be found in the card box of the researcher who wrote it, and the scholar studying it assimilates it into his own card index ... Writing, advanc[es] ever more deeply into the graphic regions of its new eccentric figurativeness ... In this picture writing, poets ... will only be able to participate by mastering the fields in which (quite unobtrusively) it is being constructed: the statistical and technical diagram.[22]

Benjamin's project was to write a book that may have been called, had it been completed and published, *Paris: Capital of the Nineteenth Century.* This

[*] http://meaningpatterns.net/benjamin-convolutes

[20] Ludwig Wittgenstein, 1953 [2001], *Philosophical Investigations*, translated by G.E.M. Anscombe, Oxford, UK: Blackwell, §129.

[21] Walter Benjamin, 1999, *The Arcades Project*, translated by H. Eidland and K. McLaughlin, Cambridge, MA: Harvard University Press, p. 29.

[22] Walter Benjamin, 1925 [1979], "One Way Street," pp. 45–106 in *One Way Street and Other Writings*, London: Verso, pp. 62–63.

is the title he gave to two summaries he sent to his project sponsors, Theodor Adorno[§AS1.4.2b] and Max Horkheimer – Jewish intellectual friends from the School for Social Research in Frankfurt. They had already left Germany and joined the New School for Social Research in New York, the "University in Exile."

In his notes and communications, Benjamin called this work the "Arcades Project." The shopping arcade was a key motif in his evocation of nineteenth-century Paris, glass-roofed pedestrian streets, bristling with the allure of commodities artfully laid out in the shop windows, window shoppers casually passing by, imagining what they might buy, or imagining themselves with what they might not be able to buy. As the research went on, the folders of notes grew thicker.[23]

Each of these folders, Adorno later gave the German word *Konvolut* – a sheaf or a bundle. The editors of the English language translation created the word "convolute" to name these bundles, "as the most evocative term for designating the elaborately intertwined collections of 'notes and materials'."[24] "Convolute A: Arcades," then thirty-five more.

The plan for the work was sorted into several iterations. Two project summaries were written. Here are some ideas in a 1935 project summary:

I

Iron, as the first artificial building material
Theory of education as the root of utopia

II

The welcoming of photography
Rear-guard action by art against technology

III

The world exhibition of 1867; triumph of cynicism
The universal extension of the commodity character to the world of things . . .

VI

The end of the arcades
The political function of fashion; critique of crinoline[25]

Then, in the summer of 1940, the Nazis invaded France and entered Paris. Benjamin's friends in New York had arranged an entry visa to the US, wanting him to join them at their University in Exile. He headed to the Spanish border.

---

[23] Ursula Marx, Gundrun Schwarz, Michael Schwarz, and Ermut Wizisla, eds., 2007, *Walter Benjamin's Archive*, translated by E. Leslie. London, UK: Verso, p. 260.

[24] Howard Eidland and Kevin McLaughlin, 1999, "Translators' Foreword," in *The Arcades Project*, Cambridge, MA: Harvard University Press, p. xiv.

[25] Ursula Marx, Gundrun Schwarz, Michael Schwarz, and Ermut Wizisla, eds., 2007, *Walter Benjamin's Archive*, translated by E. Leslie, London, UK: Verso, p. 229.

There he and some other exiles, including a Mrs. Gurland and her son, found people who could show them a path over the Pyrenees.

Lisa Fittko tells "The Story of Old Benjamin," though he wasn't old. He was 48.

I do remember everything that happened; I think I do ... Is it possible to step back into those times when there was no time for remembering what normal life was like, those days when we adapted to chaos and struggled for survival? ...

Mrs. Gurland's son, José – he was about fifteen years old – and I took turns carrying the black bag; it was awfully heavy ... Old Benjamin: under no circumstances would he part with his ballast, that black bag; we would have to drag the monster across the mountain ... José and I took him between us; with his arms on our shoulders, we dragged him and the bag up the hill. He breathed heavily, yet he made no complaint, not even a sigh. He only kept squinting in the direction of the black bag ...

We passed a puddle. The water was greenish slimy and stank. Benjamin knelt down to drink.

"You can't drink this water," I said, "it is filthy and contaminated." ...

"I do apologize," Benjamin said, "but I have no choice. If I do not drink, I might not be able to continue to the end." ...

"Listen to me," I said, " ... You will get typhus".

"True, I might. But don't you see, the worst that can happen is that I can die of typhus AFTER crossing the border. The Gestapo won't be able to get me, and the manuscript will be safe."[26]

When the Spanish border post came into sight in the valley below, Lisa Fittko turned back and Benjamin walked on to the border with the others in the small party.

New orders from Madrid, the border guards said, no entry to Spain without a French exit visa, the group was to be sent back to France. That night, Benjamin took an overdose of morphine. The next day, shaken by the death, the guards let the rest of Benjamin's party through.

No bag, no manuscript was found. Gershom Scholem, Benjamin's closest friend, said (ambiguously, contradictorily), "There is no manuscript ... Until now, nobody knew such a manuscript existed."[27]

We're interested in the materiality of text, as well as what it said, or might have said. There was something more ordinarily weighty in this bag, if there was a bag. Meanwhile, to keep them from falling into the hands of the Gestapo,

[26] Lisa Fittko, 1980 [1999], "The Story of Old Benjamin," pp. 946–54 in *The Arcades Project*, edited by H. Eidland and K. McLaughlin, Cambridge, MA: Harvard University Press, pp. 946, 950, 952.

[27] Walter Benjamin, 1999, *The Arcades Project*, translated by H. Eidland and K. McLaughlin, Cambridge, MA: Harvard University Press, p. 953.

librarian Georges Bataille hid the convolutes away in the *Bibliothèque Nationale*.[28] Adorno brought them to New York in 1947.

§0c   *Bundling*

Walter Benjamin's *Arcades* project[§0b] is richly evocative, not only for its explorations of the materiality of streets and buildings and shopping and commodities in the iconic city of the nineteenth century, but also for its intricate material formlessness. From these quotidian raw materials, Benjamin was going to shape a philosophical history of modernity. Each object, so ordinary, was to illuminate deeper meanings. However, we are left today to read a book that does not exist. Benjamin left a kind of a ruin, a miniature version of the ruin of Europe left by his nemesis, the Nazis.

This is how we have been left to decipher the bundles of notes. They are a fertile place to imagine what Benjamin's masterwork may have said. We read the summary and the categories of classification for clues. We read the cryptic insights that may have later become continuous prose. The richness of meaning in this philosophy of ordinary things arises as we try to fill in the absences.

Benjamin's meanings are important for us, for their insights into objects and their seeing, into media, and the persistent understanding he and his Frankfurt School colleagues developed. The structures of inequality, and their necessary occlusions, lay at the heart of the travesty, the betrayal of human possibility that was modern life.

In the book you are reading now we've collected examples of meaning and discussions by significant thinkers about meaning and put them in five bundles, in this introductory part, then at greater length in the parts that follow and its companion volume, *Adding Sense*. We have put together examples of the ways in which ordinary meanings are manifest and the concepts they exemplify, highlighting the multimodal play between texts, images, spaces, bodies, gestures, sounds, and speech. We interrogate their ordinariness by juxtaposing the ideas of thinkers who have striven to make sense of, and beyond, the ordinary.

And, as much as we are committed to theoretical work in the spirit of Benjamin, we're also constrained by the affordance of text (as was he, in the works he finished), where one word unforgivingly follows another. But the interconnections run every which way, like a card index – or a database. Benjamin's convolutes presciently foretell the database, where today we have machines to help us to assemble sense from scraps of information.

---

[28] Hannah Arendt, 1968 [1973], "Introduction," in *Walter Benjamin*, edited by H. Arendt, London, UK: Fontana, p. 17.

In our rough bundling, we gesture towards multilinear connections that defy straightforward textual rendering, but there are innumerably more, including many that you, dear reader, may notice but we have not.

§0d   Supermarket Order

Most of the time, the things in a supermarket[§AS2.3f] are only put in one place, alongside other things that it makes a kind of rough sense to be near. It makes sense that you might find the yoghurt somewhere near the milk. Less obviously perhaps, experience and instinct also tell you that you are more likely to find the dishwashing detergent nearer the pet food than the milk. We know that some things more or less go together.[*]

Benjamin's convolutes were, by accident of genocide, never synthesized into a book. In the Arcades Project, we are left with the contiguities of a card index, each card distinct but left at one place in the convolute according to its rough-best fit. The space of the supermarket and the medium of the card index demand selection of a single location – physically, practically. In ordinary life, the meaning connections are of course much less definitive than the logic of singular contiguity that such spaces and media practically demand.

In sifting through the ways meanings of ordinary life are expressed, this book creates the same oversimplifications as the supermarket or card index. Our medium demands that we put things alongside each other. The best we can do is throw things together into a rough-best fit. So, in our five parts about meaning functions (Fig. 0d(i)), we put reference beside agency, agency beside structure, structure beside context, and context beside interest. All five always happen together, but to make the analytical distinctions we have to discuss one at a time. Each of these pairs seems, more or less, to go together, though there are a myriad of cross-connections.

This book is organized around these meaning functions, which is why the meaning forms (text, image, space, object, body, sound, and speech) are mixed up across the parts of this book, appearing as exemplifications of the meaning

Meaning Functions
Reference
Agency
Structure
Context
Interest

Fig. 0d(i): Meaning functions

[*] http://meaningpatterns.net/supermarket-order

functions in the five parts (Fig. 0d(ii)). We might have also sorted them into supermarket order, and if we had, we would have placed text beside image, image beside space, space beside object, object beside body, body beside sound, sound beside speech – this is the way we organized the *Literacies* book.[29] There, we deliberately put speech a long way away from text – and we do this again now – if only to make a point contrary to much conventional wisdom, that these two modes

Meaning *Forms*	Text	Image	Space	Object	Body	Sound	Speech

Fig. 0d(ii): Meaning forms

are as different from each other as any of the meaning forms. In fact, in important respects, text is more like image (it is image) which is close to space; and speech is more like sound (it is sound) which is close to body.

These seven meaning forms support representation (making sense to oneself) and communication (making sense to others). They are the stuff of representation and communication. They render, they embody, they express, meanings. To render is to make manifest, in the mind or using media. Meaning forms are renderings of our thinking, or resources for thinking. They are forms of action. They are kinds of work, mental and physical. They are objects that we make in material or mental reality, at the same time as they are expressions of our will and identities as subjects.

Then there are the processes of transposition that tie forms and functions together. Meanings can be re-represented and re-communicated across the different forms, though never in the same way – this is why we must have multimodality.

And functions are simultaneous, kinds of attention to meaning that are always open to transposition, one perspective on meaning for one moment, then another for a different moment. Then, within each of the functions, meanings are always ready to move. For example: a single instance is always ready for transposition when classified into a multiplicity captured by concepts;[§1.1] or "I" transposes for "you"[§2.2] in the case of empathy.[§AS2.5b]

More than ready, meanings beg transposition. This is written into their nature.

---

[29] Mary Kalantzis, Bill Cope, Eveline Chan, and Leanne Dalley-Trim, 2016, *Literacies* (Edn 2), Cambridge, UK: Cambridge University Press.

§0.1   Participation

> **Participation.** *The making of meaning in the context of the social relations of its sharing – whether it is representation (making meanings for oneself); communication (making meanings that are accessible to others); or interpretation (making sense of meanings in the found objects of multimodal communication).*

Making sense involves three kinds of action: representing, communicating, and interpreting.[*] These are not merely things of the mind or sign systems. They are kinds of social participation.[§AS1.2]

They also require work. They use material tools and media for their work, as is the habit of our species, otherwise known as *homo faber*. They are things you do to mean, and the things you need to use for that meaning, in the context of shared conditions of sociability.[§AS2.4]

Participation is a series of anticipations of imminent movement. Representation is ever-ready for its communication, and representation is always ripe for its interpretation. The meaning of each dimension of participation is in the begging-to-be-transposed that runs across the three. However, these meanings, though connected, can never be quite the same. Transposition makes for transformation.

§0.1.1   Representation

> **Representation.** *Doing things to make sense for oneself, in thought and action – where individual bodies and minds re-enact the social and manipulate material media either in physical realty or their minds' eyes in order to make personal meaning.*

Representation[§AS1.2.1] is the process of making meanings for oneself, using meaning forms that are rendered in externalized media, or internalized patterns of reflection that recreate these meaning forms in the mind. The process of meaning-making always entails representation, where the meaning forms work as cognitive prostheses, externalized media or internalized mental reflections that rehearse the using of externalized media, patterning action and extending memory.

Externalized media: one might make or use, just for oneself, a list, a diagram, a wayfinding path through a building, a tool, a gesture, a sound connected with action, or one might talk or gesture to oneself in silent speech. These are internalized mental reflections working in concert with externalizing media.

---

[*] http://meaningpatterns.net/participation

Or perhaps this is just a matter of playing through the externalizations in one's mind's eye, ear, or body. Then, these are mental constructs, cognitive renderings that nevertheless derive from a life experience of renderings in tangible media – thinking of a written word, a mental image, an anticipation of space, the to-be-expected feel of an object, a sense of embodiment, an expectation of sound, or silent speech.

In these ways, the philosophy of ordinary meanings underpinning our multi-modal grammar is also a theory of processes of thinking, where we use externalized media as cognitive tools, and where our internalized mental representations are derivative of practices that have in the first instance developed using externalized media. This book is an account of these acts of meaning. It connects with and adds to a science of the mind, developing a social psychology grounded in a socio-historical account of human meaning-making practices.

Wittgenstein[§2.1.1a] calls the meanings we have named representations, "private."[30] But they are hardly that to the extent that the forms and functions of representation are the products of social life and human history. Another person may more or less anticipate your private meanings based on shared experience or knowable differences in experience. Or they may get it wrong, or never know. But when they fail to know, the reasons are more interestingly social than their apparent privateness.

Representation always comes before communication. Already, a lot of meaning has been made, and without (yet) communication. Representation happens without (necessary) communication.

§0.1.2 Communication

> **Communication.** *Encounters with the material traces of meanings made by others – texts, images, spaces, objects, bodies, sounds, speech. The forms of these traces that can be received by others as meaningful.*

Communication[§AS1.2.2] happens when one meaning-maker encounters meaning forms made by another. The externalized artifacts of one meaning-maker may be encountered by others, by accident or design, by one or many others.

Communication is an event analytically distinct from representation, even though representation and communication may happen, not just serially and separately, but in parallel or unitary spaces and times. For instance, you often think just before you speak (representation before communication), and then of course you keep thinking as you speak (representation during communication).

---

[30] Ludwig Wittgenstein, 1953 [2001], *Philosophical Investigations*, translated by G.E.M. Anscombe, Oxford, UK: Blackwell, §§243, 358.

§0.1.3   Interpretation

> ***Interpretation.*** *Making sense of found objects of communicated meaning, an act of re-representation where the communicated meaning is never a matter of unmediated transmission; rather the meaning is in what we make of the object of communication, a relation between that object and the interpreter's making of it.*

Interpretation[§AS1.2.3] is the process of making sense of meanings when they are encountered, be they human-made or natural.

Communication is never straightforward transmission of meaning. It involves re-representation, this time by an other. This other encounters the first other's externalized artifact of representation, the meaning form they have rendered or made manifest in media: text, image, space, object, body, sound, speech. Representation always precedes communication, and interpretation of communicated meaning entails another representation.

Interpretation, or re-representation, never aligns precisely with the original representation, and the nature and extent of the disjunction becomes a focal point for uncertainty and bad faith. "Communication" never lives up to its promise.

Nor does a human agent have to be involved as the communicator. Nature "speaks," in the form of patterns of matter, movement, and life that we may encounter and interpret. In other words, interpretation does not necessarily follow human communication. There is a great deal of meaning without human communication.

We say this because, in the history of linguistics, visual analysis, and media studies, there is a lot of emphasis on communication. We want to rebalance the emphasis to encompass also representation and interpretation.

§0.2   Meaning Form

> ***Meaning Form.*** *The means by which meaning is made, the media through which representation or communication occurs, where thinking or thinkable things are expressed in text, image, space, object, body, sound, and speech.*

Meaning takes shape through a series of actions that connect thinking with material media.[§AS1.0.1] Text uses writing instruments, representing phonemes and ideographs in graphemes on paper or screen. Image creates two-dimensional visual meanings on canvas, or paper, or screen. Space and object create three-dimensional meanings. Meanings are made in and by bodies. Sound and speech present meanings in hearable form.

§0.2.1   Text

> **Text.** *Meanings made by combining graphemes, the elemental, character-level components of writing, as documented in Unicode. Graphemes can be phonemic, referencing sounds, or ideographic, referencing an idea or material thing.*

The textual form[§AS1.4.7] is represented and communicated in written script. Many definitions of text are broader than this. Images, for instance, are by some conceived as text, or an integral part of text. Our conversations might be conceived as texts. If we went broader still, metaphorically speaking, life is a text. But by this time we are eliding just too many things for the word "text" to be particularly helpful.

We want to narrow our definition because there are some important distinctions that we would like to make between the various meaning forms, and particularly between writing and speech. Writing is very different from speech, in fact as different from speech as it is from image. Of course there are parallels, and that is what this grammar of multimodality is about – the major functional parallels that we call reference, agency, structure, context, and interest. But the parallels between speech and writing are no stronger than any of the others.

For the digital age, we can rely on a very precise definition of textual form: those meanings that can be encoded using the elemental components of meaning-rendering documented in Unicode.[§0.2.1a]

The elemental component of text is a grapheme, the minimally meaningful constrastive unit in text. Graphemes can refer either to a sound (a phoneme, such as the letter "a"), or to an idea or a material thing (an ideograph, such as the number "7," a Chinese character, an emoji).

§0.2.1a Unicode

Unicode is a comprehensive character set documenting all systems of written text.[31] Of the 136,755 characters in Unicode version 10, a few are: a, A, 7, ?, @, 威, ی and ☺. For writing that is principally alphabetic, graphemes mostly represent sounds. In other scripts characters mainly represent ideas, such as in Chinese where each character is an ideograph – although the distinction is not so clear, because for writers in mainly alphabetic languages 7, @ and ☺ are ideographs, and utterable sounds can be represented in Chinese. Unicode includes symbolic scripts that range from Japanese dentistry symbols to the

---

[31] http://unicode.org/

recycle symbol, and 2,623 emojis.[§AS1.1.1a] It also includes obscure historical scripts, like Linear A, an as-yet undeciphered written script of Ancient Greece.[*]

Unicode was a name coined by Joseph Becker in 1988, a researcher in the Xerox lab in Palo Alto, California.[32] In 1984, he had written a seminal article for *Scientific American* on multilingual word processing,[33] and in 1987–88 was working with a colleague at Xerox, Lee Collins, and Mark Davis at Apple. A Unicode Working Group formed in 1989, Microsoft, Sun, IBM, and other companies soon joining, creating today's Unicode Consortium in 1991. At its first release in October 1991, Unicode consisted of 7,161 characters. The June 2017 release added 8,518 new characters, bringing the total to 136,755.[34]

In a manner that has become typical of the global governance of digital meanings, companies have eschewed competition to form non-profits that they control so singular and universal agreement can be reached about the means of production, distribution, and exchange of meanings. Representatives from Facebook, Google, Amazon, and Adobe are now on the Unicode Consortium's board of directors.[35]

The details of the Unicode standards have been thrashed out in volunteer subcommittees and conferences since 1991, but the basis of their work is to catalogue thousands of years of human writing practices, as well as new practices such as the use of emojis.[§AS1.1.1a] The participants argue the merits of new candidates for the compendium in obsessively careful detail. The end result is that, for all our apparent uncertainties about meaning in the modern world, there is just one definitive list of the elementary components of all writing, ever – and this is it.

Today, everybody uses Unicode on their phones, web browsers, and word processors. Only the aficionados argue, but even then, the arguments are limited to details and are readily resolvable by consensus. Such are the manners that the players are sometimes able to keep in the backrooms of digital governance.

Most Unicode characters are ideographs; just a few are phonemes, even if the relatively few phonemes in the character set still get a lot of use. By the time we reach dentistry symbols and emojis in Unicode, we encounter ways of meaning that are getting close to image. There has been a tendency in the digital age to move our character set towards ideographs – not only numbers, but symbols and emojis of internationalization in our contemporary multilingual spaces, the navigational icons in user interfaces, and visual design that marks the larger

---

[*] http://meaningpatterns.net/unicode

[32] Joseph D. Becker, 1988, "Unicode 88," Palo Alto, CA: Xerox Corporation.
[33] Joseph D. Becker, 1984, "Multilingual Word Processing," *Scientific American* 251(1):96–107.
[34] www.unicode.org/history/summary.html.   [35] www.unicode.org/consortium/directors.html.

textual architectures of the page and the screen. "We are all becoming Chinese,"[36] says Jack Goody,[§AS1.4.7a] anthropologist of writing, flowers, and love, if only half in jest.

One of the underlying reasons for this convergence with image is that the digitized images of characters are manufactured in the same way as all other images, by the composition of pixels. These are invisible to the casual viewer, only to become visible as conceptual wholes – as a character in writing or a picture. The fact that writing and images are today made of the same stuff brings them closer together for the most pragmatic of reasons in the media of their manufacture and distribution. They can easily sit beside each other on the same screen or digitally printed surface, or they can layer over each other.

These are some of the mundanely practical reasons why, in the era of digital meaning, we put text beside image in our listing of meaning forms, and not speech as might be conventionally expected. And there are other reasons, the most profound of which is that we see writing but hear speech. Writing is close to image, whereas speech is close to sound. This has always been the case. But today the conjunctions are closer than ever, providing a practical rationale for why today we need to disaggregate "language" in a grammar of multimodality.

§0.2.1b Learning to Read

There is a conventional idea in the practice of teaching literacy in alphabetic scripts, that writing is a transliteration of speech. The twenty-six letters of the English alphabet, plus letter combinations, transliterate forty-four possible sounds. Learning to read is a matter of learning to decode letters (graphemes) into sounds (phonemes). Then, you'll be able to read! Or so the advocates of phonics tell us, in their rhetorical "basics" of literacy.

The reality is different. The range of sounds and sound combinations formed in English syllables runs to thousands. The forty-four sounds of phonics instruction are only a crude rendering of writing into speech.[37]

Nor could a person read by sounding out every letter in every word. This would be impossibly slow and laborious. It would interfere with the flow of meaning to the point of making reading nearly impossible. So, we learn to see the shape of whole words.[38] In reality, we have a character set of thousands because the elementary unit of reading is the whole word – just like Chinese.

---

[36] In conversation, at our Third International Conference on New Directions in the Humanities, Cambridge University, August 2–5, 2005.

[37] Catherine E. Snow, M. Susan Burns, and Peg Griffin, eds., 1998, *Preventing Reading Difficulties in Young Children*, Washington, DC: National Academy Press, p. 22; Jeanne S. Chall, 1967 [1983], *Learning to Read: The Great Debate*, New York, NY: McGraw-Hill.

[38] Frank Smith, 2004, *Understanding Reading: A Psycholingustic Analysis of Reading and Learning to Read*, Mahwah, NJ: Lawrence Erlbaum, pp. 143–46; Alan H. Schoenfeld and P. David Pearson, 2009, "The Reading and Math Wars," pp. 560–80 in *Handbook of Education*

Then there is another pressure in the digital era pushing writing away from the phonics of alphabetical languages. This is the phenomenon of powerful symbolic languages that underlie our digital representations and communication – computer code, the mathematics of algorithmically generated meanings, and the semantics of textual markup (HTML, XML, and such like).[§AS1.4.7d] These represent their meanings with elementary units or graphemes that work as ideographs, not phonemes. Again, we're all becoming Chinese, kind of.

§0.2.2   Image

> **Image.** *Two-dimensional meanings made in line, form, and color in a range of media, reproducible and renderable digitally through the array of pixels.*

Beside textual form, for these reasons, we have placed image[§AS1.4.6] or visual form, by which we mean two-dimensional renderings of the world-as-seen. Elemental components of imaging include line, form, and color. Using externalized media, we diagram, we draw, we paint, we photograph. In our mind's eye, we see mental images. By various tricks of rendering and interpolation, we represent three-dimensionality on a two-dimensional plane – with linear perspective, for instance,[§2.2b] or in plans. In the digital era, all two-dimensional images can be manufactured in "pixels," or picture elements across a color spectrum.[§1.3.1h]

"The mountains loomed large," we might write, and we can show a picture too.[§0] And when we do, we may mean the same mountains. Anything that can be written can also be shown, hence the parallelism between writing and pictures. All the functions of meaning that can be rendered in writing – reference, agency, structure, context, and interest – can also be rendered in image.

Yet there are also irreducible differences. As Gunther Kress[§AS2c] tells us, speaking consists of sequential meaning elements, moving forward relentlessly in time, one word after the other. Reading also prioritizes time, because its line-by-line presentation takes us through time. Image, by contrast, presents to us a number of meaning-elements simultaneously. Its viewing path prioritizes space.[39] (Actually, reading is not so timebound, and to the extent that it is closer to image, also is architected around vision – hence tables of contents and indexes,

Policy Research, edited by G. Sykes, B. Schneider, and D.N. Plank, New York: Routledge; Mary Kalantzis, Bill Cope, Eveline Chan, and Leanne Dalley-Trim, 2016, *Literacies* (Edn 2), Cambridge, UK: Cambridge University Press, pp. 255–60.

[39] Gunther Kress, 2009, *Multimodality: A Social Semiotic Approach to Contemporary Communication*, London, UK: Routledge, p. 99.

or speed reading versus close reading, the image-alignment of text thus affording greater flexibility in time than listening.)

Notwithstanding their priorities, writing and image are equally capable of representing time and space. But they do it differently, the one at times with greater ease than the other. When we put both together, we may attain a fuller, more nuanced meaning, or for that matter, a less settled meaning, perhaps perceptively so, or deceptively.

We may pay the price of redundancy of meaning, or live its insights and pleasures. Such are the dangers and rewards of multimodality.

§0.2.3   Space

> **Space.** *Three-dimensional meanings, navigable by human actors, and that can be represented and rendered digitally in 3D design and geosurvey.*

When we consider space[§AS1.4.5] as a meaning form, we want to make a simple distinction between the two-dimensional renderings of image and the three-dimensional renderings of space. A building renders meaning according to its spatial affordances – a house differently from a classroom, differently from a shop, differently from a library.

We internalize spatial meaning in our anticipations of action (representation). Spatial meaning is communicated at the point at which the shape of our action is patterned by the resistances and openings in the space, expected or unexpected. The same happens on a larger scale in landscapes and with travel.

Elements of space include volume, boundary, layout, proximity. In a larger frame of reference, we encounter geographies, landscapes, and ecosystems. Stasis, flow, and wayfinding offer dimensions of time to the experience of space. If space is analogous to vocabulary, flow is analogous to syntax.

We place space alongside image in our metaphorical supermarket or convolute[§0d] because image renders three-dimensional space by many means – using perspective in a picture, for instance, or in plans that are coordinated with projections, or with glasses for 3D cinema.

In the digital era, 3D design, GPS,[§AS1.3.2b] and digital geosurvey technologies offer unprecedented capacities to represent space.

§0.2.4   Object

> **Object.** *Three-dimensional meanings, tangible and useable things, produced digitally in three-dimensional renderings.*

Next to space in our metaphorical "supermarket"[§0d] of meanings we place object,[§AS1.4.4] because these objects are located in space and share with space their three-dimensionality. Objects have meaning to us, and give meaning to us by their presence or in their application – the utensils or tools we use, the food we eat, the furniture which positions our bodies, the toys we play with, the objects around which games are centered, and the pencils or phones or computers by means of which we make meanings across time and distance. We see, touch, smell, and taste objects. We feel temperature, pressure, texture, and pain. Objects have surfaces, edges, and textures. They have shapes and sizes.

Viscerally, we grasp, manipulate, and use objects as extensions of ourselves. They are material extensions of our bodies, and when anticipating imminent or imagining possible use, they serve as cognitive prostheses. We use them as props in rituals. Objects may be ours, or they may be someone else's. They may be the products of human artifice, and in this sense they become represented, communicated, and interpreted meanings. Or they may be objects of nature where the meaning is in our interpretation as a relationship to that object. In the digital era, objects may be represented and communicated in a variety of ways, from 3D printing to the "internet of things."[§1.1.1g]

§0.2.5 Body

> *Body. Meanings made by configuring human bodies, where wearable devices now ubiquitously record and communicate bodily meanings across time and space.*

To the extent that objects are bodily extensions, we place body[§AS1.4.3] beside object in our catalogue of meaning forms. The body is where subjectivity meets objectivity, where the person full of feeling meets things that might be felt, literally and figuratively. There is not a separable world of objects, as if "objectivity" could be truth-in-a-thing. Because objects become integral parts of our selves through the processes of our meaning them, there cannot be separable realms of subjectivity and objectivity.

Direct object extensions of the body include fashion, cosmetics, and jewelry. Expressions of bodily meaning include gesticulation, facial expression, gaze, posture, gait, and demeanor. Feelings and emotions are bodily representations of meaning. In the larger frame of reference of a grammar of multimodality, these may be characterized as gesticulation, appearance, and enactment.

In the era of ubiquitous digital "wearables," devices such as smart phones, smart watches, and fitness trackers represent the recordable body in ways that allow us to add layers of interpretation about bodily movement, place, time, and human interconnection. Ubiquitous image- and video-recording devices, geo-location and activity measurement, attached by alerts to any of the billions of bodies with one of these devices, represent and communicate the nuances of embodied location, bodily action, gesture, and demeanor across space and time.

§0.2.6   Sound

> **Sound.** *Hearable meanings, renderable digitally in recordings and transmissions from synthetically created or sampled sound.*

Sound,[AS1.4.2] like object, is experienced viscerally. It is not only hearable but feelable as vibration. The meaning-universe of sound consists of audible alerts, ambient sounds, sounds incidental to action, and music. Aural meanings may be the products of human artifice, or the sounds of nature. The dynamics of sound include pitch, volume, tempo, rhythm, directionality. Digital renderings of sound may take the form of synthetic sounds, or recordings of sound based on sampling of sound signals.

§0.2.7   Speech

> **Speech.** *Voiced meanings, spoken according to phonemic conventions, renderable digitally in recordings and transmissions from synthetically created or sampled sound.*

We put speech[AS1.4.1] beside sound because both are heard. And, since the invention of analogue and now digital technologies for recording and transmission of sound, both use the same technologies for representation and communication across time and space.

Again, we want to separate speaking from writing. Writing is imaging of sorts, and in the digital era both writing and image render in pixels. Speaking is sounding of sorts, and in the digital era both sound and speech render from synthetically created or sampled sound waves. Practically speaking, in the logistics of putting multimodal meanings together, we are more likely to put image with writing, and sound with speech, than speaking with writing. This is simply because image and writing are made of the same stuff, and sound and speech the same stuff.

More profoundly though, the affordances are different: image and writing render in space; sound and speech render across time. Of course, in our deeply multimodal being, writing and speaking are closely related in manifold ways and digitization provides a common platform for them all. But the relations between speech and writing are no closer than to the other meaning forms. We're going to this much trouble to place them apart because we wish to unsettle conventional wisdoms about language in linguistics and other social sciences.

Speech is intrinsically close to sound for the obvious reason that it is rendered in sound. Writing is unable to capture the full, audible dimensionality of intonation, accent, and dialect. A comma can never tell you how poignant the pause, a question mark how insistent the question, underlining how stressed the emphasis. Tonic prominence or sound emphasis tells you the point of a clause (given information/subject), contrasted in a word cluster with audibly more prominent new information/predicate.

Technology also decouples writing and speaking. Until radio, telephone, and the gramophone, writing was the only way language could transcend the limits of time and space for the purposes of representation and communication. Before recording and transmission of sound, it seemed that writing served speech by breaking its intrinsic parochialness. This is what writing uniquely achieved, its defining characteristic as a form of meaning. So speech and writing had this special complementarity. This is one reason why linguists and others were likely to think that writing must mostly be a transliteration of speech. Speech needed writing as an extension of is capacities to span space and time. However, with recording and transmission, speech is just as readily communicable over distance, and representable across time, from the past and into the future. Writing then lost its privileged relation to speech. There could no longer be any illusion that writing serves speech in the ways that were esteemed in the past.

§0.2.7a *M.A.K. Halliday on the Differences Between Speech and Writing*

Speech and writing are different in the very processes of their representation and communication. Their grammars, M.A.K. Halliday[0.3a] says, are fundamentally different. Speech, he says, strings information units one after the other, connecting them with words that link roughly equivalent things (such as "and," "or," "then") and logical connectives that link things where a difference needs to be highlighted (such as "until," "as," "to," "because," "if," "to," "which").

Writing, on the other hand, uses nominalization, packing an idea that might have been a whole spoken clause into a noun or a noun phrase inside a written clause. "People should be able to bring" in an oral text about opportunities to bring their capacities to a task, becomes "provides an outlet" in the written text. Writing performs the logical task of connecting ideas in a way quite different from speaking. Each is just as intricate as a meaning-design. It is just that they are very different kinds of intricacy. They are different ways of seeing the world and thinking about the world.

There are also characteristic differences in the orientations of meaning-makers to the world. Speaking is full of statements like "I think," "in my opinion," "I'm sure," "you see?," and "you know?" which make the interactive stance of the participants more visible than is mostly the case for writing. Speech will more often use the active voice, in which who is doing what to whom is directly stated. ("I went to the party yesterday, and I found it interesting to meet lots of new people.") In these and other ways, speaking makes the interest-laden role of the speaker more explicit.

A writer, on the other hand, is more likely to choose the passive voice, and is also more likely to choose third person to refer to events. The writer may be referring to the same thing as a speaker, but writers tend to create the impression that objects and events have a life of their own. ("Yesterday's party was well attended, with many new faces.") This is how writing has an aura of objectivity while speaking has an aura of subjectivity. Writing, explains Halliday, is inclined to represent the world more as a product; speaking more as a process. Speech is more spun out, flowing, choreographic, and oriented to events (doing, happening, sensing, saying, being). It is more process-like, with meanings related serially. Writing is dense, structured, crystalline, and oriented towards things (entities, objectified processes). It is product-like and tight, with meanings related as components.[40]

Of course, when writing has this aura of objectivity, this is more a matter of rhetorical effect,[§AS2.1] an impression you are expected to get, rather than an intrinsic reality. Information writers may want you to think that they are speaking facts or expert argument, though just to be writing they must have a lot invested personally and subjectively. Speakers, by comparison, are mostly more explicit about their subjective, immediate, here-and-now connection with their meanings. "You know, I reckon …, " they might characteristically say when they frame a statement. When the speaker is in the presence of the listener, it is hard for them not to make explicit their personal investment in what they are saying.

There are also important differences in the ways speaking and writing make reference and point to context. In oral conversation, "I" or "you," "this" or "that," "here" or "there," "today" or "yesterday" are all relative to the speaking participants, their time, and their place. In terms of our classification of functions, oral meaning is carried by context. Writing, however, first has to name "I", "you," "this," "that," "here," "there," "today," and "yesterday" before these

---

[40] M.A.K. Halliday, 1987 [2002], "Spoken and Written Modes of Meaning," pp. 323–51 in *On Grammar*, The Collected Works of M.A.K. Halliday, Volume 1, edited by J.J. Webster, London, UK: Continuum, pp. 327–35, 344, 350.

words can be used. In terms of our classification of functions, written meaning is carried to greater extent by structure, or internal reference, than by context, or external reference.[41]

Then there are other fundamental differences in the manner of construction of speech and writing, which in practical ways determine their architecture. Speech is full of repetitions and errors that are corrected audibly and on-the-fly. A writer removes repetitions and erases errors visually. Speech is linear because sound is rendered in time, clause stitched onto preceding clause, one stitch at a time. Writing is multilinear because it is rendered visually. "She" refers to a woman named some place earlier in the text, and multiple "she"s point back to the same reference – visualize pronoun references as lines across the text, and you will see the multilinearity.

Hierarchical information architectures are created in written text by clauses that are nested into sentences into paragraphs into sections into parts or articles into books or magazines. These are explicitly marked in an essentially visual arrangement. The logical structures of information texts, arguments, and narratives can also be diagrammed demonstrating that they too do not simply work in linear and sequential ways. These are some of the underlying reasons why writers keep writing over text, backwards and forwards, eliminating redundancy, refining the logic of their text by revising the spatial presentation of their meaning.

Planning is followed by drafting and editing. Visual arrangement takes priority over the sequence of text-making actions. If writing were to be like speaking, the reader would replay the writer's keystrokes, revealing the hesitations and the changes. This would get in the way of communication, and surely the writer would not want the distracting messiness of their interim thinking to be made visible. Writing is carefully arranged in a visual form across the canvas of space, where speech is sound, tied to the arrow of time.

Today, the multilinear and visual processes of text construction are intensified by digitization, affording writers the infinite flexibility and efficiencies of being able to work back over text without having to rekey a single character unnecessarily. Written digital text is more visual and more framed by multilinear processes of construction than ever. It is more different from speaking than ever.

Now, something has crept up on us in the drift of this argument. In this grammar we're not going to need to talk about a thing called "language" that crosses speech and writing. In fact, to speak of language is to conflate some crucial distinctions – distinctions that are all-the-more important in the era of

---

[41] Mary Kalantzis, Bill Cope, Eveline Chan, and Leanne Dalley-Trim, 2016, *Literacies* (Edn 2), Cambridge, UK: Cambridge University Press, pp. 409–14.

digital media. You'll hear almost nothing of language for the rest of this book, and the one that follows.

§0.2.8 Multimodality

> ***Multimodality.*** *Meanings that simultaneously render in more than one meaning form (text, image, space, object, body, sound, and speech), motivated by shared meaning functions (reference, agency, structure, context, and interest).*

Text, image, space, object, body, sound, and speech are distinct meaning systems. They have different "grammars," to extend by metaphor a word that usually refers to the syntax of text. By "grammar," we mean "meaning pattern."

Anything and everything can be meant in each meaning form. However, each meaning form has distinctive affordances. Each has relative strengths for particular kinds of meaning-making. Each has habitual tendencies.

Meanings are transposable across forms – the same meaning can be expressed in multiple forms. But in the transposition, the meaning is never quite the same. Each form is partial. Its media have affordances, which offer both opportunities for meaning and constraints. This is why we need multimodality,[§AS1.0.3] why we habitually transpose meanings. Multimodal transposition is in our natures.

Notwithstanding the differences between the forms of meaning and the practical necessity of multimodality, there are strong relations between contiguous meaning forms in our list, between text and image, image and space, space and object, object and body, body and sound, and sound and speech.

In the everyday realities of representation and communication, meaning forms are layered into each other, simultaneously supporting each other – not just contiguous meanings, but a wide range of deeply integrated layerings, right across the spectrum. They meld into each other. They have close dependencies and integral hybridities.

Just to look at the forms, this process is additive, text with image, or object in space, or gesture with speech. The meanings may be complementary in their angles on meaning. Or they may be redundant (helpfully or wastefully) in their repetitive framing of meaning, in one form as well as another.

Theories of multimodality often just describe how this goes with that, and they do this in a simply additive way. In our grammar of multimodality, we want to build an integrative account, explaining the dynamics of "multi" in the underlying shared patterns of meaning function and their transpositions. In any one moment of meaning, multimodality is driven by a shared attention to reference, agency, structure, context, and interest. Meaning forms are combined to achieve these shared ends.

§0.2.9 Synesthesia

> **Synesthesia.** *Representational processes of reframing a meaning from one meaning form to another.*

We want to use the word "synesthesia" to characterize the representational process of reframing a meaning from one form to another. In psychology, the term is used narrowly to describe a condition where a person associates one sensation with another, a sound with a color, for instance. We use the word more broadly, as the cognitive and practical process of transferring a meaning from one form to another.[42]

Multimodality and synesthesia are essential to our expressively human natures. However, notwithstanding the realities of contiguous, overlapping, hybrid, and crossover forms, the analytical distinctions still need to be made between forms. Each has an archetypical grammar.

To return to the example of written and oral forms,[§0.2.7a] there are many crossover forms – reading aloud, music lyrics, theater dialogue, technical or academic talk, text messaging, instant messages, social media activity stream posts, tweets, emails, or quoted direct speech, for instance. This does not undermine the strong distinction we want to make between speaking and writing as meaning forms. These hybrid meaning-practices do not reduce the canonical differences. Rather, they are examples of multimodality, where two quite different meaning forms are brought together and for the most practical of reasons, the very differences in form that make for complementarity in multimodal meaning.

Digital technologies of representation and communication intensify these processes of multimodality and synesthesia. They offer, as never before in the history of media, a common platform for the construction and rendering of meaning in multiple forms. The forms become more permeable and more malleable than ever. A wider range of forms becomes accessible to a wider of range of people for their practices of representation and communication. But for the greater access, the gains we seem to be making as a partly self-made species seem small.

§0.2.9a *Alexander Bogdanov's* Philosophy of Living Experience

Alexander Bogdanov's *Philosophy of Living Experience* was published in three Russian editions between 1913 and 1923, after which for a century it disappeared into obscurity. It was not translated into English until 2016.[43] This idea,

---

[42] Ibid., pp. 233–4.
[43] Alexander Bogdanov, 1923 [2016], *The Philosophy of Living Experience: Popular Outlines*, translated by D.G. Rowley, Leiden, NL: Brill.

"living experience," is a central one for us in this book. Our account of meaning, our transpositional grammar, is a philosophy of living experience and its ordinary meanings.

Born Alexander Alexandrovich Malinovsky, Bogdanov joined Russia's underground Social Democratic Labor Party in the 1890s and changed his surname to a pseudonym. "Bogdanov" was his wife's middle name. Fellow revolutionary Vladimir Ilich Ulianov changed his name to "Lenin" at about the same time.

In 1897, Bogdanov wrote *A Short History of Economic Science*, analyzing the authoritarian inequalities of the past and forecasting a future when human toil would be relieved by "automatically regulating machines," a time when people would also travel in "dirigible aircraft," when "the perfection of wireless telegraphy and telephony will create the possibility for people to communicate with each other under any condition, over any distance," and with this, "the gradual abolition of all standards of compulsion."[44] His predictions about flying and communications were prescient, though the communist revolutions of the twentieth century failed to abolish compulsion. Lenin said in a review, "Mr. Bogdanov's book is a remarkable manifestation in our economic literature."[45] Through many editions, the *History of Economic Science* became a leading text in the revolutionary call-to-arms.

The Russian Democratic Labor Party was also a place of endless and raucous dispute – arguments, for instance, about whether the party should take an insurrectionary route to revolution, or a parliamentary one. At the second party congress of 1903, Bogdanov sided with Lenin and joined a newly formed, radical splinter group called the Bolsheviks ("majority"). He was arrested and thrown into prison by the Tsarist government during the failed revolutionary attempt of 1905.

From about 1900, Bogdanov became interested in the work of the Austrian scientists and philosophers Ernst Mach and Richard Avenarius who had argued that the human mind perceives the natural world through bodily sensations. Bogdanov adopted these ideas, and called them "Empiriomonism." He wrote numerous articles, then a three-volume treatise published in 1904–06.[46] *Philosophy of Living Experience* was written in 1910–11 as a more accessible, synoptic account, hence its subtitle: *Popular Outlines*.

---

[44] Alexander Bogdanov, 1919 [1925], *A Short History of Economic Science*, London, UK: Communist Party of Great Britain, pp. 379, 380, 387.

[45] V.I. Lenin, 1898 [1964], "Book Review: A. Bogdanov, a Short Course of Economic Science," pp. 46–54 in *Lenin: Collected Works*, Moscow: Progress Publishers.

[46] Michael M. Boll, 1981, "From Empiriocriticism to Empiriomonism: The Marxist Phenomenology of Aleksandr Bogdanov," *The Slavonic and East European Review* 59 (1):41–58.

"The task of philosophy," says Bogdanov, "consists in harmoniously system-atizing experience, ... clarifying its interconnectedness." In a grammar of experience, the subject is "the collective, humanity"; the predicate is human "effort, activity, labor"; and the object is the "matter" of the world. "An idea is always the product of a certain *abstraction*, i.e. the attenuation and schematiza-tion of experience, the distancing of itself from the living concreteness of experience." "The task of cognition consists in expediently organising experience."

In order to determine the basic tendency of a series of phenomena, it is necessary to "abstract" – i.e. to detach from them, in practice or intellectually – all incidental tendencies connected with their specific variable conditions. For this it is necessary cognitively to *break down* phenomena, to distinguish their general from their particular conditions, and to "analyse" them. In consequence, this method is also called the *"analytic"* method.[47]

In 1905, Bogdanov sent Lenin – then in exile in Finland – the first volume of *Empiriomonism*. Lenin wrote a long, angry letter. Bogdanov returned the letter saying that, for the sake of political unity, he would pretend he had never read it.[48] But Lenin was not going to pretend back.

It was obvious from reading Marx and Engels, said Lenin, that "things and their mental pictures or images arise exclusively from sensations ... Materialism, in full agreement with natural science, takes matter as primary and regards consciousness, thought and sensation as secondary."[49] Lenin spent nearly four hundred pages furiously refuting the heretic Bogdanov, and along with him, the bourgeois sources of Bogdanov's inspiration, Mach and Avenarius.

Bogdanov swallowed the bait of professorial philosophy ... that sensations are func-tions of man's central nervous system ... [and the] absurd denial that the visual image of a tree is a function of the retina ... A philosophy which teaches that physical nature itself is a product [of its conceptualization], is a philosophy of the priests, pure and simple ... The 'empirio-criticists' fill scores of pages with such unutterable trash ... Bogdanov ... has abandoned the materialist standpoint and has thereby inevitably condemned himself to confusions ... Bogdanov's denial of objective truth is agnosticism and subjectivism ... Bogdanov thinks that to speak of the social organisation of experience is 'cognitive socialism.' This is insane twaddle ... Experience is experience. And there are people who take this quasi-erudite rigmarole for true wisdom! ... Bogdanov's philosophy contains nothing but a reactionary muddle ... Bogdanov *absolutely does not know* the history of philosophy ... empty "philosophical" acrobatics ... a stupid and

---

[47] Alexander Bogdanov, 1923 [2016], *The Philosophy of Living Experience: Popular Outlines*, translated by D.G. Rowley, Leiden, NL: Brill, pp. 46, 56, 62, 206, 107.
[48] McKenzie Wark, 2015, *Molecular Red: Theory for the Anthropocene*, London, UK: Verso, p. 5.
[49] V.I. Lenin, 1908 [1947], *Materialism and Empirio-Criticism*, Moscow: Foreign Languages Publishing, pp. 34, 38.

fruitless occupation ... a senseless jumble ... pseudo-erudite quackery ... outrageous distortions of Marxism.[50]

Bogdanov was never able to respond, given the subsequent course of history.

We picked up our copy of Lenin's *Materialism and Empirio-Criticism* online from a second-hand bookstore in Nashville, Tennessee specializing, its website says, in Civil War, Antique Maps, Religion, Genealogy, African Americans, Southern Fiction, Southern History, Children's Literature, First Editions, and Nashville History.[*]

It's not clear how Lenin's book might have ended up there, an arcane tract from the old USSR. Our edition was published in 1947, at the height of Joseph Stalin's rule. Stalin carefully cultivated the cult of the state's founding philosopher-ruler. Only this can explain the frequent republication of such a peculiar tract. Who knows what ordinary Russians or ordinary communists might have made of this long and rambling diatribe, the sole purpose of which was to vilify a long-deleted person.

In the April of 1908, the writer Maxim Gorky brought Lenin, Bogdanov, and other Bolshevik leaders to his villa on the Island of Capri. They fought out their factional differences in conversation and chess. Lenin must have been writing *Materialism and Empirio-Criticism* at this time, because its preface is dated September of that year. Lenin had "the sound of a Hooligan," said Gorky when he read the manuscript.[51] Bogdanov and Lenin by then had differences in revolutionary strategy too. Bogdanov was considered a potential rival leader of the party. He was thrown out of the party in 1909, by which time Lenin had produced plenty of theory to support that decision.

Now out of political action, Bogdanov wrote two science fiction novels set on already-socialist Mars, *Red Star* (1908) and *Engineer Menni* (1913). When the Russian revolution came in October 1917, he was partly rehabilitated. For a time he became a member of the Presidium of the Socialist Institute of Scientific Philosophy attached to Moscow State University. He was the general editor of a new Russian edition of the three volumes of Marx's *Capital* and allowed to set up "Proletarian Culture" schools to train workers in a socialist version of philosophy and history, but this was soon taken away from him when the regime decided to focus on literacy. As the regime hardened its grip, it became suspicious of grassroots initiatives.

In 1924, Bogdanov started a series of scientific experiments with blood transfusion, a suitably apolitical endeavor – he had originally trained as

---

[*] http://meaningpatterns.net/bogdanov

[50] Ibid., pp. 85, 233, 163, 51, 121, 234, 147, 234, 223, 35, 86, 371, 336.
[51] Robert C. Williams, 1986, *The Other Bolsheviks: Lenin and His Critics, 1904–1914*, Bloomington IN: Indiana University Press, p.138.

a doctor. Transfusion was supposed to be a source of bodily and mental rejuvenation. In 1926 he was allowed to start an Institute for Hematology and Blood Transfusions. Bogdanov himself enthusiastically took part in the experiments. In 1928 he contracted tuberculosis following a blood exchange from a student at the institute who carried the disease, but in whom it was currently inactive. Bogdanov died but the student survived.[52]

Bogdanov's *Philosophy of Living Experience* was based on lectures he gave in the socialist worker schools in Bologna and Capri where he taught in 1910–11.[53] Avenarius and Mach, he explained, were overly narrow in their empiricism when they claimed that meanings were singularly derived from sensations of the material world. To this, Bogdanov added the idea, which he attributed to Marx, "that objectivity does not have an absolute but a *socially-practical* meaning."[54] The meanings of material reality do not simply present themselves to us; they are as much constructed by our social and historical frames of reference. Experience is socially organized. Socially practical meaning is layered over sensations of the objective world. Or to rephrase this in contemporary terms, meaning is an act of social cognition.

[C]onsider how *in practical terms* an axe, as a physical body, is distinguished from an axe, as a psychical complex – i.e. a perception or psychical image of it. The axe as a physical body serves to cut wood, but what about the axe as a psychical image? You would say, of course, that it is not useful for cutting wood, and you would be essentially right, but this is not all that could be said . . . But the axe-body . . . [is] located in the same moment of time and at the same point in space both for you and for other people with whom you communicate; it is composed of the same parts and possesses the same qualities, and, in general, presents the same elements in the same interconnectedness. The experience of people regarding it is *socially agreed upon* or – what is the same thing – *socially organised*. But one cannot say that the corporeal axe is identical for all people. For the lumberjack who is working with it all the time, it has a greater sum of qualities than for a tailor who almost never works with it. For a scholar learned in physics and chemistry, it contains a greater number and a greater variety of elements . . . But even so, in the experience of these people there is . . . sufficient agreement for it to be assumed that for the entire collective the corporeal axe is "the same thing." This experience is *socially valid* or *objective* . . . Now the inner meaning is clear to us: the objectivity of physical experience is its social organisation.[55]

So, how does this social process of meaning-making work? "[T]hought operates with the elements of experience according to the technological and cognitive goals that are in hand," says Bogdanov.[56] These tools do not just reflect experience. They extend experience. "An idea is always the product of

[52] McKenzie Wark, 2015, *Molecular Red: Theory for the Anthropocene*, London, UK: Verso, pp. 57–58.

[53] Alexander Bogdanov, 1923 [2016], *The Philosophy of Living Experience: Popular Outlines*, translated by D.G. Rowley, Leiden, NL: Brill, p. xiii.

[54] Ibid., p. 215.   [55] Ibid., pp. 211–12.   [56] Ibid., p. 210.

a certain *abstraction*, i.e. the attenuation and schematisation of experience, the distancing of itself from the living concreteness of experience."[57] This extension of meaning is according to practical social interests, using tools for conceptualization that have developed through human history.

At this point in his argument, Bogdanov introduces the idea of "substitution," or practices of cognitive work and social meaning that progressively generate broader and deeper meanings in living experience.

We usually observe the sun in the form of a shining yellow circle on a blue field. This is a purely visual form, and if primitive people consider the form to be a material body, then this is an unconscious substitution of the elements of hardness – as perceived by touch – for the elements of colour and form – as perceived by sight. Very early on – apparently even before the birth of scientific astronomy – people began to guess that the sun is not a flat circle, as it appears to the eye, but is a sphere.[58]

The processes of multimodal meaning that we analyze in this book entail substitution more or less in Bogdanov's sense. The word we use for this is "transposition." When we see the sun, we extend that meaning by speaking its name, locating its sight within a repertoire of mental images, associating its feeling with bodily experiences of a particular warmth on one's skin, locating the sun in the space of the sky, perhaps linking it also to ideas about the sun that we have learned from scientific texts, such as its three-dimensional spherical character which is not otherwise obvious. So, we mean the sun with text, image, and body. Meaning is a system of substitutions, a process of meaning transpositions tied together in a multimodal experience.

Bogdanov continues:

The origin of substitution lies in the symbolics of human communication. In place first of other people's words and gestures, and later of various artistic symbols, written signs, etc., people substitute, as the "content" of those things, various forms of consciousness, feelings, desires, and thoughts ... In this way, people "understand" one another, mutually "explain" the meaning and correlation of their actions, and anticipate to a degree other people's actions ... [P]eople transfer this accustomed method to various other facts of experience with the goal of achieving an "explanation" of them that provides "understanding" and anticipation.[59]

§0.2.10 Transposition of Forms

> ***Transposition of Forms.*** *Making sense of living experience by using historically evolved and socially learned forms of meaning: the mental and physical work of moving across and between the meaning forms of text, image, space, body, sound, and speech.*

[57] Ibid., p. 62.   [58] Ibid., p. 222.   [59] Ibid., p. 63.

For the grammar that we are developing in this book, we begin with the spirit of Bogdonov's notion of substitution,[§0.2.9a] but also shift it somewhat. We share with Bogdanov the idea that the substitution of meaning is a process involving shifts in meaning activity within and between social mind and material world. However, we want to use the word "transposition" rather than substitution, because the relationship is not one of replacement. It is more a matter of multimodal overlay where a sense-maker builds a composite meaning, using one form then another to repeat and extend their meaning, in succession or simultaneously.[§AS1.0.1]

In the first instance, transposition is the meaning-act of the singular person as a distinct bodily and cognitive entity, making meaning by moving between embodied mind and sensuous experience. The systems of transposition that we use are not simply individual; they are also socially learned products of human history. In our terminology, text, image, space, object, body, sound, speech are the elementary forms of meaning by means of which we move across and between embodied mind and sensuous experience. These forms of meaning are kinds of practical action, the shape of which is determined by the materiality of their media.

Each of the forms of meaning and their multimodal realization extends immediate experience with social meaning. These extensions are both cognitive and material. They are tools of the mind and matter with which we make sense of experience. Every piece of writing, for instance, connects with previous experiences of pages and screens, as seeable objects and media. Every act of speaking connects with previous experiences of sound and speech, as hearable objects and media. These are artifacts of socially-practical meaning, of social cognition. They are the material traces of work which has simultaneously been mental (thinking in writing, for instance) and physical (pushing the pen or tapping on the keyboard).

Transposition occurs on two dimensions, across meaning forms and meaning functions.[§0.3.6] On the dimension of meaning forms, one meaning form can transpose for another (be swapped out, juxtaposed, layered over), because they serve a shared meaning function. Through mental and physical work, the objects of thought can be transposed by the artifacts of text, image, space, object, body, sound, and speech. This work, simultaneously or in turn, (re)shapes our thinking. Meaning forms can be envisaged; they can take shape in our minds; and our minds can be shaped by these forms as tangible objects and the associated work we put into their representation. Cowan and Kress call this process "transcription" or "transduction" – the re-materialization or reconstitution of meanings.[60]

---

[60] Katharine Cowan and Gunther Kress, 2019, "Documenting and Transferring Meaning in the Multimodal World: Reconsidering 'Transcription'," pp. 66–77 in *Remixing Multiliteracies: Theory and Practice from New London to New Times*, edited by F. Serfini and E. Gee, New York, NY: Teachers College Press.

Returning to his astronomy example, Bogdanov speaks to the role of technologies as media:

> The path to [further understanding] was cleared by *technological* substitution, based in the present case on optical instruments. Galileo's telescope already magnified the optical image more than a thousand times ... Technological substitution reveals the social origin of physical experience to us with particular persuasiveness. With the naked eye you see a not very vivid star, unflickering and with an imprecise and dull cast – the planet Saturn. With a telescope, a strikingly strange, mysterious picture appears before you – a bright sphere with stripes and spots, circled by three or four flat rings ... [T]he entire guarantee of "objectivity" of the phenomena observed by you with the help of the telescope is contained in that sum of systematically applied labour of other people which has been socially crystallised in this instrument ... Thus the process of substitution unfolds, penetrating ever more deeply into the depths of phenomena. We see that in place of more simple, definite, and stable complexes there are substituted elements that are ever more complicated and richer ... [A] coherent and holistic organisation of experience can be achieved only by applying substitution.[61]

Our understanding is mediated by our artifacts of seeing and the historical experience of having seen that, in Bogdanov's example, we have learned as science.

Meanings – the same meanings – can be made in text, image, space, object, body, sound, speech. Here we have Mary and, for the purposes of this example, not Bill: in text ("Mary" on this page); image (Mary in a photo); space (Mary in a room); object (a figurine of Mary,); body (Mary's gesticulations and appearance); sound (the sound of Mary's footsteps approaching); or speech (Mary speaking or being spoken of).

Each form of meaning is a relationship between thinking and by material media with which we are able to think, these are cognitive prostheses. Each is social, but each is also a thing in the material world, ultimately connected through however many steps of human work, to the natural world. We have learned to think with and through these forms of meaning. We have acquired our social and personal capacities for meaning through our practical engagement by working with the material media in which these forms are expressed, through our lives of meaning-action. This is a socio-historical and personal legacy we bring to every new moment of meaning when, yet again, we make these forms work for us, in representation (meaning for ourselves), communication (meaning for others), or interpretation (the meaning of others and things).

It's the same Mary we were just meaning, but the meanings are never quite the same because the different forms of their meaning can never mean in the same ways. Our picture of Mary can never capture what we can say in our speaking of her. These are distinct systems of meaning, with their own

---

[61] Alexander Bogdanov, 1923 [2016], *The Philosophy of Living Experience: Popular Outlines*, translated by D.G. Rowley, Leiden, NL: Brill, pp. 223–29.

affordances, their characteristic opportunities to mean as well as constraints on meaning. As everyday practice and experience, the forms of meaning are profoundly different from each other. Each has its peculiar meaning affordances. For practical purposes much of the time, none is adequate by itself, so we put them together. Some forms of meaning it is even impossible in most circumstances to separate – text from image, for instance, or in-person speech from body. Hence: multimodality.

This movement across and between forms of meaning, and their layering over each other, we call transposition.[§AS1.0.4]

§0.3   Meaning Function

> **Meaning Function.** *The uses to which meaning is put, as evidenced in the social and natural-material experience of its making, always involving reference, agency, structure, context, and interest.*

The five meaning functions that we propose in this transpositional grammar – reference, agency, structure, context, and interest – can be understood as focal concerns in meaning. All are always present in every meaning. We can focus the attention of our analysis on one, then another, of these meaning functions.[§AS1.0.2] With each shift in focus we will see different things in a meaning, perhaps complementary or conflicting.

Linking forms and functions into a matrix, Fig. 0.3 is a map of our philosophy of living experience, our grammar of multimodal meanings.

In this book and its companion volume, we'll fill out the blank cells in this matrix with extended definitions, related thinking, and a range of examples. In so doing, we aim to outline a conceptual framework that accounts for the creation and reception of meaning across all forms. We aim to do this with the same rigor and practical applicability as already well-elaborated linguistic accounts of speech and text, but at a more broadly encompassing level of generality.

However, our most important theme is not what we can put into each of the cells of this matrix, but the transpositions – in this visualization, the horizontal

		Text	Image	Space	Object	Body	Sound	Speech
Meaning Functions	Reference							
	Agency							
	Structure							
	Context							
	Interest							

Fig. 0.3: Matrix for a transpositional grammar

movements across and between forms of meaning, and the vertical shifts of attention across and between functions of meaning.

More than this, the rigid spatiality of a table deceives, because forms are much of the time layered over each other, and all five functions are always present, even though for practical purposes we may choose to attend to just one function at a time. Nor can meaning be neatly put away in a cell of the matrix, because if it is not already somewhere else at the same time, it is begging to go there.

§0.3a   M.A.K. Halliday and Ruqaiya Hasan's Systemic-Functional Grammar

A note about the origin of this notion, "function."[§AS0.2] We started to develop this idea as a consequence of our engagement with the "systemic-functional" approach to linguistics developed by M.A.K. Halliday, Ruqaiya Hasan,[*] and their colleagues. We first met Michael Halliday when we were working in Sydney and he was head of the Linguistics Department at the University of Sydney. Mary had studied linguistics and semiotics at Macquarie University with Ruqaiya Hasan.

Inspired by their work, we have tried to extend its applicability, first in genre approaches to literacy.[62] Then, developing the notion of "Multiliteracies"[63] with our colleagues and good friends in the New London Group, we attempted to apply notions of "system" and "function" to multimodal meanings and contrasting texts from different socio-cultural contexts – meanings that require us to go beyond writing or speech in their canonical forms and to range wider than the discipline of linguistics. Many others have begun to work on these agendas in the new field of "multimodality" over the past several decades. Notable among these and most influential on our thinking is our dear friend and colleague, Gunther Kress.[64]

---

[*] http://meaningpatterns.net/halliday-hasan

[62] Bill Cope and Mary Kalantzis, eds., 1993, *The Powers of Literacy: Genre Approaches to Teaching Writing*, London, UK: Falmer Press and Pittsburgh, PA: University of Pennsylvania Press.

[63] New London Group, 1996, "A Pedagogy of Multiliteracies: Designing Social Futures," *Harvard Educational Review* 66(1):60–92; Bill Cope and Mary Kalantzis, eds., 2000a, *Multiliteracies: Literacy Learning and the Design of Social Futures*, London, UK: Routledge; Bill Cope and Mary Kalantzis, 2009b, "'Multiliteracies': New Literacies, New Learning," *Pedagogies: An International Journal* 4:164–95; Mary Kalantzis and Bill Cope, 2012a, "Multiliteracies in Education," in *The Encyclopedia of Applied Linguistics*, Wiley; Mary Kalantzis, Bill Cope, Eveline Chan, and Leanne Dalley-Trim, 2016, *Literacies* (Edn 2), Cambridge, UK: Cambridge University Press.

[64] Gunther Kress, 2009, *Multimodality: A Social Semiotic Approach to Contemporary Communication*, London, UK: Routledge; Gunther Kress and Theo van Leeuwen, 2006, *Reading Images: The Grammar of Visual Design*, London, UK: Routledge.

We stick faithfully with Halliday and Hasan's notions of system and function, but we extend the range of their analysis in several ways. To the systems of speech and writing, we add analyses of systems of image, space, object, body, and sound – and most importantly, the inevitable processes of multimodality where speech and writing rarely happen by themselves. We also want to make the case that speech and writing never make much sense as a unified pair. They need to be seen as integrally connected into the inevitably multimodal, living experience of meaning-making, where speech is closely associated with sound and writing with image, and more so than ever in today's digital communications environments.

When it comes to meaning functions, we also want to extend Halliday. He proposed three "metafunctions" for the analysis of speaking and writing: ideational, interpersonal, and textual.[65] Ideational meanings are constituted by the theme or the field of a meaning. Interpersonal meanings establish the tenor of the relationships between participants in a meaning. Textual meanings refer to the mode of construction and presentation of a meaning and the forms of its coherence.

We rename these metafunctions, revise their contents, and add two more. Our "reference" is more or less Halliday's "ideational" metafunction, but we have moved considerations of time, place, cause, and effect to our "context" function. Our "agency" is more or less Halliday's "interpersonal" metafunction, but we are just as interested in the impersonal and the broadly social. And our "structural" is more or less Halliday's "textual," but we want to recognize systems of meaning which move beyond "text" narrowly understood as writing or transcribed speech.

Then, we add two more functions: "context," or the larger frame of reference of a meaning, as analyzed for speech in the traditional linguistic subdiscipline of pragmatics,[66] and "interest," the analytical focus of critical discourse analysis[67] and many areas of social theory.[68]

Following Halliday, we want to say that all functions are present in every moment of meaning. A functional analysis offers us a set of conceptual tools with which to examine meanings, and the meanings of meanings.

---

[65] M.A.K. Halliday and Christian M.I.M. Matthiessen, 2014, *Halliday's Introduction to Functional Grammar* (Edn 4), Milton Park, UK: Routledge.

[66] For instance: Stephen C. Levinson, 1983, *Pragmatics*, Cambridge, UK: Cambridge University Press; Yan Huang, 2014, *Pragmatics*, Oxford, UK: Oxford University Press.

[67] For instance: Norman Fairclough, 1995, *Critical Discourse Analysis*, London, UK: Longmans; James Paul Gee, 2005, *An Introduction to Discourse Analysis: Theory and Method*, New York, NY: Routledge.

[68] For instance: Jürgen Habermas, 1968 [1971], *Knowledge and Human Interests*, translated by J.J. Shapiro, Boston, MA: Beacon Press.

§0.3.1   Reference

> *Reference. The identification of entities and actions, in particular instances or as general concepts, and their properties, including qualities and quantities.*

The function of reference[1] is to delineate particular beings and events, in writing or speaking in the form of nouns to represent entities such as persons, things, or states, or verbs to represent actions. In images, particular instances may be delineated with line, form, and color; in space by volumes and boundaries; in tactile representations by edges and surface textures; in gesture by acts of pointing or beat. Reference can establish properties: adjectives or adverbs in language; or visual attributes in images.

Reference may also be to a general concept for which there are many instances: a word that refers to an abstract concept; an image that is a symbol; a space that is characterized by its similarity with others; or a sound that represents a general idea. There is an enormous cognitive and practical difference between referring to one instance (the beings "Mary" or "Bill") and referring to more than one instance ("people") – singular and plural; one instance and multiple instances that, notwithstanding their differences-in-singularity, can be counted. $1+1 = 2$. Instance + instance = concept.

The concept is related to the instance, but is remarkably different, a transposition that works both by way of reduction and extension of meaning. These processes of reduction and extension become critical dilemmas in the digital era, where particular things are relentlessly recorded and aggregated as general things, and their meanings algorithmically manipulated for the purposes of interpretation.

§0.3.2   Agency

> *Agency. Identification of meaning in human and natural activity, offering an account of their causes in terms of patterns of action.*

The function of agency[2] identifies meaning in terms of the range of kinds of human action. In every act of meaning we establish roles: speaker/listener, writer/reader, designer/user, maker/consumer, gesturer/observer, and soundmaker/hearer. We direct or encounter events: interpersonal relations in language, first/second/third person and direct/indirect speech; in image, placement and eyelines; in gesture, pointing to self, others, and the world. We encounter different modulations of agency: in language, voice, mood, and transitivity; in image, focal planes of attachment and engagement; in space, openings and barriers. We discover a range of interpretative potentials: directive or turn-taking gestures; spaces which determine flows deterministically and others that allow a range of alternatives. And our meanings express conditionality: assertion, requirement, and possibility.

§0.3.3 Structure

> **Structure.** *Networks of interconnection across meaning that create coherence in text, image, space, object, body, sound, and speech. Structure is realized in systems that can be characterized by their ontology or connections in the universe to which they refer, their explicit and implicit internal relations, their designs and the relations in their ordering.*

Structure[§3] is to be found in meanings-in the world. This is the stuff of ontology, both philosophically speaking, but more specifically in the era of digital text, the classification schemes that drive databases and the semantic web.

However, these are not simply meanings-in the world. They are humanly constructed meanings-for the world, culturally specific forms of our figuring. Structures of meanings-in and meanings-for are in continuous, dialectical interplay.

Structure manifests itself in the distinctive organization of meaning forms: text, image, space, object, body, sound, and speech. Structure is manifest in techniques for creating internal coherence that make meanings distinguishable as such. These are the processes of binding that hold together a meaning and that also define where that meaning more or less starts and ends: a book, or a picture, or a building, or a utensil, or an embodied person, or an aural alert, or an utterance.

Structure consists of the devices used to create internal cohesion, coherence, logic, and boundedness in meanings. Each form of meaning composes atomic meaning units (graphemes, picture elements, physical components, structural materials in the constructed environment, strokes in gesture) in a certain kind of order. There are internal pointers: pronouns or connectives in language; keys and arrows in images; wayfinding markers in space; cadence and rhythm in sound. There is sectioning: sequence in text; positioning of picture elements in images; the functional mechanics of tangible objects. There is logic that affords reasoning and reasonableness to a structured, composite meaning.

We also want to highlight here the processes of multimodality, or the restructuring of meaning through the overlay of different meaning forms, and synesthesia, or the always-possible transposition of one form for another. Here we encounter in the processes of meaning design the wellsprings of human identities, personal voice and creativity. Meanings are both conventional (using available designs for meaning) and inventive (the process of designing). As a consequence, no two designs of meaning are ever quite the same. Every moment of meaning is a moment of world transformation.

§0.3.4   Context

> **Context.** *The meanings around acts and artifacts of meaning. The relation of meaning to context varies according to the dynamics of its materialization in likeness (resemblance), directedness (pointing), and abstraction (symbolism). Context is determined in part by kinds of participation in meaning, according to the uses to which meanings are put in acts of representation, communication, or interpretation. Meanings are positioned in time and space. Media are materials drawn down from context to make meanings. Associations are the kinds of connections that make meanings cohere. And genres are similar kinds of meaning pattern.*

The function of context[§AS1] is to locate meaning in its surroundings. Meanings never mean by themselves. They are as much creatures of context as they are products of binding through structure. A distinguishable meaning is never just a matter of what it is, a thing itself. It is at least as much a matter of where, when and how it is in the surrounding universe of meanings.

To the extent that context makes meaning, it is a part of the meaning. A label on a packet points to the contents of the packet, and speaks to the supermarket where it is for sale. A text message speaks to the geolocation of the conversants and the tagging of the images that are posted with it. A kitchen relates to living areas in a house which in turn fits into larger patterns of everyday suburban life. Bells and electronic "dings" can mean all manner of things, depending on their context.

Context is established in different kinds of connection: likeness, directedness, and abstraction. Context is also established in the forms of participation of meaning-makers and meaning objects: representation, communication, or interpretation.

Surroundings of time and place supplement meanings: the invisible concentric circles of time and space, extending from the contiguous present across contextual distances of present and future; and progressively more distant places. In the era of digital meanings, time is measured according to coordinated Universal Time (UTC)[§AS1.3.1b] and spaces are definitively located by global positioning coordinates, and aligned with place names at GeoNames.[§AS1.3.2b]

Context also establishes relations: prepositions or possessives in language; collocation or contrast in image. Context may be marked by absence as much as presence. Context entails comparison, including juxtapositions or metaphors, in words, image, sound, or space.

Across all modes, meanings are framed. They refer to other meanings by similarity or contrast, such as motif, style, genre. It encompasses the patterns of causality and emergence that constitute history, from its micro local and momentary instantiations to the macro frames of world and natural history.

Finally, meanings use tangible media, available meaning-resources in the world, and the materiality of these media in part determines structure; the materiality of rendering itself shapes the functions of structure: handwriting, speaking, drawing, photographing, making material objects, building, making music, or gesturing. Distinctive edge features serve as a kind of skin for these structures of meaning that link these media into the universe of meanings: metadata, addresses, covers, and frames, for instance.

§0.3.5   Interest

> *Interest. The purposes participants in meaning bring from their context of meaning to each situation of meaning; and the meaning-work that participants do to negotiate their inevitable differences.*

Now to the function of interest[§AS2] or the wider and deeper human meaning of meanings. What, emotions, social impulses, and reasoning motivate meaning? How does rhetoric work, in text, image, or gesture? How do subjectivity and objectivity work in written and visual texts? How are interests embodied? How are interests served and shaped in the spaces of nature and the constructed environment?

In explorations of interest, we might interrogate meanings not simply for their agreements and congruence, but also for their cross purposes, concealments, dissonances, and a range of failures to understand or communicate. We can explore the dynamics of ideologies, be these explicit or implicit, propagandistic or pseudo-informational. For this we need critique, or the methods used to uncover interests that may have been left unstated by way of deliberate or unconscious concealment.

If the functions of reference, agency, structure, and context reveal how we show and are shown the world, an analysis of interest offers us tools with which to reveal deeper and wider purposes in the world, and in the revelation, to change the world.

§0.3.6   Transposition of Functions

> *Transposition of Functions. Making sense of living experience by using historically evolved and socially learned functions of meaning: understanding experience by turns as reference, agency, structure, context, or interest; and within each function, the always-shifting possibilities for meaning.*

In this grammar, there are two axes of movability: form and function. Meanings are always on the move, along and across both axes. We call this movement transposition.[§AS1.0.4]

However, the dynamics of movement along the axis of function is quite different from the axis of form.[§0.2.10] Having more than one form in a meaning situation is normal; having all forms is possible, but not necessary.

But having all functions in a meaning situation is obligatory. The transposition between the five major functions is a change in our attention, not a change in the meaning. However, within functions, there is constant movement where the meaning is always changing. Each meaning is not only what for the moment it seems to be, but also its immanent movability.

So, when we parse our making sense by its meaning functions – meanings as reference, agency, structure, context, and interest – every meaning is answerable to each one of these functions. If our sense-making is always shifting, this is because we are understanding meaning one way or the other in any moment.

At a more granular level in this transpositional grammar, within each function the meanings are always moving. Within reference, for example, the singular instance[§1.1.1] is always ready to become the countable concept.[§1.1.3] Within agency, the sense of the other[§2.2.2] can be substituted into an imagined self,[§2.2.1] in the case either of empathy[§AS2.5b] or cruelty. And many more such functional transpositions as the grammar unfolds.

Across form and function, a transpositional grammar is not about meanings as they are, but anticipating what any moment now they could be. Its focus is not structures that have been categorically frozen, but patterns of changeability.

§0.4   Grammar

> **Grammar.** *Patterns of meaning in the forms of text, image, space, object, body, sound, and speech. Patterns of meaning in the functions of reference, agency, structure, context, and interest. The activity of parsing these patterns, making sense of their meanings. When we parse, we uncover designs.*

The subtitle of this book mentions "a grammar of multimodal meanings." But, in a way, we don't really need grammars. We can live our lives practically without looking deeply in the meanings of our meanings, and without giving technical names to those meanings.

Yet experts and teachers make it their life's practice to undertake the exercise of precisely naming and finely relating the names in theories or disciplines. "It's useless," or "it's wantonly obfuscatory," say annoyed users, or patients, or students, or populists in moments of anti-intellectual pique. They say this not only of traditional grammars of text, but theories in general.

"Grammar" is a specialized naming scheme that is conventionally used to describe writing, and less frequently, speaking. It's of more concern for the deliberative process of "correct" style in standardized forms of writing than in speech, where inconsistencies of non-standard speech are useful markers that point to personal voice, life experience, geographical origins, social status, and culture.

In the conventional scheme of things, grammar is not "lexis," or vocabulary. It's not "semantics," or meaning. It's not "pragmatics," or the context of use. These are some of the other subdisciplines of linguistics. Grammar is just "syntax," or how we systematically and correctly string words together and correctly apply the morphology of words, creating agreement by enforcing consistencies about things like time (tense), number (singular/plural), and person (first/second/third). Teachers and copy editors learn these rules well enough in order to attain their self-appointed right to enforce them.

We like the word "grammar" because it is about identifying and naming patterns in meaning. But the patterns of syntax are not separable from the patterns of lexis, semantics, and pragmatics. And text is almost invariably layered into larger patterns of meaning involving also image, space, object, body, sound, and speech. Across all these modes, there are shared patterns of meaning that we call meaning functions. This is why we want to stretch the meaning of the word, and create a bigger scope for it – hence, a "grammar of multimodality."

§0.4a   Pāṇini's Aṣṭādhyāyī

The earliest extant grammar is *The Aṣṭādhyāyī of Pāṇini*, created in India in somewhere between 350 and 250 BCE. *Aṣṭādhyāyī* means "eight books" in Sanskrit. Its author, Pāṇini, acknowledges other grammarians, but their works have been lost. His grammar consists of 3,959 *sûtras* or rules for the proper use of Sanskrit.

We managed to locate online a scan of the bilingual edition published in 1897 in that great center of Hindu religious theory and practice, Benares (today, Varanasi). A masterpiece of letterpress typography,[*] the University of Toronto Library must have purchased this copy in 1967 from a library in Varanasi.[69]

---

[*] http://meaningpatterns.net/panini

[69] Srisa Chandra Vasu (translator), 1897, *The Aṣṭādhyāyī of Pāṇini*, Benares, India: Sindhu Charan Bose.

Most of Pāṇini's *sûtras* are no more than a few lines long. As well as documenting phonemic forms and syntactic relations, they also extend to underlying semantic relations such as "agent," "goal," and "location."[70] They are remarkably dense, as technical texts tend to be, where the power and elegance of writing is in part in its systems of abbreviation and cross-reference, its formal consistency and its economy of expression. With all its glosses and accretions over subsequent centuries, plus parallel translation into English, the edition we have used runs to 1,681 pages.

Here is a paraphrase of Sûtra 49, Chapter 1, Book 5. When referring to the causal relationship between giving food to the *Brahmans* (ascetics or priests) "for the sake of" securing entry to "the next world," the giver acquires grace "by substitution," where the grace that the Brahman has acquired by his austerity is transferred by the act of giving to the food giver. "The gift of food produces effect in the next world," but only when the ritual is undertaken correctly, formally expressed in Sanskrit.[71]

We have here several parallel transpositions; the transpositions in Sanskrit which can express a relation to the next life or not; the formalized forms of words in Sanskrit transposing for patterns of ritual action; the ritual actions of the giver of food transposing for the austerity of the ascetic; and the gift transposing for the knowledge that would provide access to the next world. In our terminology, this is a multimodal grammar that involves formalized speech, symbolic objects, and embodied ritual action. Pāṇini's meta-formalization in writing re-formalizes the linguistic and cultural formalizations.

Scholars have long noted the enormous intellectual achievements of Pāṇini's grammar, in some respects not rivaled until modern times.[72] The founder of modern structuralist linguistics, Ferdinand de Saussure,[3d] wrote his doctorate on Sanskrit, and this remained his primary area of expertise and teaching for the rest of his life as professor at the Universities of Paris and Geneva.[73] Only after his death was the *Course in General Linguistics* (1916) published from lecture notes taken by his students. The layers of abstraction and interpretative power of Pāṇini's grammar, surely, lie behind Saussure's achievement two millennia later, whose academic work began with his studies of Sanskrit.

---

[70] Paul Kiparsky and Frits Staal, 1969 [1988]. "Syntactic and Semantic Relations in Pāṇini," pp. 184–218 in *Universals: Studies in Indian Logic and Linguistics*, edited by F. Staal, Chicago, IL: University of Chicago Press, p. 185.

[71] Srisa Chandra Vasu (translator), 1897, *The Aṣṭādhyāyī of Pāṇini*, Benares, India: Sindhu Charan Bose, p. 1061.

[72] Staal, Frits. 1972, *A Reader on the Sanskrit Grammarians*, Cambridge, MA: MIT Press.

[73] Ferdinand de Saussure, 1881 [2017], *On the Use of the Genitive Absolute in Sanskrit*, translated by A. Sukla, Champaign, IL: Common Ground Research Networks.

Leonard Bloomfield[§1.2.2a] introduced structuralist ideas to the United States. He too was a student of Sanskrit, exploring excruciatingly fine points of possible inconsistency between Pāṇini's *sûtras*.[74] Bloomfield's *Introduction to the Study of Language* was published in 1914 while he was a professor at the University of Illinois, where he taught from 1910 to 1921. He revised this and published a new edition in 1933, simply called *Language*, serving as an introduction to modern, structuralist approaches to linguistics. "The grammar of Pāṇini," he says in the opening pages of *Language*, "is one of the greatest monuments of human intelligence."[75]

Then, half a century later, another dominating figure in the development of the discipline of linguistics, Noam Chomsky,[§3.1.2f] writes in the first paragraph of his 1964 *Aspects of a Theory of Syntax*, "The idea that a language is based on a system of rules determining the interpretation of its infinitely many sentences is by no means novel ... Pāṇini's grammar can be interpreted as a fragment of such a 'generative grammar,' in essentially the contemporary sense of this term."[76]

To these testimonials we would add that the system of meanings Pāṇini described was also by extension multimodal, codifying rules of meaningful action, as well as their expressions in text and speech.

"Language," explains Bloomfield, "plays a great part in our life. Perhaps because of its familiarity, we rarely observe it, taking it rather for granted, as we do breathing and walking."[77] Why then, did Pāṇini, and his predecessors in the Vedic tradition, set out on the massive project of systematic codification of Sanskrit, which in turn was the medium for the codification of the lessons of social and spiritual life in the Vedas? And why Sanskrit, by then a language no longer spoken in everyday life? Bloomfield again: "Long after it had ceased to be spoken as anyone's native language, it remained (as classical Latin remained in Europe) the artificial medium for all writing on learned or religious topics."[78]

The word "Veda" is derived from the Sanskrit word for "knowledge." The four major Vedas consist of spiritual wisdoms, religious benedictions, chants, instructions for ritual practices, and insights into mathematics, science, and philosophy. Thought to have been created between 1500 and 500 BCE, the Vedas have come to us as written texts, though they are full of metrical

---

[74] Leonard Bloomfield, 1927, "On Some Rules of Pāṇini," *Journal of the American Oriental Society* 47:61–70.

[75] Leonard Bloomfield, 1933, *Language*, New York, NY: Henry Holt and Company, p. 11.

[76] Noam Chomsky, 1964, *Aspects of the Theory of Syntax*, Cambridge, MA: MIT Press, p. v.

[77] Leonard Bloomfield, 1933, *Language*, New York, NY: Henry Holt and Company, p. 3.

[78] Ibid., pp. 11, 63.

mnemonics to assist recitation and singing. This also indicates that their origins lie deep in an earlier world of orality.

Writing first comes to India in about 2200 BCE with the as-yet undeciphered, ideographic Harrapan script. But this writing system appears to have died out before the adaption to Sanskrit of a form of the Semitic alphabet brought to India by Aramaic merchants from the Middle East in about 600 BCE. The Vedas were the written texts of the Brahman ruling class, also to be memorized and chanted from memory.[79] This is the context in which Pāṇini wrote his grammar, documenting the formal, written text of Sanskrit and prescribing its correct forms of pronunciation and recitation from memory.

Pāṇini's Sanskrit was the preserve of the members of an elite who ascribed to themselves the exclusive right to know and practice the arcane textual, spoken, and ritual code of the Vedas. The Vedas had been divinely ordained, and the Brahmans were the mediators of the divine. The Sanskrit of the Vedas and the practices described therein enforced a separation of a liturgical discourse and philosophical knowledge from the everyday experience of the peasant masses.[§3.3d] To the masses, the Vedas and their interlocutors held out the promise of rewards such as going to heaven, attaining power, or controlling the labor of others.[80] This was, to use Bernard Cohn's words, a "theater of power managed by ... priests and ritual preceptors."[81]

So, to return to our Sûtra 5.1.49, the person who works to grow food gains grace by giving food to a higher-caste person who does not do such profane work. Redistribution of the fruits of labor from the lower-caste farmer to the Brahman is a matter of obligation, expressed multimodally in sacred text and ritual exchange. In unequal societies, this is typical of many such obligations whereby the poor are charged or taxed in one way or another by the rich. This is one of the ways in which inequality was made tolerable, such was the power of the separation of meaning forms, and the institutionalization of functional inequality in the caste system. Both the Vedas and Pāṇini's grammar were embedded in this system of inequality. If the Vedas mediated between Gods and Brahmans, and Brahmans and the masses, Pāṇini's text was a mediation on the mediations.

Our edition of Pāṇini's grammar has a dedication by its translator, "To the Hon'ble Sir John Edge, Rt.Q.C., Chief Justice of the North-Western

[79] Jack Goody, 1987, *The Interface between the Written and the Oral*, Cambridge, UK: Cambridge University Press, pp. 113–22.

[80] Romila Thapar, 2013, *The Past before Us: Historical Traditions of Early North India*, Ranikhet, India: Permanent Black, pp. 87–106.

[81] Bernard S. Cohn, 1996, *Colonialism and Its Forms of Knowledge: The British in India*, Princeton, NJ: Princeton University Press, p. 3.

Provinces, this work is, with his Lordship's permission and in respectful appreciation of his Lordship's services to the cause of administration of justice and of education in these provinces, dedicated by his Lordship's humble servant, the translator." Until independence in 1947, the British Imperial Civil Service in India consisted of about a thousand civil servants. The "heaven born", they were called, and Sir John was numbered among them. Until the last years of the British Empire, they were almost exclusively Englishmen, ruling 300 million people in 250 provinces from today's Myanmar, to Sri Lanka, to Pakistan. Like the Brahmans, they were trained at the Universities of Oxford and Cambridge in the arcane ancient languages of Europe, and sometimes also Sanskrit. The parallel inequalities worked nicely for the British Empire, an imperial bureaucracy with an inaccessible and ostensibly superior knowledge, ruling colonized illiterate masses.[82] To honor Sanskrit was a mark of the mutual respect of one intensely hierarchical edifice of social meanings for another.

While we may maintain an ever-vigilant suspicion of discourses and knowledge systems that generate inequalities, we can also acknowledge their achievements. Contemporary thinkers acknowledge Pāṇini's achievement, manifestly not his alone because he acknowledges predecessors. The tradition he documents produced a grammar that is a structured system of knowledge representations, progressively becoming more abstract from an object language that references things in the world, to a metalanguage with metarules, *paribhâsâ*, or rules about rules.[83]

Some have gone so far as to say that Pāṇini's grammar prefigures modern computational thinking, with its density, technicality, and depths of recursiveness. Kadvany notes the "modern idea that computation can be expressed in any media you like, with software an abstraction independent of any hardware implementation ... Computing languages, like structured grammars, require the tiered, hierarchical structures of symbolic forms found first in Pāṇini."[84] These are akin to the "modern idea of algorithmic thinking as generic procedural exactness," something that, in the context of the Vedas, applied as much to "recursive combinations of chants, marches or offerings in a larger composite ritual," as to written text or memorized oral utterance.[85] Even more closely related, we would argue, are the markup languages, from

---

[82] Ibid., pp. 16–56.
[83] Frits Staal, 1975, "The Concept of Metalanguage and Its Indian Background," *Journal of Indian Philosophy* 3(3/4):315–54; P.G. Patel, 1996, "Linguistic and Cognitive Aspects of the Orality-Literacy Complex in Ancient India," *Language and Communication* 16(4):315–29.
[84] John Kadvany, 2016, "Pāṇini's Grammar and Modern Computation," *History and Philosophy of Logic* 37(4):325–46, p. 344.
[85] John Kadvany, 2007, "Positional Value and Linguistic Recursion," *Journal of Indian Philosophy* 35(5/6):487–520, p. 489.

HTML$^{\S AS1.4.7d}$ to XML,$^{\S 3.3b}$ that drive the semantic annotation practices and mechanisms of the contemporary internet.[86]

§0.4b   Michael Reddy's Conduit Metaphor

Grammar works for us at two levels. Whether we are in the moment conscious of it or not, our meanings are constituted in patterns. The patterns are there, even when we don't care to name them. Mostly we don't need to name them. Notwithstanding our relative disinterest, the patterns of meaning are not just circumstantially present – they are profoundly so, they are essentially so, and in their astounding complexity. Complex and multilayered patterns of meaning drive our meanings, even when unspoken and unthought as patterned. This is the first or primary level at which grammar operates.

Then, there is a second level, when the patterns are named and when we begin to think reflectively and then more or less systematically about them. There is a folk or everyday version of this practice of reflection, which begins to appear when we try to account for misunderstandings, or when we are struck by moments of exceptional clarity. For example, in communication, we might note a person's ineffectiveness or effectiveness in "getting the message across."

Michael Reddy identifies such expressions in spoken English, all mundane, and all appearing with remarkable frequency. "It's very hard to *get an idea across* in a hostile atmosphere." "Your real feelings are finally *getting through* to me." "The man's thought is *buried* in these terribly difficult and dense paragraphs." "I'm *cramming* history for tomorrow's exam." These are moments of explicit self-reflection on the processes of meaning.[87]

Reddy goes on to identify the self-deceptive, "biasing" power that is frequently built into these self-understandings. He identifies the frequency of "container" and "conduit" metaphors to account for the processes of meaning in English. Perhaps 70 per cent of references to communication in English use metaphors of this kind, he says. "This model of communication objectifies meaning in a misleading and dehumanizing fashion. It influences us to talk and think about thoughts as if they had [some] kind of external, intersubjective reality." Moreover, "to the extent that the conduit metaphor does see communication as requiring some slight expenditure of energy, it localizes that expenditure almost totally in the speaker or writer."[88]

---

[86] More at §3.3a; Bill Cope and Mary Kalantzis, 2004, "Text-Made Text," *E-Learning* 1(2):198–282.

[87] Michael J. Reddy, 1993, "The Conduit Metaphor: A Case of Frame Conflict in Our Language About Language," pp. 164–201 in *Metaphor and Thought*, edited by A. Ortony, Cambridge, UK: Cambridge University Press, pp. 189–197; 177.

[88] Ibid., p. 186.

Here we have a case where, in our practices of meaning, although we do have ways of speaking about meaning, they may be systematically flawed. They are biased towards self-deception about our role as meaning-makers and the transportability of meanings in the act of communication. We only start to realize this at points of apparent failure to communicate.

A comprehensive theory of meaning entails representation (including levels of unawareness), communication, and re-representation in moments of interpretation (including systematic patterns of seeing different things into a meaning, and failing to see). Such a theory may serve to undo the naive and egocentric assumptions about communication intrinsic to our folk "grammar."

Within our second level of meaning, where we explicitly name and acknowledge patterns and processes in meaning, there are in fact multiple sub-levels. In Reddy's case, there is a folk level and a scientific level by means of which the systematic occlusions in the folk level of self-understanding are revealed.

So, we have these two principal levels of operation of grammar, the unacknowledged but nevertheless powerfully efficacious grammar in everyday life at a first level, and explicit acknowledgments of the presence of this grammar, across a scale of increasing abstraction from folk self-representation to systematic observation and conceptualization that might warrant the term "science."

These two levels Michael Halliday[§0.3a] wants to call "grammar" and "grammatics," to make the distinction abundantly clear.[89] Grammar is our practice. Grammatics is its explicit naming and explanation. Between everyday self-reflections on the processes and patterns of meaning and the convoluted intricacies of formalized representations of these meanings in the various branches of linguistics (lexis, syntax, pragmatics, semantics), then even more abstractly in formal logic, computer science, and semiotics, there are numerous middle spaces.

One such space is a "grammatics" for language study in schools. This needs to be technical enough to render usable insights for learners and to provide teachers with conceptual tools for their instructional trade. In the words of Mary Macken and her co-authors, teachers need to turn the conceptual apparatus of "knowledge about" meaning into the practical capacities of "know-how."[90]

We started this journey with Mary Macken, Gunther Kress, Jim Martin, and Joan Rothery, attempting to translate Hallidayan linguistics – impractically over-complicated for children, and quite unnecessarily so for the purposes of

---

[89] M.A.K. Halliday, 1996 [2002], "On Grammar and Grammatics," in *On Grammar*, The Collected Works of M.A.K. Halliday, Volume 1, edited by J.J. Webster, London, UK: Continuum.

[90] Mary Macken-Horarik, Kristina Love, and Len Unsworth, 2011, "A Grammatics 'Good Enough' for School English in the 21st Century: Four Challenges in Realising the Potential," *Australian Journal of Language and Literacy* 34(1):9–23, p. 11.

pedagogy – into a program for the teaching of writing.[91] Our overarching frame was the notion of "genre," or different kinds of text structure for different social purposes.[92]

We're not going to mark the "grammatics" distinction with a special term, in part because the borderline between grammar as namable patterns of meaning and conscious naming of the patterns is blurred. It's hard to tell where thinking in patterns ends and thinking about the patterns begins. Also, there is a succession of steps, where in a first step, reflection on meaning is practically inseparable from the activity of meaning, even in folk meaning; to more formalized and institutionalized practices in media and teaching; to, at another extreme, the arcane intricacies of academic specialisms. It's all grammar, as object and reflection.

But why take this journey between object and reflection, why travel this distance, however far? Our answer is in the usefully insightful processes of identifying deeper meanings which may cast doubt on immediate impressions or folk understandings. The world, at first glance, does seem flat. Inequalities, at first glance, do seem normal. Communication, at first glance, does seem to be a conduit for meaning.

Occluding ideologies may seem to speak truth to the practical reality. But when you look carefully, things are more complex than they at first seem. We need to uncover the complexities in order to develop a truer realization. This is one reason why we might do grammar, to uncover the less immediately obvious, more complex and deeper truths.

However, now we encounter a paradox. For every moment when grammars uncover complexity, they can also simplify things for us. Their generalizations about meaning encompass multiple instances, and are potentially transferrable to instances yet to be encountered or possibly encounterable. This also makes them helpful. Such reflections might prompt us to conceive meanings that are possible but, for the moment at least, purely imaginary.

This makes grammar in our broad sense the basis for creativity that extends the bounds of human possibility. The design concepts that architects, or writers,

[91] Mary Macken, Mary Kalantzis, Gunther Kress, Jim Martin, Bill Cope, and Joan Rothery, 1990d, *A Genre-Based Approach to Teaching Writing, Years 3–6*, Book 1: *Introduction*, Sydney, AU: Directorate of Studies, N.S.W. Department of Education; 1990c, *A Genre-Based Approach to Teaching Writing, Years 3–6*, Book 2: *Factual Writing: A Teaching Unit Based on Reports About Sea Mammals*, Sydney, AU: Directorate of Studies, N.S.W. Department of Education; 1990b, *A Genre-Based Approach to Teaching Writing, Years 3–6*, Book 3: *Writing Stories: A Teaching Unit Based on Narratives About Fairy Tales*, Sydney, AU: Directorate of Studies, N.S.W. Department of Education; 1990a, *A Genre-Based Approach to Teaching Writing, Years 3–6*, Book 4: *The Theory and Practice of Genre-Based Writing*, Sydney, AU: Directorate of Studies, N.S.W. Department of Education.

[92] Bill Cope and Mary Kalantzis, eds., 1993, *The Powers of Literacy: Genre Approaches to Teaching Writing*, London, UK: Falmer Press and Pittsburgh, PA: University of Pennsylvania Press.

or artists bring to bear in their work allow them to create new buildings, or writings, or artworks. They facilitate knowledge transfer and scaffold creativity.

§0.4c   Edmund Husserl's Pure Phenomenology

Edmund Husserl's[*] *Ideas* was published in 1913, a masterwork of modern philosophy. The First World War began the following year. One of Husserl's sons was killed, then one of his most talented students, then his other son was badly injured. This was the war that was supposed to end all wars. Instead of peace, the war was followed by revolutionary crisis, and fascism, and after that, an even more horrible war. Such is the terrible history of the twentieth century.

Little wonder that the large intellectual project of the European Enlightenment was abandoned, given its manifold failures in social practice. But not by Husserl. Husserl was the last philosopher to contemplate the universalizing power of essential ideas. In the postwar age of intellectual modesty, nay pessimism, the subtitle to *Ideas* is startling: *General Introduction to Pure Phenomenology*.[93]

Husserl's *Phenomenology* stands in the confidently human-centered tradition of Western Philosophy. For Plato, the highest form of knowledge was to be found in "ideas" or "forms" that captured the essence of worldly realities.[§AS1.0.1] For Descartes, there was at least one grounding certainty that mitigated against productive doubt, and that was *cogito ergo sum*: "I think, therefore I am."[§3.1.2g] For Kant, human understanding can be traced to pure concepts, or the categories of the mind in terms of which all thinking occurs: quantities, qualities, relations, and modalities.[§3.3e] Husserl works firmly in this tradition, perhaps its last philosopher.

Husserl's first book had been published in 1891, *Philosophy of Arithmetic*, elaborating on themes from his doctorate. After this, his thought began to range wider, to explore the nature of thinking that underlay mathematics and all sciences. His massive six-part work, *Logical Investigations*, was published in 1901.

"The mathematician, the physicist and the astronomer," he says, "need not understand the ultimate grounds of their activities in order to carry through even the most important scientific performances ... Significant metaphysical propositions ... underlie all those sciences that are concerned with actual reality ... time, space, math, cause." These conceptual presuppositions are

---

[*] http://meaningpatterns.net/husserl

[93] Edmund Husserl, 1913 [2002], *Ideas: General Introduction to Pure Phenomenology*, translated by W.R.B. Gibson, London, UK: Routledge.

the grounding of science. So, Husserl set out to reflect on "the relationship between the subjectivity of knowing and the objectivity of the known content." This was to be the basis of "a new, purely theoretical science," a "theory of theory," a "science of sciences," a "phenomenology of experiences in general," a "universal ... grammar ... [of] laws which determine the possible forms of meaning."[94]

Then there was a hiatus in Husserl's philosophical output for over a decade, before his *Ideas* was published. At this point, Husserl's ambition became even more expansive, to trace the path of thinking from grounded experience to the most transcendental truths of science.

[The] first outlook on life ... [is] the natural standpoint. I am aware of the world, spread out in space endlessly, and in time becoming and become, without end. I am aware of it, that means, first of all, I discover it immediately, intuitively. I experience it. Through sight, touch, hearing etc., in the different ways of sensory perception, corporeal things somehow spatially distributed are for me simply there, in verbal or figurative sense "present," whether or not I pay them special attention by busying myself with them, considering, thinking, feeling, willing.[95]

The sciences of the empirical world expand these everyday horizons. They address "the World [as] the totality of objects that can be known through experience, known in terms of orderly theoretical thought on the basis of direct, present experience ... justif[ying their] claim to transcend the narrow framework of direct empirical given-ness." These are "grounded systems of knowledge, so rich and so ramified."[96] Hence the achievements of the natural sciences, history, and applied mathematics, as they document the empirical world.

However, "every factual science (empirical science) has essential theoretical bases in ... objectivity in general," a higher level of truth. For instance, "in pure geometry, we judge as a rule ... 'straight,' 'angle,' 'triangle,' or 'conic section,' ... about universal triangles in general, conic sections in general. Such universal judgments have the character of essential generality, of 'pure,' or as one says, of 'rigorous,' absolutely 'unconditioned' generality." These generalities don't apply only to the discernible empirical world. They also apply to other worlds, not yet the objects of experience. These are "constructions of a syntactico-logical kind: ... substantive meaning, relation, constitutive quality, unity, plurality, numerical quantity, order, ordinal number, and so forth."[97]

---

[94] Edmund Husserl, 1913 [2001], *Logical Investigations*, Volume 1, translated by J.N. Findlay, London, UK: Routledge, pp. 15–16, 2, 152, 166; Edmund Husserl, 1921 [2001], *Logical Investigations*, Volume 2, translated by J.N. Findlay, London, UK: Routledge, p. 49.

[95] Edmund Husserl, 1913 [2002], *Ideas: General Introduction to Pure Phenomenology*, translated by W.R.B. Gibson, London, UK: Routledge, p. 51.

[96] Ibid., pp. 10, 20.   [97] Ibid., pp. 20, 15, 25, 24.

The process of ascending from the natural standpoint, to empirical science, to the syntactico-logical constructions of phenomenology, is a process of progressive "disconnexion" from the specifics of the empirical world. Husserl calls this "bracketing." This "renders 'pure' consciousness accessible to us." Now we reach "the free outlook upon 'transcendentally' purified phenomena" and "pure or transcendental phenomenology, established not as a science of facts, but as a science of essential Being."[98]

If we wanted to step back from the grandiosity of this claim in order to trace a path towards transcendental knowledge, we might paraphrase it as this: things of experience are not just how they immediately seem to be. If we work diligently at our examination of experience, and move our investigation to the level of experience in general, we can come to a point where we understand aspects of experience that are not immediately obvious in the circumstantial, empirical moments that are a-spot-in-time and/or a place of happen-to-be. Albeit on a far more modest scale, this is the kind of project we now are attempting in this transpositional grammar.

Ideas was the first of Husserl's works to be translated into English by W.R. Boyce Gibson, Professor of Mental and Moral Philosophy at the University of Melbourne. Boyce spent his sabbatical leave with Husserl at the University of Freiburg in 1928, working on the translation.[99]

While Boyce remained faithful to the text and spirit of Husserl's phenomenology, some of the students he inspired did not. As editor of the *Yearbook for Philosophy and Phenomenological Research*, Husserl published *Being and Time*[100] in its 1927 volume, the work of his assistant and, for a time, close friend, Martin Heidegger. But when, after publication, Husserl finally found the time to read Heidegger's full text carefully, he was angered and disappointed by the extent of its revision of his ideas. Jean-Paul Sartre also took phenomenology in a different direction, so different that it needed another name: existentialism.[101] Husserl's most famous followers abandoned him, and the project of the European Enlightenment.

Husserl, a Jew by Nazi racial classification but not religious persuasion, was suspended from the University of Freiberg in 1933 and banned from teaching or publishing in Germany. Not that his ideas were any particular threat to the new Nazi state, as they might have been if he were a communist. Heidegger joined the Nazi party and become the Rector of the University.

---

[98] Ibid., pp. 61, 63, 3.
[99] S.A. Grave, 1988, "Gibson, William Ralph Boyce (1869–1935)," in *Australian Dictionary of Biography*, Melbourne, AU: Melbourne University Press.
[100] Martin Heidegger, 1926 [1962]. *Being and Time*, translated by J. Macquarrie and E. Robinson, Oxford, UK: Blackwell.
[101] Jean-Paul Sartre, 1943 [1993], *Being and Nothingness: An Essay on Phenomenological Ontology*, translated by H.E. Barnes, New York, NY: Washington Square Press.

Husserl died in 1938, before he could become a victim of the Holocaust. His voluminous papers were smuggled out of Germany in 1939.

§0.4d   *Jacques Derrida's* Of Grammatology

Four years after Husserl's death, a twelve-year-old Algerian schoolboy, Jacques Derrida,* was called to his principal's office. It was the first day of his school year, in 1942. "You are going to go home, my little friend, your parents will get a note."

Algeria was at the time still a French colony, and by order of the Vichy government of Nazi-occupied France, quotas had just been set limiting the number of Jewish students allowed to attend school. The only other option for him, "a little black and very Arab Jew," was a Jewish school which he didn't much want to attend. So, he skipped school for a year and read voraciously. After the war he went to high school in Paris and after that to university. There, he studied Husserl, writing his master's thesis on "the problem of genesis in Husserl's philosophy."[102]

For the whole of his illustrious academic career, Derrida kept coming back to Husserl as a reference point, if mostly an antithetical one. Where Husserl wanted to find consistent patterns of meaning in an attempt to get closer to the depths of meaning in general, Derrida's life project came to be one where he would question the possibility of anything being consistently meaningful, or finding meanings that are systematically structured, or all-encompassing. Derrida accorded Husserl the respect he deserved, but as a counterpoint, in order to show that the characteristic project of Western philosophy and science was neither possible nor desirable. After the horrors of the twentieth century, intellectual pessimism, or at least circumscribed caution, was the preferred intellectual tone.

Derrida traced in Husserl a relation between "expression forms," such as speech and writing, and the underlying "indications" to which they point, their "non-sensory mental aspects." For Husserl, speech and writing "exteriorize" thought.[103] Underneath the purely grammatical aspects of language, says Derrida, Husserl posits a pure logic of ideal thought, and by transposition, the presence in "the living present" of a "transcendental life" such that systematic truths are waiting to be uncovered by means of bracketing or phenomenological reduction.[104]

---

* http://meaningpatterns.net/derrida

[102] Benoît Peeters, 2010 [2013], *Derrida: A Biography*, Cambridge, UK: Polity Press, p.19.
[103] Jacques Derrida, 1967 [1973]a, "Form and Meaning: A Note on the Phenomenology of Signs," in *Speech and Phenomena, and Other Essays on Husserl's Theory of Signs*, Evanston, IL: Northwestern University Press, p. 113.
[104] Jacques Derrida, 1967 [1973]b, *Speech and Phenomena, and Other Essays on Husserl's Theory of Signs*, translated by D.B. Allison, Evanston, IL: Northwestern University Press, p. 6.

In earlier times, these systematic truths may have been named God. After modern science and philosophy, after the European Enlightenment, these truths come to be reframed and renamed "reason." Such is the failed project of metaphysics, says Derrida, aiming to discover the essences of knowledge and being, whether that be a theology of theologies or a philosophy of philosophies.

Derrida refers to a long tradition of such metaphysical "reductions" in Western thought, where speech and writing are secondary to essential thought. Indeed, writing is often secondary to speech, because, he says, speech seems closer to the human heart. So, Aristotle had said, "Spoken words are symbols of mental experience and written words are the symbols of spoken words." And Rousseau: "Languages are made to be spoken, writing is nothing but a supplement of speech ... thought is made through speech ... the art of writing is nothing but a mediated representation of thought." Saussure found behind the signifier (an artifact of meaning), a signified (an idea that sits in a structure of inter-related, mental meanings).§3d In this long tradition, speech is an exteriorization of thought, and writing a secondary representation of speech. Husserl, Derrida says, is yet another thinker caught within this tradition.[105]

In his riposte, Derrida claims that any such appeals, reducing meaning to underlying and ultimately discoverable reason, are misguided. No longer can there be any metaphysics. There are just traces of meaning, chained together by similarities perhaps, but also by their differences. Writing does not simply represent speech which in turn represents thought. Speech and then writing are transpositions which may refer back, but which are also different to the extent that they are moments of supplementation or transformation of meaning.[106]

Writing is not simply a conduit for speech, nor speech simply a conduit for thought, though traces remain. The traces interconnect by means of "assemblages," where a trace of meaning connects back to other meanings, and differs from them in the moment of their re-representation. Each new trace happens in a new space, a new time, and it never quite expresses what has come before, either in thought or antecedent expression. This is "movement by which language, or any code, any system of reference in general, becomes 'historically' constituted as a fabric of differences." The result is an "incessant synthesis that is constantly led back upon itself, back upon its assembled and assembling self, by retentional traces and protentional openings."[107]

---

[105] Jacques Derrida, 1967 [1997], *Of Grammatology*, translated by G.C. Spivak, Baltimore, MD: Johns Hopkins University Press, pp. 30, 295, 31–34.

[106] Ibid., pp. 70–71, 54.

[107] Jacques Derrida, 1968 [1973], "Differance," in *Speech and Phenomena, and Other Essays on Husserl's Theory of Signs*, Evanston, IL: Northwestern University Press, pp. 141, 153.

For this reason, Derrida replaces "grammar," in the sense of uncoverable patterns of essential meaning, with "grammatology," mapping contingent chains of traces, traceable similarities, but also the differences that occur in the transpositions.[108] He replaces analysis of the generalizable patterns that constitute structures of meaning with "deconstruction" of trace-to-trace genealogies, "interweaving" circumstantial similarity and with contingent difference.[109] Derrida's agenda becomes a critique of (not coincidentally Western, male, imperialistic) "logocentrism" – word-centeredness and reason-centeredness.

But then he pushes his analysis over an edge where meaning disintegrates. "The radical dissimilarity of ... the graphic and phonic ... exclude[s] derivation," he says. "Writing is not mere supplement, addition, *techne*. It adds only to replace."[110] Meaning "continually breaks up in a chain of different substitutions."[111] And so, in the "absence of the referent ... there is nothing outside of the text." Such is the "irreducible complexity" of meaning "which metaphysics cannot think,"[112] producing a "transcendental disquietude."[113] "Signs are all there is ... a play, which is the absence of the transcendental signified." Such is "the game of the world,"[114] where there is "no depth to be had for this bottomless chessboard where being is set in play."[115] And so, with this "undoing of logocentrism ... there is no origin, no essence" of meaning.

Then, an abyss: "there have never been anything but ... substitutive significations which could only come forth in a chain of differential references; ... language is writing as the disappearance of natural presence." The transposed meaning "comes in a place of lapse, a nonsignified or a nonrepresented, a nonpresence. There is no present before it, it is not preceding by anything but itself." And "[t]he concept of repression is thus, at least as much as that of forgetting, the product of philosophy (of meaning)."[116]

---

[108] Jacques Derrida, 1967 [1997], *Of Grammatology*, translated by G.C. Spivak, Baltimore, MD: Johns Hopkins University Press, p. 60.

[109] Jacques Derrida, 1967 [1973]a. "Form and Meaning: A Note on the Phenomenology of Signs," in *Speech and Phenomena, and Other Essays on Husserl's Theory of Signs*, Evanston, IL: Northwestern University Press, p. 111.

[110] Jacques Derrida, 1967 [1997], *Of Grammatology*, translated by G.C. Spivak, Baltimore, MD: Johns Hopkins University Press, pp. 54, 144–45.

[111] Jacques Derrida, 1968 [1973], "Differance," in *Speech and Phenomena, and Other Essays on Husserl's Theory of Signs*, Evanston, IL: Northwestern University Press, p. 159.

[112] Jacques Derrida, 1967 [1997], *Of Grammatology*, translated by G.C. Spivak, Baltimore, MD: Johns Hopkins University Press, pp. 158, 167.

[113] Jacques Derrida, 1967 [1973]b, *Speech and Phenomena, and Other Essays on Husserl's Theory of Signs*, translated by D.B. Allison, Evanston, IL: Northwestern University Press, p. 14.

[114] Jacques Derrida, 1967 [1997], *Of Grammatology*, translated by G.C. Spivak, Baltimore, MD: Johns Hopkins University Press, p. 50.

[115] Jacques Derrida, 1968 [1973], "Differance," in *Speech and Phenomena, and Other Essays on Husserl's Theory of Signs*, Evanston, IL: Northwestern University Press, p. 154.

[116] Jacques Derrida, 1967 [1997], *Of Grammatology*, translated by G.C. Spivak, Baltimore, MD: Johns Hopkins University Press, pp. 159, 303, 286.

Humorous Derrida, endlessly clever Derrida, who sets out to defeat word-centric reason with word games, logic with logical inversions, capital "R" Reason with smart scholarly reason. Not that he's unaware that these apostasies may also be hypocrisies. "The enterprise of deconstruction always in a certain way falls prey to its own work." "Only half in jest" does he speak.[117]

Some of Derrida's peers in the business of theorizing meaning were not impressed. Says Noam Chomsky[§3.1.2e] of Derrida, "I thought I ought to at least be able to understand his *Grammatology*, so I tried to read it. I could make out some of it, for example, the critical analysis of classical texts that I knew very well and had written about years before. I found the scholarship appalling, based on pathetic misreading; and the argument, such as it was, failed to come close to the kinds of standards I've been familiar with since virtually childhood."[118]

And John Searle:[§2.3.1b] "I believe that Derrida's work, at least those portions I have read, is not just a series of muddles and gimmicks;" also it is a "text [that] is written so obscurely that you can't figure out exactly what the thesis is." And it falls into the trap of taking metaphysics seriously.[119]

A joke that has for some time done the rounds in academe, goes like this: "what do you get when you cross a deconstructionist and a mafioso? You get a proposition you can't understand."[120] But of course, Derrida is understandable, his meanings, a revulsion in the face of the terrors of Enlightenment.

Perhaps Chomsky and Searle don't want to understand Derrida, or perhaps they can't understand him because he lays down a challenge that is outside what is thinkable in their intellectual systems. Derrida positions himself as an outsider to these systems, and stays an outsider, though a figure who nevertheless manages to find himself on the inside of some fancy academic institutions.

Still, just before we go over a cliff where patterned meaningfulness disappears, there are some productive insights in Derrida. These we want to capture with the notion of "design,"[§0.4.1] as we attempt to get past Derrida's philosophical apostasies, nay philosophical hypocrisies.

§0.4e   Mr. He's Gypsy China Chairs

A note about the cover picture we have chosen for this book.[*] For the reasons we explained earlier in this part,[§0.0] we have decided not to put any pictures in

---

[*] http://meaningpatterns.net/gypsy-china-chairs

[117] Ibid., pp. 24, 216.
[118] http://mindfulpleasures.blogspot.com/2011/01/noam-chomsky-on-derrida-foucault-lacan.html
[119] John R. Searle, 1983, "The Word Turned Upside Down," *New York Review of Books* (October 27).
[120] Peter L. Berger, 1996, *Redeeming Laughter: The Comic Dimension of Human Experience*, Berlin, Germany: Walter de Gruyter.

the book. Instead, we have created a slideshow of images and other media objects and put them on the web at meaningpatterns.net. But publishers like to have pictures on the cover. So, we have chosen a photograph of an image that we made, *Gypsy China Chairs* (2010).

The image comes with a story, indicative of the notion of transposition, a term which we use as an alternative to Derrida's notions of "trace" or "supplement"[§0.4d] or Bodganov's concept of "substitution."[§0.2.9a] Some tormented transpositions come with this image, symptomatic of the kinds of things that we want to be able to parse in our grammar of multimodality, something we want to be able to use to make sense of such things. Several of the transpositions have already arisen in our awkward language. An "image" – but why couldn't we say "painting"? And "we made" – why couldn't we name the artist straight off, as the little labels beside the paintings or photographs in galleries do with such (apparent) directness?

To trace a genealogy of transpositions, Mary was born in Greece in that old house in the mountains we mentioned earlier when we said "the mountains loomed large."[§0] We go there often, to stay in the house to experience the silver-green shimmering of the leaves of the olive trees in the wind. (This is just the beginning of a chain of existential associations, but we digress too far?)

Gypsies come to the village every now and then, their trucks with loud speakers on the roof, and a haunting chant of whatever they have for sale. It sounds a bit like the Imam's call to prayer, if this were a Muslim village (but it is not). Theirs is just a commercial call to partake in the practicalities of saleable things: watermelons or potatoes, floor mats or plastic chairs. The plastic chairs are reliably five euros each, reliably white, reliably made in China, reliably ubiquitous in Greece. And unexpectedly – if you care to notice, or at least we think so – they are elegant.

From Bill and Mary's experience, sitting in a café one day, Bill takes a photo. We are moved to notice something of the elegance, something of the ubiquity, something of Greece-ness of this ordinary and not-so-very Greek thing. Also, we've been working to evaluate a Roma education project run by our dear colleagues at the Aristotle University of Thessaloniki.[121]

"Gypsy" has slightly pejorative connotations, so the word we used in our report is "Roma," which means "man" in the language of the same name. (But do we digress?) Thinking about the way the people in the village view the people who sell them these chairs, "Gypsy" seems a word closer to our experience, though the root of the word "Γύφτος" is "Egyptian", from where this "race,"[§AS1.4.3c] this

---

[121] Mary Kalantzis and Bill Cope, 2016, "Learner Differences in Theory and Practice," *Open Review of Educational Research* 3(1):85–132; Mary Kalantzis, Bill Cope, and Eugenia Arvanitis, 2015, "Evaluation Report of the Project, Education of Roma Children in Central Macedonia, West Macedonia and East Macedonia and Thrace," Thessaloniki, Greece: Aristotle University; Evangelia Tressou, Soula Mitakidou, and Panagiota Karagianni, eds., 2015, *Roma Inclusion – International and Greek Experiences: Complexities of Inclusion*, Thessaloniki, Greece: Aristotle University.

people, was supposed in the middle ages to have come (incorrectly, as it happens). (We digress?)

Anyway, we thought (or at least we think now, because our thinking at that time has been overwritten by the way we've told the story since) just then about our in-law Nicola who is working in Hong Kong. She's been getting oil paintings copied at a village in southern China that does such things (... we don't know its name). So we think, or to be more honest to ourselves about this, we now think we thought, to send the photo to the artists in this village, through a Chinese friend of Nicola's, to have it painted as an oil painting. This would be an ironical honoring of this absolutely mundane and absolutely ubiquitous thing.

The painting gets done, then it arrives in a roll in the mail. Now we find some rococo moldings from a demolished building in a second-hand store where we live in Champaign, Illinois, and make a very fancy but also somewhat ramshackle frame, for what? To laugh at framing, to exaggerate the irony, to direct attention to the many symbolisms of Gypsy, China, chairs. And of course, a nice recursion, the oil painting is made in China. A return to a source of meaning and making.

Now we're writing this book and thinking about the idea of transposition, and more pragmatically, wondering what we might ask the publisher to put on the cover. So Bill emails Nicola, and says, could you ask Vivienne (the Anglicized version of her Chinese name that we, for convenience, use) more about that painting? For the intervening years, the painter had been unknown to us and unnamed by us. Is that because we thought this thing, this idea, was ours? Now, shamefully perhaps, we care to find out some other truths.

Nicola emails Vivienne, Vivienne writes back, Nicola forwards the email to Bill, in English except for the footer: "從我的 iPhone 傳送."

Dear Nicola,

Here is the information of the painter: Mr. He Wei Jiang, born in 1966, focused on creative arts painting after the graduation from Guangzhou College of Art at the age of 30.

Mr. He was deeply influenced by his family culture since childhood. He was once the student of the renowned Chinese traditional painting teacher, Mr. Liao Ji Xiang and Mr. Wu Kang in ceramic art painting before graduation from college. His paintings was awarded in different Chinese arts painting contests in the last 20 years.

Besides he established the trading business in 2008 targeted on the markets in Europe and N. America; he extended the hand-crafted painting expertise in interior design area to 5 star hotels in Macau, China and Middle East – walls and roof top, and residential. He started his workshop in Shenzhen, China in 2011 to extend/share his experience and technique with his colleagues and students.

Besides, I also email you the website of the village where the painter was: www.cndafen.com

Hope this helps!

Best

Vivienne[122]

Thank you, Vivienne, for tracking back six years to find this out. She also sends us a photo of Mr. He, very much the artist. Thank you too, Mr. He (belatedly, shamefully).

If you go to the website of Mr. He's village, you'll find out about the awards the artists have won and the paintings they have made. In a culture that disparages some kinds of copying as "fake," you might see some van Goghs and Michaelangelos here. But in these paintings, there's no dissembling that might warrant such an accusation. And here were we, thinking that the painting was a mere copy of the photo, which of course it was, but also it wasn't because that's why we had it painted.

Oh, and the name of the place is Da Fen,

a village under the jurisdiction of Buji Neighborhood Committee of Longgang District, Shenzhen City. It is with 4 square kilometers and over 300 aboriginal people. In 1989, Mr. Huang Jiang, a Hong Kong artist came to Da Fen. He rented the residential buildings and hired arts students and artists to do the creation, imitation, collection and export of the oil paintings, thus, bringing the special industry of oil paintings to Da Fen Village and "Da Fen Oil Paintings" have become the well-known cultural brand at home and abroad.[123]

More than well known, an estimated 60 percent of the world's oil paintings are created in Dafen.[124]

Who is this revered Mr. Huang Jiang, this artist's artist? And what of the aboriginality of his artists and their well-known cultural brand? Where does this fit in the long history of human inequality?

Enough! There is a lot more we could find out, and a lot more that might be said, but where does analysis end and digression start? What, for the sake of analysis, can we make of the transpositions in our *Gypsy China Chairs*?

Reference: There can be no neatly congruent meaning of "Gypsy," and its symptomatic slippages, its failures as reference, are as important as what the word straightforwardly seems to mean.[125] And much more.

[122] Email, October 31, 2016.   [123] www.cndafen.com/index.php?s=/Index/index.shtml

[124] www.artsy.net/article/artsy-editorial-village-60-worlds-paintings-future-jeopardy

[125] Mary Kalantzis and Bill Cope, 2016, "Learner Differences in Theory and Practice," *Open Review of Educational Research* 3(1):85–132.

Agency: Bill, Mary, Nicola, Vivienne, Mr. He, and Mr. Huang Jiang are all at work in their visioning, but who speaks in the image? Who and what are the first, second, and third persons? And much more.

Structure: The frames of old paintings are one of the delights of galleries, and what of our frame, at once formal and scrappy? What is the picture doing as it claims its edges? And much more.

Context: Greece? China? USA? The 2010 of the painting? The 2016 of the email? And much more.

Interest: Greece-ness, at one level, the ironies of globalization at another, the refractions of global inequality, and a thousand other possible interests.

These are questions that open the painting to its parsing. And the answers? It's complicated.

§0.4.1   Design

> **Design.** *An account of patterns in meaning: the patterns of conventional meaning that are our design resources; the transformation of meaning through designing action that brings into play patterns of differing, where the new meaning draws from available resources for meaning, nevertheless transforming these; and the traces of meaning left in the world that are the residues of design.*

Here are some seemingly straightforward patterns in meaning. Signifier (a word, for instance) represents signified (the idea behind the word). Form (a picture, for instance) communicates meaning (the pictured). Text (a particular piece of writing) expresses grammar (replicated patterns of meaning in speech). Expressions of meaning (for instance speech and, some say secondarily, writing) exteriorize patterns in thought.

The specifics of experience can be synthesized by such moves in theories of meaning, and theory of their theories. In these formulations, we might hear the voices of Husserl, Pāṇini, Aristotle, Halliday, Saussure, Bloomfield, or Rousseau. In the parts to come, we'll also have Chomsky, Frege, and a whole host of others speak to us in similar ways.

These ideas offer us powerful insights about meanings that are straightforwardly congruent in the sense that they strive to be more or less "true" to "reality." Here's the word "smile," here's the emoji ☺, here's a picture of a smiling person, and here we see an embodied smile, in a space where the person's body is oriented our way. In a straightforward grammar of multimodality, all of these things stand for a congruent meaning. They "signify," "communicate," "express", "exteriorize." This is how the forms of meaning can be conceived to be true to some underlying meaning. The transpositions are congruent, as between signifier and signified, form and meaning, text and grammar, expression and thought – to this extent transposition falls from view, and becomes a trivial or unnecessary method of analysis.

Yes of course in a way these meanings are congruent, but no, we also want to say, in some important ways also they are not. In the transposition, differences present themselves, as well as similarities. The similarities first: of course there are powerful traces of meaning, vectors of origin. Husserl,[0.4c] for one, gives us a way to track back from immediate origins in the living present, to patterns of meaning inherent to that present, to the patterns in the patterns, and ultimately to transcendental meanings, or the all-encompassing meaning of meanings. This methodology offers us an account of how patterning reproduces itself, how conventions of meaning make sense based on their predictability, and how we can anticipate meanings based on the repetition of previously learned rules for meaning.

But this does not give us an adequate account of the differences. Things change from meaning trace to meaning trace. But how do we make sense of this? Derrida[0.4d] tells us that we can track back over the path of meaning, and in so doing we can see how meaning differs. But then he concludes that all we can do is look at the traces, piecemeal, and deconstruct their immediate cultural and historical contingencies. The circumstantial differences are such that we can't find larger patterns of meaning. When people have tried to find universal patterns, like Husserl, they end up on the fool's errand of metaphysics, a futile attempt to find transcendent patterns in the patterns. Or worse still, a moral lapse, the Western hubris that Derrida calls "logocentrism." Difference is all there is.

We want to have both these things in our theory of meaning: sameness and difference. The sameness is inherited patterns of conventionality; the difference is in the constant remaking of these patterns. The transpositions are in a certain sense and in limited ways congruent; but in transposition there are also always differences. However, in the differences – and this is one of the main ideas of this book – there is another series of patterns, or patterns of incongruence.

Here are some vectors of transposition where we can trace difference as well as similarity. Representation is only ever a partial "take" on the world, but how so? we will ask. Communication always varies according to interpretation, but how so? There are parallels in meaning between different forms, because anything and everything can be said in text, image, space, object, body, sound, and speech. But from meaning form to meaning form, the affordances are different, and so the meaning is never (quite) the same. How so? Then, taking a perspective of meaning function, here is the contradictory play: the functions are not only an account of universal patterns of meaning. They open up for us an account of patterns of difference. How so?

Briefly, some examples. "Reference": there is a distinction between a single instance (represented in a person's name) and the concept ("person"), but in the transposition, while similarities are retained, differences are symptomatically erased. We may be able to transpose a quasi-noun (the abstract entity that is "running") for a verb (the concrete action of "she runs"). This is a matter of congruence in meaning, but also patterned incongruence. In the transposition, the meaning shifts . . . somewhat. So singular does not simply become plural by the grammatical addition of one thing to another, nor are verbs intrinsically different from nouns. They are transpositions for each other, or complex relations of similarity and difference. How so?

Then "agency" explains different perspectives in and of meaning. "Structure" points to the affordances of different forms of meaning that themselves have some degree of influence over the meanings. "Context" points to the infinities of time and space. From the present to the past and future, and from the local to the global, these can be put to work to frame meaning in any which way, though not quite "any." How so? "Interest" suggests that we interrogate the influence of purpose on meanings, of certain kinds of truth and other kinds of deceptions that present themselves in the making of meaning. How so?

The meaning functions, in other words, all bend patterned congruence away from its quest for straightforward truth-in-meaning. But, unlike Derrida, we want to keep our sights on overall meanings. Having begun to follow his socio-historical line of reasoning, deconstructing the provenance of differings, we do not give up on larger patterns. Rather we find another series of patterns that beg analysis. These are the patterns of differing, second-order patterns that undo the first-order patterns, but only in part, and where the undoing itself is patterned. Transposition bends convention as it maintains convention and creates another order of convention. Conventionality explains continuities in human experience. The patterns of differing provide us ways to interpret change. The word we give to this process is "design."§3.2

"Design" has a fortuitous double meaning. On the one hand, design exists in all things in the world. Represented meanings have designs. Their parts can be identified, and also the way these parts fit together: nouns and verbs; hyperlinks and navigation paths; visual frames and focal points; the designs of bodies; the designs of objects, spaces, and nature. Design in this sense is the study of form and structure in the meanings that we make. This is "design" used as a noun.

On the other hand, design is also a sequence of actions, a process motivated by our purposes. This is the kind of design that drives representation as an act of meaning-for-oneself and message-making as an act of communication oriented to others. Design in this sense refers to a certain kind of agency. It is something you do. This is "design" used as a transitive verb. What, then are the processes of design-the-verb, the consequences of which are design-the-noun?

There are three parts to the process of design, themselves indicative of the processes of transposition in all meaning: "design" the noun, "design" the verb, and "design" the noun again. Or:

$$design \Leftrightarrow designing \Leftrightarrow designed$$

Design (patterns): Patterns of meaning in found objects (human and natural) and lived experience. There are first-order patterns, "rules" of meaning in the designs of found meaning-objects that can be applied by way of partial replication.

Designing (actions): The mental and physical work of meaning in the amalgam of ideas and materialized action (praxis). We can mean an infinity of things, even though our field of vision is also constrained by the here-ness and now-ness of experience. We can develop an account of this selection in terms of our identities, and our identities in terms of the unique history of living experience in each of us. Then, our forms of meaning or the mental and material tools we use to represent and communicate our meaning, bending our meaning in ways that are characteristic of these forms (text, image, space, object, body, sound, and speech). We bend our meanings according to the affordances of form, and the forms of our meanings bend us. An analysis of the meaning functions across different modes provides an account of the patterns in the bending, these second-order patterns.

Designed (artifacts): Something made, a trace of the thinking and bodily effort put into meaning. Now we are back to first-order meanings (design), but with traces of second-order meanings (designing). We can track the genealogy of this artifact of meaning back to the design patterns found in the world and lived in experience. We can track the bending of these patterns in the process of designing, providing an account of selection from an infinity of meaning options and the affordances of meaning forms. In parsing a designed artifact we have a theory that accounts both for congruence (the patterns replicated), and incongruence (the impossibility of faithful replication, and the patterns of divergence).

Lo, the world has been redesigned. A completely new meaning has been made, albeit within the social and material conditions of meanability. This can now return to the world as a template for renewed meaning. These are the wellsprings of personal voice, creativity, and human identities. Meanings are both conventional (using available designs for meaning) and inventive (the process of designing). As a consequence, no two designs of meaning are ever quite the same.

The world meant is both the world repeated and the world transformed. Now we have a theory that traces change as well as continuity. Then we can ask, what are the patterns in the transformation?

§0.4.2   To Parse

For the rest of this book and its companion volume, *Adding Sense*, we parse. We suggest that five questions can reasonably be asked about the meaningfulness of something, its functions as meaning (Fig. 0.4.1a(i)). Here we make a bold claim: all five questions can always be asked of anything, and these questions can produce answers that (potentially, if we had the time) address everything about meaning.

When "it" is something that might be meaningful ...	Function
What is it about?	Reference
Who or what is doing it?	Agency
What holds it together?	Structure
What else is it connected to?	Context
What's it for?	Interest

Fig. 0.4.1a(i): Five questions about meaning

Meaning always, inevitably, happens in all five ways simultaneously. Ask these questions of what you will – of printed words, images on screens, buildings or open spaces, objects, bodily gestures, sounds, or spoken utterances. No matter what the form of meaning (text, image, space, object, body, sound, speech), these five questions are always askable, always answerable.

First to the multimodality of forms.[§AS0.1] We often put forms of meaning together – text with image, speech with body, sound with space, for instance. Not only is this a matter of convenience. Much of the time it is impossible not to do. How could you do science without image? How could in-person conversation be without bodies? How could you do buildings without objects? The different forms of meaning go together. They rely on each other. This is why we need a multimodal grammar. In fact, this is reason enough to say that separated scholarly practices such as linguistics, visual communication, architecture, medicine, music, and such like, along with focused insight, bring narrowness of sense, even systematic occlusion.

However, we want to add another element to the theory of multimodality – not only do the forms of meaning go with each other in our daily practices of meaning. The forms of meaning are always ready to become each other.

So, to the word transposition, the main idea of this book, and why we are calling this a "transpositional grammar." We can mean something in text, image, space, object, sound, or speech. And we can always swap out the way we mean. Everything can be meant any which way, though the meaning is never quite the same because of the humdrum materiality of each of the forms – its scope for meaning, its distinctive affordances. The mundane materialities of the different forms of meaning both open and constrain possibilities for meaning. Transposition is how we are always able, and why we are always ready, to swap out one form of meaning for another, as well as to supplement one form of meaning with another, even when this is at the expense of some amount of redundancy. Transposition of meaning-form presents itself as an ever-present readiness.

And to this we will add a second dimension of transposition, of meaning-function.$^{§AS0.2}$ This is what we address in the five questions about meaning. We are suggesting that these questions, these five functions of meaning, are always there, if we care to look. They are five universals. The five functions are integrally with each other, in each other. However, in a practical sense, when we parse, it's best to examine each independently before connecting them. The five functions are perspectives on meaning. The transposition happens by changing the focus of one's meaning-attention.

After this, the idea of transposition becomes all-the-more relevant within each of the functions. In each of the five functions, one kind of meaning is always ready to become another. Nothing is categorically straightforward because, in a flash, there can be functional transposition: a third person by empathy becomes a first; a concept is instantiated; time becomes place; entities act and actions become manifest in entities. These are several of the transpositions we explore in the pages that follow. Within each meaning function, one kind of meaning is always impatiently wanting to slip over into another.

Gone now are the categorical stabilities of traditional grammars, because the key to meaning is in the immediate possibility of movement. Transposability is imminent because it is immanent.

Finally, design. Where nothing sensible is stable, every sense is in the (re)making and nothing is replicated without change. But for all the newness, every meaning has a history, which means that we can always trace sources, though they be heterogeneous. The historical work of finding patterns and tracing their origins, we say, is "to parse."$^{§AS2.5.1}$

In anticipation of our parsing, Fig. 0.4.1a(ii) provides an overview of where we will be travelling for the rest of this book (the first three functions), and its companion, *Adding Sense* (the final two):

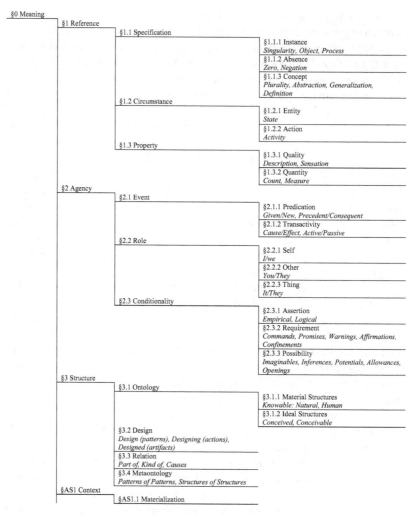

Fig. 0.4.1a(ii): A transpositional grammar

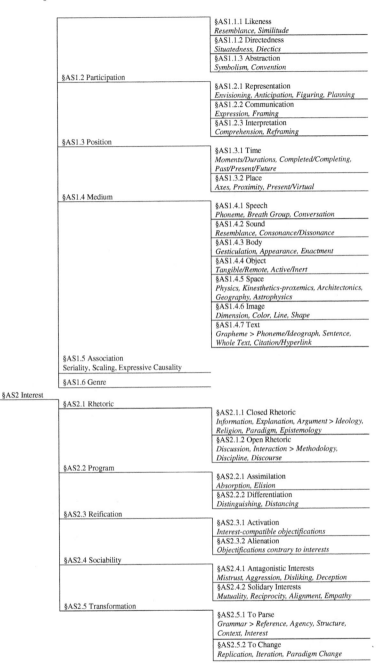

§AS1.2 Participation

§AS1.1.1 Likeness
Resemblance, Similitude

§AS1.1.2 Directedness
Situatedness, Diectics

§AS1.1.3 Abstraction
Symbolism, Convention

§AS1.3 Position

§AS1.2.1 Representation
Envisioning, Anticipation, Figuring, Planning

§AS1.2.2 Communication
Expression, Framing

§AS1.2.3 Interpretation
Comprehension, Reframing

§AS1.4 Medium

§AS1.3.1 Time
Moments/Durations, Completed/Completing, Past/Present/Future

§AS1.3.2 Place
Axes, Proximity, Present/Virtual

§AS1.4.1 Speech
Phoneme, Breath Group, Conversation

§AS1.4.2 Sound
Resemblance, Consonance/Dissonance

§AS1.4.3 Body
Gesticulation, Appearance, Enactment

§AS1.4.4 Object
Tangible/Remote, Active/Inert

§AS1.4.5 Space
Physics, Kinesthetics-proxemics, Architectonics, Geography, Astrophysics

§AS1.4.6 Image
Dimension, Color, Line, Shape

§AS1.4.7 Text
Grapheme > Phoneme/Ideograph, Sentence, Whole Text, Citation/Hyperlink

§AS1.5 Association
Seriality, Scaling, Expressive Causality

§AS1.6 Genre

§AS2 Interest

§AS2.1 Rhetoric

§AS2.1.1 Closed Rhetoric
Information, Explanation, Argument > Ideology, Religion, Paradigm, Epistemology

§AS2.1.2 Open Rhetoric
Discussion, Interaction > Methodology, Discipline, Discourse

§AS2.2 Program

§AS2.2.1 Assimilation
Absorption, Elision

§AS2.2.2 Differentiation
Distinguishing, Distancing

§AS2.3 Reification

§AS2.3.1 Activation
Interest-compatible objectifications

§AS2.3.2 Alienation
Objectifications contrary to interests

§AS2.4 Sociability

§AS2.4.1 Antagonistic Interests
Mistrust, Aggression, Disliking, Deception

§AS2.4.2 Solidary Interests
Mutuality, Reciprocity, Alignment, Empathy

§AS2.5 Transformation

§AS2.5.1 To Parse
Grammar > Reference, Agency, Structure, Context, Interest

§AS2.5.2 To Change
Replication, Iteration, Paradigm Change

Fig. 0.4.1a(ii): (cont.)

Part 1 Reference

§1.0 Overview of Part 1

Reference is a phenomenon both of experience and thinking. It happens when a focal point for meaning is selected by the meaning-maker from the infinities of the world. The meaning – taking form as a mental representation, an act or object of communication, or an interpretation – "stands for" something in the world.

But the "standing for" is never unequivocal or straightforwardly congruent. Immediately it can be transposed for an infinity of contiguous, and not-so-contiguous meanings. In the case of reference, some potential transpositions include between a particular instance and a general concept (or for that matter, an absence), between entities and the actions whereby they are both constituting and constituted, and between properties referenced by quality or quantity. A meaning is always ready to become something else, by act of transposition. Our meaning attentions are ever ready to wander.

Fig. 1.0 provides a schematic overview of the part that follows:

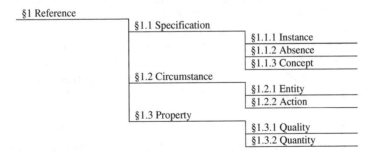

Fig. 1.0: Functions of reference

§1 REFERENCE

> *Reference. The specification of particular instances and general concepts, their circumstances as entities or actions, and their properties as qualities or quantities.*

Things in the world might be identified as entities or actions, though by transposition actions may be construed as entities, and entities as actions. Entities and actions can be particular – a single instance – or multiple, defined in their generality as concepts. By transposition, by way of conceptualization, instances can be connected to the general. This connection of the instance to the general is by means of shared properties, including qualities and quantities.

There are the two vectors of transposition in a grammar of multimodality. One is a depth dimension (to use a spatial metaphor), between functions, where we can alternate the level of our attention between reference, agency, structure, context, and interest. However, these are only alternatives in perspective. All five functions are always to be found. They are always available for the parsing. A layered analysis can bring to our notice different aspects of our attending to meaning.

If all five functions are obligatory, within each function there is considerable fluidity. In the case of reference, instances are ever-ready to become concepts and concepts instantiated. Entities are ever-ready to be sites of action and actions manifest themselves in entities. And everything referenceable has properties, at once qualitative and quantitative, where qualities can be enumerated and quantities can reference qualities.

The other vector we will characterize as horizontal, a breadth dimension. Transposition occurs across meaning forms, when the affordances of text, image, space, object, body, sound, and speech give partly parallel but always differently modulated meanings for us. In this part of the book we will ask, across a breadth dimension, how does reference work across these forms of meaning? What are the parallels? What are the differences? What stays the same and what changes in the transposition from one form to another?

These are the foundations of a "theory of human experience," to apply Halliday's[§0.3a] wording. For these are the very instruments of meaning that we "think with." They are how "we pursue or everyday lives."[1] With Halliday, this is what we mean by "grammar."

---

[1] M.A.K. Halliday, 2000 [2002], "Grammar and Daily Life: Concurrence and Complementarity," pp. 369–83 in *On Grammar*, The Collected Works of M.A.K. Halliday, Volume 1, edited by J.J. Webster, London, UK: Continuum, pp. 369–70.

§1a   *Gottlob Frege's* Sense and Reference

Some thinkers, including those in the twentieth-century tradition of Analytical Philosophy, say that Gottlob Frege[*] founded the modern philosophy of language with his 1892 article "Sense and Reference."[2] Or more, Frege laid the basis for the application of mathematics, logic, and algorithmic thinking that is the basis of modern computing.[3]

For an article that is supposed to be foundational, this one is notable for its haziness, and often remarked to be such by the very philosophers of language who deem it foundational.[4] It is nevertheless a useful starting point for our discussion of the notion of "particular things" or "instantiations," because it sits in a place where we want to make some distinctions that Frege half makes or fails to make.

Here is our paraphrase of the article, addressing the elemental raw material of meaning upon which we want to start to build our transpositional grammar. There are things in the world to which we may refer – referents. We give them a sense, or a meaning-to-us. The process of making sense, of reference, connects the sense we are making to the thing we are making sense of, a referent.

So, to Frege's example, there is a bright star in the sky in the evenings that we call the Evening Star. And there is bright star in the morning we call the Morning Star.[5] The ancients didn't realize it, nor do people today who don't know astronomy, but this is the same star. And in another sense it is not even a star. It is the planet Venus. We have the same referent but different senses. The astronomical referrer has added a layer of inferential reasoning to come to their more scientific senses.

When two people speak of Venus, they not only have the same referent; they have also achieved the same sense. Then we might say, using direct quotes, that the bright star in the evening that we sometimes call the "Evening Star" is in fact the planet called "Venus," which is the same as the "Morning Star."[6] By placing these words inside inverted commas, our referents now have become

---

[*] http://meaningpatterns.net/frege

[2] Gottlob Frege, 1892 [1948], "Sense and Reference," *The Philosophical Review* 57(3):209–30.
[3] Jean-Luc Chabert, ed., 1994 [1999], *A History of Algorithms*, translated by C. Weeks, Berlin, Germany: Springer, p. 455.
[4] Colin McGinn, 2015b, *Philosophy of Language: The Classics Explained*, Cambridge, MA: MIT Press, pp. 5–18; Michael Dummett, 1973, *Frege: Philosophy of Language*, New York, NY: Harper and Row; John McDowell, 1977, "On the Sense and Reference of a Proper Name," *Mind* LXXXVI(342):159–85; Mark Textor, 2011, *Frege on Sense and Reference*, London, UK: Routledge, pp. 103ff.
[5] Gottlob Frege, 1892 [1948], "Sense and Reference," *The Philosophical Review* 57(3):209–30, pp. 212, 215.
[6] Ibid., p. 211.

our sense and we are speaking grammatically – to use this word in the broad way we do in this book, as a process of thinking reflectively about the function of our meaning.

Here Frege is talking about exactly the things that interest us for a transpositional grammar, mainly the connection between our externalizable practices of thinking (and to the words "Morning Star," "Evening Star," and "Venus," we also want to add visualizing, and objectifying, and embodying and other meaning forms) and the world to which these meaning-making practices refer. But pushing the analysis beyond this, Frege becomes vague.

Frege calls the elemental unit of reference, the process of making sense of a referent, a "proper name," a "definite object."[7] But, in English proper names (nouns) are capitalized. "The planet" is also a "proper name" for Frege, though not in our regular understanding of this phrase in traditional grammar. In Frege, there is no definition of "proper name," so its distinction from other semantic units can be based on no more than intuitive recognition of the existence of singularly determinate objects.[8]

Frege encounters several symptomatic problems. He has an "Aristotle" problem, where there can be a number of senses given to this proper name: the student of Plato, the teacher of Alexander the Great, the person born in Stagira, but "so long as the referent remains the same, such variations in sense may be tolerated."[9] But tolerability is a very rough and ready measure. Here, Frege is eliding practices that we will later in this part call attribution of quality (studentness, teacherliness, biographical description, and an infinity of such possible attributions) that add meaning to an instantiation, but do not define the instantiation. The word "Aristotle" and his marble bust are both instantiations, before we add however many of their qualities and his.

So, we need not despair of making sense of "Aristotle," which Frege does to this extent that so many of his senses of the person may be possible: "Comprehensive knowledge of the referent would require us to be able to say immediately whether every given sense belongs to it. To such knowledge we never attain." In a transpositional grammar, the specifiability of a singular referent is not to be confused with the infinite range of describable qualities that might be attributed to that referent.

Then, Frege has an "Odysseus" problem. The sentence "Odysseus was set ashore in Ithaca while sound asleep," has no reference.[10] Homer or his people (we may presume) made it up. However, this highlights something for us about

---

[7] Ibid., p. 210.

[8] Michael Dummett, 1973, *Frege: Philosophy of Language*, New York, NY: Harper and Row, pp. 54–55.

[9] Gottlob Frege, 1892 [1948], "Sense and Reference," *The Philosophical Review* 57(3):209–30, p. 210.

[10] Ibid., p. 215.

human design. We can conjecture possibilities in the form of referents that may later be discovered to exist (the elementary Higgs Boson particle for instance[11]), or we may fail to find them because they don't exist or we can't find them. Or we can imagine things that may be fictional, or half-fictional in the nice way that fictions are always part-true in their characteristic manner of indirectness. Such modes of reference should not give us trouble. In fact, these varied modulations of reference can be specified in our transpositional grammar as ontology.[§3.1]

Next, Frege has a fundamental problem with something variously translated from his German as "identity" or "equality."[12] This is the opening sentence of his now-famous article: "Identity gives rise to some challenging questions which are not altogether easy to answer." At the end of this sentence, a footnote points to this: "I use this word strictly and understand 'a=b' to have the sense of 'a is the same as b' or 'a and b coincide'."[13] Evening Star/Morning Star; "a" can be substituted for "b." Venus can substitute for both. "What else," he asks, "but the truth value could be found, that belongs quite generally to every sentence concerned with the referents of its components and remains unchanged by substitutions of the kind in question?"[14]

We can see two transpositions here, but we are not sure Frege can: one is sense for referent, the thing you see in the sky with one of these three names for it; and the other is sense for sense, or one word for another. But none of these transpositions is ever a matter of identity or equality. Different senses reflect different frames of reference, and in the case of the two stars versus the planet, profoundly so.

And the thing you see in the sky is not in any sense the same as the word. The perceptible thing has a visual and spatial meaning, and the word a spoken or written meaning. Nor is it just the word that is the meaning. Both are acts of meaning, seeing and speaking. Acts of meaning transposition are different in their processes and meaningful effects. We may trace genealogies that account for the similarities in the design process that makes for transposition, but the source and the meaning transposed to another destination are never the same.

And another major problem for us in Frege: what is the difference between the "sense" of his "proper name" and the sense that defines a concept? He issues a "warning against apparent proper names having no referents" because "this leads to demagogic abuse ... 'The will of the people' can serve as an example; for at any rate there is no generally accepted referent for this expression."[15]

---

[11] www.sciencealert.com/cern-discovers-higgs-like-particle
[12] Susanna Schellenberg, 2012, "Sameness of Fregean Sense," *Synthese* 189(1):163–75.
[13] Gottlob Frege, 1892 [1948], "Sense and Reference," *The Philosophical Review* 57(3):209–30, p. 209.
[14] Ibid., p. 217.   [15] Ibid., p. 222.

However, herein lies a fundamental difficulty – "the will of the people" is a concept, not a proper name.

Of course, "the will of the people" as a general concept is always deserving of considerable qualification, in every moment of its specification, as well as the generality of the process. Here is a sentence we have just made up: "The will of the people was expressed in the German Election of 1933." What to make now of this "proper name"? Frege mixes two things where we want to make a fundamental distinction. We will name this as the distinction between an "instance" and a "concept."

On these (it seems) shaky foundations, Frege builds an elaborate logical-mathematical superstructure of inference and truth conditions so things like planets and stars can get sorted. This superstructure is designed to be capable of inferential reasoning that will address "truth values."

A very short version of the story that follows runs like this: Frege builds a logical-mathematical edifice in his monumental two-volume *Basic Laws of Arithmetic*. Bertrand Russell writes him a letter, pointing out that his system is radically incomplete.[16] Frege acknowledges this, in an appendix to his Volume 2. "Hardly anything more unfortunate can befall a scientific writer than to have one of the foundations of his edifice shaken after the work is finished. This was the position I was placed in by a letter of Mr. Bertrand Russell, just when the printing of this volume was nearing its completion."[17] Then, with Alfred North Whitehead, Russell constructs a three-volume monument, *Principia Mathematica*, famously proving after 362 pages that $1 + 1 = 2$.[18] In 1931, Kurt Gödel demonstrates that their mathematical/logical system is also radically incomplete, and perhaps that all such systems must always be incomplete.[19] The paths to transposition are not straightforward, even in their mechanical extension through the rule-based equivalences of logic and mathematics.

Frege was by reputation an austere person, a mechanic of reason who did not give much away about his personal views and life. He taught Gershom Scholem, who became a scholar of Jewish mysticism, and was a close friend of Walter Benjamin. Frege's most significant translator and interlocutor into the world of Anglophone academe was Jean van Heijenoort, former Soviet leader

---

[16] Robert Brandom, 1994, *Making It Explicit: Reasoning, Representing and Discursive Commitment*, Cambridge, MA: Harvard University Press, pp. 436–37.

[17] Gottlob Frege, 1893/1903 [2016], *Basic Laws of Arithmetic*, Oxford, UK: Oxford University Press.

[18] Alfred North Whitehead and Bertrand Russell 1910/1912/1913 [1927], *Principia Mathematica*, Cambridge, UK: Cambridge University Press, Volume 1, p. 362.

[19] Kurt Gödel, 1931 [1962], *On Formally Undecidable Propositions of Principia Mathematica and Related Systems*, Volume 38, translated by B. Meltzer, New York, NY: Basic Books.

Leon Trotsky's bodyguard, secretary, editor, and translator in the years of his exile from 1932 to 1939, and one of artist Freda Kahlo's lovers.[20]

Another great Frege exegete was Analytical Philosopher and anti-racism activist Michael Dummett. Late in his career, Dummett discovered Frege's diary which shows him "to have been a man of extreme right-wing political opinions, bitterly opposed to the parliamentary system, democrats, liberals, Catholics, the French, and above all, Jews, who he thought ought to be deprived of political rights and, preferably, expelled from Germany. When I first read that diary ... I was deeply shocked, because I revered Frege as an absolutely rational man, if, perhaps a not very likeable one."[21]

Scholem and van Heijenoort may never have come to know Frege in the sense Dummett came to know him. But the context of his meaning does help us with Frege's sense of "the will of the people."

§1.1   Specification

> **Specification.** *The identification of something, either in its singularity (an instance) or its generality in more than one instance (a concept); also absences or meaningful non-specification.*

Somewhat more serviceable than Frege's notion of "proper name" is the distinction between singular and plural, or things marked in English by the definite article "the" in contrast to the indefinite article "a."

However, for a grammar of multimodality, we need to escape a framework grounded in speech or writing. Whether it be in writing or any other mode, we want to distinguish kinds of specification, and we do this with the notions of an instance as a matter of singularity and a concept that applies to more than one instance. We also want to note the meaning of absence, or non-specification.

§1.1.1   Instance

> **Instance.** *One thing – an object or process – meaningfully denominated by its singularity and to which our attention may be drawn.*

---

[20] Anita Burdham Feferman, 1993, *From Trotsky to Gödel: The Life of Jean Van Heijenoort*, Natick, MA: A.K. Peters; Jean van Heijenoort, 1978, *With Trotsky in Exile: From Prinkipo to Coyoacán*, Cambridge, MA: Harvard University Press.

[21] Michael Dummett, 1973, *Frege: Philosophy of Language*, New York, NY: Harper and Row, p. xii.

In the specification of a singular thing, the process of its identification we call "instantiation." Using the term "instantiation," rather than "proper name," or "singular," or "definite article," allows our theory of sense-making to escape the conceptual confines of language. Instantiation is but one aspect of reference. It is the process and consequence of specifying a single thing.

An instance is not always uniquely identified, but it is open to identification. If not, as it happens, already instantiated, it is instantiable or at-any-moment-ready to be instantiated. And conversely, something that is posited as instantiable but not yet instantiated (a single Higgs Boson particle, for instance, initially no more than a figment of theory[22]), may later be found to be instantiated (as was the presence of a Higgs Boson particle, found in the Large Hadron Collider in Switzerland on March 14, 2013[23]).

"Instance" stands by way of distinction from "concept." An instance is a single identifiable thing, whereas a concept is more than one thing identifiable by their shared criterial features. It may seem, from the perspective of arithmetic, that 1 and 2 are similar objects. But, from the point of view of our practices of making sense, they are radically different. In fact, the most fundamental of distinctions is not between 1 and 2, but between 1 and any number other than one. Whether that other number is 2 or 2,345 is trivial from the point of view of a grammar of multimodality.

Signs of reference to an instance in written text and speech include proper nouns (marked in written English text by capitalization, but unmarked in speech), definite articles, and noun phrases in the singular. "Mary Kalantzis" and "Bill Cope" are singularly persons and for that reason capitalized in writing. Other family members have had the same names, and so do strangers, known and unknown. The capitalized names are not enough to instantiate definitively. To do that we also need date of birth, and perhaps more if the coincidences go further.

Signs of reference to an instance in image are things that can only have been supposed to exist in one place and one point of time, as photographs always suggest. Images are more straightforward, because there is something always unambiguous about the specificity of the pictured – a person (say, Jean-Paul Sartre), or a thing (say, his pipe), or a place (say, the Pont des Arts, Paris).[*] Signs of reference to an instance of a space are in the one-and-onlyness of a space – this museum, or this kitchen. Signs of reference to an instance of object, this camera in my hand, named in its specificity perhaps by a serial number. Signs of reference to an instance of embodied meaning may be

[*] http://meaningpatterns.net/sartre-pic

[22] Brian Cox and Jeff Forshaw, 2011, *The Quantum Universe: Everything That Can Happen Does Happen*, London, UK: Allen Lane, pp. 203–11.
[23] www.sciencealert.com/cern-discovers-higgs-like-particle

a gesture or bodily appearance in a moment, showing signs of similarity with other gestures and kinds of bodily experience perhaps, but always uniquely expressed in that moment. Or there may be a performance of sound, or spoken utterance, uniquely instantiated because said in one, unrepeatable time and place.

Forms of meaning are proxies for each other, where the meaning of a single person, for example, is their instantiation in a name, image, embodied presence, a statue even. In a transpositional grammar, cross-reference is the meaningful connection between one form of meaning and another. Instantiation is a process of always-being-about-to-become: a thing that is ready to be named, or a name in search of its possible object; a picture whose object is about to be found, or a found object that could be pictured; an event that could be indicated by a sound, or a sound indicating an event. Instantiation is sometimes a traceable actuality; at other times it is the absolute possibility of its meaning to appear as an instance. These are form/form transpositions. They are things that, from one form of meaning to another, stand for each other.

In this analysis, "language" is not a higher form of meaning that defines our human-ness. Nor do the abstractions of theory, logic, and the mechanics of quantification overlie language alone. They may also be rendered visually, in diagram, geometry, and mathematical formula, for example. It is the habit of Analytical Philosophers and theorists of "the language turn" to privilege the ways in which written or spoken words overlie visual, sounded, material, and embodied meanings. Then the logicians and mathematicians layer over language progressively deeper abstractions.

We want to give equal credence to journeys in the other direction, where just as readily we may transpose an object for a word, or a visualization for a number. This is as powerfully meaningful a vector of transposition, just as important as language. It is the patterns of transposition across meaning forms that define our human-ness. We are not mainly a "language animal"[24] or even a "symbolic species"[25] whose peculiar bent is to abstract in verbal concepts.[AS§1.1.3a] We are a species of meaning-transposers – as for that matter are other species, though in their different ways.

As well as form/form transpositions, there are also always-possible function/function transpositions, one of which is the transposition of instance with concept, or one with more than one. Whichever direction we go, form/form or function/function, these transpositions are the product of a meaning act (designing), whose patterned genealogy is traceable to found meaning artifacts (available designs), and whose consequence is always new, transformed

---

[24] Charles Taylor, 2016, *The Language Animal: The Full Shape of the Human Linguistic Capacity*, Cambridge, MA: Harvard University Press.

[25] Terrence W. Deacon, 1997, *The Symbolic Species: The Co-Evolution of Language and the Brain*, New York, NY: W.W. Norton.

meaning (the redesigned).$^{§0.4.1}$ Every such act is equally and in concert a mental act and a materially manifest act. It is a never-to-be-repeated conjunction of transposition across meaning forms and meaning functions.

"Instance," to restate this in somewhat different terms, stands in contrast with "concept." These are the two canonical forms of specification. If a concept stands for something general, something of which two or more instances may exist, an instance stands only for itself. It is just one thing. For the moment at least, an instance is irreducible in its singularity, its uniqueness. Here is a proper noun written down, "Mary Kalantzis," or we could show you a photo that is unmistakably just her, or you may experience her bodily presence if you happen to be in the same space and time, or you may see and hear that bodily presence in a video. A related concept is "person," which may be two if she is speaking to another one, or billions if we consider all those alive today.

Consider, then, the map of multimodal specification in Fig. 1.1.1, anticipating ideas that will be outlined in greater detail as this part unfolds:

Form / Function: Specification	Text	Image	Space	Object	Body	Sound	Speech
Instantiation	A singular noun or noun phrase, capitalized proper noun, "the" something, an alphanumeric identifier	An intelligible sight or image of something	Some-where, a particular space	A present object, some-thing, an item	A corporeal person	Some sound or distinguishable cluster of sounds that can stand for something	A speech act
Conceptual-ization	A plural noun or noun phrase, a generalizing common noun, "a," "any," or "all" something, a classifier of alphanumeric identifiers	An image standing for a kind of thing, or more than one thing	A kind of space	A kind of object, a product	Persons, people in the generalities of more than one	A repeated sound, a symbolic sound	A way of speaking, a kind of speech act

Fig. 1.1.1: Specification

On the horizontal axis, through the process of specification, forms can be transposed for each other. Or transposable forms can be juxtaposed, creating both redundancy by virtue of the parallelism and supplementary meaning by virtue of the irreducibly unique affordances of each form of meaning.

The rule of both instantiation and conceptualization is meaningful minimalism. Some redundancy is helpful, but there can be too much, so specify just enough for the transposition to indicate either one-ness and singularity, or multiplicity and generality. Specify just enough to be definite in the determination of this particular instance or general concept; just enough to disambiguate; and no more than is necessary.

On the vertical axis, within the function of reference, its possibilities are always on the move; each possibility can be transposed for another. An instantiation is ever-ready to be framed as an instance of a concept, or a concept is ever-ready to be manifest and exemplified in an instance. A concept is defined by criterial aspects that are worthy of our attention across more than one instance. And here arises another rule of meaningful minimalism: the fewer the criterial features, the more serviceable the concept.

§1.1.1a Henri Cartier-Bresson's The Decisive Image

If we know today the look of this indisputably singular person, Jean-Paul Sartre, it is often through one, remarkable photograph by Henri Cartier-Bresson.* It's numbered Image 60, *The Decisive Image*, and indexed, "Jean-Paul Sartre on the Pont des Arts, Paris, 1946."[26] The name can transpose for the image (tracking a form/form move in our grammar of multimodality), or the image for the name.

I had just discovered the Leica. It became an extension of my eye, and I have never been separated from it since I found it. I prowled the streets all day, feeling very strung up and ready to pounce, determined to "trap" life – to preserve life in the act of living . . . Of all the means of expression, photography is the only one that fixes forever the precise and transitory instant.[27]

Instantiation is realized in an instant, and from the point of view of context, the instance is one that is never quite repeatable. But the instantiation always fixes something quite definitive. In this case, at this instant in 1946, the singularity of Sartre was "trapped." It's unequivocally, unambiguously Jean-Paul Sartre, so we are told, and of course, the famous Jean-Paul Sartre and none other. There is no reason to disbelieve his singularity, represented here in name and image, the one confirming the other.

The casualness, the context-laden-ness also speaks to a certain facticity. Such was Cartier-Bresson's art.

I infinitely prefer, to contrived portraits, those little identity-card photos which are pasted side by side, row after row, in the windows of passport photographers. At least there is on those faces something that raises a question, a simple factual testimony.[28]

---

* http://meaningpatterns.net/sartre-pic

[26] Henri Cartier-Bresson, 1952 [2014], *The Decisive Moment: Photography by Henri Cartier-Bresson*, Göttingen, Germany: Steidl.

[27] Ibid., Introduction, unnumbered pages. [28] Ibid., Introduction, unnumbered pages.

We don't know who Sartre was speaking to in Cartier-Bresson's photograph. We might presume that the photographer knew, and even if it happened that he did not, we can also be certain of their namability, their findability in a register of births, and other traces of acts of instantiation that might demonstrate without a shadow of doubt their specific personhood. Cartier-Bresson, of course, may also have known this person, or not; but for the purposes of visual representation, they are not named. So, they stand out of frame, a meaningful absence pointing to the general concept of an interlocutor in existential conversation – another philosopher or a student, perhaps.

This is how particulars are ever-ready to become generalities, and how a concept might transpose for an (only possible) instantiation in an image.

§1.1.1b The Leica M3

Cartier-Bresson used one kind of camera for his whole career as a photographer, a 35mm Leica. As cameras went in the pre-digital era, it is small and unassuming.[*] The first Leicas were made in 1913, but the one that Cartier-Bresson used for the longest time was the M3, a model manufactured from 1954 to 1966.

All Leicas have serial numbers, and these are laboriously listed on a website for collectors who want to find out exactly when a particular camera was manufactured. The number sequence of M3s is listed, along with a description of the hundred or so permutations: the batch of 300 black M3s produced in 1963 (#s 1078501 to 1078800); the batch of five M3s with green enamel manufactured in February 1967 (#s 1158996 to 1159000). We counted the rows – there were 110 permutations of the M3. Then we added up the Batch column: 227,608 M3s were manufactured.[29] That's 227,608 instantiations. One of these, or perhaps several, would have been Cartier-Bresson's. We don't know the serial number of his camera, but it would have had one, and this is how we might be able to know without ambiguity that a particular camera was his.

It's a definitive list, but at the same time ramshackle, typical of lists like this that keep getting added to over time. The numbers are not consecutive, because a new batch would often (but not always) start with 01 in the final position in the number, which meant there was a gap in the numbering whenever a batch was less than 100. The first model in the M series was the M3; the M1 and M2 came later. #1000070, our list tells us, was accidentally numbered thus on two

---

[*] http://meaningpatterns.net/leica

[29] www.cameraquest.com/mtype.htm

cameras. The cameras NASA took into space are not listed; if they had numbers, the website says, they are presently unknown.

The M7 was the last film camera Leica made. Digital Ms have been manufactured since 2006, and by 2017 the model iterations had reached M10. But the details of the story, if you care to go into them, are much messier than this. For all the efforts to document the inconsistencies, one thing remains clear – every M is instantiable, and necessarily so if you are a collector purchasing one, or a store worker accounting for inventory, or insuring a camera, or reporting a theft to the police.

Here's the Leica M3 schema in terms of our grammar of multimodality. The instantiation happens at a level we call "item," whose meaning is established in the transposability of the irreducibly singular object, the camera, with its "proper name" (if you like, to use Frege's flawed term,[1a] but only by way of language metaphor) – in this case serial number. We could also do the equivalent of proper naming with image. Sellers on eBay do this by providing photos of the particular configuration of scratches, marks, or other unique features of well used cameras.

The instantiation is the camera numbered or pictured or held in the hand. The concept is a level that we might call the "product," definable at a number of levels of generality: Leica M3 batch → Leica M3→ Leica M → Leica → camera.

§1.1.1c Everyday "Identifiers"

In late modernity, we find ourselves doing more instantiation than ever before. It is a sign of our times. The modern story of instantiation comes in two episodes. In a first episode, we develop a proclivity to instantiate that comes with private property and the marketable commodity, an episode now several centuries old and ongoing. In a more recent episode, in the era of digitized meanings we have a phenomenon popularly called "the internet of things." This is a standardized and massively generalized sociotechnical system of instantiation, and in which many objects now "speak" their names, albeit in ways that are limited by the affordances of calculability: scannable products instantiated at a point of sale; bags instantiated at the airport with bag tags; objects connectable to sensors in the internet of things.

First, to explore the older tradition in modernity. The difference between a product number and a serial number is the difference between a product and an item, or in the terms of our grammar, between a concept and an instantiation. A lithographic print may say 7/50, where the title/artist/date/print run is the concept and the number in the print run is the instantiation. A book may have an ISBN, but a single item in the library may be marked "copy 2," or a special edition may be numbered, or a second-hand book may have a particular configuration of features ("signed by the author") or flaws that are documented at a point of sale. In the case of a rare book, a narrative of provenance may be needed to prove this book is not a forgery or stolen. A packet of cereal may have a barcode using encoding EAN-13 number, a unique product number, but a single packet may be instantiated in a product safety inspection, or when it is linked to a purchaser in the moment of scanning at the supermarket checkout, or when that purchaser returns that product because it is flawed.

Products worthy of theft, from Leica cameras to iPhones and cars, have serial numbers at the item level as well as product numbers. Some of these are now so rigorously tracked that theft has been radically reduced because there is little or no resale value for items whose ownership history is traceable. Banknotes have serial numbers. Virtual money transactions have record numbers. Downloaded software can have a serial number, recording a single purchase. A suitcase wending its way through the luggage sorting system at an airport is, for this episode of travel at least, uniquely identifiable by the barcode on a bag tag. These are all grammatical acts of instantiation, of meaningful transposition which produces the effect of "one," of singularity.

In a universe that is today called "metadata," there is a mandatory field called "identifier" which may speak either to a concept (the product) or the instances (an item). The atomic unit of data is the item identifier.

Persons are identifiable via the same grammatical process as any other "thing." Crossing today's borders, the process identification via transposition moves between inarguably singular bodily presence, and the instantiation of that presence by cross-reference to other records of unambiguous bodily presence (biometric indicators such as finger prints, iris recognition, or face IDs), country/passport number, name/date of birth/place of birth, and facial photograph. There is enough transposition in each case for the instantiation to be considered definitive.

In dealings with governments or employers our identifiers may be social security numbers, or tax file numbers, or driver's license numbers, or some other such government-issued ID. In online accounts an email address is often enough, because no two email addresses in the world can be the same, and even if you have more than one, each will always point to a singular account holder. Including international area codes (a standard established in 1960, now regulated by the International Telecommunication Union), phone numbers are unique – and with the now-ubiquitous mobile phone, these are directly attached to bodies. Credit cards point directly to persons and their financial credibility, and no two credit card numbers in the world can be the same.[30]

These are all systems of definitive instantiation – global in their reach and universal in their application. These alphanumeric names perform the function

---

[30] David L. Stearns, 2011, *Electronic Value Exchange: Origins of the Visa Electronic Payment System*, London, UK: Springer-Verlag.

formerly served by proper nouns, and with greater success in terms of the reliability of their instantiation. There is no way to live a life that avoids this all-but-absolute, mostly unequivocal instantiation.

If it wasn't enough that each scheme insists on unique identification of persons, there is the constant triangulation of one scheme of instantiation against others. Organizations ask people with whom they interact to supply various combinations of credit card information, email address, mobile phone number, or government ID. Then they periodically check these triangulations with authentication routines. If there is any shadow of ambiguity, you will be peremptorily excluded from any social contract that you, for the moment or in the future, might wish to enter.

§1.1.1d Numbers as Text

Less and less used, usable, and useful these days are instantiations formerly achieved by speech or in text. Iris recognition is less ambiguous than your proper name. A product and serial number is more definitive than "my iPhone." We need to be able to instantiate definitively to get down to (serious) business.

Numbers are text, in our Unicode definition.[§0.2.1] They are certainly not speech, because they are mostly in a practical sense unspeakable. They are only for transcription, or writing. Here is another illustration of the profound differences between speech and writing, a difference that has been intensified in the age of digital representation and communication of meaning. In a language like English that purports to be phonemic, numbers are graphemes. They are in this respect closer to image than other forms of writing.

Increasingly also, machine-readable numbers present as images, mainly today the abstractions of barcodes and QR codes that are unreadable by humans, but nevertheless images and not writing.[*] The identifier is the connection between an item (instantiation) or product (concept) and a universe of items and products, and an identifier is not separable from an item lest it confuse or lose its identity. In the case of products, the identifier is not simply inscribed on the item; it becomes part of the item. Its product-ness is established by its unique identification in a matrix of interconnections between other items and products, records of which are kept that offer supplementary confirmation of its individual item-ness and conceptual instantiation as a product. The data and the metadata are at one.

We have taken to using text and images (of these particular sorts – numbers and machine-readable visualizations of number), as well as biometric indicators of bodily presence – because they are so much clearer in their instantiation than conventional alphabetical names or speech. No longer can we live our ordinary lives without them.

---

[*] http://meaningpatterns.net/numbers-as-text

§1.1.1e Penelope Umbrico's Sunset Portraits

The gallery that exhibited this work[*] by the artist Penelope Umbrico called it an "installation." In our grammar, it's an instantiation. The evidence is in its presence at an exhibition and the metadata that testifies to its specificity: "*Sunset Portraits from 27,700,711 Sunset Pictures on Flickr on 05/04/15.* 2015. 1,625 machine c-prints. Each 4in x 6in. Installation view at Sextant et plus, FOMO, Marseille, France."[31] We define this instantiation by its singularity.

But in a cleverly reflexive way, the work instantiates in order to reflect on the processes of instantiation. It's clever-funny (just imagine, such ordinary pictures are art?) as well as clever-serious. 1,625 sunset photos are here instantiated in this instantiation of apparent sameness, but profoundly, no two are the same. The 1,625 must have been selected in an arbitrary kind of way from 27,700,711 instantiations Umbrico says were so labeled by Flickr on that day, because we know the artist could have not looked at all of them. The classification has been conceptual, and at this scale, the conceptualizing work has been done by the original photographers if they have tagged their pictures, or perhaps by the artificial intelligence of the image recognition software that has read their images.[§AS1.4.6c]

For Sunset Portraits I found images where the technology of the camera is exposing for the sun, not the people in front of it, thereby erasing the subjectivity of the individual. I use the entire photograph for this work, thinking of the relationship between the collective and the individual, the individual assertion of 'I am here' in the process of taking the photograph, and the lack of individuality that is ultimately expressed, and experienced, when faced with so many assertions that are more or less all the same.[32]

But every picture has been unambiguously instantiated. Every one will be unequivocally instantiated like this one, a picture of the artist taken at an exhibition in 2015: https://www.flickr.com/photos/thealdrich/16807094213/in/photolist-rBbKyr-6oucUz-4PmdeU-8mnSgq-Ddcu95-ar41bm-axKY1y-cqV1Cw-nFmUmP-nHoNCM-7NZSAn-cCbJvC-bq4EL8-dQzxqe-bbyZf8-e64emg-6oucVc-f7BKaH-7vFnLz-da9Wop-fgSrJ5-a3Hk5r-cqV6Au-8jR1Z3-f7yLYt-9XRpzo-fm15cn-fSQcgA-fm1esZ-7WkVuH-8zGQxu-f7PaaQ-8JeFPq-fgCrLR-fmfibQ-f7yW3c-f7yWmP-fm187F-fm1dba-fgCuVB-fmfd43-f7P2s1-fm14na-fgCs5D-6z2cwo-fm17gv-f7yW5t-fmfnCA-bgB1hk-fgCuHt

This is not a word because it can't be spoken or even realistically written. We couldn't type this and be sure we get it right. We had to "paste" it in – a nice metaphorical association with scrap-booking images. It's a machine-readable grapheme. This is what proper nouns or noun phrases of yore used to do, but

---

[*] http://meaningpatterns.net/umbrico

[31] http://penelopeumbrico.net/index.php/project/sunset-portraits/   [32] Ibid.

which they can't do given the clarity of instantiation that we have found today we must have.

§1.1.1f URLs and TCP/IP

Every URL or Uniform Resource Locator on the web must be unique. It must succeed at instantiating web pages, and with that incidentally the thing to which the web page refers. It does this with a precision that makes the grammatical work of natural language decidedly inadequate to our times.

There are of course antecedents in earlier modern classification, cataloguing, and numbering systems. However, URLs demand a more rigorous and global system of instantiation than any of their predecessors. There is no other system of instantiation in the world of digitized meaning. There is no differentiation in the naming system whether the meaning form on the destination web page is written text (including dynamic data represented in Unicode$^{\S0.2.1a}$), image, representations of 3D space, embodied meanings captured on video, audio, or recorded speech. This uniform, universal, always unequivocally singular mode of instantiation crosses all meaning forms. The URL does not just name an object of representation. When it takes the form of a link, the name is "active"; it will take you to the object.

URLs have their own internal structure: "http://" is the name of the universal naming protocol, "hypertext transfer protocol." The domain name is a unique address that can be written in natural language: "cgscholar.com." This is the domain name for our multimodal web writing platform, Common Ground Scholar. Then sections of digital data are delineated with hierarchical file path syntax: "/community/profiles/william-cope".

Paul Mockapetris is credited with conceiving the domain name system in 1987.[33] For the next decade, Jon Postel, an academic at UCLA and after that the University of Southern California, managed the domain name system. Since 1998, the singularity of domain names is regulated by the Internet Corporation for Assigned Names and Numbers (ICANN), a not-for-profit corporation based in Los Angeles.

Underlying the domain name system is a technology dating from 1974, Transmission Control Protocol/Internet Protocol (TCP/IP), where every device connected directly into the internet or a gateway server that connects other devices has an address in the form of a never-to-be-replicated number.[34] Domain names are proxies for IP address numbers. The IP address for http://cgscholar.com is

---

[33] Paul V. Mockapetris, 1987, "Domain Names: Concepts and Facilities," Network Working Group (https://tools.ietf.org/html/rfc1034).

[34] Vinton G. Cerf and Robert E. Kahn 1974, "A Protocol for Packet Network Inter-communication," *IEEE Trans. Comm. Tech.* COM-22(V5):627–41.

"206.221.145.251."[*] After reaching cgscholar.com at this address, there are then (in this case) hundreds of thousands of pages, each with its own unique name. After reaching gmail.com, there are one billion accounts, every one accessible via a unique email address.[35] Emails sent to <bill.cope@cgnetworks.org> find their way into an inbox at Gmail.

TCP/IP became the standard for all computers on ARPANET,[§AS1.4.7e] the network of research computers whose development had been funded by the US Department of Defense. All these computers were set to work on TCP/IP as of January 1, 1983.[36] Since 1986, the internet has been "governed," to use an anachronistic term, by the Internet Engineering Task Force, a not-for-profit, voluntary coalition of experts who develop technical standards via a process quaintly called "Request for Comments." Says one of its founders, David Clark, "We reject kings, presidents and voting. We believe in rough consensus and running code."[37]

Never before has there been a singular system of proper naming that operates across all languages, all states, all forms of meaning. This is a unique creature of the universe of digitized meanings.

§1.1.1g The Internet of Things

Then comes the "Internet of Things," where ordinary objects transmit data from sensors. The first time this happened was in a Coke vending machine, modified by researchers at Carnegie Mellon University in 1982 to report its inventory via the internet.[38] Today, such objects include cars, homes, products, and wearable devices attached to our bodies, including "smart" watches and phones.

Objects in the Internet of Things are not just waiting to be read, as was the case for barcodes or QR codes. These are objects that can speak, transmitting data through the internet in one way or another – a transmitted video of a person at the door in the case of an internet-connected doorbell; the number of steps taken in the case of a fitness tracker; or the location of an item in the case of products fitted with a miniaturized RFID (Radio Frequency Identification)

---

[*] http://meaningpatterns.net/url

[35] http://expandedramblings.com/index.php/gmail-statistics/

[36] Barry M. Leiner, Vinton G. Cerf, David D. Clark, Robert E. Kahn, Leonard Kleinrock, Daniel C. Lynch, Jon Postel, Larry G. Roberts, and Stephen Wolff, 2009, "A Brief History of the Internet," *SIGCOMM Computer Communication Review* 39(5):22–31; Ulysees Black, 2000, *Internet Architecture: An Introduction to IP Protocols*, Upper Saddle River, NJ: Prentice Hall.

[37] Paul Hoffman, 2012, "The Tao of Ietf: A Novice's Guide to the Internet Engineering Task Force": Internet Engineering Task Force. (www.ietf.org/tao.html).

[38] www.cs.cmu.edu/~coke/history_long.txt

chip.[*] And every time such objects speak, they must speak their name; to be meaningful, the object must identify itself as a singular instantiation or conceptually as an instance of the product it represents.

This development, as well as the dramatic extension of access to the internet (46 percent of the world's population in 2016, compared to 17.6 percent a decade before[39]), has produced new challenges for the universal naming system of TCP/IP. Since 1983, the underlying numbering system for all networked devices has been specified in a protocol called "IPv4." However, this faces the imminent threat of address space exhaustion, as only 4.3 billion addresses are available in this naming scheme.[40]

When the internet was mainly "pages," this was enough slots for unique names. But now that it extends to a myriad of devices and "things," the naming scheme has to be extended. To address this problem, a voluntary group of experts, the Internet Engineering Task Force, has since 1992 been working on a successor protocol, IPv6, launched as a parallel scheme in 2012. IPv6 will support 3.4×10^{38} addresses.[41] Or to put this another way, that's an increase from 4,300,000,000 possible proper names to 340,000,000,000,000,000,000,000,000,000,000,000,000 internet-wide proper names.

Behind these are many more proper names that have been created locally by way of extension to these IP addresses – the pathway of forward slashes after the domain name in a URL, or the email address, or the device identifier on the other side of a gateway. And if the scope for proper naming here becomes not enough, experts will surely agree to revise the top-level TCP/IP naming scheme once again, while of course preserving the integrity of the older one. There might be resistances to scaling, called in the trade "address exhaustion." But these are just that, resistances that are never insurmountable.

So here are the social facts: we have just one global system of proper naming of computer-networked meanings and, by extension, the things to which they refer. Now we are proper-naming more and more things (in our grammar, specifying instances). These are objects, moreover, that can speak to their data, but they only speak meaningfully when they also speak to their unambiguous specificity.

Nor is there anything particularly mathematical about the numbers; you can't add the number that instantiates the sensor at your doorbell with the sensor on your wrist. Every number points to an incalculable singularity. It is a name and not a quantity in a grammatical sense. And of course, in terms of our theory of meaning-transpositions, instantiations could also be named in words, uniquely

---

[*] http://meaningpatterns.net/internet-of-things

[39] www.internetlivestats.com   [40] https://en.wikipedia.org/wiki/IPv4
[41] https://en.wikipedia.org/wiki/IPv6

as is the case for URLs that are not impracticably long, or vaguely as is the case for "Mary's iPhone."

§1.1.1h Lewis Carroll's Alice

Alice, in this book unmistakably written by a professor of logic, is talking to a gnat (as you do, in Wonderland).

" – then you don't like all insects?" the Gnat went on . . .
    I like them when they can talk," Alice said. "None of them ever talk, where *I* come from."
    "What sorts of insects do you rejoice in, where *you* come from?" the Gnat inquired.
    "I don't *rejoice* in insects at all," Alice explained, "because I am rather afraid of them – at least the large kinds. But I can tell you the names of some of them."
    "Of course, they answer to their names?" the Gnat remarked carelessly.
    "I never knew them to do it."
    "What's the use of their having names," the Gnat said, "if they won't answer to them?"[42]

In Alice's journeys into enchantment,[§3.1.1b] all kinds of things answer to their names.[*] So today do many other things, though not yet insects.

§1.1.1i "Big Data"

The techno-enthusiasts and idea peddlers are breathless in their optimism about the potential of an internet where things speak their names. The founder of a company called Ambient Devices calls the instantiations on the internet of things "enchanted objects" that will "respond to our needs, come to know us, or learn to think ahead on our behalf."[43]
    Here is another author who predicts that, after a period that can apparently be called "Pax Americana," we are destined to have a "pax technica," or "a political, economic, and cultural arrangement of social institutions and net-worked devices in which government and industry are tightly bound in mutual defense pacts, design collaborations, standards setting, and data mining."[44]
    A "big data" revolution, exhorts a professor from the Oxford Internet Institute and his co-author, will "transform how we live, work and

---

[*] http://meaningpatterns.net/alice

[42] Lewis Carroll, 1872 [2000], *The Annotated Alice: Through the Looking Glass*, edited by M. Gardner, New York, NY: W.W. Norton, p. 173.

[43] David Rose, 2014, *Enchanted Objects: Design, Human Desire, and the Internet of Things*, New York, NY: Scribner, dustjacket blurb.

[44] Philip N. Howard, 2015, *Pax Technica: How the Internet of Things May Set Us Free or Lock Us Up*, New Haven, CT: Yale University Press, pp. 145–46.

think."[45] And here is a non-fiction author whose quest for futurism has produced a string of best sellers: "Connecting everyone and everything in a global network driven by extreme productivity moves us ever faster and faster toward an era of nearly free goods and services and, with it, the shrinking of capitalism in the next half century and the rise of the collaborative columns as the dominant model for organizing economic life."[46]

This is the "new digital age, transforming nations, businesses and our lives" say the Executive Director of Google and his Director of Google Ideas, in the title of their book.[47]

But there is every reason to be skeptical about such claims.[48] A commission led by John Podesta in the Obama White House qualified his group's optimism for the future of commodity capitalism with a measure of circumspection: "The fusion of many different kinds of data, processed in real time, has the power to deliver exactly the right message, product, or service to consumers before they even ask. Small bits of data can be brought together to create a clear picture of a person to predict preferences or behaviors ... Unfortunately, 'perfect personalization' also leaves room for subtle and not-so-subtle forms of discrimination in pricing, services, and opportunities."[49] And of course, surveillance by corporations and states, and lack of privacy.

A report commissioned by the US Department of Defense paints a bleaker picture of possibility:

If the United States executes wisely, the IoT could work to the long-term advantage of the domestic economy and to the US military ... Ability to fuse sensor data from many distributed objects could deter crime and asymmetric warfare ... On the other hand, we may be unable to deny access to networks of sensors and remotely-controlled objects by enemies of the United States ... Massively parallel sensor fusion may undermine social cohesion if it proves to be fundamentally incompatible with Fourth-Amendment guarantees against unreasonable search.[50]

[45] Viktor Mayer-Schönberger and Kenneth Cukier, 2013, *Big Data: A Revolution That Will Transform How We Live, Work, and Think*, New York, NY: Houghton Mifflin Harcourt.

[46] Jeremy Rifkin, 2014, *The Zero Marginal Cost Society: The Internet of Things, the Collaborative Commons, and the Eclipse of Capitalism*, New York, NY: Palgrave Macmillan, p. 16.

[47] Eric Schmidt and Jared Cohen 2013, *The New Digital Age: Transforming Nations, Businesses, and Our Lives*, New York, NY: Vintage Books.

[48] Phillip Kalantzis-Cope, 2016, "Whose Data? Problematizing the 'Gift' of Social Labour," *Global Media and Communication* 12(3):295–309.

[49] John Podesta, Penny Pritzker, Ernest Moniz, John Holdern, and Jeffrey Zients, 2014, "Big Data: Seizing Opportunities, Preserving Values," Washington, DC: Executive Office of the President, p. 7.

[50] SRI Consulting Business Intelligence Consulting, 2008, "Disruptive Civil Technologies: Six Technologies with Potential Impacts on US Interests out to 2025," Washington, DC: National Intelligence Council, p. 27.

§1.1.1j   Joseph Kusuth's Real

> **Real** ... *adj.* ... **1.** existing or happening as or in fact; actual, true, objectively so, etc.; not merely seeming, pretended, imagined, fictitious, nominal, or ostensible. **2.** authentic, genuine. **3.** in *law*, of or relating to permanent, immovable things: as *real* property; opposed to *personal*. **4.** in *mathematics*, not imaginary: said of a number or quantity. **5.** in *optics*, of or relating to an image made by the actual meeting of light rays at a point. **6.** in *philosophy*, existing objectively; actual (not merely possible or ideal), or essential, absolute, ultimate (not relative, derivative, phenomenal, etc.) *n.* anything that actually exists, or reality in general (with *the*). *adv.* ... very. – *SYN.* see true.[51]

We found an instantiation of this text in what was described by the artist Joseph Kusuth or his curator as "mounted photograph," *'Titled (Art as Idea as Idea) [real],'* 1968. "Courtesy of the artist and the Sean Kelly Gallery," says the curator's inscription to its left while the work was in the National Gallery of Art, in Washington, DC. Doubtless, the work is catalogued to be certain of its provenance, testifying to the "real"-ness of the work for the purposes of exhibition or sale by the gallery representing the artist. This instantiation must, of proprietorial necessity, be completely unambiguous.

Actually, there are two instantiations we would like to mention here, one we saw that day in the National Gallery, and another in the form of IMG_7177. JPG, taken on Bill's iPhone, date stamped Oct 19, 2016, 1.56pm.[*] The precise geolocation is identified as a pinpoint on a map, but more vaguely named in words by the phone as "National Mall" and "Pennsylvania Ave NW, Washington DC." This instantiation, too, is completely unambiguous. When it comes to the instantiation of meaning, this is as real as it gets.

Words are, by and large, pretty bad at instantiation. However, you might think that there could be no word more grounded, specifiable, identifiable – in sum instantiable – than "real." Take this work, "Real." It has been taken (we presume) from some (unacknowledged) dictionary. Or did the artist know the genre of dictionary well enough to write the definition? A Google search on combinations of words in this definition does not turn up a "real" source. However, it does turn up similarities in the definitions for "actual," "pre-existing," "synchronous," "present," and "potential."

Also, the text in the work is white on black, not a practice of "real" dictionaries. Perhaps this is to unsettle our conventional images of dictionaries. And of course, it is bigger; we can read it from half a room away. "Unrealistically" too, there is no word before or word after. Then there are the six definitions offered for "real," where the brevity deceives

---

[*] http://meaningpatterns.net/kusuth-real

[51] Joseph Kusuth, *'Titled (Art as Idea as Idea) [real]'*, Mounted photograph, 1968.

because the person in search of a meaning has to be acquainted with a whole universe of social practice to be able to know what it would be to be "not imaginary" in mathematics, or "merely phenomenal" in philosophy. This creates some almost insurmountable problems for the computability of language, which our Google search in this case showed. Not only could we not find the source. Reverse engineering the definition, we found the wrong words.

The curator's blurb on the wall of the gallery starts out, "Kusuth argued that ideas alone could exist as art." But what we learn – and this may or may not have been the artist's intention – is that the sources of "real" are exceedingly complex, even elusive.

Because the meaning of "real" is so fraught, we are left with just two things that were indubitably real, instantiations in the multimodal grammar of modernity: "Joseph Kusuth *Titled (Art as Idea as Idea) [real],'* 1968" and "IMG_7177.JPG" on Bill's iPhone. And now there is a third instantiation circling this work, this paragraph on this page in a book that has both an ISBN (International Standard Book Number) and a DOI (Digital Object Identifier). And of course there are countless other possible instantiations.

§1.1.2   Absence

Absence. *Meaningful non-instantiation.*

Here is not-real (or, if "real," then in a qualitatively different, indeed paradoxical, kind of way): zero,[52] "no"/"not" (text); something notably out-of-the picture (image) or missing (object); emptiness (space); a poignant nonpresence (body); silence (sound and speech).

This type of not-real is always something (a thing, or a kind of thing) that is absent in a meaningful way. Unmeaningful absence is utterly unseeable, unhearable, insensible, unspeakable, unthinkable. Absence becomes meaningful in the moment of its noticing. However, everything not yet noticed is a potential absence, something that may be noticed or called to attention. But nothing (even) becomes an absence until it is noticeable.

Fig. 1.1.2 shows a rough map of absences.

---

[52] Brian Rotman, 1987, *Signifying Nothing: The Semiotics of Zero*, Stanford, CA: Stanford University Press.

Form Function: Absence	Text	Image	Space	Object	Body	Sound	Speech
Absence	Ellipsis, the unmarked	Blank space, something missing in an image	Empty place, something missing in an image	An object not present	Non-presence of an embodied person, or reference to their body in transposition	Silence, or in a soundscape, a missing sound	Mute, speechless, the unmentioned

Fig. 1.1.2: Absence

§1.1.2a John Cage's 4'33"

John Cage's *4'33"* was first performed in public by pianist David Tudor on August 29, 1952.[53] The performer walks to the piano, the keyboard cover is open, and he opens the score. Then he closes the cover and starts a stop watch. Then this again for each of three movements, totaling four minutes and thirty-three seconds of silence. The silence is not true silence, because for a hearing person this can never be. We hear the sounds of people in the audience coughing, the piano cover being opened and closed, the stopwatch started and stopped. The audience claps, the pianist bows.[*] The notable absence is the playing of the piano, and this absence not only points to itself, but other presences that may otherwise have gone unremarked.

By way of multimodal transposition, the sound of 4'33" can be represented visually as a conventional musical score in which silence is represented as "rests." John Cage created a version of the score using his "proportional notation," now in the collection of the Museum of Modern Art in New York. This is a nicely hand-titled and signed sequence of pages, blank but for a vertical line of time marked with the duration of each movement.

There is no absence of sound that is total – unless you are deaf. The non-playing in a context where playing would normally be expected is a meaningful absence.

"The Earth's Quietest Place Will Drive You Crazy in 45 Minutes," says a headline in the *Smithsonian Magazine*. An anechoic chamber created in the Orfield Laboratories in Minnesota is so quiet that you don't hear anything. The threshold of hearability for an average human is 0 decibels. The Orfield Lab registers –9.4 dBA. Total silence is impossible, so places quieter than this lab are theoretically possible, though to be quieter still is practically irrelevant in terms of human physiology. After your ears adjust in the Orfield Lab, you begin to hear your own heartbeat. "In the anechoic chamber, you become the sound."[54]

---

[*] http://meaningpatterns.net/cage

[53] John Biguenet, 2015, *Silence*, London, UK: Bloomsbury, pp. 49–51.
[54] Rose Eveleth, 2013, "Earth's Quietest Place Will Drive You Crazy in 45 Minutes," *Smithsonian Magazine* (December 17).

There is no absence – silence, for instance – until it is noticeable. When we want it to be, we have many ways to direct notice to silence – ellipses in transcriptions of speech, a person noticeably missing from a dialogue, rests in musical scores, a finger pressed over lips, or digitized measurements of decibels below the threshold zero.

Reading mostly happens in silence, and conversation is the sound of speech punctuated by meaningful silence (meaning, "I can speak now") – marking yet another of the dramatic differences between these two forms of meaning.

Other silences in speech, when noticed, might also be symptomatic of absences. Bessie Dendrinos and Emilia Robeiro Pedro studied gender difference in giving directions in Greece and Portugal. When a man and woman together are approached by a stranger to give directions, the man mostly speaks while the woman remains silent, a dynamic of presence and absence that points to the wider context of gender inequalities.[55] The absence is noticeable if not always noticed, so, marking another presence.

In his "Lecture on Nothing," John Cage says, "I am here, and there is nothing to say . . . What we require is a silence; but what silence requires is that I go on talking."[56]

§1.1.3 Concept

> **Concept.** Representation of more than one thing, a set of things meaningfully denominated by its generality, a group of beings or events defined by shared criterial features.

Meaning forms – text, image, space, object, body, sound, and speech – have two parallel but inextricably intertwined lives: one is cognitive, the other is in an externalized object designed to support the thinking process. There is thinking and there are the tools we have learned to use to help us think – "cognitive prostheses," we call them.

Each life of meaning is a creature of the other. The artifacts of meaning can be envisaged before they become present: text, image, space, object, body, sound, and speech. They can be mentally enacted. Lev Vygotsky and Aleksandr Luria[§1.1.3a] speak at length about "inner speech,"[§AS1.2.1a] talking to oneself, as

---

[55] Bessie Dendrinos and Emilia Robeiro Pedro, 1997, "Giving Street Directions: The Silent Role of Women," pp. 215–38 in *Silence: Interdisciplinary Perspectives*, edited by A. Jaworksi, Berlin, Germany: Mouton de Gruyter.

[56] John Cage, 1961 [1966], *Silence: Lectures and Writings*, Cambridge, MA: MIT Press, p. 109.

a tool for thinking.[57] "Mindsight" or mental images, to use a term of Colin McGinn's,[§3.1.2b] is a way to think in images based in perception but nevertheless quite distinct from perception in its mental processes. (To see the Eiffel Tower in one's mind's eye is quite different from seeing it in reality or in a photograph.)[58] Or, navigating a space – a shopping mall compared to a lecture theater, for instance – we envisage its spatial "program"[§AS1.4.5b] in order to navigate it meaningfully.[59] We do this even before we start to interact with the space. Or we might envisage our embodied presence and its gesturings. Or we might imagine how to use a tool or what to do with an object.

We use these mental tools for thinking, whether this thinking is for ourself (representation)[§AS1.2.1] or whether this thinking reaches others in a meaningful way by means of its material realization (communication).[§AS1.2.2] Even if we don't end up communicating our meaning, the cognitive life of a meaning begins as a silent and at first intangible mental representation which may appear in our mind's eye as text, image, space, object, body, sound, and speech. But these envisionings are only possible because we have learned the arts of making text, image, space, object, body, sound, and speech for the purposes of thinking and action.

This is not to commit a dualism, where mind is separate, as it is in Descartes'[§1.3a] or Kant's[§3.3e] humanism, where our human-ness is defined by the prior mental categories with which we make the world. Rather, it is a socio-historical process whereby the cognitive shape of our minds has been made in a social dialectic, where the social practices and material media for making text, image, space, object, body, sound, and speech progressively become tools for envisioning an externalized representation of the world for ourselves. We are what we can mean, and meaning is that which is materializable.[§AS1.4]

Luria has a nice phrase for this – it is not a separation between the mind and the tools of the mind, but a "doubling of the world."[60] Reference is one such doubling. There is a referable world; our common sense irrefutably tells us that. Then there is a world that can be represented in text, image, space, object, body, sound, and speech. Our practice with these meaning forms is not just in the tangibility of these as activities engaging with externalized media, but our envisioning of these as forms of action (anticipating, planning, hoping, expecting).

---

[57] Lev Semyonovich Vygostky, 1934 [1986], *Thought and Language*, Cambridge, MA: MIT Press, pp. 224–35; Aleksandr Romanovich Luria, 1981, *Language and Cognition*, New York, NY: John Wiley and Sons, pp. 103–13.

[58] Colin McGinn, 2004, *Mindsight: Image, Dream, Meaning*, Cambridge, MA: Harvard University Press.

[59] Christopher Alexander, 1979, *The Timeless Way of Building*, New York, NY: Oxford University Press.

[60] Aleksandr Romanovich Luria, 1981, *Language and Cognition*, New York, NY: John Wiley and Sons, p. 35.

Reference is one such kind of envisioning (a meaning function, we have called it). Instantiating is a kind of reference, which doubtless many other sentient creatures can do, though not to the degree of endless and stable specification now possible for humans in the era of digital meaning.[3.4b] Conceptualization is harder. Other creatures can do this to some degree – primates, for instance,[AS1.1.3a] and perhaps also ants who will know another ant-in-general from a spider-in-general.

In Luria's words, "mediated responding to the world becomes an intra-psychic process. It is through this interiorization of historically determined and culturally organized ways of operating on information that the social nature of people comes to be their psychological nature as well."[61]

§1.1.3a Lev Vygotsky and Aleksandr Luria's Higher Psychological Processes

"Instance," in our grammar of multimodality, stands for one thing. "Concept" stands for more than one thing, linked to each other by means of generality.

Soviet psychology is a useful place to begin to explore the notion of "concept." The key thinkers whose ideas we want to examine are Lev Semyonovich Vygotsky and Aleksandr Romanovich Luria.[*] Vygotsky and Luria offer a cultural-historical account of the ontogenesis of concepts in the lives of children, and the phylogenesis of concepts in the course of human history.

As Jews, Vygotsky and Luria would have found it near impossible to have become researchers and university professors in the Russia of the Tsars. The revolution of 1917 opened new possibilities for them both. In gratitude, they embraced its secular faith. "My entire generation was infused with the energy of revolutionary change," says Luria, looking back on his life from the vantage point of the 1970s, "the liberating energy people feel when they are part of a society that is able to make tremendous progress in a very short time."[62]

The stifling conditions of the tsarist period are difficult for modern people to understand. Prerevolutionary Russian Society comprised strictly divided classes: workers and peasants, intellectuals (physicians, teachers and engineers), merchants and business-men, and the gentry (aristocrats and high government officials). The repressive nature of the regime was reflected in the educational system, which was designed to see to it that everyone stayed in his or her "natural" station in life and nothing changed . . . Of course, the revolution changed all this. It broke down the barriers between classes and gave all of us, no matter what our social class, new perspectives and new opportunities.[63]

---

[*] http://meaningpatterns.net/vygotsky-luria-psychology

[61] Michael Cole, Karl Levitin, and Alexander R. Luria, 1979 [2006], *The Autobiography of Alexander Luria: A Dialogue with the Making of Mind*, Mahwah, NJ: Lawrence Erlbaum, p. 45.
[62] Ibid., p. 17.   [63] Ibid., p. 18.

Luria started work as a laboratory assistant at the Institute for the Scientific Organization of Labor in his home city, Kazan. There he studied the effect of hard work on the mental activity of foundry workers. His work soon attracted the attention of Professor K.N. Kornilov, the director of the Moscow Institute of Psychology. Moving to Moscow in 1923, he "joined a small group of scholars who were charged with reconstructing Russian psychology in order to bring it into accord with the goals of the Revolution."[64] Vygotsky joined the Institute in 1924, and the two began a close working relationship which lasted a decade, until Vygotsky died of tuberculosis in 1934, aged 37. The rest of Luria's life and work was a homage to his friend and colleague.

Luria and Vygotsky's starting point was a critique of the "bourgeois" schools of psychology in the West, and an attempt to create a new, Marxist psychology. On the one hand, American behaviorists[§3.1.2d] limited themselves to what Luria and Vygotsky considered to be mechanistic interpretations of elementary behavioral phenomena, many of which humans shared with animals. On the other hand, there was a tradition of philosophical idealism starting with René Descartes[§3.1.2g] in the seventeenth century and Immanuel Kant in the eighteenth.[§3.3e] This tradition posited an abstract humanism where "the loftiness of man's ideas are present in the child at the moment of their birth,"[65] which subsequently became manifest in consciousness. The distinguishing feature of the human mind was its unique capacity to classify and categorize sensory experience, then to reason on the basis of these conceptualizations. And this, as if it were a purely voluntary act of the individual.

Unlike the American behaviorists, Vygotsky and Luria wanted to be able to examine "higher psychological processes, including consciously controlled action, voluntary attention, active memorizing, and abstract thought."[66] However, unlike the metaphysical speculations of philosophers about intrinsic human consciousness, they wanted to start with the everyday conditions of material existence and to consider individual consciousness as a phenomenon of human history. Here, "material conditions [are] constantly changing, ceaselessly in movement, although this movement sometimes experiences leaps, breaks, discontinuities."[67]

Two such leaps are the leap into conceptual thinking by the growing child (the ontogenesis of conceptual meaning), and the historical development of

---

[64] Ibid., p. 28.

[65] Lev Semyonovich Vygostky, 1930 [1999], "The Problem of Practical Intellect in the Psychology of Animals and the Psychology of the Child," pp. 3–26 in *Collected Works of L.S. Vygotsky*, Volume 6, edited by R.W. Rieber, New York, NY: Kluwer Academic, p. 80.

[66] Michael Cole, Karl Levitin, and Alexander R. Luria, 1979 [2006], *The Autobiography of Alexander Luria: A Dialogue with the Making of Mind*, Mahwah, NJ: Lawrence Erlbaum, p. 41.

[67] Aleksandr Romanovich Luria, 1925 [1977], "Psychoanalysis as a System of Monistic Psychology," *Soviet Psychology* 16(2):7–45, p. 9.

conceptual thinking (the phylogenesis of conceptual meaning). The latter[§1.1.3d] proved to be more problematic than the former.[§1.1.3b]

§1.1.3b Lev Vygotsky and Aleksandr Luria on Children's Concept Development

While using the research and insights of Vygotsky[*] and Luria to define "concept," we are going to slip between our terminology and theirs. First ours, to provide an account of ontogenesis. Young children start off learning to distinguish instances: the sights, objects, people, gestures, and spoken words that represent and communicate the specificities of their immediate, concrete experience. Later they learn to conceptualize, layering generalizations over the specifics of experience. These are fundamentally different modes of thinking and action.

Now (mostly) in Vygotsky and Luria's words. After a "pre-intellectual phase"[68] where they learn to feel, see, and hear distinguishable things as would any other animal, children begin "symbolic activity," using objects, images, and words to make meaning.[69] This is an essentially multimodal process of meaning-making, in which children move beyond mere stimulus and response that governs activity and learning for all animals, to the use of artifacts that mediate activity and meaning.[70]

Take toys: "A pile of clothes or a piece of wood becomes a baby in a game because the same gestures that depict holding a baby in one's hands or feeding a baby can apply to them. The child's self-motion, his own gestures, are what assign the function of a sign to an object and give it meaning."[71] Or take images: "Often children's drawings not only disregard but also directly contradict the actual perception of the object . . . For instance, a child will draw legs that grow straight out of a head, omitting the neck and torso . . . Children do not strive for representation; they are very much more symbolists than naturalists."[72] Spoken words similarly symbolize.

Despite the differences in their forms of meaning, these tools for meaning, these mediators of meaningful activity are equally "mnemono-technic symbols."[73] Objects, speech, and gestures are meaning-making tools of the

---

[*] http://meaningpatterns.net/vygotsky-luria-concept

[68] Lev Semyonovich Vygostky, 1934 [1986], *Thought and Language*, Cambridge, MA: MIT Press, pp. 86–7.
[69] Lev Semyonovich Vygostky, 1930 [1999], "The Problem of Practical Intellect in the Psychology of Animals and the Psychology of the Child," pp. 3–26 in *Collected Works of L.S. Vygotsky*, Volume 6, edited by R.W. Rieber, New York, NY: Kluwer Academic, pp. 14–15.
[70] Lev Semyonovich Vygostky, 1962 [1978], *Mind in Society: The Development of Higher Psychological Processes*, Cambridge, MA: Harvard University Press, p. 39.
[71] Ibid., p. 108.   [72] Ibid., p. 112.   [73] Ibid., pp. 54, 115.

same cognitive order. And all are the products of socio-cultural context, presenting opportunities for meaning based on their available designs (to return for a moment to our terminology). We learn to become through the designs that are available in these historically evolved forms of meaning – the objects, gestures, and words we have at hand.

In the development of the child, the journey towards conceptualization occurs through a number of phases. From a world of circumstantially co-located instances, the child moves step by step into the world of concepts. First, the instances go into "unorganised congeries" or "heaps ... consisting of disparate objects, grouped together ..., inherently unrelated objects linked by chance in the child's perception ... Many words," Vygotsky says, "have in part the same meaning to the child and the adult, especially words referring to concrete objects in the child's habitual surroundings."[74] Luria calls these "associative meanings," the dog with its leash, with its bark, linking the experience of a single dog with things associated in the child's experience. The word "dog" brings to mind a succession of instantiations.

But the adult who speaks that word may be using it conceptually, referring to dogs in general, or with even more conceptual precision, as a species.[75] Returning to Vygotsky, "The child's and the adult meanings of a word often 'meet,' as it were, in the same concrete object, and this suffices to ensure mutual understanding."[76] This meeting becomes the source of subsequent learning, and progressive induction into an adult world of mediators that conceptualize – in image, writing, and the other forms of meaning.

In another phase of development, children begin to think in "complexes" with "the unification of scattered impressions; by organising discrete elements into groups, it creates the basis for later generalizations." A "child's use of 'quah' to designate first a duck swimming in the pond, then any liquid, including the milk in his bottle; when he happens to see a coin with an eagle on it, the coin is also called a 'quah,' and then any round, coin like object. This is typical of a chain complex [one amongst a number of varieties of thinking in complexes] – each new object included has some attribute in common with another element, but the attributes undergo endless changes."[77]

---

[74] Lev Semyonovich Vygostky, 1934 [1986], *Thought and Language*, Cambridge, MA: MIT Press, p. 110.

[75] Aleksandr Romanovich Luria, 1981, *Language and Cognition*, New York, NY: John Wiley and Sons, p. 52.

[76] Lev Semyonovich Vygostky, 1934 [1986], *Thought and Language*, Cambridge, MA: MIT Press, p. 111.

[77] Ibid., pp. 135, 127.

Then finally, concepts, or "categorical behavior," to emphasize that this is a practical activity, and not just a manner of thinking.[78]

A concept is more than the sum of certain associative bonds formed by memory, ... a concept embodied in a word represents an act of generalization. But word meanings evolve. When a new word has been learned by the child, its development is barely starting; the word at first is a generalization of the most primitive type; as the child's intellect develops, it is replaced by generalizations of a higher and higher type – a process that leads in the end to the formation of true concepts. The development of concepts, or word meanings, presupposes the development of many intellectual functions: deliberate attention, logical memory, abstraction, the ability to compare and to differentiate. These complex psychological processes cannot be mastered through the initial learning alone.[79]

§1.1.3c Aleksei Leontyev on the Psyche

Now the words of a third important participant in the development of what is today called "activity theory," Aleksei Nikolaevich Leontyev.[*] He had worked with Vygotsky and Luria since the 1920s, and in 1966 became the first Dean of the Faculty of Psychology at Moscow State University, where Luria also spent the last decades of his career.

Man does not know the world like a Robinson Crusoe making independent discoveries on an uninhabited island. He assimilates the experience of preceding generations of people in the course of his life; that happens precisely in the form of his mastering of meanings and to the extent that he assimilates them. Meaning is thus the form in which the individual man assimilates generalised and reflected human experience ...

Psychological analysis demonstrates that inner, ideal activity has the same structure as practical activity. In thinking, too, we should consequently distinguish between activity, acts, and operations proper, and the functions of the brain realising them. It is precisely because of the commonness of the structure of inner theoretical activity and outward practical activity that their separate structural elements can and do pass into one another, so that inner activity is constantly embracing separate external acts and operations, while developed external, practical activity incorporates inner, thought actions and operations ...

At a certain, relatively late stage of evolution activity may be interiorised, i.e. may also acquire the form of an inner activity of ideas, but it remains a process implementing the real life of a real subject and does not become 'purely' mental, opposed in principle

---

[*] http://meaningpatterns.net/leontyev

[78] Aleksandr Romanovich Luria, 1981, *Language and Cognition*, New York, NY: John Wiley and Sons, pp. 25–27, 37.
[79] Lev Semyonovich Vygostky, 1934 [1986], *Thought and Language*, Cambridge, MA: MIT Press, pp. 149–50.

to external, directly practical activity ... This approach thus rejects the dualist opposing and isolation of inner, theoretical activity from outward, practical activity.[80]

In this spirit, Luria and Vygotsky wanted to account for the social process in the acquisition of cognitive capacities in humans, including "higher" capacities such as conceptualization. They did this with two historical accounts: the first is an account of the life history of every thinking human;[§1.1.3b] the second, the history of our species.[§1.1.3d] Children learn to conceptualize by play, by drawing, by speaking and later by writing. Progressively, something that appears in their world as an instance becomes a concept – where things can be represented in their generality, as more than one thing of the same kind, or something that is repeatable.

But when they came to account for the development of higher capacities in the history of the species, Luria and Vygotsky's interpretation runs into difficulties.[§1.1.3e]

§1.1.3d Aleksandr Luria in Uzbekistan

In 1931 and again in 1932, Aleksandr Luria set out on expeditions into Uzbekistan in Soviet Central Asia to explore the thinking of people whose lives were only now being touched by modernity.[*] The project had been planned by Lev Vygotsky and Luria together, but Vygotsky was not well enough to travel.

In Uzbekistan, Luria and his research team tested the conceptualizing capacities of two groups of people. The first group consisted of illiterate peasants living in remote villages, where women were still isolated from social life by what Luria characterizes as the conservative teachings of Islam.

The second group consisted of people who, after the revolution, had become workers on the new, self-managed collective farms and who had participated in the social planning of production and also undertaken some formal education, if only short courses.[81] These were men and women who, "by participating in the socialist economy had gained access to the new forms of social relations and the new life principles accompanying the changes, [and so] had experienced the conditions necessary to alter radically the content and form of their thought."[82]

---

[*] http://meaningpatterns.net/uzbekistan

[80] Aleksei Nikolaevich Leontyev, 1947 [2009], "An Outline of the Evolution of the Psyche," pp. 137–244 in *The Development of Mind*, edited by M. Cole, Pacifica, CA: Marxists Internet Archive, pp. 202, 223, 243.

[81] Aleksandr Romanovich Luria, ed. 1974 [1976], *Cognitive Development: Its Cultural and Social Foundations*, Cambridge, MA: Harvard University Press, p. 15.

[82] Michael Cole, Karl Levitin, and Alexander R. Luria, 1979 [2006], *The Autobiography of Alexander Luria: A Dialogue with the Making of Mind*, Mahwah, NJ: Lawrence Erlbaum, p. 62.

Rakmat, age thirty-nine, an "illiterate peasant from an outlying district; has seldom been in Fergana [a nearby town], never in any other city." He was shown pictures of a hammer, saw, log, and hatchet. Which is a different kind of thing? he was asked. The conceptualizing answer: hammer, saw, and hatchet are "tools."

But no, he said:

"They are all alike. I think all of them have to be here."

"Which of these things could you call by one word?"

"How's that? If you call all three of them a 'hammer,' that can't be right either."

"But one fellow picked three things – the hammer, saw, and hatchet – and said they were alike."

"A saw, a hammer, and a hatchet all have to work together. But the log has to be there too!"

"Why do you think he picked these three things and not the log?"

"Probably he's got a lot of firewood, but if he left without firewood, we won't be able to do anything."

This is what Luria and Vygotsky characterized as complex or associative thinking, or thinking in terms of juxtaposed instances of things – this log, this saw – without being able to move forward via generalization and abstraction to the concept of "tool."[83]

Rejecting "the Cartesian notion of the primacy of self-consciousness" and focusing instead on meanings "shaped through social activity," Luria traced "fundamental psychological shifts that had occurred in human consciousness during a vigorous revolutionary realignment of social history – the rapid uprooting of class society and a cultural upheaval creating hitherto unimagined perspectives for social development."[84] For Luria, socialism was a higher form of human development, so illustrating its role in "the transition from sensory to rational consciousness, a phenomenon that the classics of Marxism regard as one of the most important in human history."[85]

Or, in the words of Nurmal, an "eighteen-year-old girl from an outlying village [who] had taken courses designed to overcome illiteracy, but was barely able to read and write":

L: What is freedom?

N: I have heard that women have got their freedom, but that's all I know. It means that the landowners oppressed them before but now they have escaped from their misery.[86]

---

[83] Aleksandr Romanovich Luria, 1981, *Language and Cognition*, New York, NY: John Wiley and Sons, pp. 55–56.

[84] Ibid., p. 19.

[85] Michael Cole, Karl Levitin, and Alexander R. Luria, 1979 [2006], *The Autobiography of Alexander Luria: A Dialogue with the Making of Mind*, Mahwah, NJ: Lawrence Erlbaum, p. 74.

[86] Aleksandr Romanovich Luria, 1981, *Language and Cognition*, New York, NY: John Wiley and Sons, p. 88.

§1.1.3e Aleksandr Luria on Cognitive Development

Aleksandr Luria gave several talks about his work in Soviet Central Asia soon after returning to Moscow, but did not publish on the subject until 1974. The research, to the extent that it had become known in the 1930s, was controversial. A book they had written together outlining their general socio-historical theory of psychology soon went out of circulation and was not republished until the 1990s.[87]

Communicating excitedly via telegram with Lev Vygotsky in Moscow a finding about the modes of visualization of their research subjects, Luria announced "Uzbeks do not have illusions." Nervous about the problem of incorporating minorities, the authorities who intercepted the message took this to be a comment about the policies of the Soviet Union. When Luria arrived back in Moscow, the party police were waiting to meet him.[88]

In a letter to the Culture and Propaganda Section of the Central Committee of the Bolshevik Party, Luria was forced to defend the work during a subsequent investigation into the Institute of Psychology by the Moscow Control Commission of Workers and Peasants Inspection. "Making a biased selection of individual facts and interpreting them incorrectly, the commission made a number of extremely grave charges, presenting our work as a specimen of colonizing research based on racist theory."[89]

Also at this time, Luria faced accusations that he was uncritically introducing "bourgeois" ideas from non-Marxist thinkers. In 1935, the director of the Institute S.G. Levit was denounced for his correspondence with American scholars and supposedly anti-Soviet views. Luria was about to defend him at a meeting, when a friend dragged him from the room. Levit was murdered in Stalin's orgy of death, as were six of the thirteen members of the Politburo, most of the 138 members of the Central Committee, and as many as 800,000 members of the Communist Party. Vygotsky, legend has it, chose not to go to a better sanatorium for his tuberculosis, preferring to die before he could face a similar fate.[90]

Luria had to leave the Institute of Psychology, and returned to medical school to train as a neuropsychologist, an area that would be less politically controversial than social-historical psychology. Here he made himself useful again to the Soviet Union, and internationally famous, for studying the effects of brain

---

[87] Lev Semyonovich Vygotsky and Aleksandr Romanovich Luria, 1930 [1993], *Studies on the History of Behavior: Ape, Primitive and Child*, translated by V.I. Golod and J.E. Knox, Hillsdale, NJ: Lawrence Erlbaum.

[88] Ibid., p. 15.

[89] Michael Cole, Karl Levitin, and Alexander R. Luria, 1979 [2006], *The Autobiography of Alexander Luria: A Dialogue with the Making of Mind*, Mahwah, NJ: Lawrence Erlbaum, pp. 260–61.

[90] Ibid., pp. 208, 248–50.

damage of soldiers injured during the Second World War. Eventually, during the thaw initiated by Stalin's successor, Nikita Khrushchev, Vygotsky and Luria were rehabilitated, and so, the Uzbekistan research was finally published.

But the historical part of their theory of concepts remains as complicated as it was when the Moscow Control Commission of Workers and Peasants Inspection made its complaints. Does the work in Soviet Central Asia posit some kinds of humans to be smarter than others – modern people compared to primitive; developed compared to underdeveloped? Traveling into Aboriginal Australia we find how unfathomably complex is the abstract and conceptualizing thinking of "first peoples" – though in ways so different that they cannot be measured on a common scale.[§AS1.1.3c]

Even if the comparative historical judgment was too hasty, this is not to contradict Luria's insight that "sociohistorical shifts not only introduce new content into the mental world of human beings; they also create new forms of activity and new structures of cognitive functioning."[91] We might add that the new forms of thinking may unjustly devalue and inhumanly erase the old, including the new pedagogical practices of "literacy" or instrumentalist epistemologies of "science." But Luria's point remains, that thinking – new or old, colonizing or cosmopolitan – is socio-historical in character.

In fact, to their shame, in their relativistic respect for difference, and to raise a preemptive point of self-defense made by Luria himself, "many students of 'backward' peoples have tried – either consciously or unconsciously – to justify existing inequalities."[92] The paths to socio-historical progress have strange twists and turns.

§1.1.3f Sergei Eisenstein's Battleship Potemkin

Walter Benjamin[§0b] visited Moscow in 1927, and spent two months there. Among his interests in the capital of the revolution, then a decade old, was Soviet film, and in particular the work of the famed director, Sergei Eisenstein. Released in 1925, *Battleship Potemkin* is Eisenstein's dramatization of a mutiny by the crew of a war ship in the failed revolution of 1905.[*] "A great film, a rare achievement," says Benjamin. "This film has solid concrete foundations ideologically; the details have been worked out precisely, like the span of a bridge."[93]

---

[*] http://meaningpatterns.net/eisenstein

[91] Aleksandr Romanovich Luria, ed. 1974 [1976], *Cognitive Development: Its Cultural and Social Foundations*, Cambridge, MA: Harvard University Press, p. 163.

[92] Ibid., p. 12.

[93] Walter Benjamin, 1927 [1999], "On the Present Situation of Russian Film," pp. 12–19 in *Walter Benjamin, Selected Writings,* Volume 2: *1927–1934*, edited by M.W. Jennings, Cambridge, MA: Harvard University Press, p. 19.

Here was one such carefully engineered detail: "The leader of the mutiny, Lieutenant Commander Schmidt, one of the legendary figures of revolutionary Russia, does not appear in the film." An oppressed social class (an abstract concept) is represented as the agent of history rather than the individual (a representative person instantiated). "That may be seen as a 'falsification of history,'" Benjamin continues, "although it has nothing to do with the estimation of his achievements... It would have been senseless to depict them as differentiated individuals ... Here, for the first time, a mass movement acquires the wholly architectonic and by no means monumental qualities that justifies its inclusion in film."[94]

Aleksandr Luria and Lev Vygotsky[§1.1.3a] met regularly with Eisenstein to discuss the ways in which the abstract concepts in Marx's philosophy of historical materialism could be embodied in visual imagery. Eisenstein was interested to get the technical assistance from the two professors of psychology, on the translation between verbal and visual concepts or what Eisenstein called the "generalized image." He was also interested to enlist their support to research the success of his films in conveying these concepts to audiences. Together, they created questionnaires for audiences of students, workers, and peasants to determine whether they had understood the concepts underlying the images. After Eisenstein died, Luria kept the great visualist's brain in a bottle in his office at Moscow State University.[95]

Even if Benjamin did not meet Luria and Vygotsky during his time in Moscow, he well understood their purposes and Eisenstein's.

The mode of mental reception of the peasant is basically different from that of the urban masses ...; serious scenes provoke uproarious laughter and ... funny scenes are greeted with straight faces ... To expose such audiences to film and radio constitutes one of the most grandiose mass-psychological experiments in the gigantic laboratory that Russia has become ... At the moment, the establishment of an "Institute for Audience Research" in which audience reactions can be studied both experimentally and theoretically, is being considered.[96]

§1.1.3g Lev Rudinev's Moscow State University

We were hosts of a conference at Moscow State University in 2012, jointly with their Faculty of Global Studies. The building where we met was an unassuming,

[94] Ibid., p. 18.
[95] Michael Cole, Karl Levitin, and Alexander R. Luria, 1979 [2006], *The Autobiography of Alexander Luria: A Dialogue with the Making of Mind*, Mahwah, NJ: Lawrence Erlbaum, pp. 207, 243; Al LaValley and Barry P. Scherr, eds., 2001, *Eisenstein at 100*, New Brunswick, NJ: Rutgers University Press.
[96] Walter Benjamin, 1927 [1999], "On the Present Situation of Russian Film," pp. 12–19 in *Walter Benjamin, Selected Writings*, Volume 2: *1927–1934*, edited by M.W. Jennings, Cambridge, MA: Harvard University Press, p. 14.

straight-up-and-down, modernist structure of ten or so floors, that must have been built in about the 1970s. It was positioned on a broad axis stretching across the Lenin Hills from the Moscow river. Walking out the door and looking left along the axis, there in the distance was the succession of peaks and spires of the main building of Moscow State University.[*]

Broadly, Soviet architecture falls into three phases: a futuristic modernism until about the mid-thirties; a period of historicist reference during the Stalin years from the mid-thirties to the mid-fifties; then, after Khrushchev's intervention at the Twentieth Party Congress of 1956 at which he condemned monumentalism, a return to modernism but this time of a mass-functionalist kind. On the Moscow State campus, the last two are palpably in play.

Lev Vladimirovich Rudnev was the lead architect on the main building, the largest of "seven sisters" constructed from the late forties to the mid-fifties and still defining the Moscow horizon. Some dimensions: 240 meters tall, 36 floors, 30,000 tons of reinforcing steel, able to house 30,000 students as well as offices and lecture halls. The structure is clad in ceramics, the spires are steel, topped with wreaths encircling red stars of the 1917 revolution.

It took 14,290 construction workers four years to build. Some of the workers were prisoners from the Soviet gulag and German prisoners of war, housed during the last phases of construction in the upper floors of the structure where they could easily be guarded. It was the tallest building in Europe from 1953 to 1990, only to be beaten then by corporate structures. It is still the tallest educational building in the world.[97]

This is a building in its singularity, its instantiation on one place on the Lenin Hills, no other building quite the same, though its sisters are insistently related, of a type. Yet it has its own layering of concepts, of "generalized images": the red star of communism, hammers and sickles for the workers and peasants. And there are other, more obtuse references. It is somewhat like the skyscrapers of Chicago and New York, idealized in Hugh Ferriss' book *Metropolis of Tomorrow*, which had been translated into Russian in the 1930s.[98] But it is also quite unlike the American skyscraper, confined as it was by the grid of the city, the cost of real estate, and the impossibility of planning on a large scale in a city divided into small rectangles of private property.

To make the point, the Soviets insisted the seven sisters were "tall buildings," not "skyscrapers."[99] There were references to classicism in the columns,

---

[*] http://meaningpatterns.net/moscow-state-university

[97] Owen Hatherley, 2015, *Landscapes of Communism*, London, UK: Allen Lane, p. 204; Gabriele Basilico, 2009, *Vertiginous Moscow*, London, UK: Thames and Hudson, p. 8.
[98] Owen Hatherley, 2015, *Landscapes of Communism*, London, UK: Allen Lane, p. 209.
[99] Gabriele Basilico, 2009, *Vertiginous Moscow*, London, UK: Thames and Hudson, pp. 4, 7; Hugh Ferriss, 1929 [2005], *The Metropolis of Tomorrow*, New York, NY: Dover Publications.

to Babylonian ziggurats in the layers, to the spires and transepts of Gothic cathedrals. If modernism rejected history, one form of its transcendence was a historicism of the kind that "closed its circle,"[100] so taking another path to historical transcendence. Later, in another abstraction, the building becomes a symbol for Moscow, as well as the things that the building itself conceptualizes.

As we got closer, the building loomed larger, then larger, then the intricate conceptual details of its façade came into clearer view and the height of the red star reached closer to the heavens. Rigorous symmetry drew us to the middle door, even though it was not particularly large. From here, we entered a dark labyrinth of corridors, marble clad walls, students scurrying past, seemingly not many of them for spaces so vast.

Somehow, we were pulled to the center, then up some marble stairs into an inner sanctum deep below the tallest of the spires. There we reached a darkened shrine with statues of Marx and Lenin, at once objects of reference to their singular personhood, and representatives of concepts of historical materialism as a system: labor, property, class, and revolution. The lights were off – turned off, we mused, on that day in 1991 when the Soviet Union was dissolved.

§1.1.3h Otto Neurath's Pictorial Statistics

In writing and speech we instantiate with "the," a proper noun, something named in the singular. We conceptualize with "a," a common noun, something namable in the plural. In realistic image, we can mark the difference with a representation of something in its inarguable singularity, compared to icons which refer only to the criterial features of more than one thing.

Now we have a picture of a singular person, Otto Neurath,[*] in a photo taken in 1919 by Heinrich Hoffman when Neurath was President of the Central Office of Economics in the short-lived Bavarian Soviet Republic. The caption in a photo booklet on the revolution printed at the time said, "Dr Neurath, Socialization Commissar."

The photographer later joined the Nazi Party, making his way eventually into Adolf Hitler's inner circle where he became the only photographer allowed to take the Führer's portrait. Republished in a Nazi newspaper in 1932, this time the photo was captioned "The Jew Neurath."[101] The contextual narrative only serves to sharpen the singularity of the person captured in the photograph

---

[*] http://meaningpatterns.net/neurath

[100] Vladimir Paperny, 2002, *Architecture in the Age of Stalin: Culture Two*, translated by J. Hill and R. Barris, Cambridge, UK: Cambridge University Press, p. 19.

[101] Christopher Burke, Eric Kindel, and Sue Walker, eds., 2013, *Isotype: Design and Contexts, 1925–1971*, London, UK: Hyphen Press, pp. 20–21.

(Neurath's embodied instantiation) and the singularity of the photograph (Neurath's instantiation in this image).

After the failure of the Bavarian revolution, Neurath was jailed in Germany for a time. Following his release, he returned to his native Vienna. In 1924 he was appointed director of a new Museum of Society and Economy, created under the auspices of the socialist city government.

For the museum, a chart was created showing the number of children offered school meals before 1922, in 1922, then in 1931. Lined in a row like a horizontal bar graph, each outline figure of a child represents 1000 children served, and the growth in provision from zero to 18,000 children is represented by repeated profiles of the children. The concept of child (in general, in their plurality) is represented by a pictogram.[102]

Otto Neurath and the visual "transformers" he employed in the museum, Marie Reidemeister and Gerd Arntz, can be credited as major figures in the development of modern visual iconography. Directly and indirectly, the fruits of their theory and practice in the visual representation of concepts are in evidence today in the proliferation of visual symbols from street and building signage, to today's web with its ubiquitous infographics, navigational icons, emojis,[§AS1.1.1a] and the ideographs in Unicode.[§0.2.1a]

The museum was founded by the Municipality of Vienna and the Viennese Chamber of Workers and Employees.[103] The city government, true to its socialist principles, was energetically building public housing, kindergartens, playgrounds, and health centers.[§AS2.3b]

Here is Neurath offering his rationale for a museum that featured social statistics: "But how, it may be asked, is it possible in any city with a democratic government to achieve so much of benefit to the masses unless the people understand what it is all about, at least in its larger outlines, and unless these enormous expenditures out of tax revenues are approved on the basis of a constant accounting to the people?"[104]

As for the visual form, "Modern man is first of all an ocular being. Advertising, the educational billboard, cinema, illustrated newspapers and magazines are broadly responsible for the education of the masses."[105] The museum is "directed in the spirit of the workers' movement . . . It is not the lies

---

[102] Ibid., pp. 40, 72.
[103] Nader Vossoughian, 2008, *Otto Neurath: The Language of the Global Polis*, Rotterdam, NL: NAi Publishers.
[104] Otto Neurath, 1973, *Empiricism and Sociology*, translated by P. Foulkes and M. Neurath, Dordrecht, NL: D. Reidel Publishing, pp. 215, 221; Otto Neurath, 1945 [2010], *From Hieroglyphics to Isotype: A Visual Autobiography*, London, UK: Hyphen Press, pp. 3–4.
[105] Otto Neurath, 1931 [2017], "Pictorial Statistics Following the Vienna Method," *ARTMargins* 6(1):108–18, p. 115.

that are the worst thing about schools, but the concealment. One does not learn from school … how bad the quality of housing is; one learns nothing of the fight for freedom. Now, a museum should not carry out propaganda in a vulgar sense – it must give plain facts! … Most museums have a dead effect because they appeal too little to the wants of people."[106] In these ways, the focus of the museum was the presentation of revelatory social facts by visualization.

Marie Reidemeister was invited by Neurath to join the museum in 1925. Her role as a "transformer" was to turn facts and statistics into visuals for display in the museum and at public events, and later also information pamphlets and books.[107] Then, in 1929 they were joined by the modernist artist Gerd Arntz, who had been creating images in the style of Cubism. Working in the museum, he perfected the "pictogram," a key feature of what came to be known as the Vienna Method of Pictorial Statistics. To achieve identical reproduction, Arnt devised a linocut process.[108]

Arnt eventually created a "picture dictionary" of about 4,000 symbols. Symbols could be qualified: a green person is an agricultural worker and red is an industrial worker; and different kinds of professions could be further qualified with an icon on their chest, a wheel on the chest of a transport worker and a hammer on the chest of an industrial worker – creating the visual equivalent of noun phrases. These "stylised symbols have been designed," Neurath explained, "to characterize social facts: men, women, cogwheels, vacuum cleaners, coffins, homes, ships, etc. … careful symbolic representation is educationally superior to … sentimental naturalism, and also to the jokes of caricature."[109] Other areas of technical innovation in the museum included mapping, including a magnetic map of Vienna where pictograms could be moved, anticipating the dynamic web maps of the digital era.[110]

---

[106] Christopher Burke, Eric Kindel, and Sue Walker, eds., 2013, *Isotype: Design and Contexts, 1925–1971*, London, UK: Hyphen Press, p. 29.

[107] Otto Neurath, 1973, *Empiricism and Sociology*, translated by P. Foulkes and M. Neurath, Dordrecht, NL: D. Reidel Publishing, pp. 215, 221; Otto Neurath, 1945 [2010], *From Hieroglyphics to Isotype: A Visual Autobiography*, London, UK: Hyphen Press, pp. 3–4.

[108] Christopher Burke, Eric Kindel, and Sue Walker, eds., 2013, *Isotype: Design and Contexts, 1925–1971*, London, UK: Hyphen Press, pp. 17, 67.

[109] Ibid., pp. 63, 65; Otto Neurath, 1973, *Empiricism and Sociology*, translated by P. Foulkes and M. Neurath, Dordrecht, NL: D. Reidel Publishing, p. 222; Otto Neurath, 1931 [2017], "Pictorial Statistics Following the Vienna Method," *ARTMargins* 6(1):108–18.

[110] Christopher Burke, Eric Kindel, and Sue Walker, eds., 2013, *Isotype: Design and Contexts, 1925–1971*, London, UK: Hyphen Press, p. 58; Christopher Burke, Eric Kindel, and Sue Walker, eds., 2013, *Isotype: Design and Contexts, 1925–1971*, London, UK: Hyphen Press, p. 38; Marie Neurath and Robin Kinross, 2009, *The Transformer: Principles of Making Isotype Charts*, London UK: Hyphen Press, pp. 23–5.

There was a manifest politics to Neurath's theory of representation and the museum's visualizations of social facts. "Statistics are a tool of the proletarian struggle," he said, "statistics are an essential part of the socialist order; statistics are joy for the international proletariat struggling hard with the ruling classes."[111] A system of visualization would also transcend different languages and cultures, "through its neutrality, and its independence of separate languages. . . . Words divide, pictures unite."[112]

§1.1.3i The Vienna Circle's Scientific Conception of the World

Otto Neurath[§1.1.3h] had another theoretical project, political in a more general way, and this was "the search for a neutral system of formulae, for a symbolism freed from the slag of historical languages." And, beyond this, "also the search for a total system of concepts. Neatness and clarity are striven for, and dark distances and unfathomable depths are rejected. In science, there are no 'depths'; there is surface everywhere: all experience forms a complex network."[113]

Here we begin to catch a glimpse of a larger agenda for conceptualization. Neurath was a leading member of the Vienna Circle, inspired by the same "bourgeois" philosopher that got Alexander Bogdanov[§0.2.9a] into trouble with Lenin, Ernst Mach. Among its members were the mathematician Kurt Gödel, and one of the founders of Analytical Philosophy, Rudolf Carnap.[§AS3.2b] In 1929, the Vienna Circle published a manifesto, *The Scientific Conception of the World*. Neurath wrote the first draft, which Hahns Hahn and Rudolf Carnap extended and revised, but the authorship was simply credited, "The Vienna Circle."[114]

The problem, said the manifesto, with "the form of traditional languages [is that they create] a confusion about the logical achievement of thought. Ordinary language for instance uses the same part of speech, the substantive, for things ('apple') as well as for qualities ('hardness'), relations ('friendship'), and processes ('sleep'); therefore it misleads one into a thing-like conception of functional concepts." The "scientific world conception," by contrast, knows

---

[111] Christopher Burke, Eric Kindel, and Sue Walker, eds., 2013, *Isotype: Design and Contexts, 1925–1971*, London, UK: Hyphen Press, p. 84.

[112] Otto Neurath, 1973, *Empiricism and Sociology*, translated by P. Foulkes and M. Neurath, Dordrecht, NL: D. Reidel Publishing, p. 215.

[113] Vienna Circle, 1929 [1973], "The Scientific Conception of the World," pp. 299–318 in *Empiricism and Sociology*, edited by P. Foulkes and M. Neurath, Dordrecht, NL: D. Reidel Publishing, p. 318.

[114] Ibid.; Thomas Uebel, 2008, "Writing a Revolution: On the Production and Early Reception of the Vienna Circle's Manifesto," *Perspectives on Science* 16(1):70–102; Jacob Struan and Otto Karl-Heinz, 1990, "Otto Neurath: Marxist Member of the Vienna Circle," *Auslegung: A Journal of Philosophy* 16(2):175–89.

with clarity just two things: "empirical statements about things of all kinds, and analytic statements of logic and mathematics."

On this basis, "the aim of scientific effort is to reach the goal, unified science, by applying logical analysis to the empirical material ... For us, something is 'real' through being incorporated into the total structure of experience." By these means it will be possible to gain "the required precision of concept definitions and of statements, and in formalizing the intuitive process of inference of ordinary thought, that is to bring it into a rigorous, automatically controlled form by means of a symbolic mechanism."[115]

This sounds rather like the relationships in the digital era between empirical objects named in the internet of things (instantiations),[§1.1.1] their classification schemes (conceptualizations),[§1.1.3] and the algorithmic processes of symbol manipulation via "artificial intelligence" that overlie them.

The Vienna Circle's project was "the arrangement of the concepts of the various branches of science into the constitutive system." It would be an incremental project, though its general shape Neurath thought evident already. "We are like sailors who on the open sea must reconstruct their ship but are never able to start afresh from the bottom. Where a beam is taken away a new one must at once be put there, and for this the rest of the ship is used as support. In this way, by using the old beams and driftwood, the ship can be shaped entirely anew, but only by gradual reconstruction."[116]

§1.1.3j   Marie Reidemeister's Isotype

In the USSR a new ship was being built, though more than one beam at a time. In 1931, the Council of People's Commissars issued a decree that "Dr. Neurath's method of graphic representation of statistics is to be applied in all schools, trade unions, public and cooperative organizations."[117] So, the All-Union Institute of Pictorial Statistics of Soviet Construction and Economy or ИЗОСТАТ (Izostat) was created. Neurath, Reidemeister, and Arntz began to spend considerable periods of time in Moscow, working with the seventy or so staff in the Institute, then regional bureaux that were created in various parts of the USSR. A book was published in Russian in 1932 written by Ivan Ivanitskii, *Pictorial Statistics and the Vienna Method.*[*] By these means, the achievements of the five-

---

[*]   http://meaningpatterns.net/isotype

[115]   Vienna Circle, 1929 [1973], "The Scientific Conception of the World," pp. 299–318 in *Empiricism and Sociology*, edited by P. Foulkes and M. Neurath, Dordrecht, NL: D. Reidel Publishing, pp. 307–09.

[116]   Otto Neurath, 1973, *Empiricism and Sociology*, translated by P. Foulkes and M. Neurath, Dordrecht, NL: D. Reidel Publishing, p. 199.

[117]   Ibid., p. 222.

year plans were represented. "Pictorial statistics should be a powerful instrument for mass agitation and propaganda in the hands of the party and for the working class," said Ivanitskii in the preface of the book.[118]

Neurath was fortunate to be working in Moscow, not Vienna, when in February 1934 he received a telegram from Marie Reidemeister, "Carnap is coming." This was code to say that the fascists had taken control of key ministries in Austria. Neurath was never to return to Vienna.

Neurath, Reidemeister, and Arntz fled to the Netherlands, where on Reidemeister's suggestion, they created a new name for their visual design group, "Isotype," or the International System of Typographic Picture Information.[119] And here, a new manifesto:

When will the Middle Ages be at an end? As soon as all men can participate in a common culture and the canyon between educated and uneducated people has disappeared ... One solution is Isotype, a method with a special visual dictionary and a special visual grammar; that is, a new visual world, comparable to our book and word world ... Visual education is related to the extension of intellectual democracy within single communities and within mankind, it is an element of international social planning and engineering.[120]

With the Nazi invasion of the Netherlands, Neurath and Reidemeister fled to England in an open boat. Initially they were interned on the Isle of Man as enemy aliens. When freed, they set up Isotype in Oxford and married in 1940. Neurath died in 1945. Reidemeister, now as Marie Neurath, ran Isotype in London until her retirement in 1971. Among her later projects were children's books and public information campaigns for illiterate populations in Africa.[121]

§1.2   Circumstance

> **Circumstance.** *Whether something is conceived in terms of its condition as an entity or the actions constituting that entity.*

---

[118] Emma Minns, 2013. "Picturing Soviet Progress: Isostat, 1931–1934," pp. 257–81 in *Isotype: Design and Contexts, 1925–1971*, edited by C. Burke, E. Kindel, and S. Walker, London, UK: Hyphen Press.

[119] Marie Neurath and Robin Kinross, 2009, *The Transformer: Principles of Making Isotype Charts*, London, UK: Hyphen Press, p. 47; Otto Neurath, 1939, *Modern Man in the Making*, New York, NY: Alfred A. Knopf.

[120] Otto Neurath, 1973, *Empiricism and Sociology*, translated by P. Foulkes and M. Neurath, Dordrecht, NL: D. Reidel Publishing, pp. 224, 247.

[121] Eric Kindel, 2011, "Reaching the People: Isotype Beyond the West," pp. 175–93 in *Image and Imaging in Philosophy, Science and the Arts*, edited by R. Heinrich, E. Nemeth, W. Pichler, and D. Wagner, Frankfurt, Germany: Ontos Verlag.

To extend our analysis of the dimensions of reference, both instances and concepts can refer to other states or actions (circumstances), as shown in Fig. 1.2(i).

Specification

	Instance	*Concept*
Entity	Presence (absence) of one entity	Presence (absence) of more than one entity, instances connected in their generality
Action	Presence (absence) of one action	Presence (absence) of repeated action, instances connected in their generality

(left side label: *Circumstance*)

Fig. 1.2(i): Circumstances specified

To illustrate how circumstances play out in multimodal practice, Fig. 1.2(ii) gives a rough map of of some of the functional transpositions between entities and actions across different forms of meaning:

Form \ Function: Circumstance	*Text*	*Image*	*Space*	*Object*	*Body*	*Sound*	*Speech*
Entity	Nouns, noun phrases	Points, volumes	Spaces	At rest, parts making wholes	Appearance (e.g. phenotypes, fashion)	Sounds of states	Naming, description
Action	Verbs, verb phrases	Vectors	Flows	In use, mechanisms at work	Gesticulation, enactment	Sounds of activity	Speech acts

Fig. 1.2(ii): Circumstances

§1.2a Gottlob Frege's "Aristotle"

Gottlob Frege[§1a] mentioned different senses of the word "Aristotle": the student of Plato, teacher of Alexander, and the person born in Stagira. Unequivocally, we can be referring to the same person (instance). It seems we can know Aristotle by a description of his personage, the years he lived, the place he lived, his famous teacher, his famous student (Alexander), his stone bust in the museum, the picture of the bust in a book, the two hefty tomes that are the complete extant works of Aristotle published by Princeton University Press ... and we can go on until a descriptive composite comes into view through multimodal transposition. This is what Saul Kripke called a "description theory," commonly found in theories of meaning, including Frege's.[122]

However, here we want to make a distinction. Concepts can be defined. Instances cannot be. However, we can specify instances in terms of concepts. A philosopher is a kind of person who thinks about thinking and being. "Philosopher" refers to many people (hence, a concept, specifying a kind of person), whose instances include not only Aristotle, but also Plato, Socrates, and a host of others. Above all Aristotle was a philosopher, and this is the reason we remember him today. Of course, we can know him descriptively, and description is potentially endless[123] – the properties of the man in terms of other aspects of his personhood and his relations in the world. But above all, we know him as a philosopher, by this conceptual classification.

We can know instances only empirically. However, we know concepts by their definition – analytically. We can get to know more about instances through their classification according to concept. We can build out rich descriptions of instances by elaborating on their properties of quality and quantity.$^{\S1.3}$ But the most efficient and effective way to navigate the meaning of multiple, more or less repeated instances is to conceptualize, or to focus attention on some criterial feature that is more salient than others.

Now, extending this picture of the processes of specification, we can differentiate an entity (in this case, an abstract state, the existence of the concept "philosophy" describing a generalizable aspect of the human experience); and an action (in this case, the practice of "philosophizing"). Actions turn into entities and entities can be seen as the unfolding of actions. Actions are the doing; entities are the evidence of doing. There is no philosophy without there having been philosophizing (concept). Aristotle, the philosopher, became that because he philosophized (the realization of the concept in an instance).

In our multimodal grammar, actions can be conceived as entities and entities as evidence of action. Nouns (philosophy) are evidence of the presence of verbs (philosophizing). Regions (entities) in our field of vision are evidence of vectors (actions), or how that field of vision came to be there. Gestures (actions) sit in the context of embodied presence (entities), and embodied presence is evidence of having actioned the form of that presence. Entities and actions are alternative perspectives on the same world.

---

[122] Saul A. Kripke, 1972, *Naming and Necessity*, Cambridge, MA: Harvard University Press, pp. 27, 30.

[123] Bertrand Russell, 1905, "On Denoting," *Mind* 14(56):479–93, p. 487.

So, for Aristotle's circumstances, some definitions. Philosophy is an artifact produced by thinking about thinking and being (entity). Philosophizing is thinking about thinking and being (action). A philosopher is a kind of person (entity) who does philosophy (action). We can't define Aristotle, because he is an instance. But we can apply a conceptual classification to him, which is to say first and foremost, he was a philosopher.

These then, are key vectors of transposition within the function of reference. Instances are always ready to be considered as concepts and concepts always ready to be instantiated. Actions are always about to be realized as entities and entities have a provenance that can only be understood in actions.

Circumstantially, all meaning is referenced in these ways. But this referencing is a matter of movement, not a business of separating into categories and fixing into structures. To take our cues from the traditional grammar of text, meanings are not to be fixed in singulars or plurals, nouns or verbs, because each is always ready to become the other. When the transposition comes, the meaning is both profoundly connected and profoundly new. Instance/concept and entity/action are conditions where each of their others is ever immanent, and for this reason, transposition always imminent.

§1.2b   Unified Modeling Language

The philosophy of ordinary things reaches a new level of complexity – and a pragmatic everyday ordinariness – with the rise of object-oriented software programming.[124] Today, computers can mediate just about every form of human representation and communication – from product purchases, to reading and writing on a screen, to learning, to walking the streets, to searching romantic matches. Software anticipates the relationships of things in patterns of action in general (concepts), as well as structuring the arrangement of things and possibilities for action in each moment of practice (instances).

In the world of the web and interoperable software, there is one widely adopted way to represent the relationship of software to the world – Unified Modeling Language, known ubiquitously by its acronym, UML. As a formal standard, UML almost has the status of law, spelling out the ways in which software functions should be presented, so developers are clear and systematic in their thinking (representation), and are able to communicate with each other about their designs no matter what their natural language or programming language. Version 2.5 of the now labyrinthine standard runs to 794 pages.[125] A version is also published by the Switzerland-based International Standards

---

[124] Erich Gamma, Richard Helm, Ralph Johnson, and John Vlissides, 1994, *Design Patterns: Elements of Reusable Object-Oriented Software*, Boston, MA: Addison-Wesley.

[125] Object Management Group, 2015, "OMG Unified Modeling Language (OMG UML)," Version 2.5 (www.omg.org/spec/UML/2.5/).

Association.[126] There would be no point in contemplating an alternative when this one is both so immediately accessible in available diagramming software and so exhaustive in its scope.

UML, to use the terminology we have adopted in this book, is a "grammar" of any and every entity and action in the world from the functional perspective of software development. Take the prosaic experience of purchasing a theater ticket.* This can be modeled structurally, where the focus is more or less on entities and their properties. Or it can be modeled dynamically with a view to behavior, where the focus is on actions and action sequences.[127]

From the perspective of entity, structural views include class diagrams connecting concept to concept, component diagrams connecting parts of the system, or deployment diagrams showing the dependencies between components – relating potential audience theatergoers to performances, to reservations, to their tickets. Taking the perspective of action, use case diagrams show actors and their actions, and sequence diagrams show the order in which actions occur – making tickets available, requesting a ticket, choosing a seat, making credit card charges, issuing a ticket.[128]

Written text or speech alone could never model the world with the systematic rigor required by software development. UML models entities and actions diagrammatically, expressing meanings in a formal visual notation of standardized boxes, lines, and arrows, with textual labels differentiated by punctuation, underlining. The available modeling labels run to hundreds of concepts, each defined in exhaustive detail. Classifiers, behaviors, properties, relationships, constraints, events, data types, roles, messages – this is a complete ontology for the representation of possible human relations to entities and forms of action.

Indeed, UML covers the whole territory of human meaning, not just elemental concepts and their instantiation, but traversing all five functions that we address in this pair of books, from reference, to agency, structure, context, and even to stakeholders and their interests.§AS2 For our function of reference, in UML the whole scene of human activity, and human–computer action, can be represented in a metamodel that roughly divides into what we would term entities and their properties (UML: structure) and actions (UML: behavior).[129]

---

* http://meaningpatterns.net/uml

[126] International Organization for Standardization, 2012, "Information Technology: Object Management Group Unified Modeling Language (OMG UML)," Part 1: Infrastructure.

[127] Object Management Group, 2015, "OMG Unified Modeling Language (OMG UML)," Version 2.5 (www.omg.org/spec/UML/2.5/), pp. 12–13.

[128] James Rumbaugh, Ivar Jacobson, and Grady Booch, 2004, *The Unified Modeling Language Reference Manual*, Boston, MA: Addison-Wesley, pp. 18–34.

[129] Ibid., p. 544.

UML 1.0 was launched in 1997. By 2006, it was estimated that ten million software developers were using it, and 70 percent of software development organizations.[130] Version 2.5 was released in 2015. It is now a ubiquitous part of software requirements specification.[131]

Today, UML speaks with law-like authority: "The words SHALL, SHALL NOT, SHOULD, SHOULD NOT, MAY, NEED NOT, CAN and CANNOT in this specification shall be interpreted according to Annex H of ISO/IEC Directives, Part 2, Rules for the structure and drafting of International Standards, Sixth Edition 2011."[132] What unfolds across its many pages are rules for modeling anything or everything in the world, for the purposes of inserting software into some part of the process:

A model is always a model *of* something. The thing being modeled can generically be considered a *system* within some *domain* of discourse. The model then makes some statements of interest about that system, abstracting from all the details of the system that could possibly be described, from a certain point of view and for a certain purpose. For an existing system, the model may represent an analysis of the properties and behavior of the system. For a planned system, the model may represent a specification of how the system is to be constructed and behave.[133]

The luminaries of UML barely get a mention in its voluminous documentation because the author is a collective, in this case a "task force" convened by the elusively named Object Management Group, an "international, open membership, not-for-profit technology standards consortium" based in Needham, Massachusetts.[134] Among the "what's trending" topics on its website, unsurprisingly perhaps, are the Internet of Things and Cybersecurity.

Lest we be under any illusion that the world of shared meanings is a place for participatory design by the masses, or even where smart philosophers of ordinary things can make their mark on the world for the uncompromised purposes of human self-understanding, let alone disinterested pragmatic utility, we learn that OMG was founded in 1989 by eleven companies, including Hewlett-Packard, IBM, Sun Microsystems, American Airlines, and Data General. Their mutual interests lie in having machines and software that connect with each other in supply chains and with customers in markets. Another OMG standard, the Semantics of Business Vocabulary and Rules™, brings us close to the point.[135]

---

[130] Andrew Watson, 2008, "Visual Modelling: Past, Present and Future," Needham, MA, p. 2.
[131] Jon Holt, Simon A. Perry, and Mike Brownsword, 2012, *Model-Based Requirements Engineering*, Stevenage, UK: Institution of Engineering and Technology.
[132] Object Management Group, 2015, "OMG Unified Modeling Language (OMG UML)," Version 2.5, p. 9.
[133] Ibid., p. 12.   [134] www.omg.org/gettingstarted/gettingstartedindex.htm
[135] www.omg.org/spec/SBVR/

OMG hosts four technical meetings per year, where the details of its standards are thrashed out. This is the strange, stateless way of semantic standards, software development, and the web. Here, in these communes of shared expertise, the agents of innovation in the representation of human meaning are anonymous to all other than each other. Voluntarily and without pay other than the regular salaries they earn working for their corporate sponsors, they serve global capitalism, offering up frameworks for the design of shared meanings. Dig deep and you'll find names for mostly overlooked luminaries – Grady Booch, Ivar Jacobson, and James Rumbaugh, to name several – and ideas that stretch back several decades before the formal launch of UML.

§1.2c   Object-oriented Software Development

Framed broadly in terms of object-oriented software development, "a system is modeled as a collection of discrete objects that interact to perform work that ultimately benefits an outside user."[136] Entities have states (data) and these can be transformed in actionable code (methods). The laws of modeling are, to emphasize the first letter of the UML[§1.2b] acronym, now "unified," across all domains of human action, semantic frameworks, programming languages, and development methodologies.[137]

Some unknown author of a line in the Wikipedia entry for object-oriented programming dryly notes that "attempts to find a consensus definition or theory behind objects have not proven very successful." A book promisingly titled *A Theory of Objects* says that the notion of modeling is based on "an analogy . . . between building an algorithmic model of a physical system from software components and building a mechanical model of a physical system from concrete objects. By analogy, the software components are themselves called *objects*."[138]

We would suggest that this is more than an analogy; rather it is a series of meaning transpositions. On the dimension of meaning form, these transpositions are between embodied action, visualized models of action in the form of UML diagramming, and the scaffolding of action by "objects" in the text of "code." On the dimension of meaning function, they are in the dynamic relationship of instances (what goes in the cells in a database table) and concepts (the column and row labels); and entities (states) and actions (interactions).

---

[136] James Rumbaugh, Ivar Jacobson, and Grady Booch, 2004, *The Unified Modeling Language Reference Manual*, Boston, MA: Addison-Wesley, p. 2.
[137] Ibid., p. 6.
[138] Martin Abadi and Luca Cardelli, 1996, *A Theory of Objects*, New York, NY: Springer-Verlag, p. 7.

The grammar we are proposing in this book can map onto UML, though we want to make some distinctions that UML blurs. Instances, for clarity's sake, we believe should be unequivocally singular, where UML can have instances that are general to the extent that they fit within a class. For UML "class," we want to use the word "concept." For UML "structure," we want to distinguish the specification,[§1.1] circumstances,[§1.2] and properties[§1.3] of elemental things. We want to distinguish circumstances we call "actions"[§1.2.2] from composites of action, which we will call "events."[§2.1] Instead of "model," or "metamodel," we use the word "ontology."[§3.1]

Notwithstanding these differences in nuance, we have one fundamental point of agreement with the spirit of UML and object-oriented programming: that modeling of entities can be transposed into models of action. Entities and actions are alternative modes of representation of circumstances. This is a key dimension of our notion of transposition.

Considering also the dimension of forms of meaning, there is a grammar of embodied meaning in getting a ticket for the theatre. We can speak about it conversationally, talking through the scenario as a "user story"[139] for the purposes of software design. We can model it visually using UML. We can test that the ticketing software works in embodied practice by walking it through in a use case, a single instance that might be taken to be indicative of many others. The transpositions between embodied action, speech, and its visual conceptualization are between parallel forms of meaning, with shared meaning functions (in this case, people and tickets as entities and going to the theater and purchasing as actions).

As a consequence of its specialized affordances, UML has become the pre-eminent, global interlocutor for software developers. Its job is to refer to the transposition of these functions and forms of meaning for the purposes of software design. Good software could not be designed on intuitions arising from conversation and embodied action alone. UML affords a rigorous, grammatical awareness of entities and actions in their multimodal relationships to embodied human practice.

§1.2.1   Entity

Entity. An object or state captured by its representation in space at a moment in time: a person, an object, a space, an abstraction.

---

[139] Phillip A. Laplante, 2013, *Requirements Engineering for Software and Systems*, Boca Raton, FL: Auerbach Publications, p. 58.

An entity is something distinguishable, such as a person, object, space, or abstraction.

Entities are the consequences of actions. Entities can act with consequences. But, for a moment at least, they might be conceived in their particularity, as instances. When someone acts to instantiate, the entity produced is an instantiation.

Also, entities can exist in their generality. When someone acts to conceptualize, the entity produced is a generalizing concept.

§1.2.2 Action

> **Action.** *A process captured by its representation as being a state of change in an entity or entities over a duration of time.*

Entities are products of action. They can also act. Entities can transpose with actions, functionally.

So, in speech, noun (instantiation/concept) can be transposed with verb (instantiate/conceptualize), and verb with noun. Actions can become entities. Entities emerge through action.

Entities and actions are the same thing by virtue of the shared focus of their referring (now instantiating action/instantiated entities, then conceptualizing actions/conceptualized entities). Yet entities and actions are also radically different orientations to reality, the same reality even.

§1.2.2a Leonard Bloomfield on Nouns and Verbs in Tagalog

Some linguists claim to have found languages that do not have distinct classes of nouns and verbs.[140] Leonard Bloomfield[§0.4a] worked for two years with Alfredo Viola Santiago, a Tagalog speaker and Filipino architectural engineering student at the University of Illinois. Starting with source texts in the form of a number of traditional stories told by his informant, Bloomfield proceeded to analyze the language, over four hundred pages in what has since been recognized as one of the masterworks of descriptive linguistics.

In Tagalog, Bloomfield points out, a word can be put to several kinds of use. The same word, *sumusulat*, can be used to refer to "the person writing" (noun), the act "he is writing" (verb), and an attribute "the writing child" (adjective). The differences between the meanings are marked by the context of the sentence.[141]

---

[140] R.M.W. Dixon, 2010b. *Basic Linguistic Theory,* Volume 2: *Grammatical Topics*, Oxford, UK: Oxford University Press, p. 37.

[141] Leonard Bloomfield, 1917, *Tagalog Texts with Grammatical Analysis*, Urbana, IL: University of Illinois Press.

This is not to say that Tagalog cannot make the distinction between an entity (in this case an abstract concept) and an action, but that the grammatical distinction is not necessarily marked in the form of a distinct word.

As for parts of speech in general, linguist Emmon Bach concludes, "differences in parts of speech only exist at a superficial level."[142] Fellow linguist Edward Sapir[§AS1.3.1c] says that parts of speech do "not merely grade into each other but are to an astonishing degree actually convertible into each other." The preposition "to" can be used to indicate place, "he came to the house" or this can also be represented as an action, "he reached the house." His conclusion? " ... that 'part of speech' reflects not so much our intuitive analysis of reality as our ability to construct reality into a variety of formal patterns ... Each language has its own scheme."

Such is the scope of linguistic diversity. Although, Sapir says, there is perhaps one universal (and here he contradicts Bloomfield and others), "no language fails to distinguish between a noun and a verb, though in particular cases the nature of the distinction may be an elusive one."[143]

The difference between entity and action may only be in the form of our representation, or what Peter Gärdenfors calls the mode of mental scanning,[144] where action is seen in the representation of things across time, and entity is a mental scan that shows the consequences of action in the constitution of some thing, conceived now as an object momentarily fixed in space.

To make things more complex, in all languages there are intermediate forms, things that are not distinctly states or actions. In English, "I write," the action, is clearly different from "the writing," the entity, and we can see the difference marked in the different words, "write" and "writing." But what is the gerund, "writing," in the sentence "writing is enlightening"? And what is the infinitive "to write" in the sentence "to write is to enlighten"? Or the gerundive nominal, "being eager," in "John's being eager to please." Or the derived nominal, "eagerness" in "John's eagerness to please."[145] These meanings lie at intermediate places as meanings move along a path between an action and an entity.

So, not only can nouns be made verbs and verbs be made nouns. There are many intermediate points across the path of transposition between nouns and verbs – or, in a more broadly framed multimodal grammar, a wide spectrum of

---

[142] Emmon Bach, 1968. "Nouns and Noun Phrases," pp. 90–122 in *Universals in Linguistic Theory*, edited by E. Bach and R.T. Harms, New York, NY: Holt, Rinehart and Winston, p. 91.

[143] Edward Sapir, 1921, *Language: An Introduction to the Study of Speech*, New York, NY: Harcourt Brace, pp. 118–19.

[144] Peter Gärdenfors, 2014, *Geometry of Meaning: Semantics Based on Conceptual Spaces*, Cambridge, MA: MIT Press, p. 13.

[145] Noam Chomsky, 1970, "Remarks on Nominalization," pp. 184–221 in *Readings in English Transformational Grammar*, edited by R. Jacobs and P. Rosenbaum, Waltham, MA: Ginn, pp. 187–8.

middle places in the everyday transpositional traffic between entities and actions.

§1.2.2b Henri Bergson's "Integral Experience"

The rise of quantum mechanics,[§AS1.3.1a] either as a supplement to or replacement of Newtonian physics, aligned nicely with the zeitgeist of the twentieth century. Matter could be transformed into energy. Particles could be conceived as waves. The uncertainty principle told us that at the smallest of scales, either position or speed can be accurately measured but not both.

When we propose to see states and actions, not as distinct things in the mechanics of ordinary experience, but as always-ready-to-be-transposed, one for the other and with many ambiguous midpoints along the way, we are suggesting something that might be conceived as a quantum grammar.[§AS1.4.4b] Where traditional grammars have conventionally identified entities and actions as two distinct and separate kinds of circumstance, making a foundational distinction between nouns and verbs for instance, we want to trace the dynamic where states and actions are always transposable, and where there are innumerable, equivocal intermediate positions. Entities and actions are not separable circumstances, but transitory orientations to circumstance. Entities and actions are integral elements of circumstance, always in a state of torsion.

If quantum mechanics upended the old physics, a parallel disquiet was created in twentieth-century philosophy. Here is a paraphrase of Henri Bergson,[*] famed philosopher at the Collège de France: the problem of philosophy to date had been to freeze reality into entities and their states for the purposes of construing it as facts (the empiricists) or concepts (the rationalists). Naming words deceive to the extent that they seem to denote changeless things. Conceptual analysis tends to freeze reality into entities. Images deceive to the extent that they freeze objects and persons in moments of time. Instead, we need to conceive reality in cinematographic terms, as movement and change.[146]

Not only are things on the move, where apparent entities present themselves as mere momentary appearances in a universe of action. The person experiencing things is always in a process of becoming, formed by the ever-changing experiences of their life where the immediate frame of experience is always changing too, and where "the same antecedents will never recur."[147] The

---

[*] http://meaningpatterns.net/bergson

[146] Henri Bergson, 1903 [1912], *An Introduction to Metaphysics*, translated by T.E. Hulme, New York, NY: G.P. Putnam, pp. 25, 30–32, 56–58, 48–49; Henri Bergson, 1907 [1944], *Creative Evolution*, translated by A. Mitchell, New York, NY: Random House, pp. 333, 357–58.

[147] Henri Bergson, 1889 [1910], *Time and Free Will*, London, UK: Muirhead Library of Philosophy, p. 199.

human species should be conceived more as *homo faber*, the creature who works to make the world, than *homo sapiens*, the creature who freezes the world in his conceptualizations, as do naming word or still image.[148] Experience is a process of "ceaseless self-creation."[149] For this, Bergson proposes a metaphysics of "integral experience" whose capacity to capture movement and change is grounded in its methods of "qualitative differentiations and integrations."[150]

To re-say this in the terms of our grammar, the world is a place of active meaning designing, where the conditions of designing – the available resources for design action and the designed outcomes of our actions – are never quite the same, where exact repetition is never possible even if the similarities of word or image might lead us to think that. It is the action of designing that is more critical to our understanding of the meaning of reality than the apparently static objects of design that are mere residues of the past or the designed objects that become the legacy for another future.

Little wonder Bergson had a preoccupation with change, as the debris of the catastrophic twentieth century fell around him. He had won the Nobel Prize for literature in 1927 for his philosophical writings.[§AS1.3.1a] But when, near the end of his life, the Nazis invaded Paris, he renounced all the French honors he had been awarded, and stood in line in inclement weather to register as a Jew.[151]

§1.2.2c *Alfred North Whitehead's* Process and Reality

Early in his long career, Alfred North Whitehead[*] had, with his former student Bertrand Russell, written the monumental *Principia Mathematica.*[§1a] Starting a second career at age 63, he moved from the University of London to Harvard University. Here, he turned his focus from mathematics to philosophy of meaning.

In 1927 he was invited to give the famed Gifford lectures. In other years, William James, Hannah Arendt, and John Dewey have lectured. Often the lecture hall had been packed, as was it was in anticipation of Whitehead's first lecture. His topic: "Process and Reality."

---

[*]   http://meaningpatterns.net/whitehead

[148]   Henri Bergson, 1934 [1946], *The Creative Mind*, translated by M.L. Andison, New York, NY: The Philosophical Library, p. 99.

[149]   Henri Bergson, 1907 [1944], *Creative Evolution*, translated by A. Mitchell, New York, NY: Random House, p. 10.

[150]   Henri Bergson, 1903 [1912], *An Introduction to Metaphysics*, translated by T.E. Hulme, New York, NY: G.P. Putnam, pp. 70–72, 92.

[151]   Jimena Canales, 2015, *The Physicist and the Philosopher: Einstein, Bergson, and the Debate That Changed Our Understanding of Time*, Princeton, NJ: Princeton University Press, p. 336.

But by the second and subsequent lectures, the numbers dwindled down to half a dozen stalwarts, the material was so dense. Had he not known who Whitehead was, said one member of the audience, he "would have suspected that it was an imposter making it up as he went along." The year before, he had given a series of five lectures at the University of Illinois, an early version of his Gifford lectures, where according to one wit, "the philosophers did not understand the lectures but hoped the mathematicians did, and the mathematicians did not understand the lectures but hoped the philosophers did."[152]

Later, Whitehead's Gifford lectures were published as a book of over four hundred pages. The first edition was riddled with typographical errors, and editors of a later edition had to go through a torturous process of trying to figure out what Whitehead had meant.[153] Late in his life and with things he urgently needed to say, Whitehead had little patience for proofreading.

Acknowledging his debt to Bergson, Whitehead addresses two contradictory biases in modern philosophy – objectivist and subjectivist orientations to experience – and maps these onto parallel biases in the everyday human representation of experience. Francis Bacon's scientific method of observation and induction tended to find static things in the world by virtue of its objectivist, empiricist orientation. So too mathematics tends to assume through oversimplification that each additional one-object is for the purpose of enumeration namable as the same object as the previous one. This is a radically revisionary thought from a co-author of *Principia Mathematica*.

Language also leads us to objectification, where the subject as an object precedes and is separated from the predicate as action. By these means, we tend to atomize "the extensive continuum of the world" into separate entities. "We analyze the world in terms of static categories." We spatialize the universe at the expense of fluency. We freeze moments in time at the expense of the life history of the object. We relegate "each item of the 'many' to its subordination in the constitution of a novel 'one'."

However, says Whitehead, in reality nothing is so static and repetitive. No subject experiences the same thing twice. Whitehead likes Locke's[§1.3a] bleak phrase; our experience of the world is one of "perpetual perishing." "We find ourselves in a buzzing world, amid a democracy of fellow creatures; whereas, under some disguise or other, orthodox philosophy can only introduce us to solitary substances, each enjoying an illusory experience."[154]

In other moments of science and everyday experience, however, we do the opposite, we tend to subjectivize. Such is the occupational hazard of

---

[152] Victor Lowe, 1990, *Alfred North Whitehead: The Man and His Work,* Volume 2: *1910–1947,* Baltimore, MD: Johns Hopkins University Press, pp. 250, 207.

[153] Alfred North Whitehead, 1928 [1978], *Process and Reality,* New York, NY: Free Press, Editor's Preface.

[154] Ibid., pp. 5–6, 12–13, 67, 209, 321, 211, 29, 210, 50.

philosophical rationalism or purely Analytical Philosophy where we can deduce meanings from the syntax of language or the logic of mathematics. (Again, this from a co-author of *Principia Mathematica*.) We make the mistake of working from the "tacit assumption of the mind as subject and of its contents as predicates." This blinds the meaning-maker to the wholeness of the world; "the selective character of the individual obscures the external totality from which it originates and which it embodies. The task of philosophy is to recover the totality obscured by the selection ... Philosophy is the self-correction by consciousness of its own initial excess of subjectivity." So too in everyday life, "we must ... avoid the solipsism of the present moment."[155]

Whitehead's philosophy of process sets an ambitious agenda, "to frame a coherent, logical, necessary system of general ideas in terms of which every element of our experience can be interpreted." It lays out "metaphysical first principles," by means of which to identify the wholeness of the world in its infinite diversity, a "flux of things" in which "all things flow." Making a part of this journey in science, "Newton ordered fluency back into the world" with his Theory of Fluxions, or the mathematics of calculus.[§1.3.2d] However, this same mathematics could slip back, only "to atomize the extensive continuum" into static, infinitesimal datapoints.

Reaching first principles in the last sentence of his lectures, Whitehead speaks to the process of experience as an "insistent craving, ... [a] zest for existence ... refreshed by the ever-present, unfading importance of our immediate actions, which perish and yet live for evermore."[156] This, in our terms, is how we live transposition.

§1.2.2d Citroën DS and Bézier Curves

A modern mechanics for representing the quantifiable relations of states to action begins with algebra, الجبر, al-jabr, or the reunion of broken parts in Islamic mathematics, a notion established by Muḥammad ibn Mūsā al-Khwārizmī (780–850). A variable in the form of a letter (say, "x") represents a possible number. A number can stand for an entity; its variability indicates that something is movable in action.

Later, a coordinate system with x and y axes is developed by René Descartes.[§3.1.2g] Coordinate geometry locates points (entities), traces lines (actions), and specifies areas and volumes on a two-dimensional plane ("x" and "y" axes) or in three-dimensional space. After that comes calculus, versions of which were invented contemporaneously by Gottfried Leibniz and Isaac Newton.[§1.3.2d] Now, the trajectory of constantly changing lines can be calculated, and the spaces around them. Calculus traces continuous change.

---

[155] Ibid., pp. 51, 15, 81.   [156] Ibid., pp. 3, 79, 208–9, 332, 351.

Indicative points on a line can be selected (entities), but the line traces movement (action).

Until the late 1950s, not every curve was representable mathematically. Two people, principally, can be credited with an innovation by means of which every curve could be mathematized. Paul de Casteljau was an engineer working at the French automaker, Citroën, but he did not publish his thinking at the time. Meanwhile Pierre Bézier was working at the competitor company, Renault, designing the first generation of computer aided design (CAD) software. De Casteljau, it seems, may have reached this point first, * but today these things are known as Bézier curves because he published first, in 1962.[157]

Citroën and Renault were in the 1950s in the business of curves, so little wonder their engineers were trying to find systematic ways to represent them. In 1955, Citroën launched the model DS, famed for its aerodynamic curves, manufacturing 1,455,746 instances before ceasing production in 1975.

Semiotician and cultural critic Roland Barthes announced the DS in these terms:

The new Citroën manifestly falls from heaven insofar as it presents itself first of all as a superlative object ... The DS (the Déesse, or goddess) has all the characteristics ... of one of those objects from another world ... We know that smoothness is always an attribute of perfection ... Christ's tunic was seamless, just as the spaceships of science fiction are of unbroken metal ... The DS has the beginnings of a new phenomenology of assembly, as if we were leaving the world of welded elements for a world of juxtaposed elements held together by the sole virtue of their marvelous shape ... Everything indicates a sort of control exerted over movement ...

In the exhibition halls, the sample cars are visited with an intense, affectionate care: this is the great tactile experience of discovery, the moment when the visual marvelous will submit to the reasoned assault of touching (for touch is the most demystifying of the senses ...) ... sheet metal stroked ... doors caressed ... Here the object is totally prostituted ...

[T]he Déesse is mediatized in fifteen minutes, accomplishing in this exorcism the entire dumb show of petit bourgeois annexation.[158]

Multimodally across image, object, and space – and viscerally – the Citroën DS represented the merger of object and movement. Functionally speaking, the dynamic movement of line and surface were captured in Bézier curves, the invitation to travel in the sleekly lined object – layers of action-in-entity and entity-in-action.

* http://meaningpatterns.net/bezier

[157] Gerald Farin, 2002, "A History of Curves and Surfaces in Cagd," pp. 1–21 in *Handbook of Computer Aided Geometric Design*, edited by G. Farin, J. Hoschek, and M.-S. Kim, Amsterdam, NL: Elsevier, pp. 5–6; Mike Kamermans, 2011–2017, "A Primer on Bézier Curves," retrieved from https://pomax.github.io/bezierinfo/.
[158] Roland Barthes, 1957 [2012], *Mythologies*, New York, NY: Hill and Wang, pp. 169–71.

Barthes was killed in a moment of automotive movement, hit by a laundry truck as he crossed the road on the way home from a lunch with François Mitterrand, future President of France – such was the fame he had acquired for his cultural prognostications. Was the truck a Citroën?

§1.2.2e Scalable Vector Graphics

Today, Bézier curves[§1.2.2d] are a key mechanism to capture movement in computer graphics. To account for their significance, we need to make a distinction between two modes for the presentation of image in the universe of digital rendering – "raster" in contrast to "vector" imaging.

In raster imaging, a visual is "bitmapped" as a series of dots. Screens are bitmaps – a series of dots (pixels) of varied colors and brightness mapped across the x and y axes of Cartesian coordinates.[§1.2.2d] Image capture is also via pixel sensors. Taking a digital photo, a sensor records hue and intensity for each pixel. Creating the image of a character or grapheme from Unicode[§0.2.1a] is to bitmap out a series of black pixels on a white ground. In this way, an image or text is decomposed into an enumerated pattern of states. This is not new to the practices of digital imaging – it was an essential element of dot-screening in photolithography, the different-sized black ink dots in the screening of black and white photographs for offset printing, or the CMYK (Cyan, Magenta, Yellow, and Black) dots of color photolithography.[§1.3.1e]

The problem with these forms of raster graphics is that they are not scalable. Increase the size of a bitmapped image and it will become pixelated. They also involve a great deal of needless repetition, often many of the same dots appearing after each other, to draw a line for instance. Vector graphics, by contrast, trace a theoretically infinite series of intermediate points, because a line or a volume is represented in a formula rather than a myriad of discrete places. This means that it is dynamically scalable and the redundancies of repetition are removed.* The difference is between enumerating a myriad of states and offering conditions for innumerability, or vectors as actionable instructions.

Given the practicalities of digital screen technologies, images all have to be rasterized by the time they are rendered. But as this happens on-the-fly at the time of rendering, it allows flexible scaling, necessary in applications such as digital maps or animations. Many images are bitmapped at their inception, such as digital photos, before being converted to scalable vector graphics.

Vector mapping (including Bézier curves) allows the transposition from dots into vectors and back to dots, or in the terms of our multimodal grammar, the transposition of states and actions. This supports interactive imaging applications

---

* http://meaningpatterns.net/svg

where the user is involved in customizing the image presentation to suit their needs and interests.[159] Not only is the image a product of movement (action); it is movable (actionable) by the viewer.

Scalable Vector Graphics (SVG) is one of the key technologies of the web, in development as a foundational standard by the World Wide Web Consortium in 1999.[160] Participants in the nominally open process of standards development include representatives from a predictable cast of corporations, including Microsoft, Adobe, Google, and Apple – also Boeing, another modern enterprise with an obvious interest in the production of curves.

All major web browsers now support SVG, as well as billions of smart phones and other digital devices. When they do, it is the same, universal engine at work. Adobe's Postscript, a page in development description language for electronic and print publishing in development since 1982, uses these vectoral principles. Adobe's Illustrator imaging program runs on vector graphics, and it is possible to convert backwards and forwards between this and the bitmap manipulation software, Adobe Photoshop. Parallel to SVG has been another web standard, Virtual Reality Modelling Language (VRML, 1994), developed in parallel with the core language of the web, Hypertext Markup Language (HTML), and since renamed X3D.[161]

Analogue cinema was an earlier moment in the transformation of the affordances of the image, shifting the focus of imaging from entities, whose primary reference point in still photography was space, to the moving image, where the primary reference point was action. Scalable Vector Graphics and related technologies take this to a new stage. Not only does the source image prioritize action; the viewer can also engage with the image as an actor who affects the form of its presentation.

§1.3   Property

> *Property. Descriptive feature of an entity or action, either in its singularity in the case of an instance at a moment in time, or in plurality when criterial features are captured within a concept in order to define the shared features of more than one entity or action. Properties may be variable in the case of an entity which is the subject of action, or capture the range of variability across instances within the scope of a concept. Properties may refer to qualities or quantities.*

[159] David Dailey, Jon Frost, and Domenico Strazzullo, 2012, *Building Web Applications with SVG*, Redmond, WA: Microsoft Press.
[160] www.w3.org/Graphics/SVG/.
[161] www.web3d.org/x3d/; Vladimir Geroimenko and Chaomei Chen, eds., 2005, *Visualizing Information Using SVG and X3D: XML-Based Technologies for the XML-Based Web*, London, UK: Springer-Verlag.

Reference to properties adds a descriptive supplement in reference to an instance or a concept. Instance: this elephant is gray; it is walking slowly. Concept: elephants are gray; their walking is slow. Properties can refer to qualities (grayness and slowness) and quantities (one or more elephants, or the enumerated speed at which they are walking).

Properties are singular and invariable (if we are to trust our senses) in the case of a manifest entity or action (as is the case when this elephant is inarguably gray, or a movement that is inarguably in a certain direction). Although properties may be invariable in an instance of an entity at a moment of time, they may vary for that entity over time as a consequence of action.

Properties may be variable in the case of a concept (as dogs may be black or brown, or the velocity of one dog running compared to another), or they may be invariable when a description is integral to a concept and universally applicable in all instances by definition (as the sides of a square are by both definition and description straight, and light may be defined in part by its invariable speed in a vacuum).

For the purposes of understanding the dynamics of meaning in a time of ubiquitous calculation, we want to make a distinction between properties referring to quality and those referring to quantity, as shown in Fig. 1.3(i).

| | | Specification | |
		Instance	Concept
Properties	Quality	Descriptive features: (a) invariable to an entity or action; (b) variable to an entity in space or action over time	Descriptive features: (a) invariable if integral to definition of an entity or action; (b) variable if not integral to definition of an entity or action
	Quantity	One (or the absence of one)	More than one (or the absence of any)

Fig. 1.3(i): Properties specified

Conventional accounts of language do not make a quantity/quality distinction grammatically, to the extent that numbers are mere adjectives (categorically, "seven" is the same part of speech as "red"), or inadequately to the extent that the plural form is an undifferentiated more-than-one.

Until the past several thousand years, human societies have not needed a finely grained sense of quantity. The social practice of extensive quantification commences with the invention of human inequality. Both quantification and inequality have intensified since the coming of industrial modernity, and this can be no coincidence.[§AS1.4.7a]

Since the third quarter of the twentieth century, quantification has come to be mediated by now-universal technologies of digitization. Until these relatively recent historical events, the human species had no need for a distinguishable system of quantities. We do today, and with a new urgency in the digital era where by processes of functional transposition, numbers denote instances, concepts, and properties – and do so with an insistent practical import for the mechanics of representation and communication, and near-universal agreement as to the objects of their reference.

With this change in our systems of sense-making comes (another) self-transformation of human nature, perhaps for the worse, perhaps for the better – there is no essential directionality in the tools of human self-transformation. It may be that we are creatures of history; we nevertheless remain responsible for the direction of our continuous self-making, our designs on ourselves, and our impacts on others.

So, to distinguish these two kinds of property, quality refers to everyday, viscerally ordinary experiences such as light, sound, and touch; and quantities refer to their enumeration – their numbered naming in an instance, their enumeration in concept classification, or numbering that adds specificity to the vagaries of speech in the specification of properties by their degree.

We manage both qualities and quantities across modes. In writing and speech, adjectives refer to the properties of entities and adverbs to the properties of action. In image, line and color refer to the properties of entities, and vectors to the properties of visible actions. In space, the properties of entities may be determined by the material form of structure, and the qualities of their use in spatially defined action.

Fig. 1.3(ii) provides a rough map of properties in a grammar of multimodality, with some examples:

Form Function: Property	Text	Image	Space	Object	Body	Sound	Speech
Quality	Adjectives, adverbs	Visible forms: color, line, directionality, volume	Material form, shape, extent	Shape, mass, composition, texture	Sensations: warmth/ coolness, pleasure/ pain, taste, smell	Pitch, volume, tempo, timbre	Phonic emphases directing to descriptive words and phrases
Quantity	Numbers, variables, math symbols, equations	Diagram, scaled map, plan	Area, distance, direction, geometry	Dimensions, volume, weight, chemistry, physics	Temperature and other quantifiable sensations	Musical notation, digitized sound recording	Rough plurality (few, many), speakable number

Fig. 1.3(ii): Properties

§1.3a   René Descartes and John Locke on Color

Our focal point in this grammar is human experience. For a philosophy of ordinary things we call this "grammar," or the patterns in our sense-making. But whence this sense? What of its making?

In the European tradition of philosophy, there are two canonical frames of interpretation, one frequently spoken for by René Descartes[§3.1.2g] and the other by John Locke. A thousand variants have since been thought up in order to rework, refine, or struggle to supersede what is in essence the same problematic. Nevertheless, all largely fail to escape entrapment within the terms of reference of the debate. Descartes' account of human sense-making prioritizes the mind; Locke's prioritizes empirical sensation.

Here is Descartes: we know that the body exists because its presence "can be perceived by touch, sight, hearing, by taste, or smell." These are sensations that in our grammar of multimodality we call "qualities." However, the body is "moved ... not ... by itself ... For ... the power of self-movement [is] quite foreign to the nature of a body." The body is moved by the soul in the form of its mind.[162] The reality of mind is more certain than the realities of bodily sensation, because things I think my body touches, sees, hears, and feels could always be dreams, imaginings, or figments of my perception. If the qualities of experience are forever questionable, the only thing we can be certain of is our thinking. So, famously, *cogito ergo sum*, "I am thinking, therefore I exist ... the first principle of philosophy."[163] This is the only reality that is finally unshakable by a skepticism arising from the intrinsic uncertainties of embodied perception.

Now, here is Locke, by way of contrast:[*]

We come by those ideas we have of yellow, white, heat, cold, soft, hard, bitter, sweet, and all those which we call sensible qualities; which when I say the senses convey into the mind, I mean, they from external objects convey into the mind what produces there those perceptions. This great source of most of the ideas we have, depending wholly upon our senses, and derived by them to the understanding, I call sensation ... If a child were kept in a place where he never saw any other but black and white till he were a man, he would have no ... ideas of scarlet or green.

So, mind follows sensible matter:

Let us then suppose the mind to be, as we say, white paper [Locke's famous *tabula rasa* or mind-as-blank-slate, as famed a formulation as Descartes' *cogito*] void of all

---

[*]   http://meaningpatterns.net/descartes-locke

[162]   René Descartes, 1641 [1984], *Meditations on First Philosophy*, translated by J. Cottingham, R. Stoothoff, and D. Murdoch, Cambridge, UK: Cambridge University Press, p. 17.

[163]   René Descartes, 1637 [1985], *Discourse on the Method of Rightly Conducting the Reason, and Seeking Truth in the Sciences*, translated by J. Cottingham, R. Stoothoff, and D. Murdoch, Cambridge, UK: Cambridge University Press, p. 127.

characters, without any ideas. How comes it to be furnished? Whence comes it by that vast store which the busy and boundless fancy of man has painted on it with an almost endless variety? Whence has it all the materials of reason and knowledge? To this I answer, in one word, from experience.[164]

Despite the canonical differences between these two philosophical stances, there are symptomatic, even surprising, convergences. Notwithstanding the fallibility of sensation, Descartes will not deny its irreducibility and role in meaning, involving as it does "pain, pleasure, light, colours, sounds, smells, tastes, heat, hardness and other tactile qualities."[165] "If someone is blind from birth, we should not be able by force of argument to get him to have true ideas of colours just like the ones we have, derived as they are from the senses."[166] At this point, Descartes is sounding very like Locke.

Locke, meanwhile, insists that experience also involves "reflection," or mental processes wherein the "mind furnishes the understanding with ideas of its own operations." These are "ideas ... being such only as the mind gets by reflecting on its own operations within itself." Now Locke is sounding like Descartes. Take color:

when the mind makes the particular ideas received from particular objects to become general ... This is called *abstraction* ... Thus the same colour being observed to-day in chalk or snow, which the mind yesterday received from milk, it considers that appearance alone, makes it a representative of all of that kind; and having given it the name whiteness, it by that sound signifies the same quality wheresoever to be imagined or met with; and thus universals, whether ideas or terms, are made.[167]

In other words, "white" is not just a sensation; it is also a mental reflection on a shared property in experience.

So, both Locke and Descartes recognize the visceral materiality of the sensations that we, in our grammar of multimodality, call qualities. They also both recognize the role of mind in giving order to these sensations. Prioritizing mind, Descartes insists that people can get colors wrong, when for instance, "after being struck in the eye, a person sees sparks and flashes, or when after looking at the sun, the impression is retained for a short time after looking away." However, he also speaks of vision "acting directly upon our soul insofar as it is united to our body, ... ordained by nature to make it have such

---

[164] John Locke, 1690 [1801], *An Essay Concerning Human Understanding*, Edinburgh, UK: Mundell & Son, Bk. II, Ch. I: s.3, 7, 2.

[165] René Descartes, 1644 [1985], *Principles of Philosophy*, translated by J. Cottingham, R. Stoothoff, and D. Murdoch, Cambridge, UK: Cambridge University Press, p. 209.

[166] René Descartes, 1628 [1985], *Rules for the Direction of the Mind*, translated by J. Cottingham, R. Stoothoff, and D. Murdoch, Cambridge, UK: Cambridge University Press, p. 56.

[167] John Locke, 1690 [1801], *An Essay Concerning Human Understanding*, Edinburgh, UK: Mundell & Son, Bk. 2, Ch. I: s.2; Bk. 1, Ch. I: s.9.

sensations."[168] Meanwhile, Locke says that experience is as much a matter of reflection as sensation, as when whiteness is taken to be a shared property of chalk, snow, and milk.

So the opposition between the two philosophers is not fundamental, or at least not to the extent that we may have been led to believe by the academic predisposition to find dispute.

Both Descartes and Locke might be considered dualists – and Descartes notoriously so – separating as they do mind and matter-sensing body. In Locke, the dualism is in the difference between sensation and reflection. But in other moments both also insist on the unity of mind and body-sensing-matter, soul united with body in Descartes' terms, or reflection integral to sensation in Locke's.

Both find themselves having to be integrationists as often as they are dualists. So, when we come to our own integrationist account of quality, we want to have our Descartes and our Locke as well.

§1.3.1   Quality

> *Quality. Reference to primordial properties of sensuous human activity, identified as sensations in the meeting of matter-sensing body with mind in human praxis.*

How do we escape mind–body dualism, and the seemingly interminable debate about the priority of mind or matter? In his *Theses on Feuerbach*, Karl Marx came up with the expansive phrase, "sensuous human activity," to capture human "practice" or "praxis" in its ineluctable wholeness, where mind meets matter in socially mediated and historically specific activity.[169]

Qualities, we suggest, are the most basic and primordial forms of reference. Babies feel and see the properties of things – as colors, textures, shapes, or tastes – before they are able to distinguish them as instances, and later still, generalize these into concepts of quality. Qualities are a first order of experience, where our minds and the world are inseparably integrated.

Mind is matter. Mind is shaped by matter. Matter is made sensible by mind. Take color ...

---

[168] René Descartes, 1637 [1985], *Discourse on the Method of Rightly Conducting the Reason, and Seeking Truth in the Sciences*, translated by J. Cottingham, R. Stoothoff, and D. Murdoch, Cambridge, UK: Cambridge University Press, pp. 167–68.

[169] Karl Marx, 1845 [1969], "Theses on Feuerbach," pp. 13–15 in *Marx & Engels Selected Works*, Moscow, USSR: Progress Publishers.

§1.3.1a Berlin and Kay's Basic Color Terms

Descartes' and Locke's accounts of sense-making tend to neglect the fact that experience and mind are cultural and historical. In other words, they are variable according to human contexts of meaning, where contexts of meaning – history – are the consequences of human practice, and cultures can be vastly different. In their trail, modern philosophy, psychology, and today neuroscience often neglect culture and history, too.[170] However, differences in historical experience and cultural mindedness are as important to our account of human sense-making as biophysical universals.

Color is a favorite topic among socio-historical linguists, psychologists, neuroscientists, and philosophers of mind alike. Often, the archetype in color analysis is the mind and body of the singular person. However, the sensible world is a place where colors are a creation of human artifice as much as they are facts of nature. Notwithstanding certain continuities in nature, including the nature of the human body, the praxis of color varies considerably. The electromagnetic spectrum and the range of human color perception may be what it is,[§1.3.1c] but human references to color and the uses to which color reference is put are widely varied.

In the sociolinguistics of color, perhaps the most celebrated work is by Berlin and Kay, the title of whose book announces their unequivocal conclusion, *Basic Color Terms: Their Universality and Evolution.* Universality: in their study of ninety-eight languages, respondents were asked to name color chips, then locate them in a Munsell Chart.[§1.3.1g] They found that there are only eleven basic color categories: white, black, red, yellow, blue, green, purple, pink, orange, brown, and gray. Evolution: some languages have words for more of these basic color categories than others, and these can be placed in an evolutionary sequence, from what Berlin and Kay term "primitive" to "advanced." [*]

Some languages only have two of the basic color terms, black and white: Dugum Dani in New Guinea; Ngombe in Congo; Paliyan in India. In evolutionary terms, Berlin and Kay call these Stage 1 languages. Stage 2 languages add a third term, red, to their color classification repertoire: Swahili in Tanzania, Poto in the United States, and Toda in South India. Stage 3 languages add green or yellow. And so on through seven stages where languages become "more evolved" by adding more basic color terms, culminating at between eight and eleven color terms in English, Spanish, and Arabic. Their conclusion? "There seems to be a positive correlation between general cultural complexity

---

[*] http://meaningpatterns.net/color-terms

[170] James Paul Gee, 1992 [2013], *The Social Mind: Language, Ideology, and Social Practice,* Champaign, IL: Common Ground.

(and/or level of technological development) and complexity of color vocabulary."[171]

Screaming to escape their conclusions is the evidence Berlin and Kay themselves provide. We ask: how could such extraordinary variety in so fundamental a quality as color be taken to indicate universality? As for evolution, why would we consider us moderns to be more evolved, because when it comes to our unusually obsessive rendering of color to walls or pages or digital screens, eleven terms is nowhere near enough? On the other hand, isn't it sufficient to say that everyone in every language has as wide a range of color terms as circumstances may require? In Berlin and Kay's own words, "every language has an indefinitely large number of expressions that denote the sensation of color." In this context, what does "basic" color term mean? Their answer is, a term that means what it does on a stand-alone basis (such as "red") as opposed to metaphorical extension ("gold") or a term extended by qualification ("light green"). However, if every color is expressible in every language, why would it matter whether they are expressed with a unique term rather an analogical one? Russian, meanwhile, seems to have two "basic" terms for blue, and what is the significance of that when in English we can with equal facility say "light blue" and "dark blue."[172] Does this make Russian more "evolved" when it comes to blue?

What, then, are the reasons for the differences? Perhaps it's not that we users of modern written languages speak in ways that are more evolved; it is just that our ways of making sense – our grammars of meaning – differ for reasons of our histories and purposes. On the one hand the cultures of first peoples may simply have not much use for some of the color terms we moderns use – and in the same way modern cultures have abandoned the labyrinthine grammar of kinship used by many first peoples[§AS1.1.3c] because, at least to this degree of intricacy, kinship no longer suits our purposes.

Then, even in languages which seem a lot less "evolved" in terms of their number of "basic" terms, when needs arise, people do a lot of color work. Quechua speakers in Peru can name 350 varieties of potato, largely distinguished by terms identifying the color of the skin or pulp of the potato, or the flowers of the potato plant.[173] In their Philippine jungle context, Hanunóo color categories distinguish levels of succulence across a scale of wetness and dryness.[174]

[171] Brent Berlin and Paul Kay, 1969, *Basic Color Terms: Their Universality and Evolution*, Berkeley, CA: University of California Press, pp. 2–3, 46–62, 16.
[172] A.E. Moss, 1989, "Basic Colour Terms: Problems and Hypotheses," *Lingua* 78:313–20; A.E. Moss, I. Davies, G. Corbett, and G. Laws, 1990, "Mapping Russian Basic Colour Terms Using Behavioural Measures," *Lingua* 82:313–32.
[173] Ralph Bolton, 1978, "Black, White, and Red All Over: The Riddle of Color Term Salience," *Ethnology* 17(3):287–311, pp. 297–98.
[174] Harold C. Conklin, 1955, "Hanunóo Color Categories," *Southwest Journal of Anthropology* 11:339–44.

Some languages don't even have a word for color.[175] There is no word for "color" in the language Yélî Dnye of Rossel Island, Papua New Guinea, and only three words that Berlin and Kay would classify as "basic color terms." This is in part because, as the linguist Stephen Levinson concludes, "color is simply of minor communication import, handled by a range of descriptive phrases," though these, he shows, are numerous and reflect subtle color variations.[176]

"We Don't Talk Much about Color Here," said the Bellonese speaker on the Polynesian island of Bellona, mystified by the linguist's questioning. Although with no word for color and only at Stage 2 on the Berlin and Kay evolutionary ladder, when contextually located color terms are taken into consideration, the Bellonese "could also be considered to have an extremely sophisticated system of color notation, with innumerable 'color words,' way beyond the Western system, and thus much more sophisticated."[177]

The point, then, is not the universality of color naming, but the extraordinary differences in such naming, across human cultures and in human history. Nor are the differences a matter of evolution. Modern color terminology is not more evolved. Color terminologies are just differently framed, for different purposes.

And if there are just eleven terms in the most advanced languages, these are inadequate to the ends of modernity. Not only do they have to be extended in modern naming schemes. In the digital era, words are extended and in many places replaced by transpositions into the properties of quantity – alphanumeric naming.[§1.1.1c] These differences and changes are the stuff of history, and given the pain and uncertainty of modernity, there is no claiming that "our" history might be in evolutionary terms ahead of "theirs." Modernity may be temporally later than the sense-making grammars of first peoples,[§2.1.2d] and it may have displaced them via colonialism and other atrocities. But it is by no means smarter.

§1.3.1b C.L. Hardin's Color for Philosophers

If Berlin and Kay[§1.3.1a] are the most cited sociolinguists of color, C.L. Hardin is perhaps the most cited philosopher of color. Hardin brings the science of optics to bear on age-old philosophers' problems of mind, body, and reality.

---

[175] Anna Wierzbicka, 2006, "The Semantics of Color: A New Paradigm," pp. 1–24 in *Progress in Colour Studies,* Volume 1: *Language and Culture,* edited by C.P. Biggam and C.J. Kay, Amsterdam, NL: John Benjamins.

[176] Stephen C. Levinson, 2000, "Yélî Dnye and the Theory of Basic Color Terms," *Journal of Linguistic Anthropology* 10(1):1–53, p. 41.

[177] Rolf Kuschel, and Torben Monberg, 1974. "'We Don't Talk Much About Colour Here': A Study of Colour Semantics on Bellona Island," *Man* 9(2):213–42, p. 241.

Like his sociolinguistic colleagues, Hardin says one thing in his headline claim, while his text seems to say the opposite. We don't see colors of things, he says; rather we see two quite different species of light – reflected light and light generated by light sources. And the three types of color-detecting cells in our eyes do not "see" primary or basic colors; our minds create these based on the mental recombination of data and our conventions of color naming. This is what he concludes: "Since physical objects are not colored . . . colored objects are illusions, but not unfounded illusions. We are normally in chromatic states, and these are neural states."[178]

So color is a figment of our neurobiology, and a mental state to the extent that the retina is considered an extension of mind. Now we are back to the version of Descartes who, for the sake of argument, has been dressed in dualist caricature.[§1.3a] Like Descartes, Hardin is a mind–sensation dualist and not even-handedly so, because the conceiving mind maintains its pre-eminence as the ultimate master of sensation.

However, to make his case, Hardin refers to a lot of stuff that would make you think that color is far from an illusion. Rather, it seems to be a phenomenon of the natural world engaged with mind, itself also a creature of natural history. Color may express complex and highly mediated relations to the material world, nevertheless in the practical business of reference, color is as real as meaning gets. We can make this case using Hardin's own evidence, extended with some more recent accounts.

§1.3.1c Isaac Newton's Spectral Decomposition of Light

Here are some facts of the materiality of color and the physiology of our human seeing. These are indicative of the ways in which the meanings of qualities are made, more generally.

The human eye captures only about one-eightieth of the electromagnetic spectrum, elementary wave-particles, photons, that travel in a vacuum at 299,792,458 meters per second. Light is visible to the human eye in the 380nm to 780nm wavelength range – a nanometer (nm) is one-billionth of a meter. Wavelengths outside this range are not visible to the human eye, and here we have X-rays, ultraviolet light, infrared rays, microwaves and radio waves. The part of the spectrum we happen to find visible is no different in physical form from the other parts of the spectrum.

---

[178] C.L. Hardin, 1988, *Color for Philosophers: Unweaving the Rainbow*, Indianapolis, IN: Hackett Publishing Company, p. 111.

Isaac Newton[§2.3a] was the first to explain the spectral decomposition of white light into the component wavelengths that we see as colors,[*] and their recomposition into white light.[179] Light may consist of a number of wavelengths in combination, all the way to white light which includes the whole spectrum of visible wave lengths. Light can be generated at its source (incandescence), or reflected so that the source light and the reflected light interact to determine color. Our eyes see light sources and reflected light entirely differently, as when the embers of a fire seem red in the dark, but gray when a light is shined on them.[180]

Then there are the complexities of diffraction (the reason the day sky appears blue), transparency, luster, and luminosity.[181] These are fundamentally different processes. In our commonsense experience, things are colored. In reality nothing is (simply) colored. Color is much more complicated than our immediate impressions seem to tell us. But it is not so complicated that we need to resort to the notion that it is an illusion, as Hardin suggests.[§1.3.1b]

The mechanisms in our seeing mean that we only see to the extent that our (also very complicated) processes of mind allow us to see. In our retina, rod cells (120 million of them) detect light and dark. Three kinds of cone cells (7 million of them) detect color at just three peaks in the electromagnetic spectrum that seem to have no distinctive character as colors: at about 440nm (a bluish yellow), 530nm (a greenish yellow) and 560nm (a greenish red). Then, through a mechanism called opponent processing, combining the input from the three different kinds of cone cell, the mind figures colors from the combinations of spectral input.[182]

Moreover, there is no reflectance profile, or measurement of wavelength on the electromagnetic spectrum, that reliably aligns with common colors – two yellows, for instance, may be indistinguishable to the eye, but with different reflectance profiles, though optical devices give us ways of distinguishing

---

[*] http://meaningpatterns.net/newton-light

[179] Isaac Newton, 1730 [1952], *Opticks, or a Treatise of the Reflections, Refractions, Inflections and the Colours of Light*, New York, NY: Dover Publications, pp. 113–17; 161–65.

[180] M. Chirimuuta, 2015, *Outside Color: Perceptual Science and the Puzzle of Color in Philosophy*, Cambridge, MA: MIT Press, pp. 60–62.

[181] C.L. Hardin, 1988, *Color for Philosophers: Unweaving the Rainbow*, Indianapolis, IN: Hackett Publishing Company, pp. 60, 63; T. van Leeuwen, 2011, *The Language of Colour*, London, UK: Routledge, pp. 34–37; 60–65.

[182] C.L. Hardin, 1988, *Color for Philosophers: Unweaving the Rainbow*, Indianapolis, IN: Hackett Publishing Company, pp. 10, 26–36; Paul M. Churchland, 2010, "On the Reality (and Diversity) of Objective Colors: How the Color-Qualia Space Is a Map of Reflectance-Profile Space," pp. 37–66 in *Color Ontology and Color Science*, Cambridge, MA: MIT Press, pp. 42–47; M. Chirimuuta, 2015, *Outside Color: Perceptual Science and the Puzzle of Color in Philosophy*, Cambridge, MA: MIT Press, p. 59.

them.[183] Colors in these ways seem to be figments of our seeing, mind adding meaning to the limited spectral receptivity of the eye.

But receptive nevertheless our eyes are. Light is real; the eye offers affordances, albeit constrained, for its seeing; the mind processes its meaning into colors. Though the scientists agree that much is still to be learned about the neuroscience of color perception, this much we know, and this is surely enough to conclude that color is more than mere mental illusion.[184]

We process light variations as brightness (dark to light), hue (color), and saturation (strength of hue). Sighted humans can distinguish about 2 million juxtaposed colors, and separately identify about thirty[185] – which means that if there are only eleven "basic" color terms,[§1.1.3a] this is never enough. We also share our fundamental mechanisms of seeing with other animals in the natural world. Some animals – birds and insects even – can see more colors than us; others fewer.[186]

There are also differences between sighted individuals, ranging from color blindness to the minor biophysical differences between individuals and among groups that one would expect in the realm of living things whose natural history proceeds on the basis of random mutation.[187] Notwithstanding these differences, there is cognitive constancy in the references humans make to color and historical consistency in the grammars of color within particular cultures.

---

[183] Paul M. Churchland, 2010, "On the Reality (and Diversity) of Objective Colors: How the Color-Qualia Space Is a Map of Reflectance-Profile Space," pp. 37–66 in *Color Ontology and Color Science*, Cambridge, MA: MIT Press, pp. 38, 57.

[184] M. Chirimuuta, 2015, *Outside Color: Perceptual Science and the Puzzle of Color in Philosophy*, Cambridge, MA: MIT Press, pp. 59–62; Clyde L. Hardin and Luisa Maffi, eds., 1997, *Color Categories in Thought and Language*, Cambridge, UK: Cambridge University Press.

[185] C.L. Hardin, 1988, *Color for Philosophers: Unweaving the Rainbow*, Indianapolis, IN: Hackett Publishing Company, pp. 25–6; 88–9; Rolf G. Kuehni, 2010, "Color Spaces and Color Order Systems," pp. 3–36 in *Color Ontology and Color Science*, edited by J. Cohen and M. Matthen, Cambridge, MA: MIT Press, pp. 4, 19.

[186] C.L. Hardin, 1988, *Color for Philosophers: Unweaving the Rainbow*, Indianapolis, IN: Hackett Publishing Company, p. 151; M. Chirimuuta, 2015, *Outside Color: Perceptual Science and the Puzzle of Color in Philosophy*, Cambridge, MA: MIT Press, p.4; Rolf G. Kuehni, 2010, "Color Spaces and Color Order Systems," pp. 3–36 in *Color Ontology and Color Science*, edited by J. Cohen and M. Matthen, Cambridge, MA: MIT Press, p. 9.

[187] C.L. Hardin, 1988, *Color for Philosophers: Unweaving the Rainbow*, Indianapolis, IN: Hackett Publishing Company, pp. 78–80; Rolf G. Kuehni, 2010, "Color Spaces and Color Order Systems," pp. 3–36 in *Color Ontology and Color Science*, edited by J. Cohen and M. Matthen, Cambridge, MA: MIT Press, p. 9; Kimberly A. Jameson, David Bimler, and Linda A. Wasserman, 2006, "Re-Assessing Perceptual Diagnostics for Observers with Diverse Retinal Photopigment Types," pp. 13–34 in *Progress in Colour Studies*, Volume 2: *Psychological Aspects*, edited by N.J. Pitchford and C.P. Biggam. Amsterdam, NL: John Benjamins, p. 14; Marc H. Bornstein, 1973, "Color Vision and Color Naming: A Psychophysiological Hypothesis of Cultural Difference," *Psychological Bulletin* 80 (4):257–85; Marc H. Bornstein, 1975, "The Influence of Visual Perception on Culture," *American Anthropologist* 77(4):774–98; Melvin Ember, 1978, "Size of Color Lexicon: Interaction of Cultural and Biological Factors," *American Anthropologist* 80(2):364–67.

Our minds make mental adjustments, composing constancy when the yellow color of a ripe lemon needs to be seen to be the same in sunlight, shadow, or under neon light. When a camera produces "bad" photos, we come to realize how different the light "really" is.

We also tell colors, not just by what they "are," but in contrast by juxtaposition in space and successive contrast across time.[188] So, the sky may not be blue in the same way that a lemon is yellow, but in our shared, embodied, natural history we can tell that the sky is differently colored from a lemon, and a ripe lemon is differently colored from an unripe one. This is the existentially ordinary stuff of the chemistry of lemons and the physics of the biosphere. The chemistry, physics, and neuroscience are complicated perhaps, but nevertheless explicable.

These days, the carefully designed observational apparatuses of science allow us to "see" the electromagnetic spectrum beyond the immediate capacities of our eyes, both within and beyond the 380nm to 780nm range. Using media, today we can put to representational and communicative use the whole of the electromagnetic spectrum, hence the uses we have for X-rays, infra-red radiation, and radio. We can also see variation within the visible spectrum not visible to unmediated eye and mind.

We have, in other words, extended the affordance of vision well beyond the native capacities of the eye. This deeper and broader seeing is an artifact of history, no less than the artifacts of seeing evident in the grammar of color that Berlin and Kay uncovered,[§1.3.1a] remarkable for their historically contingent differences and notwithstanding their claim to universalism.

§1.3.1d Leonardo da Vinci's Color Mixing

Leonardo da Vinci's *Treatise on Painting** was for centuries regarded by art teachers and their students to be the great artist's own work, though more recent research shows that it is a patchwork of his precepts stitched together over a century after his death.[189] Born in 1452, this was a special moment in early modernity, because over the Alps in Mainz, Germany, Johannes Gutenberg was part way through his momentous three-year-long project, printing his 42-line Bible, revolutionizing the process by means of which written text is rendered as image.[§AS1.4.7b]

On his side of the Alps, not only did the polymath da Vinci paint. He participated in another revolution in visualization, in his case developing the theories and

---

* http://meaningpatterns.net/leonardo

[188] C.L. Hardin, 1988, *Color for Philosophers: Unweaving the Rainbow*, Indianapolis, IN: Hackett Publishing Company, pp. 49–51; M. Chirimuuta, 2015, *Outside Color: Perceptual Science and the Puzzle of Color in Philosophy*, Cambridge, MA: MIT Press, pp. 81–86.
[189] Francesca Fiorani, 2012, "Leonardo Da Vinci and His Treatise on Painting," Charlottesville, VA: Rector and Visitors of the University of Virginia (www.treatiseonpainting.org/intro.html).

practices of optics. "Black and white," Leonardo said, "are not reckoned among colours; the one is representative of darkness, the other of light: that is, one is the simple privation of light, the other is light itself." There are four colours, properly speaking: yellow, green, blue, and red. Together with black and white, "the mixture of colours may be extended to an infinite variety."[190]

Mixing of base colors becomes the fundamental mechanism for the creation of color in modernity. It was da Vinci's genius to have theorized and put into practice this manufacturing principle – though his four were later reduced to three "primary" colors, aligning (although only indirectly) with the trichromacy of the human eye.[§1.3.1c] However, given the chemistry of color creation, the range of colors that can be so generated in any particular medium – its "gamut" – is broad though not infinite.

For the centuries following Leonardo, color mixing was always "subtractive" because coloring was for viewing of objects and images illuminated by reflected light. The ground for the image (the page or the canvas) was white. "Additive" color processes are based on seeing colors in a light source, where the ground for the image is black. Additive coloring does not happen at scale until the mid-twentieth century, when there is a radical shift to viewing light sources, first with analogue televisions and later with digital displays. Seeing a light source is for the human eye quite a different process from seeing reflected light.[§1.3.1b]

§1.3.1e Pantone Matching and Digitized Color

In the twentieth century, the processes for subtractive mixing are extended and elaborated in two different ways – the mixing of pigments for paints and inks, and the optical fusion of colored dots.

The colors of mixed inks were standardized to their most elaborated form in the Pantone Matching System (PMS).[*] A creation of Lawrence Herbert in the mid-1950s, 1,114 colors were generated by mixing 12 base pigments in specified proportions. The advertising and design industries had come to demand design consistency, and each color was assigned a number. Kodak standardized its yellow packaging with PMS 1235. Coca Cola likes to say its formulae are secret, the red of its branding as well as the ingredients of its sweetened drink – but the red is PMS 485, or close enough.[191]

---

[*] http://meaningpatterns.net/pantone

[190] Leonardo da Vinci, 1651 [1835], *A Treatise on Painting*, translated by J.F. Rigaud, London, UK: J.B. Nichols and Son, pp. 125–27.
[191] Roberta Schultz Santos, 2014, "Pantone: Identity Formation through Colours," Master of Arts in Contemporary Art, Design and New Media Art, OCAD University, Toronto, Canada, pp. 23–25, 29.

With the widespread adoption of four-color offset printing in the second half of the twentieth century, the CMYK system was created, where tiny dots of Cyan, Magenta, Yellow, and Black, almost invisible without a magnifying glass, are overprinted in different sizes, depending on the contribution each needed to create the composite color effect. Black is added to the three colors, because although in theory the three colors when overprinted solid should produce black, it is never black enough. Not all colors in the PMS pigment mixing system can be represented in CMYK, and for this reason inks generated by mixing pigments are placed side by side with CMYK renderings in the PMS swatches. They are noticeably different.

With the coming of analogue color television, for the first time humans begin reading images from light sources that use additive color processes. Using continuous voltage signals to modulate color on a phosphorescent screen, these have an infinite number of intensities. Quality has not yet been transposed into quantity. Digital screens, however, have a fixed and numbered range of intensities, moving us radically into a world where properties are ubiquitously transposed between quality and quantity.

This is how the additive process of a digital screen works. Each pixel (a picture element) is a combination of three juxtaposed subpixels: red, green, and blue. These are not normally visible separately, but they become fused as a color given the limited affordances of our vision. When rendered with 24-bit encoding, the industry standard since 2005, each subpixel can be projected with an intensity of 0 to 255: zero when it is turned off; 255 when it is as bright as it can be. The effect of all three RGB subpixels at brightness 255 is to create a white pixel; at zero a black one. This means that 256^3 or 16,777,216 color variations are possible.

If the human eye can only distinguish about 10 million colors for the practical purposes of everyday seeing, there is no point in going further than 24-bit encoding.

§1.3.1f The Colors "Greige" and "YInMin Blue"

Today we find we often have to deal with finely calibrated colors – when it comes to the printed page, the painted wall, the face with makeup of particular shades, or the fashion fabric. In speech, there may be only eleven basic color terms,[§1.3.1a] and thirty words that we can remember that describe color differences when encountered alone, without comparison by juxtaposition. But in writing there are thousands, illustrating once again the radical divergence of speaking and writing in a multimodal grammar.

To tell us "black is beautiful,"[§AS1.4.3c] Pantone experts suggest[*] Chestnut (19–1118 in its extended numbering scheme), Jet Set (19–5708), Silver Cloud (15–4502), and Ecru Olive (17–0836).[192] The names are pretty meaningless. From the hearing of the word, they are of little help if we want to conjure up a color in our mind's eye, and in a way that is reliably identifiable from viewer to viewer. They are too numerous for more than a few to be sufficiently memorable to be usable in speech.

Or, as one wit on the web, Steven Markow, said of that year's Pantone "colors of the year," now we have 15–3919, "*Serenity* – you will quickly achieve nirvana surrounded by this utterly forgettable light blue," and 16–1109, "*Greige* – no way, you're telling me grey and beige had a kid together? Is it as totally fucking boring as its parents?"[193]

And then there is the conversation on Reddit where the Color Marketing Managers at PPG Architectural coatings talk about the 500 new names they have added to the 7,700 paint colors in their repertoire including "Black Flame" and "Millennial Pink." To which commenters suggested the addition of others, like "Accidental Brown" and "Spotless Mind."[194]

Meanwhile, the range of colors is by no means limited to the gamut of CMYK or RGB recomposition. While researching new materials that could be used in electronic circuitry, Oregon State University materials scientist Mas Subramanian and his students accidentally discovered a new blue, by combining the elements yttrium, indium, manganese, and oxygen.[195] With the seriousness you would expect of chemists, they called this YInMin Blue, after its elements. Now it's the color of a Crayola crayon.

Artist Anish Kapoor created a furore in the art world when he purchased exclusive rights to that blackest black, "Vantablack," created by Nanosystems, an English nanotechnology company that had been working on coatings for military uses, including stealth bombers. Made of carbon nanotubes, Vantablack absorbs 99.96 percent of the light that reaches its surface.[196]

---

[*] http://meaningpatterns.net/black-blue

[192] Leatrice Eiseman and Keith Recker, 2011, *Pantone: The 20th Century in Color*, San Francisco, CA: Chronicle Books, p. 125.

[193] https://medium.com/slackjaw/pantone-color-names-v-what-they-actually-look-like-3361033 af61a#.1cyzyny6p

[194] www.reddit.com/r/IAmA/comments/3tyt69/we_create_the_names_of_paint_colors_for_a_living/

[195] Gabriel Rosenberg, 2016, "A Chemist Accidentally Creates a New Blue. Then What?," in *National Public Radio* (www.npr.org/2016/07/16/485696248/a-chemist-accidentally-creates-a-new-blue-then-what?t=1560853665108).

[196] Henri Neuendorf, 2016, "Anish Kapoor Angers Artists by Seizing Exclusive Rights to 'Blackest Black' Pigment," *Artnet News*, 29 February.

When another artist, Stuart Semple, created what he thought might be the world's pinkest pink, he made it available in 50g bottles for £3.99 through his webstore – to everyone except Anish Kapoor, @anishKapoor #ShareTheBlack.

§1.3.1g *Alfred Munsell's* Color Notation

When spoken words fail us, as a matter of habit we now transpose properties that we experience as qualities into reference by means of quantity. This happens in text, unspeakable in the sense that numbering schemas can't be remembered for the purposes of spontaneous speech. Here we encounter further support for our case to abandon a notion of "language" and replace it with separate grammars of text and speech, where in the spirit of our times we have defined text as anything that can be represented in Unicode.[§0.2.1a]

The first widely used numbered elaboration of color is the Munsell Color System.[*] Albert A. Munsell first published *A Color Notation* in 1905. "Cramped by the poverty of color language," Munsell classified and numbered 320 colored swatches according to their hue (color), value (light to dark), and chroma (color strength).[197] When presented in a two-dimensional array as it was by Berlin and Kay in their research,[§1.3.1a] hues (red, yellow, green, purple, blue, and intermediate chroma) are numbered 1–40 across a horizontal axis. On a vertical axis, values each have a letter, B–I. (A is reserved for white and J for black, in a parallel grayscale that has ten gradations.) So, at hue number 17, a green, we have 8 green values: 17C is a light green, and 17H a dark green.[198]

Munsell's purpose was to "standardize" color and to rectify the lack of clarity in spoken color language, as if there could be a standard measure: a "normal" viewer viewing light reflected from a "standard" light source. The question of course immediately arises whether there can ever be a standard or a normal when viewing is forever subject to the vagaries of context and viewer. These will generate infinite variety of empirical color experiences such that no two experiences are ever quite the same.

---

[*] http://meaningpatterns.net/munsell

[197] A.H. Munsell, 1905, *A Color Notation*, Boston, MA: Geo. H. Ellis Co, pp. 9, 14–15; A.H. Munsell and T.M. Clelland, 1921, *A Grammar of Color*, Mittineague, MA: Strathmore Paper Company, pp. 13–17; A.H. Munsell, 1915, *Atlas of the Munsell Color System*, Boston, MA: Albert H. Munsell; Anna Wierzbicka, 2006, "The Semantics of Color: A New Paradigm," pp. 1–24 in *Progress in Colour Studies,* Volume 1: *Language and Culture,* edited by C.P. Biggam and C.J. Kay, Amsterdam, NL: John Benjamins, p. 18.

[198] Mikael Vejdemo-Johansson, Susanne Vejdemo, and Carl-Henrik Ek, 2014, "Comparing Distributions of Color Words: Pitfalls and Metric Choices," *PLoS ONE* 9(2: e89184), doi:10.1371/journal.pone.0089184; C.L. Hardin, 1988, *Color for Philosophers: Unweaving the Rainbow*, Indianapolis, IN: Hackett Publishing Company, pp. 159–62.

However, we don't want to accept defeat, and to assume as Hardin[§1.3.1b] does in his critique of the ostensibly normal viewer that color is no more than a figment of our minds.[199] Rather, we want to claim that it is possible to create a complex account of such variabilities. This we do in our notion of design as active meaning-making. Every color is uniquely designed in its creation and viewing; however, the patterning of the design can be accounted for, both in its conventionality and its unique modulations in the moment.

§1.3.1h ICC Color Profiles

Now that we have entered the digital era, we have a single standard for defining color, against which the main historical schemas and rendering processes are matched: the ICC Profile. This is a creation of the International Color Consortium.

Here we encounter another one of these perversely democratic yet undemocratic instruments that come to power in the digital era for the purposes of governance in the sundry territories of our human meanings. Unbeknown to the multitude, the ICC has become our global government of color.

Formed in 1993 by eight companies including Adobe, Agfa, Apple, Kodak, and Microsoft, by 2014 ICC had sixty-one member companies. A not-for-profit, ICC is headquartered in the intellectual heartland of the US military-industrial complex, down the road from the US National Security Agency in Reston, Virginia. First released in 2001, version 4 was published in its 2010 iteration as ISO 15076–1:2010. ICC profiles create color matches through an intermediate profile connection space based on the wavelength profiles of light readable in spectrophotometers. With these profiles, it is possible to match color from device to device, software system to software system, and color rendering system to system such as CMYK[§1.2.2e] to RGB.[200]

The result, according to the ICC website, is "an open, vendor-neutral, cross-platform color management system architecture."[201] This kind of disinterested global governance on a plane elevated above self-interest and competition provides essential grease for the proverbial wheels of commerce in the digital era. The class of citizen-corporations afforded the right to participate in this democracy consists of a select few. The processes of discrimination are not so unlike those that separated the citizens of Ancient Athens from the classes of slaves, women, and foreigners that excluded them from decision-making and

---

[199] C.L. Hardin, 1988, *Color for Philosophers: Unweaving the Rainbow*, Indianapolis, IN: Hackett Publishing Company, pp. 76–80.

[200] Phil Green, ed., 2010, *Color Management: Understanding and Using ICC Profiles*, Chichester, UK: John Wiley & Sons.

[201] www.color.org/abouticc.xalter

denied them freedom. But what if the excluded classes cared to be citizens in Athens, or if ordinary people today were to care about the finer points of color and its commerce?

When there is this much finely calibrated measurement of quality and universal agreement about ascribable alphanumeric names – company to company, device to device, medium to medium – color is no illusion, no matter how peculiar and historically circumstantial the manner of coming to that agreement. Color is real in the complex relation of the biomechanics of our species to the electromagnetic spectrum.

It is also real in the sense that the theoretical frameworks for alphanumeric naming and the technical apparatuses for rendering – now singular and universal by means of the interoperability effected by ICC Profiles – are practical and circumstantial products of history. History is as real as the photon wavelengths measured by spectrophotometers. It is as real as the governance structures that transcend capitalist competition in the service of securing profit from color.

§1.3.2 Quantity

> **Quantity.** *Naming, counting, and measuring of instance, concept, and quality by transposing numbers, letters, and symbols for sensuous human experience.*

We have contemplated the quality of color[§1.3.1a] as an example of properties in general – to which we could add a myriad of other qualities that are the raw materials of human, sensuous activity, including our experiences of the properties of sound, shape, movement, and chemistry. Before the "civilizations" of calculated inequality,[§AS1.4.7a] and before the intensification of calculation in the era of digital technologies, we may not have needed to treat quantity as a property analytically separate from quality. But now, by force of historical necessity, we must.

Our questions are these: what is the nature of the transposition of instance to concept, one to counted more-than-one, and quality into measurable quantity? What is gained and what is lost in these transpositions? What, in other words, are the affordances of quantity?

Quantity has three subsidiary functions: to name instances and concepts (our house is number 4018); to count (there are 25 houses in the street); and to measure (the street is 800 m long). (In the digital era there is another major function of quantity, and that is to render on screens, pages, audio players, video, 3D printers, but in our grammar we have located this as a function of medium[§AS1.4] rather than reference.)

To name: instances, concepts, and qualities are named in alphanumeric terms. Some, such as street addresses, can be spoken. Others in the digital era cannot, such as web links[§1.1.1f] and mathematical formulae. Some may be conceived as ordinal numbers, but mostly these are not even that, findable only by search for their alphanumeric name, but unsortable, unlistable, and so, not meaningfully orderable.

We use alphanumeric names for qualities, for instance, because they do the job of specifying with more finely granular precision than is possible in speech. In the case of color, we started alphanumeric naming of quantity before the digital era, hence Munsell's 17C[§1.3.1g] and Pantone's PMS 485.[§1.3.1e] ICC color profiles radically extend and universalize this naming process.[§1.3.1h] These terms of quantification by name are not in themselves calculable. It makes no sense to add ICC profile numbers.

Extensive alphanumeric naming is possible only in writing, highlighting another area where speech and text are today radically different. When they are long, the names become unspeakable. Even a regular expert colorist would not likely remember too many PMS and Munsell numbers – let alone ICC profiles – nor for this reason will they be able to say them in spontaneous speech. This is writing for reference, where written alphanumeric names support a system of cognitive prosthesis. These require that we use multimodal externalizations of meaning; image and text must be juxtaposed to have workable meaning, in color swatches and the like.

We use these alphanumeric naming systems for naming qualities because, in their expansive detail, we have become lost for meaningful words. For the purposes of modern life and media, we want to use a broader range of colors than spontaneous speech can support. This is why we resort to the written language of enumeration, or at most short-term oral renditions of the written, reading out an alphanumeric name.

Not only properties, but a whole host of other things such as instances and concepts are discoverable by their alphanumeric name. Much of the hype about so-called "artificial intelligence" is little more than a relatively trivial phenomenon that might be called "lookupability," a system of naming and classification, a mere extension of our native capacities to name instances, concepts, and qualities, and to recall them, previously supported by indexes and catalogues, now assisted by machines.

To count: an instance is one; multiple instances can be classified and counted by concept. In the digital era, we can use our digital cognitive prostheses to do more counting than would be practically possible in speech. When we come to what are now popularly called big data, machine learning, and artificial intelligence, we are at root only counting, albeit on a scale that would not be practicable without calculating machines doing most of the work for us. But the counting would not happen without the alphanumeric naming and classification of countable things: instances, concepts, and qualities. Much of the power is in the meanings and not the math, the ontologies[3.4] and not the algorithms.

To measure: by transpositions of quality, quality can be measured as quantity. "Fast" and "slow," quantifiable relations of time to distance, can be measured on the same scale and with peculiar numbered precision, for an elephant or a rocket. Turned into number, it is possible to measure qualities on a scale more finely calibrated than the expressions of quality possible in speech.

Things are also now finely measurable across a range, using quantities to array qualities along a scale. These can be so minutely differentiated that we are able dramatically to extend our bodily limits. We can "see" beyond light on the electromagnetic spectrum, with X-rays for instance. The nanometers of the electromagnetic spectrum allow us to see greater detail within that spectrum than would normally be possible with our three-coned retinas.[1.3.1c]

In the "internet of things,"[1.1.1g] sensors pervasively name qualities including not only color[1.3.1h] and brightness, but geoposition,[AS1.3.2b] the time of a recorded event,[AS1.3.1b] proximity, motion, pressure, force, strain, torque, temperature, humidity, moisture, chemical composition, flow, acoustic characteristics, and electrical characteristics.[202] These may be points namable by number across scales of quality. Or by calculus,[1.2.2d] these may be projections of trends capable of determining an infinity of possible intermediate points across scales of quality.

Here, the fundamental differences between speech and text come up again, in the form of the practically limited affordances for quantification in speech. We reach the limits of quantification in speech with vague plurals, and small or round numbers. Most modern quantification can only happen by transposition into text – uncountable names and unspeakable calculations.

In the middle of these digital meaning processes, even to find an alphanumerical name, there is calculation. Between the keyboard on which this sentence is being typed and your reading it, there is calculation. Between speaker and a voicemail there is calculation. Between the scene, the camera, and the digital image, there is calculation. This is ubiquitous, and the calculation is all being done in the zeros and ones of base two.

"Digital," we call such calculations in text, image, and sound today, though this is a terrible misnomer. Ten digits are a mere accident of natural history. This is how many fingers our species happens to have, so this has become how we like to see our numbers. But there is nothing intrinsically digital about electronically-mediated meanings, whose elemental technology is an on/off switch. Fundamentally, the

---

[202] Matthew Montebello, 2019, *Ambient Intelligent Classroom: Beyond the Indispensable Educator*, Dortmund, Germany: Springer, p. 25.

underlying technology of calculation is an opposing pair. "Binary" would be a more truthful name for today's electronic technologies of representation and communication, and to name our times, now so deeply shaped by them.

§1.3.2a *Ada Lovelace's Notes on the Analytical Engine*

> Ada! Sole daughter of my house and heart?
> When last I saw thy young blue eyes they smiled,
> And then we parted . . .

So said Lord Byron, English aristocrat and romantic poet, in the third canto of a work that made him famous and also made him a fortune. Byron was a terrible father, abandoning wife, Anne Isabella Noel Byron, the eleventh Baroness Wentworth, and child Ada when the girl was three months old. He was never to see either of them again.[203]

Like her mother, Ada had mathematical inclinations. Byron had dismissively called his wife "Princess of Parallelograms." Also like her mother, Augusta Ada Byron was to marry within the English aristocracy, though to a man more settled and less unsettling than her father, and supportive of his wife's mathematical studies. Augusta Ada King-Noel, Countess of Lovelace, she was thenceforth to be known, or Ada Lovelace.

Ada and her mother first met Charles Babbage one evening in June 1833, before she married. She was eighteen, and Babbage twenty-four years her senior. He had studied at Cambridge University at about the same time as both her father and future husband, and was a leading light in the Analytical Society, devoted to replacing Newton's notation for the calculus with Leibniz's.[§1.3.2d] A famed inventor, Babbage held regular soirées at his home, attended by thinkers and dignitaries from engineer Isambard Kingdom Brunel[§2a] to novelist Charles Dickens, to natural scientist Charles Darwin, to Queen Victoria's consort, Prince Albert. This was one of those soirées.

On display in the house was Babbage's "Difference Engine," an elaborate mechanical calculator.[*] It was designed to mechanize the labor-intensive process of manually creating logarithmic tables, used for the multiplication of large numbers.[204] A friend of her mother said that while most visitors stared at the

---

[*] http://meaningpatterns.net/lovelace

[203] James Essinger, 2014, *Ada's Algorithm: How Lord Byron's Daughter, Ada Lovelace, Launched the Digital Age*, Brooklyn, NY: Melville House, p. 6.

[204] Charles Babbage, 1889 [2010], *Babbage's Calculating Engines: Being a Collection of Papers Relating to Them; Their History, and Construction*, Cambridge, UK: Cambridge University Press; Charles Babbage, 1864 [1994], *Passages from the Life of a Philosopher*, New Brunswick, NJ: Rutgers University Press; Bruce Collier, 1970, "The Little Engines That Could've: The Calculating Machines of Charles Babbage," Ph.D., Department of History of

machine in perplexed awe, "Miss Byron, young as she was, understood its working, and saw great beauty in the machine."[205]

Pursuing her interest in things mechanical and analytical, in the following year Ada Byron and her mother toured English factories, including cloth factories using punched cards to manufacture elaborate patterns in fabric and lace.[206] The mechanical loom had also been an interest of her father's, though of a different kind. In his maiden speech to the house of Lords in 1812, three years before Ada was born, Lord Byron had taken the opportunity to protest a bill that would have made the wave of machine-breaking a capital crime.[207]

"By the adoption" of such machines, he said, "one man performed the work of many, and the superfluous labourers were thrown out of employment, [being] . . . left in consequence to starve." It would seem that "the maintenance and well doing of the industrious poor, were objects of greater consequence than the enrichment of a few individuals," the owners of the mechanical looms. The protestors were left "liable to conviction, on the clearest evidence, of the capital crime of poverty."[208]

Ada, now married to the Earl of Lovelace, pursued her mathematical studies over the decade following her first meeting with Babbage, met him frequently, and corresponded with him at length.[209] By 1842, his work was at a crossroads. Despite substantial government funding, he had failed to produce a complete Difference Engine. To the annoyance of his sponsors his plans had moved on to a seemingly more fanciful and never-to-be-built Analytical Engine. Babbage even met British Prime Minister Sir Robert Peel in person in a failed attempt to appeal for further funding.[210] "What shall we do to get rid of Mr. Babbage and his calculating Machine?" Peel asked in desperation.[211]

Science, Harvard University, Cambridge, MA; Bruce Collier and James MacLachlan, 1998, *Charles Babbage and the Engines of Perfection*, New York, NY: Oxford University Press.

[205] Christopher Hollings, Ursula Martin, and Adrian Rice, 2018, *Ada Lovelace: The Making of a Computer Scientist*, Oxford, UK: Bodleian Library, p. 45.

[206] James Essinger, 2004, *Jacquard's Web: How the Hand-Loom Led to the Birth of the Information Age*, Oxford, UK: Oxford University Press.

[207] Sadie Plant, 1997, *Zeros + Ones: Digital Women + the New Technoculture*, New York, NY: Doubleday, p. 15.

[208] https://api.parliament.uk/historic-hansard/lords/1812/feb/27/frame-work-bill

[209] Dorothy Stein, 1985, *Ada: A Life and a Legacy*, Cambridge, MA: MIT Press. 41ff.; James Essinger, 2014, *Ada's Algorithm: How Lord Byron's Daughter, Ada Lovelace, Launched the Digital Age*, Brooklyn, NY: Melville House, pp. 95ff.

[210] James Essinger, 2014, *Ada's Algorithm: How Lord Byron's Daughter, Ada Lovelace, Launched the Digital Age*, Brooklyn, NY: Melville House, pp. 156–61; Maboth Moseley, 1964 [1970], *Irascible Genius: The Life of Charles Babbage*, Chicago, IL: Henry Regnery Company; Doron Swade, 2000, *The Difference Engine: Charles Babbage and the Quest to Build the First Computer*, New York, NY: Viking.

[211] John Fuegi and Jo Francis, 2003, "Lovelace & Babbage and the Creation of the 1843 'Notes'," *IEEE Annals of the History of Computing* 25(4):16–26, p. 16.

Hopes dashed in England, Babbage visited Italy. There his proposed Analytical Engine attracted the attention of Luigi Menabrea, Professor of Mechanics in the Military Academy of the University of Turin, later to be Prime Minister of Italy. Menabrea was sufficiently impressed with Babbage's plan for the Analytical Engine to write an article about it in French.

Upset and annoyed by Babbage's partly self-inflicted failures to secure support for the project – when he met Prime Minister Peel, instead of showing gratitude for past support, he complained that his work had been unappreciated – Lovelace offered to translate Menebrea's article, and add some explanatory notes. Perhaps this would breathe life back into the project.

The translated article, "Sketch of The Analytical Engine Invented by Charles Babbage, By L. F. Menabrea, with Notes upon the Memoir by the Translator," was published in 1843. The translated part is just over 10,000 words; Lovelace's notes, simply signed A.A.L., run to over 22,000 words.[212]

In the notes, Lovelace goes far beyond Babbage in addressing what is for us a critical question, the transposability of meanings by machines of calculation. Today we call such machines "computers." Where Babbage saw his machines as primarily mathematical, Lovelace saw broader potentials.

Lovelace makes a distinction between what would today be called software and data: "In studying the action of the Analytical Engine, we find that the peculiar and independent nature of the considerations which in all mathematical analysis belong to operations, as distinguished from the objects operated upon and from the results of the operations performed upon those objects, is very strikingly defined and separated."[213]

However, Lovelace casts the net of "operation" far wider than mathematics in the abstract, to any calculable meanings in the world: "It may be desirable to explain, that by the word operation, we mean any process which alters the mutual relation of two or more things, be this relation of what kind it may. This is the most general definition, and would include all subjects in the universe." By mathematical representation and calculation, it may be possible to "express the great facts of the natural world, and those unceasing changes of mutual relationship which, visibly or invisibly, consciously or unconsciously to our immediate physical perceptions, are interminably going on in the agencies of the creation we live amidst."[214]

---

[212] A.A. Lovelace, 1843, "Sketch of the Analytical Engine Invented by Charles Babbage, by L.F. Menabrea, with Notes Upon the Memoir by the Translator," pp. 666–731 in *Scientific Memoirs Selected from the Transactions of Foreign Academies of Science and Learned Societies*, Volume 3, edited by R. Taylor, London, UK: Richard and John E. Taylor.

[213] Ibid., p. 692.   [214] Ibid., pp. 693, 696.

The model for such mechanical possibility, Lovelace went on, was "the principle which Jacquard devised for regulating, by means of punched cards, the most complicated patterns in the fabrication of brocaded stuffs." The Analytical Engine was also designed to run on the same kinds of punched cards she and her mother had seen at work in the factories they had toured. "[T]he Analytical Engine weaves algebraical patterns just as the Jacquard-loom weaves flowers and leaves." In these ways, "not only the mental and the material, but the theoretical and the practical in the mathematical world, are brought into more intimate and effective connexion with each other."[215]

However, Lovelace adds an important proviso: "to guard against the possibility of exaggerated ideas that might arise as to the powers of the Analytical Engine ... It can follow analysis; but it has no power of anticipating any analytical relations or truths. Its province is to assist us in making available what we are already acquainted with." Any such machine's capacity is limited to "devising for mathematical truths a new form in which to record and throw themselves out for actual use." To this extent and no more its contribution is "extensions of human power, or additions to human knowledge."[216]

We rephrase: the limits of calculated meaning were to be the limits of calculability, its affordances in terms of the constraints as well as the potentials for transposing other meaning functions (such as instances, concepts, qualities) into quantities, and quantities into other meaning functions.

A.A.L.'s translation and its notes were received to great acclaim, and congratulations poured in. Babbage signed off a letter of appreciation to her, "Ever my fair Interpretess, Your faithful slave."[217]

Then the paper was forgotten for the best part of a century.

§1.3.2b Alan Turing's "Mechanical Intelligence"

"Can machines think?" asked Alan Turing[*] in his celebrated 1950 article, "Computer Machinery and Intelligence." His answer was that, some day in the not-too-distant future, in a certain sense they might: "I believe that at the end of the century the use of words and general educated opinion will have altered so much that one will be able to speak of machines thinking without expecting to be contradicted."[218]

---

[*] http://meaningpatterns.net/turing

[215] Ibid., pp. 696–97.   [216] Ibid., pp. 722–23.
[217] John Fuegi and Jo Francis, 2003, "Lovelace & Babbage and the Creation of the 1843 'Notes'," *IEEE Annals of the History of Computing* 25(4):16–26, p. 24; Betty Alexandra Toole, ed., 1992, *Ada, the Enchantress of Numbers: A Selection from the Letters of Lord Byron's Daughter and Her Description of the First Computer*, Mill Valley, CA: Strawberry Press.
[218] A.M. Turing, 1950, "Computing Machinery and Intelligence," *Mind* 59:433–60, p. 442.

Then Turing works over a number of possible objections to his prediction. "Lady Lovelace's Objection: ... she states, 'The Analytical Engine has no pretensions to originate anything. It can do whatever we know how to order it to perform'."[§1.3.2a] But perhaps, says Turing, the Analytical Engine had the potential to "think for itself" to the extent that it could come up with surprising answers to mathematical problems.[219]

Turing proposes an "imitation game" where a computer gives answers that seem as smart as a person.[§1.3.2c] Such a game might require, say, 10^9 binary digits. "At my present rate of working I produce about a thousand digits of programme a day, so that about sixty workers, working steadily through the fifty years might accomplish the job, if nothing went into the waste-paper basket." Meanwhile, "[p]arts of modern machines which can be regarded as analogues of nerve cells work about a thousand times faster than the latter ... Machines take me by surprise with great frequency . . ., largely because I do not do sufficient calculation."[220]

Perhaps, Turing says in a footnote, in this sense Lovelace was not so wrong. Her statement about machines doing what we tell them, he says, does not include the word "only." "There was no obligation on [Lovelace or Babbage] to claim all that could be claimed."[221] Nor, on the other hand, was Turing's claim ever so grandiose as to suggest what is now popularly called "artificial intelligence."[§AS1.4.6c] His claim was not to anything more than "mechanical intelligence," that computers could produce surprising mathematical results with fast calculation. Lovelace surely would have agreed.

Turing first brought these ideas to print in his 1936 paper, "On Computable Numbers." He had been appointed a fellow of Kings College Cambridge University just two years before, at the remarkably early age of 22.

"On Computable Numbers" is in some respects a strange paper, not just for its mathematical tangle written in obscure German Gothic type, but for talking about what seem to be two quite tangential things that add up to an apparently contradictory proposition. The rest of its title was " ... with an Application to the *Entscheidungsproblem*," or the problem of decidability in mathematics.[222] German mathematician David Hilbert had famously argued in 1928 that mathematics was complete, that it was consistent, and that every problem it posed was decidable in the sense that every one of its propositions could be proved or disproved. Kurt Gödel had by 1931 shown that mathematics was neither complete nor consistent.[§1a] Turing was now able to show that not every problem was decidable, so bringing down the last pillar of Hilbert's mathematical edifice.

---

[219] Ibid., p. 450.   [220] Ibid., pp. 455, 450.   [221] Ibid., pp. 459, 450.

[222] A.M. Turing, 1936, "On Computable Numbers, with an Application to the Entscheidungsproblem," *Proceedings of the London Mathematical Society* 42(2):230–65.

But, here is the apparent contradiction: incidental to making this case, Turing imagined a machine that would be able to deal with things in mathematics that were still absolutely decidable, though not feasibly decidable by humans. "According to my definition, a number is computable if its decimal can be written down by a machine."[223] This leaves a lot of scope for definitive decidability, including calculations that are well beyond what is practically possible for humans and without the errors to which they are prone.

Turing's imaginary machine worked like this. It would run by reading a paper tape with a sequence of squares each capable of carrying a symbol. As the machine is fed the tape, it scans each symbol and is able to remember some of the symbols it has already scanned. It can print calculations onto blank squares, so remembering the steps it is taking. It can, in other words, write down the interim results of its calculations in a kind of working memory, then act on these. In this way, the machine emulates a sequence of minimal states of mind, breaking a sequence of mathematical operations into their most elementary steps.[224]

"Let us imagine the operations performed by [a person computing] to be split up into 'simple operations' which are so elementary that it is not easy to imagine them further divided," said Turing. Now, "the two-dimensional character of paper is no [longer] essential of computation. I assume then that the computation is carried out on one-dimensional paper, i.e. on a tape divided into squares." By this means, and far from being undecidable, "[i]t is my contention that these operations include all those which are used in the computation of a number."[225]

Now, we find that we have a machine capable of making calculations beyond the practical realm of human decidability. "[A]n an Arabic numeral such as 17 or 999999999999999 is normally treated as a single symbol ... The differences from our point of view between the single and compound symbol is that the compound symbols, if they are too lengthy, cannot be observed at one glance ... We cannot tell at a glance whether 9999999999999999 and 999999999999999 are the same." But by laborious emulation of elementary "states of mind," a machine of the hypothetical kind he was describing would be able to deal quickly and with precision with calculations that a human could only do with such difficulty as to make them impracticable. With such a machine a whole lot more could become decidable, and definitively. "It is possible to invent a single machine which can be used to compute any computable sequence," he concluded.[226]

Turing offered his first lecture course at Cambridge in 1939, "Foundations of Mathematics," in which the final examination question was to come up with a solution to the *Entscheidungsproblem*. In that year, the famed philosopher of

---

[223] Ibid., p. 230.   [224] Ibid., p. 230.   [225] Ibid., pp. 250, 249, 232.   [226] Ibid., pp. 250, 241.

language, Ludwig Wittgenstein,[§2.1.1a] offered a course with the same name. Turing was one of fifteen people who attended Wittgenstein's course.

> TURING: You cannot be confident about your calculus until you know there is no hidden contradiction in it ...
> WITTGENSTEIN: ... Why should [people] be afraid of contradictions inside mathematics? ...
> TURING: The real harm will not come in unless there is an application, in which a bridge may fall down or something of that sort.[227]

Or perhaps, to imagine a further question and its answer, why even bother with the *Entscheidungsproblem?* Because it tells of a whole lot more that is definitively decidable by calculation, even if much of what is possible cannot be done without the help of a machine. We calculate, machines help us to calculate, and bridges mostly stay up.

As it happened, a professor at the Institute of Advanced Study at Princeton University, Alonzo Church, had at the same time come to the same conclusion as Turing about the *Entscheidungsproblem*, though his method of proof was different and his version of the idea he called "effective calculability."[228] Turing acknowledged Church in his paper, and for his part Church recognized the ingenuity of Turing's hypothetical apparatus by calling it a "Turing Machine."[229] The principles of calculability have come to be known as the "Church–Turing thesis."

The Institute of Advanced Study was where the intellectual action was – not only were Church and Gödel there, but at various times, other key figures in the creation of computing, including John von Neumann and Claude Shannon. Turing spent time there in 1936–38, writing his PhD on ordinal numbers.

In 1938 Shannon come up with the idea that, instead of paper tape, relay circuits or on/off switches could represent mathematical symbols as zeros and ones, and do the work of calculation electrically. Applying the elementary logic of nineteenth-century mathematical philosopher George Boole, he suggested that when the circuit is closed a proposition could be considered false, and when it is open, it could be considered true: "any circuit is represented by a set of equations, the terms of the equations corresponding to the various relays and switches in the circuit. A calculus is developed for manipulating these equations by simple mathematical processes."[230] Such an electronic machine would

---

[227] Andrew Hodges, 1983, *Alan Turing: The Enigma*, New York, NY: Simon and Schuster, p. 254.
[228] Alonzo Church, 1936, "A Note on the Entscheidungsproblem," *The Journal of Symbolic Logic* 1(1):40–41.
[229] Alonzo Church, 1937, "Review of 'on Computable Numbers, with an Application to the Entscheidungsproblem' by A.M. Turing," *The Journal of Symbolic Logic* 2(1):42–43.
[230] Claude E. Shannon, 1938, "A Symbolic Analysis of Relay and Switching Circuits," *Transactions of the American Institute of Electrical Engineers* 57:471–95, p. 471; Claude E. Shannon and Warren Weaver, 1949, *The Mathematical Theory of Communication*, Urbana,

work sequentially through a series of yes/no binaries: no decision problems or contradictions here.

By the mid-2010s, a smart phone would have over three billion such switches, performing exactly the kinds of humanly impractical calculations that Lovelace and Turing had both anticipated, though on a scale unimaginably larger again. Perhaps these things should be called Lovelace-Turing Machines.

§1.3.2c The "Turing Test"

The Second World War came, and Turing's work turned to cryptography, decoding the messages sent by the German military through its Enigma enciphering machines. Working in an old house in the English countryside, Bletchley Park, Turing and his colleagues used a mix of hand-written mathematics and mechanical calculating machines to decipher German war commands.[231]

At Bletchley Park, and now also in Princeton, deceptively encoded meanings became the focus during this stage of the development of the meaning encipherment and decipherment machines that would later be called "computer." It is a nice irony – or perhaps not – that the impetus for this foundational work was as much as anything about meanings deliberately hidden by calculation.

Then came the Cold War, and the focus shifted to the mathematic modeling of thermonuclear explosions. The first nuclear weapons – the atom bombs dropped on Hiroshima and Nagasaki,[§2.0a] and then the hydrogen bombs of the 1950s, were built with the help of computers in the Los Alamos National Laboratory in New Mexico. The most advanced in the world, these used punched cards like those in Jacquard looms and proposed for Charles Babbage's Analytical Engine.[§1.3.2a] The Mathematical and Numerical Integrator and Computer created there came to be known by the unfortunate acronym MANIAC. For a decade, from the beginning of the second World War and into the Cold War, computing research and development was cloaked in militaristic secrecy. Without scholarly publication, it becomes hard to tell who contributed what in the development of these first electronic machines of calculation.[232]

IL: University of Illinois Press; Jimmy Soni and Rob Goodman, 2017, *A Mind at Play: How Claude Shannon Invented the Information Age*, New York, NY: Simon and Schuster.

[231] Dermot Turing, 2015, *Prof: Alan Turing Decoded, a Biography*, Brimscombe Port, UK: The History Press, pp. 113–47; George Dyson, 2012, *Turing's Cathedral: The Origins of the Digital Universe*, New York, NY: Pantheon Books, pp. 253–57.

[232] George Dyson, 2012, *Turing's Cathedral: The Origins of the Digital Universe*, New York, NY: Pantheon Books, pp. 7, 64ff., 257–59.

After the war, the Illinois Automatic Computer ILLIAC was installed at the University of Illinois, a first generation replicant of MANIAC and the first electronic computer to be owned by a university. Its design had been mapped out by John von Neumann in 1945.[233] A former doctoral student of David Hilbert, then professor at the Institute of Advanced Study where Turing had worked for two years, von Neumann moved to Los Alamos to work on nuclear weapons. When he drove through Urbana in 1951 on one of his frequent trips between Princeton and Los Alamos, he stopped at the University to give a talk about the new machine, which was of course also being used for "secret government work."[234]

Like so many of his colleagues at the Institute of Advanced Study, von Neumann was a Jewish refugee. Born into a wealthy Hungarian family, he was "violently anti-communist ... since I had about three months taste of it in Hungary in 1919."[§AS2.4.2b] So the Cold War project suited him in a way that it did not necessarily suit other scientists and Jews who had also signed up to fight Nazis during the war. Prominent among these was Robert Oppenheimer, who pulled out of the venture when the bombs he and Neumann had created in Los Alamos were dropped on civilian populations.

Not von Neumann: of all his intellectual projects ranging from the game theory of an idealized capitalist market[235] to computer design,[236] nuclear "shock waves were von Neumann's first love." He is credited with the development of the doctrine of "mutually assured destruction" (MAD) where the US and the Soviet Union had piled up enough nuclear weapons to be able to destroy each other and the world. This, so the theory went, would be sufficient to keep the Soviets at bay while also creating a disincentive to use them.[237]

John Bardeen, inventor of the transistor, came to Illinois in the same year that von Neumann visited, winning the Nobel Prize in Physics for this achievement in 1956, and a second Nobel Prize in 1972. The pieces for the creation of modern computing were now all in place, Turing's logic and Bardeen's semiconductors. As the supposedly foolproof HAL 9000 computer dies in Arthur C. Clarke's 1968 novel and Stanley Kubrick's film *2001: A Space Odyssey*, he reminisces about his construction and training in Urbana, Illinois.[238] In another Kubrick movie, *Dr. Strangelove or: How I Learned to Stop Worrying and Love*

---

[233] John von Neumann, 1945, "First Draft of a Report on the Edvac," Philadelphia, PA: Moore School of Electrical Engineering, University of Pennsylvania.

[234] George Dyson, 2012, *Turing's Cathedral: The Origins of the Digital Universe*, New York, NY: Pantheon Books, pp. 287–88.

[235] John von Neumann and Oskar Morgenstern, 1953 [2007], *Theory of Games and Economic Behavior*, Princeton, NJ: Princeton University Press.

[236] John von Neumann, 1958, *The Computer and the Brain*, Yale, NH: Yale University Press.

[237] George Dyson, 2012, *Turing's Cathedral: The Origins of the Digital Universe*, New York, NY: Pantheon Books, pp. 42, 95, 298.

[238] Arthur C. Clarke, 1968, *2001: A Space Odyssey*, New York, NY: Signet, p. 156.

the Bomb, a von Neumann caricature is the star of the show, barely able to restrain a spontaneous Nazi salute.*

But beyond military decipherment and designing thermonuclear explosions, what could all this mean? What could be the use of computing machinery? Like Lovelace, Turing was ready to dream forward. He is better known today for his philosophy of the machine and his theory of its meaning capacities, than his work on the machines themselves.

The war was over and the Bletchley Park team was disbanded. Turing joined the National Physical Laboratory, whose director was Sir Charles Darwin, grandson of the natural scientist. Turing and the team to which he belonged made slow progress on the machine, the Automatic Computing Engine (a nod to Babbage's "Engines"). In the meantime, Turing wrote a speculative report, "Intelligent Machinery."

Turing made the reference point for his report the human brain. A hypothetical Universal Logical Computing Machine would be able to do more than calculate according to instructions; it would also be able to apply the answers it came up with as new instructions to itself. "Whenever the content of [the machine's] storage was altered by the internal operations of the machine, one would naturally speak of the machine 'modifying itself.'" By this process, the machine would also be able to teach itself in a way analogous to children's learning, using a system of rewards and punishments for right and wrong answers.[239] (Behaviorism[§3.1.2i] was at the time the psychological theory of choice.)

"The electrical circuits which are used in electronic computing machinery seem to have the essential properties of nerves," Turing said. Without having to go through the cumbersome process of creating a body, an electronic brain could be given organs of sight (television cameras), speech (loudspeakers), and hearing (microphones), by means of which it could learn games, languages, translation of languages, and mathematics, though he wondered about language because this was rather too dependent on locomotion. Compared with these large promises, the report was also at times rather more circumspect, the machine merely "mimicking education," learning only by laboriously undertaking an enormous number of minimal mathematical steps.[240]

Sir Charles Darwin was not impressed: "a schoolboy's essay . . . not suitable for publication" was his verdict.[241] Considering him useless to the ACE

---

* http://meaningpatterns.net/turing-test

[239] A.M. Turing, 1948, "Intelligent Machinery," A Report to the National Physical Laboratory, pp. 8, 13–14.

[240] Ibid., pp. 9–10, 11.

[241] Dermot Turing, 2015, *Prof: Alan Turing Decoded, a Biography*, Brimscombe Port, UK: The History Press, pp. 203, 213.

project, Darwin sent Turing back to Cambridge for a year's sabbatical. The report was not published until after Turing's death.

By the time the sabbatical was over, Turing had a new job, at the University of Manchester. As it happens, this was where Ludwig Wittgenstein[§2.1.1a] had begun his mathematical and philosophical journey.

In Manchester, they had started to build an electronic computer using seven tons of surplus parts delivered there from the scrapped Bletchley Park machines. "Manchester 1" had 1024 bits of random access memory, with paper-tape input and output – this last mechanism had been Turing's suggestion. By 1949, announced *The Times*, "the mechanical brain" in Manchester had done something that was practically impossible to achieve in paper. It had found some previously undiscovered, extremely large prime numbers.[242]

Turing decided it was time to try again with the theoretical ideas that had been so cursorily consigned to the proverbial dustbin by Sir Charles Darwin. In 1950, he published "Computing Machinery and Intelligence" in the philosophy journal, *Mind*. His question: how would you be able to determine when a machine was intelligent? His answer has come to be called the "Turing Test."

Turing proposed an "imitation game," where a machine and a person are behind a screen. Each is asked questions, with the source of the answers masked by a teleprinter. If the smartness of answers are indistinguishable to the human questioner, the machine might be deemed as intelligent as a person.

Playing such a game, the machine had certain advantages. The number of discrete states of which the Manchester machine was capable was, said Turing, about $10^{50,000}$. Moreover, a universal machine was able to conduct any kind of operation depending on how they were programmed. And more: "By observing the results of its own behaviour it can modify its own programmes so as to achieve some purpose more effectively." By calculation based on its own previous calculations, such a machine can learn. It can be "used to help in making up its own programmes ...; a machine undoubtedly can be its own subject matter."[243]

To this extent, computing machinery could perform some of the same operations of calculation as humans, though much faster. "Parts of modern machines which can be regarded as analogues of nerve cells work about a thousand times faster than the latter." So, the "view that machines cannot give rise to surprises is due, to a fallacy ..., the assumption that as soon as a fact is presented to a mind all consequences of that fact spring into the mind

[242] Ibid., pp. 212–17.
[243] A.M. Turing, 1950, "Computing Machinery and Intelligence," *Mind* 59:433–60, pp. 441, 449.

simultaneously with it."[244] Things can present themselves as surprises after a lot of working over data, and some of the working over that machines can do is too laborious for manual calculation. Today, these methods are called "machine learning" and "artificial intelligence."[§AS1.4.6c]

Having specified these capacities, Turing reframed the question that began the paper. With these capacities, "the question 'Can machines think?' should be replaced by 'Are there imaginable digital computers which would do well in the imitation game?'"[245]

Philosopher of language John R. Searle[§2.3.1b] was to mount what has become the best known challenge to Turing, in the hypothetical case of the Chinese room. Two people are behind Turing's screen; the first one knows Chinese and the second doesn't but has a dictionary. A third person asks each the meaning of words, and will get correct answers from both. The two people behind the screen seem equally smart because they can both type out the right answers. Like the second person, computers cannot know Chinese; they can only seem to know Chinese.[246]

The target of Searle's critique was "artificial intelligence." But Turing never made such an overblown claim. His claim was to no more than "mechanical intelligence,"[247] and this intelligence was in fact a trick. Turing had a dry sense of humor, and with some of its absurd counter-arguments, "Computing Machinery and Intelligence" can be read as a humorous text. The computer, he said, exhibited no more than a semblance of intelligence. If it was smart enough, it would be able to trick a gullible user in an "imitation game." The computer itself was the joker. Perhaps Turing had Wittgenstein's "language game" in mind, though Wittgenstein had not been joking.[§2.3.2a] Sir Charles Darwin was not joking, either.

Here is our re-reading of Turing. Calculation is one narrowly circumscribed function of meaning, a function which in our multimodal grammar we have called quantity. By transposition into quantity we can reduce a Chinese character to the zeros and ones that lie behind Unicode.[§0.2.1a] The character makes sense as something in the world expressed in our sensuous experience though non-quantitative functions. Or we have the word for the character spoken in voice synthesis that also reduces the word represented by that character to zeros

---

[244] Ibid., p. 451.   [245] Ibid., p. 442.

[246] John R. Searle, 1980, "Minds, Brains, and Programs," *Behavioral and Brain Sciences* (3):417–57, pp. 417–18; John R. Searle, 2014, "What Your Computer Can't Know," *New York Review of Books*; Daniel C. Dennett, 1998, *Brainchildren: Essays on Designing Minds*, Cambridge, MA: MIT Press, p. 5; Stevan Harnad, 1989, "Minds, Machines and Searle," *Journal of Theoretical and Experimental Artificial Intelligence* 1:5–25; Hubert L. Dreyfus, 1992, *What Computers Still Can't Do: A Critique of Artificial Reason*, Cambridge, MA: MIT Press.

[247] George Dyson, 2012, *Turing's Cathedral: The Origins of the Digital Universe*, New York, NY: Pantheon Books, p. 310.

and ones, albeit a totally different set of zeros and ones from text. Because, even in the binary world the instruction tables for text and speech are fundamentally different and can only be aligned by probabilistic statistics.

The zeros and ones in the middle, between creation and rendering, are an extremely narrow species of written text, completely unreadable except by a machine. When, following an instruction to calculate, they come out of the machine, and they are mechanically reconstructed as text or sound. In the middle is a huge amount of very fast calculation, but the elemental textual units are far too minimal and too many for the human mind to be able to read, even for their mathematical meaning.

Now we're back to routines like those developed in Bletchley Park to fight the German War Machine: encipherment > practically unintelligible, mathematically expressed text > decipherment. The stuff between encipherment and decipherment is no more than calculation, the logic of which humans have created by clever reduction, and the speed of which has been mechanized to beyond mortal capacities. We are back with Lovelace.

Nor is the computer so very different from other novel inventions of Lovelace's time. When in 1825 the steam locomotive first went faster than a person walking or a horse pulling a stage coach, people marveled – would a human body disintegrate at twenty miles per hour, a speed until then thought possible only for angels?[248] Bodies moving fast, numbers adding fast. Such are the powers of the mechanical prostheses of modern invention.

The question, then, is what is the scope of transposition into quantity? What are its affordances? Our answer, in sympathy we believe with the insights of both Lovelace and Turing: only things that are countable. By counting, instances can become concepts.[§1.1] By counting across a grade, qualities[§1.3.1] can be measured and named. By relating variables, curves can be drawn.[§1.2.2d] By counting the pixels and numbering their colors, an image can be deconstructed then reconstructed.[§1.2.2e] By numbering time and place, we can organize our days and find our way.[§AS1.3] And by giving a huge number of things a huge number of mostly unspeakable alphanumerical names, we have created for ourselves an unfathomably long list of things to count. That's a lot, but also, that's about all.

Turing's mortal fate was to be determined by another kind of decidability, born of a different series of binaries. On 7 February 1952, he reported to the police a burglary at his house. When the case came to court, Turing confessed, "I tried to mislead you about my informant . . . I picked him up in Oxford Street,

---

[248] Wolfgang Schivelbusch, 1977 [2014], *The Railway Journey: The Industrialization of Time and Space in the Nineteenth Century*, Berkeley, CA: University of California Press.

Manchester ... I have been an accessory to an offense in this house ... I had an affair with him."

The informant's friend had stolen Alan's things, but that was soon ignored, and Turing was committed to trial on three charges of indecency. He wrote a grimly jokey letter about it to a friend, signing off:

> Turing believes machines think
> Turing lies with men
> Therefore machines do not think
>   Yours in distress
>   Alan[249]

He was sentenced by the court to undergo "treatment," and this included estrogen implants whose effect was chemical castration.[250]

Turing was found dead from poisoning on 7 June 1954. He had a small lab in the house where he used cyanide to conduct electrical experiments. The coroner's court ruled suicide, but his mother, whom he had never liked but who went on to write for him a hagiography, insisted the death was accidental.[251]

§1.3.2d Gottfried Leibniz: "Let us Calculate"

Gottfried Leibniz, courtier to the German House of Hanover in the last quarter of the seventeenth and first quarter of the eighteenth century, was the first to prefigure the ideas and machines of Charles Babbage, Ada Lovelace,[§1.3.2a] and Alan Turing.[§1.3.2b] He seized on the idea of binary numbers, inspired in part by the Yin and Yang of the Chinese *I Ching* or "Book of Changes."[252] He created a mechanical calculator.[*] He envisaged the reduction of the elements of meaning ("monads"[253]) to elementary, calculable symbols and their logical relations. And this insight:

I have found an astonishing thing, which is, that we can represent all sorts of truths and consequences by Numbers ... [T]here are certain primitive Terms which can be posited if not absolutely, at least relatively to us, and then all the results of reasoning can be

---

[*] http://meaningpatterns.net/leibniz

[249] Dermot Turing, 2015, *Prof: Alan Turing Decoded, a Biography*, Brimscombe Port, UK: The History Press, pp. 246–47.

[250] David Leavitt, 2006, *The Man Who Knew Too Much: Alan Turing and the Invention of the Computer*, New York, NY: W.W. Norton.

[251] Sara Turing, 1959 [2012], *Alan M. Turing*, Oxford, UK: Oxford University Press, pp. 114–18.

[252] Maria Rosa Antognazza, 2009, *Leibniz: An Intellectual Biography*, Cambridge, UK: Cambridge University Press, pp. 433–36.

[253] Gottfried Wilhelm Leibniz, 1898, *The Monadology and Other Philosophical Writings*, translated by R. Latta, Oxford, UK: Oxford University Press.

determined in numerical fashion, and even with respect to those forms of reasoning in which the given data do not suffice for an absolute answer to the question, we could still determine mathematically the degree of probability.

Followed by this utopian flourish: " ... and where there are disputes among persons, we can simply say, Let us calculate, without further ado, in order to see who is right."[254]

"Let us calculate" has been revived as a slogan in the era of computer-mediated meaning. Today, we calculate incessantly, though the monads of our calculation involve peculiar transpositions between quantity from other meaning functions, transpositions which are one of the subjects of this grammar.

For all his prescience about the trajectory of modernity, Leibniz also found himself caught in some practical and intellectual dead-ends. One was to apply his prodigious scientific and mathematical capabilities to the problem of draining the water from the Duke of Hanover's silver and lead mines. Six years of calculation and design of windmill-powered pumps came to nothing.[255]

Then, consuming him for another six years at the end of Leibniz's life there was the debilitating dispute with Isaac Newton about which of them had been the inventor of the calculus, a huge breakthrough in the technology of calculability. Newton claimed that Leibniz had plagiarized his idea. The consensus judgment of peers was that indeed he had, though scholars now believe that each invented the calculus independently because their systems of notation were so different.[256] Long after he died, Leibniz's system came to be the preferred one. In Newton's old school, Cambridge University, Charles Babbage[§1.3.2a] became one of Leibniz's strongest advocates.[257]

Meanwhile, Newton, though a great physicist and mathematician, wandered into his own dead ends of calculation. When Cambridge University economist John Maynard Keynes[§AS2.4a] received a tip that a trove of Newton papers was to come up for sale at Sotheby's London auction house in 1936, he was there to purchase them. In his lifetime, Newton had written about two million words that are pivotal achievements of the Western scientific canon, but the auction brought to light another seven million words.[258]

[254] Gottfried Wilhelm Leibniz, 1951, *Leibniz: Selections*, translated by P.P. Weiner, New York, NY: Charles Scribner's Sons, pp. 50–51.

[255] Maria Rosa Antognazza, 2009, *Leibniz: An Intellectual Biography*, Cambridge, UK: Cambridge University Press, pp. 210–12; 227–30.

[256] Ibid., pp. 486–88, 495–97; Richard S. Westfall, 1980, *Never at Rest: A Biography of Isaac Newton*, Cambridge, UK: Cambridge University Press, pp. 698ff.

[257] James Essinger, 2014, *Ada's Algorithm: How Lord Byron's Daughter, Ada Lovelace, Launched the Digital Age*, Brooklyn, NY: Melville House, pp. 106–7.

[258] Sarah Dry, 2014, *The Newton Papers: The Strange and True Odyssey of Isaac Newton's Manuscripts*, Oxford, UK: Oxford University Press.

"Newton was not only the first of the age of reason," said Keynes after he started to read them, and the full scope of Newton's calculations became clear to him. "He was the last of the magicians." Most of what he had purchased at the auction was "wholly devoid of scientific value."[259]

The world had long known about Newton's mathematics, physics, and optics,[§1.3.1c] but not his chemical and metaphysical calculations. The chemical calculations are today dismissed as "alchemy." The metaphysical ones attempted to calculate the time of the realization of prophesies made in the Bible's most obscure books, Daniel and Revelation.[260] "Of the Vision of the Four Beasts; ... Of the ten Kingdoms represented by the ten horns of the Fourth Beast; ... Of the power of the eleventh horn of Daniel's fourth Beast, to change times and laws; ... Of the Prophecy of the Seventy Weeks" – these are some of the chapter heads, in one of the few of his religious manuscripts to be published. This was Newton at work, calculating "The design of God."[261]

Calculation had frustratingly reached its limits in Leibniz's mine pumps and Newton's prophetic revelations. Calculation alone is not enough. It needs a schema for what is calculable and worth calculating, or what we call ontology.[§3.1] It is not enough that the quantities add up. The calculations are no more than transpositions from other meanings into quantities and back again to humanly sensible meanings. The calculations themselves mean not much, unless they can make broader kinds of sense, multimodal sense, ontological sense.

So now to our era of ubiquitous calculation. Three centuries after Newton, here is the editor-in-chief of *Wired* magazine, Chris Anderson, forecasting the latest version of "Let us calculate":

Out with every theory of human behavior, from linguistics to sociology. Forget taxonomy, ontology, and psychology ... This is a world where massive amounts of data and applied mathematics replace every other tool that might be brought to bear ... With enough data, the numbers speak for themselves.[262]

No, we would say. Though the calculations of the computers connected to our fingers and minds are fast and helpful, we need ontologies to make sense of them. If computers work for us today, the calculation part of their work is

---

[259] Ibid., pp. 158–59; Daniel Kuehn, 2013, "Keynes, Newton and the Royal Society: The Events of 1942 and 1943," *Notes and Records of the Royal Society of London* 67(1):25–36.

[260] Iliffe Robert, 2017, *Priest of Nature: The Religious Worlds of Isaac Newton*, Oxford, UK: Oxford University Press, pp. 219ff.; James E. Force and Richard H. Popkin, 1990, *Essays on the Context, Nature, and Influence of Isaac Newton's Theology*, Dordrecht, NL: Kluwer.

[261] Isaac Newton, 1733 [1922], *Sir Isaac Newton's Daniel and the Apocalypse, with an Introductory Study of the Nature and Cause of Unbelief, of Miracles and Prophecy*, edited and translated by W. Whitla, London, UK: John Murray, pp. xvi, 306.

[262] Chris Anderson, 2008, "The End of Theory: The Data Deluge Makes the Scientific Method Obsolete," *Wired*, 16 July.

trivial. But what they are calculating may be profound, because any such meanings are made by transposition, where the inputs and outputs make more than just mathematical sense.

Today, the fundamental source of the practicality of calculated meanings lies in one aspect of calculation, and that is the by now exhaustive, universal, and dynamic but relatively stable scheme of alphanumeric naming.[§3.4b] The names are ordered into ontologies, supporting the lookupability of instances, concepts, qualities, and a whole host of other things. Modernity has created for itself a vast theory of everything, and this book is a theory of these theories. Only after this can we calculate, and with meaning.

Part 2 Agency

---

§2.0   Overview of Part 2

If reference is that to which meaning "speaks" (metaphorically, because this is a multimodal grammar), agency is the patterning of action. Reference is the addressed; agency is the addressing.

In this part, we are going to focus on three prominent features of agency: event, role, and conditionality. These are thoroughly named and analyzed in linguistics, though the complexities at times confound. They are not so thoroughly analyzed in the other forms of meaning that are also of concern to us. However, our focus is at a broader level of generality, one that crosses multiple forms.

Fig. 2.0 provides a rough and schematic outline of our theory of agency, and the organizational scheme for this part.

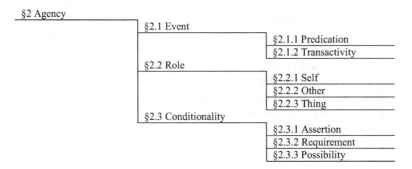

§2 Agency

- §2.1 Event
  - §2.1.1 Predication
  - §2.1.2 Transactivity
- §2.2 Role
  - §2.2.1 Self
  - §2.2.2 Other
  - §2.2.3 Thing
- §2.3 Conditionality
  - §2.3.1 Assertion
  - §2.3.2 Requirement
  - §2.3.3 Possibility

Fig. 2.0: Functions of Agency

Agency is constituted in events (predication by means of which entity into action fold into each other; and transactivity or the relations of entities-in-action to each other). Agents assume roles (as self, other, or thing). Different nuances of

173

conditionality are established in the relations of entities and action (assertion, requirement, and possibility).

Our renaming at this level of generality is not only in order to identify parallels across forms of meaning. It is also to analyze affordances – opportunities to mean, as well as constraints in meaning – that always prompt multimodality and necessary transposition from form to form.

We are also interested to trace functional transpositions, where patterns of the meanings of events are always ready to change, roles can be revised or reversed, and conditionalities can change. These kinds of always-readiness for change indicate that, like all meaning functions and in spite of their momentary appearances, they have within them the immanent and imminent possibility of change; and change inevitably comes. They mean, as much as themselves, their vectors of changeability.

§2.0a   Errol Morris' Fog of War

In human life natural events can be more or less human. The sun rose into a perfectly clear sky in Hiroshima on August 6, 1945. The sun rising and the processes of nuclear reaction in the sun that generated the light and warmth on that morning are natural events, though of course, the meanings of any sunny morning are layered into our feeling and our thinking.

The perfect clarity of that morning came to be defined at 8.15am by another nuclear reaction, the explosion of an atom bomb in the sky above the center of the city. Both events, the sun rising on that day and the explosion of the bomb, had human meanings. Both were events in nature to the extent that nuclear reactions are physical events. But the structure of agency in each case was different.

The natural historical event that is life on earth is dependent upon nuclear reaction in the sun, a fact of both natural and human history. Death on that day, perhaps 90,000, perhaps 150,000 souls, was inflicted upon natural creatures who perish under such conditions, and so this occurred in a structure of agency also involving both natural history and human history.[*]

"LeMay spoke in monosyllables. I never heard him say more than two words in sequence," Robert McNamara recalled. "It was basically 'Yes,' 'No,' 'Yup,' or 'The hell with it.'"

General Curtis LeMay was McNamara's commanding general during the Second World War, and McNamara later became US Secretary of State during the Vietnam War.

"LeMay said, 'If we'd lost the war, we'd all have been prosecuted as war criminals.' And I think he's right. He, and I'd say I, were behaving as war criminals. LeMay recognized that what he was doing would be thought

---

[*] http://meaningpatterns.net/morris

immoral if his side had lost. But what makes it immoral if you lose and not immoral if you win?"[1]

"He," "I," "We," "It" (the sun on that day or the bomb on that day) are some pointers in the direction of agency. LeMay's limited facility with speech alone fails to capture the pattern of agency in this event. We need a transpositional grammar for that.

§2 AGENCY

> *Agency. Identification of meaning in human and natural activity, offering an account of causes in terms of patterns of action.*

Agency is a process of causing. Causes may be human, or they may be natural. In human experience, mostly they are both, in a complex relation. The range of variation in this relation is a central concern for our grammar of multimodality.

Human meaning is a phenomenon of natural history, in its particularities, an outcome of our species emergence – not that other creatures cannot mean, but this book parses meaning for our species. Nature is humanly apprehensible and, to different degrees, humanly remade. Agency is naturally humanized and humanly naturalized.

Agency is always there, in and through meanings made in text, image, space, object, body, sound, and speech. Agency happens in events, where agents have roles, the meaning of which we can experience in different sense orientations, and the endless variability of meanings can be accounted for in the design process.

There are two sources of agency – human and natural events; though in our now hugely fabricated ecosphere, the two are mostly intertwined in our practical experiences. Indeed, they are by now so intertwined as to warrant the naming of our species-presence on the earth as an event of geological scale, the "Anthropocene."[2]

But even this is too much to grant to human agency alone. There is no human action that is not natural in the sense that the human species, though self-made, is a creature of a natural history. The architecture of our sentience is not so fundamentally different from many other creatures. Insects live event patterns

---

[1] www.scripts.com/script.php?id=the_fog_of_war%253A_eleven_lessons_from_the_life_of_rob ert_s._mcnamara_8370&p=9

[2] McKenzie Wark, 2015, *Molecular Red: Theory for the Anthropocene*, London, UK: Verso; Jesse Ribot, 2014, "Cause and Response: Vulnerability and Climate in the Anthropocene," *The Journal of Peasant Studies* 41(5):667–705, doi: 10.1080/03066150.2014.894911.

driven both by motivation to work and the sociabilities of reproduction and cooperation.

Nor is there any human action that does not involve the materials of nature – objects, light, and sound for instance, no matter how "artificial" in terms of the degree to which nature has been reworked by humans.

§2a   *J.M.W. Turner's* Rain, Steam and Speed

To reference an instantiation and some of its properties: *Rain, Steam and Speed: The Great Western Railway*, J.M.W. Turner, oil on canvas, 91 × 121.8 cm, 1844, National Gallery, London, NG538.[*] In Part 1, we spoke of meanings in this sense as reference: here, the painting and the scene pictured.

For the purposes of distinguishing reference from agency as another aspect of our transpositional grammar, and now speaking for it out loud, here is the event: "The train is quickly passing by in the storm; soon, train and storm will be gone." In speech, we need clauses to express an event structure, a relationship of a noun to a verb, and a subject ("the train") to its predicate ("is quickly passing by"). Or to move the analysis to the level of generality we want to capture in our grammar, entity ("the train") predicates action ("is quickly passing by").

Then, clause by clause we say what happens first, then next: "soon, train and storm will be gone." In an image, the entities are volumes (the locomotive, the train, the rail line, the bridge, the sky, and more that we may not have included in the spoken words), and action is marked by vanishing point and vector (the vanishing point of the train's origin, the vector the direction of the railway line).

We mean the same train in our speaking now as Turner did in his picturing then, but the two forms of its meaning are fundamentally different. Speech presents in time, where the speaker places word after word, clause after clause. As the listener hears "the train," they haven't yet heard "is quickly passing by," and later they will hear "soon, train and storm will be gone."

Image presents in space, so that when the eye falls upon the painting – from a distance walking into the room where it is hung in the National Gallery in London, or pulling up a digital copy on your computer screen (other events) – first you see the ominous swirl of a storm, then you make out the locomotive and the train, then if you look longer, you may be able to make out details such as the scared hare running away from the train, the farmer ploughing a field, the arch of the bridge, and people watching from the riverside.

There is a necessary temporal order in the meaning when presented in speech, but no necessary spatial arrangement. There is a necessary spatial order in the meaning when presented in image, but no necessary temporal

---

[*] http://meaningpatterns.net/turner

sequencing. Speech affords agency to the listener to configure space in their mind's eye. Image affords agency to the listener to configure time in their mind's eye – imagining the origins and destination of the train, the fate of the hare scurrying out of harm's way, the comparative speed of the plough in the field, the people at the river's edge who will still be there when the train has passed, until they, at their own pace, have time to go their way.

What did Turner mean to communicate about agency in *Rain, Steam and Speed?* A woman who boarded the Great Western Railway in Exeter was later to tell the story of how she found herself in a compartment on the train, sitting opposite an old man. "The weather was very wild, and by-and-by a violent storm swept over the country, blotting out the sunshine and blue sky, and hanging like a pall over the landscape. The old gentleman seemed strangely excited at this, jumping up to open the window, craning his neck out, and finally calling her to come and observe a curious effect of the light. A train was coming in their direction, through the blackness, over one of Brunel's bridges." The old gentleman, apparently, was Turner.

And another witness report, from a man who was nine at the time and watching Turner working on the canvas at the Royal Academy: "He used very short brushes, a very messy palette, and standing very close up to the canvas, appeared to paint with his eyes and nose as well as his hand. Of course, he repeatedly walked back to study the effect . . . He talked to me every now and then, and painted the little hare running for its life in front of the locomotive."[3]

After meanings have been transposed from representation into communication, there can only be slippery uncertainties. The woman and the man were speaking when the painting had become famous, and these were their brief encounters with fame. First exhibited at the Royal Academy in 1844, the painting has been in the National Gallery since 1865.

To the extent that the painting instantiates, part reality or part imagination, the Great Western Railway was new when the painting was made, opened in 1838. People marveled at its modernity, the audaciously broad 7'1/4" gauge rail lines, the longest tunnel in the world at Box Hill, the magnificent iron and glass arches spanning the platforms of its London terminus in Paddington, and here in Turner's painting, the bridge over the Thames at Maidenhead. With its long, gently elliptical arches, many observers thought the Maidenhead Bridge would not hold up, even the contractor who was supplying the bricks.[4]

[3] John Gage, 1972, *Turner: Rain, Steam and Speed*, New York, NY: Viking Press, pp. 16, 19.

[4] Isambard Brunel, 1870, *The Life of Isambard Kingdom Brunel, Civil Engineer*, London, UK: Longmans, Green, and Co, pp. 96, 172–74; L.T.C. Rolt, 1957, *Isambard Kingdom Brunel*, London, UK: Longmans, Green and Co. Colin Maggs, 2016, *Isambard Kingdom Brunel: The Life of an Engineering Genius*, Stroud, UK: Amberley.

The railway was an expression of the engineering genius of Isambard Kingdom Brunel and the hard labor of tens of thousands of "navvies" who dug the tunnels and filled the embankments with shovel and wheelbarrow. The express trains on the Great Western averaged 43 miles per hour, but Brunel prophesized that one day trains would travel at one hundred.

What might Turner have been thinking in his seeing? Beyond the canvas, we know a little from the title of the painting, but further than this it is hard to know, and the meaning of the painting is in part in the space it leaves for alternative meanings. Of the concept of "railway," contemporary interpretations varied. The poet Wordsworth asked in anger, "Is there no nook of English ground secure/From rash assault?"[5] In Turner's painting, English ground surrounds. The hare is alarmed, the ploughman slowly treads his furrows at the speed of his horse, and we might be able to imagine his ambivalence.

But here is a John Francis, by profession "of the Bank of England," by vocation a writer of history books. In his 1851 *History of the English Railway*, he quotes a commentator whose exuberance was common in those heady days that were at the time called the "railway mania." "The length of our lives, so far as regards the power of acquiring information and disseminating power, will be doubled, and we may be justified in looking for the arrival of a time when the whole world has become one great family, governed in unity by like laws."[6]

If this sounds like the heady rhetoric in a later century about the powers of the internet, it is because the phenomenon is in essence the same. The vectors of social transformation in both cases are lines of communication, whether they be the railway lines that send bodies and letters from station to junction to station, or the cables and wireless beams that send packages of information from computer to router to computer. In our multimodal grammar, the compression of human activity in the time and space of modernity is the same historical phenomenon whether it's a letter or a body on the move in a train, or in the era of the internet, text sent via email or body image, gesture, and speech sent via Skype, Google Meet or FaceTime. Of course, these media of communication are also different in the specific nuances that are their affordances.

The parallel in the 1840s to the breathless IPOs of the internet era was the "railway mania" of the 1840s. By a law of the English Parliament, the Joint Stock Companies Act of 1844, a registry had been created where new companies could be listed and public companies traded on the stock exchange. Railways became the focal point of speculative frenzy. "The most cautious were deceived by this apparent prosperity; and men esteemed good citizens and sound moralists were drawn into acts which avarice urged but conscience

---

[5] John Gage, 1972, *Turner: Rain, Steam and Speed*, New York, NY: Viking Press, p. 28.
[6] John Francis, 1851, *A History of the English Railway: Its Social Relations and Revelations, 1820–1845*, Volume 2, London, UK: Longman, Brown, Green & Longmans, p. 139.

condemned ... They pledged their purses and their persons to a great delusion ... They entered the whirlwind and were carried away by the vortex."[7]

And then the crash. Turner was painting a storm of nature while whirling around him was the metaphorical storm of industrial capitalism's first great crisis, a crisis of already global proportions. The vector of the train was accompanied by the abstract vectors of capitalism. Turner could have been saying any or all of these and other things, or not.[8]

The train in the picture is unnervingly still. The weather is the same in every viewing of the painting. We have to work to interpret the image as event, because all we can see is entities, and actions are conjectural. We can project action from the orientation of the vanishing point and the vector of the railway tracks. The train must have come from somewhere; it must be moving to be going somewhere; and it will soon pass into a future of uncertain weather that lies behind us viewers. Although the hare is scared, it will likely not be killed, and the trajectory of the tracks assures viewers that we will survive the train's passing.

The train in the image could possibly have stopped, but the words of the title tell us definitively that it has not. And it can't have stopped in the words of our second, made-up clause, "soon, train and storm will be gone." In words, we can also be assured that the storm ends soon.

If we struggle with time in images, we struggle with envisionable spatial detail when our representation or communication is in spoken words. You could talk about the visible contents of the image and the spatial arrangement of the scene for a lot longer than would normally be reasonable, without ever exhausting its detail. To supplement or break free from the affordances of pictures, we title paintings or caption and label diagrams and make movies. To supplement or break free from the affordances of speech, we juxtapose pictures.

Image is action stilled and represented conjecturally in vectors and vanishing points. Speech predicates action on the presence of entities in hypothetical space, where circumstances are separated into the antinomies of noun and verb, subject predicating object, disconnecting from their having been actioned then reconnecting them. These are radically different configurations of event, even though we want to insist that we mean these to be the same events, the agencies of nature and people as the train passes, or the railway mania that was its larger frame of world-historical agency.

[7] Ibid., pp. 144–45.
[8] Gerald Finley, 1999, *Angel in the Sun: Turner's Vision of History*, Montreal, Canada: McGill–Queens University Press, pp. 138–43.

§2.1   Event

> **Event.** Agency as expressed in the relationships of entities to action, and entities-in-action to each other.

An event happens when entities[§1.2.1] connect through action.[§1.2.2] Predication is a relation of a setting (the given, the found, a starting point), and the subsequent (what happens, effects, consequences). Transactivity is patterns of action, the kinds of relations established between entities in action.

Fig. 2.1 provides a rough map of event across the forms of meaning.

Form / Function: Event	Text	Image	Space	Object	Body	Sound	Speech
Predication	Subject → predicate; theme → rheme; given → new	The seeable → the seen; ground → figure	A spatial program → its navigation; wayfinding	Presence → use, solidity	Actor → action; Gestural preparation → stroke; position → change; disposition → re-orientation	Silence, meaningless noise → meaningful sounding	Prosody of scene-setting; prosody of new information
Transactivity	Transitivity (in/transitive); case (nominative, accusative etc.); voice (active, passive, etc.).	Volumes in relation to vectors; visible patterns of interaction	Explicit/inexplicit spatial causers; openings/barriers	Affecting → affected objects	Embodied action/its effects	Sounding → its responses	Markers in prosody of transitivity, case, voice

Fig. 2.1: Event

§2.1.1   Predication

> **Predication.** The relation of entities as focal points for attention to the action that gives cause for that attention.

Edward Sapir, who is otherwise famed for proposing that different languages express different social realities,[§AS1.3.1c] nevertheless thought there were some universals. "There must be something to be talked about and something must be said about this subject of discourse once it is selected."[9]

---

[9] Edward Sapir, 1921, *Language: An Introduction to the Study of Speech*, New York, NY: Harcourt Brace, p. 119.

In the clauses of speech we may name this difference as subject and predicate: between something that is the object of our attention, and our saying about this something. The same difference across other forms of meaning may be realized in something to be seen and what is salient now about its seeing, an object ready to be used and the process of its use, a space to be navigated and its navigating, in embodied gesticulation with its preparation followed by a stroke, a foreshadowing of sound and what follows in its sounding, in the clause and sentence structures of written text. These are all instances of predication, expressing meaning in the traffic between entities and actions in events.

"The category of Subject ... has always been one of the most obscure and controversial categories in western grammatical theory," says M.A.K. Halliday.[10] Three functions might be identified, say Halliday and Matthiessen, but these are of such different semantic orders that they almost do not bear classification into an overarching category: to establish a concern (the psychological subject); as the premise for an argued truth (the grammatical subject); and as the doer of an action (logical subject)[11] – though, to underline the slipperiness of any such demarcation, argued truths could be considered logical and logic might be better described as a pattern of action.

In the grammars of text there are numerous ways to name this relation, each meaning something different despite the overlap. For subject contrasted with predicate, we could also contrast theme with rheme,[12] given with new,[13] actor with action, topic with comment,[14] constant with variable,[15] nominative with accusative plus verb, force vector with result vector.[16] Every one of these distinctions addresses a subtly different aspect of predication – or confusingly, to the extent that frames of reference mean somewhat different things even though they are often taken to be more or less synonymous.[17]

Nevertheless, says Halliday,

---

[10] M.A.K. Halliday, 1984 [2002], "On the Ineffability of Grammatical Categories," pp. 291–322 in *On Grammar*, The Collected Works of M.A.K. Halliday, Volume 1, edited by J.J. Webster, London, UK: Continuum, p. 298.

[11] M.A.K. Halliday and Christian M.I.M. Matthiessen, 2014, *Halliday's Introduction to Functional Grammar* (Edn 4), Milton Park, UK: Routledge, pp. 78–80.

[12] M.A.K. Halliday, 1984 [2002], "On the Ineffability of Grammatical Categories," pp. 291–322 in *On Grammar*, The Collected Works of M.A.K. Halliday, Volume 1, edited by J.J. Webster, London, UK: Continuum, pp. 299–300.

[13] M.A.K. Halliday, 1967a, "Notes on Transitivity and Theme in English: Part 2," *Journal of Linguistics* 3(2):199–244, pp. 205, 211–12.

[14] M.A.K. Halliday and Christian M.I.M. Matthiessen, 2014, *Halliday's Introduction to Functional Grammar* (Edn 4), Milton Park, UK: Routledge, p. 89.

[15] Ronnie Cann, 1993, *Formal Semantics*, Cambridge, UK: Cambridge University Press, p. 27.

[16] Peter Gärdenfors, 2014, *Geometry of Meaning: Semantics Based on Conceptual Spaces*, Cambridge, MA: MIT Press, pp. 65, 267.

[17] Charles J. Fillmore, 1966, "Toward a Modern Theory of Case," Columbus, OH: Ohio State University, p. 60; Jerrold J. Katz, 1972, *Semantic Theory*, New York, NY: Harper & Row, p. 113.

the category of Subject is no less "meaningful" (semantically motivated) than other functional categories ... in the grammarian's pharmacopoeia. It would be easy to pour scorn on the whole enterprise of trying to gloss such categories at all ... But there are sound and respectable reasons for wanting to do so. The original impetus for semantic glosses on the grammar comes from the desire to explain observed formal patterns: why is this particular element in the nominative case, or in the genitive? Why is this element put first or after that one?[18]

One argument we want to make in this multimodal grammar is that these glosses on patterning can be devised for all of text, image, space, object, body, sound, and speech. And the affordances of speech and text are not just a matter of opening out opportunities to mean; with their systematic constraints, they also shape the scope of meaning. For this reason the conceptual glosses in grammars of writing or speech do not necessarily or completely transfer to other forms. Then, once we have created our multimodal grammar, we look back to find that we need different grammars for speech and text, a broader and recalibrated view of their patterning. And as soon as we do this, we begin to notice the limitations of speech and text, the skewing of their meanings that we have called their "affordances."

Our other key argument is about functional transposition, the immanent and imminent movability of meanings. My subject may at any time soon become my predicate. Or your subject may become my predicate; any moment now I may be able to experience your meaning more like the way you do.

Halliday calls this, in the title of his paper, "the ineffability of grammatical categories," and with good reason, because transposability makes stable categorization impossible.

§2.1.1a Ludwig Wittgenstein's Tractatus

One day in the fall of 1911, while Bertrand Russell was taking tea in his rooms at Trinity College, Cambridge with a student, C.K. Ogden,[§AS1a] an "unknown German" arrived.[19] Ludwig Wittgenstein said he had come to see them because he was interested in mathematics and logic. He had been studying engineering at the University of Manchester, focusing his work on aeronautics.

We want to explore Wittgenstein's thinking as a way to elaborate what we mean, somewhat differently, by "predication."

By way of context, Wittgenstein and Adolf Hitler had both been born in Vienna in 1889, six days apart. They went to the same school but Hitler fell

---

[18] M.A.K. Halliday, 1984 [2002], "On the Ineffability of Grammatical Categories," pp. 291–322 in *On Grammar*, The Collected Works of M.A.K. Halliday, Volume 1, edited by J.J. Webster, London, UK: Continuum, pp. 299–300.

[19] Ray Monk, 1990, *Ludwig Wittgenstein: The Duty of Genius*, New York, NY: The Free Press, pp. 38–39.

behind a year and Wittgenstein moved ahead a year, so they ended up two grades apart. There is some chance that they knew each other, though they were divided by social class and school-defined ability. Wittgenstein was a son of the second most wealthy family in Austria, after the Rothschilds. His family had made their money investing in steel.[20]

While studying engineering in Manchester, Wittgenstein's interest had been piqued by the meaning of the mathematics. He had become aware of the writings of Bertrand Russell and Gottlob Frege.[§1a] He visited Frege at the University of Jena in the summer of 1911, who advised him to see Russell.

Wittgenstein stayed in Cambridge after that initial meeting and went to Russell's lectures. They were poorly attended, often with only three or four students. This gave Wittgenstein ample opportunity to interact with Russell.

"My German engineer is very argumentative & tiresome ... He thinks nothing empirical is knowable ... He wouldn't admit that there was not a rhinoceros in the room ... [and] as usual maintained his thesis that there is nothing in the world except asserted propositions."[21] Russell nevertheless offered his encouragement to Wittgenstein, who decided to give up engineering for philosophy.

Wittgenstein started working on a thesis on logic. He submitted it for his BA degree in 1913, but it was rejected because the regulations required that an academic text include referencing in order to distinguish what was original from ideas drawn from scholarly sources and requiring attribution.

Wrote Wittgenstein to the professor who had submitted it on his behalf:

Dear Moore,

Your letter annoyed me. When I wrote Logik [its title at the time] I didn't consult the Regulations, and therefore I think it would only be fair if you gave my degree without consulting them so much either! ... If I am not worth your making an exception for me even in some STUPID details then I may as well go to HELL directly; and if I am worth it and you don't do it, then – by God – you might go there ...

L.W.[22]

An exception was not made.

Then the First World War came, and that was hell on earth. Wittgenstein joined the Austro-Hungarian army, served on the front line, and was taken a prisoner of war. After the war he became a primary school teacher in a small Austrian village.

[20] Brian McGuinness, 1988, *Wittgenstein: A Life; Young Ludwig 1889–1921*, Berkeley, CA: University of California Press, p. 51.
[21] Ray Monk, 1990, *Ludwig Wittgenstein: The Duty of Genius*, New York, NY: The Free Press, pp. 39–40.
[22] Ibid., p. 103.

Finally he finished the work that he had submitted unsuccessfully as his BA. It was published in German in 1921. He sent it to Russell and Ogden in England to see whether it could be published in English as a book.[23] Ogden worked on the translation with a young student, F.P. Ramsay, and it was published in 1922 under the Latin title that Ogden had suggested, *Tractatus Logico-Philosophicus*, a riff on the title of Baruch Spinoza's[§3.1.1a] *Tractatus Theologico-Politicus* of 1677.[24]

The *Tractatus* was just 75 pages long. Along with a small children's dictionary and one article, this was all Wittgenstein published during his lifetime. It is of interest to us as we work through our grammar of multimodality, partly because, in a way that became very typical of social theory by the end of the twentieth century, it grants so much to language as the core of human meaning. Or perhaps it doesn't, and to this extent its meanings become lost in its depths of ambiguity – self-contradiction, even.[§2.3.2a]

Here is our gloss on an elusive text, drawing out just those things that might help us elucidate our notion of predication. ("Elucidate" is Wittgenstein's word for the role of philosophy in addressing the ordinary world, reduced to its bare bones after what he considered to be the declarative "nonsense" of metaphysics, aesthetics, and ethics – and this idea we do like. "Philosophy is not a theory but an activity," he said.[25])

In the *Tractatus*, the world consists of facts, and facts consist of objects that are logically connected with each other. "The object is the fixed, the existent; the configuration is the changing, the variable."[26] Logic is expressed in language in the form of a proposition. "The proposition *shows* how things stand, *if* it is true. And it *says*, that they do so stand."[27] This is all that is thinkable.

"All propositions of our colloquial language are actually, just as they are, logically completely in order . . . not a model of the truth but the complete truth itself."[28] As a consequence, *"The limits of my language mean the limits of my world."*[29] And of the logic that language expresses, "logic fills the world: the limits of the world are also its limits."[30]

Wittgenstein's "objects" we call entities, and their "configuration" or "variables" we call action. Entities and actions come together in events.

However, from the start, we are unhappy with Wittgenstein's idea that the world is held together by mere configuration, or logic, as expressed via propositions in language. The world is more than things and their relations. And we mean something more active and varied than logic.

In our grammar, the world is held together by dynamics that can be activated across a number of quite different meaning functions. In this part of the book,

[23] Ludwig Wittgenstein, 1973, *Letters to C.K. Ogden*, Oxford, UK: Basil Blackwell.
[24] Ludwig Wittgenstein, 1922 [1933], *Tractatus Logico-Philosophicus*, London, UK: Routledge.
[25] Ibid., §4.112.   [26] Ibid., §2.0271.   [27] Ibid., §4.022.   [28] Ibid., §5.5563.   [29] Ibid., §5.6.
[30] Ibid., §5.61.

we address agency in events that involve predication and transitivity connecting entities through patterns of action. To us, Wittgenstein's view of reality has rather a static feel. There is then a lot more than logic that holds the world together, and we need more than logic to think that holding-togetherness.

Then, in our grammar – and in fact this is the very reason why we need a transpositional grammar – there is much meaning in the world that happens beyond or beside language and logic, in image, space, object, bodies, and sound. Language is only able to represent these meanings by transposition, and only partially given its affordances. We need multimodality to fill out or complement the meanings of language. And we need a theory of transpositions to explain the traffic between language and the world that gives language its meaning. Language has limited meaning by itself. To invert Wittgenstein's now-famous formulation, the limits of my meaning are the limits of the affordances of my forms of meaning-making, and there is much awaiting my meaning that is beyond the scope of any one form.

Adding to our problem of Wittgenstein's limiting meaning to language is a categorical problem about the form of meaning to which Wittgenstein ascribes limits. "Language," as we have argued,$^{§0.2.7a}$ is an unhappy aggregation of speech and writing. It would be simply impossible to represent or communicate the logical sections of the *Tractatus* in speech; these of necessity take the characteristic form of writing, closely aligned as it is to visual representation.[*] So, if anything, Wittgenstein should more accurately refer in his theory to writing, rather than language.

Having found the limits of meaning in language, Wittgenstein admits, beyond that "there is indeed the inexpressible. This *shows* itself; it is the mystical." The *Tractatus* ends in a self-contradiction. It is an anti-metaphysical metaphysics. It is a work of logic that drops much of our ordinary experience into the nonsensical, then the mystical. Then even philosophy. Having spoken declaratively for seventy-five pages, of his own propositions he now says, "he who understands me finally recognizes them as senseless, when he has climbed out through them, on them, over them. (He must so to speak throw away the ladder, after he has climbed up on it.)"[31] His last words: "Whereof one cannot speak, thereof one must be silent."[32]

Wittgenstein sent a copy of the book to Frege, who replied, "You see, from the very beginning I find myself entangled in doubt as to what you want to say, and so make no proper headway." Russell wrote a foreword, which Wittgenstein felt misunderstood his main arguments, some of which Russell privately considered "a curious kind of logical mysticism."[33]

---

[*] http://meaningpatterns.net/wittgenstein-tractatus

[31] Ibid., §6.54.   [32] Ibid., §7.
[33] Ray Monk, 1990, *Ludwig Wittgenstein: The Duty of Genius*, New York, NY: The Free Press, pp. 163, 165.

Silence followed, or at least written silence. Wittgenstein's next book, *Philosophical Investigations*, was not published until after his death, more than thirty years later.[§2.3.2a]

§2.1.1b Wittgenstein's Handles

Vienna III, Parkasse 18 (summer 1927)

My dear Keynes, . . . (I have) taken up architecture. I am in the process of building a house in Vienna. This is causing me considerable worry and I am not even certain that I won't botch it.

As ever, yours, Ludwig

Vienna III, Kundmanngasse 19 (1928)

Dear Keynes, I have just finished my house, which has occupied me entirely over the past two years . . . I enclose a few photos and hope that you don't find its simplicity too offensive.

As ever, yours, Ludwig[34]

Ludwig Wittgenstein is writing to the economist, John Maynard Keynes,[§AS2.4a] with whom he had become friends while he was at Cambridge.

The house Wittgenstein was building was for his sister, Margarete (Gretl) Stonborough,* at Kundmanngasse 19, Vienna. He had given his share of the family's phenomenal wealth to his siblings in 1918. This was Gretl's money, and no expense would be spared.

At first, Gretl had commissioned architect Paul Engelmann, student of the modernist architect and architectural theorist, Adolf Loos. "Ornament is crime!" Loos declared in a widely quoted essay of 1908.[35] Wittgenstein had known Loos for some years.[36] Engelmann created the initial plans, then Wittgenstein took over. A working drawing of November 1926 has Engelmann and Wittgenstein both listed as architects. But when it was finished, Engelmann said, "he was actually the architect and not myself. Although when he started working on the

---

* http://meaningpatterns.net/wittgenstein-handles

[34] Bernhard Leitner, 2000, *The Wittgenstein House*, New York, NY: Princeton Architectural Press, p. 22.

[35] Adolf Loos, 1998, *Ornament and Crime: Selected Essays*, translated by M. Mitchell, Riverside, CA: Ariadne Press, pp. 167–76.

[36] David Macarthur, 2014a, "Working on Oneself in Philosophy and Architecture: A Perfectionist Reading of the Wittgenstein House," *Architectural Theory Review* 19(2):124–40, p. 125. doi: 10.1080/13264826.2014.951869; David Macarthur, 2014b, "Reflections on 'Architecture Is a Gesture' (Wittgenstein)," *Paragrana* 23(1):88–100; Allan Janik and Stephen Toulmin, 1973, *Wittgenstein's Vienna*, New York, NY: Simon and Schuster, p. 92.

project the plans had already been completed, I view the result as his and not my achievement."[37]

"Ludwig Wittgenstein, Architect." This is how he signed off in letters he wrote at the time.[38] To the one book of philosophy published in his lifetime, we can add one building, competed in 1928 after two years of hard work.

A small entryway was followed by an anteroom with a cloakroom (and off that WC and a washroom), then ten steps up into a wide central hallway. To the left, tall glass doors opened out onto a terrace, and doors to a dining room which also opened onto the terrace. Ahead was an alcove in which Gretl placed a sculpture of a discus thrower. Behind the wall was a stair to the upper levels, encircling an elevator in a glass-walled shaft. To the right were a salon, and off this a library and another terrace.

The effect of the entry and hallway was reminiscent of Viennese palace architecture, and the house came to be called among family members, "Palais Stonborough." Chronicler of the fraught history of the house, Bernhard Leitner, takes a phrase "family resemblance" from Wittgenstein's posthumous *Philosophical Investigations*, but there is no evidence that the architect-philosopher had any such thought at the time. Leitner fought to have the house saved from demolition in the 1970s, but not disfiguration when it was purchased in 1976 and remodeled for the Embassy of the People's Republic of Bulgaria.[39]

Apart from the hallway and its overall size (Gretl lived in the house with her husband and two sons, a cook, two girls who assisted her in the kitchen, three maids, a lady's maid, a governess, and a chauffeur), there was nothing palace-like about the building. All the surfaces were artificial: the walls plastered in a pale stuccolustro with touches of ochre and red; the almost-black polished concrete slabs on the floor; the varnished steel windows, doors, and window screens. Every line was rigorously straight. Chandeliers were forbidden; instead there were unadorned light bulbs. Carpets were forbidden too, and also curtains, in place of which Wittgenstein designed heavy steel screens. Defying their weight of over one hundred kilograms, these rose effortlessly from the floor with a block and tackle system of pulleys and counterweights. And the handles . . .

---

[37] Bernhard Leitner, 2000, *The Wittgenstein House*, New York, NY: Princeton Architectural Press, p. 23; Nana Last, 2008; *Wittgenstein's House: Language, Space and Architecture*, New York, NY: Fordham University Press, p. 92; Bernhard Leitner, 1976, *The Architecture of Ludwig Wittgenstein: A Documentation*, New York, NY: New York University Press.

[38] Bernhard Leitner, 2000, *The Wittgenstein House*, New York, NY: Princeton Architectural Press, p. 32.

[39] Ibid., pp. 26–28, 64–69, 39–46.

Wittgenstein spent a year agonizing over the door handles. They were lever mechanisms, austerely simple, placed quite high on the door, and, though in the same style, of different size and at different heights on the door depending on its proportions.[40] Because the doors were steel, there was no rosette. Wittgenstein arranged for them to be cast in bronze to his design.[41]

Predication: the handle begs the opening of the door. The meaning function of the entity transposes with the action for which it has been designed. The meaning form of the handle transposes with embodied movement in space. The handle acts when acted upon. Agency in the case of objects reveals itself in their workability, their utility, and the nuances of their feel.

Here Wittgenstein was working with meanings that are beyond the limits of language. Though of course, we can name these meanings, albeit awkwardly because text about Wittgenstein's handles is by affordance less than the experience of feeling the handles in one's hand. This, we can no longer do, because they were thrown away in the 1976 renovation. We are left with pictures, and text, and our mental images of feeling and opening – strangely high on the door. As smooth as modernity, they must have been.

"Remember the impression one gets from good architecture, that it expresses a thought. It makes one want to respond with a gesture."[42] Almost thirty years after his death, this enigmatic aphorism was published in a book of scraps from Wittgenstein's notebooks. And this one: "Working on philosophy is really like working on oneself – as is often true of working on architecture. Working on one's own perception, on how one sees things (and what one demands of them)."[43]

§2.1.1c HandleSets.com

"TECNOLINE® is an independent private limited company that has been manufacturing and supplying exclusive, fine-quality switches and fixtures since 2002." We find this background information at the "About" page on the company's website, www.bauhaus-fittings.com. Producing fittings designed by Bauhaus greats Wilhelm Wagenfield and Walter Gropius, the site goes on, "TECNOLINE® is licensed to market these products under the name of the

---

[40] Nana Last, 2008; *Wittgenstein's House: Language, Space and Architecture*, New York, NY: Fordham University Press, pp. 106, 112.

[41] Bernhard Leitner, 2000, *The Wittgenstein House*, New York, NY: Princeton Architectural Press, pp. 170–79.

[42] Ludwig Wittgenstein, 1931–44 [1980], *Culture and Value*, edited by G.H. von Wright, translated by P. Winch, Chicago, IL: University of Chicago Press, 22e.

[43] Ibid., 16e.

original designers, i.e. it actually produces **original articles**" [emphases by the site creators].

Among the "original" products for sale are "door and window handles designed by Ludwig Wittgenstein."[*] However, unlike the handles Wittgenstein made for his sister's house, we notice that they have rosettes, and there may be other differences. "**TECNOLINE®**['s] . . . solid brass fixtures are manufactured and finished exclusively in Germany. In our view, Germany is the only location that can ensure the necessary degree of exclusiveness and sustainability."[44] It is hard to see how Wittgenstein might be classified "Bauhaus" by way of direct affiliation, though there is a family resemblance between his handles and theirs, created at about the same time.

The US-based HandleSets.com is uncommitted when it comes to handle design and offers no provenance that might be called "original" or named by famous designers. "Make an Impression with these Hardware, Lock, Door Lever and Handleset Categories," exhorts the site's home page. Among the 2,214 kinds of handleset for sale, shoppers can make their choice from "Themes: Traditional (882), Contemporary (7), Transitional (653), Modern (819), Rustic (98), Craftsman (13), Crystal (120), and Vintage (251)." The categories don't add up to the total, because unlike a bricks-and-mortar store, things can be put in more than one "place."

Then there are multiple options to "Narrow Your Results: Handleset Type: (Handleset; Mortise Lock); Handleset Function (Keyed Entry, Keyless Entry, Dummy Set, Passage, Privacy, Single Dummy)" . . . and hundreds of other variables under the macro categories "Cylinder Type, Finish, Brand, Mount, Style, Price," and finely graduated ranges of dimension and door thickness. Because within each Handleset there are often multiple finishes (for instance, "Aged Bronze, Matte Black, Polished Chrome, Polished Nickel, Satin Chrome and Satin Nickel"), there are possibly 10,000 different handleset products in this store.[45]

And naturally, working our way through all this categorical choice, we find that several among the 267 lever handles in the "Modern" style look rather like Wittgenstein's. We find the "Omnia 11/00F.PA32D Brushed Stainless Steel Passage Door Leverset from the Stainless Steel Collection Featuring a 2–7/16" Round Rose" and immediately see that "People Who Viewed Omnia 11PA Also Viewed" . . . the "Emtek S100KL-SS Brushed Stainless Steel Kiel Stainless Steel Passage Leverset," and the "Delacora DHDW101OS-32D Satin Stainless Erie Passage Door Lever Set." This naming works in writing, but cannot work in speech, because the names to differentiate ten thousand handlesets are all but unspeakable in a way that "Wittgenstein's Handles" are not. Here is still further evidence of the separation of text and speech in digital modernity.

On the Omnia page, a reviewer who gives the handleset a five-star rating says, "Growing up in Europe, I could never get friendly with door knobs (try that with grocery bags in both of your hands) or the knob replacement levers . . . The Omnia levers have a clever mechanism that converts a short stroke on the lever to a long stroke on the latch. With this you get the convenience of a door knob installation with the feel and function of a mortise lock . . . The Omnia levers cost more than a simple knob replacement lever, but it's well made, installs quickly and feels so much better."

The reviewer who selected these options explained his rating: "Met Expectations. Packaged Well. Easy to Install/Use. Easy to Clean. Sturdy." The page offers options to rate the review for its helpfulness, or to report abuse of the review function which evidently is not otherwise moderated. A whole lot of technical information is also provided, as well as a three-page PDF with the assistance of which a non-expert, so the site suggests, should be able to install the handle.[46]

Launched in 2003, HandleSets.com must be the biggest handle retailer in the world. It is the Amazon of handlesets. (Amazon also offers thousands of handles too, but fewer than HandleSets.com and without such finely grained naming, tagging, and filtering.) No bricks-and-mortar store could offer this many products. An ordinary mortal walking down the aisles of any such imaginary store would be overwhelmed, and even in the warehouse, doubtless items would only be locatable by inventory location look-up in a database. Meanings made by spatial juxtaposition of items in the physical store are replaced by meaning that must be made by textual mediation through look-up.

On so many levels, this is a radically new patterning of agency in the meanings of objects. Wittgenstein had worked with a brass foundry in Vienna. He had engineering experience from his days designing propellers during his aeronautics studies at the University of Manchester. He had the time on his hands to be able to spend a year on the handles. He had the benefit of a sister who was able to spare no expense.

The Omnia, however, costs just $70.50, "Originally $94, You Save 25%." If Wittgenstein had gone to a hardware store, his choices would have been limited for practical reasons. The store would have been local, and from locality to locality in Austria, the choices would in all probability not have varied much. Today, he could have just gone to the online store, and surely, among the ten

---

[46] www.handlesets.com/omnia-11pa-passage-door-leverset-from-the-stainless-steel-collection-featuring-a-2-7-16-round-rose/p1742352

thousand options, something would have worked for him and, by his proxy, for Gretl.

The first online purchase was on August 11, 1994, a copy of Sting's CD, "Ten Summoner's Tales," at netmarket.com for $12.48, plus shipping costs.[47] Amazon.com was founded in the same year.[48] In 2016, 79 per cent of Americans shopped online.[49] Amazon is one of the four most valuable companies in the world by capitalization, up there with Apple, Alphabet/Google, and Microsoft.[50] And there is really only one place where you can shop in full knowledge of your handleset options, and that is HandleSets.com.

Such is the tendency to concentration of informational and physical capital in the era of the database-driven warehouse. This may also spell the end of the urban. Wittgenstein could be discerning in his handle selections in Vienna, as could others in cities where they were in proximity to fancy stores or brass foundries.

Today, anyone and everyone can contemplate and get every imaginable handleset no matter where they may be because there is no place, on or off the grid, inaccessible to a delivery van, and soon, we are promised, a delivery drone. In geospatial terms, the consequence of these textually and image-enabled social changes is enormous, as we move from an economics and sociability of spatial contiguity to one of virtual contiguity.[51] And with this also, unhappy possibilities for the commodification, reification,[§AS2.3] alienation,[§AS2.3.2] and impersonalization of the stuff that was until recently somewhat closer to the lifeworld of human sensuous activity.

Shopping by database involves a peculiar patterning of multimodal transpositions. Explicitly, we explore concepts (the products), filtering them by their properties. At HandleSets.com, the site, text, and image are generated algorithmically and on-the-fly, and products can be compared side by side. The consumer is an information co-designer.

Then, when we purchase an instantiation, the number of instantiations available in the warehouse drops by one – we can see that happen before our very eyes as we purchase. The database knows the date of purchase of that instantiation when it comes to the returns policy (30 days for a refund, 31–60

[47] Alorie Gilbert, 2004, "E-Commerce Turns 10," c|net, 11 August.
[48] James Marcus, 2004, Amazonia: Five Years at the Epicenter of the Dot.Com Juggernaut, New York, NY: The New Press; Richard L. Brandt, 2011, One Click: Jeff Bezos and the Rise of Amazon.Com, New York, NY: Penguin; Brad Stone, 2013, The Everything Store: Jeff Bezos and the Rise of Amazon, New York, NY: Little, Brown and Company.
[49] Sarah Perez, 2016, "79 Percent of Americans Now Shop Online," TechCrunch, 19 December.
[50] FT500, Financial Times. https://markets.ft.com/data/dataarchive/ajax/fetchreport? reportCode=GMKT&documentKey=688_GMKT_170401
[51] Bill Cope and Mary Kalantzis, 2015, "Extraurbia, or, the Reconfiguration of Spaces and Flows in a Time of Spatial-Financial Crisis," pp. 219–46 in Smart Cities as Democratic Ecologies, edited by D. Araya, New York, NY: Palgrave.

days for a store credit), or the warranty (this varies by manufacturer, the site tells us).

The returns policy offers yet another multimodal transposition. In addition to the text and image on the site, you can get the object into your hands, see whether it aligns with the function and feeling in your mind's eye, and send it back if it doesn't. Ron Scollon calls this "mediated discourse" in the "nexus of practice."[52]

HandleSet.com is full of text, mostly in title case, sentences that are also headings, nouns with verbs assumed, entities always ready to predicate action. Text and image anticipate the predication in the handles themselves, the begging to be opened or closed, and the opening or closing – these are functional transpositions. The site and the process of product delivery helps users through a multimodal transposition, anticipating then delivering the function and feel of opening and closing a door for any one handleset, compared to the ten thousand-odd others.

Everywhere, we sense the nuances of predication, entity related to action, in user reviews, and in the product itself, as we decide to keep it or send it back. And anyone can become a handleset installer because its engineering principles are clearly spelled out. In addition to the PDF on every product page, there are the endless instructional videos on YouTube, where a search on "installing handlesets" generates "about 11,500 results."

Today, you might be led to think, everyone can be their own Wittgenstein. Though maybe not.

§2.1.1d Picture Theory in Vienna

While working on his sister's house in Vienna, Wittgenstein established an uneasy connection with the Vienna Circle.[§1.1.3i] In their weekly meetings, the Circle discussed the *Tractatus* at length. Wittgenstein never attended the formal meetings, but he did meet with members of the Circle informally. When they published their *Scientific Conception of the World* manifesto in 1929, they declared their debt to the "far-reaching ideas of Wittgenstein."[53]

Moritz Schlick, sponsor and coordinator of the Circle and a Professor of Philosophy at the University of Vienna, first met Wittgenstein early in 1927.[54]

---

[52] Ron Scollon, 2001, *Mediated Discourse: The Nexus of Practice*, London, UK: Routledge; Ron Scollon, 2000, "Action and Text: Toward an Integrated Understanding of the Place of Text in Social (Inter)Action," pp. 139–83 in *Methods in Critical Discourse Analysis*, edited by R. Wodak and M. Meyer, London, UK: Sage; Ron Scollon and Suzie Wong Scollon, 2004, *Nexus Analysis: Discourse and the Emerging Internet*, London, UK: Routledge.

[53] Vienna Circle, 1929 [1973], "The Scientific Conception of the World," pp. 299–318 in *Empiricism and Sociology*, edited by P. Foulkes and M. Neurath, Dordrecht, NL: D. Reidel Publishing, p. 311.

[54] Brian McGuinness, 1985, "Wittgenstein and the Vienna Circle," *Synthese* 64(3):351–58, pp. 351–52.

After this, he and his protégé, Friedrich Waissmann, began to meet Wittgenstein regularly, sometimes also with other members of the group.[55] Many in the group, mainly Otto Neurath[§1.1.3h] and Rudolf Carnap,[§AS2.2b] were skeptical. Their intellectual agenda was Logical Positivism, and where Wittgenstein appeared strong on the logical part of this methodological label, he could hardly be considered positivistic for his lack of attention to empirical science.

Wittgenstein's pronouncements, said Carnap, were "similar to those of a religious prophet or a seer." And Neurath: "We do not need a metaphysical ladder of elucidation. On this point we cannot follow Wittgenstein."[56] Wittgenstein returned his disdain when meeting several members of the larger group – still informally – by turning his back on them and reading from the Bengali poet, Rabindranath Tagore.[57]

Nevertheless, strong connections were formed. Waissmann and Wittgenstein commenced a joint book project in 1929, which mainly consisted of Wittgenstein dictating and Waissmann taking notes. Under the notional title *Logic, Language, Philosophy*, the project continued sporadically until Wittgenstein broke it off in 1934. The English translation of the notes and draft manuscript were published in 2003, running to 515 pages.[58] In 1936, Neurath, who was by then living in the Netherlands, began negotiations with the Dutch publisher Springer Verlag to have the book published. A full, final manuscript was submitted in 1937 under Waissmann's name alone, but never published because the war came. The manuscript was lost in the fire-bombing of the publisher during a Nazi air raid.[59]

One convergence in these Vienna years was an area that Wittgenstein had in the *Tractatus* called "picture theory." While Wittgenstein was working on Gretl's house and after that, writing with Waissmann, Otto Neurath and Marie Reidemeister were working on their own version of picture theory in the Museum of Society and Economy.[60]

---

[55] Ludwig Wittgenstein and Friedrich Waissmann, 2003, *The Voices of Wittgenstein: The Vienna Circle*, translated by G. Baker, M. Mackert, J. Connolly, and V. Politis, London, UK: Routledge, p. xviii.

[56] Rudolf Haller, 1991b, "Two Ways of Experiential Justification," pp. 191–202 in *Rediscovering the Forgotten Vienna Circle: Austrian Studies on Otto Neurath and the Vienna Circle*, edited by T.E. Uebel, Dordrecht, Germany: Kluwer Academic Publishers, p. 197.

[57] Ray Monk, 1990, *Ludwig Wittgenstein: The Duty of Genius*, New York, NY: The Free Press, pp. 244, 234.

[58] Ludwig Wittgenstein and Friedrich Waissmann, 2003, *The Voices of Wittgenstein: The Vienna Circle*, translated by G. Baker, M. Mackert, J. Connolly, and V. Politis, London, UK: Routledge.

[59] Ibid., pp. xxix–xxx, xxii.

[60] Karl H. Müller, 1991, "Neurath's Theory of Pictorial-Statistical Representation," pp. 223–54 in *Rediscovering the Forgotten Vienna Circle: Austrian Studies on Otto Neurath and the Vienna Circle*, edited by T.E. Uebel. Dordrecht, Germany: Kluwer Academic Publishers, p. 246; Rudolf Haller, 1991a, "On Otto Neurath," pp. 25–31 in ibid., p. 27.

Neurath's quest was "the search for a neutral system of formulae, for a symbolism freed from the slag of historical languages ... the search for a total system of concepts." The problem with "the form of traditional languages [is that they create] a confusion about the logical achievement of thought." The "scientific world conception," by contrast, knows with clarity just two things: "empirical statements about things of all kinds, and analytic statements of logic and mathematics." This was the theory of "Logical Positivism."

In their Museum, Neurath and Reidemeister were but turning the theory of Logical Positivism into practice, where visualizations express social concepts, their logical relations, and the mathematical characteristics of these relationships. In so doing, they were "formalizing the intuitive process of inference of ordinary thought, that is to bring it into a rigorous, automatically controlled form by means of a symbolic mechanism."[61]

Like the Vienna Circle, Wittgenstein starts the *Tractatus* with the idea of fact, in order to build logic on this foundation. "The world is the totality of facts, not of things."[62] "An atomic fact is a combination of objects (entities, things)."[63] But for the rest, he shows little interest in the constitution of facts, beyond the assertion that they simply show themselves.

Then comes Wittgenstein's picture theory:[64] "We make to ourselves pictures of facts."[65] "The elements of the picture stand, in the picture, for the objects."[66] "To the objects correspond in the picture the elements of the picture."[67] "That the elements of the picture are combined with one another in a definite way, represents that the things are so combined with one another."[68] In this way, pictures have a propositional and logical character. "Thus the picture is linked with reality; it reaches up to it."[69] "The representing relation consists of the co-ordinations of the elements of the picture and the things."[70]

This idea, Norman Malcolm recalls in his biographical memoir, came to Wittgenstein while he was serving in the Austrian Army in the First World War. "He saw a newspaper article that described the occurrence and location of an automobile accident by means of a diagram or map. It occurred to Wittgenstein that this map was a proposition and that therein was revealed the essential nature of propositions – namely, to picture reality."[71] "The logical picture of the

[61] Quoted at §1.24.
[62] Ludwig Wittgenstein, 1922 [1933], *Tractatus Logico-Philosophicus*, London, UK: Routledge, §1.1.
[63] Ibid., §2.01.
[64] Michael A. Peters and Jeff Stickney, 2018, *Wittgenstein's Education: 'A Picture Held Us Captive'*, Singapore: Spring Nature.
[65] Ludwig Wittgenstein, 1922 [1933], *Tractatus Logico-Philosophicus*, London, UK: Routledge, §2.1.
[66] Ibid., §2.131.   [67] Ibid., §2.13.   [68] Ibid., §2.15.   [69] Ibid., §2.1511.   [70] Ibid., §2.1514.
[71] Norman Malcolm, 1958, *Ludwig Wittgenstein: A Memoir*, Oxford, UK: Oxford University Press, pp. 68–69.

facts is the thought,"[72] Wittgenstein concludes. And so, "The totality of true thoughts is a picture of the world."[73]

But elsewhere, Wittgenstein says language is all there is.[§2.3.2a] Where does this leave pictures? In one view, they simply correspond with reality. "The picture is a fact."[74] They just show reality in such a way that the form of their showing is unanalyzable. Like facts themselves, they just are. "The picture . . . cannot represent its form of representation; it shows it forth."[75] It is what it is.

This is not a terribly satisfactory theory of picturing. It does not tell us how a picture might be different from reality, or to use our terminology, how object and space transpose into image. It does not tell us how language and pictures relate, or even whether they are in any essential ways different. Are pictures just what one sees in one's mind's eye as you speak – another mere correspondence?

We want to say once again that this view of objects that are logically-propositionally related is a pretty static view of the world of facts and their corresponding representations. Predication, in our terminology, is dynamic, where subjects are to be found begging predicates, and objects begging their use. It is where the one is always ready to transpose into the other. Our patterns of transitivity are not merely indicative (this is how the world is), as a correspondence theory of picturing would have us think. They are transactional.

Then, there is all the stuff of which Wittgenstein enigmatically could not speak and of which, presumably, neither language nor pictures could speak either. But what is in this other realm, and by what means is that conceivable? It certainly includes metaphysics, Wittgenstein says, and it may also have included door handles.[§2.1.1b]

One possibility, if one is inclined to read consistent sense into what Wittgenstein is saying (though why should we, when Frege and Russell could not?), is that he is just leveraging picture as a metaphor, when in the thought of a fact, objects and their logical connections to the world are expressed in one's mind's eye while speaking to oneself. Pictures, then, are just the metaphorical mental seeing that goes with language. Or possibly Wittgenstein "really" means pictures, in which case his theory of picturing has nowhere near the sophistication of Neurath's.

As we are trying to demonstrate in our grammar, pictures do not unproblem-atically show the world. As much as they reflect, they also refract. Picturing has its affordances, and these are different from the affordances of text, or object, or space. Though sharing some of its features across forms of meaning – for instance when visual array meets text in the representation of formal logic in the *Tractatus* – picturing is also different. As much as it opens out meaning

---

[72] Ludwig Wittgenstein, 1922 [1933], *Tractatus Logico-Philosophicus*, London, UK: Routledge, §3.
[73] Ibid., §3.01.   [74] Ibid., §2.141.   [75] Ibid., §2.172.

through its affordances, picturing's same affordances also constrain meaning. We cannot leave the world simply said (the names of facts in the world that Wittgenstein leaves unquestioned) or shown (in his picture theory). We need an account of saying and showing which can explain our ever-shifting forms of meaning, while prioritizing none. This is our theory of transposition, the stuff of human, sensuous activity. Meaning is a transpositional practice.

In 1929, Wittgenstein decided to return to Cambridge. Keynes fetched him at the railway station. "Well, God has arrived. I met him on the 5.15 train."[76] He had been away from Cambridge for sixteen years, and ten years away from philosophy except for the textual revisions for the publication of the *Tractatus* and the ideas he had dictated to Waissmann in Vienna. Officially, still, he was only an advanced student, and this even though he did not yet have a first degree.

He offered the *Tractatus* for examination, this time for the degree of Ph.D. It was examined by Russell and the same philosophy professor, G.E. Moore, who had unsuccessfully tried to have the earlier version submitted for a BA in 1913.[§2.1.1a] After some questions from the examiners, the proceedings were ended by Wittgenstein. He clapped each of the examiners on the shoulder: "Don't worry, I know you'll never understand it."

Moore said in his report, "I myself consider that this is a work of genius; but, even if I am completely mistaken and it is nothing of the sort, it is well above the standard required for the Ph.D. degree." Wittgenstein was appointed a lecturer and fellow of Trinity College.[77] He worked at Cambridge on and off for the rest of his life.

He was not happy there, though. According to friend and colleague Henrik von Wright, "in general he was not fond of English ways of life and he disliked the academic atmosphere of Cambridge."[78] In 1935, Wittgenstein got Keynes to write to the Soviet Ambassador in London, explaining that he was "anxious to find a means of obtaining permission to live more or less permanently in Russia. Dr Wittgenstein, ... a distinguished philosopher, is a very old and intimate friend of mine, and I should be extremely grateful for anything you could do for him ... He is not a member of the Communist Party, but has strong sympathies with the way of life which he believes the new regime in Russia stands for."

Wittgenstein visited Russia later that year, and again in 1939. He was offered a teaching post at Moscow University which he intended to accept, but the offer

---

[76] Ray Monk, 1990, *Ludwig Wittgenstein: The Duty of Genius*, New York, NY: The Free Press, p. 255.
[77] Ibid., pp. 272–73.
[78] Norman Malcolm, 1958, *Ludwig Wittgenstein: A Memoir*, Oxford, UK: Oxford University Press, p. 16.

was later withdrawn as Germans were regarded with increasing suspicion in Russia.[79]

Meanwhile, in Vienna, things were not going well. Wittgenstein accused members of the Vienna Circle of plagiarism, including Rudolf Carnap and Moritz Schlick.[80] Schlick was murdered in 1936 by a Nazi sympathizer, who after ranting in court about the degeneracy of the Vienna Circle spent only two years in jail. The members of the Circle fled Vienna, including Waissmann, who lectured for a time at Cambridge and was interned as an enemy alien. Wittgenstein would forbid his students from attending Waissmann's lectures because he considered these ideas to be his.[81]

After the annexation of Austria by the Nazis in 1938, Wittgenstein, the secular, non-sectarian Austrian citizen, came to be classified as a German Jew. Keynes arranged a permanent university post for Wittgenstein, and a solicitor to secure for him British citizenship.[82]

Meanwhile, Ludwig's siblings faced danger in Vienna. They had three Jewish grandparents. Most of the family's enormous fortune was already in Swiss banks. Ludwig had given all his money to his siblings two decades before. Now a British citizen, he shuttled between Berlin and Vienna to arrange for the money to be transferred to the Nazis, in return for *Mischling* or half-Jewish status for the family so his sisters could stay in Vienna. This needed the consent of the Führer himself, which Hitler gave on the very day in 1939 when the Germans invaded Poland. Of 2,100 such applications, only 12 were granted.[83] Perhaps Hitler remembered his fellow student.

Ludwig's sisters Hermine and Helene, now half Aryans, were able to stay in Vienna through the War. Gretl and her family went to the United States, but returned after the war. The money that had been confiscated by the Nazis was given back to them, and Gretl lived with her entourage of servants in Palais Stonborough[§2.1.1b] until she died in 1958. The house remained empty and unchanged from her death until 1976 when it was purchased from her son by the People's Republic of Bulgaria.

---

[79] John Moran, 1972, "Wittgenstein and Russia," *New Left Review* (I/73):85–96, pp. 88, 91.

[80] Ray Monk, 1990, *Ludwig Wittgenstein: The Duty of Genius*, New York, NY: The Free Press, p. 324; Norman Malcolm, 1958, *Ludwig Wittgenstein: A Memoir*, Oxford, UK: Oxford University Press, pp. 58–59.

[81] Ludwig Wittgenstein and Friedrich Waissmann, 2003, *The Voices of Wittgenstein: The Vienna Circle*, translated by G. Baker, M. Mackert, J. Connolly, and V. Politis, London, UK: Routledge, p. xxi.

[82] Ray Monk, 1990, *Ludwig Wittgenstein: The Duty of Genius*, New York, NY: The Free Press, p. 395.

[83] Ibid., pp. 398–400; Alexander Waugh, 2008, *The House of Wittgenstein: A Family at War*, New York, NY: Doubleday, pp. 250–55.

§2.1.2   Transactivity

Transactivity. *Patterns of agency – action, cause and effect – in the relation of entities in action.*

In his work on transitivity in speech, Halliday has a John opening the door.[84] So does Charles Fillmore in his structural semantics of case.[85] In Palais Stonborough,[§2.1.1b] Ludwig Wittgenstein had his sister Gretl opening the door, and of course over the life of the house and its doors, so did many other people.

For the sake of exemplification we say it was Gretl in this scene – a scene that we will in the general terms of our multimodal grammar call "transactivity," encompassing notions that are in the grammar of speech often named: "transitivity" (transitive, intransitive, and possibly other things); "voice" (active, passive, and possibly other permutations); and "case" (nominative, accusative, and others).

For grammatical ideas that sound so definitive in their naming, these are surprisingly slippery, inextricably interconnected, overlapping, and controversial in their translation into ordinary practice – even when attached to the apparently straightforward practice of opening doors. Some of these features are thought to pertain to verbs (voice and transitivity); and some to nouns (case). But the verbs make no transactive sense without the nouns, and the nouns none without the verbs, hence the essentially clausal nature of meaning in speech.

Or, to put it another way, meanings are not intrinsic to elemental units; they are transpositional. This is why they seem so slippery. This is why we need a theory of the slipperiness, instead of attempting to tie things down into categories and structures.

§2.1.2a   Charles Fillmore on Case

To Gretl Stonborough[§2.1.1b] first, by way of example, then to Charles Fillmore for analysis, and also to M.A.K. Halliday.[§0.3a] (See Fig. 2.1.2a.)

All three fragments of speech in this example – "Gretl opened the door," "the door opened," and "the door was opened" – are "indicative" in their mood. In Wittgenstein's rather unsatisfactory terms, these are the kinds of propositions we ideally use to picture reality. In the *Tractatus*, Wittgenstein does not get

---

[84] M.A.K. Halliday, 1968, "Notes on Transitivity and Theme in English: Part 3," *Journal of Linguistics* 4(2):179–215, pp. 183–84.

[85] Charles J. Fillmore, 1968, "The Case for Case," pp. 1–88 in *Universals in Linguistic Theory*, edited by E. Bach and R.T. Harms, New York, NY: Holt, Rinehart and Winston, pp. 25–27.

	Gretl opened the door	the door opened	the door was opened
Mood	Indicative	Indicative	Indicative
Voice	Active-Operative	"Middle" [Halliday]	Passive-Receptive
Transitivity	Transitive	Intransitive	Transitive
Case	Nominative (Gretl) → Accusative (door)	Nominative (door) [at first glance but "ergative"perhaps]	Nominative (door) [and if an accusative follows, it is omitted by way of ellipsis]

Fig. 2.1.2a: Transactivity

much beyond declarative propositions of fact, and even more narrowly, he prefers for his facticity active and transitive versions of indicative propositions. He does not seem interested to distinguish these kinds of indicative proposition,[§2.1.1d] so neglecting large stretches of the universe of agency that we want to capture under the concept of transactivity.

The first of the three fragments is a proposition that Wittgenstein would readily be able to picture. "**Gretl**," the subject/theme, "opened the door," something we have already called predication.[§2.1.1] The subject of the statement (a noun in the nominative case, the causer of the action and its subsequent impact on another entity) is marked by tonic emphasis – in this transcription, the bolded words. The predicate includes both a verb referencing action and a noun referencing what has been acted upon (the object, with the noun in the accusative case). For its having a "direct object," an explicit accusative, the sentence is taken to be in the active voice.

We are not going to look at the second speech fragment quite yet because it is the most problematic. For the moment, we are going to move to the third of the fragments, the passive voice. We have changed the subject, from Gretl to the door. The door was opened by someone, it seems – Gretl perhaps, and we might be able to assume this from the context of the speaking or the situation. In this case, we could have said, "the door was opened by Gretl," but as it happened, we didn't. There is no direct object, no accusative, and the door mysteriously becomes the agent. Or perhaps there is a mysterious agent behind the agent.

Speech has allowed us to make a statement where we have left something out, meaningfully for the sake of economy where context clearly speaks, or just as meaningfully because we would rather not say. Speech allows us to commit omission, for one reason or another, and the reason is never immediately clear. The omission may be a matter of redundancy within speech (it's a waste of time to say it again because it's already been said, and it may be inelegant to repeat the obvious), or pragmatics (we share the same context, so it should be obvious from that, even if it is not obvious from the speech), or ignorance, or malice. These are all forms of (non-)meaning-by-ellipsis, or omission.

Now we come to the second and most vexing of the three fragments of speech, "the door opened." Here, "open" has become an intransitive verb, or so it seems, in defiance of the seemingly neat grammatical distinction between one kind of verb and another. In the case of transitive verbs, action involving one entity extends to another (Gretl and the door). In the case of intransitive verbs, the action does not extend to another entity. Something just happens. This is what appears to be the situation when "the door opened."

The suggestion is that there is no agent. However, here arises another type of agency, called the ergative,[§2.1.2d] mostly found in speech when a verb can either be transitive or intransitive and the nouns in subject and object share the same case. In fact, this presents a third option. (Halliday calls it "middle," between transitive and intransitive.) Instead of a straightforward actor, action, and goal where the action is represented in a transitive verb, we have a different kind of agency, that of cause and effect, though the causer is omitted by a process of ellipsis in this fragment. However, there must have been a causer. If not Gretl, then perhaps a gust of wind blows the door open, or the way the door was hung on its hinges means that it seems to open itself. This kind of ellipsis is different from the ellipsis that occurs in the passive voice.

So, even these simplest of actions give us trouble in our account of agency. Fillmore focuses his analysis on the grammatical case of the entities: the "ergative" case is neither nominative nor accusative. It is marked overtly in some languages, but not English. Equally troublesome in terms of slippages between cases, Fillmore points out that the ergative case is frequently connected in English to what would at first glance be considered the simplest of verbs, including "break," "connect," "continue," "develop," "increase," and many others.[86]

Halliday, in his analysis, focuses more on the transitivity of verbs than the case of the nouns to which these verbs are connected, where transitive verbs link action and goal, but the ergative links cause to effect.

The operative/receptive forms then contain a second, optional participant whose function might be labelled, for purposes of the discussion, the "causer"; the causer is the subject in the operative and the agent in the receptive, *John* in both *John opened the door* and *the door was opened by John*. The causer is present in the operative/receptive but not in the middle form; in other words, there is an opposition of features middle/non-middle such that the non-middle is interpretable as embodying external causation, the existence of a causer that is not identical with, or at least is treated as discrete from, the affected.[87]

---

[86] Charles J. Fillmore, 1966, "Toward a Modern Theory of Case." Columbus, OH: Ohio State University, pp. 5–7.

[87] M.A.K. Halliday, 1968, "Notes on Transitivity and Theme in English: Part 3," *Journal of Linguistics* 4(2):179–215, pp. 182, 185.

We use the ergative in speech because the cause is unknown, or not wanting to be disclosed, or because the causer is too complex a mix of natural and human causes to bear the immediate trouble of representation. Behind the wind is a window left open by someone, Gretl perhaps? Behind the door that swings open by itself when unlatched is a tradesperson who made it that way, perhaps, or someone who had been working with Ludwig who designed it that way, perhaps? The "perhaps" is the ellipsis.

The ergative refers to cause but buries it, so avoiding having to account for it. But cause nevertheless we know there must be, natural and/or human. Behind every entity is a lineage of action, Alfred North Whitehead would remind us.$^{§1.2.2c}$ To this, we would now add that there must be agency, natural and/or human, whether or not this is disclosed in particular frames of partiality by one pattern of transactivity or another.

Fillmore's solution to the lack of conceptual clarity in conventional grammars of speech is to suggest a radically different configuration of cases. He suggests, in the interim at least, agentive (animate instigator), instrumental (inanimate force), dative (animate being affected), factitive (object affected), locative (place where affected), objective (things affected by an action). And, he says, "additional cases will surely be needed."[88] His conclusion: theories of grammatical case capture the relations of nouns to verbs poorly.[89]

Halliday, for his part, proposes a different system of transitivity where agency is expressed in six clause types: "extensive clause with 'action' process-type; effective clause with 'directed action' process-type; operative clause with 'directed action,' subject as actor; receptive clause with 'directed action,' subject as goal; descriptive clause with 'non-directed action' process-type; intensive clause with 'ascription' process-type."[*] "Transitivity," he says, "is thus being defined in terms of paradigmatic and syntagmatic relations in the clause, not by the classification of verbs as 'transitive' or 'intransitive.'"[90] Nor, we should add, by the grammatical case of nouns – though of course verbs and nouns in speech work together to create these larger, intrinsically relational units of meaning.

Something happened with that door, if we care to trust any of the three fragments we presented in the figure at the beginning of this section. Let's assume the same matter of happening to which each fragment refers. However,

---

[*] http://meaningpatterns.net/halliday-transitivity

[88] Charles J. Fillmore, 1968, "The Case for Case," pp. 1–88 in *Universals in Linguistic Theory*, edited by E. Bach and R.T. Harms, New York, NY: Holt, Rinehart and Winston, pp. 24–25.

[89] Charles J. Fillmore, 1977, "The Case for Case Reopened," *Syntax and Semantics* 8:59–82, pp. 70–71.

[90] M.A.K. Halliday, 1967b, "Notes on Transitivity and Theme in English: Part 1," *Journal of Linguistics* 3(1):37–81, pp. 40, 52.

each configures agency in its own way. Each has its own mode of revelation and occlusion. Such meaning-selectivity Halliday calls "construal." Each, by transposition, could easily slip into the other and still be true to door-ness and opening, meaning the same thing but slightly differently.

Or, to use the language we have been developing for our grammar, between the door opening (itself a design of meaning) and the fragments of speech that are its transposition, there has been a redesign according to the affordances of speech, necessarily limiting meaning. This involves acts of omission of one kind or another, explicable according to the pragmatics of representational economy, or ignorance, or deception. Without multimodal parsing, it is hard to know the reasons for these ellipses, as well as the dynamic possibilities for meaning that have been elided. The meaning is in the immanent elisions, and their imminent revisability.

So we must say in reply to Wittgenstein[§2.1.1a] that there is much more to my meanings than my language, and the limits of the affordances of my language are consciously or unconsciously leveraged for reasons that language itself often does not disclose.

To get beyond these limits of language, Fillmore proposed a "frame semantics."[91] Late in his career, he and several colleagues started to turn their theory of frames into a semantic markup language,[92] expressed in Standard Generalized Markup Language (SGML),[§AS1.4.7d] but the project was left incomplete with the rise of primarily statistical approaches to mechanical language processing.[§AS2.2.1a] Frame semantics was intended to be a program by means of which the limitations of language could be supplemented. Such a project still waits to be addressed in the era of computer-mediated meaning.

Language does not readily confess its unremarked features, because ellipsis is one of its key strategies, pragmatically to avoid ponderous over-explicitness, or as a cover for referential laziness, or as a sign of ignorance, or as a matter of deceit. We need a wider examination of frames of meaning to unveil these (non-) meanings.

A multimodal grammar always needs to move beyond speech to give a fuller account of meaning. Multimodal transposition can fill in the dots of the ellipses that are an intrinsic affordance of speech.

§2.1.2b *Jacques Tati's* Mon Oncle

In his 1958 film *Mon Oncle*, director Jacques Tati plays Monsieur Hurlot, denizen of grubby old Paris. His nephew Gérard lives in an estate of ideal houses,

---

[91] Charles J. Fillmore, 1976, "Frame Semantics and the Nature of Language," *Annals of the New York Academy of Sciences* 280(1):20–32.

[92] Collin F. Baker, Charles J. Fillmore, and John B. Lowe, 1998, "The Berkeley Framenet Project," paper presented at the COLING '98 Proceedings of the 17th International Conference on Computational Linguistics, August 10–14, Montreal.

portending the future. A person rings at the gate, Gérard's mother rushes to the door to press the switch that opens the gate. Her pretentious instinct is to turn on the fish-fountain in the courtyard first, before pressing the switch that opens the door, even though there is no need for the fountain because it is only her husband returning from work – he is the manager of a plastic hose factory.

Gérard's mother had mistaken her husband for a stranger who needed impressing. We laugh at her misconstrual in one moment, and for her "correct" construal in another. The play of interactivity in agency in the routine of house entry works perfectly well when her bourgeois friend arrives. Her earlier misconstrual was in the context of ellipses in meaning.[§2.1.2a]

When the uncle brings Gérard home from school one day, his sister is entertaining the bourgeois friend. The gate-opening routine is one thing, but M. Hurlot takes fright at the fish-fountain, fleeing the house and its modernity.

Today, we might have an intercom or a camera at the door to avoid such mistakes. In this case, the mistake when her husband came home was caused by limitations she experienced in the affordances of space, object, and body. "The door opened" – in speech, we have problems with ellipses in meaning. Gérard's mother had different kinds of problem in the multimodal event of opening her modernist compound.[*]

If we need to know more about something so straightforward – and problematic for the construal of meaning both in speech and space/object/body – if we need to recover further meaning, today we can, and to an unprecedented degree because so much of ordinary life today is incidentally recorded. We live in a future that not even Jacques Tati could have imagined.

Here, for the twenty-first century, is a rough typology of "smart locks": RFID (Radio Frequency Identification) locks trigger door opening from a fob on a keyring; Bluetooth enabled locks allow you to open a door from a phone; biometric entry uses a fingerprint or iris recognition.[93] We always know who is at the door – or whether the person is a stranger – because these locks are linked to definitive instantiations of this door and that person via unique identifiers, such as a GMail address in the case of locks connected to a Google account or the number of a smartphone.

Then, we can supplement this information coming from our doors with indoor navigation, leveraging smart phones and security systems to track and record movements in finely granular detail.[94] Smart cameras can recognize

---

[*] http://meaningpatterns.net/mon-oncle

[93] www.safewise.com/resources/electronic-door-locks-buyers-guide
[94] Davide Carboni, Andrea Manchinu, Valentina Marotto, Andrea Piras, and Alberto Serra, 2015, "Infrastructure-Free Indoor Navigation: A Case Study," *Journal of Location Based Services* 9 (1):33–54. doi: 10.1080/17489725.2015.1027751.

people and follow their movements in real time. Comprehensive real-time transmission of activity is possible, and historical records are stored using Google Home or Apple HomeKit.

Nest IQ is connected with Google:

Nest Cam IQ is a best-in-class indoor security camera with top-of-its-class brains. Get an alert when Nest Cam IQ spots a person. Open the Nest app to follow them as they walk across the room, then grab their attention with the built-in speaker and mic. It's a sharper way to look after home.[95]

In an earlier modernity speech was mostly ephemeral. Writing and drawing were the primary technologies for retaining meanings across time and space. And then there were the necessary and unnecessary but deliberate ellipses in writing. In the twenty-first century everything can be continuously "written," to speak metaphorically of persistent multimodal recording. In the past, we were captive to fallible memories of having seen and the spoken hearsay of witnesses.

Today, in the era of the Internet of Things,[§1.1.1g] multimodal meanings are recorded incidental to experience. The vast bulk of this is quite unnecessarily recorded, only to be recovered from the digital archive with the benefit of hindsight – to trace the identity and actions of an intruder, for instance. The ellipses of speech and the unreliability of memory make speech and memory less significant for our recovery of meaning.

Any of these technologies would have avoided Gérard's mother's error of construal. She was fumbling part way along the journey of modernity, and we can laugh at that.

Jacques Tati's Monsieur Hurlot would have taken even greater fright today – as did KiloSierraAlpha, a web reviewer of Nest Cam IQ:

1984 Camera. Stay creepy Google! There isn't a company I trust less.

§2.1.2c Dyirbal Scrub Hen Song

The Dyirbal people of a place now named North Queensland, Australia, had no doors in need of opening, at least not until sometime after 1863, when the processes of colonial "discovery" and "settlement" began and their lives were forever changed.

But this is to begin the way colonizers have traditionally started their understandings of the colonized, by bewildering absences in the other's meaningful world. We are going to turn this habit of observation and orientation to knowledge around the other way, to look for things that "they" have and that "we"

---

[95] www.youtube.com/watch?v=2C0V9d6HVRo

native speakers in the English-dominated universe of digital modernity do not. This, in order to find out some things about ourselves.

One of these things to be found in the meaning-making practices of Dyirbal people is finely specified, and thus acutely felt, relations of transactivity.

> ŋayi wulŋuru bula bundabunda
> ŋayi dagu bundabunda
> ŋayi wulŋuru bula bagal-ŋa-nyu
> ŋayi wulŋuru dagu bagal-ŋa-nyu

> The two of them can be heard making a big noise
> The scrub hens are making a big noise
> Two birds are making a big noise clapping their wings
> Scrub-hens are making a big noise clapping their wings[96]

Jimmy Murray – his Anglicized name – sang these words at the last corroboree or traditional communal meeting in October 1963.[*] It was nearly two centuries after first contact with the British colonizers, one century after their settlements began in the region, and now the end of a tradition tens of thousands of years old. By the time linguist Robert Dixon recorded the song, there were only about one hundred speakers of Dyirbal. They had managed to retain their language and social practices where other, neighboring peoples had lost theirs, mainly because their country was rainforest, good for them but hard for the colonizer to turn to his modern use.

All the peoples of North Queensland knew at the time that Captain Cook and his crew had been past in their ship in 1770, stopping for seven weeks in the mouth of a river Cook named after his ship, the Endeavour River. They were there to make repairs after the ship had been damaged on coral reefs. But it took the Dyirbal longer to find out that in his moment of "discovery" Cook had also claimed Australia for the British Empire. They found this out with a vengeance after 1864 when the Queensland settlers established a port at a place they called Cardwell. The first sugar plantations appeared soon after, using slave laborers captured in the South Sea Islands.

Neighboring peoples would sometimes walk for four or five days to a corroboree, which could last for up to a week. This was not a society that needed a great deal of time to work for subsistence, perhaps an average of twenty hours per week, leaving a great deal of time for purely "cultural" activity. The Dyirbal people spoke six different dialects, and other peoples attending the corroboree would be speakers of mutually unintelligible languages. Everyone, however, was multilingual.

---

[*] http://meaningpatterns.net/dyirbal

[96] R.M.W. Dixon and Grace Koch, 1996, *Dyirbal Song Poetry: The Oral Literature of an Australian Rainforest People*, Brisbane, Australia: University of Queensland Press, p. 81.

Jimmy Murray's song was one of hundreds in the Dyirbal repertoire. On the page, we have presented it as a poem, and using phonetic and orthographic practices developed by linguists in order to turn first or indigenous peoples' speech into writing. This means that the text presented here is many steps removed from the meaning-reality to which it now refers.

It is also isolated into a single meaning form, text. This never happened – Dyirbal poems were always sung. They were always danced, and by a number of dancers in unison. The dancers were painted in red, yellow, and white clays. They used props to support their performance – feathers, branches, tools, ritual objects. Boomerangs were clapped and skin drums tapped to a constant beat. Deeply synesthetic multimodality was the norm, in contrast with the world of literacy where for half a millennium at least we have artificially struggled to isolate forms of meaning.[97]

In the corroboree, each song/poem/embodied performance references a single image – mating scrub hens about to build their nest, or some other meaningful animal, natural, or human phenomenon. Songs have two or four lines, each "line" has either nine or eleven syllables. In performance, the lines are repeated in complex patterns a dozen or so times. In Jimmy Murray's singing on October 26, 1963, the four lines were performed as follows (numbers reference the four lines; commas are stops for breath; equals signs are where the song stops to repeat): 131, 314, 1313, 1331, 3141= 313, 1141, 4141= 141= 3232= 323, 2323.[98]

Many song-poems are a single clause,[99] which means that a lot of meaning turns on the nuance of its transactivity. When we parse this song-poem, it consists of several clauses elaborating upon a single event from several different perspectives of transactivity. Much is known from shared context. Singers and hearers would know by multimodal transposition into everyday experience that wing clapping happens at nest-building and mating time. Nor is the wider narrative explicit, at least there is no narrative to be found in speech alone. The narrative is deeper and pervasive. It is what surrounds, in the contextualized meanings of totemic animals and places, and in the cosmology of past and present, of people and nature.

A scrub hen may be a living person and a spirit ancestor. The living person is, by transposition, the spirit ancestor incarnate. The meaning of one is the meaning of the other. The singers and the listeners know this in the hearing and the seeing. This is the origin of the universe, where animals are spirit ancestors who created the world in its various aspects. This is law in the form of moral rule and its juridical application. This is personal identity for people so named or associated by totem. This is homage to material life in the bountiful rainforest.

---

[97] Ibid., pp. 3–6, 17–18.   [98] Ibid., pp. 14, 81.   [99] Ibid., pp. 40–41.

The colonizers created a word in English to capture this cosmology – unsatisfactorily – the "dreamtime."[100] With the sense-making resources we have in a modern world of fractured institutions and alienation from nature, it is difficult to capture the deep simultaneity, the integral totality, of these multi-modal transpositions of time, place, person, material life, and cultural practice.

Dixon parses the speech of the scrub hen performance. "The two of them . . ., " it begins. This he points out is, a dual form. Where we in English have two pluralities, singular and plural, Dyirbal has three: singular, dual, and plural. It is also in a grammatical case that we don't notice in English, which he classifies, not as the familiar nominative, but (obscurely in this naming) "absolutive." Then the verb "clapping" uses a grammatical voice which he names "anti-passive," again obscurely.

Dyirbal, like many other languages of first peoples, allows free word order (this is good for poetical meter and rhythm in song), but has a phenomenally extensive system of noun and pronoun case-marking, classificatory prefixing, and verb conjugation.[§AS1.1.3c] This encompasses meaning functions of such subtlety that speakers of modern languages can barely grasp them. The grammatical intricacy of these languages makes them almost impossible for non-native speakers to learn with anything like proficiency, capturing as they do finely calibrated nuances of meaning that have no direct parallels – let alone to comprehend the logics of transactivity that sustain their deepest cosmologies.[101]

§2.1.2d R.M.W. Dixon's Ergativity

Robert Dixon went to the University of Edinburgh in 1961 to study linguistics. M.A.K. Halliday[§0.3a] was teaching there at the time. "After about four months of learning about phonemes and morphemes, I went to Halliday and said that I wanted a language of my own – some interesting and complicated tongue that was in need of study." Dixon had been reading the extensive literature on Native American languages, and the "linguistic relativity" thesis[§AS1.3.1c] which suggests that very different language forms reflect very different ways of thinking and being human.

"No," said Halliday, "leave those to the Americans. What you want is an Australian language."

That language ended up being Dyirbal. Dixon's journey took him from the depths of linguistic theory – attending a debate at MIT in 1962 between two of

---

[100] R.M.W. Dixon, 1980, *The Languages of Australia*, Cambridge, UK: Cambridge University Press, pp. 47–48.
[101] R.M.W. Dixon and Grace Koch, 1996, *Dyirbal Song Poetry: The Oral Literature of an Australian Rainforest People*, Brisbane, Australia: University of Queensland Press, pp. 81–82.

the great linguistic paradigm-setters, Chomsky and Halliday – to the heights of the Australian rainforest in 1963.[*]

Not at MIT, but in the rainforest, he found something perplexing. "When I returned . . . and explained the structure of Dyirbal to M.A.K. Halliday, he told me that these unusual-looking grammatical patterns I had uncovered were 'ergative'." Dixon went on to document Dyirbal in a landmark book,[102] then to write the definitive text on ergativity across a number of languages,[103] then to develop his own comprehensive theory of speech, developing a frame of reference different again from Halliday's and Chomsky's.[104]

Ergativity in Dyirbal, to speak in Dixon's technical terms, is the existence not only of the nominative and accusative cases that are familiar aspects of English transitivity, but ergative and absolutive cases where "the subject of an intransitive clause is treated in the same way as the object of a transitive clause, and different from a transitive subject." In such situations, the ergative marks the transitive subject, contrasting with an absolutive which marks both the intransitive subject and transitive object[105] – the bush hen in the poem/song performed by Jimmy Murray.[§2.1.2c] In such constructions, the parallel to passive voice is called, again obscurely, the "anti-passive" – here, the bush hen clapping its wings.

Meanings of agency are never so carefully and clearly distinguished in English. But Charles Fillmore[§2.1.2a] nevertheless attempts to find them hiding in the opening of doors. In the clauses "the door will open" and "the janitor will open the door," there is a relation between door and open that is the same in both sentences, the first sentence intransitive where the door would seem to be nominative case, and the second intransitive where the door would seem to be in the accusative case. If this parsing is to be revised to capture the shared reality of the door in both sentences, door would need to be another case (absolutive) and janitor also another case (ergative).

These, Fillmore argues, are things that Noam Chomsky[§3.1.2f] neglects because he starts with the grammar of English in order to extrapolate an ostensible universal grammar applicable to all languages. Chomsky's grammar

---

[*] http://meaningpatterns.net/ergativity

[102] R.M.W. Dixon, 1972, *The Dyirbal Language of North Queensland*, Cambridge, UK: Cambridge University Press.
[103] R.M.W. Dixon, 1994, *Ergativity*, Cambridge, UK: Cambridge University Press.
[104] R.M.W. Dixon, 1991, *A New Approach to English Grammar, on Semantic Principles*, Oxford, UK: Oxford University Press; R.M.W. Dixon, 2010a, *Basic Linguistic Theory*, Volume 1: *Methodology*, Oxford, UK: Oxford University Press; R.M.W. Dixon, 2010b, *Basic Linguistic Theory*, Volume 2: *Grammatical Topics*, Oxford, UK: Oxford University Press; R.M.W. Dixon, 2012, *Basic Linguistic Theory*, Volume 3: *Further Grammatical Topics*, Oxford, UK: Oxford University Press.
[105] R.M.W. Dixon, 1994, *Ergativity*, Cambridge, UK: Cambridge University Press, p. 1.

is limited by its starting point. Some of these nuances in agency may be captured by elaboration in preposition phrases ("The janitor will open the door with this key." "This key will open the door.")[106] But prepositions like "with" are notoriously polyvalent, ambiguous, and for these reasons demand a great deal of shared contextual meaning[§AS1] to make sense. Just because English speech does not recognize these nuances of agency in an explicit way does not mean that such agency cannot exist in our experiences and meanings. It's only that English speech doesn't do them very well. We have to rely on multimodal transpositions to make sense, and to mitigate the risk of error in communication and interpretation.

So what do people mean, so carefully and clearly in Dyirbal and other such languages? University of Chicago linguist Michael Silverstein suggests a seven-step hierarchy across case combinations in languages that are both nominative/accusative and ergative/absolutive, ranging from first and second person actors to inanimate things.[107] As for the meaning of the distinction between accusative and ergative, Anna Wierzbicka concludes that differentiating nominative/accusative from ergative/absolutive indicates that the speaker is more acutely aware of his own agency or subjecthood in relation to others. "The ergative encodes the role of someone who is causing things to happen to other people or objects."[108] It distinguishes the incidental agency of immanent effect.

William McGregor comes to parallel conclusions following a study of the phenomenally complex North West Australian language, Gooniyandi.[109] In this language, a distinction is made between accusative patterns in which direct agents and indirectly causing actors behave alike, and differently from undergoers; compared to ergative patterns in which indirect agents and undergoers are classed similarly.[110] This leads him to develop a theory of agency ranging through the most direct forms of agency (such as body moves, vocalizations) to the most indirect or immanent (attribution, existence).[111]

---

[106] Charles J. Fillmore, 1966, "Toward a Modern Theory of Case." Columbus, OH: Ohio State University, pp. 1–7.

[107] Michael Silverstein, 1976, "Hierarchy and Features of Ergativity," pp. 112–71 in *Grammatical Categories in Australian Languages*, edited by R.M.W. Dixon, Canberra, Australia: Australian Institute of Aboriginal Studies.

[108] Anna Wierzbicka, 1981, "Case Marking and Human Nature," *Australian Journal of Linguistics* 1(1):43–80, pp. 50, 76.

[109] William McGregor, 1990, *A Functional Grammar of Gooniyandi*, Amsterdam, NL: John Benjamins.

[110] William B. McGregor, 2009, "Typology of Ergativity," *Language and Linguistics Compass* 3 (1):480–508, p. 481. doi: 10.1111/j.1749-818x.2008.00118.x.

[111] William B. McGregor, 1997, *Semiotic Grammar*, Oxford, UK: Oxford University Press, pp. 110–11.

Fillmore suggests six or more cases.[§2.1.2a] Halliday proposes a taxonomy of transitivity spanning material, behavioral, mental, verbal, relational, and existential processes.[112] Dixon builds out a taxonomy of verbs based on qualitative differences in kinds of agency.[113]

Explicit ergativity, Dixon estimates, occurs in about a quarter of the world's languages: in Europe only in Basque, a rare survivor of the colonization of Eurasia by Indo-European speakers in Neolithic times; in some languages of the Caucasus; but mostly in the languages of first peoples of Australia, Melanesia, and the Americas.[114] Traces of explicit ergativity can also sometimes be found in the archaic progenitors of today's European languages.[115]

Such delicate construals of agency must surely be connected to the forms of life of first peoples. In English, by failing to make these distinctions clearly, we can elide different kinds of power and responsibility, perhaps lazily, perhaps deceptively. Methodologically, this much is clear: when our grammars use words like "subject" and "object," related in a clause via a verb through a highly restricted set of options for voice (active/passive) and transitivity (transitive/intransitive), and when we have so few case and number markers, our tools for making sense are decidedly inadequate. Languages like Dyirbal can show us what we are missing.

Indeed, for these seemingly so-very-ordinary things – opening doors in one cosmology, or the clapping of the bush hens' wings in another – we have in English grammar surprisingly limited tools for analysis.

When the linguists try to get to the bottom of the nuances, Halliday, Chomsky, Dixon, Silverstein, Wierzbicka, and McGregor all come up with systems that are, for what one would think to be such obvious everyday things, surprisingly different. The more elaborated their arguments, the more their theories diverge. Not only this, the more they work over these things, the more they seem to collapse in on themselves with qualifications and complexities. The 387 pages of the first edition of Halliday's grammar became the 786 pages of his fourth.[116] John Searle argues that Chomsky's universal grammar eventually becomes so complex that it implodes upon itself.[117] This speaks to the ultimate failure of structuralist projects that attempt to distinguish components of meaning and order them into essentially static systems. The reality of meaning is the constant movement that we call transposition, where the

[112] M.A.K. Halliday and Christian Matthiessen, 2004, *An Introduction to Functional Grammar*, London, UK: Routledge, p. 65.

[113] R.M.W. Dixon, 1991, *A New Approach to English Grammar, on Semantic Principles*, Oxford, UK: Oxford University Press, pp. 94–204.

[114] R.M.W. Dixon, 1994, *Ergativity*, Cambridge, UK: Cambridge University Press, pp. 2–5.

[115] Eleni Karantzola and Nikolaos Lavidas, 2014, "On the Relation between Labilizations and Neuter Gender: Evidence from the Greek Diachrony," *Linguistics* 52(4):1025–59.

[116] M.A.K. Halliday and Christian M.I.M. Matthiessen, 2014, *Halliday's Introduction to Functional Grammar* (Edn 4), Milton Park, UK: Routledge.

[117] John R. Searle, 2002, "End of the Revolution," *New York Review of Books* 49(3).

patterning occurs across vectors of transposability and the potentially endless range of possibilities these offer.

For all their technical finery, these minutely elaborated structuralist theories fail to engage anyone other than their own technical kind: neither ordinary first peoples nor their everyday colonizers; neither ordinarily living first peoples nor moderns without carefully considered pasts. Worse, they rarely get to the meanings of the differences, and these surely, we all should know.

§2.1.2e Paddy Biran and Jack Murray Sing Destruction of Our Country

We lived in Townsville for a number of years, just down from Dyirbal country, where we created the Institute of Interdisciplinary Studies at James Cook University. In those years, we traveled the vast and beautiful countries of Indigenous Australia in the problematic name of government-funded "literacy research."[118] We also became fellow travelers in Indigenous politics.

Eddie Koiki Mabo had been a gardener on the university grounds, and when our friend and colleague, historian Henry Reynolds, told him that in British colonial law Indigenous peoples had rights as subjects of the Crown, he began a fight for recognition of ownership of his ancestral lands in the Torres Straits. His case went all the way to the High Court of Australia, which he and with him all Indigenous Australians won in a milestone decision of 1992.[119]

By the time the judgment was handed down, Eddie had died. When his gravestone was desecrated in 1995 by racist thugs, with his widow, Bonita Mabo, we organized a rally attended by a thousand people.[*] The Deputy Prime Minister, Brian Howe, flew from Canberra to attend.[120]

A year after the last corroboree, in 1964, Dixon recorded Paddy Biran and Jack Murray singing a newly composed song about the fate of their country, the grammatical intricacy of which is such that it takes Dixon and his Dyirbal co-translators several pages to parse. Created under the full force of modernity, the song is longer than would traditionally have been the case.

In 1963 the Queensland Government granted a pastoral lease to the American-owned King Ranch Pastoral Company, covering vast swathes of Dyirbal country. The company paid $2 per acre for rainforest, $5 per acre for scrubland. A pastoral lease is a compromised form of property title which

---

[*] http://meaningpatterns.net/dyirbal-land

[118] Bill Cope, 1998, "The Language of Forgetting: A Short History of the Word," pp. 192–223 in *Seams of Light: Best Antipodean Essays*, edited by M. Fraser, Sydney, Australia: Allen and Unwin.

[119] High Court of Australia, 1992, "Mabo and Others V Queensland (No. 2)," Vol. 175 CLR 1.

[120] Bill Cope and Mary Kalantzis, 2000b, *A Place in the Sun: Re-Creating the Australian Way of Life*, Sydney, Australia: Harper Collins, pp. 150–53.

begrudgingly recognizes limited indigenous rights. Compromised or not, the company set about clearing the forest with bulldozers and flattening the contours of rock formations with dynamite. Many Dyirbal sacred sites were destroyed. Such was the simple nominative-to-accusative power of the colonizers' transitivity. Or, to shift into the register of our grammar, such is the brutally direct relation of entities to action in colonizing transactivity.

These were places from which, in the Dyirbal people's lived grammar, people's spirits arose, and where they returned upon their death.[121] The person is a timeless spirit, is a place – by way of seamless transposition. This is how the Dyirbal world makes sense.

One such place was called Guymaynginbi.

> *bungi-ŋu gumburru*
> *wudu guymayŋinbi*
> *ban-bu marrgal-bi-ŋu*
> *marrgal-bi-ŋu ban-bu*
> *balŋa-balŋa-bi-ŋu*
> *ŋaygu-rru bulu-nya*
> *bayal-i-ruu naja*
> *ban-bu nyararriŋiny*

> Mist which lies across the country
> A bulldozer nosing into Guymaynginbi
> It becoming just a cleared place
> The place really becoming cleared
> My father's father's country
> I had to sing about it
> That which was my home[122]

§2.2   Role

Role. *Kinds of actor and acted upon – self, other, and thing.*

In the speech of many modern languages, there are three canonical roles for acting and being acted upon, commonly named first, second, and third person. First person is the human self in the singular, in English "I," and self and one or more others conjointly, "we." Second person is the human other, "you," with no

[121] R.M.W. Dixon, 1984, *Searching for Aboriginal Languages: Memoirs of a Field Worker*, Chicago, IL: University of Chicago Press, pp. 70, 80–81.

[122] R.M.W. Dixon and Grace Koch, 1996, *Dyirbal Song Poetry: The Oral Literature of an Australian Rainforest People*, Brisbane, Australia: University of Queensland Press, pp. 220–22.

distinction in English made for singular and plural, and no distinction made between formal and informal forms of address. Third person includes thing, "it," and a distant person marked by gender, "he, she" (one of the few gender markings in English); and in the plural no distinction is made between objects and persons, "they."

This is a vague and inconsistent account of roles in the world, and one that places serious limits on the potential of language-based artificial intelligence,[AS1.4.7d] particularly in English. Beyond pronouns (references to particular or conceptual entities or actions), roles are barely specified in English, except for singular/plural on nouns and third person/non-third on most verb inflections. We have to rely on cross-reference or context outside of language. Other, more highly inflected languages specify roles with greater clarity, and the languages of first peoples particularly.[AS1.1.3c]

For these reasons, we propose an alternative classification into self, other, and thing, able more meaningfully to span forms of meaning. "Self" is quite different in speech than it is in text: the co-present self in speech compared to the distant, reporting self of writing. Here is another substantial difference which separates the grammars of speech and writing.

So too with "other." The co-present other of speech is different from the distant other of writing. We are going to include grammatical third persons within "other," because we can distinguish the other of existence from the other of command in the grammar of conditionality.[2.3] This "other" includes creatures whose sentience the sense-maker recognizes – pets, for instance, or wild animals, or insects.

Finally we have things, insentient "it" and "they," nevertheless capable of acting naturally and being acted upon.

Then we live in a series of transpositions, between the presence and non-presence of actors in different roles (see Fig. 2.2(i)).

When the writer says "I," or the image-maker positions their "I"/eye, they are placing "you" or "they" into the position of "I." The writer or image-maker are meaning that for the moment, you are able to transpose "I" and "you" for the purposes of standing in their metaphorical shoes, to replay the transactivity of their meaning in more-or-less the same terms. Same with "other" – the in-person "you" is transposed into the distant "them." And for things, there is

	Immediate presence	Presence transposed across time and place
Self	The in-person, meaning and acting "I" or "we"	Representation of distant meaning or acting "I" or "we"
Other	The in-person addressee, "you"	Representation of the distant "he"/"she"/"they"/ "you" (="one")
Thing	Inanimate present object, "it," "they"	Inanimate /abstract distant object; scenes

Fig. 2.2(i): Roles over time and place

a grammatical difference between the tangible, seeable, present thing and its distant representation.

Typically in theories of semantics and semiotics, the distancing character-istic of transposition across time and place[§AS1.3] is taken to be a process of symbolization, of standing for. This, for these theories, captures the essence of characteristically human communication. Our theory is flat: there is no differ-ence in the symbolic depth of meaning between present and non-present mean-ings. There is no distinction between meanings-in and meanings-of. We simply have transpositions across a plane of meaning, in this case, role transpositions – same role in different forms of meaning on one axis of transposition, and different roles transposing into each other on the functional axis. In form, for instance, a spoken role can be supplemented by embodied presence. Or a meaning in person can become a meaning at a distance. On the functional axis, a meaning that was an "I" in person can become a transposed, replayed meaning for "you" or "them" in text or image.

Here, we encounter some important differences in the affordances of forms of meaning. The radical differences between the grammars of speech and text come into view once again. The in-person "I" of speech is typically present. The at-a-distance "I" of writing demands a transposition of agency into "you" or "them" in the replay of meaning. In these senses, text is more like image than speech. In image, the embodied act of sight (the seeing "I"/eye), an image demands a transposition of agency into "you" and "them" as the viewer takes the position of the image-maker. The reader and the viewer are required to assume the position of the writer and artist.

Form / Function: Role	Text	Image	Space	Object	Body	Sound	Speech
Self	First person text (distant)	I look; I see through another's "I"/eye	I see and move in space	I sense a thing	I gesture; I see my own gesture	I hear	First person speech (present)
Other	Second person and third person text (distant)	To see you or them looking; I see another looking at another	To see you seeing and moving in space	To sense you sensing a thing	To gesture "you" or "her, him, them;" you gesture to position "me," "he," "she," or "they"	To notice you hearing	Second and third person speech (present or distant)
Thing	Third person text (distant)	To see a thing	To see things in space, and moving in space	A thing exists	Gesturing to inanimate "it" or "they."	To notice something making or reacting to sound	Third person (present or distant)

Fig. 2.2(ii): Roles

§2.2a   Four Marys

"Alone of all her sex"[123] she was, Mary mother of Christ, the sole virgin mother, impossible except for God. So she was declared to be by the Council of Ephesus in 431, not mere Χριστοτόκος or "Christ-bearer," because that would be to diminish the divinity of Christ, but Θεοτόκος or "God-Bearer." "Therefore, because the holy virgin bore in the flesh God who was united hypostatically with the flesh, we call her the mother of God."[124] Though not a substantial figure in the gospels, from this time Mary became on object of holy adoration in her own right, a centrally placed holy "she" in a theological narrative otherwise dominated by men.

A sequence of four images spanning nearly a thousand years of Mary-worship speaks to the evolution of ways of seeing the mother of Christ and, with her, the imaged world.

Perhaps the earliest extant icon of Mary is from the sixth century, found in Saint Catherine's Monastery in the Sinai Desert, Egypt.* She is depicted sitting on a throne, looking somewhat obliquely past the viewer, who must nevertheless be at least peripherally in her field of vision. On either side, a saint looks out directly to the viewer. Behind her, two angels, one on either side of the picture, look up in awe. We can only see the hand of God reaching down to Mary. The angels must be able to see more. Mary, the saints, and the Christ child sit on the same plane. Some shading of the face reveals a limited three-dimensionality. The angels stand behind on a second plane, looking slightly forward while looking up, leading the viewer to think that the hand of God is above Mary. The only evidence of a second plane is the fact that the angels' bodies are partly covered by the saints in the front row with Mary.

Next, Cimabue's *Santa Trinita Madonna* of about 1290.[125] Mary is again on a throne holding the Christ child, this time slightly forward of her, eight angels surrounding but layered behind each other on multiple planes. Three-dimensionality is marked by an architectural frame, with Jewish prophets in alcoves below. Jeremiah and Isaiah look up in anticipation of the coming of the Messiah. Notwithstanding a move in the direction of more realistic, multi-dimensional representation, Mary and the prophets we know are not of the same time, and she is scaled larger than the other persons in the image. Her face is still styled in the elongated fashion of Byzantine icons. Her body has no

---

* http://meaningpatterns.net/four-marys

[123] Marina Warner, 1976, *Alone of All Her Sex: The Myth and Cult of the Virgin Mary*, New York, NY: Alfred A. Knopf.
[124] Norman P. Tanner, ed., 1990, *Decrees of the Ecumenical Councils*, Volume 1: *Nicea I to Lateran V*, London, UK: Sheed and Ward, p. 58.
[125] Eugenio Battisti, 1963, *Cimabue*, Milan, Italy: Institutio Editoriale Italiano.

notably human shape. The folds in the fabric of her clothes are uniform lines. The angels look obliquely into abstract space.

Giotto di Bondone was a student of Cimabue's, and by the time he painted *Ognissanti Madonna* in about 1310, a change had come in ways of seeing. Mary is still surrounded by saints and angels. The gold filigree background abstracts the image into some heavenly location in the tradition of iconography. Mary remains unnaturally over-scaled. But her face is more realistically human. The fabric of her clothing has fine gradations of light and dark. The profile of breasts can be seen and the shape of her body is now womanlier, and the alcove in which she sits on her throne is defined by perspective as a three-dimensional space. The angels look to Mary in adoration, suggesting that the viewer should too. Renaissance art and architecture theorist Lorenzo Ghiberti[§2.2b] writes about this painting in the next century, noting its pivotal place in the evolution of linear perspective.[126] So does art historian Vasari in the century after that, also using the image to exemplify progress towards the realism of the greats, Leonardo and Michelangelo.[127] Dante says, "Once Cimabue was thought to hold the field/In painting; now it is Giotto's turn/The other's fame lies buried in the dust."[128]

Now to our fourth Mary, Sandro Botticelli's *Madonna of the Book* of about 1482.[129] Mother and child sit in a corner of an ordinary room. She reads the *Book of Hours*, a book of prayers widely available in the Middle Ages. The infant looks up at his mother as she reads, and there is nothing particularly holy in such a gesture. An unknown book sits at an angle on the shelf where it casually happens to have been left, beside a nondescript wooden box. The shelves recede into the corner of the room. A bowl of fruit sits on top of some other books lying on the table. Behind Mary, a window, and beyond, a horizon of trees meets a sky at twilight. The gratuitously everyday detail, the linear perspective, the visual realism of light and shadow, the consistent scaling, the absence of saints and angels, all point to a new way of seeing. Though elements of the old supernaturalism remain: the gold filigree halos, the child holding three gold nails of the cross and wearing the crown of thorns as a bracelet – these refer to a later part of the Christ child's life only knowable by the viewer. This is how we know that the "she" of the image is the singularly holy Mary.

[126] Richard Krautheimer, 1956, *Lorenzo Ghiberti*, Princeton, NJ: Princeton University Press.
[127] Giorgio Vasari, 1550 [1969], *Lives of the Most Eminent Painters, Sculptors, and Architects*, translated by G.D.C. de Vere, New York, NY: The Modern Library.
[128] Quoted by Norman Bryson, 1983, *Vision and Painting: The Logic of the Gaze*, New Haven, CT: Yale University Press, p. 2.
[129] Lionello Venturi, 1937, *Sandro Botticelli*, Oxford, UK: Oxford University Press; Sandra Legouix, 1987; *Botticelli*, London, UK: Bloomsbury; Timothy Verdon, 2005, *Mary in Western Art*, Manchester, VT: Hudson Hills, pp. 131–35.

§2.2b   Leon Battista Alberti's Commentaries

While the painters were transforming their visual practices, three Florentine thinkers were developing a new theory of seeing – goldsmith and sculptor Lorenzo Ghiberti (1378–1455), architect Filippo Brunelleschi (1337–1446), and priest, architect, artist, and thinker Leon Battista Alberti (1404–1472).

Ghiberti is known for the gilded bronze doors he designed and made in his goldsmith's shop for the *Battistero di San Giovanni* in Florence,[*] depicting in relief Old Testament scenes (1425–1452).[130] On the doors, Ghiberti sized persons according to their distance from the front of the scene. He used architectural settings as a visual framework for three-dimensionality, placing biblical personages against the receding colonnades of buildings and streetscapes that reduce into the distance. For their visual brilliance, Michelangelo called these doors *The Gates of Paradise*. Ghilberti theorized his art and the art of others in his *Commentarii*. Of the baptistery doors he said, "I strove to observe every measure of proportion, seeking the closest possible imitation of nature ... The figures are relieved against the planes so that the nearer figures appear larger than those further out, just as they are in reality."[131]

Brunelleschi was an architect, designer of the dome of the Duomo in Florence, constructed between 1447 and 1461. The drawings are now lost, but his 1425 demonstration of linear perspective outside the Florence Baptistery is the stuff of legend. According to the West's self-understanding of its history of imaging, this was the founding moment of realism as technique. Using a canvas with a peephole and a mirror, he showed the diminishing size of the walls of the building the more distant they became. The central point in a hypothetical distance was the "vanishing point," a centering line of sight oriented to the horizon. The relative sizes of seen objects could be figured mathematically.[132] Concluded his fellow architect and biographer, Antonio Manetti, this was a crucial contribution to the science of perspective, "setting down properly and rationally the reductions and enlargements of near and distant objects as perceived by the eye."[133]

---

[*]   http://meaningpatterns.net/linear-perspective

[130]   Richard Krautheimer, 1956, *Lorenzo Ghiberti*, Princeton, NJ: Princeton University Press.

[131]   Lorenzo Ghiberti, c.1447 [1948], *The Commentaries*, London, UK: Courtald Institute of Art, pp. 24–25; Hans Belting, 2008 [2011], *Florence and Baghdad: Renaissance Art and Arab Science*, translated by D.L. Schneider, Cambridge, MA: Harvard University Press, pp. 150–54.

[132]   Giulio Carlo Argan, 1946, "The Architecture of Brunelleschi and the Origins of Perspective Theory in the Fifteenth Century," *Journal of the Warburg and Courtauld Institutes* 9:96–121; Brian Rotman, 1987, *Signifying Nothing: The Semiotics of Zero*, Stanford, CA: Stanford University Press, pp. 14–22; Erwin Panofsky, 1924 [1997], *Perspective as Symbolic Form*, translated by C.S. Wood, New York, NY: Zone Books, pp. 63–64.

[133]   Hans Belting, 2008 [2011], *Florence and Baghdad: Renaissance Art and Arab Science*, translated by D.L. Schneider, Cambridge, MA: Harvard University Press, p. 165; Antonio di

Another architect, Alberti, was the first to theorize the new art and science of imaging in his *De Pictura* of 1435. Imagine a series of visual rays running from the eye to the objects it sees, he says. "Among these visual rays there is one which is called the centric." This ray points in the direction of what we know to be the vanishing point of linear perspective. Surrounding this ray, a "visual pyramid" can be conceived, around which objects are arranged "in a definite place in respect to the observer." Then, to draw, "I inscribe a quadrangle of right angles . . . which is considered an open window through which I see what I want to paint." Now, the act of visualization has been moved away from the eye to an intermediate plane, "a thin veil, finely woven, with larger threads [marking out] as many parallels as you prefer. This veil I place between the eye and the thing seen, so the visual pyramid penetrates through the thinness of the veil. This veil . . . always presents to you the same unchanged plane. Where you have placed certain limits, you quickly find the true cuspid of the pyramid."

The result is both naturalism and supernaturalism. Naturalism: "the studious painter will know from nature, and he will . . . be wide awake with his eyes and mind in this investigation and work . . . discovering and learning beauty." And still, supernaturalism: "Painting contains a divine force which not only makes absent men present, [and] the dead seem almost alive . . . [P]ainting is most useful to that piety which joins us to the gods and keeps our souls full of religion."[134]

§2.2c   *Erwin Panofsky's* Perspective as Symbolic Form

To transpose three-dimensional spaces, objects, and bodies onto a two-dimensional plane – this is one of the moves that we need to trace in a grammar of multimodality. Linear perspective, it would seem, is an act of realism, a mathematical/scientific discovery of the early modern West: to reference things accurately in image in such a way that the image truthfully captures the empirical world for the way it in fact looks.[135]

No, says Erwin Panofsky, this is a "symbolic form," a peculiarly Western way of seeing and thus thinking that was invented by artists and theorists of optics in the European Renaissance.[136] No, says Norman Bryson too, this is

Tuccio Manetti, 1497 [1970], *The Life of Brunelleschi*, translated by C. Enggass, University Park, PA: Pennsylvania State University Press.

[134] Leon Battista Alberti, 1435 [1956], *On Painting*, translated by J.R. Spencer, New Haven, CT: Yale University Press, pp. 46, 47, 51, 56, 68–69, 92, 63; Michael Baxandall, 1988, *Painting and Experience in Fifteenth Century Italy*, Oxford, UK: Oxford University Press.

[135] Mark Jarzombek, 1990, "The Structural Problematic of Leon Battista Alberti's 'De Pictura'," *Renaissance Studies* 4(3):273–86.

[136] Erwin Panofsky, 1924 [1997], *Perspective as Symbolic Form*, translated by C.S. Wood, New York, NY: Zone Books.

a characteristically Western form of "the gaze," an historically and culturally specific way of seeing, a mode of symbolic representation, as distinct from intrinsic being-in-the-world.[137]

We want to frame the human artifice that underlies naturalism in somewhat different terms. We do not want to offer a different or privileged place for symbolization, a term commonly used to classify what may be considered as second-order, abstracting, cognitively constructed systems and practices of representation such as writing and imaging.[§AS1.1.3a] In such a conventional view, our primary engagements in and with space, object, and body are viscerally experiential and in this sense non-symbolic. Symbols reference these experiential meanings, as well as systematically referencing each other. Symbols in this view are meanings-of, as distinct from meanings-in.

Instead, we want to argue that meaning by image or text is of the same order as meaning by object and space and body. No distinction should be made between meanings-of and meanings-in. We don't want to distinguish what might be considered symbolic from non-symbolic meaning. Besides, of symbols, Marshall McLuhan famously said, "the medium is the message";[138] meaning-in is meaning-of. Conversely, spaces, objects, and bodies are just as able as text and image to "stand for" singular or generalizable meanings, if that's what we take symbolization to mean. Again, meaning-in is meaning-of.

So, if we dethrone symbolization from its privileged place, what we experience in the meaning practices of multimodality is a series of transpositions between forms of meaning, shunting backwards and forwards, meaning taking one form then another, each form with its own affordances. We are always shunting because the affordances of each form not only offer new opportunities to mean; their forms also circumscribe those meanings. This is why we constantly find a need to call upon multimodal supplementation.

To address now the affordances of image, is linear perspective true to reality? Is it a "correct" representation of the spatial, object-filled, and embodied world as seeable and seen? This is what it suggests of itself, and though in some ways it is true to its promise, it is also more, and less. It is a method of transposing three-dimensional space, object, and body into two-dimensional image, and in the process a fundamental transformation of form. Here are some of the differences.

Linear perspective is the line of sight of a single eye, but we are binocular creatures. Since stereoscopic photographs, we have known that a three-dimensionality can be captured more than linear perspective on a single plane allows. Then there is the fact that our field of vision is spherical, so straight lines

---

[137] Norman Bryson, 1983, *Vision and Painting: The Logic of the Gaze*, New Haven, CT: Yale University Press.

[138] Marshall McLuhan, 1964 [2001], *Understanding Media: The Extensions of Man*, London, UK: Routledge.

curve, but linear perspective corrects this because we "know" that things like walls, windows, and doors should be straight.[139] It is horizontally oriented, and it is not until the era of tall buildings* that a vertical axis of scaling is added and parallels on the vertical axis are abandoned.[140]

As for the objectivity of the image, this is only deceptively the case, because we are by fiat of the artist's selection placed where they want us to be, most of the time conventionally at the height of an adult person, looking towards an horizon. We see through the picturer and for the picturer what they have chosen us to see. What seems to be an objective representation is in fact a deeply intersubjective transposition of the artist's eye with the viewer's.[141] The body is central – the body of the artist and the body of the viewer; but the body itself has disappeared in the seeing. This produces an in-body experience that is also weirdly out-of-body.

Or rather, we are led to believe that the body is central in viewing the picture (and centrally invisible), for even this is an optical illusion. As Alberti so insightfully points out, the image is not in the place of the eye of the artist or the viewer. Rather it is created on a visual plane between the artist and the world, and between the viewer and the world the viewer is seeing through the work of the artist. This plane is literally framed, edges defined to include chosen spaces, bodies, and objects and exclude absent others. It is composed, with pictured things arranged across a series of layers receding to a vanishing point on the horizon.[142]

For all the apparent anthropomorphism in viewing positions, the image itself is not located at the point of the eye, but on a plane placed between the eye of the artist or viewer, and the scene they are "seeing." Alberti's veil metaphor[§2.2b] is a nice one, because the image plane conceals as much as it reveals. Feigned naturalism conceals artifice. Ostensible objectivity conceals the subjectivities of the representing artist and the interpreting viewer; viewing occurs not at the eye but an intervening plane removed from the eye. Deeply architected, this plane is more like a window than an eye, based perhaps in habits of mind that became ubiquitous after the invention of glass window panes.

And another difference: the image is constituted both in its carefully considered making and in its at least half-careful viewing. This is "the gaze,"

---

* http://meaningpatterns.net/realism

[139] Erwin Panofsky, 1924 [1997], *Perspective as Symbolic Form*, translated by C.S. Wood, New York, NY: Zone Books, pp. 32–33.
[140] Rod Bantjes, 2014, "'Vertical Perspective Does Not Exist': The Scandal of Converging Verticals and the Final Crisis of Perspectiva Artificialis," *Journal of the History of Ideas* 75 (2):307–38.
[141] Norman Bryson, 1983, *Vision and Painting: The Logic of the Gaze*, New Haven, CT: Yale University Press, pp. 102–12.
[142] Gordana Korolija Fontana Giusti, 1999. "The Cutting Surface: On Perspective as a Section, Its Relationship to Writing, and Its Role in Understanding Space," *AA Files* (40):56–64; James A.W. Heffernan, 1996, "Alberti on Apelles: Word and Image in 'De Pictura'," *International Journal of the Classical Tradition* 2(3):345–59.

sustained looking that configures in systematic arrangement what is seen by artist or viewer. Gaze is quite different from seeing, which is a series of glances or "saccades," as the eye jumps across three-dimensional spaces, objects, and bodies. When seeing images that have transposed three-dimensional things into a two-dimensional plane, the eye jumps from the most prominent things and the vanishing point to which it is directed, to less prominent and peripheral things. The image is fundamentally different from seeing, and seeing an image is fundamentally different from seeing the world. The image ties a hypothetical, all-seeing eye to a fixed point, while in viewing reality the eye constantly darts around, every which way.

Apparent naturalism also achieves its effects by lighting scenes artificially. How could Botticelli's *Madonna*[§2.2a] be so perfectly lit? More likely in ordinary experience, mother and child would be dark figures against the natural light coming through the window, and if not, the outside world would be overexposed. Our eyes adjust for differences in the intensity of light within a scene – this is another aspect of three-dimensional seeing, something that cannot happen in two-dimensional seeing.

And the presence of gratuitous detail: the book leaning at an angle on the shelf and the fruit bowl are unnecessary to picturing of virgin and son, except that their irrelevance speaks to the realism of the scene. They are things you might see and wonder about only upon careful looking. Might they symbolize something? Perhaps, but not as obviously as the sacred meaning of Madonna and child. We see the book and the bowl in a kind of peripheral vision. There, they speak more to realism of the focal bodies than any intrinsic meaning in these things.

Finally, of style: in their regularized artificiality, Byzantine icons[§2.2a] show manifest style, a consistently applied lack of realism that distinguishes them as holy reference. Chinese landscape paintings, with their stylized brushstrokes and unrealistic arrangement of trees and peaks, speak to the presence of the artist and their work with the medium.[143] Realism attempts to hide its style, to speak truth to the visual powers of nature – and, as Alberti said, God as well, if He is nature's meaning.

By these means, the three-dimensional world is distanced through an optical illusion, though the distance is by the artifice of image removed, transposed onto a two-dimensional plane where there is in fact no distance. This is how the world of depth is made virtual, and the virtual is a story that can only seem to be true. The world is laid out here to see on the image plane, but what it is showing is not there.

---

[143] Norman Bryson, 1983, *Vision and Painting: The Logic of the Gaze*, New Haven, CT: Yale University Press, pp. 89–92.

Realism is in these ways a technique of illusion, a series of tricks and tropes for the transposition of three-dimensional meanings to two. Its picturing, notwithstanding its disavowal of style, is itself a style, and more. It is a series of *trompe l'oeil*, manipulations, deceptions even, by means of which you are led to think the real has been represented. As it has, but also not.

§2.2.1   Self

> *Self.* The agent of representation, the communicator, the interpreter, the actor and the acted upon from their own, embodied perspective.

In the first three of our Mary images,[§2.2a] the eye/I of Mary looks out at you and the world, and you look back at her, in need of her blessing. We see her looking at us. Or more to the point, we assume the position of the image-maker seeing her looking at them, for them in the first instance, and then us, as the image-maker seems to suggest. Mary the "I"/eye has two "you"s, the "you" of the artist, and the "you" who that artist has positioned in her proposed line of sight.

In the fourth image,[§2.2a] we are onlookers. We are merely vicarious partici-pants. We may notice in the seeing of each other by mother and child an intimacy between their two selves. But they do not look at us. It is as if we are an other that does not exist. They don't beckon us to look. They are a distanced "she" and "he."

On our two axes of transposition, form and function, this is what we now have: the self can be transposed from the forms of meaning that are body/space/object (the seen, the artist, the viewer), into image (by way of transposition from three dimensions to two), into speech (the "I" of the immediate speaker), to text (the "I" removed in time and space).

As for meaning functions, the "I" of the self is ever ready to be transposed as another's "you" or "s/he." Every "you" or "s/he" is always waiting to be figured as another's "I." The meaningful self is only ever temporary, fleeting.

§2.2.1a Al-Hasan ibn al-Haytham's Book of Optics

We know that Lorenzo Ghiberti[§2.2b] had read in translation Alhacen's great work on the science of optics,[144] because he summarized it at length in the *Commentarii*.

---

[144] A. Mark Smith, 2001a, "The Latin Source of the Fourteenth-Century Italian Translation of Alhacen's 'De Aspectibus'," *Arabic Sciences and Philosophy* 11(1):27–43.

Born in Basra in 965, Al-Hasan ibn al-Haytham, or Alhacen as Ghilberti and his Florentine contemporaries called him, came to Cairo in 1021 to work in the court of the Caliph. A mathematician, logician, and scientist whose genius was widely known, his task was to design a way to control the flow of the Nile. When this proved impossible, several biographers report, he was imprisoned, feigned madness, and on release lived the rest of his life in the spartan conditions of a tent in the grounds of the Azhar mosque. There, he wrote and tutored.

Among Alhacen's many books were works on logic, metaphysics, and theology, but he is best known for his *Kitāb al-Manāẓir* or *Book of Optics*[*] – over 200,000 laboriously expounded words, completed in about 1030.[145] In 1200, it was translated into Latin as *De Aspectibus* and the author's name Latinized to Alhacen, then translated into Italian in the fourteenth century. Ghiberti had read the Italian edition.[146]

Alberti's centric ray Alhacen had already identified as the central ray in a "cone of vision." Credited by some to be the inventor of the *camera obscura*, a box with a pinhole at one end in which an inverted image is projected at the other, Alhacen conducted a series of experiments proving the physical existence of light. He showed that it traveled in straight lines along pathways, and that it follows a geometrical course when reflected or refracted. This was a radical reversal of the ancient Western idea that the eyes emitted visual rays and these were the source of our seeing. In Alhacen's theory, eyes are a site of reception rather than emission.[147] However, he added that "vision is not achieved by pure sensation alone, that it is accomplished only by means of discernment and prior knowledge."[148]

---

[*] http://meaningpatterns.net/alhacen

[145] Al-Hasan ibn al-Haytham, *c.*1030 [1983], *Kitāb Al-Manāẓir, Books I–II–III, "on Direct Vision"*, Kuwait: National Council for Culture, Arts and Letters.

[146] Al-Hasan ibn al-Haytham, *c.*1030 [1989], *The Optics of Ibn Al-Haytham, Books I–II–III, "on Direct Vision"*, Volume 2: *Introduction, Commentary, Glossary, Concordance, Indices*, translated by A.I. Sabra, London, UK: The Warburg Institute, pp. xix–xxiv; A. Mark Smith, 2001b; *Alhacen's Theory of Visual Perception: A Critical Edition, with English Translation and Commentary, of the First Three Books of Alhacen's De Aspectibus, the Medieval Latin Version of Ibn Al-Haytham's Kitāb Al-Manāẓir*, Volume 91, Philadelphia, PA: American Philosophical Society, pp. ix–xvi, cvii; Jim Al-Khalili, 2015, "Book of Optics," *Nature* 518:164–65.

[147] David G. Lindberg, 1976, *Theories of Vision from Al-Kindi to Kepler*, Chicago, IL: University of Chicago Press, pp. 61–66.

[148] Al-Hasan ibn al-Haytham, *c.*1030 [1989], *The Optics of Ibn Al-Haytham, Books I–II–III, "on Direct Vision"*, Volume 2: *Introduction, Commentary, Glossary, Concordance, Indices*, translated by A.I. Sabra, London, UK: The Warburg Institute, pp. liv–lv; Abdelhamid I Sabra, 2003, "Ibn Al-Haytham's Revolutionary Project of Optics: The Achievement and Obstacles," pp. 85–118 in *The Enterprise of Science in Islam: New Perspectives*, edited by J.P. Hogendijk and A.I. Sabra, Cambridge, MA: MIT Press, p. 91.

Alhacen made several major methodological innovations, extending and transforming the theories of optics of the Greeks, principally those of Galen and Ptolemy. He was the first to offer an image or picture-oriented theory of vision based on mathematical principles, and to achieve this by combining experimental methods of empirical observation with geometry and mathematics. He was also the first to propose a sophisticated psychology of vision, where what is seen is as much a cognitive matter as one of empirical sensation, requiring, in addition to vision itself, inference and interpretation.

The ancient visual ray theory had placed the viewer as an unmediated agent in seeing – this was a seemingly straightforward way to explain the eye's capacity to detect distance. What Alhacen proposed aligns more closely with modern theories of vision. For him the properties of things were at play in the detection of distance: the size of the object, the angle of its edges in the visual field, and its distance. But these mathematically determinable variables in vision were not enough. In addition to the light the eye sees, he says that an interpretation of the meanings of objects and distances must be based on learned experiences of things and spaces.

So Alhacen's theory is at once objectivist, at least compared to the anthropocentrism of the visual ray theory, and subjectivist, where the viewer is positioned as an interpreter who makes meaning by adding meaning to what they see.

It was not just the centric ray that the fourteenth-century Florentine image theorists took from Alhacen. It was also this dialectic of objectivism and subjectivism: an outside world that acts in ways which are apprehensible (objects, spaces, light), and the reciprocal relation of our making sense of that world in a culture of imaging.§2.2c

§2.2.1b Islam's Imaging

Notwithstanding these profound and direct lines of influence, the cultures of imaging in classical Islam and Renaissance Catholicism were poles apart. While Western Catholic and Eastern Orthodox Christians profusely represented the personages of their faith in icons – Mary and others – Islam forbad the representation not only of sacralized persons, but any people or animals at all.

The Qur'an itself has nothing to say about images, other than to condemn idolatry in the form of statuary when the statue itself was made an object of worship.[149] This was the same injunction condemning pagan polytheism that

---

[149] Oleg Grabar, 1975, "Islam and Iconoclasm," pp. 45–52 in *Iconoclasm: Papers Given at the Ninth Spring Symposium of Byzantine Studies, University of Birmingham, March 1975*, edited by A. Bryer and J. Herrin, Birmingham, UK: Centre for Byzantine Studies, University of Birmingham, p. 54.

was to be found elsewhere in the Abrahamic tradition. "Thou shalt not make unto thee any graven image, or any likeness of any thing that is in heaven above, or that is in the earth beneath, or that is in the water under the earth. Thou shalt not bow down thyself to them, nor serve them: for I the Lord thy God am a jealous God."[150]

None of the Abrahamic religions have adhered strictly and consistently to the letter of this law; all have adhered partially. Christians have been sharply divided about statuary and imagery. Jews adhere more closely, rarely representing in image persons from their holy narrative.

Islam's stricter-than-usual visual code arises from the post-Qur'an texts of the Hadith, a record of oral tradition written in the first centuries of the new religion. In the Hadith, to make images of persons or animals with breath is deemed a sin, and to look at such images is also a sin. Imaging raised the danger that the artist or viewer may consider the images to be in some senses real, to counterfeit life whose only source can be God. Images are a forgery of God's creation. They are an attempt to escape time, to transcend mortality, and this is God's prerogative alone. In their vision of sentient life, images deign to displace God as the source of life. For these reasons, they are a blasphemy; they are forbidden transpositions. The severest application of this injunction in recent times was the Taliban regime in Afghanistan which banned photography for five years in the 1990s and in 2001 dynamited the two enormous Buddhas of Bamiyan, carved into a stone cliff-face nearly fifteen hundred years before.[*]

From an Islamic perspective, not only Buddhism and Hinduism, but other Abrahamic monotheisms look like regressions into polytheism, which surely in some senses they are – Catholic and Eastern Orthodox Christianity, for instance, with their images and statues of God incarnate in Christ and the pantheon of prophets, apostles, and saints. The rise of Mary worship after 431 is perhaps one of the clearest examples of this.[§2.2a]

When Alberti[§2.2b] comes to justify the achievement of realism in linear perspective, he recognizes the same qualities in naturalistic imaging as Islam, except in his theology he will attribute divinity to the very processes that Hadith condemn as apostasy. It must be God who is working through artists and viewers transposing past and distant persons into holy presence.

Of course, it is complicated because some of the story is never pictured in Christianity – at most, God is a hand, but never more.[§2.2a] And Islamic imagery routinely portrays other marvels of God's creation, the twisting tendrils of plants in decorative arts for instance. So Islamic imagery is not strictly speaking

---

[*] http://meaningpatterns.net/islam-imaging

[150] *Exodus* 20: 4–5. King James Version.

iconophobic, iconoclastic, or aniconic[151] – words that are all used at various times to describe religiously orthodox imaging practices in Islam. Nor is Islam non-representational in the senses we define in this grammar, because the Qur'an, the Hadith, and classical Islamic poetry vividly reference in text the Prophet's and others' experiences, both earthly-human and holy.[152] And in Arabic calligraphy, this text is stunningly, alluringly visual – a textual iconography.

So, in Islamic art we are left with beautiful abstractions, marking the absence of things that in the post-Florentine world have been credited as realism, naturalism, mimesis, and verisimilitude. Imaging is all concept and no instance.

And if, following Peirce and Deacon,[153] the abstraction of the arbitrary sign is a higher cognitive form than iconic or indexical representation (a proposition with which we must disagree$^{§AS1.1.3a}$), then Islamic culture strives to a higher level than the "realism" of iconography.

If not anti-iconic or non-representational, then we may perhaps interpret what is distinctive about Islamic visual practice as its particular way of framing the self. This self is not just human, but also applies to the selves of sentient creatures granted animacy equivalent to humans because they breathe. Instead of the "anti-" or "non-" of European realism, now we may see this reaction to Islam to be a peculiar construction. We can interpret Islamic traditions of imaging as a mode of positioning of the self which, incidental to a view of the human and divine, is uninterested in realistic imaging. This is the case for all cultures in human history before modernity – including Anmatyerre$^{§0.0a}$ – until the strange sleight of hand that is the invention of realism and its underlying techniques of linear perspective.

It is a nice irony that the Western invention of the technology of realistic imaging was inspired by Arabic optical science – though Alhacen himself figured the science purely in the abstractions of light, and the geometry of reflection and refraction.[154] What the Florentine Renaissance takes from Islamic science is the mathematics of light in space and the dialectical psychology of subjective self as see-er in relation to externalized space/object/other,

[151] Oleg Grabar, 1975, "Islam and Iconoclasm," pp. 45–52 in *Iconoclasm: Papers Given at the Ninth Spring Symposium of Byzantine Studies, University of Birmingham, March 1975*, edited by A. Bryer and J. Herrin, Birmingham, UK: Centre for Byzantine Studies, University of Birmingham, p. 51; Marshall G.S. Hodgson 1964, "Islâm and Image," *History of Religions* 3 (2):220–60, p. 221.

[152] Marshall G.S. Hodgson 1964, "Islâm and Image," *History of Religions* 3(2):220–60, pp. 240–42.

[153] Terrence W. Deacon, 1997, *The Symbolic Species: The Co-Evolution of Language and the Brain*, New York, NY: W.W. Norton.

[154] Hans Belting, 2008 [2011], *Florence and Baghdad: Renaissance Art and Arab Science*, translated by D.L. Schneider, Cambridge, MA: Harvard University Press, pp. 1–11.

objectified in its counter-position against the subject. Meaning is a dialectic of conceptually separated subject–object antinomies.

The difference between Islam and Florence is in the positioning and trans-position of self and other, human and divine, where absence is powerful presence – not unlike the naming taboos affecting reference to certain relatives and the dead in the speech of first peoples,[§AS1.1.3c] or the presence of the womanly body under the Islamic veil. These are transpositions of self and other which simultaneously amount to pointed affirmations, representational denials that exaggerate always-imminent transposability.

Here we also encounter the problematic notion of the icon,[§AS1.0b] or a non-arbitrary meaning that stands for something else, contrasted with an arbitrary meaning (such as a word of text) which means something only by convention. Objects and images can have arbitrary meanings (a wedding ring, for instance), and text non-arbitrary (onomatopoeia, for instance[§3d]).

Besides, the form of a representation, no matter how "literal" it seems at first glance, can never exhaust its meaning – let alone its interpretation, which will be even more polymorphous. So this distinction between the iconic and the anti-/aniconic is never so clear. There are just differences in the cultures of transposition from object, body, and space to text or images, where some affordances are favored, others unused or unnoticed, still others proscribed.

The Christian tradition has also had its moments of iconoclasm, where images are literally smashed for their apostasy. The Orthodox Christian Empire of Byzantium banned images between 726 and 843, also on the rationale that image worship was a form of idolatry.[155] There seem to be no direct connections, only a generalized zeitgeist of monotheism, for this was at the same time as the rise and spread of Islam.[156] Protestantism later rejects religious imagery in favor of the purely textual Word of God, inciting on this principle the wholesale destruction of statues, icons, and stained glass windows in England and parts of protestant Europe in the seventeenth century.[157]

In more recent times, aficionados of the modern have developed other aversions to realism, as if to renege on modernity's own invention. Modern movements in art from impressionism, to cubism, to abstract expressionism, scorn the apparent simple-mindedness of realism. With no further pretense to visual objectivity, these art forms return the manifest hand and eye of the artist. They make style and medium shockingly visible in order to express emotional

---

[155] Cyril Mango, 1975, "Historical Introduction," pp. 1–6 in *Iconoclasm: Papers Given at the Ninth Spring Symposium of Byzantine Studies, University of Birmingham, March 1975*, edited by A. Bryer and J. Herrin, Birmingham, UK: Centre for Byzantine Studies, University of Birmingham.

[156] Oleg Grabar, 1975, "Islam and Iconoclasm," pp. 45–52 in ibid., pp. 45–46.

[157] Christopher Hill, 1972, *The World Turned Upside Down: Radical Ideas During the English Revolution*, London, UK: Temple Smith; Christopher Hill, 1993, *The English Bible and the Seventeenth Century Revolution*, London, UK: Penguin.

abstractions. Such renditions of the modern consign to kitsch countless re-renderings of Mary by the Catholic faithful, and with equal disdain the heroic worker in the realism of the socialist faithful.

In digital modernity, moreover, there are still large areas of absent images, or at least images that are hidden for some because they are forbidden for others. Nakedness and sex acts are a case in point, ubiquitous in embodied experience, but whose images are proscribed. A largely walled-off shadow internet exists for pornography, away from "mainstream" search and social media.

Here is Facebook, drawing a visual line between what can happen in embodied experience and what can be represented: "We remove photographs of people displaying genitals or focusing in on fully exposed buttocks. We also restrict some images of female breasts if they include the nipple ... Explicit images of sexual intercourse are prohibited."[158] We can have these things in ordinary embodied experience, we can even mention them politely in speech or text, but we can't image them.

§2.2.2   Other

***Other.** A person represented as non-self, the "you" of present address, or the "them" of address that is distanced by time and space.*

We are going to use "other" to refer to an addressable other, a person or a creature (such as a dog, a horse) able to be meaningfully addressed. Close by, we may speak of "you." At a distance, we may speak of "them" or an inanimate "it."

§2.2.2a *John Berger's* Understanding the Photograph

Realistic painting and linear perspective[§2.2b] anticipated photography in the "camera obscura" method of transferring light from a scene onto a screen in order to calculate relative sizes and positions that would represent depth two-dimensionally. The innovations of Nicéphore Niépce, Louis Daguerre, and Henry Fox Talbot in the 1820s and 1830s apply chemistry to the surface of the screen in order to record and preserve an image beyond its moment. The chemistry of the photograph, says Roland Barthes, means that "the photograph is literally an emanation of the referent."[159] But the invention of the underlying

---

[158] www.facebook.com/communitystandards#nudity
[159] Roland Barthes, 1980 [2010], *Camera Lucinda: Reflections on Photography*, translated by R. Howard, New York, NY: Hill and Wang, p. 80.

mechanics and culture of perspective-based visualization was Alberti's, or before that, Alhacen's camera obscura.[§2.2.1a]

To transpose a three-dimensional world of bodies, objects, and spaces onto a two-dimensional plane, the affordances of photography are in some fundamental respects the same as realistic painting; in other, finely nuanced respects, they are quite different.[§2.2.2a]

The things that are the same first: the camera is just as one-eyed as the painter, compared to the three-dimensional world as seen in binocular vision. Occasionally, stereoscopic images are created with two-lens cameras and binocular viewers, but these are exceptions rather than the rule. The camera also conventionally transposes self and other at standing head height, with a vanishing point at the horizon, though in the era of planes, spacecraft and drones, we have also learned to see images in variations of plan perspective.

Lenses correct for "barrel distortion," or the curved appearances of things like buildings that we know are straight even if we don't really see them as straight – or some lenses do, while others, such as "fish eye" lenses, see a spherical world that is closer to vision, though photographs taken with these tend to offend our conventional expectation of the image. In photography also, as in painting, we try to balance the intensity of reflected light that in three-dimensional reality has more contrast – by getting the sun behind us, or using artificial lighting or a flash.

Then there is the frame: the conventionally square or rectangular edges which establish a plane for the image ahead of where the eye would be, an out-of-body abstraction. A frame is like a window, standing away from the viewer, restricting their field of vision. The literal frame of the painting is taken metaphorically into photography, where it becomes an act of meaning: framing.

And like painting, photography freezes event into a moment, in which entities are manifest but action needs to be inferred, what is happening in time. The moment of the image can implicate possible action before and after, and no more than that. Entities are visible; action demands more effort on the part of the viewer.

"Images," says Vilém Flusser, "are not 'denotative' (unambiguous) complexes of symbols (like numbers for example) but 'connotative' (ambiguous) complexes of symbols: They provide space for interpretation."[160] Most in need of interpretation in a still photograph is action over time.

A photograph is "a moment taken from a continuum," says John Berger. "What it shows invokes what is not shown."[161] In vision of the pictured scene, moreover, there would have been glances in dynamic time, tracing action as

---

[160] Vilém Flusser, 1983 [2000], *Towards a Philosophy of Photography*, London, UK: Reaktion Books, p. 8.

[161] John Berger, 1967 [2013], *Understanding the Photograph*, London, UK: Penguin, p. 20.

much as entity. But in both painted and photographed image we gaze into a moment that has been frozen in time, and our saccades of glancing methodically compose space at the expense of time. Flusser again: "While wandering over the surface of an image, one's gaze takes in one element after another and produces temporal relationships between them."[162]

Then there are the same transpositions in photography as realistic painting – both artist and photographer feign disappearance in the interest of naturalism. But we also know that they have put us in the picture. Our selves are their other. Their other we make our selves. "The camera never lies," we say wryly, because we know it always does. Such is the culture of modernity: feigned objectivism, hidden subjectivism, and manipulative transposition of self and other.

§2.2.2b *Susan Sontag's* On Photography

Photography is also different from realistic painting. (The role transpositions in cinema and video are very different again from both painting and photograph, because they capture movement in time, albeit still from the eye of the camera and on principles of linear perspective.)

"Painting," says Susan Sontag, "was handicapped from the start by being a fine art, with each object a unique, handmade original. A further liability was . . . the exceptional technical virtuosity" required then, no longer required with photography.[163] Photography mechanizes realistic imaging, so making it accessible to the masses. There is no need to use grids to calculate relative size and position because the lens calculates relative size in an image to render the effect of depth.

The non-technical multitude have just a few things to learn: focus, aperture, shutter speed, and framing. Or even less in mass market cameras from the Box Brownie of 1900 to the Instamatic of 1963 that offered fixed focus, just one shutter speed, and few if any aperture options. "You press the button, we do the rest," promised the Eastman Kodak company in its advertisements for the Box Brownie. "Just point and shoot," they said of the Instamatic. With digital cameras, all you have to do now is frame.

Realistic painting by comparison requires premeditation and methodical attention to the effects of perspective and detail. Details add realism – the bowl and the books casually leaning at an angle on the shelf in Botticelli's *Madonna of the Book*.[§2.2a] Every such gratuitous detail the painter must have meant to be there because he put it there. Realism is a conscious device. But in

---

[162] Vilém Flusser, 1983 [2000], *Towards a Philosophy of Photography*, London, UK: Reaktion Books, pp. 8–9.
[163] Susan Sontag, 1977, *On Photography*, New York, NY: Farrar, Strauss and Giroux, p. 47.

the case of details in a photograph, we don't know whether they are there accidentally, having been un-noticed by the photographer, or noticed to be there and included in the frame by design.

Also, although time is sliced into frozen moments both by painting and photography, the photographic moment passes in the instant that is imaged; the painter's image is slow to compose. A photograph is made in the instant that it freezes. Its start is its end. Painting happens in a longer timeframe, and the disjunction between the start and the end if its making affords space for premeditation and imagination.

Photography slices time and vision less methodically, in the impulsive moment of a shutter release. This is a different kind of agency on the part of the I-eye. It is an "art of chance."[164] It is more open to accident, with a greater unnoticed surplus, and so more open to re-interpretation both by image maker and viewer, recovering things that were in the first instance unnoticed.

Sontag: "Unlike the fine-art objects of pre-democratic eras, photographs don't seem deeply beholden to the intentions of an artist. Rather, they owe their existence to a loose cooperation (quasi-magical, quasi-accidental) between photographer and subject – mediated by an ever-simpler and more automated machine, which is tireless, and which even when capricious can produce a result that is interesting and never entirely wrong."[165]

Sontag again: "Photographed images do not seem to be statements about the world so much as pieces of it, miniatures of reality that anyone can create." For these reasons, "a photograph . . . seems to have more innocent, and therefore more accurate relation to visible reality than do other mimetic objects . . . To photograph is to appropriate the thing photographed. It means putting oneself into a certain relation to the world that feels like knowledge."

This process of transposition (to insert our term) is far from innocent. The printed word, by comparison, "seems a less treacherous form of leaching out the world, of turning it into a mental object, than photographic images, which now provide most of the knowledge people have of the look of the past and the reach of the present."[166]

Photography becomes a pervasive part of a disingenuous dialectic of objectivism and subjectivism that is new to modernity itself, transposing self, other, and object – the eye of the photographer with the eye of the viewer, the object or other with its representation fixed in time and two-dimensional image plane.

These practices of sense-making now pervade a whole series of genres and transformative social practices of memorializing.

---

[164] Robin Kelsey, 2015, *Photography and the Art of Chance*, Cambridge, MA: Harvard University Press.
[165] Susan Sontag, 1977, *On Photography*, New York, NY: Farrar, Strauss and Giroux, pp. 48–49.
[166] Ibid., pp. 3, 5, 3.

Family photographs: "Photography becomes a rite of family life just when, in the industrializing countries of Europe and America, the very institution of the family starts undergoing radical surgery. As that claustrophobic unit, the nuclear family, was being carved out of a much larger family aggregate, photography came along to memorialize, to restate symbolically, the imperiled continuity and vanishing extendedness of family life. Those ghostly traces, photographs, supply the token presence of dispersed relatives."[167]

Tourism: "Photographs will offer indisputable evidence that the trip was made, that the program was carried out, that the fun was had. Photographs document sequences of consumption carried on outside the view of family, friends, neighbors."[168]

§2.2.2c Félix Nadar's When I was a Photographer

The photographer can vicariously take others to places they would not normally venture, communicating spaces, objects, and bodies outside of ordinary experience, offering a proxy experience of viewing as if another of their selves could have been there, at least retrospectively, at least two-dimensionally.

Pioneering photographer Félix Nadar[*] shot his photographs of the Paris sewers between 1861 and 1864, an underground system created during the nineteenth-century modernization of Paris commanded by Baron Haussmann for Emperor Napoleon III.[169] Above ground, great avenues cut their way through old neighborhoods. Below ground, sewers engineered by Eugène Belgrand efficiently removed liquid detritus from the now hygiene-proud city.[170]

Before then, says Walter Benjamin, recording a quote from Victor Hugo, the people of Paris referred to the sewers, which also doubled as catacombs and ossuaries for remains of the dead, as the "Stink-Hole," the "fetid arches. Nothing equaled the horror of this old voiding crypt, . . . cavern, grave, titanic molehill, in which the mind seems to see prowling through the shadow . . . that enormous blind mole, the past."[171]

Benjamin's Convolute Y,[§0b] collated for his great unfinished work on Paris in the nineteenth century, was on photography. Here he quotes from Nadar's book,

---

[*] http://meaningpatterns.net/nadar

[167] Ibid., p. 8.   [168] Ibid., p. 8.
[169] Félix Nadar, 1900 [2015], *When I Was a Photographer*, translated by E. Cadava and L. Theodoratou, Cambridge, MA: MIT Press, pp. 75–96.
[170] Shao-Chien Tseng, 2014, "Nadar's Photography of Subterranean Paris: Mapping the Urban Body," *History of Photography* 38(3):233–54, p. 247.
[171] Walter Benjamin, 1999, *The Arcades Project*, translated by H. Eidland and K. McLaughlin, Cambridge, MA: Harvard University Press, p. 412.

When I was a Photographer, and his "splendid description of his photographic work" in the sewers.

With each new camera setup, we had to test our exposure time empirically; certain of the plates were found to require up to eighteen minutes ... I had judged it advisable to animate some of these scenes by the use of a human figure – less from considerations of picturesqueness than in order to give a sense of scale, a precaution too often neglected by explorers of this medium and sometimes with disconcerting consequences. For these eighteen minutes of exposure time, I found it difficult to obtain from a human being the absolute, inorganic immobility I required. I tried to get around this difficulty by means of mannequins, which I dressed in workman's clothes and positioned in the scene with as little awkwardness as possible.[172]

Nadar sent Belgrand twenty-three of his photographs, and Belgrand immediately ordered a second set.[173]

"For the first time," says Benjamin of Nadar's sewers, "discoveries were demanded of the lens."[174] The use of mannequins by Nadar is telling. His photographs required people, not only in order to offer scale and perspective, but for the essential anthropomorphism of the photographer's program. This was a space into which the viewer was unlikely ever to venture. Its others, the object of the viewing self, were the anonymous worker, keeping the sewers operational, and the absent engineer Belgrand whose design was the ultimate source of animation in the scene. The mannequin not only underlines the anonymity of a worker, the fact that there was no need that their image be personified; they also indicate the conditions of othering that are the nature of photography. "The absolute, inorganic immobility ... required" by Nadar was a function of time exposure; in regular light, the effect is created in the fraction of a second of the open shutter.

Hence the transpositions from self to other: Nadar's I/eye becomes I/eye of the view constrained by the two-dimensional, of-an-instant, entity-at-the-expense-of-action biased eye/I of the viewer. Nadar's I/eye transposes by admiration the vision of the famous engineer. Nadar's mannequin prompts appreciation for the workman who keeps the sewers working; I the viewer could have been that other, though I am not, and I know not his identity. Self to other, these are not simple polarities, they are positions where the one is ever able to have been the other. They are vectors of transposability.

Then there are things: the tunnels, the machines, the unhygienic waste water. These are not simply objectivized "it." They are self- and other-like,

---

[172] Ibid., pp. 673–74.
[173] Adam Begley, 2017, *The Great Nadar: The Man Behind the Camera*, New York, NY: Tim Duggin Books, p. 133.
[174] Walter Benjamin, 1939 [1999], "Paris, Capital of the Nineteenth Century," pp. 14–26 in *The Arcades Project*, edited by H. Eidland and K. McLaughlin, Cambridge, MA: Harvard University Press, p. 6.

metaphorical arteries and veins that clear the urban body. But more literally, more directly, these things are in an intimate relation to their personhood, whether that be an I or they, a self or other.

The tunnels' having-been-designed prompts us to credit M. Belgrand, Baron Haussmann, and Emperor Napoleon III. Their having-been-built prompts us to credit anonymous underground tunnel builders. Their operation prompts us to acknowledge the workers referenced as mannequins in Nadar's photographs. The miasmic flow of waste prompts us to acknowledge the people defecating, urinating, flushing, and washing their bodies. We also recognize the social concept, others in the plural and the general. The sewer is a social precondition for healthy life, a gift of modernity, a promise that the consequences of our elemental bodily functions will be managed for us systemically, remotely, while demanding minimal agency on the part of our selves.

This is how we gain insight into impossible spaces, objects, and bodies, how we see into the practically unseeable. (The sewers of Paris are not totally unseeable. Today, there is a museum of the Paris sewers in a sewer itself that can be entered from a service stair beside the Seine. To insist on the technical marvels of treatment and hygiene, waste water flows past the displays.)

In the same way, medical imaging allows us to see into our own selves, creating views that are impossible without surgery or mortal danger to the patient. When the x-ray or the MRI image is presented to us, it seems that we have become other, and our bodies made thing-like. Which indeed we have by fiat of photograph, at once and at the same time our body as self, other, and thing.

"Technological reproduction," Benjamin tells us of reproducible images, "can place the copy of the original in situations which the original itself cannot attain. Above all, it enables the original to meet the recipient half way."[175]

Microscopes and telescopes, and the images taken for the epistemic record by the experts who are able to use them, tell us things we could never otherwise have known or seen. Things inaccessible to visible experience become mundanely real to us. They mean empirical things that would not have been possible without the affordances of the photographic image. They transpose self, other, and thing in fantastic and previously impossible ways.

---

[175] Walter Benjamin, 1936 [2008], "The Work of Art in the Age of Its Technological Reproducibility," pp. 19–55 in *The Work of Art in the Age of Its Technological Reproducibility and Other Writings on Media*, edited by M.W. Jennings, B. Doherty and T.Y. Levin, Cambridge, MA: Harvard University Press, p. 21.

§2.2.3   Thing

> **Thing.** *An object without sentience, but which may nevertheless act by force of nature or circumstance of event; or which may act because a person has caused it to act.*

Things and images of things like the Paris sewers[§2.2.2c] only exist in a relation to human agency. Things are equally able to act, and act on their own. In fact, they can be depended upon to act – sewage will flow down a gentle incline. Things can also act on our selves. The smell of the sewer has a thingish effect on us. These are a few of many self–other–thing transpositions we may want to note in a sewer.

We make meaning, not by isolating each role as a singular canonical meaning; rather, the meaning is in the processes of swapping out, where the one role is always ready and able to stand for another. The meaning of the roles is in their integral transposability.

Sewers are not just things – objects and spaces – they stand for human agency in the interplay of selves and others with things. Photographs[§2.2.2a] do not just picture things; they capture things always in relation to persons in their selfhood or otherhood. Photographs do not just picture persons; they are representations of people alienated as objects.

Photography has a bias towards things. But this comes at a price; that price is agency. Entities are clearly placed but their trajectories and destinies require interpretation. Vectors provide clues, as did the rail line in Turner's *Rain, Steam and Speed*,[§2a] but we don't know for sure whether the train may for some reason have stopped. Persons are objectified because their living, moving, transitory bodies are taken from them by the image and frozen in their physicality at a moment in time. Then there are all the other manipulations that the photography imposes on the viewer by restricting their field of vision. Affordances constrain meaning, image-makers manipulating others as they transpose themselves into the putative position of the viewer.

§2.2.3a   Eadweard Muybridge's Images of Movement

As much as they constrain, the affordances of meaning forms also create new opportunities for meaning.

In the 1880s, Eadweard Muybridge took in rapid succession a celebrated series of frozen frame photos of a man running and a horse galloping,[*] offering insights into

---

[*]   http://meaningpatterns.net/muybridge

movements that pass too quickly to be noticed in embodied reality.[176] The observational gaze froze an entity into one moment in time, so offering new perspectives on the relationship between entity/body and action/movement. (This also suggested that the images might be played back at the same speed at which they were taken, and Muybridge may be credited as an inventor of cinema.)

So, what to make of the meaning of photographic meaning, its revelations as well as its occlusions? Here are two theories of the photograph, utterly opposed but both true. First, Kaja Silverman: "Photography ... shows us that there really is a world, that it wants to be seen by us, and that it exceeds our capacity to know it." She quotes Walt Whitman from *Leaves of Grass*: "A vast similitude interlocks all/ All spheres, grown, ungrown, small, large, suns, moons, planets, ... / All distances of place however wide,/ All distances of time, all inanimate forms ... "[177] Photography suggests verisimilitude. It records light and space in one place, and presents its findings in another. Like text, it transports meaning across time and space. A photograph's meanings are intelligible for their recognizability from similarities in the experience of the viewer, and informative for their unsettling, disruptive dissimilarities.

"Photography," Silverman goes on to say, undermines Descartes' notion of the *cogito*, which placed man the meaning-maker at the relational center of the universe. There are photographers and viewers of photographs, for sure, but photography is also a medium through which the world presents itself to us, "demonstrating that it exists ... an ontological calling card."[178] Photography shatters any illusion that the meaning self is the center of the world. Rather, photography transposes the meaning self with others – the other of the photographer, and the others in the image who could well be, or have been, self.

Now a second theory, of Jean Baudrillard, railing against "this confusion, this diabolical seduction of images. Above all, it is the reference principle of images ..., this strategy by means of which they always appear to refer to a real world, to real objects, and to reproduce something which is logically and chronologically anterior to themselves. None of this is true." Images tell tales; they deceive; they manipulate. Photographers are guilty and viewers are innocently led astray by this "telescoping of images into reality," this "collusion between images and life."[179]

---

[176] Rebecca Solnit, 2003a, *Motion Studies: Eadweard Muybridge and the Technological Wild West*, London, UK: Bloomsbury; Rebecca Solnit, 2003b, *River of Shadows: Eadweard Muybridge and the Technological Wild West*, New York, NY: Viking; Philip Brookman, 2010, *Helios: Eedweard Muybridge in a Time of Change*, Göttingen, Germany: Steidl/ Corcoran Gallery of Art; Brian Clegg, 2007, "The Man Who Stopped Time," Washington, DC: National Academies Press.

[177] Kaja Silverman, 2015, *The Miracle of Analogy, or the History of Photography, Part 1*, Stanford, CA: Stanford University Press, p. 11.

[178] Ibid., pp. 10–11, 1.

[179] Jean Baudrillard, 1984, *The Evil Demon of Images*, translated by P. Patton and P. Foss, Sydney, Australia: Power Institute Publications, pp. 13, 25–26.

Both theories capture the affordances of images, their contradictory truths. Benjamin: "No matter how artful the photographer, no matter how carefully posed his subject ... the beholder feels an irresistible urge to search ... a picture of the tiny spark of contingency ... to find the inconspicuous spot where in the immediacy of that long-forgotten moment in the future nest so eloquently that we, looking back, may rediscover it."[180]

So, we encounter two truths in complicated play, the truths of recorded reality (spaces, bodies, objects), and the truths of always-transposing agency between self, other, and thing.

§2.3   Conditionality

> *Conditionality. Modulations in relationships of agency between selves, others, and things according to the qualities of these relationships: assertion, requirement, or possibility.*

Then, there are different kinds of agency, connecting selves, others, and things. In grammars of text, these are called mood: indicative (entities acting in roles that have been, are, and will be); imperative (actions that must happen); and subjunctive (actions that might happen). In a language like English where there is minimal inflection, conditionality in text is marked by auxiliaries such as "is," "has," "can," "may," "might," "will," "ought," "could," "would," and "should."

Grammarians and semantic theorists have come up with systems of conditionality that, for such ordinary aspects of human meaning, are alarmingly at variance with each other.[181] In the latest version of Halliday's system, mood has become impossibly complex,[*] so complex in fact that the analysis inadvertently shows that exceedingly complex is still not complex enough.[182]

Jennifer Coates comes up with a diagram listing modal auxiliaries on one side, classifying their underlying semantics on the other: obligation, inference, possibility, ability, permission, volition, prediction, hypothesis, quasi-subjective. The arrows linking the deceptively simple words crisscross the diagram in bewildering confusion. After running her computer across a corpus of 545,000 words of English text, justifiably she concludes

---

[*] http://meaningpatterns.net/conditionality

[180] Walter Benjamin, 1931 [1999], "Little History of Photography," pp. 507–30 in *Walter Benjamin: Selected Writings,* Volume 2: *1927–1934,* edited by M.W. Jennings, H. Eiland, and G. Smith, Cambridge, MA: Harvard University Press, p. 510.

[181] John Lyons, 1977, *Semantics,* Volume 2, Cambridge, UK: Cambridge University Press, p. 792.

[182] M.A.K. Halliday and Christian M.I.M. Matthiessen, 2014, *Halliday's Introduction to Functional Grammar* (Edn 4), Milton Park, UK: Routledge, p. 162.

that "the 'untidiness' of the data has involved a recognition of indeterminacy."[183]

In our transpositional grammar, we are going to distinguish three general forms of conditionality in agency: assertion, requirement, and possibility. These are not neatly separated buckets, because the one kind of meaning is always ready to slide into the other. We're more interested in transposability across a vector of conditionality than finding points that can be fixed, no matter how finely specified.

Form〱 Function:〱 Conditionality	Text	Image	Space	Object	Body	Sound	Speech
Assertion	Indicative	Array of entities	Presence in space	Existence of an object	Presence in person	Sounds telling of presence	Presence in speech or that spoken of
Requirement	Imperative	Inference about essential action	Directions for movement or stasis	Necessary ways to use an object	Directive gestures	Alerts	Speech act (e.g. commanding, expecting)
Possibility	Subjunctive	Inference about potential actions and entities	Openings allowing movement	Usability of an object	Potential embodied actions	Anticipation in sound sequences	Modality expressed in tone, intonation

Fig. 2.3: Conditionality

Fig. 2.3 presents a rough map of conditionality across the forms of meaning we have been describing in this book.

Take an object, for instance a tool. It exists in its presence, composition and structure (assertion). The tool has an immanent action structure that requires its user to interact with it in particular ways (requirement). And it opens out potentials for use that are both open to variety and constrained by the tool's affordances (possibility). When sentient creatures encounter and use objects in their lives – ants collecting and carrying food back to a nest, for instance – they have at their disposal the same range of immanent meanings.

A problem that arises here for a text-based theory of conditionality is the ambiguity of its most basic terms. "May" can mean both permission to act (in relation to a requirement) and empirical hypothesis (possibility). "Must" can mean both command (requirement) and certain consequence (assertion). The semantics of conditionality does not clearly map onto text. Semanticists tackle this problem by distinguishing epistemic from deontic conditionality, or reference to the conditions of knowing compared to the conditions of acting.[184] But

---

[183] Jennifer Coates, 1983, *The Semantics of Modal Auxiliaries*, London, UK: Croom Helm, pp. 5, 3.

[184] John Lyons, 1977, *Semantics*, Volume 2, Cambridge, UK: Cambridge University Press, pp. 791, 841–42.

this distinction is not so clear: to act is to know, and knowing is grounded in action.

Then there are interrogatives and negatives that push meanings in a different semantic direction than the unqualified auxiliary. "Must you?" pushes the requirement "must" in the direction of possibility. "Can not" pushes the possibility "can" in the direction of requirement. These cut across assertion, requirement, and possibility, not just turning conditionalities into questions or negatives of the same kind, but changing their kind.

If these distinctions are so very unclear in text, it means that in order to make sense of conditionality we have to rely on things other than words. We have no alternative but to resort to multimodality, where text is in integral relation to meanings in image, space, object, body, sound, or speech. And on the dimension of functional transposition, instead of trying to subclassify fine gradations of conditionality, we can look for movement across and between the larger differences between assertion, requirement, and possibility.

§2.3a   Isaac Newton's Opticks

"My Design in this Book is not to explain the Properties of Light by Hypotheses," says Isaac Newton[§1.3.1c] in the opening sentence of his *Opticks*, "but to propose and prove them by Reason and Experiments."[185] White light, he proceeds to show, is composed of a range of spectral hues, and all colors are formed in combinations of these hues.[*]

In his own terms, Newton makes two kinds of move, the one empirical, the other theoretical. Here is the empirical move in Experiment 9, Book 1:

The Sun shining into a dark Chamber through a little round hole in the Window-shut, and his Light being there refracted by a Prism to cast his coloured image in PT [in Fig. 5] upon the opposite Wall: I held a white Paper V to that Image in such a manner that it might be illuminated by the coloured light reflected from thence ... And I found that when it was equally or almost distant from all the Colours, so that it might be equally illuminated by them all it appeared white.[186]

And now, here is his other move, Reason:

For it has been proved ... that the changes of Colours made by Refractions do not arise from any new Modifications of the Rays impress'd by those Refractions, and by the various

---

[*] http://meaningpatterns.net/newton-science

[185] Isaac Newton, 1730 [1952], *Opticks, or a Treatise of the Reflections, Refractions, Inflections and the Colours of Light*, New York, NY: Dover Publications, p. 1; Charles Bazerman, 1988, *Shaping Written Knowledge: The Genre and Activity of the Experimental Article in Science*, Madison, WI: University of Wisconsin Press, pp. 119–27.
[186] Isaac Newton, 1730 [1952], *Opticks, or a Treatise of the Reflections, Refractions, Inflections and the Colours of Light*, New York, NY: Dover Publications, p. 117.

Terminations of Light and Shadow ... It has been shewed also, that as the Sun's Light is mix'd of all sorts of Rays, so its whiteness is a mixture of the Colours of all sorts of Rays ... [I]t may be concluded, that the white Colour of all refracted Light at its very first Emergence, where it appears as white as before its Incidences is compounded of various Colours.[187]

In the terminology we are proposing in this grammar, these are both assertions. They are statements of scientific fact in the form of observed evidence on the one hand, and generalizable, theoretical proposition on the other.

Generalizable proposition is an epistemological marker of modern science. In the history of Western science, Newton is one of the founders of a way of framing conditionality that in this grammar we call assertion. Indeed, on the scale of conditionality, to assert is to state a certain kind of definitive, ostensibly objective (un)conditionality. This is one of the ways Newton does this in his text: to assert with objective effect, he turns actions and processes into abstract things: not "colours change" but "changes of Colours;" not "light refracts" but light's "Refractions;" not "light terminates" but "Terminations of Light;" not "colours mix" but a "Mixture of Colours;" not "white emerges" but white light's "Emergence."

M.A.K. Halliday calls this process "nominalization," and the replacement of verb with noun he calls "grammatical metaphor," where one grammatical form (a verb) is substituted by another (a noun). In each case, the verb Halliday considers to be the congruent meaning; the noun is the metaphorical substitution.[188]

This is how, to use J.R. Martin's nice turn of phrase, by framing "life as a noun," science "arrests the universe."[189] This way to "construe experience" becomes one of the characteristic textual moves of science, or what Halliday calls "a general drift ... towards 'thinginess'."[190] Or, in the terms we have been developing in this grammar, the "I" of the experiment has, from the moment of experimental possibility, been transposed into the assertive "it" of science.

We also find that the aura of textual authority in science works its way even into the most ordinary recesses of modern life. The care label Halliday chances upon on an item of clothing does not say, as it might congruently, "I say as its maker, that if you expose this item, it will deteriorate." Rather it says by way of

---

[187] Ibid., pp. 138–39, 127.

[188] M.A.K. Halliday, 2004, *The Language of Science*, The Collected Works of M.A.K. Halliday, Volume 5, edited by J.J. Webster, London, UK: Continuum, pp. 19–21; M.A.K. Halliday and Christian M.I.M. Matthiessen, 1999, *Construing Experience through Meaning: A Language-Based Approach to Cognition*, London, UK: Continuum, p. 238; M.A.K. Halliday, 1989 [1993], "Some Grammatical Problems in Scientific English," pp. 69–85 in *Writing Science: Literacy and Discursive Power*, edited by M.A.K. Halliday and J.R. Martin, London, UK: Falmer Press, pp. 79–82.

[189] J.R. Martin, 1993. "Life as a Noun: Arresting the Universe in Science and the Humanities," pp. 221–67 in ibid.

[190] M.A.K. Halliday, 2004, *The Language of Science*, The Collected Works of M.A.K. Halliday, Volume 5, edited by J.J. Webster, London, UK: Continuum, p. 77.

grammatical metaphor, "Prolonged exposure will result in rapid deterioration of the item."[191] This sounds like a suitably objective assertion. Science speaks, instead of a fallibly interested person.

In the terms we have been developing in our grammar, science characteristically transposes actions into entities, selves into things, possibilities into assertions. Such construal does not simply represent the world objectively, as one might be led to think from the tenor of the texts of science. It is to apply objectivity to the world as an ascribed meaning, fixing entities in order to classify them, measure them, and generalize about them, pretending this objectively to be the case.

This kind of science does not merely describe things in the world. When its texts are transposed back onto objects and bodies, for instance, it does things in the world – it becomes modern technology and medicine. Science is not just a way of seeing; it is a way of making meaning with and for objects and bodies. Notwithstanding the tenor of its assertions, science does not merely state the existence of entities and objectified actions. It re-orients the meanings attributed to objects and bodies.

§2.3.1   Assertion

> **Assertion.** Something that is posited to be; propositions about empirical things and states of affairs that may be true or proven untrue: statements in text; arrays of entities and implied action in image; presences in space; existing objects; or presences in body, sound or speech.

Newton's *Opticks*[§1.3.1c] uses diagrams as well as text to represent its science. Inconveniently, these are different sections of the book because the quite different technologies of offset typography and lithography of that time did not lend themselves to putting image and text on the same page. So, the connections are made by numbered figures and lettered labels.* In the words of Bruno Latour, this kind of science is a matter of "simple craftsmanship," central to which are the practices of textuality and visualization.[192]

In both scientific visualization and text, we see the same representational transposition at work that we saw before in the case of other two-dimensional imaging,[§2.2c] including photography.[§2.2.2a] Entities are represented at the expense of actions. Image and text are complementary ways by means of

---

* http://meaningpatterns.net/newton-science

[191] Ibid., p. 102.
[192] Bruno Latour, 1988, "Drawing Things Together," pp. 19–68 in *Representation in Scientific Practice*, edited by M. Lynch and S. Woolgar, Cambridge, MA: MIT Press, p. 22.

which actions are thingified. Diagram and text in Newton's *Opticks* equally become media of objectified assertion. Such objectivity works for its intricate, abstract density – too intricate, in fact, to be spoken, indicating once more the substantial differences between the affordances of text and speech.[193] But it also comes at the cost of the kinds of delicate attention to nuances of action reflected in the finely modulated transactivity of first languages.[§2.1.2d]

As powerful as science has proven to be, the affordances of its characteristic forms of meaning occlude as well as reveal. As well as opening meaning, science constrains meaning. More than a neutral craft, science is by transposition a way to remake the world, at the same time opening out and limiting the scope of our meanings, for better and at times for worse.

The most consistently objectifying of modern science has no "I." Nevertheless, agency there must always be. While in his experimental mode, Newton's "I" does things and observes things.[§2.3a] "I held a white paper ... " But then when he moves into the theoretical mode, the patterning of agency changes: "It has been proved ... It has been shewed ... It may be concluded," says Newton, transposing his experimental experience into theory.

If the action has been removed from nature, it is replaced by the epistemic actions of the scientist, and by the time scientific reason is applied, it is hidden by an "it." Something or someone must be able to act for clauses to be grammatical. The actor who remains is the reasoning scientist, though Newton and the scientists who have followed in his vocation habitually try to cover the tracks of their own agency with things that act and the passive voice of abstracted acting.

On the cusp of the revolution in human consciousness that is modernity, Newton still in places expresses a conditionally experimental "I." He tells of the things he did on his path to objectivity. Much modern science will try even to erase these tracks.

Then, to the modern reader, there comes a jarring show of subjectivity: "By this way of arguing I invented almost all the Phænomena described in these Books, beside some others less necessary to the Argument; and by the successes I met with in the Trials, I dare promise, that to him who shall argue truly, and then try all things with good Glasses and sufficient Circumspection, the expected Event will not be wanting."[194]

As if Newton invented colors! Now his "I" jarringly goes too far, at least from the perspective of a later scientific modernity.[§1.3.2d] Though of course, in a sense he did invent something, along with the other "giants" on whose shoulders he recognized he stood, and that is a characteristically modern way of transposing

---

[193] James Paul Gee, 2004, "Language in the Science Classroom: Academic Social Languages as the Heart of School-Based Literacy," pp. 13–32 in *Crossing Borders in Literacy and Science Instruction*, edited by E.W. Saul, Arlington, VA: NSTA Press; Jay L. Lemke, 1990, *Talking Science: Language, Learning and Values*, Westport, CN: Ablex.

[194] Isaac Newton, 1730 [1952], *Opticks, or a Treatise of the Reflections, Refractions, Inflections and the Colours of Light*, New York, NY: Dover Publications, p. 115.

text, image, and object, applying this in the science of light and color. And to the particular point of the *Opticks*, as a consequence of his (and others') "invention" we now do things with colors that otherwise may not have been.

The assertive function of science has taken us to new places, not just in text and image, but by dint of the transpositions of its textual and visual insights backwards and forwards into space, object, and body. Science not only has us conceive in new ways. It also has us act in new ways. Its distinctive modes of assertion have opened us to new meanings in the natural and social worlds. However, by "thingifying" the world, our modes of textuality, visioning, and embodied presence have also constrained our meanings to narrowly instrumental forms of reason.

§2.3.1a *J.L. Austin's* How to Do Things with Words

"For Dagmar," says philosopher of language John R. Searle. These two words stand out because they are on a page all of their own between the contents page and the Preface in his 1969 book, *Speech Acts*.[195] We may read around them something like, "I, the author, hereby dedicate this book to Dagmar" who may have been, we suppose, his support or inspiration. Dagmar does not have a surname, so the debt, we may also suppose, must be personal and profound.

Now, another clue, footnote 1 beside the title of a 1977 article by Searle. This takes us to the end of the text where we read: "1. I am indebted to H. Drefus and D. Searle for discussion of these matters." "D," we may guess, is for "Dagmar," but this time without the whole word, so it is not a personal dedication. It is a recognition of intellectual debt, necessary it seems.[196]

Here, in these terse statements, Searle states some requirements. He feels compelled by circumstances of life and work to acknowledge Dagmar or D. Searle. Now he compels us by way of dedication or acknowledgment to recognize his compelling. These are variants of performatives, or illocutionary acts in the terminology of his teacher at Oxford, J.L. Austin.

Austin would call what we have termed "assertion" a "locutionary act," a statement used to describe some state of affairs, or to state a fact that might be true or false. By contrast, illocutionary acts "do things with words," to use the title of his seminal book in a tradition of language theory that came to be known as Analytical Philosophy.

"I do," says each partner in a marriage ceremony. "I name this ship . . . " says the dignitary as they smash a bottle onto the stern on the slipway. "I give and bequeath . . . " says a person anticipating death in a will. "I bet you sixpence . . . "

---

[195] John R. Searle, 1969, *Speech Acts: An Essay on the Philosophy of Language*, Cambridge, UK: Cambridge University Press; also: John R. Searle, 1995, *The Construction of Social Reality*, New York, NY: Free Press.

[196] John R. Searle, 1977, "Reiterating the Differences: A Reply to Derrida," *Glyph*:198–208, p. 208.

says someone wagering that something or other will happen. These are speech acts, or performatives, where the words do not just describe the world; they require that something in the surrounding action be recognized for the meaning that it has.[197] "I dedicate ... " or "I acknowledge ... " Searle was saying of his Dagmar/D, referring to something that surrounded his writing in an essential way.

Austin's book, *How to do Things with Words*, is about these kinds of words, and by the end he classifies them into a taxonomy of requirements (to use our terminology): giving a verdict, exercising power, making promises, social behaviors such as apologizing or congratulating, and expressing a view such as affirming and denying.[198] To use our terminology again, this is a different species of conditionality from assertion. If assertion states the way things are, and often in ways which in the era of science tend to exaggerate their objectified thinginess, requirement refers to a chain of human action which explicitly directs the agent.

We don't want to use "speech act" or "illocution" to name these things, because this is to give speech more credit as a focal point of meaning than it is due. The "I do" of a wedding vow is meaningless outside of the bride's dress and the groom's suit, the processional, the presence of a congregation, the exchange of rings, and the signing of a certificate – or some such collocation of speech with body, space, object, and gesture. If some of the congregation are unable to hear the utterance, the rest will be enough for them. We are completely dependent on multimodality and form-to-form transpositions to make a sense that we may conceptualize as the word "marriage." And "I do" can mean many other things.

Although Austin's analysis is of spoken words, and notwithstanding the smart title of his book, he manages to highlight the remarkable inadequacy of words of requirement. Such words rarely make sense alone. This kind of sense can only be made in a transpositional grammar, a grammar where meanings can swap out for each other, at least in part. His book is not really about doing things with words; it is about how things like requirement can't be done with words alone, and can also be done perfectly well without them.

We need a transpositional grammar because all forms of meaning can require, without having to be connected to speech. Warning signs (a red light, for instance) and sound alerts equally communicate requirements. Requirements of this kind can happen in text too, as we saw in the case of Searle's invocation of Dagmar/D. Written warning notices communicate requirements.

---

[197] J.L. Austin, 1962 [1975], *How to Do Things with Words: The William James Lectures Delivered at Harvard University in 1955*, Cambridge, MA: Harvard University Press, pp. 1–5, passim.

[198] Ibid., pp. 151–64.

The rule of law is a series of quintessentially textual requirements – to talk like legislation or a contract would not only sound ridiculous; it can't be done unless the text is read aloud or memorized, but this is not really speech at all. The textual requirements of law transpose into embodied reality in the form of court judgments spoken by a judge and the rigid spatial requirements of prisons. A more accurate if inelegant title for Austin's book might have been *How Spoken Words Alone Often Fail, and How to Get Things Done, With or Without Them.*

Austin's test of words that are illocutionary compared to ones that are merely locutionary comes in the peculiar ways in which illocutionary words fail to mean truly. Illocutionary speech, for Austin, can't be correct or incorrect in the descriptive manner of locution. But it can, Austin says, be "infelicitous."* The outcomes of a speech act can be unhappy when the expression of the speaker's intention is in one way or another betrayed. The marriage may be a sham. The ship may be incorrectly named. The will may bequeath things that by the time of death the deceased has already disposed of. The wagerer may not honor their bet. In our terms, a requirement is communicated, but that requirement does not comport with experience, already or eventually. Dagmar/D may not have been adequately or reliably honored.

We live in a world where we are ever-alert to a requirement that may prove to be an empty promise, bad faith, deception, insincerity, dissemblance, perfunctoriness, polite avoidance, hollow praise, evasive formality, or best-but-defeated intentions – and this is just to begin a list of travesties that could become long. For every class of speech act, there can be any number of such infelicities.

In fact, infelicity may often itself be the meaning of a requirement. If the words are opaque, it may be because intentions are duplicitous and were destined to be thus. Words and other forms of requirement can by virtue of their very opacity support us in our deceptions, be these immediately conscious or unconscious self-deceptions, or merely circumstantial turns of event. The limitations in the affordances of requirement support our duplicities and missteps as to their meaning.

Searle laments that his mentor died too young, and so Austin himself was unable to extend the system of speech acts. Taking on the mantle of speech act theory, Searle presses forward. His refined, more rigorously principled classification covers: representatives (I believe, hypothesize, boast, complain); directives (I command, request, plead); commissives (I favor, undertake); expressives (I congratulate, apologize, deplore); declarations (I resign, announce, banish).[199] On this

---

* http://meaningpatterns.net/austin

[199] John R. Searle, 1975, "A Taxonomy of Illocutionary Acts," *Language, Mind, and Knowledge* 7:344–69, pp. 354–61.

foundation, he goes on to develop a "calculus of speech acts," a logical system of intention.[200]

What was that dedication to Dagmar in Searle's book? What was the footnote of acknowledgment in his article? A representative, an expressive, a declaration? If we are to have a calculus of speech acts, the variables are slippery and for this reason, hard to classify. Transposability is more revealing than classifications that might for a moment be fixed.

§2.3.1b John R. Searle's Reply to Derrida

In the 1970s, John Searle[§2.3.1a] started to get into a tangle with a new wave of thinking flagged by the neologisms "poststructuralism" and "deconstruction." It began with a talk Jacques Derrida[§0.4d] gave at a conference in Montreal in 1971, in which, towards the end, he discussed the speech act theory of Searle's teacher, J.L. Austin.[§2.3.1a] The talk was later translated into English and published in a short-lived journal of poststructuralist thought, fittingly titled *Glyph*. "Continental Philosophy," so called, had at last engaged with Anglo-American "Analytical Philosophy" on questions of language and meaning that were of apparently common concern. However, there was to be no felicitous meeting of minds.

Derrida was disturbed by the suggestion that "communication is that which circulates a representation as an ideal content (meaning)."[201] In the case of speech acts reported by Analytical Philosophers, such ideal meaning resides in the intentions of the speaker situated in a sequence of actions in which the speech act itself is embedded. Reiterating Austin, these conditions of a felicitous speech act are as follows (think of marriage vows or the verdict in a court case): that the speech act occurs in a context where conventional procedures are agreed by the parties and have a shared meaning; that the speech act is appropriate to this context; that the performance is enacted correctly so that the speech act appears in the right way at the right place in the procedure; that the participants intend the procedure to have its usually anticipated effects; and that subsequently the speech act and its surround does in fact prove to have had those intended effects.[202] Anything else is infelicity.

Such felicity, Derrida says, depends on the speech act having "an exhaustively definable context" within the whole performance, agreed by all its

---

[200] John R. Searle and Daniel Vanderveken, 1985, *Foundations of Illocutionary Logic*, Cambridge, UK: Cambridge University Press, p. 27.

[201] Jacques Derrida, 1971 [1988], "Signature Event Context," pp. 1–23 in *Limited Inc*, edited by G. Graff, Evanston, IL: Northwestern University Press, p. 6.

[202] J.L. Austin, 1962 [1975], *How to Do Things with Words: The William James Lectures Delivered at Harvard University in 1955*, Cambridge, MA: Harvard University Press, pp. 14–15, 25–38.

agents, with meaning carrying forward beyond the performance itself. Furthermore, he goes on, if intention is the measure of felicity and infelicity is thwarted intentions, what is this thing intention and who was its owner?

Derrida mocks the possibility of "a free consciousness present to the totality of the operation, and of absolutely meaningful speech, [a] master of itself: the teleological jurisdiction of an entire field whose organizing center remains intention."[203] Things, for Derrida, are more complicated than mere intention and its realization. Contexts change over time, interpretations differ, and intentions may be at cross-purposes, to a point where the myriad of such differences may themselves become the meaning of the speech act.

One other problem for Derrida, who writes extensively about writing – and this becomes the epigraph for his paper – is that Austin says that he is confining himself "for simplicity to the spoken utterance." Quotation in a novel or reciting lines from memorized text in a play become for Austin merely "parasitical" on normal speech acts because the intentions of the writer/actor are not those of the ostensibly original speaker.[204]

However, such iterability is in the nature of all speech. The "I do" at a wedding or "I pronounce you guilty" in a court case are as much a matter of social iterability as individually expressed intention. What do these words really mean when they are so often repeated? For their formulaic feel, such speech acts are always at least to one degree or another wanting of authenticity and sincerity. Quoting and iterability, for Derrida, are by no means anomalous or derivative. They are the norm.

So, a speech act is never just an act of volition, in and of a moment. It has a social provenance. It is a ubiquitous process of taking out of one context and moving to another meanings that can never be quite the same but whose provenance can nevertheless be traced ("deconstruction"). It is a transposition. Conventionality there is, but also change. Agency there is, but also society. In our grammar, we call this process "design," a tension in meaning between the social sources of meaning and the scope for individual agency in moments of re-meaning.

Because Austin was by then dead, Searle took it upon himself to defend his Analytical master in the face of Continental attack. "It would be a mistake," says Searle, "to regard Derrida's discussion of Austin as a confrontation between two prominent philosophical traditions. This is not so much because Derrida has failed to discuss the central theses in Austin's theory of language but rather because he has misunderstood and misstated Austin's position at several crucial points, as I will attempt to show, and thus the confrontation

---

[203] Jacques Derrida, 1971 [1988], "Signature Event Context," pp. 1–23 in *Limited Inc*, edited by G. Graff, Evanston, IL: Northwestern University Press, p. 15.

[204] Ibid., pp. 1, 16–17.

never takes place."[205] One should expect at least some such "misunderstanding" in any speech act.

Searle's response is to reiterate his version of Austin, now tidied up and more systematic. Nevertheless "there is no getting away from intentionality" in speech acts, and where "in serious literal speech the sentences are precisely the realizations of intentions: there is no gulf at all between the illocutionary intention and its expression."[206] This, for Searle, is the uncomplicated truth of what we are now calling requirement.

Searle's conception of what we call assertion was just as uncomplicated as what he attributed to his master, based in the premise that there is an external reality unmediated by human frames of meaning: "there is a reality totally independent of us . . . [and] of our representations of it . . . Having knowledge consists in having true representations for which we can give certain sorts of justification or evidence."

This was the agenda – at once truism and untrue for its oversimplification of meaning – of the eponymous John Searle Center for Social Ontology at the University of California, Berkeley. Derrida, Searle argues by way of contrast, makes the "apparently spectacular declaration that there is nothing outside of texts" on the basis of "the banality that everything exists in some context or other! What is one to do then, in the face of an array of weak or even non-existent arguments for a conclusion that seems preposterous?"[207]

Derrida replies with a quote from Searle's reply: "Copyright © 1977 by John R. Searle." Before jumping to the conclusion that this has illocutionary force, before deciding whether it should be considered a speech act on Searle's part, Derrida asks,

how can I be absolutely sure that John R. Searle himself (who is it?) is in fact the author [of the copyright statement]? Perhaps it is a member of his family, his secretary, his lawyer, his financial adviser, the "managing editor" of the journal, a joker or a namesake. Or even D. Searle (who is it?), to whom John R. Searle acknowledges his indebtedness . . . in the first of a series of four footnotes . . . located not in the text but the title, on the boundary, and is directed, curiously enough, at my name, "Reply to Derrida[1]" – If John R. Searle owes a debt to D. Searle . . . then the "true" copyright ought to belong (as is indeed suggested along the frame of this *tableau vivant*) to a Searle divided, multiplied, conjugated, shared.[208]

Searle's reply to Derrida had been ten pages long. Derrida's reply to Searle's reply was eighty-one pages, also published in *Glyph*. Derrida calls his reply to

---

[205] John R. Searle, 1977, "Reiterating the Differences: A Reply to Derrida," *Glyph*:198–208, p. 198.

[206] Ibid., p. 202.

[207] John R. Searle, 1995, *The Construction of Social Reality*, New York, NY: Free Press, pp. 149, 159–60.

[208] Jacques Derrida, 1977 [1988], "Limited Inc Abc . . .," pp. 29–110 in *Limited Inc*, edited by G. Graff, Evanston, IL: Northwestern University Press, p. 31.

the reply to the reply, "Limited Inc. abc," after the pseudo corporation that wrote the text attributed to Searle, and the social iterations that resulted in the text signed © by Searle. He starts with section "d" presumably because he has already used "abc" in the title, raves humorously for all these pages, including some paragraphs so breathless that they run for several pages, and ends at section "z," presumably only closing his case there because the alphabet has run out.

One thing that can be said about the difference between "Analytical" and "Continental" philosophies of language and meaning is that the former are humorless, grinding away with assertions cloaked in torturously-languaged logic. Such logical objectivism amounts to a relentless insistence on being right, an insistence that we might read as such in terms of our grammar of requirement. Derrida, at least is a humorist, living and laughing as we all do in a world where things are never quite right.

Though Austin, just for a moment, does lapse into dry, self-deprecating humor: "Clearly there are these six possibilities of infelicity ... " the analyst says, but then is quick to equivocate, "even if it is uncertain which is involved in a particular case ... And we must at all costs avoid oversimplification, which one might be tempted to call the occupational disease of philosophers if it were not their occupation."[209]

When Northwestern University Press asked Searle for permission to reprint his reply in a 1988 book, he refused. By then, Derrida's response to Searle's non-response had become somber:

What I call "text" implies all the structures called "real," "economic," "historical," socio-institutional, in short: all possible referents ... "There is nothing outside the text" ... does not mean that all referents are suspended ... But it does mean that every referent, all reality has the structure of a differential trace, and one cannot refer to this as "real" except in interpretative experience.[210]

It's a pity Derrida calls everything "text," because this concept usually refers to something narrower – as it does for us,[§0.2.1] indeed very narrowly in this grammar. But if we can get past his strange nomenclature, or for that matter believe what he is now saying about text given the writing-centered focus of his work, we want to bring into our transpositional grammar some of Derrida's ideas: of ever-changing context, interpretative frames, and the play of provenance of conventionalized designs yet renewal in redesign – Derrida's "traces."

---

[209] J.L. Austin, 1962 [1975], *How to Do Things with Words: The William James Lectures Delivered at Harvard University in 1955*, Cambridge, MA: Harvard University Press, p. 38.
[210] Jacques Derrida, 1988, *Limited Inc*, edited by G. Graff, Evanston, IL: Northwestern University Press, p. 148.

But now comes infelicity in relation to Dagmar/D,[§2.3.1a] and the realization that this is a phenomenon too delicately named.

"Lawsuit alleges that a UC Berkeley professor sexually assaulted his researcher and cut her pay when she rejected him," was the headline in the *Los Angeles Times*, March 23, 2017.[211] Here comes a complaint filed by Joanna Ong, student age 24, against Searle, professor age 84, with the court in Alemedia County, California, referring to a sequence of speech acts.* Searle, according to the statement, groped Ong in his office after he told her "they were going to be lovers." He also said he had an "emotional commitment to making her a public intellectual," the complaint states, and that he was "going to love her for a long time."[212] After this, there was a confidential settlement,[213] and, it was reported, the "professor ... abruptly stepped down from teaching his undergraduate philosophy course."[214]

Next came the news of revised requirements for speech and action at the university. "After years of bad news about sexual harassment and assault involving professors within the University of California, its Board of Regents voted this week to strengthen the systemwide Faculty Code of Conduct's policies against such behavior."[215] And after that, to avert further possibility, another requirement by dint of speech act issued by the President of the University. Other complainants had come forward. "John Searle, formerly a professor emeritus in UC Berkeley's Department of Philosophy, has had his emeritus status revoked ... his action permanently removes him from the university community."[216]

As for Dagmar/D, to swear to faithfulness to a promise or to honor an intellectual debt in the calculus of speech acts is also to forewarn the possibility of unfaithfulness and dishonor. Assertion is transposable with other possibilities. Speech may or may not align with embodied reality.

---

* http://meaningpatterns.net/searle

[211] www.latimes.com/local/education/la-essential-education-updates-southern-lawsuit-alleges-a-uc-berkeley-philosophy-1490299535-htmlstory.html

[212] Joanna Ong v. the Regents of the University of California et al., case number RG-17-854053, in the Superior Court of the State of California, County of Alameda (www.documentcloud.org/documents/3523114-34060351.html#document/p1).

[213] www.law360.com/articles/1092658/berkeley-prof-can-t-avoid-harassment-settlement-judge-told

[214] www.buzzfeed.com/katiejmbaker/famous-philosophy-professor-accused-sexual-harassment?utm_term=.mebPE4p65#.jkm2pv6kx

[215] www.insidehighered.com/news/2017/03/17/u-california-strengthens-faculty-policies-against-sexual-harassment-and-assault

[216] http://dailynous.com/2019/06/21/searle-found-violated-sexual-harassment-policies/

§2.3.2 Requirement

> **Requirement.** *Something that, between agents, must be, but which those agents*
> *nevertheless expect from the start may not necessarily be, including for instance:*
> *imperatives in text; images that warn; spaces that confine; objects whose*
> *essential use is framed by their function; gestures that command; warning*
> *sounds; authoritative tones of voice.*

J.L. Austin[§2.3.1a] knows that meanings taking the form of requirements often
don't align, which is why he acknowledges the always-possible anomaly of
infelicity. But felicity of truth to intention as agreed among the co-agents is not
necessarily the measure of success in sense-making. Some speech acts are
infelicitous by nature; they are designed to be infelicitous, that is their paradoxical success, their disagreeableness to some but not others, their conflict of
intents. Take curses or blasphemy,[217] for instance.

Then there are speech acts where one person's truth is another's travesty, or
one person's expressed intention is another's harassment: "American imperi-
alism? Oh boy, that sounds great, honey! Let's go to bed and do that right now!"
This is what Joanna Ong reported John Searle to have said in her case against
him.[218] Joanna Ong did not see the encounters with Searle, or her subsequent
dismissal, the same way he did.[§2.3.1b] Their intentions, as it transpires, did not
align. And as participant in this speech – albeit unequally in the case of sexual
harassment – she was herself capable of agency, because she did make
a complaint.

Nor was this mere infelicity. This is something that has been reported to be
all-too-frequently "normal" in male-dominated philosophy departments.
Sexual harassment is endemic. At the University of California, it has been de-
normalized in newly articulated requirements for academic conduct. Ms Ong
went on to quote these speech acts, and precisely because there was
a profound difference in the participants' intentions. This difference is the
point. Such differences are not anomalous; they are systemic in a world of
unequal power. Far from being parasitical, quoting is a way to highlight these
differences.

There are also speech acts that are insincere or dishonest, where professed
and actual intention do not align (at least to the extent that professed intent is

---

[217] Giorgio Agamben, 2011, *The Sacrament of Language*, translated by A. Kotsoko, Cambridge,
UK: Polity Press, pp. 43, 48.

[218] Joanna Ong v. the Regents of the University of California et al., case number RG-17-854053, in
the Superior Court of the State of California, County of Alameda (www.documentcloud.org
/documents/3523114-34060351.html#document/p1).

intelligible and actual intent is determinable, which is of course hard-to-impossible work). Again, in these cases infelicity is the rule, not the exception.

In fact, the words that Austin and Searle call "performative" are trickily inadequate, where the meaning is not in the words but in their dissembling. The trickiness is in the affordance of the speech act, the possibility in the slippery ambiguity of the words to say one thing but in the context of action to mean another. We may mouth requirements, and if we don't mean to dodge them immediately, we may end up dodging them later, by circumstance of changed context or changed intentions. The meaning then is failure to mean truly in words. Requirements themselves anticipate these possibilities, some agents sometimes forgiving their breach by way of explanation or excuse, other agents not.

"Who ya going to believe," asked Chico Marx, dressed up as his brother Groucho, "me or your own eyes?"[219] Or an even nicer rewrite of the line by comedian Richard Pryor, "Who you gonna believe, me or your lying eyes?"[220]

And one more thing, we are always about to slip from one function of conditionality to another. A speech act or illocution, or in our multimodal terms, a requirement, is always ready to be, or could just have been, a condition of assertion or possibility. Not only are these meaning functions transposable; they are always begging to be transposed. We move from requirement to assertion in order to reveal the facticity of an action. We move to possibility to explore other things that could have been, could be now, or could still be.

Searle, perhaps, intended to mean it when he said "Let's go to bed," or at least that's what Joanna Ong alleges in her pleadings. The speech act is surrounded by assertions, about the location, and the fact that the speech act "Let's go to bed" in fact occurred, presented as a quote in her pleadings. There were requirements – Searle's and the University's – and then possibilities, of sex and dismissal, some of which may have been realized in fact, others not. There was an attempt to forestall future possibilities in the University of California's new requirements and Searle's removal from the University.[221]

The meanings of assertion, requirement, and possibility are not just in what they are, singularly and categorically, but also in what they could have been, might be, and could yet be, then or now or after. Such functional transpositions of meaning are always ready to happen. This kind of dynamic is at least as important as the categorical fixities created in Analytical Philosophy.

---

[219] www.script-o-rama.com/movie_scripts/d/duck-soup-script-transcript-marx.html; www.you tube.com/watch?v=cHxGUe1cjzM

[220] www.quora.com/Where-did-the-phrase-who-are-you-going-to-trust-me-or-your-lying-eyes-originate

[221] http://dailynous.com/2019/06/21/searle-found-violated-sexual-harassment-policies/

§2.3.2a Elizabeth Anscombe's Compilation of Wittgenstein Notes,
  On Certainty

In the last two years of his life, Ludwig Wittgenstein[§2.1.1a] lived in Cambridge with Elizabeth Anscombe and her husband, Peter Geach, both former students of his, both of whom were to become influential Analytical Philosophers in their own right. On Wittgenstein's death in 1951, Anscombe was appointed his literary executor. She went on to translate his second major work, *Philosophical Investigations*, published in 1953, then other papers.

In 1969, with G.H. von Wright and Denis Paul as co-editors and translators, Anscombe collated and translated some texts of Wittgenstein's written in the last year and a half of his life, twenty sheets of loose pages he had left in her house, and fragments of his notebooks. The title she gave them was startling: *On Certainty*. Or, at the very least, this is a startling title given the overall tenor of Analytical Philosophy, with its focus on minutely detailed logical argument, where the ordinary, assertive language of things and their relations meets less-than-ordinary formal, textual, propositional reasoning. This was the territory that had been worked over by Frege,[§1.2a] Russell, Whitehead,[§1.2.2c] the Vienna Circle,[§1.1.3i] Wittgenstein,[§2.1.1a] and Austin[§2.3.1a] – notwithstanding their nuanced differences.

Analytical Philosophy eschews world-encompassing philosophies that tackle the meaning of the human, the natural, or the historical – typically of the "continental" variety, from Hegel, to Marx, Husserl, and Derrida. Instead, the Analytical movement adopted a frame of reasoning grounded in the logic of language. At times it is quasi-mathematical, affording it an aura of assertiveness about the nature of things. It works in an objectifying technics that reads at times like science. Something as straightforward as certainty in a world beyond its immediate, self-referential calculation – this is outside the usual frame of reference of Analytical Philosophy. The essentials of meaning are to be found in language and its propositional logic; there were no certainties outside of this.

Wittgenstein had in these final years of his life returned to a 1925 article of G.E. Moore's, "A Defense of Common Sense." Moore had been the professor with whom Wittgenstein had been annoyed in 1913 because Cambridge University would not grant him a BA for an early version of the *Tractatus*.[§2.1.1a] Then Moore was on his committee in 1929 when he was awarded a Ph.D. for the now-published version – where the proceedings ended with Wittgenstein slapping Bertrand Russell and Moore on the shoulder, "Don't worry, I know you'll never understand it."[§2.1.1d]

Moore's argument in the article ran along these lines. There is nothing to refute a commonsense view of the world that things in the world exist, independent of our thinking or naming them. So, for instance, "There exists at present a living human body, which is *my* body" is a commonsense statement that does not warrant any attempt to doubt. And the expression "'The earth has existed for many years past' is ... an unambiguous expression."[222] But when Wittgenstein had attended Russell's class at Cambridge he had refused to admit Russell's assertion that there was not a rhinoceros in the room.[§2.1.1a] The *Tractatus* had reiterated his commitment to all discussable meaning being located in the propositional logic of language, beyond which, there was only mystery.

But by the end of his life, Wittgenstein had softened his view. In *Philosophical Investigations* he introduces several main ideas that he admitted disrupted the basic propositions of the *Tractatus*. "It is interesting to compare the multiplicity of the tools in language and of the ways they are used, the multiplicity of kinds of word and sentence, with what logicians have said about the structure of language. (Including the author of the *Tractatus Logico-Philosophicus*.)"[223]

One of his new ideas was that words only roughly classify concepts. Logicians had oversimplified things, finding a clarity in words and their relations that does not in truth exist.

Consider for example the proceedings that we call "games." I mean board-games, card-games, ball-games, Olympic games, and so on. What is common to them all? – Don't say: "There must be something common, or they would not be called 'games'" – but look and see whether there is anything common to all. – For if you look at them you will not see something that is common to all, but similarities, relationships, and a whole series of them at that. To repeat: don't think, but look! ... And the result of this examination is: we see a complicated network of similarities overlapping and crisscrossing ...

I can think of no better expression to characterize these similarities than "family resemblances"; for the various resemblances between members of a family: build, features, colour of eyes, gait, temperament, etc. etc. overlap and crisscross in the same way. – And I shall say: "games" form a family.[224]

And a second main idea: that the otherwise slippery meanings of words can only make sense to the extent that they are embedded in "forms of life."[225] Then a third major thought, connecting back to the first, that language is itself a game, where these forms of life are enacted.[226]

We could imagine a language in which all statements had the form and tone of rhetorical questions; or every command the form of the question "Would you like to...?" Perhaps it will then be said: "What he says has the form of a question but is really a command," – that is, has the function of a command in the technique of using the language. (Similarly

---

[222] George Edward Moore, 1925 [1959], "A Defence of Common Sense," pp. 106–33 in *Philosophical Papers*, London, UK: George Allen and Unwin, pp. 33, 36.
[223] Ludwig Wittgenstein, 1953 [2001], *Philosophical Investigations*, translated by G.E.M. Anscombe, Oxford, UK: Blackwell, §23.
[224] Ibid., §66–67.   [225] Ibid., §17.   [226] Ibid., §7.

one says "You will do this" not as a prophecy but as a command. What makes it the one or the other?) . . .

But how many kinds of sentence are there? Say assertion, question, and command? – There are countless kinds: countless different kinds of use of what we call "symbols," "words," "sentences." And this multiplicity is not something fixed, given once for all; but new types of language, new language-games, as we may say, come into existence, and others become obsolete and get forgotten . . . Here the term "language-game" is meant to bring into prominence the fact that the speaking of language is part of an activity, or of a form of life.[227]

Wittgenstein was now conceding to a far greater extent than before that much of meaning is constituted outside of language. Meaning is framed in forms of life, where assertion, question, and command – ideas within a frame of reference that we call conditionality – are forever slip-sliding into each other, the one ever ready to become the other, and even in some moments of life the one masquerading as the other. Life makes sense of language, not language of life. The sense of language is often not congruently true to life; indeed its "truth" is often the reverse.

Nevertheless, in *Philosophical Investigations* Wittgenstein still frequently falls back into his old language-centric self. "It is only in language that I can mean something by something."[228] "The meaning of a word is its use in the language."[229] "If 'X exists' is meant simply to say: 'X' has a meaning, – then it is not a proposition which treats of X, but a proposition about our use of language, that is, about the use of the word 'X'."[230] "You learned the concept 'pain' when you learned language."[231] (No, you learned the concept pain when you experienced it for the second and subsequent times. The concept is not just the word, but the bodily experience to have felt it once and then again.)

On Certainty is startling because, even though *Philosophical Investigations* shows Wittgenstein nudging away from language-centrism, he has until now mainly stayed bound to language and its games. Now at last, we have a certainty that goes beyond language and mind.

Take the moon, for instance: "Everything that I have seen or heard gives me the conviction that no man has ever been far from the earth. Nothing in my picture of the world speaks to the opposite."[232]

Suppose some adult told a child that he had been on the moon. The child tells me the story, and I say it was only a joke, the man hadn't been on the moon; no one has ever been on the moon; the moon is a long way off and it is impossible to climb up there or fly there . . . But a child will not ordinarily stick to such a belief and will soon be convinced by what we tell him seriously . . .

---

[227] Ibid., §21, 23.   [228] Ibid., footnote, p. 16e.   [229] Ibid., §43.   [230] Ibid., §58.
[231] Ibid., §384.
[232] Ludwig Wittgenstein, 1969, *On Certainty*, translated by D. Paul and G.E.M. Anscombe, New York, NY: Harper and Row, §9.

If we are thinking within our system, then it is certain that no one has ever been to the moon. Not merely is nothing of the sort ever seriously reported to us by reasonable people, but our whole system of physics forbids us to believe it.[233]

This brings us back to forms of life that include not only language but a whole host of other forms of meaning. "I did not get my picture of the world by satisfying myself of its correctness" – in language or logic, for instance – "nor do I have it because I am satisfied of its correctness. No: it is the inherited background against which I distinguish between true and false."[234]

"My convictions ... form a system, a structure."[235] They are a "definite world picture ... learned ... as a child."[236] This is something that "stands fast for me and many others."[237] "Only the accustomed context allows what is meant to come through clearly."[238] Then "My life consists of being content to accept many things."[239] And finally, "If you are not certain of any fact, you cannot be certain of the meaning of your words, either."[240]

At last, we can agree with Wittgenstein about the ordinary, socially constituted, pictured, embodied, materially felt, holistic experience that is meaning. But, rather than leave this to vaguely specified "inherited backgrounds" or "forms of life," we want to use our grammar to trace the sources of these meanings in history and to parse their forms and functions in and beyond language: the pictures in life and mind, the embodied experiences, the visceral experiences of object, space, and sound – and of course also, the forms and functional limits of our texts and speech. We want to account for the traffic between these forms of meaning, without needing to privilege any. We also want to say that assertion, requirement, and possibility are always predicated on the likelihood at any moment of the one slipping into the other, if that hasn't happened already.

Wittgenstein was at his philosophical and architectonic best with doors.[§2.1.1b]

"I am leaving the room because you tell me to." "I am leaving the room, but not because you tell me to." Does this proposition describe a connexion between my action and his order; or does it make the connexion? Can one ask: "How do you know that you do it because of this, or not because of this?" And is the answer perhaps: "I feel it"?[241]

Or, as we would say in our parsing of this transposition between speech and object, this is a matter of requirement or not.

[233] Ibid., §106, 108.   [234] Ibid., §94.   [235] Ibid., §102.   [236] Ibid., §167.   [237] Ibid., §116.
[238] Ibid., §237.   [239] Ibid., §344.   [240] Ibid., §114.
[241] Ludwig Wittgenstein, 1953 [2001], *Philosophical Investigations*, translated by G.E.M. Anscombe, Oxford, UK: Blackwell, §487.

§2.3.3   Possibility

> **Possibility.** *Something that could have been, could be or could still be, including for instance: subjunctives in text; images that reference potential; openings in space that allow movement; the scope of usability of an object; bodily potential; possible connections between one sound and other in a sequence; or tones of voice that express uncertainty.*

H.G. Wells had imagined the possibility[*] of visiting the moon in his 1901 book, *The First Men in the Moon*.[242] Alexander Bogdanov had ventured farther afield, establishing his 1908 imagined socialist utopia on Mars.[§0.2.9a] But Wittgenstein (at last) was certain, about the moon at least.[§2.3.2a]

However, certainty in one moment does not preclude possibility in another. *On Certainty* was published in 1969, the year Neil Armstrong walked on the moon, then in the following three years, eleven other men.

Every certainty can be undercut by other possibility, and this in turn may presage a new certainty. And when a new certainty arrives, there may still be doubt that may yet undo certainty, or not.

Here comes another philosopher, James H. Fetzer, Distinguished McKnight University Professor Emeritus in the philosophy of science at the University of Minnesota, Duluth. He is the author of many books, including a 1981 book, *Scientific Knowledge: Causation, Explanation, and Corroboration*, published in the Springer series, Boston Studies in the Philosophy and History of Science. Also, a co-edited 2016 book, *And I Suppose We Didn't Go to the Moon, Either?* Says the blurb of the more recent publication, "this book demonstrates – with scientific argument and empirical proof – that Man did not go to the Moon, that Paul McCartney was replaced after his death in 1966 and that the official narrative of the Holocaust cannot be sustained."[243]

Those crystal clear, 6cm x 6cm film images of the moon taken on the best cameras money could buy in 1969, Hasselblad 500 EL/Ms – these, you might think, would be sufficient to clinch this matter, or the live television footage. But Fetzer, and 6 percent of his fellow Americans according to a Gallup poll,[244] can't believe what they have seen. Fetzer combs over a selection of the approximately 5,000 images taken during the Apollo moon missions between 1969 and 1972 in

---

[*]   http://meaningpatterns.net/moon-truth

[242]   H.G. Wells, 1901, *The First Men in the Moon*, London, UK: George Newnes.
[243]   https://books.google.com/books/about/And_I_Suppose_We_Didn_t_Go_to_the_Moon_E.html?id=CdBljwEACAAJ&source=kp_cover
[244]   http://news.gallup.com/poll/3712/landing-man-moon-publics-view.aspx

search of evidence that they were faked – the way shadows are cast, anomalous footprints, flags flapping when they couldn't have been.[245] A Wikipedia page earnestly goes over these images, as if the faking were possible.[246]

Fetzer also directs his reader to evidence of how the television images were doctored, a video on YouTube where the people on the film set of the fake landing have not been edited out. The video links to moontruth.com, and when you take the link we are directed to an advertising click validator. A DNS lookup tells us the domain name is owned by an Australian company, Fabulous. com Pty Ltd, a domain name registrar, and this company is in turn owned by Dark Blue Sea Pty Ltd, and this in turn by Photon Pty Ltd, a graphic design services company.

To prove the moon fakery, it is the photographs and video footage rather than words to which the conspiracy theorists dedicate their efforts. These days, there is more truth in images than words. Not so many people would just believe "NASA says ... "

If 94 percent of Americans end up certain about the moon landings, why is this? How do we end up knowing in the kinds of common sense ways suggested by G.E. Moore and more or less agreed by Wittgenstein in his last days? It is by virtue of the ordinary, everyday, incontrovertible materiality of our forms of meaning, the general reliability of their multimodal transpositions (where the words must be true if there are all these pictures), and the sociability of sense that is common. Together, these mean that some things are as good as certain, provisionally at least.

---

[245] https://archive.org/details/youtube-Fx4dOViBqe0 Also: https://deeppoliticsforum.com/for ums/showthread.php?4948-Fetzer-Burton-Moon-Landing-Debate-Finale#.WgmN5oZrwUw
[246] https://en.wikipedia.org/wiki/Examination_of_Apollo_Moon_photographs

Part 3 Structure

§3.0   Overview of Part 3

Meaning directs our attention to things – in Part 1, we called this "reference." Meaning tracks our activity as sensuous creatures – in Part 2, we called this "agency." Meanings also hang together, with networks of interlinkage that create coherence, where every meaning is greater than the sum of its parts. In this part, we are going to name this coherence, "structure."

Analysis of the holding together in structures, we call "ontology," or the philosophy of what things are, their being. We identify two kinds of binding, two kinds of ways in which things hold together, in the work: in material structures (the meanings-in things themselves), and ideal structures (the meanings-for those things, the meanings we attribute to them). The process of interconnecting the material and the ideal, we call design.

In forensics that analyze ontologies and their designs, we look for specific relations. This is to make our analysis more granular. However, heading the other way, towards ontologies with higher levels of generality, we find ontologies encompassed by more general ontologies, or metaontologies. Structures can nest within structures.

Fig. 3.0 provides a conceptual map of this part of our grammar.

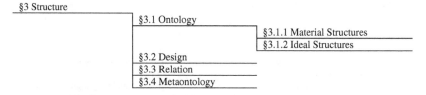

Fig. 3.0: Functions of structure

§3.0a   Ibn Jinnî's Kha â'i *(Origins of Speech)*

Grammarian and philosopher of language, Abû l-Fath 'Uthmân Ibn Jinnî, was not a native speaker of Arabic but Greek by birth, son of Byzantine slaves. Born in Mosul in about 932, he lived for a while in Aleppo, but spent the most influential part of his life in Baghdad, where he died in 1002.

Now no less devout a Muslim than his peers, in his *Kha â'i* (Origins of Speech), Ibn Jinnî nevertheless asks,

> Is the origin of speech [divine] revelation or [human] agreement? This is a subject that requires a lot of consideration, although there is a consensus among most speculative philosophers that the origin of speech is mutual agreement and convention rather than revelation and inspiration. On the other hand, 'Abû 'Alî [al-Fârisî, another grammarian] – may he rest in peace! – said to me one day: "It comes from God." He argued by referring to God's words [in the Qur'an] "He taught Adam all names." But this verse does not put an end to the controversy, because it may be interpreted in the sense that He enabled Adam to give names.[1]

For centuries, the intellectual and cultural universe of Islam struggled to reconcile the strictly congruent sacredness of its authoritative text – the truth of God as revealed in the Qur'an[§3a] – with the fluid, historical, and to this extent humanly contingent character of meaning.

Ibn Jinnî's Baghdad was at the time the largest city in the world, with a population perhaps of a million people. For all its riches, this was also a city of periodic famine, disease, rioting, and intercommunal conflict. It was nevertheless a place of intellectual ferment. Under the patronage of powerful caliphs and wealthy viziers, thinkers debated and teachers taught science, philosophy, theology, and grammar.

There were numerous bookstores and libraries, including the largest library the world had yet seen, the "House of Wisdom," with some 400,000 volumes.[*] This had been made possible in part by the technology of paper, invented in China[§AS1.4.7b] and introduced to the Arabic-speaking world in about 800. By 1000, a large amount of previously written knowledge, mainly the Greek classics, had been translated into Arabic and could be found in the libraries of Baghdad.[2] It was little wonder that thinkers should also be prompted to think, not just about the meanings in their intellectual work, but also the meanings of these meanings.

---

[*] http://meaningpatterns.net/ibn-jinni

[1] Kees Versteegh, 1997, *The Arabic Linguistic Tradition*, London, UK: Routledge, p. 75, quoting Ibn Jinnî's treatise on grammar, *Kha â'i.*

[2] Jack Goody, 2010, *Renaissances: The One or the Many?*, Cambridge, UK: Cambridge University Press, pp. 21–23, 103–7; Joel L. Kraemer, 1986, *Humanism in the Renaissance of Islam: The Cultural Revival During the Buyid Age*, Leiden, NL: E.J. Brill, pp. 26–27, 47–49, 55–57.

Ibn Jinnî opens up what other grammarians of his time, al-Fârisî included, would consider heresy. In a tradition already lasting centuries, they had developed grammars on the premise that speech had its origins in *tawqîf*, "revelation," as expressed in the ideal form of the Arabic of the prophet Muhammad and the forms of his native Bedouin speech.

Strict grammarians guided users towards idealized speech and away from error in everyday speech. A person might say somewhat ungrammatically or inelegantly, "it was Amr that Zayd hit," and when this happened, the grammarians would remind the speaker of an underlying agent–verb–object structure in order to direct them toward correct usage.[3]

Rather than attribute the source of correct meaning to revelation, Ibn Jinnî argued that speech was contingent, varying according to human *tawâ u*, or "agreement." Speakers have the freedom to modify their speech according to their capacities as agents of meaning. They have scope for error.

For, unless granted free will, how could people be held to account for their sins? Without free will, how could they be held responsible to correct their speech? One who speaks, brings his own meanings into being.[4] This position was consistent with Ibn Jinnî's rationalist "Mu'tazilite" theology, a view that stood opposed to more orthodox Islamic understandings of the revealed meanings of God and the ideal of a reverential and obedient humankind.

§3 STRUCTURE

> **Structure.** *Networks of meaning interconnection that create coherence in text, image, space, object, body, sound, and speech. In a functional sense, structure is realized in systems that can be characterized by their ontology or connections in the universe to which they refer, their explicit and implicit internal relations, their designs, and the relations in their ordering.*

Inspired by Ibn Jinnî,[§3.0a] we are going to address the question of the sources of coherence in meaning and the scope for human agency to mean.

Ibn Jinnî's revisionism we would call the heresy of human design. A millennium later, various "structuralisms" and "behaviorisms" have in their own ways also restricted the scope for human agency. Among others in this part, we will consider the cosmologies (spiritualities Ibn Jinnî might have called them) of Saussure,[§3d] Skinner,[§3.1.2d] and Chomsky,[§3.1.2f] each with their modes of fixity, each with their forms of immovable revelation, and each in their own way framing or even constraining possibilities for meaning and living.

---

[3] Kees Versteegh, 1997, *The Arabic Linguistic Tradition*, London, UK: Routledge, pp. 80, 77.
[4] Ibid.

§3a   Sîbawayh's Kitâb *(Grammar)*

In 610, an illiterate merchant in the Arabian town of Mecca announced that the Angel Gabriel had appeared to him in a cave above the city, revealing the word of God. This was the same Gabriel who had appeared for Daniel in the holy book of the Jews, and before the Virgin Mary in the holy book of the Christians. Today, we can name the recipient of this revelation – Muhammad – but not picture him.[§2.2.1b] This is just one moment in a long tradition that, since the invention of writing, would prioritize speech and text over image.

Muhammad began to preach of his revelations, and his followers memorized what he said. After his death in 632, his words were recorded in writing and collected into the 114 chapters of a book titled the Qur'an, or "recitation." A definitive text of the Qur'an had been created by about 650.[5] Now, text was prioritized over speech, and its sources in speech subsumed as if text were a mere transliteration of speech – another moment in another long tradition.

After intense conflicts with local powers who still followed the older gods, the armies of Muhammad finally assumed control of the cities of Mecca and Medina in 630. Following the death of the prophet, Arabic-speaking Muslims rapidly conquered Egypt, Mesopotamia, and Syria. In 762 the seat of power moved to Baghdad and the Abbasid caliphs assumed control. The city became the center of an Islamic empire that lasted nearly 500 years and that at the height of its powers spanned from today's Spain to India and beyond, far larger than the empires of the Greeks, Romans, or Byzantines before.

Following the conquest of so many lands, the speech of the formerly nomadic Bedouin became the text of empire. Arabic split into two forms, a high form of "eloquent, correct" speech, and a low variety, a "language of the people."[6] The high form was the *lingua franca* of imperial government and the Qur'an. The differences between these forms of speaking and writing delineated essential inequalities in the framework of empire.

Two hundred and something years before Ibn Jinnî,[§3.0a] an encounter with the higher form of the language by another non-native speaker, Sîbawayh (750–793), became a reason for the writing of the first Arabic grammar, the *Kitâb Sîbawayhi*, or the "Book of Sîbawayh."[*] Sîbawayh was a Persian who had come to Baghdad to study Islamic law.

In a celebrated incident, he joined a public debate in the court of a prominent vizier. The question for discussion was the correct construction of a sentence

---

[*] http://meaningpatterns.net/sibawayhi

[5] Jonathan Owens, 1990, *Early Arabic Grammatical Theory: Heterogeneity and Standardization*, Amsterdam, NL: John Benjamins, pp. 5–6.

[6] Kees Versteegh, 1997, *The Arabic Linguistic Tradition*, London, UK: Routledge, p. 2; M.G. Carter, 2004, *Sibawayhi*, New Delhi, India: Oxford University Press, pp. 29–33.

about whether a hornet's sting was more or less painful than a scorpion's. Sîbawayh argued that one particular construction was correct. Then four Bedouin, native speakers of Arabic, told him he was wrong.[7] On his own measure, Sîbawayh was humiliated, his social origins betrayed. So, he decided to write a grammar in order to master thoroughly a textual form beyond his original station in life.

This, legend has it, was the origin of the *Kitâb Sîbawayhi*. After the Qur'an, this was the first scholarly book to be written in Arabic, and probably the first work in Arabic to be called a "book." As Arabic was the language chosen by God for his revelation to Muhammad, it was the task of the grammarian to analyze and describe its perfect forms. This Sîbawayh did via structural analysis of speech – its phonology, morphology, and syntax. He made into an explicit science the system in its highest, most authentic, and original practice, the speech of Muhammad and the Bedouin.

Sîbawayh introduces a concept of meaning, *ma'nâ*, into his grammar, where meaning is established by the interconnection of the various elements of speech in its expression – its structure. The purpose of his grammar then is to establish compliance with the rules of correct speech, as reflected in its structurally determined rules. And behind this, there was authority that demands compliance – to the correct forms of expression established by an imperial ruling class and to the textual forms of divine revelation in the Qur'an and its practices of recitation.

§3b   Mattâ ibn Yûnus' "Logic"

In 932, another famous debate takes place in the salon of a vizier to the caliph in Baghdad, this time between a traditional Arabic grammarian and an exponent of the "Greek sciences." Here, Mattâ ibn Yûnus, a Syrian Christian and advocate of Greek logic, debates 'Abû Sa'îd as-Sîrâfî, a theologian and grammarian. Mattâ places logic in opposition to grammar:

I mean by "logic" a linguistic tool by which correct speech can be distinguished from incorrect, and false meaning from true . . . [L]ogic investigates those intentions that can be understood and those meanings that can be grasped, by studying the impulses of the mind and the motions of the soul. In the intelligible things all people are alike. Don't you see that "four plus four equals eight" and similar statements are alike for all nations? . . . [G]rammar is something I have not studied, because a logician does not need it, whereas the grammarian needs logic very much: logic investigates the meaning, and grammar investigates the expression. If the logician comes across the expression, it is by accident,

---

[7] Kees Versteegh, 1997, *The Arabic Linguistic Tradition*, London, UK: Routledge, p. 37; M.G. Carter, 2004, *Sibawayhi*, New Delhi, India: Oxford University Press, pp. 56–57, 61–63, 12–15.

and if the grammarian stumbles upon the meaning, that too is by accident. Meaning is nobler than expression and expression is humbler than meaning.[8]

Sîrâfî responds by saying that the world is directly intelligible in conventional language, and the path to knowledge begins with the study of the forms of language. Ordinary language offers a tool for reasoning that is accessible to all.[9]

§3c   Al Fārābī's "Meaning"

It was to take another of the great thinkers of the time, Abū Naṣr Muḥammad ibn Muḥammad Al Fārābī (872–950), to resolve the opposition between logic and grammar,[3b] and in so doing to extend the notion of *ma'nâ*, "meaning." Of Persian background, Al Fārābī's thinking was a blend of Aristotle's logic and Arabic grammar, and at the same time an original re-synthesis. This was a part of his wider conception of human knowledge, which in his overall scheme consisted of: linguistic sciences (grammar, syntax, writing, reading, and poetry); logic; mathematics (arithmetic, geometry, optics, astronomy, music, technology, and mechanics); physics; metaphysics; and politics (including jurisprudence and theology).[10]

Al Fārābī argued that grammar and logic were complementary. Grammar provides the rules for vocal forms, exteriorized spoken discourse, which is in its nature specific to various peoples. Logic analyzes the interior discourse of the mind, providing the underlying rules for all exteriorized discourses, shared by all peoples. Because logic can only be grasped in vocal form, there can be no logic without grammar. However, vocal form is, by itself, limiting in part because logic is not always well expressed in vocal form. Logic and grammar need each other.[11]

Arabic-speaking philosophers had by now developed a finely elaborated theory of meaning, where patterns can be traced in human speech around its distinctive components and their combination, and these in turn may be expressions of a deeper and more generalizable human reasoning. Behind the specifics of meaning are deducible larger patterns, in speech and the thought that speech expresses. These secular acts of meaning either realize the revealed

[8] Kees Versteegh, 1997, *The Arabic Linguistic Tradition*, London, UK: Routledge, pp. 39–40.

[9] Mushin Mahdi, 1970, "Language and Logic in Classical Islam," pp. 51–83 in *Logic in Classical Islamic Culture*, edited by G.E. von Grunebaum, Wiesbaden, Germany: Otto Harrassowitz, pp. 58, 62; Gerhard Endress, 1977, "The Debate between Arabic Grammar and Greek Logic in Classical Islamic Thought," *Journal for the History of Arabic Science* 1(2):320–22.

[10] Joel L. Kraemer, 1986, *Humanism in the Renaissance of Islam: The Cultural Revival During the Buyid Age*, Leiden, NL: E.J. Brill, p. 9.

[11] Peter Adamson and Alexander Key, 2015, "Philosophy of Language in the Medieval Arabic Tradition," pp. 74–99 in *Linguistic Content*, edited by M. Cameron and R.J. Stainton, Oxford, UK: Oxford University Press, pp. 83–85.

meanings in the word of God, or in the moment of their expression add an element of human volition and thus responsibility.

Here we encounter a paradox: these discussions of the purity of Arabic as a conduit of religious truth-in-text became debates about meaning that were essentially humanistic. And so, in Baghdad and the other cities of the Arab empire, there emerged an intellectual milieu antecedent to, indeed, arguably a direct predecessor of, the humanism of the European Renaissance.[12] In tension with the reverential meanings of religious orthodoxy, we encounter the power of epistemic self-reflection in a culture of reasoning about meanings, and the meanings of meanings.

In this milieu, other great epistemic advances were made, following a generalizing path of the same order as the one from specific expressions in speech, to the generalizable patterns in grammar, to logic. Some of these advances were in mathematics and mechanics. "Arabic" numbers were an extension of the Indian decimal system, adding the decimal point to express parts of wholes.[13] The conceptual break (beyond Roman numerals, for instance), was in the infinite extensibility of numbering via replicated spatial placement of just ten numerals into tens, hundreds, thousands, and tenths, hundredths, thousandths.

And another innovation: in his *Compendious Book on Calculation by Completion and Balancing*, Muḥammad ibn Mūsā al-Khwārizmī (780–850) gave us the word "algebra," or *al-jabr* meaning "restoration" through the consolidation of terms on both sides of an equation.* A Latinized version of al-Khwārizmī's name gave us the word "algorithm," or a series of step by step procedures.[14]

Such procedures were not simply conceptual. Their meanings could also be transposed into engineered objects, such as a mechanical flute, an "instrument that plays by itself," as described by the brothers bin Shākir in about 850,[15] and by al-Jazari in 1206.[16] Arguably, this is the first programmable machine.[17]

---

* http://meaningpatterns.net/algorithm

[12] George Makdisi, 1990, *The Rise of Humanism in Classical Islam and the Christian West*, Edinburgh, UK: Edinburgh University Press, pp. 32, 294, 348–49.

[13] Jim Al-Khalili, 2011, *The House of Wisdom: How Arabic Science Saved Ancient Knowledge and Gave Us the Renaissance*, New York, NY: Penguin Press, pp. 99–112.

[14] Jean-Luc Chabert, ed., 1994 [1999], *A History of Algorithms*, translated by C. Weeks, Berlin, Germany: Springer, pp. 1–2.

[15] Banū Mūsa bin Shākir, c.850 [1979], *The Book of Ingenious Devices*, translated by D.R. Hill, Dordrecht, NL: D. Reidel, p. 76.

[16] Ibn al-Razzaz al-Jazari, 1206 [1974], *The Book of Knowledge of Ingenious Mechanical Devices*, translated by D.R. Hill. Dordrecht, NL: D. Reidel Publishing Company, pp. 170–72.

[17] Jim Al-Khalili, 2011, *The House of Wisdom: How Arabic Science Saved Ancient Knowledge and Gave Us the Renaissance*, New York, NY: Penguin Press, p. 74.

Here – in the Islamic grammar, logic, mathematics, and mechanics of these centuries – we find the foundations of modern designs of meaning that eventually become modern scientific thought and computable meaning.[§1.3.2d] In this moment, conscious analysis of structure becomes an instrument with which to consider meanings-in and meanings-for[§0.3.3] the world.

§3d   *Ferdinand de Saussure's* Course in General Linguistics

Ferdinand de Saussure[*] is widely credited as the founder of the modern discipline of linguistics. His scheme for human meaning plays through ideas that take much the same form they did for the Arabic grammarians a millennium before. There is, however, no evidence that he knew these grammarians or their thinking.

But as a student of Sanskrit, Saussure of course knew Pāṇini,[§0.4a] and this much older idea of doing grammar in order to explore the structures of meaning.[18] The Arabic grammarians of intellectual Islam went beyond Pāṇini to say for the first time things about the connections of structures of meaning in language and the meaning of these structures in the logic of the world. Saussure brings us to these questions again.

Saussure creates a series of dichotomies. Where Al Fārābī had distinguished logic from vocal form,[§3c] Saussure distinguishes a concept from its manifestation in a spoken word. The concept, Saussure calls "signification," and the sound pattern of the spoken word, its "signal." Together, these two components form a "sign."

Then come some large generalizations. First, the relationship between signal and signification is arbitrary: the sound pattern "tree" in English or "arbre" in French is purely a conventional relationship to meaning (Ibn Jinnî's notion of "agreement"[§3.0a]). Mattâ ibn Yûnus had called the relation of meaning to expression "accidental."[§3b]

And a second generalization: the meaning of language is in its systematic patterning of contrasts, where different sounds in speech mark out conceptual distinctions, akin to Al Fārābī's "logic."[§3c] So, "a language is a system based on psychological contrasts between these auditory impressions." And: "a language is a system in which all the elements fit together, and in which the value of any one element depends on the existence of all the others; . . . all the words which express neighbouring ideas help define one another's meaning." From this perspective, "in language itself, there are only differences, . . . phonetic differences matched with a series of conceptual differences."[19]

---

[*]   http://meaningpatterns.net/saussure

[18]   Ferdinand de Saussure, 1881 [2017], *On the Use of the Genitive Absolute in Sanskrit*, translated by A. Sukla, Champaign, IL: Common Ground Research Networks.

[19]   Ferdinand de Saussure, 1916 [1983], *Course in General Linguistics*, translated by R. Harris, London, UK: Duckworth, pp. 67, 33, 113–14, 118.

Over this, Saussure layers some more dichotomies: the meaning-value of signification is immaterial, though the sound of the signal is material; the system of language is collective, though speech is individual; the language system is a site of social passivity, repeating received meanings, though its vocalization is a matter of individual will; the structure of language has a coherence at a single moment in time, though speech changes over time, affecting the system in evolutionary ways that are accidental and not noticeable to its speakers.[20]

In each of these dichotomies, linguistics is more interested in the immaterial, social conformity, system, and coherence in a moment of time than the materiality of meaning, individual agency, change, and history. These, in the last analysis, were also the proclivities of the Islamic grammarians, in their case for reasons of divine revelation and in order to privilege the textual powers of an imperial elite.

In our notion of "design," we want to suggest something different. We are as interested in structures where unique meanings can be made by persons, where change is as important as replication, and where we enact our meanings in a history whose future remains open. In our notion of "transposition," we want to track patterns of dynamic change, tracing microhistories of meaning within meaning functions and across meaning forms. The imminent transformability of one meaning into another is just as important as the paradigmatic logic of a stable system-in-the-moment.

Saussure's ambition was to found a science that went beyond language. He proposed that such a science might be called "semiology," anticipating a possibility with the scope of our multimodal, transpositional grammar. "A language is a system of signs expressing ideas, and hence comparable to writing, the deaf-and-dumb alphabet, symbolic rites, forms of politeness, military signals, and so on. It is simply the most important of such systems." Semiology was to be "a science which studies signs as a part of social life. It would form a part of social psychology."[21]

"Comparable to writing" is a revealing statement, showing Saussure's bias towards speech. "Deaf-and-dumb alphabet" is a strange notion when deaf signing is ideographic rather than phonemic, another indication of his bias towards speech. Language in the form of speech is for him unapologetically the "most important of such systems" of meaning as a consequence of the extent of its arbitrariness, its abstract, immaterial autonomy from the world of materialized meanings.

---

[20] Ferdinand de Saussure, 2002 [2006], *Writings in General Linguistics*, edited by S. Bouquet and R. Engler, translated by C. Sanders and M. Pires, Oxford, UK: Oxford University Press, pp. 201, 209.

[21] Ferdinand de Saussure, 1916 [1983], *Course in General Linguistics*, translated by R. Harris, London, UK: Duckworth, p. 15.

For this reason, onomatopoeia presents Saussure with a problem, or the non-arbitrary relation of the sounds of speech to the sounds of actions they reference – the "rustle" of leaves, the "chirp" of a bird, the "bang" of a colliding object, the "click" of a computer mouse, the "tap" on a door. Then there are what M.A.K. Halliday calls "phonaesthetic series," where a particular sound is associated with an area of meaning, so displaying another kind of non-arbitrariness – for instance the "-ump" in "hump," "bump," "lump," "rump," "plump," "stump," and "clump."[22]

For this reason, Saussure has to say that onomatopoeia is never an organic element of the linguistic system[23] – but surely, that can only be the case because he has positioned arbitrariness so centrally in his conception of the system, meanings that dissociate themselves from material reality by virtue of the strength of their structural relations. He privileges language as the highest form of meaning because so much of it is arbitrary, and so symbolic-abstract.

Meanwhile, many of the meanings represented in the unlanguaged world are arbitrarily connected to their referents – wedding rings, clothing styles, gestures, or visual conventions on maps, for instance. Or, considering by way of example the difference between chopsticks and a fork, the relations of object form to eating function are relatively arbitrary. So if we want to make arbitrariness the measure of semiotic sophistication, this is by no means the exclusive preserve of speech.

In this perspective, language has no special place in meaning, or at least not one that is distinguished by its arbitrariness. And for that matter, what is so special about arbitrary compared to non-arbitrary meanings? We discussed this earlier as a distinction between meanings-in and meanings-of.[§0.3.3] We have no reason to privilege the one kind of meaning over the other.

Saussure dismisses writing. At best, the purpose of writing is to represent speech, where "a spatial line of graphic signs is substituted for a succession of sounds in time."[24] At worst, says Saussure, writing "obscures our view of language," with, for instance, "irrational spellings" – as if writing were ideally a mere transliteration of speech.[25] No, we would respond, text is very different from speech, non-linear in much of its writing and reading in ways that speech can never be.

---

[22] M.A.K. Halliday, 1977 [2003], "Ideas About Language," pp. 92–115 in *On Language and Linguistics*, The Collected Works of M.A.K. Halliday, Volume 3, edited by J.J. Webster, London, UK: Continuum, p. 108.

[23] Ferdinand de Saussure, 1916 [1983], *Course in General Linguistics*, translated by R. Harris, London, UK: Duckworth, pp. 69, 175.

[24] Ibid., pp. 24, 70.   [25] Ibid., p. 29.

§3e   *Sebastiano Timpanaro's "Structuralism and its Successors"*

Sebastiano Timpanaro,[*] philologist and philosopher of materialism, published in 1970 a sustained critique of the broader movement that Saussure[§3d] founded, "Structuralism and its Successors." Here, he analyzes the inherent biases of structuralism, though he concedes greater complexity and balance to Saussure than to his successors.[26]

Timpanaro was by profession an editor and by training a philologist. His *magnum opus* explored the changes that occurred in the centuries of hand-written transcription of classical texts before the invention of the printing press, tracing the incremental errors and conscious or unconscious "improvements" made to texts by scribes.[27] Timpanaro's focus was on the tangible manifestation of texts, and the agency of scribes who might otherwise have been expected merely to repeat text true to its source. His analysis reveals the fluidly changing character of texts and the historicity of their meanings.

So too in his reading of Saussure and his successors, Timpanaro questions the abstract separation of language system and structure from language behavior, where we find "language basking in its own internal coherence," "a system unto itself." This amounts to a dematerialization of meanings, "setting the 'psychic' off from the 'physiological'."[28] It also means Saussure neglects things that are crucial to our grammar of multimodality where the "physiologies" or material practices of speech[§AS1.4.1] and writing[§AS1.4.7] are very different, and so too are their affordances.

In the title of his 1972 book, Frederic Jameson calls structuralism a "prison-house of language"[29] – where received, static systems of meaning determine our social being. This was before the rise of poststructuralism – Derrida and others.[§0.4d] But its weakness also is to over-emphasize language, even when framed more broadly as "discourse." The danger in both cases is when, either in structural analysis or poststructuralist "deconstruction," the structure of meaning in the abstract floats away from its points of reference in the material practices of meaning.

The aim of a transpositional grammar is to demonstrate the necessary traffic between text, image, space, object, body, sound, and speech – without

---

[*] http://meaningpatterns.net/timpanaro

[26] Sebastiano Timpanaro, 1970 [1975], *On Materialism*, translated by L. Garner, London, UK: New Left Books, pp. 135–220.

[27] Sebastiano Timpanaro, 1981 [2005], *The Genesis of Lachmann's Method*, translated by G.W. Most, Chicago, IL: University of Chicago Press.

[28] Sebastiano Timpanaro, 1970 [1975], *On Materialism*, translated by L. Garner, London, UK: New Left Books, pp. 142, 151, 161.

[29] Fredric Jameson, 1972, *The Prison-House of Language: A Critical Account of Structuralism and Russian Formalism*, Princeton, NJ: Princeton University Press.

privileging any of these forms of meaning. Even in domains where a lot of meaning is purely arbitrary or conventional, meanings are expressed and limited by the materiality of media[§AS1.4] – the constraints of time in speech, and space in image, for instance.

Today we are only able to read Saussure, not hear him speak. Saussure had notoriously postponed writing. When he died, loyal students hastily compiled their lecture notes into the *Course in General Linguistics*. The transcription of his speech was marked by the same "irregularities" of redesign identified by Timpanaro in the work of scribes in the medieval scriptoria, refining or "improving" the text where it appeared this was needed.[30]

In 1996 a stash of notes was found in the Saussure family home that seem truer to his intentions for being in his own hand.[31] (It's also ironical that lost, fragmentary, and partially reconstructed texts attract the interest they do – in this book, we have already worked over parts of the Walter Benjamin and Ludwig Wittgenstein legacies.)

In one of Saussure's notebooks, there is the draft of an unfinished letter to a notoriously anti-Semitic Paris newspaper, eviscerating "these swarms of parasites," Jews who had entered France from Germany. Perhaps this was a letter dictated by his father, a strident anti-Semite who was losing his eyesight. Perhaps it was written by his brother, Léopold, with whom Ferdinand was close and whose handwriting was similar. Léopold had written a book, *The Psychology of Colonization*, arguing that the peoples of the French colonies could and should never be assimilated to French civilization.[32]

So we might ask of Ferdinand, could some language systems be conceptually superior to others? Or we could ask more neutrally, what is the nature of their differences? Some argue that compromising references to race and ethnicity may have been edited out by Ferdinand's loyal students.[33] In Saussure's classification of "Aryan" and "Semitic" languages, the former were posited to be superior. Loyalists today argue that surely, none of this could be true.[34]

---

[30] John E. Joseph, 2012, *Saussure*, Oxford, UK: Oxford University Press, pp. 633–35.

[31] Ferdinand de Saussure, 2002 [2006]. *Writings in General Linguistics*, edited by S. Bouquet and R. Engler, translated by C. Sanders and M. Pires, Oxford, UK: Oxford University Press.

[32] John E. Joseph, 2012, *Saussure*, Oxford, UK: Oxford University Press, pp. 415–16, 440–45.

[33] Robert J.C. Young, 2002, "Race and Language in the Two Saussures," pp. 63–78 in *Philosophies of Race and Ethnicity*, edited by P. Osborne and S. Sandford, London, UK: Continuum, p. 67.

[34] Michael Lynn-George, 2004, "Writers, Intellectuals, Heroes: The Case of Ferdinand De Saussure," *The International Journal of the Humanities* 2:1243–49, p. 1246.

§3.1   Ontology

> ***Ontology.*** *How things are in the world. The relationship between the patterning*
> *of meanings and the patterning of the world. We make sense of the world through*
> *our inherited structures of meaning in the forms of text, image, space, object,*
> *body, sound, and speech, and their multimodal manifestations. But there is more*
> *to the structure of the world than the sense that we can for the moment make in*
> *these forms. There are excesses of meaning in the world – things we do not yet*
> *know but that are discoverable. And there are excesses of meaning not yet in the*
> *world, things that are imaginable and possibly realizable.*

The classical Arabic grammarians,[3a] as well as modern thinkers about semiotics or meaning structures – Saussure[3d] and Timpanaro,[3e] for instance – draw us, even if at times inadvertently, toward the overarching question of the connections between the patterns in meaning and the patterns in the world. This is a question of ontology, or the relation of the meanings of being (manifest in the patterns of text, image, space, object, body, sound, and speech, and their multimodal overlays), to being itself. Fig. 3.1 provides a rough map.

Form / Function: Ontology	Text	Image	Space	Object	Body	Sound	Speech
Ontology	Syntax, lexis	Visual structures, as represented in keys, and patterns of arrangement	Architectonic and natural spatial structures, as represented in plans, maps	Bounded objectness, the bonds that hold objects together and make them meaningful or usable wholes	Medical accounts of body; patterns of gesture, appearance, and enactment	Sound patterns as analyzed musical notation, or sampled for digital sound recording	Pragmatics

Fig. 3.1: Ontology

In the modern history of philosophy, there have been two main ways to frame the structuring of meaning. One is "idealism," or the notion expressed by René Descartes,[3.1.2g] that we make sense of the world by imposing human patterns of thought, or ideas. The other is "materialism," or the idea expressed by John Locke,[1.3a] that the world has intrinsic structures of meaning that our minds acquire through experience. This is a handy stereotypical distinction, though it is one that is hardly fair to Descartes and Locke, each of whose positions is more smartly balanced.

We want to argue that the material of the world and the ideal of our sense-making are never separate, as the stereotypers would for simplicity's sake want us to think. Call this a materialism if you will, because all sense-making is in, of, and through the material world. Or call it an idealism, because the material world is figured in our sense-making. We want to call this play of the material and the ideal "ontology," not only philosophically but also because we encounter this word in the practices of digital meaning, and this is what we will have it mean there too.[§3.1]

For there is more to the material than we have so far been able to experience – hence the possibility to discover, not only things that have hitherto been outside of our experience, but also things that may have been before our very eyes that we have not yet come to notice, and which with attentional effort we may still notice. And there is more to the ideal than what we have until now encountered in the real – actual possibilities that can be achieved humanly and in nature, as well as ideas that may prove practically impossible or wildly fictional. The starting point for such ideas many be the actual, but also ideas that may exceed the actual, for a while at least.

Capturing both the material and the ideal, we are going to parse the processes of ontology – the play of material and ideal – in the notion of design.[§0.4.1] Design is morphology, the identifiable structures of things. These are meanings-in the material, structures inherent in the actual. Design is also agency, or the scope for action which may exceed the hitherto-existing actual, in small or large ways. These are meanings-for, realizing the ideal.

When in this book we seem to tend towards materialism, it is because all sense-making is embedded in nature, society, and history, and its truths are discoverable. We are creatures of these determinations. And when we seem to tend towards idealism, it is because we are creatures who can by our actions determine, going beyond the actual to design the imaginable and create the new.

§3.1a   *Roy Bhaskar and Mervyn Hartwig's* Enlightened Common Sense

Roy Bhaskar is a materialist who absorbs idealism. His common sense is in the first instance as grounded and plain speaking as G.E. Moore's.[§2.3.2a] To this he adds "enlightened," exceeding the actual of what we are, in order to posit what might be.

Here comes another unfinished text (after Saussure's, Benjamin's, and Wittgenstein's), but not in this case because this author had writer's block, but because he published so much, across a sprawling oeuvre covering meanings in nature,[35] society,[36] human knowledge,[37] and the

---

[35] Roy Bhaskar, 1975 [2008], *A Realist Theory of Science*, London, UK: Routledge.
[36] Roy Bhaskar, 1998, *The Possibility of Naturalism: A Philosophical Critique of the Contemporary Human Sciences*, London, UK: Routledge.
[37] Roy Bhaskar, 1989, *Reclaiming Reality: A Critical Introduction to Contemporary Philosophy*, London, UK: Verso.

spiritual.[38] Nothing within the scope of ontology – the being of every-thing and the meaning of that being – did Bhaskar, it seems, neglect. This makes it hard to see the whole.

Bhaskar's last project before he died was to write an accessible synopsis, a summing up of his life's works and thoughts. The work was rushed; his energies were flagging. He dictated some over the telephone. His colleagues hastily typed. When he died in 2014, the manuscript was incomplete. So the colleagues decided to complete and edit the manuscript. Several set to work, but it finally fell to Mervyn Hartwig to "help Roy" by fleshing out the text.[*] This he did by trying to write as "as if I were Bhaskar." So a rough manuscript of 70,000 words became a final manuscript of 92,000 words.[39] The book was published in 2016 with the title *Enlightened Common Sense*.

Bhaskar's system came to be called "critical realism," where the claim to "realism" is that the world exists independently of the meanings we attribute to it. He and Hartwig encounter a world that is differentiated. It is structured, where the different parts of the world are in patterned relations, and where the patterns are stratified across many scales, from small and localized to global or cosmic. The world constantly changes. Its meanings can reveal themselves to us, and more, they can impose themselves on us.[40]

This world is both natural and historical. The natural part is historical, as Darwin's and other "natural histories" tell. And the historical is natural – human history has its eminently material forms and material effects, "presence of the past in our built environments, constitutions, institutions, problem-fields, practices, languages and ideas."[41] The natural and the historical are impossible to disentangle.

We would add, this is because humans are a species which emerged in natural history, whose sentience and sociability had already been prefigured in animals, from insects to primates. There is no humanity without animal existence – focusing our attentions, realizing intentions, moving in perceptual space, making sounds, using objects, eating, interacting with others in the species, birth/reproduction/death and a myriad of other natural intra- and inter-actions. These are multimodal meanings.

Nature and history are the ontology part of Bhaskar's system, where mean-ings are to be discovered. He complements this with an epistemology part,

---

[*] http://meaningpatterns.net/bhaskar

[38] Roy Bhaskar, 2000, *From East to West: Odyssey of a Soul*, London, UK: Routledge; Roy Bhaskar and Mervyn Hartwig, 2010, *The Formation of Critical Realism: A Personal Perspective*, London, UK: Routledge.

[39] Roy Bhaskar, 2016, *Enlightened Common Sense: The Philosophy of Critical Realism*, London, UK: Routledge, p. xiii.

[40] Ibid., pp. 7, 17, 24, 57, 83–84.   [41] Ibid., p. 69.

where meanings are to be made. In different societies with different histories, they are made differently. So, alongside ontological realism, he proposes an epistemological relativism.[42] Our historically evolved meaning systems affect the ways in which we understand the world. However, to the extent that they are historical – natural historical and human historical – the epistemological is a creature of the ontological; the ideal can be explained in terms of the real.

Bhaskar argues that Wittgenstein[§2.1.1a] allows the ideal to become disconnected from the real, in abstract figurations of structure which can float away from reference to reality.[43] "[T]reat of the network and not what the network describes,"[44] says the Wittgenstein of the *Tractatus*, unable yet to believe that there might not be a rhinoceros in the room.[§2.1.1a] This was before he began to agree with G.E. Moore about some material certainties.[§2.3.2a]

And before Wittgenstein there was Descartes,[§3.1.2g] who in his *cogito* prioritizes mind over matter, individual over society, humans over other species and nature, and egocentric agent over acted-upon others and things.[45] Such are the unfortunate habits of one strand in Western sense-making. However, despite these illusions, Bhaskar says ontology is always present, implicit even.[46] Pure idealisms are impossible.

For this reason, Bhaskar wants to abolish the dualisms that separate the ideal from the material, and the epistemological from the ontological: structure/agency, individual/collective, meaning/behavior, conceptuality/materiality.[47] This means that practically, in everyday commonsense experience, war is not just a concept; it is bloody. Homelessness is not just an idea; it is not having a roof over one's head.[48] War and homelessness are matters both of structure and agency, lived as individuals and in collectives. Warfare and housing are things to which we can attribute meaning and experience as behavior. They are events we can name conceptuality and experience materiality. The ideal is immanent in the real. This is common sense. And the truths of the real are discoverable in a potentially never-ending reflexive dialogue, a process of learning.[49]

Then Bhaskar brings us to the "critical" part of critical realism. He takes from Kant[§3.3e] the notion of "transcendental," or the overarching question of "what must be the case for some feature of our experience to be possible?"[50] Kant, an idealist, wants an answer not so far removed from Descartes, in the

---

[42] Ibid., p. 25.   [43] Ibid., p. 23.
[44] Ludwig Wittgenstein, 1922 [1933], *Tractatus Logico-Philosophicus*, London, UK: Routledge, §6.35
[45] Roy Bhaskar, 2016, *Enlightened Common Sense: The Philosophy of Critical Realism*, London, UK: Routledge, p. 177.
[46] Roy Bhaskar, 2000, *From East to West: Odyssey of a Soul*, London, UK: Routledge, p. 24.
[47] Roy Bhaskar, 2016, *Enlightened Common Sense: The Philosophy of Critical Realism*, London, UK: Routledge, pp. 8, 48–49.
[48] Ibid., pp. 12, 57, 171.   [49] Ibid., pp. 64, 121–24, 167.   [50] Ibid., p. 25.

fundamental categories of mind. Bhaskar's transcendental is grounded in the common sense of material being, its immanent structures that pattern the natural and social world, and where these patterns can be seen at many levels and in many perspectives – immediate and deeper, narrower and broader. With epistemological effort, the patterning in the levels and scales comes into view, coheres, makes sense.

What becomes discoverable in these deeper and broader views is not just the meaning of war and homelessness but the scandals of a "crisis system":[51] the scandal of inequality, the scandal of human damage to nature, the scandal of existential meaning in the society of the commodity. In these crises, common sense must become critical and enlightened. Reality speaks to ethics, demanding "transformative praxis" and "emancipatory change."[52] Humans have the capacity to exceed their historical selves, in a "desire to be free,"[53] an ideality that exceeds the actual. The excess of the ideal is rooted in our very natures as meaning-makers, "the transcendence involved in human creativity." For "Every human act is not only a transformation of what pre-existed but also *de novo*, a novelty, a new beginning."[54]

In our transpositional grammar, we call these new beginnings – small and large, incremental or revolutionary – design.[§3.2] Bhaskar, quoting Hartwig, quoting Eluard: this is to reach for a transcendental where "there is another world, but it is this one."[55]

§3.1.1   Material Structures

> **Material Structures.** *The patterning of meanings in nature, society, and history. Immanent order in the world.*

Nature has immanent material structures that are discoverable. So do human society and history, where Roy Bhaskar's bloody war and cold homelessness[§3.1a] speak to immanent structures that are inarguably material. To invoke our forms of meaning, this is irrefutable common sense – label-able, see-able, move-able, feel-able, listen-able, and speak-able. These are experienced as meanings-in.

The scope and sense of our meanings may be determined through text, image, space, object, body, sound, and speech, and their multimodal manifestations – these have human histories offering both openings for, and constraints

---

[51] Ibid., pp. 70, 204.   [52] Ibid., pp. 17, 5.   [53] Ibid., p. 71.
[54] Roy Bhaskar, 2000, *From East to West: Odyssey of a Soul*, London, UK: Routledge, p. 49.
[55] Roy Bhaskar and Mervyn Hartwig, 2010, *The Formation of Critical Realism: A Personal Perspective*, London, UK: Routledge, p. 66.

of, meaning. But always, these meaning practices are in a reflexive or dialectical relation to patterns of meaning-in material reality.

There is also a more direct, prosaic materiality to meaning. Text, image, space, object, body, sound, and speech all happen in physical and physiological media.[§AS1.4] We need to make matter to make meaning, and the matter gives form to the meaning. This is unavoidable in the case of communication.[§AS1.2.2] In the case of representation,[§AS1.2.1] we often use the matter of media as cognitive prostheses, tools that we use to help ourselves think. Even when we are just thinking, we are re-enacting in our minds forms of meaning that were in the first instance material – acts of writing, viewing, moving in space, experiencing object, feeling body, gesturing, hearing sound, and enunciating speech.

§3.1.1a Elizabeth Grosz's Incorporeal

If Roy Bhaskar[§3.1a] is a materialist who absorbs idealism, then Elizabeth Grosz[*] is an idealist who absorbs materialism. If Bhaskar discovers materialism in the impossibility of straightforward idealism, Grosz discovers idealism in the impossibility of straightforward materialism. Both end up in about the same place, though by different paths.

Grosz traces a line of thinking that she argues is solidly grounded on materialism, but which nevertheless uncovers meaning that exceeds the material. She starts her narrative with the Stoics of Ancient Greece, moving on to Baruch Spinoza, a contemporary of Descartes,[§3.1.2g] then to Friedrich Nietzsche in the nineteenth century, and Gilles Deleuze in the twentieth. The thread of continuity she calls "the incorporeal."

Meanwhile, she points out, it is "almost impossible to find a credible idealism today." Nevertheless, she asks "What intellectual maneuvers must materialism develop to hide what it must assume – concepts, processes, frames, that are somehow different from and other than simply material? ... How do materialists understand meaning or sense in terms beyond their materiality as sonorous or written trace?"[56]

---

[*] http://meaningpatterns.net/grosz

[56] Elizabeth Grosz, 2017, *The Incorporeal: Ontology, Ethics, and the Limits of Materialism*, New York, NY: Columbia University Press, pp. 17, 18. Some instances of the "new materialism": Franco "Biffo" Beradi, 2015, *And: Phenomenology of the End, Sensibility and Connective Mutation*, Pasadena, CA: Semiotext(e); Ian Bogost, 2012, *Alien Phenomenology, or What It Is Like to Be a Thing*, Minneapolis, MN: University of Minnesota Press; Ray Brassier, 2007, *Nihil Unbound: Enlightenment and Extinction*; London, UK: Palgrave Macmillan; Diana Coole and Samantha Frost, eds., 2010, *New Materialisms: Ontology, Agency, and Politics*, Durham, NC: Duke University Press; Graham Harman, 2016, *Immaterialism*, Cambridge, UK: Polity; Galen Strawson, 2013, "Real Naturalism," *Proceedings of the American Philosophical Association* 86(2):125–54; Quentin Meillassoux, 2006 [2008], *After Finitude: An Essay on the Necessity of Contingency*, London, UK: Continuum.

Spinoza, Grosz argues, offers an alternative to Descartes' dualism, where body and mind are two separate substances, thinking and things. Rather, there is a single indivisible substance where meanings are immanent, pervasive, indivisible. "Descartes is thus mistaken, according to Spinoza ... for matter must necessarily have a conceptual equivalent, an idea, not in opposition to ... but as one of the attributes of substance ... Substance is both material and incorporeal."[57]

For his heretical idea that God might be pervasively present in the world (Grosz's "incorporeal"), Spinoza was twice charged with heresy and convicted, first by the Portuguese-speaking Jewish community of his birth in Amsterdam, and later by the Catholic Church when his writings were listed in the *Index of Banned Books*. "The Lord shall blot out his name from under heaven,"[58] said the rabbis of his Amsterdam congregation. It was precisely these kinds of separations that Spinoza said were impossible, of heaven from earth, of a speaking God from spoken-to humanity, of language from living.

In the twentieth century Gilles Deleuze[§3.1.1b] also draws inspiration from Spinoza, whose "substance" Deleuze renames the "plane of immanence." Instead of conceptual oppositions between mind and body, or material and ideal, he finds "entwinement of ideality or conceptuality with materiality or corporeality – the nature of the world, substance – is folded in on itself through life and the process of becoming-alive." This, says Grosz, is "an incorporeal order of sense that enables and conditions thought."[59] The material and the ideal lie together in tension, a state of becoming, the one never separable from the other.

This is where, to slip across to the terminology we use for our transpositional grammar, the material has its as-yet-unrealized meanings-in, and the ideal or incorporeal is capable of exceeding the already-real, of creating meanings-for.

§3.1.1b Gilles Deleuze's Logic of Sense

As well as Spinoza, Gilles Deleuze draws inspiration from Lewis Carroll's *Alice*.[§1.1.1h] In *Alice*, Charles Dodgson exceeds the reason he teaches as professor of logic at the Oxford University,[60] to be reincarnated as the imaginary-real Lewis Carroll.

---

[57] Elizabeth Grosz, 2017, *The Incorporeal: Ontology, Ethics, and the Limits of Materialism*, New York, NY: Columbia University Press, pp. 6–7, 54–55, 61.

[58] Steven Nadler, 1999, *Spinoza: A Life*, Cambridge, UK: Cambridge University Press, p. 120.

[59] Elizabeth Grosz, 2017, *The Incorporeal: Ontology, Ethics, and the Limits of Materialism*, New York, NY: Columbia University Press, pp. 164–65.

[60] Charles Dodgson (*nom de plume*, Lewis Carroll), 1896 [1977], *Symbolic Logic*, New York, NY: Clarkson Potter.

"When *I* use a word," Humpty Dumpty said in rather a scornful tone, "it means just what I choose it to mean – neither more nor less."

"The question is," said Alice, "whether you *can* make words mean so many different things."

"The question is," said Humpty Dumpty, "which is to be master – that's all."

"They've a temper, some of them – particularly verbs, they're the proudest – adjectives you can do anything with, but not verbs – however, *I* can manage the whole lot of them! Impenetrability! That's what *I* say!"

"Would you tell me, please," said Alice "what that means?"

"Now you talk like a reasonable child," said Humpty Dumpty, looking very much pleased. "I meant by 'impenetrability' that we've had enough of that subject, and it would be just as well if you'd mention what you mean to do next, as I suppose you don't mean to stop here all the rest of your life."

"That's a great deal to make one word mean," Alice said in a thoughtful tone.[61]

Carroll brings us, says Deleuze,[*] an elaborate "play of sense and nonsense." "Humpty Dumpty (whose waist and neck, tie and belt, are indiscernible) lacks common sense as much as he lacks differentiated organs." He "opposes ... the impenetrability of incorporeal entities without thickness to the mixtures and reciprocal penetrations of substances, ... the 'pride' of verbs to the complacency of substantives and adjectives. Impenetrability also means the frontier between the two – and that the person situated at the frontier, precisely as Humpty Dumpty is seated on his narrow wall, has both at his disposal." Concludes Deleuze: "Things and propositions are less in a situation of radical duality and more on the two sides of a frontier represented by sense."[62]

Or to hear Humpty Dumpty through our notion of design,[§0.4.1] nouns and verbs can, if we so wish, be left to their regular tempers, their commonsense meanings. Nouns, by transposition, can be made verbs. Their tempers are changeable. Penetrating can become penetration, or in its absence, impenetrability. We can also make a noun – "impenetrability" – mean what we will, from meaning, to non-meaning, to meaning, to ending the discussion. We can manage meaning. Design is a matter of meanings-for as much as it is meanings-in.

Back to Deleuze (this time writing with Félix Guattari): "The concept is incorporeal, even though it is incarnated or effectuated in bodies." And, "the plane of immanence is ... the image thought gives itself of what it means to think, to make use of thought, to find one's bearings in thought."[63] This,

---

[*] http://meaningpatterns.net/deleuze

[61] Lewis Carroll, 1872 [2000], *The Annotated Alice: Through the Looking Glass*, edited by M. Gardner, New York, NY: W.W. Norton, p. 213–14.

[62] Gilles Deleuze, 1969 [1990], *The Logic of Sense*, translated by M. Lester, New York, NY: Columbia University Press, pp. xiii, 80, 25, 24.

[63] Gilles Deleuze and Félix Guattari, 1991 [1994], *What Is Philosophy?*, translated by H. Tomlinson and G. Burchill, New York, NY: Columbia University Press, pp. 21, 37.

Deleuze calls "transcendental empiricism,"[64] as if to create an oxymoron as clear in its paradoxical meaning as Humpty Dumpty's "impenetrability," where the grounded and specific is at the same time universal, a place where the actual and the virtual[65] are at one.

Deleuze traces this part of his thinking back to another materialist philosopher who also allowed that thinking could exceed the material, Alexius Meinong.[66] "The totality of what exists," said Meinong in 1904, "including what has existed and will exist, is infinitely small in comparison with the totality of the objects of knowledge."[67] This excess of meaning, things that could be meant but which do not materially exist – fictions, conjectures, imaginary possibilities and the like – later came to be called "Meinong's jungle."

Speaking less elliptically than either Deleuze or Humpty Dumpty, Elizabeth Grosz[§3.1.1a] calls for an ontology not only of what is, but what might be. We know there are things that we do not know. Ideality is our "ability to direct, orient, and internally inhabit materiality ... Ideality provides the cohesion of form, the orientation or direction toward which material things tend, the capacity for the self-expansion of material things and relations into new orders." For "without ideality, a plan, a map, a model, an ideal, a direction, or a theme, materiality would not realize itself." In this ideality, moreover, there is "no definitive break between animals and humans and between animals, plants, and inanimate objects." Our focus then should be the "material constitution of an ordered world in which the connections between things, between entities and events, come to or always already have meaning."[68]

Or, to rephrase in terms of our grammar of multimodality, our ontology of structure, there are no meanings that are not at once material and ideal, meanings-in that are also meanings-for. Yet material structures can exceed the ideal, the actually but as-yet unmeant. And ideal structures can exceed the material, the meanable but as-yet materialized. To which we add a caveat: the meanable is not just by humans, but any sentient creature, and for that matter any insentient entity that may act.

[64] Gilles Deleuze, 1995 [2001], *Pure Immanence: Essays on a Life*, translated by A. Boyman, New York, NY: Zone Books, p. 25.
[65] Gilles Deleuze and Claire Parnet, 1977 [2007], *Dialogues II*, New York, NY: Columbia University Press, pp. 148–52.
[66] Gilles Deleuze, 1969 [1990], *The Logic of Sense*, translated by M. Lester, New York, NY: Columbia University Press, p. 35.
[67] Alexius Meinong, 1904 [1981], "The Theory of Objects," pp. 76–117 in *Realism and the Background of Phenomenology*, edited by Roderick M. Chisholm, Atascadero, CA: Ridgeview, p. 79.
[68] Elizabeth Grosz, 2017, *The Incorporeal: Ontology, Ethics, and the Limits of Materialism*, New York, NY: Columbia University Press, pp. 2–3, 12–13.

Alice is the perfectly well tempered inhabitant of the world. She encounters nonsense, and makes of it what she can, always testing it against her common sense, as if the imaginable could be true. She is ever-ready to contemplate the possibility that meaning might exceed experience. She encounters the smile of the Cheshire Cat that can linger after its body has vanished. She heeds the advice of the Queen to think of six impossible things before breakfast. She is subject to arbitrary but mercifully ineffectual calls to injustice. "Off with her head," orders the Queen, but for all the times she has barked this order, there has never been an execution.

Alice is cautious but never conquered by fear of the unknown. She is careful and at the same time courageous. She remains curious, tolerant of difference, and self-reflective about the comparative conditions of her knowing. She is always willing to move between sense and nonsense, where nonsense is a test of possibility and imagination is a journey into knowability.

Leaving Humpty Dumpty, Alice says,

"Good-bye!" ... and, getting no answer to this, she quietly walked away: but she couldn't help saying to herself as she went, "Of all the unsatisfactory – " (she repeated this aloud, as it was a great comfort to have such a long word to say) "of all the unsatisfactory people I *ever* met – " She never finished the sentence, for at this moment a heavy crash shook the forest from end to end.[69]

§3.1.2   Ideal Structures

> *Ideal Structures. Possible and impossible patterns of meanings-in nature, society, and history, not certain for common sense but nevertheless conceivable or inconceivable, and so capable of representation and communication as such. The ideal is figured as meanings-for.*

The meanings-in material structures are conjecturable, discoverable, namable. If not yet meant, they lie waiting as meanings capable of representation and communication. When discovered, material structures may well be found to be ordered.

But just as likely, we will encounter disorder, unpredictability, arbitrariness, or events that are merely circumstantial. We may find perplexing contradiction and dissonance. We may find endless complexity whose meaning is, for the moment at least, and maybe much longer, impenetrable. If so, with Humpty Dumpty[§3.1.1b] we

---

[69] Lewis Carroll, 1872 [2000], *The Annotated Alice: Through the Looking Glass*, edited by M. Gardner, New York, NY: W.W. Norton, pp. 219–20.

must end the discussion, at least for a while. Such are the dimensions of material immanence, where the material frequently proves less than ideal.

The multimodal practices of science use the ideal to push ahead with the meaning of the material in nature – hypotheses, theories, mathematical formulae, diagrams, models. The multimodal practices of the humanities, the arts, and politics use the ideal to push the meanings of the material that is socio-historical life – agendas, incremental change, ideal lives, utopias even. We create likely and unlikely stories, and test sense with conjecture that may prove either sense or nonsense when we try things out in our imaginations or in material practice.

We need to work at this sense-making. Deleuze:[§3.1.1b] "Sense is never a principle or an origin; . . . it is produced."[70] Ontology is design, playing material structures against ideal structures, where the material and the ideal must always be immanent in each other, and the one can always exceed the other. These excesses offer us reason to mean, because though the material and the ideal can never be separated, there is greater meaningful possibility in the world than what we immediately encounter – more in material structures, and more in ideal.

For this reason the immanent need not rigidly determine the imminent. Things can change and we can make them change. Design figures immanence, meanings-in. Design*ing* figures imminence, meanings-for.

§3.1.2a Errol Morris' Unknown Known

MORRIS: Let me put up this next memo.
RUMSFIELD : You want me to read this?
MORRIS: Yes, please.
RUMSFIELD:
        "February 4, 2004.
Subject: What you know.
There are known knowns.
There are known unknowns.
There are unknown unknowns.
        But there are also unknown knowns. That is to say, things that you think you know that it turns out you did not. I wonder if in the future public figures will write as many memos as I did. I doubt it. I must have gotten in the habit of dictating things that were important."[71]

We know of US Secretary of Defense Donald Rumsfield's war in Iraq,[*] in a way that must be as certain as Bhaskar of war's material bloodiness.[§3.1a] For the

---

[*] http://meaningpatterns.net/morris-unknowns

[70] Gilles Deleuze, 1969 [1990], *The Logic of Sense*, translated by M. Lester, New York, NY: Columbia University Press, p. 72.
[71] Errol Morris (Director), 2013, *The Unknown Known* (www.springfieldspringfield.co.uk/movie_ script.php?movie=the-unknown-known).

war's now-certain materiality, the ideal exceeded the material. There were no weapons of mass destruction. (Though this could have been known.) There was no workable plan after the invasion. (This too could have been known.) One person's ideal may be another person's material. Such are the occlusions of interest.[§AS2]

Iraq was a tenuous link to the larger "war on terror." The so-called "torture memos" authorized "enhanced interrogation" of terror suspects held without trial in the jail at Guantanamo Bay in Cuba. Did these notions also find their way into the Abu Ghraib prison on the edge of Baghdad where suspected enemies were held? Rumsfield says no, not this kind of "unbelievably bad, illegal, improper behavior."

A formal report of the Red Cross said that the interrogation techniques in Abu Ghraib were "tantamount to torture." The report was leaked to the *Wall Street Journal*, which posted it online, in full.[72] But the world took no notice. So long as these meanings were in words, they remained largely unknown.

Only later did what was already known to the Red Cross become more widely known through a series of digital photos taken by US military personnel. The word "tantamount" was not as real, not as indisputably material, as these images.

Here is Rumsfield again, working around the now-indisputably known, trying to find his way about in Meinong's jungle:[§3.1.1b]

Well, we know that in every war there are things that evolve that hadn't been planned for or fully anticipated and that things occur which shouldn't occur . . .

If you take those words and try to connect them in each way that is possible . . . There was at least one more combination that wasn't there: The unknown knowns. Things that you possibly may know that you don't know you know . . .

Yeah, I think that memo is backwards. I think that it's closer to what I said here than that. Unknown knowns. . . .

Oh, my goodness, . . . I can't believe some of the things I wrote. I don't know where all those words came from.[73]

§3.1.2b Colin McGinn's Mindsight

Rumsfield's "unknowns"[§3.1.2a] and Humpty Dumpty's "impenetrability"[§3.1.1b] – these words mark excesses of the ideal over the material. We can find a parallel excess in the grammar of image.

---

[72] *The American Journal of International Law*, 2004, "U.S. Abuse of Iraqi Detainees at Abu Ghraib Prison," 98(3):591–96, p. 594.

[73] Errol Morris (Director), 2013, *The Unknown Known* (www.springfieldspringfield.co.uk/movie_script.php?movie=the-unknown-known).

In image, the excess of the ideal arises experientially in the difference between seeing with the body's eye (perceiving), and seeing with the mind's eye (envisioning). Take the Eiffel Tower, says philosopher Colin McGinn[*] in his book, *Mindsight*. If you are there, you can see it. But if you are not, you can envision it. "Seeing requires the presence of the object, while visualizing does not."[74]

There are profound differences between perceiving and envisioning. In the form of image, this is the difference between encountering material structures of meaning, and figuring ideal structures. The visual field, says McGinn looking at the Eiffel Tower, consists of a center and periphery; it has a fuzzy perimeter; it exists in a spatial relation to the observer in a perceiver-centered space that has a foreground and a background; dimensionality is created by binocularity; we concentrate consecutively on parts of what we see.[75] We encounter an infinity of the seeable, the overflowing of potential detail in perception, says Jean-Paul Sartre in another among the few philosophies of the image[76] – few, we suggest, because of our modern obsession with language. If you looked at the Eiffel Tower for long enough you could see every piece of wrought iron, and every intersection between one piece and another. For impractical purposes, this is an infinity of seeability.

Envisioning, seeing the Eiffel Tower in one's mind's eye, is a completely different thing. The mental image is no longer saturated with an infinity of detail. We call to mind only the criterial features, the things that make the Eiffel Tower different from other agglomerations of wrought iron, or other tall things, like trees or mountains. Mental images are selective and abstracting. They desaturate the seeable world. Beyond the mental image, there is no more detail than that immediately called to mind. Much that could have been attended in perception is now unattendable.[77]

And another difference: "images can be willed but percepts cannot." Mental images are reincarnated visual images, a metamorphosis of meaning that is creative and transformative.[78] Sartre: envisioning is "shot through with creative will, ... a synthetic act of consciousness."[79] And Merleau-Ponty[§AS1.4.3d]

---

[*] http://meaningpatterns.net/mcginn

[74] Colin McGinn, 2004, *Mindsight: Image, Dream, Meaning*, Cambridge, MA: Harvard University Press, p. 7.
[75] Ibid., p. 22.
[76] Jean-Paul Sartre, 1940 [2004], *The Imaginary: A Phenomenological Psychology of the Imagination*, translated by J. Webber, London, UK: Routledge, p. 9.
[77] Colin McGinn, 2004, *Mindsight: Image, Dream, Meaning*, Cambridge, MA: Harvard University Press, pp. 23–25, 35.
[78] Ibid., pp. 12, 35.
[79] Jean-Paul Sartre, 1940 [2004], *The Imaginary: A Phenomenological Psychology of the Imagination*, translated by J. Webber, London, UK: Routledge, pp. 15, 7.

on the kind of structures in such envisionings: these reflect "the intrinsic coherence of my representations."[80]

John Locke[§1.3a] directed his philosophy to perception, where the structures of the material world determine the structures of our thinking. René Descartes directed his philosophy to envisioning, where the mind's eye gives order to the material world. However, we need both these orientations, and Locke and Descartes[§3.1.2g] were each more nuanced than their caricatures usually allow.

Of course, despite their profound differences, direct perception and mental images are inextricably connected in the dialectical experience of everyday life. There is never one without it already having been the other. This, Sartre calls the "paradoxical simultaneity of percept and image," seeing with the eye and seeing with the mind's eye.[81]

The Eiffel Tower is recognizable when you see it in reality because the mind's eye has captured its criterial form in previous experience, or the mediated social experience of pictures. "Tantamount to torture" is the meaning we bring to the images of the Abu Ghraib prison,[§3.1.2a] after we have seen them for the first time or when we see them again. Sartre again: "In perception, knowledge is formed slowly; in the [mental] image, knowledge is immediate."[82] Material structures and ideal structures of visual meaning are irrevocably interconnected, and in the dialectical play, the one always learning from the other. Experientially, however, they are profoundly different.

Though inseparable, the material can exceed the ideal, which is why we always need to keep looking – in the grammars of science, the humanities, arts, and politics. There is endlessly more to be seen in the infinity of the seeable. And the ideal exceeds the material. This Sartre calls "the imaginary," a kind of "surpassing."[83] McGinn again: "cognitive imagination can outstrip sensory imagination in its representational content ... Cognitive imagination takes us into alternative worlds ... The image liberate[s] the mind from the domination of perception."[84]

Then there is the complicated dynamic of the picture, where someone has recreated the seeing for you, as if the naturalistic painting were truthful or the camera never lied. But this is an optical illusion, as full of visual tricks as it is also true. It is a series of *trompe l'oeil*, giving off the impression of being present, of virtually being there when in fact all you are seeing is a picture.[§2.2c]

[80] Maurice Merleau-Ponty, 1945 [2002], *Phenomenology of Perception*, translated by C. Smith, London, UK: Routledge, p. xi.

[81] Jean-Paul Sartre, 1940 [2004], *The Imaginary: A Phenomenological Psychology of the Imagination*, translated by J. Webber, London, UK: Routledge, p. 11.

[82] Ibid., p. 9.   [83] Ibid., pp. 186–87.

[84] Colin McGinn, 2004, *Mindsight: Image, Dream, Meaning*, Cambridge, MA: Harvard University Press, pp. 129, 138.

The impression of knowing the Eiffel Tower or "tantamount to torture" even without seeing either tower or torture is another moment where the ideal exceeds the material, though our sociable and mostly trusting common sense assures us that the image, one way or another and however mediated, references material reality. The ideal structure of the image that stays in our mind's eye, we trust, is connected to material structures of meaning.

Pictures themselves can transpose the excess of the ideal in the materiality of their practices, transferring the selectivity of the mind's eye into the media of cartoons, plans, or abstract expressionism. Images can also render material impossibilities that could only have been generated in the mind's eye and not reality – the visual paradoxes and "strange loops"[85] of M.C. Escher's lithographs or the unconceivable survival of characters through the hurly-burly of Disney[§AS2.5.1b] animations.

From ordinary seeing and envisioning, McGinn went on to write about the human hand, and how "we are handlers by nature: we take hold, reach and grasp, seize, stroke, poke, squeeze, probe, and rub." The anticipation of such meanings he calls "prehension," not so unlike the way perception anticipates envisioning, while envisioning anticipates perception. The way we recognize the Eiffel Tower when we see it is from our previous experiences of seeing it or seeing images made by other people who have seen it. So it is with our hands. Our use of them creates meaning in our bodies and material objects. "We are great big hands extended toward the world around us."[86]

Then this in 2011: McGinn, now aged 61, writes to a graduate student, Monica Morrison, aged 26. He says, "thank you, dearest ... I send you a hand squeeze." Later he told her he "had a hand job imagining you giving me a hand job."[87] Just envisioning, he said, nothing had materialized, nothing that might be an object of perception in embodied reality. But the emails were real and for the student and the administration at the University of Miami. They amounted to sexual harassment, both student and administration said, so McGinn resigned.

[85] Douglas R. Hofstadter, 1979, *Godel, Escher, Bach: An Eternal Golden Braid*, New York, NY: Basic Books, pp. 10–15.

[86] Colin McGinn, 2015a, *Prehension: The Hand and the Emergence of Humanity*, Cambridge, MA: MIT Press; Colin McGinn, 2008, *Mindfucking: A Critique of Mental Manipulation*, Stocksfield, UK: Acumen.

[87] https://slate.com/human-interest/2013/10/colin-mcginn-sexual-harassment-case-was-the-philosophy-profs-story-that-clear-cut.html; www.dailymail.co.uk/news/article-3289180/What-Britain-s-philosopher-thinking-sent-400-racy-emails-pretty-student-30-years-junior.html

§3.1.2c John Watson's Behavior

Ontology is the play of the material and ideal. What is its psychology? How do structures of meaning in the material connect with structures of meaning in the ideal? To begin to address this question, we turn to founding moments in the modern discipline of psychology. At first, we get an answer grounded in ordinary, material life, one which does not privilege humans and their speech.

Among the founders of psychology were experimental scientists whose interest was in the ways in which animals and humans react to environmental stimuli – Ivan Pavlov in Russia, and Edward Thorndike and John B. Watson[*] in the United States. Watson became a standard-bearer of what came to be called the behaviorist approach with his 1913 manifesto in *Psychological Review*, "Psychology as the Behaviorist Views it,"[88] then his 1914 book, *Behavior: An Introduction to Comparative Psychology.*[89]

Watson does not just define an approach to psychology that neutrally sits alongside others. He says that other major approaches are scientifically unsound. Studying the stuff of the mind – complex mental states and consciousness – via methods of "introspection" is too self-referential. How can one use the mind to work out what is happening inside the mind without coming to self-confirming conclusions? (One could make parallel arguments about studying the internal conceptual architectures of language systems – from structuralism to Analytical Philosophy.)

Instead, Watson proposes that psychologists study the reactions of animals and humans to their environments, the things they manifestly do and the environmental reasons they do them. This, instead of speculation about the workings of mind. "Psychology as the behaviorist views it is a purely objective experimental branch of natural science ... [I]ts starting point [is] the observable fact that all organisms, man and animal alike, do adjust themselves to their environment ... Certain stimuli lead organisms to make ... responses ... [G]iven the responses, the stimuli can be predicted; given the stimuli, the responses can be predicted."[90]

On this basis, and contrary to the commonly held views at the time about innately unequal intelligence, Watson concluded that a change in environmental conditions can produce a change in social outcome:

---

[*] http://meaningpatterns.net/watson

[88] John B. Watson, 1913, "Psychology as the Behaviorist Views It," *Psychological Review* 20:158–77.
[89] John B. Watson, 1914, *Behavior: An Introduction to Comparative Psychology*, New York, NY: Henry Holt and Company.
[90] Ibid., pp. 1, 7.

Give me a dozen healthy infants, well-formed, and my own specified world to bring them up in and I'll guarantee to take any one at random and train him to become any type of specialist I might select – doctor, lawyer, artist, merchant-chief and, yes, even beggar-man and thief, regardless of his talents, penchants, tendencies, abilities, vocations, and race of his ancestors.[91]

§3.1.2d B.F. Skinner's Verbal Behavior

A sentence about a scorpion had prompted Sîbawayh to write his grammar of Arabic.[§3a] Another sentence about a scorpion prompted psychologist B.F. Skinner to write his book, *Verbal Behavior*. Skinner was to become one of the best-known psychologists of the twentieth century, a leading proponent of what was for a time its leading school – "behaviorism,"[§3.1.2c] or the theory that human activity and thought are products of environmental conditioning. To rephrase this in the terms we are proposing for an ontology of structure, for the behaviorists, material structures of meaning precede and determine ideal structures. Behaviorists are the Locke[§1.3a] of caricature.

Attending a dinner at the Harvard Society of Fellows in 1934, Skinner was still a young, relatively unknown researcher. He was excited to find himself sitting beside Professor Alfred North Whitehead.[§1.2.2c] The famed philosopher and mathematician was, with Bertrand Russell, author of the monumental, three-volume investigation of the underlying meanings of mathematics, *Principia Mathematica*.[§1a] "I began to set forth the principal arguments of behaviorism with enthusiasm," Skinner tells us in the closing pages of *Verbal Behavior*.

Verbal behavior was surely different from other kinds of behavior, said Whitehead. "Let me see you account for my behavior as I sit here saying, 'No black scorpion is falling upon this table.'" This sentence was one that could not have been grounded in any direct, antecedent behavioral experience. In our phraseology, the ideal exceeded the material. So, Skinner says, "The next morning I drew up the outline of the present study."[92] His *magnum opus* was not completed and published until 1957, nearly a quarter of a century after this moment of its inspiration.

Skinner's principal contribution to the research and social agenda of behaviorism was to develop the concept of "operant conditioning," where behavioral response is determined by anticipated outcomes in the form of reward (reinforcement) or punishment. This idea he elaborated in his 1938 book, *The Behavior of Organisms: An Experimental Analysis.*[*]

---

[*] http://meaningpatterns.net/skinner

[91] John B. Watson, 1925, *Behaviorism*, New York, NY: W.W. Norton, p. 82.
[92] B.F. Skinner, 1957, *Verbal Behavior*, New York, NY: Prentice Hall, pp. 456–57.

The organism Skinner chose to test and demonstrate this principle was the white rat. "It has the advantage over man of submitting to the experimental control of its drives and routine of living."[93] The hungry rat is put in a box, with a lever at one end. Pressing the lever releases food. The rat is trained to learn that a certain stimulus produces a reward in the form of food. "The work is 'mechanistic,'" Skinner concludes, "in the sense of implying a fundamental lawfulness or order in the behavior of organisms."[94]

"Instead of going to a drinking fountain," Skinner says on the first page of *Verbal Behavior*, "a thirsty man may simply 'ask for a glass of water' – that is, he may engage in behavior which produces a certain pattern of sounds which in turn induces someone to bring him a glass of water."[95] By the next page, he proposes to replace the term "language" and the discipline of "linguistics" with the study of "verbal behavior." This was to mark his recognition of the primacy of social practices and human activities without which language is meaningless and linguistics a disconnected abstraction. The last part of the previous sentence is not quite the way Skinner would have put it. It is our paraphrase, signaling in advance our sympathies with some of the premises of behaviorism. Or to push the paraphrase further, behaviorism affirms the foundational presence of material structures of meaning, and their integral connection with the ideal.

Of course, after the horrors of concentration camps, gulags, and places like Abu Ghraib,[§3.1.2a] we take fright at the idea of putting rats in boxes, then extrapolating from this to the human experience, or even the more general ideal of placing people in institutional boxes of one kind or another, figuratively when not literally. However, with Skinner, in this grammar of multimodality we also abandon notions of "language" and "linguistics," for some similar as well as some different reasons.

But let's continue our historical narrative. Because now a protagonist with the honorific "linguist" enters the drama, in the personage of Noam Chomsky.[§3.1.2f]

§3.1.2e Noam Chomsky's Review of Verbal Behavior

Within a few short years of its publication, an angry upstart just down the road in Cambridge at Massachusetts Institute of Technology in one fell swoop demolished not only *Verbal Behavior*, but the whole behaviorist edifice. Or so, at the time, it seemed. But maybe Noam Chomsky's[§3.1.2f] book review in the journal *Language*[*] was just a tipping point, marking a shift of academic

---

[*] http://meaningpatterns.net/chomsky-skinner

[93] B.F. Skinner, 1938, *The Behavior of Organisms: An Experimental Analysis*, New York, NY: Appleton Century Crofts, p. 47.
[94] Ibid., p. 433.   [95] B.F. Skinner, 1957, *Verbal Behavior*, New York, NY: Prentice Hall, p. 1.

sensibilities in favor of cognitivism and "the language turn," as well as popular revulsion at the prospect of behaviorist control in real or metaphorical "Skinner boxes."[§3.1.2i]

How is it possible, asks Chomsky, that a child's brain could absorb something so complex as Chinese or English, just from the environment and just through cycles of reinforcement? And how is it that we can "constantly read and hear new sequences of words, recognize them as sentences, and understand them?"

This also returns us to the question of the black scorpion which, as Whitehead pointed out, was not falling on his and Skinner's dinner table.[§3.1.2d] How can humans make sense of things that have not yet been experienced in material reality, and for that matter, may not ever be?

Chomsky's answer: "It appears that we recognize a new item as a sentence not because it matches some familiar item in any simple way, but because it is generated by the grammar that each individual has somehow and in some form internalized." ("[I]n some form internalized" – this is a strangely vague formulation.) Early in their acquisition of speech, a young learner has acquired the "ability ... to distinguish sentences from nonsentences, detect ambiguities," and this "apparently forces us to the conclusion that this grammar is of an extremely complex and abstract character, and that the young child has succeeded in carrying out what from the formal point of view, at least, seems to be a remarkable type of theory construction."[96]

This is strangely unclear – the learner has constructed the grammar, remarkably, or is it so remarkable that they could never themselves have constructed it? Or, if not "internalization" or "construction," perhaps some mystery source? – "a variety of motivational factors about which nothing serious is known in the case of human beings."[97]

Behaviorism had set out to account for the sources of human meaning in terms of the patterns of ordinary experience – perhaps unconvincingly, or even scarily at times. But Chomsky's alternative mechanisms to account for the sources of speech are not at all clear.

As we will see, this vagueness proves troublesome.[§3.1.2j] Half a century later, Chomsky is still struggling for answers to the question of what makes grammaticalness and the sources of human meaning. He is still working in a region that Watson would have considered to be the self-referential space of consciousness. This turns out to be the self-enclosed space of a static language system, not dissimilar in its essential form to the structuralist system of meaning theorized by Saussure.[§3d] Chomsky and Saussure alike build ideal

---

[96] Noam Chomsky, 1959, "Review of 'Verbal Behavior,' by B.F. Skinner," *Language* 35 (1):26–58, pp. 44, 56, 57.
[97] Ibid., p. 43.

geometries of meaning whose origins are obscure and that are disconnected from the meanings-in the material world.

§3.1.2f Noam Chomsky's Syntactic Structures

Noam Chomsky is said to have commenced a revolution in the discipline of linguistics. His *Syntactic Structures* was published in 1957 – the same year as Skinner's *Verbal Behavior*.[§3.1.2d] Until this point linguistics had been a mostly empirical science. There were few notable exceptions, prominent among which was Saussure's *Course in General Linguistics*.[§3d] Scholars described languages in practice, frequently choosing for their point of empirical reference an as-yet undocumented language of an indigenous people. Or they traced the history of language and the interconnections between languages using the techniques of philology and historical linguistics. Sometimes they projected circumstantial similarities between languages, and other times they found striking differences indicating the presence of different language families.

Studying under Zellig Harris, a philologist of Semitic languages at the University of Pennsylvania, Chomsky's honors and then masters dissertations were cast in his adviser's mold, analyses of Hebrew. With their focus on grammar, they also gestured towards his future work.[98]

However, Chomsky's Ph.D. broke the mold decisively. *The Logical Structure of Linguistic Theory* was a remarkably ambitious title for a dissertation.[§AS2.2a] Chomsky's first book, *Syntactic Structures*, was based on a small part of his doctoral dissertation, presenting twenty-six grammatical rules that could be summarized into just four pages in the appendix.[99]

With *Syntactic Structures*, Chomsky turned linguistics upside down. Or, at least that was the effect of his version of linguistics and the version adopted by those who would become his followers. If the old linguistics had been the study of many particular languages in the rich empirical differences of their practice and their history, Chomsky's focus was every language, and in theory. His quest: to find the universal mechanisms of grammar. And his measure: we shall call it "grammaticalness."

The words and phrases of a language, Chomsky points out, can be arranged in an infinite number of combinations. He calls this general theoretical language "L." Then, "the fundamental aim in the linguistic analysis of a language L is to separate the *grammatical* sequences which are the sentences of L from the *ungrammatical* sequences which are not sentences of L and to study the structure of the grammatical sequences." Sentences can be broken up into their

---

[98] Randy Allen Harris, 1993, *The Linguistics Wars*, Oxford, UK: Oxford University Press, p. 38; Robert F. Barsky, 2011, *Zellig Harris: From American Linguistics to Socialist Zionism*, Cambridge, MA: MIT Press, pp. 41–43.

[99] Noam Chomsky, 1957, *Syntactic Structures*, Amsterdam, NL: de Gruyter Mouton, pp. 111–14.

components, and the grammar of their combination analyzed. "The man" (noun phrase) + "hit the ball" (verb phrase). Next, the phrases can be broken into "the" + noun, and so on.[*]

Sentences can be grammatical but meaningless. ("Colorless green ideas sleep furiously.") Different sentences can have the same underlying structure. The passive of "John loves Mary" has the same underlying structure as "John is loved by Mary." In his simplified, essential "kernel," Chomsky suggests an approach to a grammar where "the passives are deleted and reintroduced by a transformation that interchanges the subject and object of the active." So, in "the simplest grammar ... we find that the kernel consists of simple, declarative, active sentences ... and all other sentences can be described more simply as transforms."

Then there are ambiguous sentences that may have the same words but more than one underlying structure. "The shooting of the hunters" might be a transformation of "the hunters shoot" or "they shoot the hunters." Grammaticalness occurs when transformations generate syntactic equivalence. Passive is equivalent to active. Ambiguous sentences have two underlying grammatical equivalences. And the measure of grammaticalness in each case? The "intuitive knowledge" that underlies what would be "acceptable to a native speaker."[100]

At first, Chomsky called his grammar "transformational-generative," meaning that there is a relatively small number of underlying grammatical rules from which all sentences in all languages are generated. And the constituent components of these sentences are an even smaller number of stable, abstract components in the form of noun phrases (for instance the/a + noun), verb phrases (for instance, auxiliary + verb), and the like. "We can represent this grammar as a machine," he says, "with a finite number of internal states." Grammar is an "abstract system ... of representation related only by general rules."[101]

But by the mid-sixties, Chomsky had changed the focus of his grammar from a grammatical "kernel" to something even more basic, which he now called "deep structure," or more plainly, "the rules that specify well-formed strings of minimally functioning units" of syntax. He also became interested in nesting structures, or recursion: "[[[the man who you met] from Boston] who was on the train]."[102]

"Deep structure" is the grammatical logic underlying language, any language, every language. Surface structure is the manifestation of grammatical

---

[*] http://meaningpatterns.net/chomsky-structures

[100] Ibid., pp. 13, 15, 77, 80, 89, 13.   [101] Ibid., pp. 37, 59.
[102] Noam Chomsky, 1964, *Aspects of the Theory of Syntax*, Cambridge, MA: MIT Press, pp. 3, 13.

logic in a particular language. But how does one work back from the hearable forms of speech to these deep structures? (Chomsky's language analysis always starts with phonemics, or speech, ignoring writing as if it were secondarily irrelevant, a mere rendering of speech.) His practice of linguistics came to demand such technical dexterity that his transformational grammar became impenetrable to all but specialists.

Whence the standard for judging the underlying grammaticalness of speech? "Linguistic theory is concerned primarily with an ideal speaker-listener, in a completely homogeneous speech community, who knows the language perfectly and is unaffected by such grammatically irrelevant conditions as memory limitations, distractions, shifts of attention and interest, and errors (random or characteristic) in applying language in actual performance."[103] In other words, the standard is one that never, in a more fallible human reality, exists.

And what is the source of the examples Chomsky uses to illustrate his theory to demonstrate what is grammatical and what is not? Where do "colorless green ideas" and other such apparently meaningless but perfectly grammatical sentences come from? "How do I know?" Chomsky responds, as if his interviewer were asking a silly question. "Because I am a native speaker of the English language."[104] Chomsky is the source, the standard. For the purposes of theory formulation, he suspends all the constraints of speech in practice. Instead he analyzes an idealized version of his own speech. He makes it all up.

The ultimate object of Chomsky's analysis, somewhat like Husserl's "bracketing,"[§0.4c] is the working of the human mind, reducible to its essentials. "Linguistic theory is mentalistic, since it is concerned with discovering mental reality underlying actual behavior." Chomsky's grammar idealizes the perfectly grammatical structures. These are what he extrapolates to be the essence of mental reality, even though actual behavior may be erratic.

Chomsky's is "a theory of linguistic intuition,"[105] be that sourced in the intuitions of the speaker that drive their syntax, or the intuitions of the linguist who disentangles their underlying logic of meaning – logics which may not have been evident even to the speaker, and of which the speaker may not be conscious.

---

[103] Ibid., p. 4.
[104] Quoted in Randy Allen Harris, 1993, *The Linguistics Wars*, Oxford, UK: Oxford University Press, p. 97.
[105] Noam Chomsky, 1964, *Aspects of the Theory of Syntax*, Cambridge, MA: MIT Press, pp. 4, 19.

§3.1.2g René Descartes' "Cogito"

Cogito ergo sum! announced René Descartes[*] in 1637.[§1.3a] "I think there-fore I am!"

In an era of intellectual self-effacement and species-doubt, this statement is often taken to be the quintessential philosophical expression of anthropo-morphic arrogance. As if humans are so importantly different in the order of nature! As if the human meaning as manifest in the mind could be a separate substance from the world! As if the mind could construct the world from some inner source through a process of human meaning-ascription! As if there could be a single rationality that might be good for all persons, notwithstanding their irreducible diversity! For better or for worse, Descartes has become a postmodern scandal, or at least the version of him presented in convenient caricature.[§1.3a]

Noam Chomsky concurs with the Descartes of caricature, that the mind is an innate source of reason, not learned experience.[106] Linguistics is a self-examination of the *cogito*. In Chomsky's terms, the deep structures of reason-ing, available only to humans as a species, account for the creative aspect of language, or the capacity of these structures to generate an infinite number of utterances. Descartes, Chomsky says approvingly, had already pointed this out in the seventeenth century. Language is infinite, even if its underlying rules are reducible to a few.[107]

Following Descartes, Chomsky's aim is to "shift the main burden of expla-nation from the structure of the world to the structure of the mind."[108] He says that this creative aspect of language use is "both unbounded in scope and stimulus-free."[109] To be "stimulus-free" – this is a remarkable riposte to Skinner[§3.1.2d] about the sources of language.

To shift the meaning of things exclusively to the structure of the mind – this is a remarkably one-sided simplification of meaning in human experience. Or, to return to our notion of ontology,[§3.1] when it comes to meaning, Chomsky says that ideal structures of meaning are for all practical purposes disconnected from the material, which has no meaning without them.

We concede, with Chomsky, that the ideal structures of meaning can exceed the material. But we also want to say that this exceeding can happen in image[§3.1.2b] and other forms of meaning as profoundly as it does

[*] http://meaningpatterns.net/descartes

[106] Ibid., pp. 48–49.
[107] Noam Chomsky, 1980 [2005], *Rules and Representations*, New York, NY: Columbia University Press, p. 220.
[108] Noam Chomsky, 1976, *Reflections on Language*, London, UK: Fontana, p. 6.
[109] Noam Chomsky, 1966 [2009], *Cartesian Linguistics: A Chapter in the History of Rationalist Thought*, Cambridge, UK: Cambridge University Press, p. 60.

in speech – which is why we move beyond linguistics and into a multimodal grammar. And, with the behaviorists, we want to say the material structures of meaning are in a minimally co-determining relation with ideal or mental structures, and that to the extent that many of its meanings are as yet unknown. In the scope of knowability, the material also exceeds the ideal.

§3.1.2h Kenneth MacCorquodale's Reply to Chomsky

B.F. Skinner[§3.1.2d] never responds to Chomsky.[§3.1.2e] But one of Skinner's students, Kenneth MacCorquodale, does.

The fact that ... children acquire grammatical behavior at a rather early age and rather suddenly (Chomsky finds its rapidity "fantastic") does not require a previously laid-down inherited grammatical nerve net nor, even, anything much in the way of a strong genetic prepotency for grammar learning ... Nothing about the reinforcement process per se requires it to be slow and painstaking as Chomsky so insistently asserts ... That a child learns certain orders, such as adjective-noun, and actor-action sequences, on the basis of a relatively small sampling from the enormous universe of such instances shows simply that a child is able to make complex abstractions and to generalize from them to diverse new instances. Chomsky's one controlling variable for speech production – grammar, rules, competence – rests locked away in the brain somewhere, inert and entirely isolated from any input variables which could ever get it to say something.[110]

MacCorquodale calls Chomsky's mystery grammar source a "nerve net." Chomsky later comes to call it a "language organ," without saying what that organ might be in physiological terms or where or even how in the brain it might be identified or located.[111] He just makes up its possibility with the same self-assured intuition that Descartes' ascribes to the *cogito*.[§3.1.2g]

The behaviorist alternative, however, is relatively straightforward – the child makes a few core generalizations from ordinary experience, with the help of tools for human meaning that are embedded in that experience, including the speech of others, the characteristic objects and spaces of their constructed environment, the sounds and sights of nature and human artifice – not just raw experience, but pre-mediated experiences that are the communicative and epistemic artifacts of human history.

Chomsky: It is implausible that a child could learn in a few months what has taken evolution perhaps millions of years.[112] Skinner: In evolutionary terms, "a verbal environment could have arisen from nonverbal sources."[113] We're with

---

[110] Kenneth MacCorquodale, 1970, "On Chomsky's Review of Skinner's 'Verbal Behavior'," *Journal of the Experimental Analysis of Behavior* 13(1):83–99, pp. 93, 95.

[111] Noam Chomsky, 2000, *New Horizons in the Study of Language and Mind*, Cambridge, UK: Cambridge University Press, p. 4.

[112] Noam Chomsky, 1964, *Aspects of the Theory of Syntax*, Cambridge, MA: MIT Press, p. 59.

[113] B.F. Skinner, 1957, *Verbal Behavior*, New York, NY: Prentice Hall, p. 470.

Skinner on this, for several reasons. One is that we haven't yet found the language organ. One day, scientists might locate the "neurological correlates of consciousness,"[114] but so little is yet known about the relation of mind to brain, that if and when clearer answers emerge, they are likely to be very different from today's best guesses.

And another reason: despite Chomsky's disbelief, we can create a plausible historical account of the sources of human meaning, ontogenetic and phyloge-netic. In the ontogenetic account, the young child has a cognitive capacity to generalize, to feel and hear and see particular things and develop general-izations. They do this through an active process of making the world mean-ingful, or the processes of learning that Vygotsky traces.[§1.1.3a] The impossible infinities of the world can be simplified by induction, and this is made feasible by the fact that the discoverable world itself is patterned.

Then, the child is supported by a rich phylogenetic inheritance, a rich resource in the form of historically developed generalizing media – words, icons, objects, spaces, physical structures, bodily gestures, the stuff we have been discussing in this grammar. These are available designs for meaning that help them to (re)make their meanings, albeit in ways that are never quite the same. We can, in other words, create a plausible account of how meanings, in their entirety, can be learned. Any such account must be developed at the intersection of life history and human history.

Skinner's terminology in *Verbal Behavior* becomes strange ("mand," "tact," "echoic," and more), and after Chomsky's demolition, nobody uses it. But Skinner does attempt to create an account of these processes based on ordinary experi-ence and grounded in the structures of meaning immanent in the material world.

In our transpositional grammar, we offer a different terminology from the behaviorists. Nevertheless our sources of human meaning, like Skinner's, are located in the materiality of nature and history (sights, objects, spaces, bodies, sounds), and the social reconfigurations of nature in different historical moments for the purposes of our species-living. Humans have enormous capacities to learn, and so do other sentient creatures to varying degrees. The processes of learning and its practical substance are the objects of our analysis, not intuition sourced in some yet-to-be discovered organ of the *cogito*.

§3.1.2i B.F. Skinner's Beyond Freedom

B.F. Skinner pushed forward with his behaviorist work as if Chomsky had not spoken. His experiments moved on from rats to pigeons, always placed in his

---

[114] Christof Koch, 2004, *The Quest for Consciousness: A Neurobiological Approach*, Engelwood, CO: Roberts and Company; Christof Koch, 2012, *Consciousness: Confessions of a Romantic Reductionist*, Cambridge, MA: MIT Press.

"Skinner boxes" in order to regulate environmental influences for experimental purposes.

Applying these principles of environmental control to humans, he designed and built a "Baby Tender" for Deborah, his second daughter. In 1945, *Ladies Home Journal* published an article he had written extolling its virtues: "walls well insulated, and on one side, which can be raised like a window, ... a large pane of safety glass." Inside, the temperature can be controlled, ideally to about 86°F so the child needed no clothing, only a diaper.

"Crying and fussing could always be stopped by slightly lowering the temperature ... A single bottom sheet operates like a roller, ... stored on a spool outside the compartment at one end and passes into a wire hamper at the other, ... ten yards long and lasts a week ... A weekly bath is enough ... " and, with this device "it takes about one and one-half hours each day to feed, change, and otherwise care for the baby." And another "advantage: ... the soundproofing also protects the family from the baby!"[*]

The editor at *Ladies Home Journal* must have been skeptical, because when the article was published, it had been given the title, "Baby in a Box."[115] Skinner found a manufacturer, who came up with a name for the product, the "Heir Conditioner." It never took off.

Skinner must have had a proclivity for boxes. Some Japanese followers created a sleeping and music listening box for him which he installed in the basement office he had in his house in Cambridge, Massachusetts, not far from his work at Harvard University. A timer buzzed at 5.00am every morning, signaling that he had to start work.[116]

Skinner's program was to demonstrate the spatial and object-oriented engineerability of animal activity, and by extension, human activity. He aimed to show the learnability of regularized behavior in controlled conditions. He demonstrated that meanings can be materially configured. Objects and spaces can be designed that make available options for activity, and offer prompts to action.

The Skinner box was a conditioning machine. "A hungry rat [can be seen] in an experimental space which contains a food dispenser; ... any behavior on the part of the rat which depresses the lever is, as we say, 'reinforced with food.'" Transferring this insight to schooling, "teaching is the arrangement of contingencies of reinforcement under which students learn ... The application of operant conditioning to education is simple and direct."[117]

---

[*] http://meaningpatterns.net/skinner-boxes

[115] B.F. Skinner, 1945, "Baby in a Box," *Ladies Home Journal*.
[116] Daniel W. Bjork, 1993, *B.F. Skinner: A Life*, New York, NY: Basic Books, plates before p. 177.
[117] B.F. Skinner, 1968, *The Technology of Teaching*, New York, NY: Meredith Corporation, pp. 61–65.

Skinner invented a "teaching machine," also neatly contained in a box, even if this time the child being conditioned was outside the box, literally though perhaps not metaphorically. A lone child was presented material, a question was posed by the machine as substitute teacher, the student gave an answer, and then she was judged right or wrong. If right, she could move on; if wrong she must answer again.[118] This was behaviorism translated into mechanized practice. Ever the aspiring entrepreneur, Skinner filed a patent application, and the home appliance company Rheem licensed from him the right to create a product they called the "Didak."[119] In the market, it was no more successful than the Heir Conditioner.

Nor was Skinner reticent to articulate his philosophy of the human. The "autonomous man," in control of his own actions, is no more than self-flattery.[120] Society was a series of engineered environmental controls, not the self-deluding *cogito* of "mentalistic accounts of thinking" where the subject is in control.[121] Emotion is an illusion, its source not some inner cause, but environmental conditioning.[122]

The consequences of the self-delusions of ego-directedness, Skinner said, produced the disasters of the modern world. "It is not difficult to demonstrate a connection between the unlimited right of the individual to pursue happiness and the catastrophes threatened by unchecked breeding, the unrestrained affluence which exhausts resources and pollutes the environment, and the imminence of nuclear war."[123] At this late point in his career, Skinner was writing a manifesto for the application of behaviorist principles to the broadly sociopolitical regulation of behavior, his best-selling book *Beyond Freedom and Dignity.*

He wrote a novel that also became a best-seller, *Walden Two* (the first Walden was Thoreau's), about an ideal community that had adopted the principles of behavioral engineering, where babies were raised communally in air cribs, property was held in common, and people earned labor credits rather than cash.[124] Among the many communal experiments of the 1960s, several tried to put into practice Skinner's behaviorist principles to create a cooperative,

---

[118] B.F. Skinner, 1954 [1960], "The Science of Learning and the Art of Teaching," pp. 99–113 in *Teaching Machines and Programmed Learning*, edited by A.A. Lumsdaine and R. Glaser, Washington, DC: National Education Association; B.F. Skinner, 1958a, "Teaching Machines," *Science* 128(3330):969–77.

[119] B.F. Skinner, 1958b. "Teaching Machine," edited by U.S. Patent Office; Daniel W. Bjork, 1993, *B.F. Skinner: A Life*, New York, NY: Basic Books, pp. 179–80.

[120] B.F. Skinner, 1971, *Beyond Freedom and Dignity*, New York, NY: Alfred A. Knopf, p. 213.

[121] B.F. Skinner, 1974, *About Behaviorism*, New York, NY: Vintage Books, p. 113.

[122] B.F. Skinner, 1953, *Science and Human Behavior*, New York, NY: Free Press, p. 160.

[123] B.F. Skinner, 1971, *Beyond Freedom and Dignity*, New York, NY: Alfred A. Knopf, p. 213.

[124] B.F. Skinner, 1948 [1969], *Walden Two*, London, UK: Macmillan.

non-competitive society. One was in Twin Oaks, Virginia; another was Los Horcones in Sonora, Mexico.[125]

What did it mean to go beyond freedom and dignity? This strange and disturbing title had been suggested by Skinner's editor at Knopf. In a time of social turmoil, it did manage to sell a lot of books. It also helped get him a scary cover on *Time* magazine, his picture surrounded by a rat in a box, a pigeon, a teaching machine, and an eerie pastoral scene. Under the masthead was the headline, "B.F. Skinner Says: We Can't Afford Freedom."[126]

Sebastiano Timpanaro[§3e] has a phrase that sums up the politics of behaviorism: "authoritarian technocratism."[127]

§3.1.2j Noam Chomsky's Kinds of Creatures

If Skinner had nothing to say about Chomsky, Chomsky still had a lot of things to say about Skinner. Since he had reviewed Skinner's *Verbal Behavior*,[§3.1.2e] he saw fit to update his critique on the publication of Skinner's *Beyond Freedom and Dignity.*[§3.1.2i] Chomsky again heaps scorn on the notion that language rules could be acquired by generalization from experience. "So far as is known, the relevant properties can be expressed only by the use of abstract theories (for example, a grammar) describing postulated internal states of the organism, and such theories are excluded, a priori, from Skinner's 'science'."[128]

Beyond this essential conceptual difference, "as to its social implications, Skinner's science of human behavior, being quite vacuous, is as congenial to the libertarian as to the fascist." For instance, "let us consider a well-run concentration camp with inmates spying on one another and the gas ovens smoking in the distance, and perhaps an occasional verbal hint as a reminder of the meaning of this reinforcer. It would appear to be an almost perfect world." However, "suppose that [humans] want to be free from the meddling of technocrats and commissars, bankers and tycoons, mad bombers who engage in psychological tests of will with peasants defending their homes," – the Vietnam War was raging at the time[§AS2.2d] – "behavioral scientists who can't tell a pigeon from a poet, or anyone else who tries to wish freedom and dignity out of existence or beat them into oblivion."[129]

---

[125] Daniel W. Bjork, 1993, *B.F. Skinner: A Life*, New York, NY: Basic Books, pp. 160–64.

[126] *Time Magazine*, 1971, "Behavior: Skinner's Utopia: Panacea, or Path to Hell?," *Time*, September 20, p. 73.

[127] Sebastiano Timpanaro, 1970 [1975], *On Materialism*, translated by L. Garner, London, UK: New Left Books, p. 14.

[128] Noam Chomsky, 1971, "The Case against B.F. Skinner," *New York Review of Books*, 17 (11):18–24.

[129] Ibid.

Meanwhile, Chomsky kept working on his "abstract theories," addressing the "postulated internal states of the organism." He kept demonstrating that nouns in noun phrases, verbs in verb phases, determiners like "the," and not too many other elemental components, generated "representations."[130] So, "John hit the boy." There is no need to consider what the elemental components reference, because one noun is substitutable for another, one verb for another. "Language consists of two components, a lexicon and a computational system." Of these two, Chomsky was only concerned with the computational system.

Over the years, in book after book Chomsky progressively reduces his grammar to a "minimalist program," examining now the "principles and parameters" that themselves underlie the specifics of grammars in particular languages. These must (surely, he conjectures) be "invariant and unlearned."[131] The reason for retreat into a minimalist program was because, as Chomsky and his followers continued to make up new sentences in English, or in different languages, "the system exploded in complexity." The only way forward was to "show that the diversity of rules was superficial."[132] Underlying all these grammars was something deeper, and Chomsky kept trying to get at that.

Well into his eighties, Chomsky remained a prolific writer. Reviewing two of his 2016 books, the writer of the "Johnson" language column in *The Economist* set out with the heading, "Noam Chomsky: The theories of the world's best-known linguist have become rather weird."[133] The minimalist program had by now been further minimized to a conceptual phenomenon called "Merge" (the capitalization is Chomsky's), or the mechanism by means of which ideas can be embedded inside each other.

"Instinctively, birds that fly, swim." Chomsky is still making up sentences. Language is hierarchical, not linear, because "instinctively" must be associated with "swim" and not "fly." Merge involves recursion, or nesting meanings inside meanings. Ultimately, ultra-minimally, this is all there is, a "single operation ... [that] takes any two syntactic elements and combines them into a new, larger hierarchically structured expression." Language only becomes sequential when it is exteriorized.[134] If the reductions are themselves to be reduced to an essence that can be reduced no further, this is it. Layering over

---

[130] Noam Chomsky, 1986, *Knowledge of Language: Its Nature, Origin, and Use*, New York, NY: Praeger, pp. 56–57.

[131] Noam Chomsky, 1995, *The Minimalist Program*, Cambridge, MA: MIT Press, pp. 168–70.

[132] Noam Chomsky, 2002, *On Nature and Language*, Cambridge, UK: Cambridge University Press, pp. 92–93.

[133] Johnson [pseudonym], 2016, "Noam Chomsky: The Theories of the World's Best-Known Linguist Have Become Rather Weird," *The Economist*, 23 March.

[134] Robert C. Berwick and Noam Chomsky, 2016, *Why Only Us: Language and Evolution*, Cambridge, MA: MIT Press, pp. 8, 103, 116–17, 10.

this essence is too much variety and complexity to be specified, and for this reason, it's best to restrict the theory to its essence.

Here now are the essential components of Merge: we have elementary word-like "atoms of computation," which Chomsky says is in the range of 30,000–50,000. As always, he referring to speech here, not writing. Then we have the computational processes of Merge which can arrange these in an infinite number of recursions, or nests within nests – "infinite because there is no longest sentence."[135] By this means, language provides the capacity to generate "an infinite range of expressions from a finite set of elements."[136]

We want to argue the opposite, that in writing and other forms of meaning the atoms of reference can go on for ever, connected by their transposability with the endlessly open knowability of structures of material meaning. We are also capable of coming to understand instances and concepts we have never encountered before. On the other hand, when it comes to syntactic structures, we fast reach a point where nesting becomes impractical. Syntax is not infinite. Sentences can get too long.

No other creature can Merge, says Chomsky, not even other primates.[137] This is a unique part of our "genetic endowment" that must have occurred at an evolutionary moment, in a sudden genetic shift, a "great leap forward" about 50,000 to 100,000 years ago.[138] The human language facility, he says, has since then remained essentially unchanged. Once formed, Chomsky's humans stay fixed by nature in a single, biological, language-*cogito* event.

How and why this great leap forward happened, says Chomsky, may forever remain a mystery. Someday, it may be that a language organ will be found and "studied in the same way as chemical, optical, electrical, and other aspects" of the human body, the biomechanics of its processes.[139] But maybe not even this. For, "if we are biological organisms, not angels, much of what we seek to understand may be beyond our cognitive limits."[140]

---

[135] Ibid., p. 66; Noam Chomsky, 2016, *What Kind of Creatures Are We?*, New York, NY: Columbia University Press, pp. 10–13, 19, 41.

[136] Marc D. Hauser, Noam Chomsky, and W. Tecumseh Fitch, 2002, "The Faculty of Language: What Is It, Who Has It, and How Did It Evolve?," *Science* 298:1569–79; W. Tecumseh Fitch, Marc D. Hauser, and Noam Chomsky, 2005, "The Evolution of the Language Faculty: Clarifications and Implications," *Cognition* 97(2):179–210.

[137] Robert C. Berwick and Noam Chomsky, 2016, *Why Only Us: Language and Evolution*, Cambridge, MA: MIT Press, pp. 85, 90.

[138] Ibid., pp. 49–50, 70–71; Noam Chomsky, 2016, *What Kind of Creatures Are We?*, New York, NY: Columbia University Press, pp. 20, 25, 3.

[139] Robert C. Berwick and Noam Chomsky, 2016, *Why Only Us: Language and Evolution*, Cambridge, MA: MIT Press, pp. 54, 56.

[140] Noam Chomsky, 2016, *What Kind of Creatures Are We?*, New York, NY: Columbia University Press, pp. 39, 52, 94, 104.

This is where Chomsky indeed becomes weird. These were precisely the kinds of mystery that behaviorism, with its pedestrian focus on the dynamics of human and animal activity in the context of environment, set out to avoid.

In the end, both Skinner and Chomsky find themselves locked into deterministic structures, offering limited scope for human agency and conscious change in the conditions of living. Skinner says that we humans cannot make more of ourselves than material conditions structured by the boxes into which we are placed. If change is possible, it is limited to what the technocrats can do to redesign the boxes.

Chomsky, for his part, says we cannot be more than the ideal structures of meaning in the neurophysiology of recursion located in speech alone; these are "invariant and unlearned" and the only freedom we have is to fill the syntactic slots with different words.

If we go with Skinner, we are trapped inside the unyielding determinism of a one-sided materialist ontology.[§3.1.2i] But if we go with Chomsky, we are figments of a one-sided idealist ontology, whose driving forces are ultimately mystical.

Today, we might recoil at the practice of putting rats, pigeons, and persons into experimental boxes. However, Skinner may also be right in principle, that we shouldn't have the arrogance to think that we are so very different from other sentient creatures. In their own ways, primates and insects also mean. Sentience is the capacity of organisms for self-control, to act in time and space, and to interact in ways that can be characterized, not only as communication, but by implication, representation.

All sentient creatures mean, by virtue of their sentience. This is a more remarkable event in natural history than our human species-peculiarities. And if there are still a few peculiarities to our species, a capacity to recognize our modest place in natural history should be one.

After a while, both Chomsky's and Skinner's projects come to a halt. They reach dead ends under the burden of their internal complexities and external limitations, and their followers fall away. Having refined their one-sided ontologies to perfection, of neurophysical rationalism in the case of Chomsky and socio-environmental determinism in the case of Skinner, each project collapses, *in extremis*.

§3.2   Design

Design. An account of patterns in meaning: the patterns of conventional meaning that are our design resources; the transformation of meaning through designing action that brings into play patterns of differing, where the new meaning draws from available resources for meaning, nevertheless transforming these; and the traces of meaning left in the world that are the residues of design.

Even if, early on, one of the speakers stopped talking, the conversation between Chomsky[§3.1.2e] and Skinner[§3.1.2d] represents one of the great debates of human self-understanding in modern times, replaying and refracting older philosophical conversations. If Chomsky's hero is Descartes,[§3.1.2g] should Skinner have thought in philosophical terms, with his focus on the materiality of experience, his hero would surely have been Locke.[§1.3a] Or at least, such affinities would be to the stereotypical personae of Descartes and Locke.

Against these polarized alternatives, we want to counterpose an ontology of design,[§0.4.1] which has a bit of both ways, and is more, and for that is neither. In an ontology of design, patterns of being (meanings-in) can never be separated from patterns of knowing (meanings-for). This applies to all sentient creatures, rats as well as humans, ants even – though of course humans are different from other sentient creatures for the extent of their knowing and the scale of their species' impact on natural being. But this is only a matter of degree. Sentient life is the ground of an ontology of design.

Then, there is the knowable, in the material structures of nature and society, but which are not yet known. This is where material structures of meaning exceed the ideal, for the moment at least, and perhaps elusively if some remain forever unknowns. And there is the imaginable, where ideal structures of

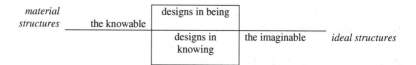

Fig. 3.2: Designs in the meeting of material and ideal structures

meaning exceed the material, for the moment at least, and forever when the ideal is unrealizable in material reality.

For this reason, structures of meaning are not stable; nor are they rigidly determined. There is always more that can be known, and knowing may unsettle our present patterns of being and knowing.

And there is always more that can be imagined, and this imagining may prompt us to change our patterns of knowing and being. More of the morphology of being and knowing is always discoverable; more is always achievable, by translating the imaginable into practice. These may be small designs in everyday personal life, or larger designs in and for society and history.

Whatever the scale, the ontology of design is the same, in the play of ideal and material structures of meaning. In every act of meaning, no matter how mundane, we interweave patterns in being with patterns in knowing; we take meanings-in and transform them into meanings-for.

We have available to us an infinity of patterns in being and knowing, and an infinity of knowable and imaginable. As a consequence, our position in time and space – the configuration material and ideal resources available for meaning – is not only patterned in conventional and predictable ways. It is also, always, circumstantially unique.

This is how, when we mean, we cast the timbre of our voice, the image of our mindsight, the nuances of our personality, and the expression of our identity grounded in history and experience. Designing meaning is always a process of remaking the world, always new in its specificity but nevertheless always a recasting of meaning from a historically available residue of meaning resources.

What is left is a world redesigned, ideally and, or, materially.

Sixto Diaz Rodriguez sings:[141]

> And you claim you got something going
> Something you call unique . . .
> And you assume you got something to offer
> Secrets shiny and new
> But how much of you is repetition?[*]

New, some. Repetition, some. Existentially, as agents of meaning, we feel there is something new to everything we mean, and that is true, not just because it is true for me in the moment, but because it is always new for all time. Never has quite this meaning been meant before. And there is repetition, as we draw on historically developed and socially available resources for meaning.

§3.2a   Intelligent Medical Objects

Structures hang together. The manner of their hanging together is their "relations."

There is a company in the Research Park at the University of Illinois that teases out the nuances of how human bodies hang together, or don't so well in the case of illness and death. The name of the company is Intelligent Medical Objects or IMO, and its business interest is not just the classification of medical objects, but the relations between these objects. The sum total of these relations amounts what we can know about the human body today, and the relations of its failing.

"Object" is a revealing word, because the manner of relating of concepts is, in the era of digital meaning, frequently called "ontology" – the terms in digital

---

[*] http://meaningpatterns.net/rodriguez

[141] https://genius.com/Rodriguez-crucify-your-mind-lyrics

ontologies purport to reference objects of the material world, in this case manifest physiological conditions. These are not mere ideas, figures of cognition, residues of "epistemology." These are "objects," arranged in some sort of order, and this order is a series of determinate relations.

"Clinicians are asked to see 6–10 patients per hour & do all the documentation," says the PowerPoint presentation that is used to sell the IMO software product. "The most expensive resource in the healthcare ecosystem is currently being used to do the bulk of documentation via the Electronic Health Record (HER). How do you extract maximal value for your investment?"

IMO offers a standardized classification scheme by means of which medical vendors can share electronic records about a patient's medical condition, preserving "the truth of clinical intent." The next reason, they say, is less important, but one wonders: the coding of conditions and relevant medical procedures for billing patients and insurance companies.[*]

Not only is there a problem of accurate coding. There are two main classification schemes, ICD (the *International Statistical Classification of Diseases and Related Health Problems*)[142] and SNOMED (*Systematized Nomenclature of Medicine*).[143] ICD exists in a succession of versions, older records in ICD-9, and newer records in ICD-10 and after that, ICD-11. IMO provides apps, accessible on computers and phones, for looking up the terminology associated with different medical conditions across ICD-9, ICD-10, ICD-11, SNOMED, and other specialized medical ontologies.

IMO also creates its own terms from synonyms that emerge in medical practice and are commonly found in medical records, and maps these to the standard ontologies. For instance, IMO has a term "abnormal excitement," which maps to ICD version 9 code 799.29, "other symptoms involving emotional state." Version 10 of ICD codes this R45.0, "nervousness." SNOMED codes it 247006004, "Over-excitement," or "Uncontrollable excitement." At this point, medical classifications begin to run into another life-defining ontology, the *Diagnostic and Statistical Manual of Mental Disorders*.[144]

In our grammar of multimodality, these are concepts,[§1.1.3] referencing things that exist or happen in more than one instance, and for that, begging classification. This is not to say that the material and the ideal align easily, the concept and its instances, the knowing and its being. Many of these concepts are matters of judgment and contention, where the ideal only roughly aligns with the material, where knowing only captures being as a matter of judgment. "Excitement," "nervousness," and "emotional states" traverse vast territories

[*] http://meaningpatterns.net/diseases

[142] www.who.int/classifications/icd/en/   [143] www.snomed.org/
[144] www.psychiatry.org/psychiatrists/practice/dsm

of human experience, and the point at which these become a medical condition as distinct from healthy life may at times become a contentious matter between patients, doctors, and insurance companies.

The official historians of ICD trace the origins of formal classification of medical conditions to registrations of the causes of death from Italy in the mid-fifteenth century and England in the mid-sixteenth. ICD had its beginnings in the International Statistical Congress which first met in Brussels in 1853, when the "CD" part of the acronym stood for "causes of death." At the 1860 meeting in Paris, Florence Nightingale used death classification statistics to show the causes of hospital deaths and how they could be reduced.[145]

The first version of the *International List of Causes of Death* was adopted at the Chicago congress of 1893.[146] Since then, ICD has gone through eleven major versions. The title "Causes of Death" was changed to "Classification of Diseases" in 1949 when the World Health Organization took responsibility for it. WHO now hosts periodical revision conferences and manages the revision process. ICD-10 was released in 1994, ICD-11 in 2018. ICD-11 expands the number of codes available to 55,000, up from the 14,400 in ICD-10.[147] Meanwhile, SNOMED, in development since 1965 and now controlled by a London-based not-for-profit, was created to describe a range of pathologies and clinical processes – 311,000 in total – not all of which are adequately captured in ICD.[148]

ICD is arranged in what we have called "supermarket order,"[§0d] where objects for practical purposes are put beside each other, only in one place, but with other things that are meaningfully associated. The practical process here is in the nature of written text – an essentially visual and spatial arrangement, where things roughly alike need to be placed near each other. Text in this respect is much more like image and space than it is like speech. There is nothing linear or temporal about the ICD text, as there is in the audio processes of speech.

Also, nobody could conceivably remember or be able to speak more than a few of 55,000 or 311,000 things, which is why IMO created the look-up app as a textual prosthesis for medical professionals. (Here again, "language" shows itself to be a singularly unhelpful concept, because text and speech are so practically unlike each other.)

[145] Mark Bostridge, 2008, *Florence Nightingale: The Woman and Her Legend*, London, UK: Viking.
[146] Iwao M. Moriyama, Ruth M. Loy, and Alastair H.T. Robb-Smith, 2011, *History of the Statistical Classification of Diseases and Causes of Death*, Hyattsville, MD: National Center for Health Statistics, pp. 1, 11–12.
[147] www.medscape.com/viewarticle/898202
[148] www.snomed.org/snomed-ct/what-is-snomed-ct/history-of-snomed-ct

ICD-10 is a carefully ordered classification scheme, in sections, marked auspiciously with roman numerals. It has sections on various bodily systems: IX "circulatory," X "respiratory," XI "digestive," IV "endocrine." Then there are some strange system conjunctions: XIII the "musculoskeletal system," and XIV "genitourinary system" – muscles are very different from bones and reproduction very different from pissing, but in the body, these things work together or are near each other.

Then there are ragbags of other things, some internal to bodies, some external, but all objects of very different orders: organs or parts of the anatomy such as VIII "eyes," VII "ears," XII "skin"; acquired conditions such as I "infectious diseases" and II "neoplasms" (cancers); external effects such as XIX "injuries"; conditions that may have been inherited in the form of XVII "congenital malformations"; conditions that may not even be medical, at least in their origins, but which might now be classified as V "mental or behavioral disorders"; and stuff that happens in XXI "contact with health systems."[149] Cross-classification clarifications are offered in the form of inclusions and exclusions. XVI "Perinatal conditions," we are told, includes conditions whose origins are in pregnancy even though the baby dies later, but they exclude congenital malformations.[150]

For all its agonizing order, and after a century and a half of institutional agonizing about its ordering, ICD still has the appearance of a ramshackle list. This is not because the ideal and our medical thinking is flawed, but because the material is varied and complex. It is as ramshackle as the particularities and relations of life itself. And it is as fallible as the politics of the construction of the medical self, where old maladies such as homosexuality are no longer that, and new conditions appear, such as post-traumatic stress disorder. "Classification systems," say Bowker and Star, "simultaneously represent the world 'out there,' the organizational context of their application and the political and social roots of that context."[151]

Then there is the frequently appearing but nevertheless disquieting notion of "other" – "other infectious diseases," "unspecified mental disorder," "neoplasms of uncertain or unknown behavior," "other ill-defined and unspecified causes of mortality," "provisional assignment of new diseases of uncertain etiology or emergency use," to mention just a few places in ICD-10.[152] If an ontology is to encompass all possibility in a domain, it has to countenance as-yet or in-the-moment unknown possibilities.

---

[149] http://apps.who.int/classifications/icd10/browse/2016/en
[150] http://apps.who.int/classifications/icd10/browse/2016/en#/XVI
[151] Geoffrey C. Bowker and Susan Leigh Star, 2000, *Sorting Things Out: Classification and Its Consequences*, Cambridge, MA: MIT Press, p. 61.
[152] http://apps.who.int/classifications/icd10/browse/2016/en: B99, F99, D37–48, R99, U00–49.

"Other" is a sleight of hand, where an ontology extends its range beyond the finite, anticipating the inevitable excesses of both the ideal and the material. While admitting its momentary finitude, the schema absorbs its certain failure to address everything that is conceivably addressable.

§3.3   Relation

> **Relation.** *The means by which structures cohere, where relations are established between kinds of things, parts of things, properties of things, and things that cause. But, despite our capacity to generalize relations, no two structures are the same, and no two relations within these structures.*

John Searle,[§2.3.1b] perhaps Noam Chomsky's[§3.1.2f] most vociferous critic, points out that linguistic competence is not just a capacity to produce grammatical sentences. It is to get things done in the world, "to make statements, ask questions, give orders, make requests, make promises, warnings, etc., and to understand other people when they use sentences for such purposes" – in other words, "semantic competence."[153]

Such competence does not just come from the arrangement of words. It comes from the meaningful context of a culture. These words do not have meanings that can be simply made up in sentences. "In order to understand the word 'bureaucrat,' for example, a child has to be introduced to a culture, a culture that includes governments, bureaus, departments, powers, employment, and a host of other things."[154]

These things are patterned, and the meaning is in their patterning of meanings in reality, not just abstract syntax. Bureaucracies in their intransigence are patterned in ways that are qualitatively different from bodies in their morbidity. It's not just a matter of swapping out words to transfer our understanding of the structures of administration to an understanding of the structures of human physiology. When we speak about them differently it is not just the syntax that has changed; it is a change in the structures of our meaning.

Or, to think the way B.F. Skinner[§3.1.2d] would, speech is only meaningful to the extent that it is embedded in reality. It is a form of human behavior inseparable from other perceptive, embodied, object-oriented, and spatially framed behaviors. Speaking about the structures of bureaucracy and its discontents is not in any essential way the same as speaking about the structures of the body and its maladies.

---

[153] John R. Searle, 1972, "Chomsky's Revolution in Linguistics," *New York Review of Books* 18 (29 June):12–29.
[154] John R. Searle, 2002, "End of the Revolution," *New York Review of Books* 49(3).

What then is generalizable, and what is variable in the grammar of structure? First the generalities, then to the ungeneralizability.

Structures cohere when one thing is a kind of another, or when it is an instance of another. "Malignant neoplasm of the breast" is a kind of "neoplasm."[155] This is the type of coherence[§3.2a] that comes with conceptualization. It can be visualized taxonomically: one thing is an instance of concept that happens more than once, such as a single case of breast cancer. Instances sit within concepts – numbers of things. And more broadly encompassing concepts can group subsets of narrower concepts – numbers of numbers. The concepts in structures are defined by characteristic properties that give them coherence relationships of similarity or difference with the properties that mark other concepts. "Benign and innocent cardiac murmur" is identifiable by its presentation.[156]

Structures also cohere when one thing is a part of another.[157] For example, "Sprain and strain of ankle" involves joints and ligaments, constituent parts of ankles.[158]

And structures are held together in patterns of action in chains of cause and effect.[159] "Whooping cough due to Bordetella pertussis" is different by dint of its cause from "Whooping cough due to Bordetella parapertussis."[160]

These then are some fundamental relations of similarity: kind of; part of; properties; causes. In their analysis of cohesion in language, M.A.K. Halliday and Ruqaiya Hasan call these endophoric relations: synonyms for associations of close similarity; antonyms for opposites; hyponyms for kinds of things; meronyms for parts of things; ellipsis for things not stated but where essential aspects of meaning can or must be filled in; conjunction identifying a range of these associations, including cause.[161]

But coherence in structures is just as much in relations of difference. Classification schemes are also about things that are different, where as much importance is afforded to: not-a-kind of; not-a-part-of; does not have certain properties; or does not cause. In medicine, differential diagnosis is the process of distinguishing the "is" from the "is-not," even though the symptoms may

[155] http://apps.who.int/classifications/icd10/browse/2016/en: C50.
[156] http://apps.who.int/classifications/icd10/browse/2016/en: R01.0.
[157] Morton E. Winston, Roger Chaffin, and Douglas Herrmann, 1987, "A Taxonomy of Part–Whole Relations," *Cognitive Science* 11:417–44.
[158] http://apps.who.int/classifications/icd10/browse/2016/en: S94.3.
[159] Judea Pearl, 2009, *Causality: Models, Reasoning and Inference*, Cambridge, UK: Cambridge University Press.
[160] http://apps.who.int/classifications/icd10/browse/2016/en A37.0, A37.1.
[161] M.A.K. Halliday and Ruqaiya Hasan, 1980, *Text and Context: Aspects of Language in a Social Semiotic Perspective*, Sophia University, pp. 74–95; M.A.K. Halliday and Ruqaiya Hasan, 1976, *Cohesion in English*, London, UK: Longman.

have created initial uncertainty. Medicine then becomes a practice of weighing evidence and categorical judgment.[162]

Differentials in medicine are close but nevertheless important differences. In structures, there are also differences that are antonyms, an "is" determined by symmetry against an "is-not." And there are differences that are just irrelevancies, informational "noise."

Then there are multiples, conjunctions of things, causes, and properties that present in ways different from each of the contributing elements. This produces particular challenges for medical practitioners.

And there is endless complexity in relations, where there is even incompleteness in structures (like mathematics[§1a]) that are by design intended to be complete. There is now a whole science of complexity, whose aim is to hunt down paradoxical, chaotic, random, fractal patterns in distributed, decentered, and emergent structures such as ant colonies, brains, markets, natural selection, economies, and the internet.[163]

Little wonder, then, that one little word capturing relations in structures – "set" – is the hardest word to define in the English language, measured at least by the length of its entry in the Oxford English Dictionary. In the first edition, its definition ran to twenty-three pages, densely typeset in three columns, covering four major meanings.[*] The one we want here, "a number or collection of things," has 154 distinguishable sub-meanings.[164] Among other contributors needed to untangle the depths of this dictionary entry was Sanskrit scholar, Philip Wittington Jacob.[165]

So far, we have stayed mostly within the bounds of repeatable relations. This is the basis of patterning, what makes for generalizable coherence in meanings across different structures. Adding to the complexity, across the forms of meaning, patterning by relations is achieved in quite different ways. Fig. 3.3 provides a rough map.

Beyond the complexity, we encounter the impossibility of perfectly replicated relations. This is a consistency Chomsky would require if his grammar

---

[*] http://meaningpatterns.net/set

[162] Samaa Haniya, Matthew Montebello, Bill Cope, and Richard Tapping, 2018, "Promoting Critical Clinical Thinking through E-Learning," pp. 5008–17 in *Proceedings of the 10th International Conference on Education and New Learning Technologies (EduLearn18)*, Palma de Mallorca, Spain.

[163] Melanie Mitchell, 2009, *Complexity: A Guided Tour*, Oxford, UK: Oxford University Press; Douglas R. Hofstadter, 1985, *Metamagical Themas: Questing for the Essence of Mind and Pattern*, New York, NY: Basic Books; Douglas R. Hofstadter, 2007, *I Am a Strange Loop*, New York, NY: Basic Books.

[164] *Oxford English Dictionary* (Edn 1), Volume 8, 1914, pp. 527–50.

[165] Simon Winchester, 2003, *The Meaning of Everything: The Story of the Oxford English Dictionary*, Oxford, UK: Oxford University Press, p. 210.

Form / Function: Relations	Text	Image	Space	Object	Body	Sound	Speech
Relations	Prepositions, case, negation	Array, orientation, spacing	Contiguity, closeness/ distance, trajectory	Form, properties	Pointing, movement	Cadence, consonance/ dissonance	Prosody

Fig. 3.3: Relations

were to be either universal or generative, if words could be swapped out while leaving the syntax the same.

No two relations are the same. We can use "kind of," "part of," "property of," and "cause of" as rough heuristics for relations. But muscles do not connect with bones in the same way that managers connect with clerks. An organization structure diagram might do for a bureaucracy, but it won't for a body. This is because the structures and relations – meanings-in – are irreducibly different.

Now, our forms of meaning, our expression of meanings-for, may also lead us into error. Bodies are only ramshackle against the measure of one form of our representation of them: the textual genre of the spatialized list. In themselves, bodies might be perfectly ordered, in sickness as well as in health.

This irreducible specificity of relations is also the reason we need big lists of things, codified and the subject of general agreement in the digital era: the International Statistical Classification of Diseases,[§3.2a] Unicode,[§0.2.1a] GeoNames,[§AS1.3.2b] Ethnologue,[166] Chemical Markup Language (ChemML),[167] Mathematical Markup Language (MathML)[168] – the list of lists in digital modernity is long, covering billions of the most useful and important things that can be meant. More meaning is to be found in the unique configurations of relations in these lists than can be found in purely algorithmic or logical work of so-called "artificial intelligence."[§AS1.4.6c] Here we find the grammar of everything, in its grounded specificity – well, nearly everything. These lists structure and refine the accumulated wisdom of human ages. Though of course, there is always more to be learned, and for this, the lists can be extended.

§3.3a   Thomas Gruber's "Ontology"

The *International Statistical Classification of Diseases and Related Health Problems*[§3.2a] is written in a format of XML (Extensible Markup Language)[§3.3b] called Classification Markup Language (ClaML). Like all markup languages, the arrangement is hierarchical, with a single root element (in this case, the name of the classification scheme), with child elements or "classes" representing different

---

[166] www.ethnologue.com   [167] www.xml-cml.org/documentation/index.html
[168] www.w3.org/Math/

levels in the taxonomy: chapters, sections, categories, and at the most granular level, codes.[*]

Intra-taxonomy relations are created by inclusions, exclusions, and cross-references.[169] The introductory text at the beginning of the standard sternly warns of the dangers of using word processing software such as Microsoft Word for storing and sharing classifications. XML rigorously represents and preserves taxonomic structures, it says, and facilitates interoperability between different medical software applications.[170]

ICD-10 is an ontology, technically speaking in the discourse of information science, and also, we would argue, philosophically as well, framing as it does meanings in the play of the ideal and the material. XML is a way to write ontologies, or schemas as they are often called.

We use the word "write" advisedly here, because this is a peculiar genre of spatialized, visually arranged writing that again demonstrates the dramatic differences between speech and writing, particularly in the era of digital text. Once more, we find reason to abandon the category "language" for its too-easy conflation of speech and writing, as if the one were a mere transliteration of the other.

Among the many mostly unnamed inventors of our forms of everyday life in the era of digital meaning is Thomas Gruber, co-creator of Siri, the voice interface that Apple bought in 2010 from his startup of the same name for a reported price of between $150 and $250 million. Like many of the other innovations in the era of digital text, his original research had been funded by the US Department of Defense.[171]

Gruber, however, may be more significant for establishing the notion of "ontology" in the emerging infrastructures of digital representation. "An ontology is an explicit specification of a conceptualization ... the objects, concepts, and other entities that are assumed to exist in some area of interest and the relationships that hold among them."[172] It is, he says, "a set of representational primitives with which to model a domain of knowledge or discourse." These are "typically classes (or sets), attributes (or properties), and relationships (or

---

[*] http://meaningpatterns.net/gruber-ontology

[169] Stefanie Weber, Egbert van der Haring, Susanne Bröenhorst, Michael Schopen, and Pieter Zanstra, 2005, "Maintaining Medical Classifications in XML: ClaML Redefined for Use with WHO-FIC Classifications," paper presented at the WHO-FIC Network Meeting, 16–22 October, Tokyo, Japan (http://apps.who.int/classifications/apps/icd/meetings/tokyomeeting/B_3–1%20Maintaining%20Medical%20Classifications%20in%20XML-ClaML.pdf).

[170] Health Informatics Technical Committee CEN/TC 251, 2007, "A Syntax to Represent the Content of Medical Classification Systems: ClaML," EN 14463:2007, Brussels, Belgium: European Committee for Standardization, pp. 5–6.

[171] www.huffingtonpost.com/2013/01/22/siri-do-engine-apple-iphone_n_2499165.html

[172] Thomas R. Gruber, 1995, "Toward Principles for the Design of Ontologies Used for Knowledge Sharing," International Journal of Human-Computer Studies 43(5–6):907–28, p. 908.

relations among class members) ... designed ... to enable the modeling of knowledge about some domain, real or imagined."[173] With the concept "ontology," Gruber managed to crystalize a number of longstanding issues in computer science about the connections between its syntax and semantics.[174]

In the terms we have been developing in this grammar, ontologies represent structures of meaning with digital text. An ontology purports both to represent meanings-in the material world (for instance, the health of bodies), and meanings-for the world in our ideal figuring so we can serve our meaning-filled interests (for instance, the practice of medicine).

This is an essentially textual practice, where the form of writing in the digital era separates itself further and further from the form of speech. When from version to version ICD terms increase more than fourfold and their differentials by an unquantifiable number, the possibility of speaking medicine spontaneously from memory becomes less and less feasible.

If "natural" language is the speech of everyday life, used for everyday bodily purposes such as medicine, for science and health's sake the textual practices of medicine have become strategically unnatural. This is why medical practitioners need their IMO apps[§3.2a] and other such digital resources on their phones or tablets. It is also why medical education needs to pay more attention to practitioners' communication with patients because the gulf is growing between their textual practice and patients' speech.

On the other hand, when you ask a question of an intelligent machine assistant such as Siri and she talks back, the speech part is not the core of the technology. It is the ontology part, or knowing what to say.

"Phone the nearest Indian Restaurant," you might ask Siri. If you get an answer, it is because the computer looks up structured text. "Sitara" is not just a word, it is marked up from ontologies as a restaurant whose property is to serve Indian food. Its address in Urbana and its phone number are not just words and numbers; these are marked up as geolocations and phone numbers. Siri's slightly stilted response is only smart because the ontologies that define structured text are smarter than what from a computer scientist's point of view is considered unstructured text. Often, Siri remains speechless, and you just get a link to a website – this is because the data is not clearly enough marked up or not structured in a processable ontology.

[173] Thomas R. Gruber, 2009, "Ontology," pp. 1963–5 in *Encyclopedia of Database Systems*, edited by L. Liu and M.T. Özsu, New York, NY: Springer-Verlag.

[174] Steven L. Lytinen, 1992, "Conceptual Dependency and Its Descendants," *Computers & Mathematics with Applications* 23(2–5):51–73; Robert I. (Bob) McKay, Nguyen Xuan Hoai, Peter Alexander Whigham, Yin Shan, and Michael O'Neill, 2010, "Grammar-Based Genetic Programming," *Genetic Programming and Evolvable Machines* 11:365–96.

Siri, the human behind the machine, is a voice actor, Susan Bennett. Working at home in Atlanta, Georgia, she took a month in 2005 to record meaningless fragments of speech for Gruber's company. Before this she had been the voice of advertisements for McDonalds, Coca Cola, and Ford. Bennett didn't know Apple was going to use Siri in iPhones until the application was launched in 2011. Now she's another ubiquitous but anonymous presence in our digital lives.[175]

§3.3b   Extensible Markup Language

In digital text, ontologies are most commonly expressed in Extensible Markup Language (XML),[176] a minimalist redesign of Standard Generalized Markup Language (SGML).[§AS1.4.7d] Notwithstanding its ubiquity, XML's authors remain largely unnamed, in this case because it was a widely collaborative invention. The World Wide Web Consortium (W3C) set up a working group of eleven, followed by an interest group of several hundred. Then, three editors created the final specification in 1998 – one of whom worked for the first-generation web browser, Netscape, another for Microsoft.[177]

This is still another example of the strangely stateless government of digital meaning, the fruit of voluntary efforts when private interests cannot themselves create the shared infrastructures of representation and communication that are nowadays required. By dint of necessity rather than philosophical commitment, coalitions of standards-setters and software developers create for their bosses something that in a strange way looks like a kind of international socialism. The market is not adequate to what the big corporations of late capitalism need, let alone its denizens.

XML is in our definition text because it is a string of characters written in Unicode.[§0.2.1a] The characters consist of markup (tags or elements) and content. We can create a tag/element <surname> in order to build a relationship between a concept and an instance, marking the beginning and the end of the string of content characters in the following way:

    <surname>
    Cope
    </surname>

Elements can be structured hierarchically: <given name> and <surname> can both be child elements of <name>. Elements can have variable attributes.

---

[175] https://en.wikipedia.org/wiki/Susan_Bennett; www.huffingtonpost.com/2013/10/04/voice-siri_n_4043134.html

[176] Jon Bosak and Tim Bray 1999, "XML and the Second-Generation Web," *Scientific American* 280(5):89–93.

[177] https://en.wikipedia.org/wiki/XML#History

And a lot more stuff in an official specification that now runs to twenty thousand words.[178]

This means that at the most basic level, XML can do things to address the fundamentals of meaning, things we have named in this grammar "instance," "concept, "property," "relation," and together, "structure." Unlike natural language, in XML these kinds of meaning are explicitly framed as such. There is no need to resort to context to work out the meaning of the same string of characters "cope," which can in a database or on a screen refer to a mental state, a priest's cloak (obscurely), a family, or one unambiguously identifiable person. Banks, employers, email recipients, and social media users need to know this unambiguously, and a string of characters is not enough.

This is why ontologies surround us these days, mechanizing our meanings with markup, a more structured and strategically unnatural shadow layer of meaning that is visible only in code. They reach us in stuff that is ordinary writing through XSLT "stylesheet transformations." This means that the mention of a name in a diary entry looks different on my device from the way it looks in an alert from Facebook.

In the lingo of digital text, structure and semantics are kept separate from rendering or presentation. Or, we would say in the terms of our grammar, the forms of meaning are separated from their functions. This is not just theoretical. It is mechanical, a technology for flexible and on-the-fly rendering of texts across multiple devices and apps.[179]

Here are some of the ontologies we live with, all expressible in XML and in practice too, mostly expressed in XML. For medicine, there are ICD and SNOMED.[§3.2a] For chemistry, there is Chemical Markup Language.[180] For places, there is GeoNames,[§AS1.3.2b] and for languages, Ethnologue.[181] There are standards for the internet of things.[182] For date and time, there is an ISO standard for which the W3C has a specification.[§AS1.3.1b] For citation and bibliography, there are MARC, Dublin Core, and ONIX.[183] And for text itself, the mundane stuff of paragraphs and headings is transferrable across platforms and renderable across multiple devices, often through XML transformations: from Microsoft Word, to LibreOffice, and to the web as HTML.[184]

And so on – there are ontologies for just about all the writable things in the world, even writing itself. In most domains, these ontologies have shaken down to

[178] www.w3.org/TR/REC-xml/
[179] Bill Cope and Mary Kalantzis, 2004, "Text-Made Text," *E-Learning* 1(2):198–282.
[180] P. Murray-Rust and H.S. Rzepa, 2003, "Chemical Markup, XML and the World Wide Web," *Journal of Chemical Information and Computer Sciences* 43(3):757–72.
[181] www.ethnologue.com   [182] www.itu.int/en/ITU-T/publications/Pages/default.aspx
[183] Bill Cope and Mary Kalantzis, 2004, "Text-Made Text," *E-Learning* 1(2):198–282.
[184] Liam Magee and James A. Thom, 2014, "What's in a WordTM? When One Electronic Document Format Standard Is Not Enough," *Information Technology & People* 27 (4):482–511.

one or two, and where there is more than one they are for somewhat different kinds of use. Specialist domains frequently get caught in the gap, and have to spend a good deal of time mapping equivalences or term-to-term "crosswalks."[185]

Ontologies are universal and translingual to the extent that their translation across different languages largely preserves their essential structures of meaning. ICD in English is not so very different from ICD in Spanish, or at least not as different as spoken English is from spoken Spanish.

Such translations are done in the ontology, not the point of rendering into text. When you select your preferred language at an ATM,[§AS2.2.2] the textual interaction which delivers cash from your bank account does so because a mixture of information you provide and information on your card has been marked up for universal banker's meaning where "natural" language is a functionally trivial condescension to the person standing at the machine. The language of the interface is functionally detached from the ontologies of banking.

And the play of ontologies, though textually arranged in visualizable schemas, is not just text. Any digital object can be so marked up, not just text, but images, video, sound, code, or datasets – hence the fundamental multimodality of the structures of digital media, notwithstanding the textual form of the tags used for its structuring.

The underlying textual forms of ontology-driven meaning are not much like the grammar of spoken sentences, or speech transliterated onto the page, or even what is spoken by Siri. Rather, this is a spatialized text of instances, concepts ordered in hierarchies of dependency, arranged in relations of difference and similarity, and ascribed properties. You can do the grammar of structures and relations in the spontaneously speakable sentence, but not with the same degree of elaborate specificity, relative lack of ambiguity, and independence from context that is possible and necessary in digital text. The functions are parallel, but the affordances of the forms make text and speech more different than ever. Multimodal transpositions like Siri or visual renderings to screen are cleverer than ever because the distance traveled in the transposition is so great.

Each of the ontologies that govern our digital meanings has a ramshackle feel to it – lists of things of uneven significance, and lists of lists, texts only roughly arranged in supermarket order.[§0d] But surely, they are no more ramshackle, their designs no more irreducibly unique in each categorical node and every relation of their structures, than the natural-historical and social-historical worlds to which they refer.

However, for all their messiness, the ontologies of digital text are no flash-in-the pan inventions of computer whizzes. They are thoroughly thought-through semantic schemas. They have their source in centuries of meticulous agonizing about the

[185] Richard Vines and Joseph Firestone, 2011, "Interoperability and the Exchange of Humanly Usable Digital Content," pp. 429–90 in *Towards a Semantic Web: Connecting Knowledge in Academic Research*, edited by B. Cope, M. Kalantzis, and L. Magee, Oxford, UK: Chandos.

structures of meaning by scientists, doctors, librarians, geographers, and such like. Collective thinking has made them unnatural, and this is the source of their peculiarly modern efficacy.[186]

The infrastructure of these ontologies has been created and is maintained in this strange, universal, stateless space of self-governing standards bodies. If there is an uber-government of digital meanings, a regulator of the framework for the making of meanings of meanings, since its founding in 1994 it has been the Word Wide Web Consortium, or W3C.[*]

Karl Marx foreshadowed the withering away of the state with the coming of socialism. In the actually existing socialisms that followed the 1917 Russian Revolution, instead of withering, the state became overbearing. Today, neoliberal capitalism is actively withering the state. In its place, these peculiar and largely invisible structures of world governance are emerging. This is an era of (un)governance by ontology.

§3.3c   *Tim Berners-Lee's* Semantic Web

Three years after the publication of the XML standard, Tim Berners-Lee, creator of the web text mechanism, Hypertext Markup Language (HTML), ventured to predict a new era of machine intelligence. Berners-Lee had coined the term "World-Wide Web" to describe his 1990 creation. When occasionally the innovators of the digital era do end up getting credit, it is more for their catchy naming. And the work itself is always more collaborative than their naming would have us think.

Now, in 2001, Berners-Lee had another catchy phrase for a next generation of XML-based text, the "Semantic Web." In a celebrated article in *Scientific American*, Berners-Lee, Hendler, and Lassila promised that "The Semantic Web will bring structure to the meaningful content of Web pages, creating an environment where software agents roaming from page to page can readily carry out sophisticated tasks for users."

So, in a hypothetical near future, Lucy, whose Mom needs physical therapy, uses the Semantic Web to check whether that is covered by her insurance, available in-plan medical providers, and doctor's schedules. Instead of having to read a whole lot of webpages, the Semantic Web will work this out for her, adding a layer of reasoning to the layer of information already available on the

---

[*] http://meaningpatterns.net/digital-governance

[186] Bill Cope, Mary Kalantzis, and Liam Magee, 2011, *Towards a Semantic Web: Connecting Knowledge in Academic Research*, Cambridge, UK: Elsevier; Allen Renear, David Dubin, C.M. Sperberg-McQueen, and Claus Huitfeldt, 2002, "Towards a Semantics for XML Markup," pp. 119–26 in *Proceedings of the 2002 ACM Symposium on Document Engineering*, McLean, VA.

web. "The Semantic Web," Berners-Lee and co-authors concluded, "will enable machines to comprehend semantic documents and data, not human speech and writings."[187] However, to do this it would need additional layers of semantic markup. With its ambiguities, context-dependencies, and a myriad of other obscurantisms, the text of natural language is fickle.[*]

Extending the structuring of names of instances and concepts in XML, Berners-Lee predicted the use of two more layers of semantic formalization using XML: Resource Description Framework (RDF) and Web Ontology Language (OWL).[188] RDF assigns every name a URL, and links three kinds of name in subject–predicate–object triples, or mini-assertions.[189] So, subject: Bill Cope > predicate: has the email address > object: billcope@illinois.edu. OWL adds a layer of reasoning based in the formalisms of description logic, where "individuals" (our instances) and "classes" (our concepts) are named as such, and their properties can be described, establishing logical connections between things.[190]

RDF and OWL have proven both too simple to capture and reason from the structure of meaning in the world, and too complicated to make practical sense. OWL rules run to 700-odd pages.[191]

In the activity areas of the W3C these were superseded in 2013 by the more modestly named "W3C Data Activity."[192] The focus now is on web data standardization, or just a lot of ontology work. A visualization created by the Linking Open Data project shows a bewildering number of ontologies across geography, government, linguistics, life sciences, media, and publishing – another ramshackle list, though this time a list of lists rather than universal semantic principles. And like all ontologies, it has the ubiquitous escape classification, "other," which it calls "cross-domain."[193]

Despite all the talk of semantic web, artificial intelligence[§AS1.4.6b] even, we really only have ontologies, whose spatialized architectures mostly pre-date the internet. The Semantic Web hasn't worked out, we would venture to say, because the structures of meaning-in the world are infinitely varied in their

---

[*] http://meaningpatterns.net/semantic-web

[187] Tim Berners-Lee, James Hendler, and Ora Lassila, 2001, "The Semantic Web," *Scientific American*, May, pp. 34–43, pp. 36, 40; Dieter Fensel, James Hendler, Henry Lieberman, and Wolfgang Wahlster, eds., 2005, *Spinning the Semantic Web: Bringing the Worldwide Web to Its Full Potential*, Cambridge, MA: MIT Press.

[188] Allen H. Renear and Carole L. Palmer, 2009, "Strategic Reading, Ontologies, and the Future of Scientific Publishing," *Science* 325(5942):828–32. doi: 10.1126/science.1157784.

[189] www.w3.org/RDF/   [190] www.w3.org/TR/owl2-overview/

[191] Christian F. Hempelmann, 2012, "NLP for Search," pp. 53–74 in *Applied Natural Language Processing: Identification, Investigation, and Resolution*, edited by P.M. McCarthy and C. Boonthum-Denecke, Hershey, PA: IGI Global.

[192] www.w3.org/2013/data/   [193] http://lod-cloud.net

specificity, and our meaning-for can exceed them, manifesting all kinds of peculiarities according to our human designs.[194]

§3.3d   Debiprasad Chattopadhyaya's Lokayata

The ancient Indian Vedas were, along with Pāṇini's grammar,[§0.4a] the first textually represented ontologies.[*]

The Vedas, says Jack Goody,[§AS1.4.7a] assumed their characteristic form as writing in Sanskrit, not speech, even though great store is laid today on their mnemonics, or the poetics of their memorization. They may have been written down as early as 500 BCE, well before writing about meaning started in the West. The oral tradition of the *mantras* (recitations) is rooted in the literate practices of an elite caste, the Brahmans, the supporting *brahmanas*, or explanatory writings. What emerges is a series of graphic devices, spatially ordered arrays of text representing meaning as elaborately structured relations. The structure of the Vedas is essentially textual, and the techniques of their memorization are secondary.[195] The *mantras* are to the *brahmanas* what Siri is to digital ontologies – a device for the multimodal transposition of meanings that are in the first instance structured in writing.

And taking one step further, this may have been the first place where the nature of ontologies was theorized – a metaontology, an ontology of ontologies, or to say this in philosophical terms, a metaphysics.

We have at other places in this book discussed the play of the material and the ideal in some recent modern thinking about ontology (Bhaskar[§3.1a] and Grosz[§3.1.1a]), as well as some earlier modern thinking (Descartes[§3.1.2g] and Locke[§1.3a]), and among theorists of language (Skinner[§3.1.2d] and Chomsky[§3.1.2e]).

In a masterwork of intellectual history covering over a thousand years and running to over seven hundred pages, Debiprasad Chattopadhyaya writes an account of the origins of Indian philosophy. He traces the emergence of what are arguably the first metaontologies. If we are to follow Chattopadhyaya's line of argument, this thinking pre-dates and then parallels metaontological thinking in the West.

Chattopadhyaya's story is an account of a struggle between the religious-idealist structures of meaning in the Vedas and materialist accounts of meaning in everyday life captured under the name of an alternative philosophical school, Lokayata. The Vedic philosophers placed self-referential spiritual consciousness

---

[*] http://meaningpatterns.net/lokayata

[194] Bill Cope, Mary Kalantzis, and Liam Magee, 2011, *Towards a Semantic Web: Connecting Knowledge in Academic Research*, Cambridge, UK: Elsevier.

[195] Jack Goody, 1987, *The Interface between the Written and the Oral*, Cambridge, UK: Cambridge University Press, pp. 110–22; Frits Staal, 2008, *The Vedas: Origins, Mantras, Rituals, Insights*, Gurgaon, India: Penguin Books.

at the center of the meaning-filled universe, making fantastic promises about immortality and reincarnation. The Lokayata, on the other hand, was a this-worldly philosophy, grounded in the practical meanings of everyday existence and the primacy of sense perception. Vedic philosophy prevailed, and the texts of Lokayata were destroyed. We only know of Lokayata now as an object of criticism in the Vedic texts.[196]

After this, within the Vedic tradition there is an ongoing intellectual struggle. On the one hand, there is Uddalaka Aruni in the eighth century BCE, who according to the great Sanskrit scholar, Walter Ruben, was the first Indian philosopher. We would argue that he was perhaps the first theorist of ontology in its modern spatio-textual forms. Uddalaka, argues Ruben, was a materialist whose thinking represented a kind of proto-science.

From the start, there was a clash between his kind of thinking and the kind of thinking represented by his nemesis, Yājñavalkya, reflecting Brahmanic ideal-ist, ritual orthodoxy. This, Ruben and Chattopadhyaya frame as a struggle between the materialist ontologies reflecting the needs and interests of the poor and oppressed, and the mystifying idealist ontologies of the Brahman caste and their ruling-class allies.[197] Chattopadhyaya also traces to these ancient sources the origins of a secular medical science, free of superstition and based instead on medical ontologies that conceptualize biophysical objects and their relations in the empirical world.[198]

These are the first inklings of the quest to define metaontology – the structures of structures of meaning – that continues today in so many places, where all too often thinkers define their position by heading to one end of the ideal/material antinomy or the other.

Our sympathies are with the materialists, but without wishing to neglect the dialectic of interplay with the ideal. The excesses of the ideal – black holes, elementary particles, and quantum mechanics – had to be imagined in theory before they were found in material reality. The excesses of immortality and reincarnation, however, remain just theories, notwithstanding the force of epistemic and institu-tional religious commitment – excesses of *cogito*, in philosophical terms, that have failed to materialize. This is not to say that the promises did not mean something, because indeed they did for a social world of painful inequality and for a species for whom death is hard to think.

This tradition continued into the first millennium of the common era, with the *Sämkhya* ("reckoning," "summing up," "numeration"), a metaontology in

[196] Debiprasad Chattopadhyaya, 1959, *Lokayata: A Study in Ancient Indian Materialism*, New Delhi, India: People's Publishing House, pp. 3–4, 28–30.

[197] Walter Ruben, 1981, "Uddalaka and Yājñavalkya: Materialism and Idealism," pp. 13–27 in *Marxism and Indology*, edited by D. Chattopadhyaya, Calcutta, India: K.P. Bagchi and Company.

[198] Debiprasad Chattopadhyaya, 1981, "Science and Society in Ancient India," pp. 231–62 in ibid.

the Vedic tradition, first committed to writing in the fourth to the sixth centuries of the common era.[199] The *Sämkhya* says

> IV. The attainment of reliable knowledge is based on ... three means: (a) perception, (b) inference, (c) reliable authority ...
> V. Perception is the selective ascertainment of particular sense-objects ...
> VI. The understanding of things beyond the senses is by means of (or from) inference by analogy.[200]

This carefully ordered text goes on to lay out distinctions between "purusa," manifest and unmanifest consciousness, and "prakrt," or materiality, consisting of "sense-capabilities" such as hearing and seeing; "action-capacities" such as grasping, speaking, and walking; "subtle elements" such as sound and touch; and "gross elements" such as space and earth. Meaning is in the interplay of the ideal ("purusa") and the material ("prakrt").[201]

Chattopadhyaya and Ruben's insights arose in an encounter between a tradition of Indian philosophy millennia long and the historical materialism of Marx.[202] They were articulated for a moment in 1980 at a strange intersection, a seminar sponsored by the Indo-GDR Friendship Society of West Bengal held in Calcutta. The society had brought Professor Walter Ruben from Humboldt University in East Berlin, so honoring his eightieth birthday.

Ruben, the book of conference papers explains euphemistically, had to flee Germany when the Nazis came to power because he had "a Jewish name" as well as communist connections. After that, he taught at universities in Turkey and Chile. At the end of the war he returned to East Berlin, where he founded the Institute of Indology at Humboldt University in 1949.

Among those participating in the seminar for Ruben were the Secretary of the West Bengal Council of the Communist Party of India, and Yuri M. Pavlov from the Department of Historical Materialism at Moscow State University,[§1.1.3g] who spoke on "Leninism and Indology." Ruben, mentioning historical materialism in his paper, footnoted Lenin's *Materialism and Empirio-Criticism*.[§0.2.9a] Chattopadhyaya had by that time been honored with membership of the Academy of Sciences of the German Democratic Republic and the USSR.

---

[199] Debiprasad Chattopadhyaya, 1959, *Lokayata: A Study in Ancient Indian Materialism*, New Delhi, India: People's Publishing House, pp. 448–56; Gerald James Larson, 1979, *Classical Sämkhya: An Interpretation of Its History and Meaning*, Santa Barbara, CA: Ross/Erikson.

[200] Gerald James Larson, 1979, *Classical Sämkhya: An Interpretation of Its History and Meaning*, Santa Barbara, CA: Ross/Erikson, pp. 256–57.

[201] Ibid., p. 237.

[202] Debiprasad Chattopadhyaya, 1964, *Indian Philosophy: A Popular Introduction*, New Delhi, India: People's Publishing House; 1990, *Anthropology and Historiography of Science*, Athens, OH: Ohio University Press; 1991, *Philosophy and the Future*, Bangalore, India: Navakarnataka Publications.

Not long after the seminar, in a crossing of paths just as peculiar, we met Mother Teresa in her convent in Calcutta. The state headquarters of the Communist Party of India was next door. The party was to govern West Bengal continuously for thirty-four years and had named one of the city's principal streets Lenin Sarani.

When we asked Mother Teresa about the relation between the needs of her poor and the political agenda of the state government, she just said that her neighbors kept their lights on very late into the night. In the nexus of the ideal and the material, it's an odd thing to have met a saint,[§AS2.5b] and one so grounded in the ephemera of the flesh.[203] After Calcutta, we traveled to East Berlin.[§AS2.3d]

§3.3e   Immanuel Kant's Critique of Pure Reason

Two and a half millennia after the Lokayata, and one and a half after the Sāmkhya,[§3.3d] we find Immanuel Kant* thinking through another metaontology, conceptualizing the play of the ideal and the material. Perhaps this is an occupational hazard for thinkers, but here again we find a philosopher favoring the ideal over the material as the final source of meaning. And once again, the kinds of structures of meaning can't easily be spoken; they need to be visualized in text.

Kant's metaphor for the work he is doing is "architectonics," taking the form of a plan of "the system of all principles of pure reason."[204] At the highest level of understanding, the system acknowledges the play of the material and the ideal. On the one hand, there is the empirical, or our relations to the world via sensation, "the effect of an object upon the faculty of representation, so far as we are affected by it." On the other hand, there are our intuitions, our understanding of experience by means of concepts.[205] However, the "bounds of sense" in Kant (to use a wonderful phrase of Strawson's which is the title of his celebrated reading of Kant) remain within the ideal. In the final analysis, Kant does not have a plausible account of the dynamics of material effect.[206]

The world, for Kant, is a product of our *a priori* mental constructs, the "pure concepts of the understanding" created according to "reason's legislative prescriptions."[207] These are reducible to four macro categories, each

---

* http://meaningpatterns.net/kant

[203] Christopher Hitchens, 1995, *The Missionary Position: Mother Teresa in Theory and Practice*, London, UK: Verso.

[204] Immanuel Kant, 1787 [1933], *Critique of Pure Reason*, translated by N.K. Smith, London, UK: Macmillan, A13/B27.

[205] Ibid., A19–20/B34.

[206] P.F. Strawson, 1966, *The Bounds of Sense: An Essay on Kant's Critique of Pure Reason*, London, UK: Methuen, p. 41.

[207] Immanuel Kant, 1787 [1933], *Critique of Pure Reason*, translated by N.K. Smith, London, UK: Macmillan, A77/B103, A832/B860.

subdivided into three: quantity (unity, plurality, totality); quality (reality, negation, limitation); relation (inherence/subsistence, causality/dependence, community/reciprocity); and modality (possibility, existence, necessity).[208]

In addition to these categories of reason where the mind at least maintains a secondary connection with the material world, the mind constructs experience as "pure intuitions," *a priori* idealities such as the dynamics of time and space. For, Kant says, there is nothing in what is represented from the world to indicate that time or space have any material reality.[§AS1.3]

In the structuring of meaning, "the concept determines *a priori* not only the scope of its manifold content, but also the positions which the parts occupy relatively to one another."[209] Kant's metaontology is founded in a process of structuring favoring mental system over material reality, as later would also the architectures of meaning proposed by Saussure in his systems of signs,[§3d] and Chomsky in his syntactic structures.[§3.1.2f]

§3.4   Metaontology

Metaontolgy. An ontology of ontologies, mapping the structure of the structures of meaning, patterns and patterns of patterns, with their repeatable commonalities and irreducible differences.

A metaontology is an ontology of ontologies.

If grammars are metalanguages or ontologies of language structure, then to the extent that we attempt to map all forms and functions of meaning, our metaphorical grammar of multimodality is an ontology[§3.1] of ontologies.[210]

So, in the spirit of Uddakala[§3.3d] and Kant,[§3.3e] this grammar is another metaontology, drawing on a long tradition in this kind of theorizing. We address, albeit in a different configuration and with different names, the elements of Kant's categorical system, and other such systems.

However, we depart from Kant (and his confreres Saussure[§3d] and Chomsky,[§3.1.2e] also the Vedas of a conventional idealist reading [§3.3d]) in two major ways. The first is that to the extent that there is an excess of the ideal over the material, it is only provisional or conjectural – provisional, for instance, when we haven't yet found a particular elementary particle but our reasoning tells us

---

[208] Ibid., A80/B106.   [209] Ibid., A832/B860.

[210] Liam Magee, 2010, "A Framework for Assessing Commensurability of Semantic Web Ontologies," *Electronic Journal of Knowledge Management* 8(1):91–102; Bill Cope, 2011, "Method for the Creation, Location and Formatting of Digital Content," U.S. Patent US7886225B2.

we may still if we keep looking, or conjectural in the realistic or unrealistic might-have-beens of fiction. Some of the ideal can be dismissed as mystification or lies, real though these may be in their effects on social life. The ideal may be materially discovered (or not), and its material effects observed no matter how disconnected from materiality. Always, we need to have the ideal in play with the material, but the material is the final measure of ideality.

The second difference we have with pure, reducible idealism is that the world of our meaning, the meanings-in natural and human materiality are infinitely complex and so always ramshackle. As we make sense of the world, no matter how much structure we attempt to impose through our meanings-for, we face the constantly changing shape of human experience as a subset of natural history and the volatility of natural history itself. Nor is the structure just in the overall patterns of macro-order, but the infinitely varied patterns of micro-order where no one relation exactly replicates any other.

And so to design. There are big patterns in our available designs of meaning, which we might for instance call "relations," where "part-of" is different from "kind-of." But every moment of design, these relations play themselves out in specific configurations that have never quite been meant this way before. No two parts-of are the same, no two kinds-of.

Ontologies do both things, laying things out using the broad patterning techniques for which text is well suited, putting these in endless spatialized array of juxtaposed specificities. And no matter how exhaustive the list, spaces can always be left for "other," allowing that, though relatively stable and comprehensive in historical practice, the lists are also infinitely extensible. The encounter between the ideal and the material is open-ended.

§3.4a   Ramanathan Guha's Schema.org

In the era of digital text, there have been attempts to create metaontologies, and also a good deal of derision directed to those who presume to think it possible. In the same special issue of the *International Journal of Human-Computer Studies* where Gruber published his celebrated piece on the idea of ontology, John Sowa had an article on "Top Level Ontological Categories."[211]

After going through the philosophical precursors, from Aristotle (but not the Indian philosophers), to Kant, Whitehead, and Peirce, John Sowa arrives at Cyc, the largest and most comprehensive of the digital metaontologies. This was 1995. In 2000, Cyc was still a centerpiece of Sowa's exhaustive book, *Knowledge Representation: Logical, Philosophical and Computational Foundations.*[212]

---

[211] John F. Sowa, 1995. "Top-Level Ontological Categories," *International Journal of Human-Computer Studies* 43(5–6):669–85.

[212] John F. Sowa, 2000, *Knowledge Representation: Logical, Philosophical and Computational Foundations*, Pacific Grove, CA: Brooks Cole.

But by 2006, Sowa was beginning to despair at the "knowledge soup," where "the best-laid plans" of ontologies, based as they are on people's "natural desire to organize, classify, label, and define the things, events, and patterns of their daily lives . . . are overwhelmed by . . . inevitable change, growth, innovation, progress, evolution, diversity, and entropy."[213]

Doug Lenat, then a professor at Stanford University, set out on the Cyc project in 1984. Later, he left academe to found Cycorp. In the words of the Cycorp website, Cyc is "a formalized representation of a vast quantity of fundamental human knowledge: facts, rules of thumb, and heuristics for reasoning about the objects and events of everyday life."[*] Today, Cyc "contains over five hundred thousand terms, including about seventeen thousand types of relations, and about seven million assertions relating these terms." Its top-level architecture consists of individuals (our instances), collections (our concepts), and functions (our relations). Then there is a myriad of "microtheories" covering all manner of domains (weather, time, geography, and such like), marked up in its own Knowledge Representation Language.[214]

Ramanathan Guha worked at Cycorp for a while, and later went to work for Google. Cyc knows stuff like, "A bat has wings. Because it has wings, a bat can fly. Because a bat can fly, it can travel from place to place." Says Guha, "It's all the things that a five-year-old knows . . . Computers still don't know that." Computers need to be told common sense, argues Lenat. "Common sense isn't written down. It's in our heads."[215]

Actually, we would respond, there is too much to be meant for it all to be in any of our heads, which is why we write it down, and record via other multi-modal means, including computer-recorded text, sound, image, visualization, and dataset. Our records need to be as complex and variegated as the meanings in the structures of materiality to which the records refer – the meanings of nature and history. Computers need to be told these things before we can have them look things up for us. To pass the Turing test (where a user can't tell the difference between the response of a person and a computer hidden behind a screen),[§1.3.2c] Lenat correctly says that a machine would have to be told a whole lot of stuff.[216]

---

[*] http://meaningpatterns.net/metaontology

[213] John F. Sowa, 2006, "The Challenge of Knowledge Soup," pp. 55–90 in *Research Trends in Science, Technology and Mathematics Education*, edited by J. Ramadas and S. Chunawala, Goa, India: Homi Bhabha Centre.

[214] www.cyc.com/kb/

[215] Cade Metz, 2016, "One Genius' Lonely Crusade to Teach a Computer Common Sense," *Wired*, 24 March; Ramanathan V. Guha and Vineet Gupta, 2016, "Communicating Semantics: Reference by Description," arXiv:1511.06341v3 [cs.CL].

[216] Douglas B. Lenat, 2016, "WWTS(What Would Turing Say?)," *AI Magazine* 37(1):97–101.

Other attempts have been made to create top-level ontologies,[217] but Cyc has been the most comprehensive. Little wonder that among the corporation's clients is the US National Security Agency, according to documents leaked by whistleblower Edward Snowdon.

Google has now created its own metaontology in the form of Knowledge Graph. Launched in 2012, Knowledge Graph presents summary text and images about a search topic in a panel on the right side of the screen. A search on "Taj Mahal musician" works because Knowledge Graph knows the difference between the person, the tomb in Agra, and Donald Trump's failed casino in Atlantic City.[218] This can only happen when digital text is driven by ontologies. One-third of Google searches now return info boxes from Knowledge Graph. This has reportedly led to a decrease in visits to Wikipedia.

Metaontologies operate at two meta-levels. One level is the distinction (in the terms we have developed in this grammar) between instances, concepts, relations, properties, and such like. At a second level this is filled out with a lot of domain-specific concepts, relations, and properties, such as that people can be musicians, tombs can be in places, and the owners of failed businesses can become presidents. Spatially arranged lists and lists of lists become the ramshackle stuff of digital ontologies. This time the "meta" part is the coverage of everything, including "other," in anticipation of new discoveries and insights.

The latest project to create a metaontology, a structure for the structures of digitized meaning, is Schema.org, initiated by Microsoft, Google, and Yahoo in 2011. Guha was one of its founders. In the Schema.org metaontology, the world consists of things, which can have names, descriptions, URLs, and images. Then these things can be arranged into item types, including persons, places, events, and creative works.[219] Over ten million websites now use ontologies marked up in the Schema.org metaontology.

Despite Sowa's pessimism about knowledge soup, much has come to pass since he and Gruber began the discussion of ontologies in 1995. These are novel forms of meaning in a number of respects. They are multimodal, where with equal ease meanings can be specified that are represented in text, image, sound, or data. However, in tagging structures and their spatial arrangement they are essentially textual, and in a largely unspeakable form where text deviates ever further from speech.

---

[217] Liam Magee, 2011, "Upper-Level Ontologies," pp. 235–87 in *Towards a Semantic Web: Connecting Knowledge in Academic Research*, edited by B. Cope, M. Kalantzis, and L. Magee, Cambridge, UK: Elsevier.

[218] Cade Metz, 2016, "One Genius' Lonely Crusade to Teach a Computer Common Sense," *Wired*, 24 March.

[219] http://schema.org/docs/full.html#datatype_tree

They also operate in a translingual semantics, where translations into differ-ent languages do not change the fundamental structures of meaning, many of which are in image or data, anyway. Ontologies and metaontologies are the Esperanto of the digital era.[220]

And this now-universal, federated structure of our meanings is governed by stateless, non-profit entities because the state is withering away, and no global state has replaced it. Corporations need shared protocols for meaning, but they can't do it for themselves. Governance is required, and with the failure of the state, corporations take the lead. Materially as well as ideally, such are the stateless dynamics of the total globalization of meanings in the digital age.

§3.4b   The Meaning of Everything

This book and its companion, *Adding Sense*, are an attempt to create a top-level ontology, a grammar that ties together in a rough, schematic way, the meaning of everything.

Sweeping territories of meaning are mapped today in vast detail in digital ontologies, examples of which we list below. We describe some of these in further detail in the sections referenced.

Mention of "NLP markers" in this table indicates that there are concepts commonly used to detect meaning in written language using Natural Language Processing technologies. These are the labels used to describe orientations of meaning either in unstructured text, or in somewhat more structured texts in the form of tags, markup, and database fields. In each functional area where we have indicated NLP might perform this task, there is considerable agreement about what to be looking for, such as informal, conventional agreement about markers of negatives and absences, role, or sentiment.

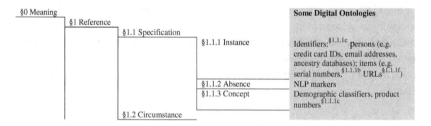

Fig. 3.4b: Some digital ontologies

[220] Bill Cope, Mary Kalantzis, and Liam Magee, 2011, *Towards a Semantic Web: Connecting Knowledge in Academic Research*, Cambridge, UK: Elsevier.

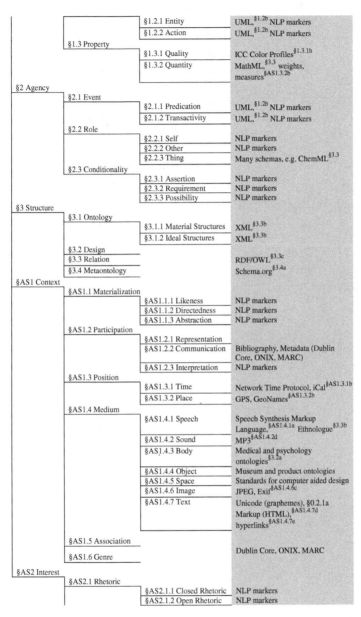

Section	Subsection	Subsubsection	Standards/Markers
§2 Agency		§1.2.1 Entity	UML,[§1.2b] NLP markers
		§1.2.2 Action	UML,[§1.2b] NLP markers
	§1.3 Property		
		§1.3.1 Quality	ICC Color Profiles[§1.3.1b]
		§1.3.2 Quantity	MathML,[§3.3] weights, measures[§AS1.3.2b]
	§2.1 Event		
		§2.1.1 Predication	UML,[§1.2b] NLP markers
		§2.1.2 Transactivity	UML,[§1.2b] NLP markers
	§2.2 Role		
		§2.2.1 Self	NLP markers
		§2.2.2 Other	NLP markers
		§2.2.3 Thing	Many schemas, e.g. ChemML[§3.3]
	§2.3 Conditionality		
		§2.3.1 Assertion	NLP markers
		§2.3.2 Requirement	NLP markers
		§2.3.3 Possibility	NLP markers
§3 Structure	§3.1 Ontology		
		§3.1.1 Material Structures	XML[§3.3b]
		§3.1.2 Ideal Structures	XML[§3.3b]
	§3.2 Design		
	§3.3 Relation		RDF/OWL[§3.3c]
	§3.4 Metaontology		Schema.org[§3.4a]
§AS1 Context	§AS1.1 Materialization		
		§AS1.1.1 Likeness	NLP markers
		§AS1.1.2 Directedness	NLP markers
		§AS1.1.3 Abstraction	NLP markers
	§AS1.2 Participation		
		§AS1.2.1 Representation	
		§AS1.2.2 Communication	Bibliography, Metadata (Dublin Core, ONIX, MARC)
		§AS1.2.3 Interpretation	NLP markers
	§AS1.3 Position		
		§AS1.3.1 Time	Network Time Protocol, iCal[§AS1.3.1b]
		§AS1.3.2 Place	GPS, GeoNames[§AS1.3.2b]
	§AS1.4 Medium		
		§AS1.4.1 Speech	Speech Synthesis Markup Language,[§AS1.4.1a] Ethnologue[§3.3b]
		§AS1.4.2 Sound	MP3[§AS1.4.2d]
		§AS1.4.3 Body	Medical and psychology ontologies[§3.2a]
		§AS1.4.4 Object	Museum and product ontologies
		§AS1.4.5 Space	Standards for computer aided design
		§AS1.4.6 Image	JPEG, Exif[§AS1.4.6c]
		§AS1.4.7 Text	Unicode (graphemes), §0.2.1a Markup (HTML),[§AS1.4.7d] hyperlinks[§AS1.4.7e]
	§AS1.5 Association		
	§AS1.6 Genre		Dublin Core, ONIX, MARC
§AS2 Interest	§AS2.1 Rhetoric		
		§AS2.1.1 Closed Rhetoric	NLP markers
		§AS2.1.2 Open Rhetoric	NLP markers

Fig. 3.4b: (cont.)

§AS2.2 Program		
	§AS2.2.1 Assimilation	Aggregating demographics, e.g. country codes, postal codes, sex
	§AS2.2.2 Differentiation	Differentiating demographic subclassifications and intersections, psychological trait schemas
§AS2.3 Reification		
	§AS2.3.1 Activation	Employment, client, and other classifications
	§AS2.3.2 Alienation	Privacy and security standards and settings
§AS2.4 Sociability		
	§AS2.4.1 Antagonistic Interests	NLP markers, Emojis[§AS1.1.1a]
	§AS2.4.2 Solidary Interests	NLP markers, Emojis[§AS1.1.1a]
§AS2.5 Transformation		
	§AS2.5.1 To Parse	NLP markers
	§AS2.5.2 To Change	NLP markers

Fig. 3.4b: (cont.)

References

Abadi, Martin and Luca Cardelli. 1996. *A Theory of Objects*. New York, NY: Springer-Verlag.

Adamson, Peter and Alexander Key. 2015. "Philosophy of Language in the Medieval Arabic Tradition," pp. 74–99 in *Linguistic Content*, edited by M. Cameron and R. J. Stainton. Oxford, UK: Oxford University Press.

Agamben, Giorgio. 2011. *The Sacrament of Language*. Translated by A. Kotsoko. Cambridge, UK: Polity Press.

al-Jazari, Ibn al-Razzaz. 1206 [1974]. *The Book of Knowledge of Ingenious Mechanical Devices*. Translated by D.R. Hill. Dordrecht, NL: D. Reidel Publishing Company.

Al-Khalili, Jim. 2011. *The House of Wisdom: How Arabic Science Saved Ancient Knowledge and Gave Us the Renaissance*. New York, NY: Penguin Press.

Al-Khalili, Jim. 2015. "Book of Optics." *Nature* 518:164–65.

Alberti, Leon Battista. 1435 [1956]. *On Painting*. Translated by J.R. Spencer. New Haven, CT: Yale University Press.

Alexander, Christopher. 1979. *The Timeless Way of Building*. New York, NY: Oxford University Press.

Anderson, Chris. 2008. "The End of Theory: The Data Deluge Makes the Scientific Method Obsolete." *Wired*, 16 July.

Antognazza, Maria Rosa. 2009. *Leibniz: An Intellectual Biography*. Cambridge, UK: Cambridge University Press.

Arendt, Hannah. 1968 [1973]. "Introduction," in *Walter Benjamin*, edited by H. Arendt. London, UK: Fontana.

Argan, Giulio Carlo. 1946. "The Architecture of Brunelleschi and the Origins of Perspective Theory in the Fifteenth Century." *Journal of the Warburg and Courtauld Institutes* 9:96–121.

Austin, J.L. 1962 [1975]. *How to Do Things with Words: The William James Lectures Delivered at Harvard University in 1955*. Cambridge, MA: Harvard University Press.

Babbage, Charles. 1864 [1994]. *Passages from the Life of a Philosopher*. New Brunswick, NJ: Rutgers University Press.

Babbage, Charles. 1889 [2010]. *Babbage's Calculating Engines: Being a Collection of Papers Relating to Them; Their History, and Construction*. Cambridge, UK: Cambridge University Press.

Bach, Emmon. 1968. "Nouns and Noun Phrases," pp. 90–122 in *Universals in Linguistic Theory*, edited by E. Bach and R.T. Harms. New York, NY: Holt, Rinehart and Winston.

Baker, Collin F., Charles J. Fillmore and John B. Lowe. 1998. "The Berkeley Framenet Project." Paper presented at the COLING '98 Proceedings of the 17th International Conference on Computational Linguistics, August 10–14, Montreal.

Bantjes, Rod. 2014. " 'Vertical Perspective Does Not Exist': The Scandal of Converging Verticals and the Final Crisis of Perspectiva Artificialis." *Journal of the History of Ideas* 75(2):307–38.

Barsky, Robert F. 2011. *Zellig Harris: From American Linguistics to Socialist Zionism.* Cambridge, MA: MIT Press.

Barthes, Roland. 1957 [2012]. *Mythologies.* New York, NY: Hill and Wang.

Barthes, Roland. 1980 [2010]. *Camera Lucinda: Reflections on Photography.* Translated by R. Howard. New York, NY: Hill and Wang.

Basilico, Gabriele. 2009. *Vertiginous Moscow.* London, UK: Thames and Hudson.

Battisti, Eugenio. 1963. *Cimabue.* Milan, Italy: Institutio Editoriale Italiano.

Baudrillard, Jean. 1984. *The Evil Demon of Images.* Translated by P. Patton and P. Foss. Sydney, Australia: Power Institute Publications.

Baxandall, Michael. 1988. *Painting and Experience in Fifteenth Century Italy.* Oxford, UK: Oxford University Press.

Bazerman, Charles. 1988. *Shaping Written Knowledge: The Genre and Activity of the Experimental Article in Science.* Madison, WI: University of Wisconsin Press.

Becker, Joseph D. 1984. "Multilingual Word Processing." *Scientific American* 251 (1):96–107.

Becker, Joseph D. 1988. "Unicode 88." Palo Alto, CA: Xerox Corporation.

Begley, Adam. 2017. *The Great Nadar: The Man Behind the Camera.* New York, NY: Tim Duggin Books.

Belting, Hans. 2008 [2011]. *Florence and Baghdad: Renaissance Art and Arab Science.* Translated by D.L. Schneider. Cambridge, MA: Harvard University Press.

Benjamin, Walter. 1925 [1979]. "One Way Street," pp. 45–106 in *One Way Street and Other Writings.* London: Verso.

Benjamin, Walter. 1927 [1999]. "On the Present Situation of Russian Film," pp. 12–19 in *Walter Benjamin, Selected Writings*, Volume 2: *1927–1934*, edited by M.W. Jennings. Cambridge, MA: Harvard University Press.

Benjamin, Walter. 1931 [1999]. "Little History of Photography," pp. 507–30 in *Walter Benjamin: Selected Writings*, Volume 2: *1927–1934*, edited by M.W. Jennings, H. Eiland, and G. Smith. Cambridge, MA: Harvard University Press.

Benjamin, Walter. 1936 [2008]. "The Work of Art in the Age of Its Technological Reproducibility," pp. 19–55 in *The Work of Art in the Age of Its Technological Reproducibility and Other Writings on Media*, edited by M.W. Jennings, B. Doherty, and T.Y. Levin. Cambridge, MA: Harvard University Press.

Benjamin, Walter. 1939 [1999]. "Paris, Capital of the Nineteenth Century," pp. 14–26 in *The Arcades Project*, edited by H. Eidland and K. McLaughlin. Cambridge, MA: Harvard University Press.

Benjamin, Walter. 1999. *The Arcades Project.* Translated by H. Eidland and K. McLaughlin. Cambridge, MA: Harvard University Press.

Beradi, Franco "Biffo". 2015. *And: Phenomenology of the End, Sensibility and Connective Mutation.* Pasadena, CA: Semiotext(e).

Berger, John. 1967 [2013]. *Understanding the Photograph.* London, UK: Penguin.

Berger, Peter L. 1996. *Redeeming Laughter: The Comic Dimension of Human Experience*. Berlin, Germany: Walter de Gruyter.

Bergson, Henri. 1889 [1910]. *Time and Free Will*. London, UK: Muirhead Library of Philosophy.

Bergson, Henri. 1903 [1912]. *An Introduction to Metaphysics*. Translated by T.E. Hulme. New York, NY: G.P. Putnam.

Bergson, Henri. 1907 [1944]. *Creative Evolution*. Translated by A. Mitchell. New York, NY: Random House.

Bergson, Henri. 1934 [1946]. *The Creative Mind*. Translated by M.L. Andison. New York, NY: The Philosophical Library.

Berlin, Brent and Paul Kay. 1969. *Basic Color Terms: Their Universality and Evolution*. Berkeley, CA: University of California Press.

Berners-Lee, Tim, James Hendler, and Ora Lassila. 2001. "The Semantic Web." *Scientific American*, May, pp. 34–43.

Berwick, Robert C. and Noam Chomsky. 2016. *Why Only Us: Language and Evolution*. Cambridge, MA: MIT Press.

Bhaskar, Roy. 1975 [2008]. *A Realist Theory of Science*. London, UK: Routledge.

Bhaskar, Roy. 1989. *Reclaiming Reality: A Critical Introduction to Contemporary Philosophy*. London, UK: Verso.

Bhaskar, Roy. 1998. *The Possibility of Naturalism: A Philosophical Critique of the Contemporary Human Sciences*. London, UK: Routledge.

Bhaskar, Roy. 2000. *From East to West: Odyssey of a Soul*. London, UK: Routledge.

Bhaskar, Roy. 2016. *Enlightened Common Sense: The Philosophy of Critical Realism*. London, UK: Routledge.

Bhaskar, Roy and Mervyn Hartwig. 2010. *The Formation of Critical Realism: A Personal Perspective*. London, UK: Routledge.

Biguenet, John. 2015. *Silence*. London, UK: Bloomsbury.

Bjork, Daniel W. 1993. *B.F. Skinner: A Life*. New York, NY: Basic Books.

Black, Ulysees. 2000. *Internet Architecture: An Introduction to IP Protocols*. Upper Saddle River, NJ: Prentice Hall.

Bloomfield, Leonard. 1917. *Tagalog Texts with Grammatical Analysis*. Urbana, IL: University of Illinois Press.

Bloomfield, Leonard. 1927. "On Some Rules of Pāṇini." *Journal of the American Oriental Society* 47:61–70.

Bloomfield, Leonard. 1933. *Language*. New York, NY: Henry Holt and Company.

Bogdanov, Alexander. 1919 [1925]. *A Short History of Economic Science*. London, UK: Communist Party of Great Britain.

Bogdanov, Alexander. 1923 [2016]. *The Philosophy of Living Experience: Popular Outlines*. Translated by D.G. Rowley. Leiden, NL: Brill.

Bogost, Ian. 2012. *Alien Phenomenology, or What It Is Like to Be a Thing*. Minneapolis, MN: University of Minnesota Press.

Boll, Michael M. 1981. "From Empiriocriticism to Empiriomonism: The Marxist Phenomenology of Aleksandr Bogdanov." *The Slavonic and East European Review* 59(1):41–58.

Bolton, Ralph. 1978. "Black, White, and Red All Over: The Riddle of Color Term Salience." *Ethnology* 17(3):287–311.

Bornstein, Marc H. 1973. "Color Vision and Color Naming: A Psychophysiological Hypothesis of Cultural Difference." *Psychological Bulletin* 80(4):257–85.

Bornstein, Marc H. 1975. "The Influence of Visual Perception on Culture." *American Anthropologist* 77(4):774–98.

Bosak, Jon and Tim Bray. 1999. "XML and the Second-Generation Web." *Scientific American* 280(5):89–93.

Bostridge, Mark. 2008. *Florence Nightingale: The Woman and Her Legend*. London, UK: Viking.

Bowker, Geoffrey C. and Susan Leigh Star. 2000. *Sorting Things Out: Classification and Its Consequences*. Cambridge, MA: MIT Press.

Brandom, Robert. 1994. *Making It Explicit: Reasoning, Representing and Discursive Commitment*. Cambridge, MA: Harvard University Press.

Brandt, Richard L. 2011. *One Click: Jeff Bezos and the Rise of Amazon.Com*. New York, NY: Penguin.

Brassier, Ray. 2007. *Nihil Unbound: Enlightenment and Extinction*. London, UK: Palgrave Macmillan.

Brookman, Philip. 2010. *Helios: Eadweard Muybridge in a Time of Change*. Göttingen, Germany: Steidl/Corcoran Gallery of Art.

Brunel, Isambard. 1870. *The Life of Isambard Kingdom Brunel, Civil Engineer*. London, UK: Longmans, Green, and Co.

Bryson, Norman. 1983. *Vision and Painting: The Logic of the Gaze*. New Haven, CT: Yale University Press.

Burke, Christopher, Eric Kindel and Sue Walker, eds. 2013. *Isotype: Design and Contexts, 1925–1971*. London, UK: Hyphen Press.

Cage, John. 1961 [1966]. *Silence: Lectures and Writings*. Cambridge, MA: MIT Press.

Canales, Jimena. 2015. *The Physicist and the Philosopher: Einstein, Bergson, and the Debate That Changed Our Understanding of Time*. Princeton, NJ: Princeton University Press.

Cann, Ronnie. 1993. *Formal Semantics*. Cambridge, UK: Cambridge University Press.

Carboni, Davide, Andrea Manchinu, Valentina Marotto, Andrea Piras, and Alberto Serra. 2015. "Infrastructure-Free Indoor Navigation: A Case Study." *Journal of Location Based Services* 9(1):33–54. doi: 10.1080/17489725.2015.1027751.

Carroll, Lewis. 1872 [2000]. *The Annotated Alice: Through the Looking Glass*. Edited by M. Gardner. New York, NY: W.W. Norton.

Carter, M.G. 2004. *Sibawayhi*. New Delhi, India: Oxford University Press.

Cartier-Bresson, Henri. 1952 [2014]. *The Decisive Moment: Photography by Henri Cartier-Bresson*. Göttingen, Germany: Steidl.

Cazden, Courtney B. 2001. *Classroom Discourse: The Language of Teaching and Learning*. Portsmouth, NH: Heinemann.

Cazden, Courtney. 2018. *Communicative Competence, Classroom Interaction, and Educational Equity: The Selected Works of Courtney B. Cazden*. New York, NY: Routledge.

Cerf, Vinton G. and Robert E. Kahn. 1974. "A Protocol for Packet Network Intercommunication." *IEEE Trans. Comm. Tech.* COM-22(V5):627–41.

Chabert, Jean-Luc, ed. 1994 [1999]. *A History of Algorithms*. Translated by C. Weeks. Berlin, Germany: Springer.

Chall, Jeanne S. 1967 [1983]. *Learning to Read: The Great Debate.* New York, NY: McGraw-Hill.

Chattopadhyaya, Debiprasad. 1959. *Lokayata: A Study in Ancient Indian Materialism.* New Delhi, India: People's Publishing House.

Chattopadhyaya, Debiprasad. 1964. *Indian Philosophy: A Popular Introduction.* New Delhi, India: People's Publishing House.

Chattopadhyaya, Debiprasad. 1981. "Science and Society in Ancient India," pp. 231–62 in *Marxism and Indology,* edited by D. Chattopadhyaya. Calcutta, India: K.P. Bagchi and Company.

Chattopadhyaya, Debiprasad. 1990. *Anthropology and Historiography of Science.* Athens, OH: Ohio University Press.

Chattopadhyaya, Debiprasad. 1991. *Philosophy and the Future.* Bangalore, India: Navakarnataka Publications.

Chirimuuta, M. 2015. *Outside Color: Perceptual Science and the Puzzle of Color in Philosophy.* Cambridge, MA: MIT Press.

Chomsky, Noam. 1957. *Syntactic Structures.* Amsterdam, NL: de Gruyter Mouton.

Chomsky, Noam. 1959. "Review of 'Verbal Behavior,' by B.F. Skinner." *Language* 35 (1):26–58.

Chomsky, Noam. 1964. *Aspects of the Theory of Syntax.* Cambridge, MA: MIT Press.

Chomsky, Noam. 1966 [2009]. *Cartesian Linguistics: A Chapter in the History of Rationalist Thought.* Cambridge, UK: Cambridge University Press.

Chomsky, Noam. 1970. "Remarks on Nominalization," pp. 184–221 in *Readings in English Transformational Grammar,* edited by R. Jacobs and P. Rosenbaum. Waltham, MA: Ginn.

Chomsky, Noam. 1971. "The Case against B.F. Skinner." *New York Review of Books,* 17 (11):18–24.

Chomsky, Noam. 1976. *Reflections on Language.* London, UK: Fontana.

Chomsky, Noam. 1980 [2005]. *Rules and Representations.* New York, NY: Columbia University Press.

Chomsky, Noam. 1986. *Knowledge of Language: Its Nature, Origin, and Use.* New York, NY: Praeger.

Chomsky, Noam. 1995. *The Minimalist Program.* Cambridge, MA: MIT Press.

Chomsky, Noam. 2000. *New Horizons in the Study of Language and Mind.* Cambridge, UK: Cambridge University Press.

Chomsky, Noam. 2002. *On Nature and Language.* Cambridge, UK: Cambridge University Press.

Chomsky, Noam. 2016. *What Kind of Creatures Are We?* New York, NY: Columbia University Press.

Church, Alonzo. 1936. "A Note on the Entscheidungsproblem." *The Journal of Symbolic Logic* 1(1):40–41.

Church, Alonzo. 1937. "Review of 'on Computable Numbers, with an Application to the Entscheidungsproblem' by A. M. Turing." *The Journal of Symbolic Logic* 2 (1):42–43.

Churchland, Paul M. 2010. "On the Reality (and Diversity) of Objective Colors: How the Color-Qualia Space Is a Map of Reflectance-Profile Space," pp. 37–66 in *Color Ontology and Color Science.* Cambridge, MA: MIT Press.

Clarke, Arthur C. 1968. *2001: A Space Odyssey.* New York, NY: Signet.

Clegg, Brian. 2007. "The Man Who Stopped Time." Washington, DC: National Academies Press.

Coates, Jennifer. 1983. *The Semantics of Modal Auxiliaries*. London, UK: Croom Helm.

Cohn, Bernard S. 1996. *Colonialism and Its Forms of Knowledge: The British in India*. Princeton, NJ: Princeton University Press.

Cole, Michael, Karl Levitin, and Alexander R. Luria. 1979 [2006]. *The Autobiography of Alexander Luria: A Dialogue with the Making of Mind*. Mahwah, NJ: Lawrence Erlbaum.

Collier, Bruce. 1970. "The Little Engines That Could've: The Calculating Machines of Charles Babbage." Ph.D., Department of History of Science, Harvard University, Cambridge, MA.

Collier, Bruce and James MacLachlan. 1998. *Charles Babbage and the Engines of Perfection*. New York, NY: Oxford University Press.

Conklin, Harold C. 1955. "Hanunóo Color Categories." *Southwest Journal of Anthropology* 11:339–44.

Coole, Diana and Samantha Frost, eds. 2010. *New Materialisms: Ontology, Agency, and Politics*. Durham, NC: Duke University Press.

Cope, Bill. 1998. "The Language of Forgetting: A Short History of the Word," pp. 192–223 in *Seams of Light: Best Antipodean Essays*, edited by M. Fraser. Sydney, Australia: Allen and Unwin.

Cope, Bill. 2011. "Method for the Creation, Location and Formatting of Digital Content." U.S. Patent US7886225B2.

Cope, Bill and Mary Kalantzis, eds. 1993. *The Powers of Literacy: Genre Approaches to Teaching Writing*. London, UK: Falmer Press and Pittsburgh, PA: University of Pennsylvania Press.

Cope, Bill and Mary Kalantzis, eds. 2000a. *Multiliteracies: Literacy Learning and the Design of Social Futures*. London, UK: Routledge.

Cope, Bill and Mary Kalantzis. 2000b. *A Place in the Sun: Re-Creating the Australian Way of Life*. Sydney, Australia: Harper Collins.

Cope, Bill and Mary Kalantzis. 2004. "Text-Made Text." *E-Learning* 1(2):198–282.

Cope, Bill and Mary Kalantzis. 2009a. "A Grammar of Multimodality." *International Journal of Learning* 16(2):361–425.

Cope, Bill and Mary Kalantzis. 2009b. "'Multiliteracies': New Literacies, New Learning." *Pedagogies: An International Journal* 4:164–95.

Cope, Bill and Mary Kalantzis. 2015. "Extraurbia, or, the Reconfiguration of Spaces and Flows in a Time of Spatial-Financial Crisis," pp. 219–46 in *Smart Cities as Democratic Ecologies*, edited by D. Araya. New York, NY: Palgrave.

Cope, Bill and Mary Kalantzis, eds. 2017. *E-Learning Ecologies: Principles for New Learning and Assessment*. New York, NY: Routledge.

Cope, Bill, Mary Kalantzis and Liam Magee. 2011. *Towards a Semantic Web: Connecting Knowledge in Academic Research*. Cambridge, UK: Elsevier.

Cope, Bill, Mary Kalantzis, Michael McDaniel, Sue McGinty, Martin Nakata, Ailsa Purdon, Nicky Solomon, and Ron Stanton. 1995. "Assessment and Access to Adult Literacy Programs for Aboriginal and Torres Strait Islander People Wishing to Participate in Vocational Education and Training." Canberra: Department of Employment, Education and Training.

Cope, Bill and Angus Phillips, eds. 2014. *The Future of the Academic Journal*. Oxford, UK: Elsevier.

Cowan, Katharine and Gunther Kress. 2019. "Documenting and Transferring Meaning in the Multimodal World: Reconsidering 'Transcription'," pp. 66–77 in *Remixing Multiliteracies: Theory and Practice from New London to New Times*, edited by F. Serfini and E. Gee. New York, NY: Teachers College Press.

Cox, Brian and Jeff Forshaw. 2011. *The Quantum Universe: Everything That Can Happen Does Happen*. London, UK: Allen Lane.

da Vinci, Leonardo. 1651 [1835]. *A Treatise on Painting*. Translated by J.F. Rigaud. London, UK: J.B. Nichols and Son.

Dailey, David, Jon Frost, and Domenico Strazzullo. 2012. *Building Web Applications with SVG*. Redmond, WA: Microsoft Press.

de Saussure, Ferdinand. 1881 [2017]. *On the Use of the Genitive Absolute in Sanskrit*. Translated by A. Sukla. Champaign, IL: Common Ground Research Networks.

de Saussure, Ferdinand. 1916 [1983]. *Course in General Linguistics*. Translated by R. Harris. London, UK: Duckworth.

de Saussure, Ferdinand. 2002 [2006]. *Writings in General Linguistics*, edited by S. Bouquet and R. Engler. Translated by C. Sanders and M. Pires. Oxford, UK: Oxford University Press.

Deacon, Terrence W. 1997. *The Symbolic Species: The Co-Evolution of Language and the Brain*. New York, NY: W.W. Norton.

Deleuze, Gilles. 1969 [1990]. *The Logic of Sense*. Translated by M. Lester. New York, NY: Columbia University Press.

Deleuze, Gilles. 1995 [2001]. *Pure Immanence: Essays on a Life*. Translated by A. Boyman. New York, NY: Zone Books.

Deleuze, Gilles and Félix Guattari. 1991 [1994]. *What Is Philosophy?* Translated by H. Tomlinson and G. Burchill. New York, NY: Columbia University Press.

Deleuze, Gilles and Claire Parnet. 1977 [2007]. *Dialogues II*. New York, NY: Columbia University Press.

Dendrinos, Bessie and Emilia Robeiro Pedro. 1997. "Giving Street Directions: The Silent Role of Women," pp. 215–38 in *Silence: Interdisciplinary Perspectives*, edited by A. Jaworksi. Berlin, Germany: Mouton de Gruyter.

Dennett, Daniel C. 1998. *Brainchildren: Essays on Designing Minds*. Cambridge, MA: MIT Press.

Derrida, Jacques. 1967 [1973]a. "Form and Meaning: A Note on the Phenomenology of Signs," in *Speech and Phenomena, and Other Essays on Husserl's Theory of Signs*. Evanston, IL: Northwestern University Press.

Derrida, Jacques. 1967 [1973]b. *Speech and Phenomena, and Other Essays on Husserl's Theory of Signs*. Translated by D.B. Allison. Evanston, IL: Northwestern University Press.

Derrida, Jacques. 1967 [1997]. *Of Grammatology*. Translated by G.C. Spivak. Baltimore, MD: Johns Hopkins University Press.

Derrida, Jacques. 1968 [1973]. "Differance," in *Speech and Phenomena, and Other Essays on Husserl's Theory of Signs*. Evanston, IL: Northwestern University Press.

Derrida, Jacques. 1971 [1988]. "Signature Event Context," pp. 1–23 in *Limited Inc*, edited by G. Graff. Evanston, IL: Northwestern University Press.

Derrida, Jacques. 1977 [1988]. "Limited Inc Abc . . .," pp. 29–110 in *Limited Inc*, edited by G. Graff. Evanston, IL: Northwestern University Press.

Derrida, Jacques. 1988. *Limited Inc*, edited by G. Graff. Evanston, IL: Northwestern University Press.

Descartes, René. 1628 [1985]. *Rules for the Direction of the Mind*. Translated by J. Cottingham, R. Stoothoff, and D. Murdoch. Cambridge, UK: Cambridge University Press.

Descartes, René. 1637 [1985]. *Discourse on the Method of Rightly Conducting the Reason, and Seeking Truth in the Sciences*. Translated by J. Cottingham, R. Stoothoff, and D. Murdoch. Cambridge, UK: Cambridge University Press.

Descartes, René. 1641 [1984]. *Meditations on First Philosophy*. Translated by J. Cottingham, R. Stoothoff, and D. Murdoch. Cambridge, UK: Cambridge University Press.

Descartes, René. 1644 [1985]. *Principles of Philosophy*. Translated by J. Cottingham, R. Stoothoff, and D. Murdoch. Cambridge, UK: Cambridge University Press.

Dixon, R.M.W. 1972. *The Dyirbal Language of North Queensland*. Cambridge, UK: Cambridge University Press.

Dixon, R.M.W. 1980. *The Languages of Australia*. Cambridge, UK: Cambridge University Press.

Dixon, R.M.W. 1984. *Searching for Aboriginal Languages: Memoirs of a Field Worker*. Chicago, IL: University of Chicago Press.

Dixon, R.M.W. 1991. *A New Approach to English Grammar, on Semantic Principles*. Oxford, UK: Oxford University Press.

Dixon, R.M.W. 1994. *Ergativity*. Cambridge, UK: Cambridge University Press.

Dixon, R.M.W. 2010a. *Basic Linguistic Theory*, Volume 1: *Methodology*. Oxford, UK: Oxford University Press.

Dixon, R.M.W. 2010b. *Basic Linguistic Theory*, Volume 2: *Grammatical Topics*. Oxford, UK: Oxford University Press.

Dixon, R.M.W. 2012. *Basic Linguistic Theory*, Volume 3: *Further Grammatical Topics*. Oxford, UK: Oxford University Press.

Dixon, R.M.W. and Grace Koch. 1996. *Dyirbal Song Poetry: The Oral Literature of an Australian Rainforest People*. Brisbane, Australia: University of Queensland Press.

Dodgson, Charles (*nom de plume*, Lewis Carroll). 1896 [1977]. *Symbolic Logic*. New York, NY: Clarkson Potter.

Dreyfus, Hubert L. 1992. *What Computers Still Can't Do: A Critique of Artificial Reason*. Cambridge, MA: MIT Press.

Dry, Sarah. 2014. *The Newton Papers: The Strange and True Odyssey of Isaac Newton's Manuscripts*. Oxford, UK: Oxford University Press.

Dummett, Michael. 1973. *Frege: Philosophy of Language*. New York, NY: Harper and Row.

Dyson, George. 2012. *Turing's Cathedral: The Origins of the Digital Universe*. New York, NY: Pantheon Books.

Eidland, Howard and Kevin McLaughlin. 1999. "Translators' Foreword." in *The Arcades Project*. Cambridge, MA: Harvard University Press.

Eiseman, Leatrice and Keith Recker. 2011. *Pantone: The 20th Century in Color*. San Francisco, CA: Chronicle Books.

Ember, Melvin. 1978. "Size of Color Lexicon: Interaction of Cultural and Biological Factors." *American Anthropologist* 80(2):364–67.

Endress, Gerhard. 1977. "The Debate between Arabic Grammar and Greek Logic in Classical Islamic Thought." *Journal for the History of Arabic Science* 1(2):320–22.

Essinger, James. 2004. *Jacquard's Web: How the Hand-Loom Led to the Birth of the Information Age.* Oxford, UK: Oxford University Press.

Essinger, James. 2014. *Ada's Algorithm: How Lord Byron's Daughter, Ada Lovelace, Launched the Digital Age.* Brooklyn, NY: Melville House.

Eveleth, Rose. 2013. "Earth's Quietest Place Will Drive You Crazy in 45 Minutes." *Smithsonian Magazine* (December 17).

Fairclough, Norman. 1992. *Discourse and Social Change.* Cambridge, UK: Polity Press.

Fairclough, Norman. 1995. *Critical Discourse Analysis.* London, UK: Longmans.

Fairclough, Norman. 2001. *Language and Power.* London: Longmans.

Farin, Gerald. 2002. "A History of Curves and Surfaces in Cagd," pp. 1–21 in *Handbook of Computer Aided Geometric Design*, edited by G. Farin, J. Hoschek, and M.-S. Kim. Amsterdam, NL: Elsevier.

Feferman, Anita Burdham. 1993. *From Trotsky to Gödel: The Life of Jean Van Heijenoort.* Natick, MA: A.K. Peters.

Fensel, Dieter, James Hendler, Henry Lieberman, and Wolfgang Wahlster, eds. 2005. *Spinning the Semantic Web: Bringing the Worldwide Web to Its Full Potential.* Cambridge, MA: MIT Press.

Ferriss, Hugh. 1929 [2005]. *The Metropolis of Tomorrow.* New York, NY: Dover Publications.

Fillmore, Charles J. 1966. "Toward a Modern Theory of Case." Columbus, OH: Ohio State University.

Fillmore, Charles J. 1968. "The Case for Case," pp. 1–88 in *Universals in Linguistic Theory*, edited by E. Bach and R.T. Harms. New York, NY: Holt, Rinehart and Winston.

Fillmore, Charles J. 1976. "Frame Semantics and the Nature of Language." *Annals of the New York Academy of Sciences* 280(1):20–32.

Fillmore, Charles J. 1977. "The Case for Case Reopened." *Syntax and Semantics* 8:59–82.

Finley, Gerald. 1999. *Angel in the Sun: Turner's Vision of History.* Montreal, Canada: McGill–Queens University Press.

Fiorani, Francesca. 2012. "Leonardo Da Vinci and His Treatise on Painting." Charlottesville, VA: Rector and Visitors of the University of Virginia. (www .treatiseonpainting.org/intro.html).

Fitch, W. Tecumseh, Marc D. Hauser, and Noam Chomsky. 2005. "The Evolution of the Language Faculty: Clarifications and Implications." *Cognition* 97(2):179–210.

Fittko, Lisa. 1980 [1999]. "The Story of Old Benjamin," pp. 946–54 in *The Arcades Project*, edited by H. Eidland and K. McLaughlin. Cambridge, MA: Harvard University Press.

Flusser, Vilém. 1983 [2000]. *Towards a Philosophy of Photography.* London, UK: Reaktion Books.

Force, James E. and Richard H. Popkin. 1990. *Essays on the Context, Nature, and Influence of Isaac Newton's Theology*, Dordrecht, NL: Kluwer.

Francis, John. 1851. *A History of the English Railway: Its Social Relations and Revelations, 1820–1845*, Volume 2. London, UK: Longman, Brown, Green & Longmans.

Frege, Gottlob. 1892 [1948]."Sense and Reference." *The Philosophical Review* 57 (3):209–30.

Frege, Gottlob. 1893/1903 [2016]. *Basic Laws of Arithmetic.* Oxford, UK: Oxford University Press.

Fuegi, John and Jo Francis. 2003. "Lovelace & Babbage and the Creation of the 1843 'Notes'." *IEEE Annals of the History of Computing* 25(4):16–26.

Gage, John. 1972. *Turner: Rain, Steam and Speed.* New York, NY: Viking Press.

Gamma, Erich, Richard Helm, Ralph Johnson, and John Vlissides. 1994. *Design Patterns: Elements of Reusable Object-Oriented Software.* Boston, MA: Addison-Wesley.

Garcia, Antero, Allan Luke, and Robyn Seglem. 2018. "Looking at the Next Twenty Years of Multiliteracies: A Discussion with Allan Luke." *Theory into Practice* 57 (1):72–78.

Gärdenfors, Peter. 2014. *Geometry of Meaning: Semantics Based on Conceptual Spaces.* Cambridge, MA: MIT Press.

Gee, James Paul. 1992 [2013]. *The Social Mind: Language, Ideology, and Social Practice.* Champaign, IL: Common Ground.

Gee, James Paul. 1996. *Social Linguistics and Literacies: Ideology in Discourses.* London, UK: Taylor and Francis.

Gee, James Paul. 2004. "Language in the Science Classroom: Academic Social Languages as the Heart of School-Based Literacy," pp. 13–32 in *Crossing Borders in Literacy and Science Instruction*, edited by E.W. Saul. Arlington, VA: NSTA Press.

Gee, James Paul. 2005. *An Introduction to Discourse Analysis: Theory and Method.* New York, NY: Routledge.

Gee, James Paul. 2017. "A Personal Retrospective on the New London Group and Its Formation," pp. 32–45 in *Remixing Multiliteracies: Theory and Practice from New London to New Times*, edited by F. Serfini and E. Gee. New York, NY: Teachers College Press.

Geroimenko, Vladimir and Chaomei Chen, eds. 2005. *Visualizing Information Using SVG and X3D: XML-Based Technologies for the XML-Based Web.* London, UK: Springer-Verlag.

Ghiberti, Lorenzo. *c.*1447 [1948]. *The Commentaries.* London, UK: Courtald Institute of Art.

Gilbert, Alorie. 2004. "E-Commerce Turns 10." *c|net*, 11 August.

Giusti, Gordana Korolija Fontana. 1999. "The Cutting Surface: On Perspective as a Section, Its Relationship to Writing, and Its Role in Understanding Space." *AA Files* (40):56–64.

Gödel, Kurt. 1931 [1962]. *On Formally Undecidable Propositions of Principia Mathematica and Related Systems*, Volume 38. Translated by B. Meltzer. New York, NY: Basic Books.

Goody, Jack. 1987. *The Interface between the Written and the Oral.* Cambridge, UK: Cambridge University Press.

Goody, Jack. 2010. *Renaissances: The One or the Many?* Cambridge, UK: Cambridge University Press.

Grabar, Oleg. 1975. "Islam and Iconoclasm," pp. 45–52 in *Iconoclasm: Papers Given at the Ninth Spring Symposium of Byzantine Studies, University of Birmingham, March 1975*, edited by A. Bryer and J. Herrin. Birmingham, UK: Centre for Byzantine Studies, University of Birmingham.

Grave, S.A. 1988. "Gibson, William Ralph Boyce (1869–1935)," in *Australian Dictionary of Biography*. Melbourne, AU: Melbourne University Press.

Green, Phil, ed. 2010. *Color Management: Understanding and Using ICC Profiles*. Chichester, UK: John Wiley & Sons.

Grosz, Elizabeth. 2017. *The Incorporeal: Ontology, Ethics, and the Limits of Materialism*. New York, NY: Columbia University Press.

Gruber, Thomas R. 1995. "Toward Principles for the Design of Ontologies Used for Knowledge Sharing." *International Journal of Human-Computer Studies* 43 (5–6):907–28.

Gruber, Thomas R. 2009. "Ontology," pp. 1963–5 in *Encyclopedia of Database Systems*, edited by L. Liu and M.T. Özsu. New York, NY: Springer-Verlag.

Guha, Ramanathan V. and Vineet Gupta. 2016. "Communicating Semantics: Reference by Description," arXiv:1511.06341v3 [cs.CL].

Habermas, Jürgen 1968 [1971]. *Knowledge and Human Interests*. Translated by J.J. Shapiro. Boston, MA: Beacon Press.

Haller, Rudolf. 1991a. "On Otto Neurath," pp. 25–31 in *Rediscovering the Forgotten Vienna Circle: Austrian Studies on Otto Neurath and the Vienna Circle*, edited by T.E. Uebel. Dordrecht, Germany: Kluwer Academic Publishers.

Haller, Rudolf. 1991b. "Two Ways of Experiential Justification," pp. 191–202 in *Rediscovering the Forgotten Vienna Circle: Austrian Studies on Otto Neurath and the Vienna Circle*, edited by T.E. Uebel. Dordrecht, Germany: Kluwer Academic Publishers.

Halliday, M.A.K. 1967a. "Notes on Transitivity and Theme in English: Part 2." *Journal of Linguistics* 3(2):199–244.

Halliday, M.A.K. 1967b. "Notes on Transitivity and Theme in English: Part 1." *Journal of Linguistics* 3(1):37–81.

Halliday, M.A.K. 1968. "Notes on Transitivity and Theme in English: Part 3." *Journal of Linguistics* 4(2):179–215.

Halliday, M.A.K. 1977 [2003]. "Ideas About Language," pp. 92–115 in *On Language and Linguistics*, The Collected Works of M.A.K. Halliday, Volume 3, edited by J.J. Webster. London, UK: Continuum.

Halliday, M.A.K. 1984 [2002]. "On the Ineffability of Grammatical Categories," pp. 291–322 in *On Grammar*, The Collected Works of M.A.K. Halliday, Volume 1, edited by J.J. Webster. London, UK: Continuum.

Halliday, M.A.K. 1987 [2002]. "Spoken and Written Modes of Meaning," pp. 323–51 in *On Grammar*, The Collected Works of M.A.K. Halliday, Volume 1, edited by J.J. Webster. London, UK: Continuum.

Halliday, M.A.K. 1989 [1993]. "Some Grammatical Problems in Scientific English," pp. 69–85 in *Writing Science: Literacy and Discursive Power*, edited by M.A.K. Halliday and J.R. Martin. London, UK: Falmer Press.

Halliday, M.A.K. 1996 [2002]. "On Grammar and Grammatics." in *On Grammar*, The Collected Works of M.A.K. Halliday, Volume 1, edited by J.J. Webster. London, UK: Continuum.

Halliday, M.A.K. 2000 [2002]. "Grammar and Daily Life: Concurrence and Complementarity," pp. 369–83 in *On Grammar*, The Collected Works of M.A.K. Halliday, Volume 1, edited by J.J. Webster. London, UK: Continuum.

Halliday, M.A.K. 2004. *The Language of Science*, The Collected Works of M.A.K. Halliday, Volume 5, edited by J.J. Webster. London, UK: Continuum.

Halliday, M.A.K. and Ruqaiya Hasan. 1980. *Text and Context: Aspects of Language in a Social Semiotic Perspective*. Sophia University.

Halliday, M.A.K. and Ruqaiya Hasan. 1976. *Cohesion in English*. London, UK: Longman.

Halliday, M.A.K. and Christian M.I.M. Matthiessen. 1999. *Construing Experience through Meaning: A Language-Based Approach to Cognition*. London, UK: Continuum.

Halliday, M.A.K. and Christian Matthiessen. 2004. *An Introduction to Functional Grammar*. London, UK: Routledge.

Halliday, M.A.K. and Christian M.I.M. Matthiessen. 2014. *Halliday's Introduction to Functional Grammar* (Edn 4). Milton Park, UK: Routledge.

Haniya, Samaa, Matthew Montebello, Bill Cope, and Richard Tapping. 2018. "Promoting Critical Clinical Thinking through E-Learning," pp. 5008–17 in *Proceedings of the 10th International Conference on Education and New Learning Technologies (EduLearn18)*. Palma de Mallorca, Spain.

Hardin, C.L. 1988. *Color for Philosophers: Unweaving the Rainbow*. Indianapolis IN: Hackett Publishing Company.

Hardin, Clyde L. and Luisa Maffi, eds. 1997. *Color Categories in Thought and Language*. Cambridge, UK: Cambridge University Press.

Harman, Graham. 2016. *Immaterialism*. Cambridge, UK: Polity.

Harnad, Stevan. 1989. "Minds, Machines and Searle." *Journal of Theoretical and Experimental Artificial Intelligence* 1:5–25.

Harris, Randy Allen. 1993. *The Linguistics Wars*. Oxford, UK: Oxford University Press.

Hatherley, Owen. 2015. *Landscapes of Communism*. London UK: Allen Lane.

Hauser, Marc D., Noam Chomsky, and W. Tecumseh Fitch. 2002. "The Faculty of Language: What Is It, Who Has It, and How Did It Evolve?" *Science* 298:1569–79.

Health Informatics Technical Committee CEN/TC 251. 2007. "A Syntax to Represent the Content of Medical Classification Systems: ClaML." EN 14463:2007. Brussels, Belgium: European Committee for Standardization.

Heffernan, James A.W. 1996. "Alberti on Apelles: Word and Image in 'De Pictura'." *International Journal of the Classical Tradition* 2(3):345–59.

Heidegger, Martin. 1926 [1962]. *Being and Time*. Translated by J. Macquarrie and E. Robinson. Oxford, UK: Blackwell.

Hempelmann, Christian F. 2012. "NLP for Search," pp. 53–74 in *Applied Natural Language Processing: Identification, Investigation, and Resolution*, edited by P.M. McCarthy and C. Boonthum-Denecke. Hershey, PA: IGI Global.

High Court of Australia. 1992. "Mabo and Others V Queensland (No. 2)." Vol. 175 CLR 1.

Hill, Christopher. 1972. *The World Turned Upside Down: Radical Ideas During the English Revolution*. London, UK: Temple Smith.

Hill, Christopher. 1993. *The English Bible and the Seventeenth Century Revolution*. London, UK: Penguin.

Hitchens, Christopher. 1995. *The Missionary Position: Mother Teresa in Theory and Practice*. London, UK: Verso.

Hodges, Andrew. 1983. *Alan Turing: The Enigma*. New York, NY: Simon and Schuster.

Hodgson, Marshall G.S. 1964. "Islâm and Image." *History of Religions* 3(2):220–60.

Hoffman, Paul. 2012. "The Tao of Ietf: A Novice's Guide to the Internet Engineering Task Force": Internet Engineering Task Force. (www.ietf.org/tao.html).

Hofstadter, Douglas R. 1979. *Godel, Escher, Bach: An Eternal Golden Braid*. New York, NY: Basic Books.

Hofstadter, Douglas R. 1985. *Metamagical Themas: Questing for the Essence of Mind and Pattern*. New York, NY: Basic Books.

Hofstadter, Douglas R. 2007. *I Am a Strange Loop*. New York, NY: Basic Books.

Hollings, Christopher, Ursula Martin and Adrian Rice. 2018. *Ada Lovelace: The Making of a Computer Scientist*. Oxford, UK: Bodleian Library.

Holt, Jon, Simon A. Perry, and Mike Brownsword. 2012. *Model-Based Requirements Engineering*. Stevenage, UK: Institution of Engineering and Technology.

Howard, Philip N. 2015. *Pax Technica: How the Internet of Things May Set Us Free or Lock Us Up*. New Haven, CT: Yale University Press.

Huang, Yan. 2014. *Pragmatics*. Oxford, UK: Oxford University Press.

Husserl, Edmund. 1913 [2001]. *Logical Investigations*, Volume 1. Translated by J.N. Findlay. London, UK: Routledge.

Husserl, Edmund. 1913 [2002]. *Ideas: General Introduction to Pure Phenomenology*. Translated by W.R.B. Gibson. London, UK: Routledge.

Husserl, Edmund. 1921 [2001]. *Logical Investigations*, Volume 2. Translated by J.N. Findlay. London, UK: Routledge.

ibn al-Haytham, Al-Hasan. *c*.1030 [1983]. *Kitāb Al-Manāẓir, Books I–II–III, "on Direct Vision"*. Kuwait: National Council for Culture, Arts and Letters.

ibn al-Haytham, Al-Hasan. *c*.1030 [1989]. *The Optics of Ibn Al-Haytham, Books I–II–III, "on Direct Vision"*, Volume 2: *Introduction, Commentary, Glossary, Concordance, Indices*. Translated by A.I. Sabra. London, UK: The Warburg Institute.

Iliffe, Robert. 2017. *Priest of Nature: The Religious Worlds of Isaac Newton*. Oxford, UK: Oxford University Press.

International Organization for Standardization. 2012. "Information Technology: Object Management Group Unified Modeling Language (OMG UML)." Part 1: Infrastructure.

Jameson, Fredric. 1972. *The Prison-House of Language: A Critical Account of Structuralism and Russian Formalism*. Princeton, NJ: Princeton University Press.

Jameson, Kimberly A., David Bimler, and Linda A. Wasserman. 2006. "Re-Assessing Perceptual Diagnostics for Observers with Diverse Retinal Photopigment Types," pp. 13–34 in *Progress in Colour Studies*, Volume 2: *Psychological Aspects*, edited by N.J. Pitchford and C.P. Biggam. Amsterdam, NL: John Benjamins.

Janik, Allan and Stephen Toulmin. 1973. *Wittgenstein's Vienna*. New York, NY: Simon and Schuster.

Jarzombek, Mark. 1990. "The Structural Problematic of Leon Battista Alberti's 'De Pictura'." *Renaissance Studies* 4(3):273–86.

Johnson [pseudonym]. 2016. "Noam Chomsky: The Theories of the World's Best-Known Linguist Have Become Rather Weird." *The Economist*, 23 March.

Joseph, John E. 2012. *Saussure*. Oxford, UK: Oxford University Press.

Kadvany, John. 2007. "Positional Value and Linguistic Recursion." *Journal of Indian Philosophy* 35(5/6):487–520.

Kadvany, John. 2016. "Pāṇini's Grammar and Modern Computation." *History and Philosophy of Logic* 37(4):325–46.

Kalantzis, Mary and Bill Cope. 2012a. "Multiliteracies in Education," in *The Encyclopedia of Applied Linguistics*. New York, NY: John Wiley and Sons.

Kalantzis, Mary and Bill Cope. 2012b. *New Learning: Elements of a Science of Education* (Edn 2). Cambridge, UK: Cambridge University Press.

Kalantzis, Mary and Bill Cope. 2016. "Learner Differences in Theory and Practice." *Open Review of Educational Research* 3(1):85–132.

Kalantzis, Mary, Bill Cope, and Eugenia Arvanitis. 2015. "Evaluation Report of the Project, Education of Roma Children in Central Macedonia, West Macedonia and East Macedonia and Thrace." Thessaloniki, Greece: Aristotle University.

Kalantzis, Mary, Bill Cope, Eveline Chan, and Leanne Dalley-Trim. 2016. *Literacies* (Edn 2). Cambridge, UK: Cambridge University Press.

Kalantzis, Mary, Bill Cope, Nicky Solomon, Allan Luke, Bob Morgan, and Martin Nakata. 1994. "Batchelor College Entry Profile and Stage Level Assessment Scales." Batchelor, NT: Batchelor College.

Kalantzis-Cope, Phillip. 2016. "Whose Data? Problematizing the 'Gift' of Social Labour." *Global Media and Communication* 12(3):295–309.

Kamermans, Mike. 2011–2017. "A Primer on Bézier Curves." Retrieved from https://pomax.github.io/bezierinfo/.

Kant, Immanuel. 1787 [1933]. *Critique of Pure Reason*. Translated by N.K. Smith. London, UK: Macmillan.

Karantzola, Eleni and Nikolaos Lavidas. 2014. "On the Relation between Labilizations and Neuter Gender: Evidence from the Greek Diachrony." *Linguistics* 52(4):1025–59.

Katz, Jerrold J. 1972. *Semantic Theory*. New York, NY: Harper & Row.

Kelsey, Robin. 2015. *Photography and the Art of Chance*. Cambridge, MA: Harvard University Press.

Kindel, Eric. 2011. "Reaching the People: Isotype Beyond the West," pp. 175–93 in *Image and Imaging in Philosophy, Science and the Arts*, edited by R. Heinrich, E. Nemeth, W. Pichler, and D. Wagner. Frankfurt, Germany: Ontos Verlag.

Kiparsky, Paul and Frits Staal. 1969 [1988]. "Syntactic and Semantic Relations in Pāṇini," pp. 184–218 in *Universals: Studies in Indian Logic and Linguistics*, edited by F. Staal. Chicago, IL: University of Chicago Press.

Koch, Christof. 2004. *The Quest for Consciousness: A Neurobiological Approach*. Engelwood, CO: Roberts and Company.

Koch, Christof. 2012. *Consciousness: Confessions of a Romantic Reductionist*. Cambridge, MA: MIT Press.

Kraemer, Joel L. 1986. *Humanism in the Renaissance of Islam: The Cultural Revival During the Buyid Age*. Leiden, NL: E.J. Brill.

Krautheimer, Richard. 1956. *Lorenzo Ghiberti*. Princeton, NJ: Princeton University Press.

Kress, Gunther. 2009. *Multimodality: A Social Semiotic Approach to Contemporary Communication*. London, UK: Routledge.

Kress, Gunther and Theo van Leeuwen. 2006. *Reading Images: The Grammar of Visual Design*. London, UK: Routledge.

Kripke, Saul A. 1972. *Naming and Necessity.* Cambridge, MA: Harvard University Press.

Kuehn, Daniel. 2013. "Keynes, Newton and the Royal Society: The Events of 1942 and 1943." *Notes and Records of the Royal Society of London* 67(1):25–36.

Kuehni, Rolf G. 2010. "Color Spaces and Color Order Systems," pp. 3–36 in *Color Ontology and Color Science*, edited by J. Cohen and M. Matthen. Cambridge, MA: MIT Press.

Kuschel, Rolf, and Torben Monberg. 1974. " 'We Don't Talk Much About Colour Here': A Study of Colour Semantics on Bellona Island." *Man* 9(2):213–42.

Lanchner, Carolyn. 2008. *Andy Warhol.* New York, NY: Museum of Modern Art.

Laplante, Phillip A. 2013. *Requirements Engineering for Software and Systems.* Boca Raton, FL: Auerbach Publications.

Larson, Gerald James. 1979. *Classical Sāmkhya: An Interpretation of Its History and Meaning.* Santa Barbara, CA: Ross/Erikson.

Last, Nana. 2008. *Wittgenstein's House: Language, Space and Architecture.* New York, NY: Fordham University Press.

Latour, Bruno. 1988. "Drawing Things Together," pp. 19–68 in *Representation in Scientific Practice*, edited by M. Lynch and S. Woolgar. Cambridge, MA: MIT Press.

LaValley, Al and Barry P. Scherr, eds. 2001. *Eisenstein at 100.* New Brunswick, NJ: Rutgers University Press.

Leavitt, David. 2006. *The Man Who Knew Too Much: Alan Turing and the Invention of the Computer.* New York, NY: W.W. Norton.

Legouix, Sandra. 1987. *Botticelli.* London, UK: Bloomsbury.

Leibniz, Gottfried Wilhelm. 1898. *The Monadology and Other Philosophical Writings.* Translated by R. Latta. Oxford, UK: Oxford University Press.

Leibniz, Gottfried Wilhelm. 1951. *Leibniz: Selections.* Translated by P.P. Weiner. New York, NY: Charles Scribner's Sons.

Leiner, Barry M., Vinton G. Cerf, David D. Clark, Robert E. Kahn, Leonard Kleinrock, Daniel C. Lynch, Jon Postel, Larry G. Roberts, and Stephen Wolff. 2009. "A Brief History of the Internet." *SIGCOMM Computer Communication Review* 39(5):22–31.

Leitner, Bernhard. 1976. *The Architecture of Ludwig Wittgenstein: A Documentation.* New York, NY: New York University Press.

Leitner, Bernhard. 2000. *The Wittgenstein House.* New York, NY: Princeton Architectural Press.

Lemke, Jay L. 1990. *Talking Science: Language, Learning and Values.* Westport, CN: Ablex.

Lenat, Douglas B. 2016. "WWTS(What Would Turing Say?)." *AI Magazine* 37 (1):97–101.

Lenin, V.I. 1898 [1964]. "Book Review: A. Bogdanov, a Short Course of Economic Science," pp. 46–54 in *Lenin: Collected Works.* Moscow: Progress Publishers.

Lenin, V.I. 1908 [1947]. *Materialism and Empirio-Criticism.* Moscow: Foreign Languages Publishing.

Leontyev, Aleksei Nikolaevich. 1947 [2009]. "An Outline of the Evolution of the Psyche." pp. 137–244 in *The Development of Mind*, edited by M. Cole. Pacifica, CA: Marxists Internet Archive.

Levinson, Stephen C. 1983. *Pragmatics.* Cambridge, UK: Cambridge University Press.

Levinson, Stephen C. 2000. "Yélî Dnye and the Theory of Basic Color Terms." *Journal of Linguistic Anthropology* 10(1):1–53.

Lindberg, David G. 1976. *Theories of Vision from Al-Kindi to Kepler*. Chicago, IL: University of Chicago Press.

Locke, John. 1690 [1801]. *An Essay Concerning Human Understanding*. Edinburgh, UK: Mundell & Son.

Loos, Adolf. 1998. *Ornament and Crime: Selected Essays*. Translated by M. Mitchell. Riverside, CA: Ariadne Press.

Lovelace, A.A. 1843. "Sketch of the Analytical Engine Invented by Charles Babbage, by L.F. Menabrea, with Notes Upon the Memoir by the Translator," pp. 666–731 in *Scientific Memoirs Selected from the Transactions of Foreign Academies of Science and Learned Societies*, Volume 3, edited by R. Taylor. London, UK: Richard and John E. Taylor.

Lowe, Victor. 1990. *Alfred North Whitehead: The Man and His Work*, Volume 2: *1910–1947*. Baltimore, MD: Johns Hopkins University Press.

Luke, Allan. 1996. "Text and Discourse in Education: An Introduction to Critical Discourse Analysis." *Review of Research in Education* 21:3–48.

Luke, Carmen. 2003. "Pedagogy, Connectivity, Multimodality, and Interdisciplinarity." *Reading Research Quarterly* 38(3):397–403.

Luke, Carmen and Jennifer Gore, eds. 1992. *Feminisms and Critical Pedagogy*. New York, NY: Routledge.

Luria, Aleksandr Romanovich. 1925 [1977]. "Psychoanalysis as a System of Monistic Psychology." *Soviet Psychology* 16(2):7–45.

Luria, Aleksandr Romanovich, ed. 1974 [1976]. *Cognitive Development: Its Cultural and Social Foundations*. Cambridge, MA: Harvard University Press.

Luria, Aleksandr Romanovich. 1981. *Language and Cognition*. New York, NY: John Wiley and Sons.

Lynn-George, Michael. 2004. "Writers, Intellectuals, Heroes: The Case of Ferdinand De Saussure." *The International Journal of the Humanities* 2:1243–49.

Lyons, John. 1977. *Semantics*, Volume 2. Cambridge, UK: Cambridge University Press.

Lytinen, Steven L. 1992. "Conceptual Dependency and Its Descendants." *Computers & Mathematics with Applications* 23(2–5):51–73.

Macarthur, David. 2014a. "Working on Oneself in Philosophy and Architecture: A Perfectionist Reading of the Wittgenstein House." *Architectural Theory Review* 19(2):124–40. doi: 10.1080/13264826.2014.951869.

Macarthur, David. 2014b. "Reflections on 'Architecture Is a Gesture' (Wittgenstein)." *Paragrana* 23(1):88–100.

MacCorquodale, Kenneth. 1970. "On Chomsky's Review of Skinner's 'Verbal Behavior'." *Journal of the Experimental Analysis of Behavior* 13(1):83–99.

Macken, Mary, Mary Kalantzis, Gunther Kress, Jim Martin, Bill Cope and Joan Rothery. 1990a. *A Genre-Based Approach to Teaching Writing, Years 3–6, Book 4: The Theory and Practice of Genre-Based Writing*. Sydney, AU: Directorate of Studies, N.S.W. Department of Education.

Macken, Mary, Mary Kalantzis, Gunther Kress, Jim Martin, Bill Cope, and Joan Rothery. 1990b. *A Genre-Based Approach to Teaching Writing, Years 3–6, Book 3: Writing Stories: A Teaching Unit Based on Narratives About Fairy Tales*. Sydney, AU: Directorate of Studies, N.S.W. Department of Education.

Macken, Mary, Mary Kalantzis, Gunther Kress, Jim Martin, Bill Cope, and Joan Rothery. 1990c. *A Genre-Based Approach to Teaching Writing, Years 3–6*, Book 2: *Factual Writing: A Teaching Unit Based on Reports About Sea Mammals*. Sydney, AU: Directorate of Studies, N.S.W. Department of Education.

Macken, Mary, Mary Kalantzis, Gunther Kress, Jim Martin, Bill Cope, and Joan Rothery. 1990d. *A Genre-Based Approach to Teaching Writing, Years 3–6*, Book 1: *Introduction*. Sydney, AU: Directorate of Studies, N.S.W. Department of Education.

Macken-Horarik, Mary, Kristina Love, and Len Unsworth. 2011. "A Grammatics 'Good Enough' for School English in the 21st Century: Four Challenges in Realising the Potential." *Australian Journal of Language and Literacy* 34(1):9–23.

Magee, Liam. 2010. "A Framework for Assessing Commensurability of Semantic Web Ontologies." *Electronic Journal of Knowledge Management* 8(1):91–102.

Magee, Liam. 2011. "Upper-Level Ontologies," pp. 235–87 in *Towards a Semantic Web: Connecting Knowledge in Academic Research*, edited by Bill Cope, Mary Kalantzis, and Liam Magee. Cambridge, UK: Elsevier.

Magee, Liam and James A. Thom. 2014. "What's in a WordTM? When One Electronic Document Format Standard Is Not Enough." *Information Technology & People* 27 (4):482–511.

Maggs, Colin. 2016. *Isambard Kingdom Brunel: The Life of an Engineering Genius*. Stroud, UK: Amberley.

Mahdi, Mushin. 1970. "Language and Logic in Classical Islam," pp. 51–83 in *Logic in Classical Islamic Culture*, edited by G.E. von Grunebaum. Wiesbaden, Germany: Otto Harrassowitz.

Makdisi, George. 1990. *The Rise of Humanism in Classical Islam and the Christian West*. Edinburgh, UK: Edinburgh University Press.

Malcolm, Norman. 1958. *Ludwig Wittgenstein: A Memoir*. Oxford, UK: Oxford University Press.

Manetti, Antonio di Tuccio. 1497 [1970]. *The Life of Brunelleschi*. Translated by C. Enggass. University Park, PA: Pennsylvania State University Press.

Mango, Cyril. 1975. "Historical Introduction," pp. 1–6 in *Iconoclasm: Papers Given at the Ninth Spring Symposium of Byzantine Studies, University of Birmingham, March 1975*, edited by A. Bryer and J. Herrin. Birmingham, UK: Centre for Byzantine Studies, University of Birmingham.

Marcus, James. 2004. *Amazonia: Five Years at the Epicenter of the Dot.Com Juggernaut*. New York, NY: The New Press.

Martin, J.R. 1993. "Life as a Noun: Arresting the Universe in Science and the Humanities," pp. 221–67 in *Writing Science: Literacy and Discursive Power*, edited by M.A.K. Halliday and J.R. Martin. London, UK: Falmer Press.

Marx, Karl. 1845 [1969]. "Theses on Feuerbach," pp. 13–15 in *Marx & Engels Selected Works*. Moscow, USSR: Progress Publishers.

Marx, Ursula, Gundrun Schwarz, Michael Schwarz and Ermut Wizisla, eds. 2007. *Walter Benjamin's Archive*. Translated by E. Leslie. London, UK: Verso.

Mayer-Schönberger, Viktor and Kenneth Cukier. 2013. *Big Data: A Revolution That Will Transform How We Live, Work, and Think*. New York, NY: Houghton Mifflin Harcourt.

McDowell, John. 1977. "On the Sense and Reference of a Proper Name." *Mind* 86 (342):159–85.

McGinn, Colin. 2004. *Mindsight: Image, Dream, Meaning*. Cambridge, MA: Harvard University Press.

McGinn, Colin. 2008. *Mindfucking: A Critique of Mental Manipulation*. Stocksfield, UK: Acumen.

McGinn, Colin. 2015a. *Prehension: The Hand and the Emergence of Humanity*. Cambridge, MA: MIT Press.

McGinn, Colin. 2015b. *Philosophy of Language: The Classics Explained*. Cambridge, MA: MIT Press.

McGregor, William. 1990. *A Functional Grammar of Gooniyandi*. Amsterdam, NL: John Benjamins.

McGregor, William B. 1997. *Semiotic Grammar*. Oxford, UK: Oxford University Press.

McGregor, William B. 2009. "Typology of Ergativity." *Language and Linguistics Compass* 3(1):480–508. doi: 10.1111/j.1749-818x.2008.00118.x.

McGuinness, Brian. 1985. "Wittgenstein and the Vienna Circle." *Synthese* 64(3):351–58.

McGuinness, Brian. 1988. *Wittgenstein: A Life; Young Ludwig 1889–1921*. Berkeley, CA: University of California Press.

McKay, Robert I., Nguyen Xuan Hoai, Peter Alexander Whigham, Yin Shan and Michael O'Neill. 2010. "Grammar-Based Genetic Programming." *Genetic Programming and Evolvable Machines* 11: 365–96.

McLuhan, Marshall. 1964 [2001]. *Understanding Media: The Extensions of Man*. London, UK: Routledge.

Meillassoux, Quentin. 2006 [2008]. *After Finitude: An Essay on the Necessity of Contingency*. London, UK: Continuum.

Meinong, Alexius. 1904 [1981]. "The Theory of Objects," pp. 76–117 in *Realism and the Background of Phenomenology*. Edited by Roderick M. Chisholm. Atascadero, CA: Ridgeview.

Merleau-Ponty, Maurice. 1945 [2002]. *Phenomenology of Perception*. Translated by C. Smith. London, UK: Routledge.

Metz, Cade. 2016. "One Genius' Lonely Crusade to Teach a Computer Common Sense." *Wired*, 24 March.

Michaels, Sarah and Richard Sohmer. 2000. "Narratives and Inscriptions: Culture Tools, Power, and Powerful Sensemaking," pp. 267–88 in *Multiliteracies: Literacy Learning and the Design of Social Futures*, edited by B. Cope and M. Kalantzis. London, UK: Routledge.

Minns, Emma. 2013. "Picturing Soviet Progress: Isostat, 1931–1934," pp. 257–81 in *Isotype: Design and Contexts, 1925–1971*, edited by C. Burke, E. Kindel, and S. Walker. London, UK: Hyphen Press.

Mitchell, Melanie. 2009. *Complexity: A Guided Tour*. Oxford, UK: Oxford University Press.

Mockapetris, Paul V. 1987. "Domain Names: Concepts and Facilities," Network Working Group (https://tools.ietf.org/html/rfc1034).

Monk, Ray. 1990. *Ludwig Wittgenstein: The Duty of Genius*. New York, NY: The Free Press.

Montebello, Matthew. 2019. *Ambient Intelligent Classroom: Beyond the Indispensable Educator*. Dortmund, Germany: Springer.

Moore, George Edward. 1925 [1959]. "A Defence of Common Sense," pp. 106–33 in *Philosophical Papers*. London, UK: George Allen and Unwin.

Moran, John. 1972. "Wittgenstein and Russia." *New Left Review* (I/73):85–96.

Moriyama, Iwao M., Ruth M. Loy, and Alastair H.T. Robb-Smith. 2011. *History of the Statistical Classification of Diseases and Causes of Death*. Hyattsville, MD: National Center for Health Statistics.

Morris, Errol (Director). 2013. *The Unknown Known* [film] (www.springfieldspringfield.co.uk/movie_script.php?movie=the-unknown-known).

Moseley, Maboth. 1964 [1970]. *Irascible Genius: The Life of Charles Babbage*. Chicago, IL: Henry Regnery Company.

Moss, A.E. 1989. "Basic Colour Terms: Problems and Hypotheses." *Lingua* 78:313–20.

Moss, A.E., I. Davies, G. Corbett, and G. Laws. 1990. "Mapping Russian Basic Colour Terms Using Behavioural Measures." *Lingua* 82:313–32.

Müller, Karl H. 1991. "Neurath's Theory of Pictorial-Statistical Representation," pp. 223–54 in *Rediscovering the Forgotten Vienna Circle: Austrian Studies on Otto Neurath and the Vienna Circle*, edited by T.E. Uebel. Dordrecht, Germany: Kluwer Academic Publishers.

Munsell, A.H. 1905. *A Color Notation*. Boston, MA: Geo. H. Ellis Co.

Munsell, A.H. 1915. *Atlas of the Munsell Color System*. Boston, MA: Albert H. Munsell.

Munsell, A.H. and T.M. Clelland. 1921. *A Grammar of Color*. Mittineague, MA: Strathmore Paper Company.

Murray-Rust, P. and H.S. Rzepa. 2003. "Chemical Markup, XML and the World Wide Web." *Journal of Chemical Information and Computer Sciences* 43(3):757–72.

Nadar, Félix. 1900 [2015]. *When I Was a Photographer*. Translated by E. Cadava and L. Theodoratou. Cambridge, MA: MIT Press.

Nadler, Steven. 1999. *Spinoza: A Life*. Cambridge, UK: Cambridge University Press.

Nakata, Martin. 2000. "History, Cultural Diversity and English Language Teaching," pp. 106–20 in *Multiliteracies: Literacy Learning and the Design of Social Futures*, edited by B. Cope and M. Kalantzis. London, UK: Routledge.

Nakata, Martin. 2007. *Disciplining the Savages: Savaging the Disciplines*. Canberra, Australia: Aboriginal Studies Press.

Neale, Margot, ed. 2008. *Utopia: The Genius of Emily Kame Kngwarreye*. Canberra, Australia: National Museum of Australia Press.

Neuendorf, Henri. 2016. "Anish Kapoor Angers Artists by Seizing Exclusive Rights to 'Blackest Black' Pigment." *Artnet News*, 29 February.

Neumann, John von and Oskar Morgenstern. 1953 [2007]. *Theory of Games and Economic Behavior* Princeton, NJ: Princeton University Press.

Neurath, Marie and Robin Kinross. 2009. *The Transformer: Principles of Making Isotype Charts*. London, UK: Hyphen Press.

Neurath, Otto. 1931 [2017]. "Pictorial Statistics Following the Vienna Method." *ARTMargins* 6(1):108–18.

Neurath, Otto. 1939. *Modern Man in the Making*. New York, NY: Alfred A. Knopf.

Neurath, Otto. 1945 [2010]. *From Hieroglyphics to Isotype: A Visual Autobiography*. London, UK: Hyphen Press.

Neurath, Otto. 1973. *Empiricism and Sociology*. Translated by P. Foulkes and M. Neurath. Dordrecht, NL: D. Reidel Publishing.

New London Group. 1996. "A Pedagogy of Multiliteracies: Designing Social Futures." *Harvard Educational Review* 66(1):60–92.

Newton, Isaac. 1730 [1952]. *Opticks, or a Treatise of the Reflections, Refractions, Inflections and the Colours of Light*. New York, NY: Dover Publications.

Newton, Isaac. 1733 [1922]. *Sir Isaac Newton's Daniel and the Apocalypse, with an Introductory Study of the Nature and Cause of Unbelief, of Miracles and Prophecy*. Edited and translated by W. Whitla. London, UK: John Murray.

Object Management Group. 2015. "OMG Unified Modeling Language (OMG UML)." Version 2.5. (www.omg.org/spec/UML/2.5/).

Owens, Jonathan. 1990. *Early Arabic Grammatical Theory: Heterogeneity and Standardization*. Amsterdam, NL: John Benjamins.

Panofsky, Erwin. 1924 [1997]. *Perspective as Symbolic Form*. Translated by C.S. Wood. New York, NY: Zone Books.

Paperny, Vladimir. 2002. *Architecture in the Age of Stalin: Culture Two*. Translated by J. Hill and R. Barris. Cambridge, UK: Cambridge University Press.

Patel, P.G. 1996. "Linguistic and Cognitive Aspects of the Orality-Literacy Complex in Ancient India." *Language and Communication* 16(4):315–29.

Pearl, Judea. 2009. *Causality: Models, Reasoning and Inference*. Cambridge, UK: Cambridge University Press.

Peeters, Benoît. 2010 [2013]. *Derrida: A Biography*. Cambridge, UK: Polity Press.

Perez, Sarah. 2016. "79 Percent of Americans Now Shop Online." *TechCrunch*, 19 December.

Peters, Michael A. and Jeff Stickney. 2018. *Wittgenstein's Education: 'A Picture Held Us Captive'*. Singapore: Spring Nature.

Plant, Sadie. 1997. *Zeros + Ones: Digital Women + the New Technoculture*. New York, NY: Doubleday.

Podesta, John, Penny Pritzker, Ernest Moniz, John Holdern, and Jeffrey Zients. 2014. "Big Data: Seizing Opportunities, Preserving Values." Washington, DC: Executive Office of the President.

Reddy, Michael J. 1993. "The Conduit Metaphor: A Case of Frame Conflict in Our Language About Language," pp. 164–201 in *Metaphor and Thought*, edited by A. Ortony. Cambridge, UK: Cambridge University Press.

Renear, Allen, David Dubin, C.M. Sperberg-McQueen, and Claus Huitfeldt. 2002. "Towards a Semantics for XML Markup," pp. 119–26 in *Proceedings of the 2002 ACM Symposium on Document Engineering*. McLean, VA.

Renear, Allen H. and Carole L. Palmer. 2009. "Strategic Reading, Ontologies, and the Future of Scientific Publishing." *Science* 325(5942):828–32. doi: 10.1126/science.1157784.

Ribot, Jesse. 2014. "Cause and Response: Vulnerability and Climate in the Anthropocene." *The Journal of Peasant Studies* 41(5):667–705. doi: 10.1080/03066150.2014.894911.

Rifkin, Jeremy. 2014. *The Zero Marginal Cost Society: The Internet of Things, the Collaborative Commons, and the Eclipse of Capitalism*. New York, NY: Palgrave Macmillan.

Rolt, L.T.C. 1957. *Isambard Kingdom Brunel*. London, UK: Longmans, Green and Co.

Rose, David. 2014. *Enchanted Objects: Design, Human Desire, and the Internet of Things*. New York, NY: Scribner.

Rosenberg, Gabriel. 2016. "A Chemist Accidentally Creates a New Blue. Then What?" in *National Public Radio* (www.npr.org/2016/07/16/485696248/a-chemist-accidentally-creates-a-new-blue-then-what?t=1560853665108).

Rotman, Brian. 1987. *Signifying Nothing: The Semiotics of Zero*. Stanford, CA: Stanford University Press.

Ruben, Walter. 1981. "Uddalaka and Yājñavalkya: Materialism and Idealism," pp. 13–27 in *Marxism and Indology*, edited by D. Chattopadhyaya. Calcutta, India: K.P. Bagchi and Company.

Rumbaugh, James, Ivar Jacobson, and Grady Booch. 2004. *The Unified Modeling Language Reference Manual*. Boston, MA: Addison-Wesley.

Russell, Bertrand. 1905. "On Denoting." *Mind* 14(56):479–93.

Sabra, Abdelhamid I. 2003. "Ibn Al-Haytham's Revolutionary Project of Optics: The Achievement and Obstacles," pp. 85–118 in *The Enterprise of Science in Islam: New Perspectives*, edited by J.P. Hogendijk and A.I. Sabra. Cambridge, MA: MIT Press.

Santos, Roberta Schultz. 2014. "Pantone: Identity Formation through Colours." Master of Arts in Contemporary Art, Design and New Media Art, OCAD University, Toronto, Canada.

Sapir, Edward. 1921. *Language: An Introduction to the Study of Speech*. New York, NY: Harcourt Brace.

Sartre, Jean-Paul. 1940 [2004]. *The Imaginary: A Phenomenological Psychology of the Imagination*. Translated by J. Webber. London, UK: Routledge.

Sartre, Jean-Paul. 1943 [1993]. *Being and Nothingness: An Essay on Phenomenological Ontology*. Translated by H.E. Barnes. New York, NY: Washington Square Press.

Schellenberg, Susanna. 2012. "Sameness of Fregean Sense." *Synthese* 189(1):163–75.

Schivelbusch, Wolfgang. 1977 [2014]. *The Railway Journey: The Industrialization of Time and Space in the Nineteenth Century*. Berkeley, CA: University of California Press.

Schmidt, Eric and Jared Cohen. 2013. *The New Digital Age: Transforming Nations, Businesses, and Our Lives*. New York, NY: Vintage Books.

Schoenfeld, Alan H. and P. David Pearson. 2009. "The Reading and Math Wars," pp. 560–80 in *Handbook of Education Policy Research*, edited by G. Sykes, B. Schneider, and D.N. Plank. New York: Routledge.

Scollon, Ron. 2000. "Action and Text: Toward an Integrated Understanding of the Place of Text in Social (Inter)Action," pp. 139–83 in *Methods in Critical Discourse Analysis*, edited by R. Wodak and M. Meyer. London, UK: Sage.

Scollon, Ron. 2001. *Mediated Discourse: The Nexus of Practice*. London, UK: Routledge.

Scollon, Ron and Suzie Wong Scollon. 2004. *Nexus Analysis: Discourse and the Emerging Internet*. London, UK: Routledge.

Searle, John R. 1969. *Speech Acts: An Essay on the Philosophy of Language*. Cambridge, UK: Cambridge University Press.

Searle, John R. 1972. "Chomsky's Revolution in Linguistics." *New York Review of Books* 18(29 June):12–29.

Searle, John R. 1975. "A Taxonomy of Illocutionary Acts." *Language, Mind, and Knowledge* 7:344–69.

Searle, John R. 1977. "Reiterating the Differences: A Reply to Derrida." *Glyph*:198–208.

Searle, John R. 1980. "Minds, Brains, and Programs." *Behavioral and Brain Sciences* (3):417–57.

Searle, John R. 1983. "The Word Turned Upside Down." *New York Review of Books* (October 27).

Searle, John R. 1995. *The Construction of Social Reality*. New York, NY: Free Press.

Searle, John R. 2002. "End of the Revolution." *New York Review of Books* 49(3).

Searle, John R. 2014. "What Your Computer Can't Know." *New York Review of Books*, 9 October.

Searle, John R. and Daniel Vanderveken. 1985. *Foundations of Illocutionary Logic*. Cambridge, UK: Cambridge University Press.

Shäkir, Banü Müsa bin. *c*.850 [1979]. *The Book of Ingenious Devices*. Translated by D.R. Hill. Dordrecht, NL: D. Reidel.

Shannon, Claude E. 1938. "A Symbolic Analysis of Relay and Switching Circuits." *Transactions of the American Institute of Electrical Engineers* 57:471–95.

Shannon, Claude E. and Warren Weaver. 1949. *The Mathematical Theory of Communication*. Urbana, IL: University of Illinois Press.

Silverman, Kaja. 2015. *The Miracle of Analogy, or the History of Photography, Part 1*. Stanford, CA: Stanford University Press.

Silverstein, Michael. 1976. "Hierarchy and Features of Ergativity." pp. 112–71 in *Grammatical Categories in Australian Languages*, edited by R.M.W. Dixon. Canberra, Australia: Australian Institute of Aboriginal Studies.

Skinner, B.F. 1938. *The Behavior of Organisms: An Experimental Analysis*. New York, NY: Appleton Century Crofts.

Skinner, B.F. 1945. "Baby in a Box: The Mechanical Baby-Tender." *Ladies Home Journal* 62:30–31; 135–36; 38.

Skinner, B.F. 1948 [1969]. *Walden Two*. London, UK: Macmillan.

Skinner, B.F. 1953. *Science and Human Behavior*. New York, NY: Free Press.

Skinner, B.F. 1954 [1960]. "The Science of Learning and the Art of Teaching," pp. 99–113 in *Teaching Machines and Programmed Learning*, edited by A.A. Lumsdaine and R. Glaser. Washington, DC: National Education Association.

Skinner, B.F. 1957. *Verbal Behavior*. New York, NY: Prentice Hall.

Skinner, B.F. 1958a. "Teaching Machines." *Science* 128(3330):969–77.

Skinner, B.F. 1958b. "Teaching Machine." Edited by U.S Patent Office.

Skinner, B.F. 1968. *The Technology of Teaching*. New York, NY: Meredith Corporation.

Skinner, B.F. 1971. *Beyond Freedom and Dignity*. New York, NY: Alfred A. Knopf.

Skinner, B.F. 1974. *About Behaviorism*. New York, NY: Vintage Books.

Smith, A. Mark. 2001a. "The Latin Source of the Fourteenth-Century Italian Translation of Alhacen's 'De Aspectibus'." *Arabic Sciences and Philosophy* 11(1):27–43.

Smith, A. Mark. 2001b. *Alhacen's Theory of Visual Perception: A Critical Edition, with English Translation and Commentary, of the First Three Books of Alhacen's De Aspectibus, the Medieval Latin Version of Ibn Al-Haytham's Kitāb Al-Manāẓir*, Volume 91. Philadelphia, PA: American Philosophical Society.

Smith, Frank. 2004. *Understanding Reading: A Psycholinguistic Analysis of Reading and Learning to Read*. Mahwah, NJ: Lawrence Erlbaum.

Snow, Catherine E., M. Susan Burns, and Peg Griffin, eds. 1998. *Preventing Reading Difficulties in Young Children*. Washington, DC: National Academy Press.

Sohmer, Richard and Sarah Michaels. 2002. "Re-Seeing Science: The Role of Narratives in Mediating between Scientific and Everyday Understanding and Explanation," pp. 167–208 in *Learning for the Future*, edited by M. Kalantzis, G. Varnava-Skoura and B. Cope. Melbourne AU: Common Ground.

Solnit, Rebecca. 2003a. *Motion Studies: Eadweard Muybridge and the Technological Wild West*. London, UK: Bloomsbury.

Solnit, Rebecca. 2003b. *River of Shadows: Eadweard Muybridge and the Technological Wild West*. New York, NY: Viking.

Soni, Jimmy and Rob Goodman. 2017. *A Mind at Play: How Claude Shannon Invented the Information Age*. New York, NY: Simon and Schuster.

Sontag, Susan. 1977. *On Photography*. New York, NY: Farrar, Strauss and Giroux.

Sowa, John F. 1995. "Top-Level Ontological Categories." *International Journal of Human-Computer Studies* 43(5–6):669–85.

Sowa, John F. 2000. *Knowledge Representation: Logical, Philosophical and Computational Foundations*. Pacific Grove, CA: Brooks Cole.

Sowa, John F. 2006. "The Challenge of Knowledge Soup," pp. 55–90 in *Research Trends in Science, Technology and Mathematics Education*, edited by J. Ramadas and S. Chunawala. Goa, India: Homi Bhabha Centre.

SRI Consulting Business Intelligence Consulting. 2008. "Disruptive Civil Technologies: Six Technologies with Potential Impacts on US Interests out to 2025." Washington, DC: National Intelligence Council.

Staal, Frits. 1972. *A Reader on the Sanskrit Grammarians*. Cambridge, MA: MIT Press.

Staal, Frits. 1975. "The Concept of Metalanguage and Its Indian Background." *Journal of Indian Philosophy* 3(3/4):315–54.

Staal, Frits. 2008. *The Vedas: Origins, Mantras, Rituals, Insights*. Gurgaon, India: Penguin Books.

Stearns, David L. 2011. *Electronic Value Exchange: Origins of the Visa Electronic Payment System*. London, UK: Springer-Verlag.

Stein, Dorothy. 1985. *Ada: A Life and a Legacy*. Cambridge, MA: MIT Press.

Stone, Brad. 2013. *The Everything Store: Jeff Bezos and the Rise of Amazon*. New York, NY: Little, Brown and Company.

Strawson, Galen. 2013. "Real Naturalism." *Proceedings of the American Philosophical Association* 86(2):125–54.

Strawson, P.F. 1966. *The Bounds of Sense: An Essay on Kant's Critique of Pure Reason*. London, UK: Methuen.

Struan, Jacob and Otto Karl-Heinz. 1990. "Otto Neurath: Marxist Member of the Vienna Circle." *Auslegung: A Journal of Philosophy* 16(2):175–89.

Swade, Doron. 2000. *The Difference Engine: Charles Babbage and the Quest to Build the First Computer*. New York, NY: Viking.

Tanner, Norman P., ed. 1990. *Decrees of the Ecumenical Councils*, Volume 1: *Nicea I to Lateran V*. London, UK: Sheed and Ward.

Taylor, Charles. 2016. *The Language Animal: The Full Shape of the Human Linguistic Capacity*. Cambridge, MA: Harvard University Press.

Textor, Mark. 2011. *Frege on Sense and Reference*. London, UK: Routledge.

Thapar, Romila. 2013. *The Past before Us: Historical Traditions of Early North India*. Ranikhet, India: Permanent Black.

The American Journal of International Law. 2004. "U.S. Abuse of Iraqi Detainees at Abu Ghraib Prison." 98(3):591–96.

Time Magazine. 1971. "Behavior: Skinner's Utopia: Panacea, or Path to Hell?" *Time*, September 20, p. 73.

Timpanaro, Sebastiano. 1970 [1975]. *On Materialism*. Translated by L. Garner. London UK: New Left Books.

Timpanaro, Sebastiano. 1981 [2005]. *The Genesis of Lachmann's Method*. Translated by G.W. Most. Chicago, IL: University of Chicago Press.

Toole, Betty Alexandra, ed. 1992. *Ada, the Enchantress of Numbers: A Selection from the Letters of Lord Byron's Daughter and Her Description of the First Computer*. Mill Valley, CA: Strawberry Press.

Tressou, Evangelia, Soula Mitakidou, and Panagiota Karagianni, eds. 2015. *Roma Inclusion – International and Greek Experiences: Complexities of Inclusion*. Thessaloniki, Greece: Aristotle University.

Tseng, Shao-Chien. 2014. "Nadar's Photography of Subterranean Paris: Mapping the Urban Body." *History of Photography* 38(3):233–54.

Turing, A.M. 1936. "On Computable Numbers, with an Application to the Entscheidungsproblem." *Proceedings of the London Mathematical Society* 42(2):230–65.

Turing, A.M. 1948. "Intelligent Machinery." A Report to the National Physical Laboratory.

Turing, A.M. 1950. "Computing Machinery and Intelligence." *Mind* 59:433–60.

Turing, Dermot. 2015. *Prof: Alan Turing Decoded, a Biography*. Brimscombe Port, UK: The History Press.

Turing, Sara. 1959 [2012]. *Alan M. Turing*. Oxford, UK: Oxford University Press.

Uebel, Thomas. 2008. "Writing a Revolution: On the Production and Early Reception of the Vienna Circle's Manifesto." *Perspectives on Science* 16(1):70–102.

van Heijenoort, Jean. 1978. *With Trotsky in Exile: From Prinkipo to Coyoacán*. Cambridge, MA: Harvard University Press.

van Leeuwen, T. 2011. *The Language of Colour*. London, UK: Routledge.

Vasari, Giorgio. 1550 [1969]. *Lives of the Most Eminent Painters, Sculptors, and Architects*. Translated by G.D.C. de Vere. New York, NY: The Modern Library.

Vasu, Srisa Chandra (Translator). 1897. *The Aṣṭādhyāyī of Pāṇini*. Benares, India: Sindhu Charan Bose.

Vejdemo-Johansson, Mikael, Susanne Vejdemo, and Carl-Henrik Ek. 2014. "Comparing Distributions of Color Words: Pitfalls and Metric Choices." *PLoS ONE* 9(2: e89184). doi: 10.1371/journal.pone.0089184.

Venturi, Lionello. 1937. *Sandro Botticelli*. Oxford, UK: Oxford University Press.

Verdon, Timothy. 2005. *Mary in Western Art*. Manchester, VT: Hudson Hills.

Versteegh, Kees. 1997. *The Arabic Linguistic Tradition*. London, UK: Routledge.

Vienna Circle. 1929 [1973]. "The Scientific Conception of the World," pp. 299–318 in *Empiricism and Sociology*, edited by P. Foulkes and M. Neurath. Dordrecht, NL: D. Reidel Publishing.

Vines, Richard and Joseph Firestone. 2011. "Interoperability and the Exchange of Humanly Usable Digital Content," pp. 429–90 in *Towards a Semantic Web: Connecting Knowledge in Academic Research*, edited by B. Cope, M. Kalantzis, and L. Magee.Oxford, UK: Chandos.

von Neumann, John. 1945. "First Draft of a Report on the Edvac." Philadelphia, PA: Moore School of Electrical Engineering, University of Pennsylvania.

von Neumann, John. 1958. *The Computer and the Brain*. Yale, NH: Yale University Press.

Vossoughian, Nader. 2008. *Otto Neurath: The Language of the Global Polis*. Rotterdam, NL: NAi Publishers.

Vygostky, Lev Semyonovich. 1930 [1999]. "The Problem of Practical Intellect in the Psychology of Animals and the Psychology of the Child," pp. 3–26 in *Collected Works of L.S. Vygotsky*, Volume 6, edited by R.W. Rieber. New York, NY: Kluwer Academic.

Vygotsky, Lev Semyonovich. 1934 [1986]. *Thought and Language*. Cambridge, MA: MIT Press.

Vygostky, Lev Semyonovich. 1962 [1978]. *Mind in Society: The Development of Higher Psychological Processes*. Cambridge, MA: Harvard University Press.

Vygotsky, Lev Semyonovich and Aleksandr Romanovich Luria. 1930 [1993]. *Studies on the History of Behavior: Ape, Primitive and Child*. Translated by V.I. Golod and J.E. Knox. Hillsdale, NJ: Lawrence Erlbaum.

Warhol, Andy. 2006. *"Giant" Size*. London, UK: Phaidon.

Wark, McKenzie. 2015. *Molecular Red: Theory for the Anthropocene*. London, UK: Verso.

Warner, Marina. 1976. *Alone of All Her Sex: The Myth and Cult of the Virgin Mary*. New York, NY: Alfred A. Knopf.

Watson, Andrew. 2008. "Visual Modelling: Past, Present and Future." (www.uml.org /Visual_Modeling.pdf).

Watson, John B. 1913. "Psychology as the Behaviorist Views It." *Psychological Review* 20:158–77.

Watson, John B. 1914. *Behavior: An Introduction to Comparative Psychology*. New York, NY: Henry Holt and Company.

Watson, John B. 1925. *Behaviorism*. New York, NY: W.W. Norton.

Waugh, Alexander. 2008. *The House of Wittgenstein: A Family at War*. New York, NY: Doubleday.

Weber, Stefanie, Egbert van der Haring, Susanne Bröenhorst, Michael Schopen, and Pieter Zanstra. 2005. "Maintaining Medical Classifications in XML: ClaML Redefined for Use with WHO-FIC Classifications." Paper presented at the WHO-FIC Network Meeting, 16–22 October, Tokyo, Japan (http://apps.who.int/classifica tions/apps/icd/meetings/tokyomeeting/B_3–1%20Maintaining%20Medical%20Clas sifications%20in%20XML-ClaML.pdf).

Wells, H.G. 1901. *The First Men in the Moon*. London, UK: George Newnes.

Westfall, Richard S. 1980. *Never at Rest: A Biography of Isaac Newton*. Cambridge, UK: Cambridge University Press.

Whitehead, Alfred North. 1928 [1978]. *Process and Reality*. New York, NY: Free Press.

Whitehead, Alfred North and Bertrand Russell. 1910/1912/1913 [1927]. *Principia Mathematica*. Cambridge, UK: Cambridge University Press.

Wierzbicka, Anna. 1981. "Case Marking and Human Nature." *Australian Journal of Linguistics* 1(1):43–80.

Wierzbicka, Anna. 2006. "The Semantics of Color: A New Paradigm," pp. 1–24 in *Progress in Colour Studies*, Volume 1: *Language and Culture*, edited by C.P. Biggam and C.J. Kay. Amsterdam, NL: John Benjamins.

Williams, Robert C. 1986. *The Other Bolsheviks: Lenin and His Critics, 1904–1914*. Bloomington, IN: Indiana University Press.

Winchester, Simon. 2003. *The Meaning of Everything: The Story of the Oxford English Dictionary*. Oxford, UK: Oxford University Press.

Winston, Morton E., Roger Chaffin, and Douglas Herrmann. 1987. "A Taxonomy of Part–Whole Relations." *Cognitive Science* 11:417–44.

Wittgenstein, Ludwig. 1922 [1933]. *Tractatus Logico-Philosophicus*. London, UK: Routledge.

Wittgenstein, Ludwig. 1931–44 [1980]. *Culture and Value*. Edited by G.H. von Wright. Translated by P. Winch. Chicago, IL: University of Chicago Press.

Wittgenstein, Ludwig. 1953 [2001]. *Philosophical Investigations*. Translated by G.E.M. Anscombe. Oxford, UK: Blackwell.

Wittgenstein, Ludwig. 1969. *On Certainty*. Translated by D. Paul and G.E.M. Anscombe. New York, NY: Harper and Row.

Wittgenstein, Ludwig. 1973. *Letters to C.K. Ogden*. Oxford, UK: Basil Blackwell.

Wittgenstein, Ludwig and Friedrich Waissmann. 2003. *The Voices of Wittgenstein: The Vienna Circle*. Translated by G. Baker, M. Mackert, J. Connolly, and V. Politis. London, UK: Routledge.

Young, Robert J.C. 2002. "Race and Language in the Two Saussures," pp. 63–78 in *Philosophies of Race and Ethnicity*, edited by P. Osborne and S. Sandford. London, UK: Continuum.

Index

Abbasid, 262
absence, 99
absolutive, syntax, 207, 208
abstract expressionism, 7, 227
abstraction, 47
Abu Ghraib prison, 282, 284
academic talk, 34
accent, 30
accusative, syntax, 208
action, 2, 45, 70, 121, 123, 125, 127, 129,
   229, 241
additive coloring, 148
adjective, syntax, 127, 136
Adobe, 24, 135, 152
Adorno, Theodor, 15
affordance, 11, 33, 42, 182
agency, 9, 44, 45, 70, 173, 175
Agfa, 152
Al Fārābī, Muhammad, 264
Alberti, Leon Battista, 218, 220, 225
al-Fârisî, 260
algebra, 132, 265
algorithm, 265
algorithmic thinking, 54
Alhacen (Al-Hasan ibn al-Haytham), 222–24
Alhalkere, 8
al-Haytham, Al-Hasan ibn, 223
alienation, 191
al-Khwārizmī, Muḥammad ibn Mūsā, 132, 265
alphanumeric naming, 90, 143, 153, 154,
   168, 172
Amazon, 24, 190, 191
American Airlines, 124
Analytical Engine, 157, 160, 163
Analytical Philosophy, 79, 83, 85, 132, 243,
   246, 253
Anderson, Chris, 171
animation, 285
Anmatyerre, 7, 226
Anscombe, Elizabeth, 253
Anthropocene, 175
anti-passive, syntax, 207

appearance, 28
Apple, 135, 152, 204, 311, 313
Arabic, 141, 260, 264, 265
architecture, 188
Arendt, Hannah, 130
Aristotle, 62, 80, 121, 264
Aristotle University of Thessaloniki, 65
Armstrong, Neil, 257
Arntz, Gerd, 115, 116
ARPANET, 94
artificial intelligence, 118, 154, 167, 213,
   310, 317
assertion, 238, 241
as-Sîrâfî, 'Abû Sa'îd, 263
associative meaning, 106
Austin, J.L., 243–45, 246, 248
Automatic Computing Engine, 165
auxiliary, syntax, 239
Avenarius, Richard, 35

Babbage, Charles, 156–59, 170
Bach, Emmon, 128
Bacon, Francis, 131
Bank of England, 178
bar graph, 115
barcode, 94
Bardeen, John, 164
Barthes, Roland, 133, 228
Basque, 210
Battleship Potemkin, 111
Baudrillard, Jean, 236
Bauhaus, 188
Bavarian Soviet Republic, 114
Becker, Joseph, 24
Bedouin, 262
behaviorism, 104, 165, 286, 287, 289, 297
Belgrand, Eugène, 232
Bellonese, 143
Benjamin, Walter, 82, 111, 232, 234, 237
   Arcades, 14–17
Bennett, Susan, 313
Berger, John, 229

Bergson, Henri, 129–30, 131
Berlin, Brent, 141–43, 151
Berners-Lee, Tim, 316–18
Bézier, Pierre, 133, 134
Bhaskar, Roy, 272–75, 276
big data, 96–97
Big Yam Dreaming, 8
biometric indicator, 91
Biran, Paddy, 211
bitmap, 134
Bletchley Park, 163, 165, 168
Bloomfield, Leonard, 52, 127
Bluetooth, 203
body, 28
Boeing, 135
Bogdanov, Alexander, 34–39, 40, 41, 117, 257
Bolshevik Party, 35
Booch, Grady, 125
Botticelli, Sandro, 216, 230
boundary, 27, 45
Bowker, Geoffrey C., 306
Box Brownie, 230
Boyce Gibson, W.R., 60
British Empire, 54
Brunel, Isambard Kingdom, 156, 178
Brunelleschi, Filippo, 217
Bryson, Norman, 218
Byron, Alfred Lord, 156, 157
Byron, Anne, 156
Byzantine icon, 215, 221
Byzantium, 227

Cage, John, 100–1
calculus, 132
Cambridge University, 156, 160, 170, 182, 196, 253
camera obscura, 223, 228
capitalism, 97, 125, 153, 179
card index, 14, 17, 18
Carnap, Rudolf, 193, 197
Carnegie Mellon University, 94
Carroll, Lewis, 96, 277
    Alice, 96, 182
Cartier-Bresson, Henri, 87–88
case, syntax, 207
Catholic Church, 277
Cazden, Courtney, 4
centric ray, 224
cgscholar.com, 94
Chattopadhyaya, Debiprasad, 318–21
Chemical Markup Language, 310, 314
Chinese, 23
Chinese landscape paintings, 221
Chinese, language, 25

Chomsky, Noam, 52, 64, 208, 293, 294, 298–301, 307, 322
    on behaviorism, 288–90
    Syntactic Structures, 290–92
Christianity, 225
Church, Alfonso, 162
Cimabue, 215
cinema, 135
circumstance, 119
Citroën DS, 133
Clark, David, 94
Clarke, Arthur C., 164
clause, 32
clause, syntax, 30
CMYK, 134, 149, 152
Coates, Jennifer, 237
Coca Cola, 148
code, computer, 125
cogito ergo sum, 58, 236, 293. *See* Descartes
cognitive prosthesis, 20, 28, 41, 101, 154
Cohn, Bernard, 53
Coke, 94
Cold War, 163, 164
Collège de France, 129
Collins, Lee, 24
colonialism, 143
color, 45, 139, 141–53
communication, 21, 41, 56, 69
complex, thinking, 106, 109
computer aided design, 133
concept, 2, 19, 45, 70, 82, 101, 104–7, 117, 118, 121, 122, 125, 136, 154, 154, 304, 308, 322
conceptualism, 7
conditionality, 46, 237
consciousness, 295
context, 9, 44, 47, 70
Continental Philosophy, 246
convolute, 15, 18
Cook, Captain James, 205
corroboree, 206
cosmetics, 28
Council of Ephesus, 215
Cowan, Katharine, 40
Crayola, 150
creativity, 71
credit card, 90
critical discourse analysis, 44
critical realism, 273
crosswalk, 315
cruelty, 49
Cubism, 116, 227
cybersecurity, 124
Cyc, 324

Da Fen, China, 67
Daguerre, Louis, 228
Dante, 216
Darwin, Charles, 156
Darwin, Sir Charles (grandson), 165
Data General, 124
database, 191
Davis, Mark, 24
de Casteljau, Paul, 133
de Saussure, Ferdinand, 51, 266–70, 289, 322
    Course in General Linguistics, 266–68, 270
de Saussure, Léopold, 270
deconstruction, 63, 64, 246, 247, 269
deep structure, 291
Deleuze, Gilles, 277–80, 281
Delmore Gallery, 10
demeanor, 28
Derrida, Jacques, 61–64, 69, 246–49
Descartes, René, 58, 102, 104, 132, 134,
    138–40, 144, 236, 271, 274, 277, 284, 293
design, 46, 64, 68, 70, 130, 247, 259, 267, 272,
    278, 301, 323
Dewey, John, 130
Diagnostic and Statistical Manual of Mental
    Disorders, 304
dialect, 30
Dickens, Charles, 156
Difference Engine, 156
diffraction, 145
direct speech, 34
directedness, 47
directionality, 29
discourse, 269
Disney, 285
Dixon, R.M.W., 205, 207–11
DOI, 99
domain name. *See* URL
domain name system, 93
dreamtime, 207
dualism, 274, 277
Dublin Core, 314
Dugum Dani, 141
Dummett, Michael, 83
Dyirbal, 204–12

ecosystem, 27
edge, 28, 45
Eisenstein, Sergei, 111–12
electromagnetic spectrum, 141, 144, 145,
    153, 155
Electronic Health Record, 304
email, 34
email address, 90, 95
emoji, 24, 68, 115
emotion, 28, 48

empathy, 2, 19
Empiriomonism, 35
enactment, 28
Engelmann, Paul, 186
Engels, Frederick, 36
English, 141
Enigma machine, 163
Enlightenment, European, 60, 62, 64
entity, 2, 45, 70, 121, 123, 125, 126, 129,
    229, 241
ergative, syntax, 200
Escher, M.C., 285
Esperanto, 326
Ethnologue, 310, 314
European Renaissance, 218, 265
event, 45, 180
experience, 38
eyeline, 45

Facebook, 24, 228
facial expression, 28
Fairclough, Norman, 4
family resemblances, 254
fashion, 28
Ferriss, Hugh, 113
Fetzer, James H., 257
Fillmore, Charles, 201–2, 208
film, 111
first peoples, 111, 143, 227
first person, syntax, 1, 212
First World War, 183
fitness trackers, 28
Fittko, Lisa, 16
Flickr, 92
Flusser, Vilém, 229
food, 28
forms of life, 254
frame, 229
frame semantics, 202
Francis, John, 178
Frankfurt School. *See* School for Social
    Research
Frege, Gottlob, 79–83, 120, 183, 185, 195
furniture, 28

gait, 28
Galen, 224
gamut, 148
Gärdenfors, Peter, 128
gaze, 28, 219, 220, 230, 236
Geach, Peter, 253
Gee, James Paul, 4
gender, 101
genre, 48, 57
geography, 27

geometry, 59
GeoNames, 47, 310, 314
gerund, syntax, 128
gesticulation, 28
gesture, 46, 121
Ghiberti, Lorenzo, 216, 217, 222
Gifford lectures, 130
Giotto di Bondone, 216
global governance, 24, 125, 152, 316, 326
God, 62, 171, 215, 221, 225, 261, 277
Gödel, Kurt, 82, 117, 160, 162
Goody, Jack, 25, 318
Google, 24, 97, 98, 135, 203, 324, 325
Gooniyandi, 209
Gorky, Maxim, 37
GPS, 27
grammar, 33, 49, 55–58, 63, 138, 263, 264, 291
grammatology, 63
gramophone, 30
grapheme, 22, 23, 26, 46, 134
grasp, 28
Great Western Railway, 177
Gropius, Walter, 188
Grosz, Elizabeth, 276–77
Gruber, Thomas, 311
Guangzhou College of Art, 66
Guha, Ramanathan, 324
Gutenberg, Johannes, 147

Hadith, 225
HAL 9000, 164
Halliday, M.A.K., 1, 2, 43, 78, 210
    ergative case, 200–1
    grammatics, 56
    metafunction, 2, 44
    mood, 237
    nominalization, 240
    on speech and writing, 30–32
    phonaesthetic series, 268
    subject, syntax, 181–82
    transitivity, 201
HandleSets.com, 189
Hanunóo, 142
Hardin, C.L., 143–44, 152
Harrapan script, 53
Harris, Zellig, 290
Hartwig, Mervyn, 272–75
Harvard University, 130
Hasan, Ruqaiya, 43
Hasselblad, camera, 257
Haussmann, Baron, 232
He Wei Jiang, 66
Hebrew, 290
Heidegger, Martin, 60
Herbert, Lawrence, 148

Hewlett-Packard, 124
Higgs Boson, 81, 84
High Court of Australia, 211
Hilbert, David, 160, 164
Hiroshima, Atomic Bomb, 163, 174
history, 273
Hitler, Adolf, 114, 182, 197
Hoffman, Heinrich, 114
Holocaust, 61
homo faber, 20, 130
Horkheimer, Max, 15
House of Wisdom, 260
Howe, Brian, 211
HTML, 26, 55, 135, 314, 316
Hugo, Victor, 232
humanism, 265
Humboldt University, 320
Husserl, Edmund, 58–61, 69, 292
hyperlink, 70

IBM, 124
Ibn Jinnî, Abû l-Fath 'Uthmân, 260–61
ICC Color Profiles, 152–53, 154
ICD (International Classification of Diseases),
    304–6, 308, 310
icon, 114, 115, 215, 224, 227
iconoclasm, 226
idealism, 272, 276, 323
ideational meaning, 44
identifier, 91
identifier (database field), 90
identity, 71
ideograph, 22, 23, 24, 26
ideology, 48, 57
idolatry, 224, 227
ILLIAC, 164
illocutionary act, 243
Illustrator, Adobe, 135
image, 26, 45, 105, 176, 195, 214, 219, 236,
    283, 285
imperative, syntax, 237
impressionism, 227
incandescence, 145
indicative, syntax, 237
inequality, 136, 153
infelicity, 245, 251
infra-red rays, 144, 147
Instamatic camera, 230
instance, 2, 19, 45, 70, 83, 118, 121, 122, 125,
    136, 154
instant messages, 34
instantiation, 191
Institute for the Scientific Organization of
    Labor, Kazan, 104
Institute of Advanced Study, 162, 164

Institute of Psychology, Moscow
    University, 110
Intelligent Medical Objects, 303–7, 312
interest, 9, 44, 48, 70
International Color Consortium, 152
International Standards Association, 123
International Telecommunication Union, 90
internet, 55, 93, 94, 95, 122, 178, 228, 309,
    317
Internet Corporation for Assigned Names and
    Numbers (ICANN), 93
Internet Engineering Task Force, 94
internet of things, 89, 94–96, 97, 118, 124,
    204, 314
interpersonal meaning, 44
interpretation, 22, 41, 69
interrogative, syntax, 239
intonation, 30
IP address, 93
IPO, 178
ISBN, 99
Islam, 260, 262
    imaging, 224
Isotype, 119

Jacob, Philip Wittington, 309
Jacobson, Ivar, 125
Jacquard loom, 159
James Cook University, 211
James, William, 130
Jameson, Frederic, 269
Jew, Jewish, 15, 60, 61, 83, 103, 114, 130, 164,
    197, 225, 270, 277, 320
jewelry, 28

Kadvany, John, 54
Kahlo, Freda, 83
Kant, Immanuel, 58, 102, 104, 274,
    322
    Critique of Pure Reason, 321–22
Kapoor, Anish, 150
Kay, Paul, 141–43, 151
Keynes, John Maynard, 170, 186, 196
keystrokes, 32
Khrushchev, Nikita, 111, 113
King Ranch Pastoral Company, 211
Kngwarreye, Emily Kame, 11
Knowledge Graph, 325
Knowledge Representation Language, 324
Kodak, 148, 152, 230
Kornilov, K.N., 104
Kress, Gunther, 4, 40, 43, 56
Kripke, Saul, 121
Kubrick, Stanley, 164
Kusuth, Joseph, 98–99

landscape, 27
language game, 254
Latour, Bruno, 241
layout, 27
Leibniz, Gottfried, 132, 156, 169–70
Leica (camera), 87–89
Leitner, Bernhard, 187
LeMay, Curtis, 174
Lenat, Doug, 324
Lenin, Vladimir, 35, 36, 117, 320
Leonardo da Vinci, 147–48, 216
Leontyev, Aleksei Nikolaevich, 107
Levinson, Stephen, 143
Levit, S.G., 110
lexis, 50
Liao Ji Xiang, 66
likeness, 47
line, 45
Linear A, 24
linear perspective, 26, 219, 225
linguistic relativity, 207
Linking Open Data project, 317
linocut, 116
literacy, 10, 25, 111
Locke, John, 131, 138–40, 271, 284
locutionary act, 243
logic, 184, 263, 264
Logical Positivism, 193, 194
logocentrism, 63, 69
Lokayata, 318
Loos, Alfred, 186
Los Alamos National Laboratory, 163
Lovelace, Ada, 156–59, 160
Luke, Allan, 4
Luke, Carmen, 4
luminosity, 145
Luria, Aleksandr, 101, 102, 103–7,
    108–11, 112
luster, 145

Mabo, Bonita, 211
Mabo, Eddie Koiki, 211
MacCorquodale, Kenneth, 294
Mach, Ernst, 35, 117
Macken, Mary, 56
Malcolm, Norman, 194
MANIAC, 163
mantra, 318
MARC, 314
Margarete (Gretl), *née* Wittgenstein, 197. *See*
    Stonborough
Markow, Stephen, 150
Martin, J.R., 56, 240
Marx, Chico, 252
Marx, Karl, 36, 37, 112, 140, 316

Mary, mother of Christ, 215–16
materialism, 272, 276, 279
Mathematical Markup Language, 310
mathematics, 52, 58, 130, 132, 158, 160,
     168, 224
   Islamic, 132
Mattâ ibn Yûnus, 263
McGinn, Colin, 102, 282–85
McGregor, William, 209
McLuhan, Marshall, 219
McNamara, Robert, 174
meaning, 11
meaning form, 12, 19, 22, 33, 40, 69
meaning function, 12, 18, 42, 49, 50, 70, 73
mechanical loom, 157, 159
media, 20, 22, 33, 40, 48, 102
   digital, 1, 6, 25, 28, 29, 30, 33, 34
Meinong, Alexius, 279
Meinong's jungle, 279
Menabrea, Luigi, 158
Merleau-Ponty, Maurice, 283
metadata, 90, 91
metaontology, 318, 322
metaphor, 47
metaphysics, 62, 64, 69, 184, 185
Michaels, Sarah, 4
Michelangelo, 216
Microsoft, 24, 135, 152, 313, 325
Microsoft Word, 311
microwaves, 144
mind–body dualism, 140, 144
minimalism, 7
MIT, 207, 288
Mitterand, François, 134
Mockapetris, Paul, 93
modernism, 7
modernity, 136
Mon Oncle (film), 202
monad, 169
Monet, Claude, 7
monotheism, 225
mood, 45
Moore, G.E., 196, 253, 258
morphology, 50
Morris, Errol, 174, 281
Moscow Control Commission of Workers and
     Peasants Inspection, 111
Moscow Institute of Psychology, 104
Moscow State University, 37, 107, 112–14,
     196, 320
Mother Teresa, 321
MRI, 234
Mu'tazilite, 261
Muhammad, 262
multilingualism, 24

Multiliteracies, 4, 43
multimodality, 33, 72
Munsell, Alfred, 151–52, 154
Murray, Jack, 211
Murray, Jimmy, 205
Museum of Modern Art, New York, 13, 100
Museum of Society and Economy, Vienna,
     115–17, 193
music lyrics, 34
Muybridge, Eadweard, 235

Nadar, Félix, 232
Nagasaki, Atomic Bomb, 163
Nakata, Martin, 4
Nanosystems, 150
NASA, 258
National Gallery, London, 176
National Gallery of Art, Washington DC, 98
natural history, 175, 273
Natural Language Processing, 326
naturalism, 219
nature, 175
navigation path, 70
Nazi Party, 14, 15, 60, 114, 130, 164, 165,
     197, 320
negative, syntax, 239
Netscape, 313
Neurath, Marie. See Reidemeister, Marie
Neurath, Otto, 114–19, 193
New London Group, 4, 43
New School for Social Research, New York, 15
Newton, Isaac, 132, 145, 156, 170–71
   Opticks, 241
Ngombe, 141
Niépce, Nicéphore, 228
Nobel Prize, 130, 164
nominalization, 30
nominative, syntax, 207, 208
noun, common, 114
noun, proper, 80, 84, 91, 92, 114
noun, syntax, 1, 30, 45, 70, 116, 121, 127, 128,
     198, 207, 240
nuclear weapons, 163

O'Keefe, Georgia, 7
object, 27
Object Management Group, 124
Object-oriented Software Development,
     125–26
Odysseus, 80
Ogden, C.K., 182, 184
ONIX, 314
onomatopoeia, 268
ontology, 46, 126, 155, 259, 271, 303, 311, 314,
     315, 325

opponent processing, 145
Oregon State University, 150
Orfield Laboratories, 100
other, 2, 22, 213, 228
Oxford Internet Institute, 96

pain, 28
painting, 218, 229, 230
Palais Stonborough, 187, 197
Paliyan, 141
Pāṇini, 266, 318
    Aṣṭādhyāyī, 50–55
Panofsky, Erwin, 218
Pantone Matching System, 148–49, 150, 154
paragraph, 32
participation, 20, 47
passport, 90
Pavlov, Ivan, 286
Pavlov, Yuri M., 320
Peel, Sir Robert, 157
People's Republic of Bulgaria, 187
personalization, 97
phenomenology, 58–60, 61
phone number, 90
phoneme, 22, 23, 24, 26, 207
phonics, 25
photography, 84, 88, 115, 147, 228, 229,
    230–34, 235, 236
    digital, 134
photolithography, 134
Photoshop, 135
pictogram, 115
pitch, 29
pixel, 25, 26, 29, 134, 149, 168
plan perspective, 229
Plato, 58, 80
plural, 45
plural, syntax, 1, 50, 70, 114, 122, 155,
    207, 213
Podesta, John, 97
Pollock, Jackson, 7
polytheism, 224
pornography, 228
possibility, 238
Postel, Jon, 93
postmodernism, 7, 293
Postscript, 135
poststructuralism, 246, 269
posture, 28
Poto, 141
pragmatics, 50
pragmatics, linguistics, 2
praxis, 71, 140, 275
predicate, 30
predicate, syntax, 181

predication, 181, 195
prehension, 285
preposition, syntax, 128
pressure, 28
Prince Albert, 156
Princeton University, 162
pronoun, syntax, 32, 46, 207, 213
propaganda, 48
properties, 45, 135
proposition, 184
Protestantism, 227
proximity, 27
Pryor, Richard, 252
psychology, 34, 104, 224, 286
Ptolemy, 224

QR code, 91, 94
quality, 121, 136, 137, 138, 139, 140, 154, 168
quantity, 121, 136, 137, 153, 167
quantum mechanics, 129
Quechua, 142
Queen Victoria, 156
Qur'an, 224, 260, 262

radio, 30, 144
railway, 178
railway mania, 178
Ramsay, F.P., 184
raster imaging, 134
reading aloud, 34
reading (learning to read), 25
realism, 222, 226, 227, 230
Reddy, Michael, 55–56
reference, 9, 44, 45, 70, 77, 78
reflectance profile, 145
reflected light, 145
Reidemeister, Marie, 115, 116, 118–19, 193
reification, 191
relation, 303, 307
Renault, 133
representation, 20, 41, 69
requirement, 238, 251
Resource Description Framework (RDF), 317
retina, 145
Revelation, 171
Reynolds, Henry, 211
RFID (Radio Frequency Identification),
    95, 203
RGB, 149, 152
rhythm, 29
ritual, 28
Robinson Crusoe, 107
Rodriguez, Sixto Diaz, 303
role, 45, 212
Roma ("Gypsy"), 65, 67

Rothery, Joan, 56
Rothko, Mark, 7
Rousseau, Jean Jacques, 62
Royal Academy, 177
Ruben, Walter, 319, 320
Rudinev, Lev, 112–14
rule of law, 245
Rumbaugh, James, 125
Rumsfield, Donald, 281
Russell, Bertrand, 82, 130, 182–84, 195, 254

saccades, 221, 230
Saint Catherine's Monastery, Sinai Desert, 215
Sämkhya, 319
Sanskrit, 50–52, 309, 319
Santiago, Alfredo Santiago, 127
Sapir, Edward, 128, 180
Sartre, Jean-Paul, 60, 83, 87, 283
Saussure. *See* de Saussure
scalable vector graphics, 134
Schema.org, 325
Schlick, Moritz, 192, 197
Scholem, Gershom, 16, 82
School for Social Research, Frankfurt, 15
science, 41, 52, 56, 58, 59, 62, 72, 111, 240, 241, 242
Scientific Conception of the World. See Vienna Circle
Scollon, Ron, 192
Searle, John R., 64, 167, 307
765.1, 765.2, 765.3, 765.4
second person, syntax, 212
Second World War, 111, 163
self, 213, 222, 226
Semantic Web, 316–18
semantics, 50
semiconductor, 164
semiology, 267
Semple, Stuart, 151
sentence, 32
SGML, 313
Shannon, Claude, 162
shape, 28
shopping, 15, 102
Sîbawayh, 262, 287
sign, 63, 266
signified, 63, 68
signifier, 68
silence, 100
Silverman, Kaja, 236
Silverstein, Michael, 209
Siri, 311, 312, 315, 318
size, 28
Skinner, B.F., 294, 295–98, 301, 307
boxes, 295–98

Verbal Behavior, 287
SNOMED (Systematized Nomenclature of Medicine), 304
Snowdon, Edward, 325
social cognition, 38
social media, 34
social psychology, 21
socialism, 108, 115
socialist realism, 228
software, 54, 158
software design, 126
song, 206
Sontag, Susan, 230–32
sound, 29
Soviet Union, 110, 111, 113, 118, 164, 196
Sowa, John, 323
space, 27
Spanish, 141
specification, 83
speech, 29, 32, 62, 176, 181, 268
speech act, 244, 252
Spinoza, Baruch, 276, 277
Stalin, Joseph, 37, 110, 113
Standard Generalized Markup Language (SGML), 202
Stanford University, 324
Star, Susan Leigh, 306
statistics, 115
Sting, 191
Stoics, 276
Stonborough, Margarete (Gretl, neé Wittgenstein), 186
Strawson, P.F., 321
structuralism, 1, 13, 51, 269
structure, 9, 44, 46, 70, 126, 279
subject, syntax, 317
subjunctive, syntax, 237
Subramanian, Mas, 150
substitution, 39
subtractive coloring, 148
Sun Microsystems, 24, 124
supermarket order, 18, 28, 305, 315
surface, 28
Swahili, 141
symbol, 194, 219
symbolic activity, 105
synesthesia, 34, 46
syntax, 50
Systemic-Functional Grammar, 43

tabula rasa. See Locke
Tagalog, 127
Tagore, Rabindranath, 193
Talbot, Henry Fox, 228
Taliban, 225

Tatehata, Akira, 7
Tati, Jacques, 202
taxonomy, 311
TCP/IP, 93, 95
teaching machine, 297
techne, 63
TECNOLINE®, 188
telephone, 30
television, 148, 149
temperature, 28
tempo, 29
tense, 50
text, 23, 32, 62, 63, 155, 214, 242, 311, 323
text messaging, 34
textual meaning (Halliday), 44
texture, 28, 45
theater dialogue, 34
thing, 213, 235
third person, syntax, 1, 212
Thorndike, Edward, 286
time, 47
Timpanaro, Sebastiano, 269, 298
tonic prominence, 30
Torres Straits, 211
tourism, 232
toys, 28, 105
transactivity, 198
transcription, 40
transduction, 40
transformational-generative grammar, 291
transitivity, 45
transparency, 145
transposition, 12, 19, 33, 40, 46, 49, 62, 65, 69, 70, 72, 85, 122, 125, 126
travel, 27
Trotsky, Leon, 83
Trump, Donald, 325
Tudor, David, 100
Turing, Alan, 159–69
   Turing test, 166, 324
Turner, J.M.W., 176–79
tweet, 34

Uddalaka Aruni, 319
ultraviolet light, 144
Umbrico, Penelope, 92–93
Unicode, 23–25, 91, 115, 134, 167, 310, 313
Uniform Modeling Language, 122–25
Universal Time (UTC), 47
University of California, Berkeley, 248
University of Chicago, 209
University of Edinburgh, 207
University of Freiberg, 60
University of Illinois, 52, 127, 131, 164, 303
University of Jena, 183

University of London, 130
University of Manchester, 166, 182, 190
University of Miami, 285
University of Minnesota, 257
University of Pennsylvania, 290
University of Southern California, 93
University of Turin, 158
URL, 93–94, 317
US Department of Defense, 94, 97, 311
user story, 126
USSR. *See* Soviet Union
Utopia station, 8, 10
Uzbekistan, 108

van Gogh, Vincent, 67
van Heijenoort, Jean, 82
vanishing point, 229
Vantablack, 150
Vasari, art historian, 216
vector, 121, 137
vector mapping, 134
Vedas, 52–53, 318
verb, syntax, 1, 70, 121, 127, 128, 198, 207, 240
Vienna Circle, 117–18, 192, 197
   Scientific Conception of the World, 192
Virtual Reality Modelling Language, 135
visual ray theory, 224
volume, 27, 29, 45
von Neumann, John, 162, 164
von Wright, Henrik, 196
Vygotsky, Lev, 101, 103–7, 108–11, 112

W3C, 313, 314, 316
Wagenfield, Wilhelm, 188
Waissmann, Friedrich, 193, 197
Warhol, Andy, 7, 13
Water Heater, 13
Watson, John B., 286–87
wayfinding, 27, 46
wearables, 28
Web Ontology Language (OWL), 317
Wells, H.G., 257
Whitehead, Alfred North, 82, 130–32, 287
Whitman, Walt, 236
Wierzbicka, Anna, 209
Wikipedia, 258, 325
Wittgenstein, Ludwig, 13, 21, 162, 166, 182–88, 189, 274
   architecture, 186–88
   On Certainty, 253–54, 255–56
   Philosophical Investigations, 187, 254–55
   picture theory, 193–95
   Tractatus, 182–86, 192, 194, 198
Wordsworth, William, 178

World Health Organization, 305
World Wide Web Consortium, 135
World-Wide Web, 316
writing. *See* text

Xerox lab, Paulo Alto, 24
XML, 26, 55, 310, 313–14
X-ray, 144, 147, 155, 234

XSLT, 314

Yahoo, 325
Yājñavalkya, 319
Yélî Dnye, 143
Yin and Yang, 169
YInMin Blue, 150
YouTube, 192